DRAMA
for Students

Advisors

Erik France: Adjunct Instructor of English, Macomb Community College, Warren, Michigan. B.A. and M.S.L.S. from University of North Carolina, Chapel Hill; Ph.D. from Temple University.

Kate Hamill: Grade 12 English Teacher, Catonsville High School, Catonsville, Maryland.

Joseph McGeary: English Teacher, Germantown Friends School, Philadelphia, Pennsylvania. Ph.D. in English from Duke University.

Timothy Showalter: English Department Chair, Franklin High School, Reisterstown, Maryland. Certified teacher by the Maryland State Department of Education. Member of the National Council of Teachers of English.

Amy Spade Silverman: English Department Chair, Kehillah Jewish High School, Palo Alto, California. Member of National Council of Teachers of English (NCTE), Teachers and Writers, and NCTE Opinion Panel. Exam Reader, Advanced Placement Literature and Composition. Poet, published in *North American Review, Nimrod,* and *Michigan Quarterly Review,* among other publications.

Jody Stefansson: Director of Boswell Library and Study Center and Upper School Learning Specialist, Polytechnic School, Pasadena, California. Board member, Children's Literature Council of Southern California. Member of American Library Association, Association of Independent School Librarians, and Association of Educational Therapists.

Laura Jean Waters: Certified School Library Media Specialist, Wilton High School, Wilton, Connecticut. B.A. from Fordham University; M.A. from Fairfield University.

DRAMA
for Students

Presenting Analysis, Context, and Criticism
on Commonly Studied Dramas

VOLUME 28

Sara Constantakis, Project Editor

Foreword by Carole L. Hamilton

GALE
CENGAGE Learning

Detroit • New York • San Francisco • New Haven, Conn • Waterville, Maine • London

GALE
CENGAGE Learning

Drama for Students, Volume 28

Project Editor: Sara Constantakis

Rights Acquisition and Management:
Margaret Chamberlain-Gaston, Aja Perales,
Robyn Young

Composition: Evi Abou-El-Seoud

Manufacturing: Rhonda Dover

Imaging: John Watkins

Product Design: Pamela A. E. Galbreath,
Jennifer Wahi

Content Conversion: Katrina Coach

Product Manager: Meggin Condino

For product information and technology assistance, contact us at
Gale Customer Support, 1-800-877-4253.
For permission to use material from this text or product,
submit all requests online at **www.cengage.com/permissions.**
Further permissions questions can be emailed to
permissionrequest@cengage.com

Gale
27500 Drake Rd.
Farmington Hills, MI, 48331-3535

ISBN-13: 978-0-7876-8124-1
ISBN-10: 0-7876-8124-5

ISSN 1094-9232

This title is also available as an e-book.
ISBN-13: 978-1-4144-4940-1
ISBN-10: 1-4144-4940-2
Contact your Gale, a part of Cengage Learning sales representative for ordering information.

Printed in Mexico
1 2 3 4 5 6 7 15 14 13 12 11

Table of Contents

The Study of Drama

We study drama in order to learn what meaning others have made of life, to comprehend what it takes to produce a work of art, and to glean some understanding of ourselves. Drama produces in a separate, aesthetic world, a moment of being for the audience to experience, while maintaining the detachment of a reflective observer.

Drama is a representational art, a visible and audible narrative presenting virtual, fictional characters within a virtual, fictional universe. Dramatic realizations may pretend to approximate reality or else stubbornly defy, distort, and deform reality into an artistic statement. From this separate universe that is obviously not "real life" we expect a valid reflection upon reality, yet drama never is mistaken for reality—the methods of theater are integral to its form and meaning. Theater is art, and art's appeal lies in its ability both to approximate life and to depart from it. For in intruding its distorted version of life into our consciousness, art gives us a new perspective and appreciation of life and reality. Although all aesthetic experiences perform this service, theater does it most effectively by creating a separate, cohesive universe that freely acknowledges its status as an art form.

And what is the purpose of the aesthetic universe of drama? The potential answers to such a question are nearly as many and varied as there are plays written, performed, and enjoyed. Dramatic texts can be problems posed, answers asserted, or moments portrayed. Dramas (trage-dies as well as comedies) may serve strictly "to ease the anguish of a torturing hour" (as stated in William Shakespeare's *A Midsummer Night's Dream*)—to divert and entertain—or aspire to move the viewer to action with social issues. Whether to entertain or to instruct, affirm or influence, pacify or shock, dramatic art wraps us in the spell of its imaginary world for the length of the work and then dispenses us back to the real world, entertained, purged, as Aristotle said, of pity and fear, and edified—or at least weary enough to sleep peacefully.

It is commonly thought that theater, being an art of performance, must be experienced—seen—in order to be appreciated fully. However, to view a production of a dramatic text is to be limited to a single interpretation of that text—all other interpretations are for the moment closed off, inaccessible. In the process of producing a play, the director, stage designer, and performers interpret and transform the script into a work of art that always departs in some measure from the author's original conception. Novelist and critic Umberto Eco, in his *The Role of the Reader: Explorations in the Semiotics of Texts* (Indiana University Press, 1979), explained, "In short, we can say that every performance offers us a complete and satisfying version of the work, but at the same time makes it incomplete for us, because it cannot simultaneously give all the other artistic solutions which the work may admit."

Thus Laurence Olivier's coldly formal and neurotic film presentation of Shakespeare's *Hamlet* (in which he played the title character as well as directed) shows marked differences from subsequent adaptations. While Olivier's Hamlet is clearly entangled in a Freudian relationship with his mother Gertrude, he would be incapable of shushing her with the impassioned kiss that Mel Gibson's mercurial Hamlet (in director Franco Zeffirelli's 1990 film) does. Although each of performances rings true to Shakespeare's text, each is also a mutually exclusive work of art. Also important to consider are the time periods in which each of these films was produced: Olivier made his film in 1948, a time in which overt references to sexuality (especially incest) were frowned upon. Gibson and Zeffirelli made their film in a culture more relaxed and comfortable with these issues. Just as actors and directors can influence the presentation of drama, so too can the time period of the production affect what the audience will see.

A play script is an open text from which an infinity of specific realizations may be derived. Dramatic scripts that are more open to interpretive creativity (such as those of Ntozake Shange and Tomson Highway) actually require the creative improvisation of the production troupe in order to complete the text. Even the most prescriptive scripts (those of Neil Simon, Lillian Hellman, and Robert Bolt, for example), can never fully control the actualization of live performance, and circumstantial events, including the attitude and receptivity of the audience, make every performance a unique event. Thus, while it is important to view a production of a dramatic piece, if one wants to understand a drama fully it is equally important to read the original dramatic text.

The reader of a dramatic text or script is not limited by either the specific interpretation of a given production or by the unstoppable action of a moving spectacle. The reader of a dramatic text may discover the nuances of the play's language, structure, and events at their own pace. Yet studied alone, the author's blueprint for artistic production does not tell the whole story of a play's life and significance. One also needs to assess the play's critical reviews to discover how it resonated to cultural themes at the time of its debut and how the shifting tides of cultural interest have revised its interpretation and impact on audiences. And to do this, one needs to know a little about the culture of the times which produced the play as well as the author who penned it.

Drama for Students supplies this material in a useful compendium for the student of dramatic theater. Covering a range of dramatic works that span from 442 BCE to the 1990s, this book focuses on significant theatrical works whose themes and form transcend the uncertainty of dramatic fads. These are plays that have proven to be both memorable and teachable. *Drama for Students* seeks to enhance appreciation of these dramatic texts by providing scholarly materials written with the secondary and college/university student in mind. It provides for each play a concise summary of the plot and characters as well as a detailed explanation of its themes. In addition, background material on the historical context of the play, its critical reception, and the author's life help the student to understand the work's position in the chronicle of dramatic history. For each play entry a new work of scholarly criticism is also included, as well as segments of other significant critical works for handy reference. A thorough bibliography provides a starting point for further research.

This series offers comprehensive educational resources for students of drama. *Drama for Students* is a vital book for dramatic interpretation and a valuable addition to any reference library.

Sources

Eco, Umberto, *The Role of the Reader: Explorations in the Semiotics of Texts*, Indiana University Press, 1979.

Carole L. Hamilton
Author and Instructor of English at Cary Academy, Cary, North Carolina

Introduction

Purpose of the Book

The purpose of *Drama for Students* (*DfS*) is to provide readers with a guide to understanding, enjoying, and studying dramas by giving them easy access to information about the work. Part of Gale's "For Students" literature line, *DfS* is specifically designed to meet the curricular needs of high school and undergraduate college students and their teachers, as well as the interests of general readers and researchers considering specific plays. While each volume contains entries on "classic" dramas frequently studied in classrooms, there are also entries containing hard-to-find information on contemporary plays, including works by multicultural, international, and women playwrights. Entries profiling film versions of plays not only diversify the study of drama but support alternate learning styles, media literacy, and film studies curricula as well.

The information covered in each entry includes an introduction to the play and the work's author; a plot summary, to help readers unravel and understand the events in a drama; descriptions of important characters, including explanation of a given character's role in the drama as well as discussion about that character's relationship to other characters in the play; analysis of important themes in the drama; and an explanation of important literary techniques and movements as they are demonstrated in the play.

In addition to this material, which helps the readers analyze the play itself, students are also provided with important information on the literary and historical background informing each work. This includes a historical context essay, a box comparing the time or place the drama was written to modern Western culture, a critical essay, and excerpts from critical essays on the play. A unique feature of *DfS* is a specially commissioned critical essay on each drama, targeted toward the student reader.

The "literature to film" entries on plays vary slightly in form, providing background on film technique and comparison to the original, literary version of the work. These entries open with an introduction to the film, which leads directly into the plot summary. The summary highlights plot changes from the play, key cinematic moments, and/or examples of key film techniques. As in standard entries, there are character profiles (noting omissions or additions, and identifying the actors), analysis of themes and how they are illustrated in the film, and an explanation of the cinematic style and structure of the film. A cultural context section notes any time period or setting differences from that of the original work, as well as cultural differences between the time in which the original work was written and the time in which the film adaptation was made. A film entry concludes with a critical overview and critical essays on the film.

To further help today's student in studying and enjoying each play or film, information on audiobooks and other media adaptations is provided (if available), as well as suggestions for works of fiction, nonfiction, or film on similar themes and topics. Classroom aids include ideas for research papers and lists of critical and reference sources that provide additional material on each drama. Film entries also highlight signature film techniques demonstrated, as well as suggesting media literacy activities and prompts to use during or after viewing a film.

Selection Criteria

The titles for each volume of *DfS* are selected by surveying numerous sources on notable literary works and analyzing course curricula for various schools, school districts, and states. Some of the sources surveyed include: high school and undergraduate literature anthologies and textbooks; lists of award-winners, and recommended titles, including the Young Adult Library Services Association (YALSA) list of best books for young adults. Films are selected both for the literary importance of the original work and the merits of the adaptation (including official awards and widespread public recognition).

Input solicited from our expert advisory board—consisting of educators and librarians—guides us to maintain a mix of "classic" and contemporary literary works, a mix of challenging and engaging works (including genre titles that are commonly studied) appropriate for different age levels, and a mix of international, multicultural and women authors. These advisors also consult on each volume's entry list, advising on which titles are most studied, most appropriate, and meet the broadest interests across secondary (grades 7–12) curricula and undergraduate literature studies.

How Each Entry Is Organized

Each entry, or chapter, in *DfS* focuses on one play. Each entry heading lists the full name of the play, the author's name, and the date of the play's publication. The following elements are contained in each entry:

Introduction: a brief overview of the drama which provides information about its first appearance, its literary standing, any controversies surrounding the work, and major conflicts or themes within the work. Film entries identify the original play and provide understanding of the film's reception and reputation, along with that of the director.

Author Biography: in play entries, this section includes basic facts about the author's life, and focuses on events and times in the author's life that inspired the drama in question.

Plot Summary: a description of the major events in the play. Subheads demarcate the play's various acts or scenes. Plot summaries of films are used to uncover plot differences from the original play, and to note the use of certain film angles or techniques.

Characters: an alphabetical listing of major characters in the play. Each character name is followed by a brief to an extensive description of the character's role in the play, as well as discussion of the character's actions, relationships, and possible motivation. In film entries, omissions or changes to the cast of characters of the film adaptation are mentioned here, and the actors' names—and any awards they may have received—are also included.

Characters are listed alphabetically by last name. If a character is unnamed—for instance, the Stage Manager in *Our Town*—the character is listed as "The Stage Manager" and alphabetized as "Stage Manager." If a character's first name is the only one given, the name will appear alphabetically by the first name. Variant names are also included for each character. Thus, the nickname "Babe" would head the listing for a character in *Crimes of the Heart,* but below that listing would be her less-mentioned married name "Rebecca Botrelle."

Themes: a thorough overview of how the major topics, themes, and issues are addressed within the play. Each theme discussed appears in a separate subhead. While the key themes often remain the same or similar when a play is adapted into a film, film entries demonstrate how the themes are conveyed cinematically, along with any changes in the portrayal of the themes.

Style: this section addresses important style elements of the drama, such as setting, point of view, and narration; important literary devices used, such as imagery, foreshadowing, symbolism; and, if applicable, genres to which the work might have belonged, such as Gothicism or Romanticism. Literary terms are explained within the entry, but can also be found in the Glossary. Film entries cover how the director conveyed the meaning, message, and mood of the work using film in comparison to the author's use of language, literary device, etc., in the original work.

Historical Context: in play entries, this section outlines the social, political, and cultural climate in which the author lived and the play was created. This section may include descriptions of related historical events, pertinent aspects of daily life in the culture, and the artistic and literary sensibilities of the time in which the work was written. If the play is a historical work, information regarding the time in which the play is set is also included. Each section is broken down with helpful subheads. Film entries contain a similar Cultural Context section, because the film adaptation might explore an entirely different time period or culture than the original work, and may also be influenced by the traditions and views of a time period much different than that of the original author.

Critical Overview: this section provides background on the critical reputation of the play or film, including bannings or any other public controversies surrounding the work. For older plays, this section includes a history of how the drama or film was first received and how perceptions of it may have changed over the years; for more recent plays, direct quotes from early reviews may also be included.

Criticism: an essay commissioned by *DfS* which specifically deals with the play or film and is written specifically for the student audience, as well as excerpts from previously published criticism on the work (if available).

Sources: an alphabetical list of critical material used in compiling the entry, with full bibliographical information.

Further Reading: an alphabetical list of other critical sources which may prove useful for the student. It includes full bibliographical information and a brief annotation.

Suggested Search Terms: a list of search terms and phrases to jumpstart students' further information seeking. Terms include not just titles and author names but also terms and topics related to the historical and literary context of the works.

In addition, each entry contains the following highlighted sections, set apart from the main text as sidebars:

Media Adaptations: if available, a list of audiobooks and important film and television adaptations of the play, including source information. The list may also include such variations on the work as musical adaptations and other stage interpretations.

Topics for Further Study: a list of potential study questions or research topics dealing with the play. This section includes questions related to other disciplines the student may be studying, such as American history, world history, science, math, government, business, geography, economics, psychology, etc.

Compare and Contrast: an "at-a-glance" comparison of the cultural and historical differences between the author's time and culture and late twentieth century or early twenty-first century Western culture. This box includes pertinent parallels between the major scientific, political, and cultural movements of the time or place the drama was written, the time or place the play was set (if a historical work), and modern Western culture. Works written after 1990 may not have this box.

What Do I Read Next?: a list of works that might give a reader points of entry into a classic work (e.g., YA or multicultural titles) and/or complement the featured play or serve as a contrast to it. This includes works by the same author and others, works from various genres, YA works, and works from various cultures and eras.

The film entries provide sidebars more targeted to the study of film, including:

Film Technique: a listing and explanation of four to six key techniques used in the film, including shot styles, use of transitions, lighting, sound or music, etc.

Read, Watch, Write: media literacy prompts and/or suggestions for viewing log prompts.

What Do I See Next?: a list of films based on the same or similar works or of films similar in directing style, technique, etc.

Other Features

DfS includes "The Study of Drama," a foreword by Carole Hamilton, an educator and author who specializes in dramatic works. This essay examines the basis for drama in societies and what drives people to study such work. The essay also discusses how *DfS* can help teachers show students how to enrich their own reading/ viewing experiences.

A Cumulative Author/Title Index lists the authors and titles covered in each volume of the *DfS* series.

A Cumulative Nationality/Ethnicity Index breaks down the authors and titles covered in each volume of the *DfS* series by nationality and ethnicity.

A Subject/Theme Index, specific to each volume, provides easy reference for users who may be studying a particular subject or theme rather than a single work. Significant subjects from events to broad themes are included.

Each entry may include illustrations, including photo of the author, stills from stage productions, and stills from film adaptations, if available.

Citing Drama for Students

When writing papers, students who quote directly from any volume of *DfS* may use the following general forms. These examples are based on MLA style; teachers may request that students adhere to a different style, so the following examples may be adapted as needed.

When citing text from *DfS* that is not attributed to a particular author (i.e., the Themes, Style, Historical Context sections, etc.), the following format should be used in the bibliography section:

> "*Our Town.*" *Drama for Students.* Vol. 1. Ed. David Galens and Lynn Spampinato. Detroit: Gale, 1998. 227–30.

When quoting the specially commissioned essay from *DfS* (usually the first piece under the "Criticism" subhead), the following format should be used:

Fiero, John. Critical Essay on *Twilight: Los Angeles, 1992. Drama for Students.* Vol. 2. Ed. David Galens and Lynn Spampinato. Detroit: Gale, 1998. 247–49.

When quoting a journal or newspaper essay that is reprinted in a volume of *DfS*, the following form may be used:

> Rich, Frank. "Theatre: A Mamet Play, *Glengarry Glen Ross.*" *New York Theatre Critics' Review* 45.4 (March 5, 1984): 5–7. Excerpted and reprinted in *Drama for Students.* Vol. 2. Ed. David Galens and Lynn Spampinato. Detroit: Gale, 1998. 51–53.

When quoting material reprinted from a book that appears in a volume of *DfS*, the following form may be used:

> Kerr, Walter. "*The Miracle Worker.*" *The Theatre in Spite of Itself.* Simon & Schuster, 1963. 255–57. Excerpted and reprinted in *Drama for Students.* Vol. 2. Ed. David Galens and Lynn Spampinato. Detroit: Gale, 1998. 123–24.

We Welcome Your Suggestions

The editorial staff of *Drama for Students* welcomes your comments and ideas. Readers who wish to suggest dramas to appear in future volumes, or who have other suggestions, are cordially invited to contact the editor. You may contact the editor via e-mail at: **ForStudentsEditors@cengage.com.** Or write to the editor at:

Editor, *Drama for Students*
Gale
27500 Drake Road
Farmington Hills, MI 48331-3535

Literary Chronology

1639: Jean Racine is born on December 22 in La Ferté-Milon in the Picardy province of France.

1667: Jean Racine's *Andromache* is published.

1699: Jean Racine dies of liver cancer on April 21 in Paris, France.

1707: Henry Fielding is born on April 22 in Sharpham, England.

1730: Henry Fielding's *Tom Thumb* is produced on April 24 at the Little Theatre in the Haymarket (Westminster, England). A slightly revised version is performed a few weeks later.

1754: Henry Fielding dies on October 8 in Lisbon, Portugal.

1824: Wilkie Collins is born on January 8 in London, England.

1857: Wilkie Collins's *The Frozen Deep* is first performed.

1882: Jean Giraudoux is born on October 29 in Bellac, France.

1885: Stephen Sondheim's *Sunday in the Park with George* is awarded the Pulitzer Prize for Drama.

1888: T. S. Eliot is born on September 26 in St. Louis, Missouri.

1889: Wilkie Collins dies of a stroke on September 23 in London, England.

1911: Dean Fuller is born on December 12 in Woodbury, New Hampshire.

1914: William Gibson is born on November 13 in New York, New York.

1930: Stephen Sondheim is born on March 22 in New York, New York.

1931: *Once upon a Mattress* lyricist and writer Marshall Barer is born on February 19 in New York, New York.

1931: *Once upon a Mattress* musical composer Mary Rodgers is born on January 11.

1931: Adrienne Kennedy is born on September 13 in Pittsburgh, Pennsylvania.

1933: Michael J. Frayn is born on September 8 in London, England.

1939: T. S. Eliot's *The Family Reunion* is published.

1944: Jean Giraudoux dies of sudden kidney failure on January 31 in Paris.

1945: Jean Giraudoux's *La Folle de Chaillot* is published and produced in Paris. *The Madwoman of Chaillot*, an English translation by Maurice Valency, is published and produced in New York in 1948.

1947: Rupert Holmes is born as David Goldstein on February 24 in Northwich, Cheshire, England.

1948: T. S. Eliot receives the Nobel Prize in Literature.

1950: John Patrick Shanley is born on October 3 in New York, New York.

1952: Emily Mann is born on April 12 in Boston, Massachusetts.

1957: William Gibson's *The Miracle Worker*, directed by Arthur Penn, is broadcast on the CBS program *Playhouse 90*.

1959: *Once upon a Mattress* is produced on May 11 at the Phoenix Theatre in New York, New York.

1959: William Gibson's *The Miracle Worker*, directed by Arthur Penn, opens at the Playhouse Theater on Broadway and runs for 719 performances.

1962: William Gibson's *The Miracle Worker*, directed by Arthur Penn, is released as a feature motion picture by Playfilms Productions and United Artists.

1963: Stephen Gregg is born on May 19 in Sacramento, California.

1963: William Gibson's *The Miracle Worker* wins Academy Awards for Best Actress in a Leading Role (Anne Bancroft) and Best Actress in a Supporting Role (Patty Duke).

1965: T. S. Eliot dies of emphysema on January 4 in London, England.

1982: Michael Frayn's *Noises Off* is published.

1984: Stephen Sondheim's *Sunday in the Park with George* is produced.

1985: Rupert Holmes's *The Mystery of Edwin Drood* is published.

1986: Rupert Holmes is awarded the Tony Award for Best Musical for *The Mystery of Edwin Drood*.

1988: Stephen Gregg's *This Is a Test* is published.

1995: Emily Mann's *Having Our Say* is produced.

1996: Adrienne Kennedy' *Sleep Deprivation Chamber* is produced.

1998: *Once upon a Mattress* lyricist and writer Marshall Barer dies of cancer on August 25 in Santa Fe, New Mexico.

2004: John Patrick Shanley's *Doubt* is produced at the Manhattan Theater Club in New York, New York.

2005: John Patrick Shanley is awarded the Pulitzer Prize for Drama for *Doubt*.

2005: John Patrick Shanley is awarded the Tony Award for Best Play for *Doubt*.

2008: John Patrick Shanley's film *Doubt* is released.

2008: William Gibson dies on November 28 in Stockbridge, Massachusetts.

Acknowledgments

The editors wish to thank the copyright holders of the excerpted criticism included in this volume and the permissions managers of many book and magazine publishing companies for assisting us in securing reproduction rights. We are also grateful to the staffs of the Detroit Public Library, the Library of Congress, the University of Detroit Mercy Library, Wayne State University Purdy/Kresge Library Complex, and the University of Michigan Libraries for making their resources available to us. Following is a list of the copyright holders who have granted us permission to reproduce material in this volume of *DfS*. Every effort has been made to trace copyright, but if omissions have been made, please let us know.

COPYRIGHTED EXCERPTS IN *DfS*, VOLUME 28, WERE REPRODUCED FROM THE FOLLOWING PERIODICALS:

America, v. 200, no. 2, January 19, 2009. Copyright © 2009 by America Press, Inc. Reproduced by permission.—*Back Stage*, v. 36, no. 6, February 10, 1995; v. 37, no. 11, March 15, 1996; v. 50, no. 35, August 27, 2009; v. 50, no. 47, November 19, 2009. Copyright © 1995, 1996, 2009 by VNU Business Media, Inc. All reproduced by permission.—*Back Stage East*, v. 49, no. 9, February 28, 2008. Copyright © 2008 by VNU Business Media, Inc. Reproduced by permission.—*Back Stage West*, v. 15, no. 4, January 24, 2008. Copyright © 2008 by VNU Business Media,

Inc. Reproduced by permission.—*Chicago Reader*, December 12, 1991. Copyright © 1991 by *Chicago Reader*. Reproduced by permission.—*Christian Century*, v. 125, no. 26, December 30, 2008. Copyright © 2008 by Christian Century Foundation. Reproduced by permission.—*Cineaste*, v. 20, no. 2, Spring 1993. Copyright © 1993 by *Cineaste*. Reproduced by permission.—*Clio*, v. 32, no. 4, 2003. Copyright © 2003 by *Clio*. Reproduced by permission.—*Commonweal*, v. 49, no. 14, January 14, 1949; v. 71, no. 10, December 4, 1959. Copyright © 1949, 1959 by *Commonweal*. Both reproduced by permission.—*Conscience*, v. 30, no. 1, Spring 2009. Copyright © 2009 by Catholics For Choice. Reproduced by permission.—*Daily Collegian Online*, March 22, 2002. Copyright © 2002 by *The Daily Collegian*. Reproduced by permission.—*Dallas Observer*, April 17, 2003. Copyright © 2003 by *Dallas Observer*. Reproduced by permission.—*Denver Post*, April 8, 2005. Copyright © 2005 by *Denver Post*. Reproduced by permission.—*Financial Times*, June 16, 2009. Copyright © 2009 by *Financial Times*. Reproduced by permission.—*French Review*, v. 48, no. 3, February 1975. Copyright © 1975 by *French Review*. Reproduced by permission.—*Insight on the News*, v. 12, no. 46, December 9, 1996. Copyright © 1996 by *Insight on the News*. Reproduced by permission.—*London Sunday Telegraph*, November 30, 2008. Copyright © 2008 by Johnston Publishing Limited. Reproduced by permission.—*Modern Drama*, v. 22, no. 2, June

1979. Copyright © 1979 by *Modern Drama*. Reproduced by permission.—*New Leader*, v. 68, November 4, 1985; v. 78, May 8, 1995. v. 80, January 13, 1997. Copyright © 1985, 1995, 1997 by *The New Leader*. All reproduced by permission.—*New Republic*, v. 120, no. 3, January 17, 1949; v. 141, no. 19, November 9, 1959. Copyright © 1949, 1959 by *The New Republic*. Both reproduced by permission.—*New York*, v. 41, no. 8, March 3, 2008. Copyright © 2008 by *New York* Magazine. Reproduced by permission.—*Palo Alto Daily News*, July 13, 2007. Copyright © 2007 by *Palo Alto Daily News*. Reproduced by permission.—*Philological Quarterly*, v. 69, no. 1, Winter 1990. Copyright © 1990 by *Philological Quarterly*. Reproduced by permission.—*Publishers Weekly*, v. 250, no. 22, June 2, 2003. Copyright © 2003 by *Publishers Weekly*. Reproduced by permission.—*Scientific Monthly*, v. 34, no. 2, February 1932, pp. 157-166. Copyright © 1932 by American Association for the Advancement of Science. Reproduced with permission from American Association from the Advancement of Science.—*Scrutiny: A Quarterly Review*, v. 17, no. 1, Spring 1950. Copyright © 1950 by Cambridge University Press. Reproduced with the permission of Cambridge University Press.—*St. Petersburg Times*, August 1, 2008; July 17, 2009. Copyright © 2008, 2009 by *St. Petersburg Times*. Reproduced by permission.—*Studies in the Novel*, v. 41, no. 3, Winter 2009. Copyright © 2009 by *Studies in the Novel*. Reproduced by permission.—*Theater Journal*, v. 1, March 1997. Copyright © 1997 by *Theater Journal*. Reproduced by permission.—*Yeats Eliot Review*, v. 23, no. 4, Fall/Winter 2006. Copyright © 2006 by Murphy Newsletter Services. Reproduced by permission.

COPYRIGHTED EXCERPTS IN *DfS*, VOLUME 28, WERE REPRODUCED FROM THE FOLLOWING BOOKS:

Harrell, Wade. From "When the Parody Parodies Itself: The Problem with Michael Frayn's 'Noises Off,'" in *From the Bard to Broadway*, Karelisa V. Hartigan, University Press of America, 1987. Copyright © 1987 by Rowman & Littlefield. Reproduced by permission.—Marshall, William H. From "The Shorter Works through 1870," in *Wilkie Collins*, Twayne Publishers, Inc., 1970. © 1997 Gale, a part of Cengage Learning, Inc. Reproduced by permission. www.cengage.com/permissions

Contributors

Bryan Aubrey: Aubrey holds a Ph.D. in English. Entries on *The Frozen Deep* and *Sunday in the Park with George*. Original essays on *The Frozen Deep* and *Sunday in the Park with George*.

Cynthia A. Bily: Bily is an instructor in literature and writing. Entry on *The Madwoman of Chaillot*. Original essay on *The Madwoman of Chaillot*.

Catherine Dominic: Dominic is a novelist, freelance writer, and editor. Entry on *The Family Reunion*. Original essay on *The Family Reunion*.

Joyce Hart: Hart is a published writer and teacher of creative writing. Entries on *Sleep Deprivation Chamber* and *Once upon a Mattress*. Original essays on *Sleep Deprivation Chamber* and *Once upon a Mattress*.

Sheri Metzger Karmiol: Karmiol teaches literature and drama at the University of New Mexico, where she is a lecturer in the University Honors Program. Entry on *Having Our Say: The Delany Sisters' First 100 Years*.

Original essay on *Having Our Say: The Delany Sisters' First 100 Years*.

David Kelly: Kelly is a college instructor of creative writing and literature. Entries on *Doubt* and *The Miracle Worker*. Original essays on *Doubt* and *The Miracle Worker*.

Laura Pryor: Pryor is a freelance writer with twenty-five years of experience in professional writing with an emphasis on fiction. Entry on *The Mystery of Edwin Drood*. Original essay on *The Mystery of Edwin Drood*.

Bradley A. Skeen: Skeen is a classics professor. Entries on *Andromache* and *Noises Off*. Original essays on *Andromache* and *Noises Off*.

Leah Tieger: Tieger is a freelance writer and editor. Entry on *Tom Thumb*. Original essay on *Tom Thumb*.

Rebecca Valentine: Valentine is a self-employed writer with an extensive background in literary analysis and theory. Entry on *This Is a Test*. Original essay on *This Is a Test*.

Andromache

JEAN RACINE

1667

In one of the greatest plays ever written, Jean Racine reshapes a classical Greek tragedy into a revenge drama worthy of Shakespeare with a simplicity and elegance that is nearly unparalleled in world literature. Racine's *Andromache* explores the psychological depth of Orestes and Pyrrhus, the sons of Agamemnon and Achilles, respectively, driven to madness and destruction by desire and an obsession with honor in a world whose order has been destroyed by the catastrophe of the Trojan War. In an honor-based society where women have little freedom, the play's antagonists vie for control of Hermione, the daughter of Helen of Troy, and Andromache, the widow of the Trojan hero Hector. First performed in 1667 at the court of Louis XIV, *Andromache* is Racine's third play and his first masterpiece. It is one of the leading works of the flourishing school of French baroque drama, which is also represented by Corneille and Molière.

The name of the title character of Racine's play, Andromache, was originally Greek and can be written in languages that use the Roman alphabet in various ways, including Andromaque. The spelling Racine chose for the original French version of the play was *Andromache*. This spelling is more common in English and is frequently used as the title of English translations of the play, including the English translation by Eric Korn that is used here.

Jean Racine *(The Library of Congress)*

AUTHOR BIOGRAPHY

Racine was born in the small French town of Ferté on December 22, 1639. His father was a royal official in charge of collecting the salt tax. Both of Racine's parents died before he was two, so he was raised by his grandparents. After the death of his grandfather in 1649, his grandmother retired with her charge to the Cistercian abbey of Port-Royal des Champs, a center of education and educational reform in baroque France that graduated the philosopher Blaise Pascal as well as Racine. The abbey was, however, a home of Jansenist heresy (a set of religious beliefs eventually condemned by the Catholic Church as being too similar to those of the Protestant theologian John Calvin), a fact that attached some scandal to Racine's name but does not seem to have materially affected his career.

While studying law in Paris, Racine began to show his poetry to leading critics of the Time, such as Nicolas Boileau, and soon had his first play, *Thébaïdes*, performed in 1664 by Molière's professional company at the Théâtre du Palais-Royal. Very quickly, Racine became the first French author to support himself financially solely through his writing.

Racine produced about a play a year for the next decade, including 1667's *Andromache*, acknowledged by modern critics as his first masterpiece. Racine's plays were as popular with the public as they were with the critics and the royal court (the three elements that determined artistic success in Louis XIV's France), but he had curiously little interest in the theater compared to contemporary playwrights like Molière or the brothers Corneille.

After what was recognized then as now as his greatest artistic triumph, *Phèdre* in 1677, Racine was happy to leave the theater and take up a position at court. At first he was styled a royal historiographer, meaning effectively that he became a librarian with the responsibility of research and writing. Once he was elected to the culturally all-powerful Académie française, he became the leading molder of France's artistic life.

Throughout the 1690s Racine was given a series of positions of increasing importance in the royal household. The wife of Louis XIV, Madame de Maintenon, persuaded Racine to write two more plays to be performed by students at the crown-sponsored school for girls at St.-Cyr, just outside Versailles. He chose as his subject matter the Biblical stories of *Esther* (1689) and *Athalie* (1691). Ill health forced Racine's retirement from court in 1697, and he died two years later, on April 21, 1699, probably of liver cancer.

PLOT SUMMARY

Act 1

SCENE 1

Orestes arrives at the court of Pyrrhus in Epirus in Northwestern Greece and meets his friend Pylades. He quickly reveals to Pylades that the real reason he is there is because he is still in love with his cousin Hermione, Pyrrhus's fiancée, and is contemplating kidnapping her to marry her himself. Orestes is also in Epirus at the behest of Menelaus, the king of Sparta, and the other Greek kings to demand that Pyrrhus surrender the Trojan prince, Astyanax. The Greeks had believed Astyanax had been killed during the sack of Troy, but his mother, Andromache, saved him. Although Pyrrhus is engaged to Menelaus's daughter Hermione, he is in love with Andromache and wants to use the life of her son to blackmail her into returning his affection. Pylades advises Orestes that he is better off if he fails to get the child. The implication is that

MEDIA ADAPTATIONS

- Many of Racine's plays were adapted as operas by contemporary French composers such as Lully and Rameau, but *Andromache* had to wait until 1780 to be set to music by André-Ernest-Modeste Grétry. This little-known opera was recorded for the first time in 2010 by H. Niquet conducting Le Concert Spirituel.

- One of Gioachino Rossini's few tragic operas, the 1819 *Ermione* is also an adaptation of Racine's *Andromache*.

- Jacques Rivette's 1969 film *L'Amour fou* follows the disintegrating marriage of a theater director and his wife/leading lady during the rehearsals for a production of *Andromache*.

if Pyrrhus does not satisfy the demands of the other Greek kings, he will become an outlaw and leave Hermione free for Orestes, who has loved her for years.

SCENE 2

Orestes demands that Pyrrhus surrender Astyanax to the Greeks. Pyrrhus refuses but grants Orestes permission to visit his cousin Hermione.

SCENE 3

Achilles's friend Phoenix acts as counselor to Pyrrhus. He reminds the king that if Orestes makes a play for Hermione, it might prove inconvenient, but Pyrrhus does not care. In fact, he wishes Orestes would abduct his cousin. That would make one less thing for him to worry about.

SCENE 4

Pyrrhus has a brief talk with Andromache while she is on her way to see her son. She is allowed only a brief daily visit. Pyrrhus boasts that he is risking war with the Greeks for the sake of her son. Will that not make her love him? If only she will love him, he will rebuild Troy for her and make her son a king, but there is nothing left for her but the memory of the dead. She indulges no longer in such fantasies. Andromache tells Pyrrhus he should go

to Hermione and boast of burning Troy and of his father killing Hector, saying that "these don't sicken her." Then Pyrrhus switches tactics and concludes that if Andromache will not love him, he must hate her and will turn Astyanax over to the Greeks after all. Andromache explains that would suit her perfectly well since she would kill herself and be reunited with her husband and child in death. Pyrrhus relents and sends her on her way, leaving the situation unresolved.

Act 2

SCENE 1

Hermione is awaiting the arrival of Orestes with her maid, Cleone. In their conversation, Hermione reveals that she is the one who sent a message to her father, Menelaus, telling him that Astyanax is still alive. She has received orders from her father in return that if Pyrrhus does not surrender the child to the Greeks, Hermione herself is to leave with Orestes because Pyrrhus would soon be attacked by the Greeks. Hermione further reveals that as much as she loves Pyrrhus because of his service in restoring the honor of her family, she is now growing angry with him over his insult to her own honor in preferring Andromache. She is willing to transfer her affection to Orestes.

SCENE 2

Orestes meets with Hermione and briefly tells her of his recent adventure. He was sent by the god Apollo to Tauris in Scythia (the Ukraine) to retrieve a statue of Artemis. He tells her also that Pyrrhus is refusing to turn over Astyanax. Hermione condemns Pyrrhus as a traitor and suggests that she might look more favorably on Orestes now that a marriage with Pyrrhus has become impossible. Orestes, who knows nothing of Menelaus's orders to his daughter, asks that she return to Greece with him. She refuses, claiming she must stay until either Pyrrhus sends her away or her father orders her to leave.

SCENE 3

In a soliloquy (a speech in which a lone character speaks aloud to the audience, explaining what he/she is thinking), Orestes decides to take Hermione away with him. He believes that Pyrrhus, who is in love with Andromache, can be easily convinced to send Hermione away from his court.

SCENE 4

Orestes encounters Phoenix and Pyrrhus, who has reconsidered his earlier plan and has decided to surrender Astyanax and immediately marry Hermione with Orestes as the witness.

SCENE 5

Pyrrhus confides to Phoenix that he has grown to hate Andromache for her treatment of him. He saw how unmoved she was by his offer to protect Astyanax's life even at the cost of war with Greece, so now he is done with her. Phoenix congratulates his king for finally breaking free of Andromache's spell but has doubts when Pyrrhus suggests immediately going to see her again to taunt her with his new decision. Phoenix fears that if Pyrrhus sees her again, the flames of love will flare up.

Act 3

SCENE 1

Orestes informs Pylades that he intends to kidnap Hermione rather than see her married. He orders Pylades to leave so that no guilt in the matter will attach to him, but Pylades volunteers to take charge of the matter, claiming that he knows the layout of the palace better than Orestes and so will be able to devise the abduction. Orestes dispatches him to brief his bodyguard of Greek soldiers about their plan.

SCENE 2

Orestes meets with Hermione, who has already found out about Pyrrhus's reversal. She now seems content to love Pyrrhus as she always had. Orestes tells her nothing of his plan to abduct her, seeing that she probably would not be willing to go along with it.

SCENE 3

Hermione dismisses Cleone's suggestion that Pyrrhus is simply bowing to the military threat from Greece. Hermione is certain that Pyrrhus, who captured Troy when the other Greeks could not, has nothing to fear from war with them and must have truly fallen in love with her at last.

SCENE 4

Andromache comes to remind Hermione that at one point during siege of Troy, the Trojans were ready to kill Helen, Hermione's mother, so angry were they over their predicament, but Andromache intervened and saved her. She begs Hermione to intervene now with her father or with Pyrrhus to save Astyanax. Hermione says Andromache must persuade Pyrrhus; if she does, Hermione will intervene with her father on behalf of Pyrrhus and the child.

SCENE 5

Cephisa, Andromache's maid, repeats Hermione's advice.

SCENE 6

Andromache makes a final appeal to Pyrrhus for mercy for Astyanax.

SCENE 7

Pyrrhus relents and tells Andromache he is ready to break his word to Orestes and save Astyanax, but she must marry him immediately place of Hermione.

SCENE 8

In conversation with Cephisa, Andromache lists all the reasons she has to hate Pyrrhus: the death of her husband at his father Achilles's hands, the murder of her father-in-law Priam by the Greeks when he sought refuge at an altar, and the first time she saw Pyrrhus himself covered with Trojan blood from the massacre at the end of the siege. In spite of all of this, she comes within a hair's breadth of sending Cephisa to Pyrrhus to tell him she accepts his proposal.

Act 4

SCENE 1

It seems to Cephisa that Andromache has undergone some kind of paranormal experience with Hector's ghost that has made her relent and look forward to life with Pyrrhus. Andromache explains that Hector's spirit has indeed inspired her to marry Pyrrhus on the condition of his first swearing to protect Astyanax. Then, as soon as the oath is sworn and the marriage vows exchanged, she will kill herself, protecting her son and still honoring Hector's memory. She orders Cephisa not to kill herself, however, since she must teach Astyanax Trojan tradition as he grows up.

SCENE 2

Informed of Pyrrhus's decision to marry Andromache, Hermione summons Orestes. Cleone is frightened by how calm her mistress seems in the face of this turn of events.

SCENE 3

Stung by the insult of her fiancé Pyrrhus's wedding to a slave, Hermione tells Orestes that if he kills Pyrrhus for her, she will marry him. When he hesitates over the propriety and details of the killing, Hermione tells Orestes that if he cares nothing for her, she will assassinate Pyrrhus herself and then take her own life. Since it seems his uncle Menelaus and the other Greek kings would approve of punishing Pyrrhus for shielding Astyanax, Orestes agrees to kill him.

SCENE 4

Hermione reconsiders the matter and decides that the pleasure of taking revenge for Pyrrhus's insult with her own hands, staining them with his blood, is almost worth any sacrifice. At last she dispatches her maid, Cleone, to catch up with Orestes and tell him to make sure that Pyrrhus knows before he dies that he is being killed for Hermione's sake.

SCENE 5

Pyrrhus comes to Hermione and explains to her that love is a force too powerful to resist and that it is forcing him to act against all propriety and his own conscience. There is little lost by canceling their wedding, he thinks. If they had wed, they would both only have been doing their duty. Hermione rages at Pyrrhus that she indeed was and still is in love with him. She demands at least that she not have to witness the wedding.

SCENE 6

Phoenix advises Pyrrhus to do as Hermione says; the Greeks will take her side.

Act 5

SCENE 1

In a soliloquy, Hermione takes an inventory of her love and hate for Pyrrhus. She still hesitates over whether she wants him dead or not.

SCENE 2

Cleone reports to Hermione that Astyanax has been taken by Phoenix to a distant fortress for safekeeping and that the wedding is underway. Pyrrhus has no guards at the wedding ceremony, but Orestes still hesitates to act. He is anxious to please Hermione but just as anxious about the possible results of assassinating a lawful king and a man of some respect. Hermione determines that she will go and kill Pyrrhus herself.

SCENE 3

Orestes reports to Hermione that his soldiers have killed Pyrrhus, striking him down when he announced during the wedding ceremony that he recognized Astyanax as king of Troy. Hermione is grief-stricken and asks Orestes how he could have

done such a thing. Orestes reminds her that he was acting on her orders. Hermione responds that he should have recognized she was mad with jealously and restrained rather than obeyed her. Hermione blames Orestes for killing the man she loves and for making Pyrrhus love Andromache in the first place, rationalizing that Orestes's advice is what made Pyrrhus choose Andromache.

SCENE 4

In a soliloquy, Orestes questions his decisions. He has broken all of the laws of diplomacy and hospitality in killing his host, and now it seems he did it for nothing. He begins to feel his grasp on reality slipping away.

SCENE 5

Pylades comes to Orestes and explains that they must leave at once, since Andromache, now recognized as queen by the Epirites, is rallying them to take revenge on the Greeks who killed Pyrrhus. Pylades also reveals that Hermione went to Pyrrhus's body and killed herself. Orestes is completely given over to madness, believing himself to be tormented by the ghosts of Hermione and Pyrrhus and by the furies, goddesses who take revenge on those who have murdered unjustly. At last he faints. Pylades has the Greek soldiers take Orestes away but has no idea what to do if he has not returned to his senses when he recovers consciousness.

CHARACTERS

Andromache

Andromache is the widow of Hector, the prince of Troy. Hector was killed in battle by Achilles, Pyrrhus's father. After the capture of Troy by the Greeks led by Pyrrhus, she was made a slave and given to Pyrrhus as part of his booty from the sack of the city. Her son Astyanax, as the rightful heir to the throne of Troy, was to be killed by the Greeks to prevent him taking revenge once he grew up, but in Racine's play, Andromache arranged to switch Astyanax for another child and then took her son to the court of Pyrrhus in Epirus.

As Pyrrhus's captive in Epirus, Andromache is completely defeated and empty. She has seen her whole civilization destroyed and witnessed the death of her husband Hector and her father-in-law Priam with her own eyes. The only meaning her existence has now is to care for her son. For this reason Pyrrhus carefully regulates her contact with Astyanax since it is the only hope he has of controlling her. Pyrrhus tries to win her affection by telling her he has refused to surrender her son to the Greeks and, if she wishes, will endure war for her sake. He claims he will go so far as to rebuild Troy and crown Astyanax as king there, but Andromache has suffered too much loss to idly dream of gain she knows will never come. When the threat to her son's life finally makes her agree to marry Pyrrhus, she determines to kill herself as soon as Pyrrhus publically pledges to protect Astyanax: she cannot betray Hector's memory by marrying again. By the same token, once Pyrrhus is killed during the wedding ceremony, Andromache must fulfill the role of dutiful widow again and starts to organize the people of Epirus to take revenge on Orestes and the other Greeks who killed him.

Cephisa

Cephisa is Andromache's maid from her time as princess of Troy. Although Andromache is technically Pyrrhus's slave, she has been permitted to keep much of her former royal status and so still has her servant. Cephisa is unquestioningly loyal to her mistress, expecting to follow her even in death when Andromache plans suicide, but ready to obey her orders not to do so.

Cleone

In France in Racine's time, royalty was attended by servants who were themselves of noble birth (a lady-in-waiting). That historical circumstance provides the best context for understanding Cleone. She is clearly Hermione's servant, but they are also more or less on an equal footing socially. They also appear to be close friends; Hermione holds back from Cleone nothing of her difficulties and grants her every confidence. Cleone's capacity as a servant is demonstrated by her acting as a messenger between Pyrrhus and Hermione.

Hermione

Hermione is the daughter of Helen of Troy and Menelaus, the king of Sparta. She is the first cousin of Orestes, since their fathers were brothers and their mothers were sisters. Before Helen was kidnapped by Paris and before the Trojan war, it had been generally understood that Orestes and Hermione would eventually marry. The wedding of cousins was a very common marriage arrangement among Greek aristocrats. During the war, with both of her parents absent from Sparta, Hermione

grew up with Orestes at the court in Mycenae. However, Menelaus promised Hermione in marriage to Pyrrhus as a battlefield honor when he led the final successful attack on Troy. Hermione was completely smitten by Pyrrhus as a war hero and king and above all, perhaps, as a stranger. His rejection of her for Andromache is a terrible blow to her vanity and her very identity. She is unable to process the overwhelming emotions she experiences and cannot separate love and the desire for revenge. Once she goads Orestes into killing Pyrrhus, however, rather than her feelings being discharged as she had hoped, she is even more profoundly overwhelmed and kills herself.

Orestes

Orestes is the son of Agamemnon, the king of Mycenae and the commander of the Greeks during the Trojan war. When Agamemnon returned to Greece after the sack of Troy, his wife Clytemnestra murdered him because she had taken a lover. Orestes murdered his own mother to avenge his father. The Furies, divine entities that punish impiety like killing a parent, drove Orestes mad, but the goddess Athena deferred the punishment because she judged that his killing of Clytemnestra was (barely) just. Apollo nevertheless ordered Orestes to expiate his sin by traveling to Tauris (the Crimea) to steal and bring back to Greece a cult statue of Artemis made from a meteorite. Once there, he discovers that his sister Iphigenia, who had supposedly been sacrificed at the start of the Trojan war to appease the wrath of Artemis, had really been transported by that goddess from the altar (where a deer was magically substituted to be sacrificed in her place) to Tauris where she was made a priestess of Artemis in charge of the statue Orestes must take to Greece. Once they recognize each other as brother and sister, she helps him steal the statue, and they flee back to Greece. By the time of the play, Orestes had assumed his rightful place as king of Mycenae. It is in this capacity that he is sent as an ambassador to Pyrrhus.

Orestes is driven in every action he carries out in the play by his love for his cousin Hermione. He had thought he had been purged of it by hatred when Hermione was pledged to Pyrrhus because she so obviously preferred him, but the feeling returns. He is ready to kill Pyrrhus to win back Hermione's love. It is very likely that such an action would be approved by the other Greek kings, but Orestes nevertheless hesitates because of his awe of Pyrrhus as the son of Achilles, as a legitimate king, and as a man who has established his own military reputation by leading the final assault on Troy, in contrast to Orestes himself, who is so far lacking in the martial achievements required of Greek kingship. As if this conflict were not enough, Orestes finds all of his expectations betrayed when he actually kills Pyrrhus (or rather when he allows his men to kill Pyrrhus). He is so overwhelmed by Hermione's rejection and then her suicide that he has a kind of mental breakdown and completely collapses.

Orestes's future is left purposefully and brilliantly unresolved by Racine. However, in Euripides's version of the play and in Greek legend, Orestes succeeds in marrying Hermione and eventually expands his kingdom by conquering several other Greek cities near Mycenae.

Phoenix

Phoenix had been the best friend and charioteer of Pyrrhus's father Achilles during the Trojan war. His role in the play is quite limited and does not go far beyond advising Pyrrhus to act on the basis of reason rather than emotion.

Pylades

Pylades has been Orestes's friend from childhood and has acted as his helper in his quests to kill his mother and to steal the statue of Artemis from Tauris. He has no role in Greek myth apart from being Orestes's companion, and this is reflected in their names: *Orestes* means mountain, and *Pylades*, which means the plain, undoubtedly coined to make a contrasting pair. His role in the play is simply to faithfully carry out Orestes's orders. He arranges almost everything Orestes does, from the plot to kidnap Hermione to the assassination of Pyrrhus and the escape afterward. He is so thoroughly subordinated to Orestes that he can hardly imagine even taking the initiative to protect Orestes from himself if he does not recover his reason after the end of the play.

Pyrrhus

Pyrrhus (frequently known in sources outside of *Andromache* by his alternative name of Neoptolemus) is the son of Achilles, the greatest hero of the Trojan war who killed Hector, the husband of Andromache and the father of Astyanax. After Achilles's death in battle, Pyrrhus himself led the final attack on Troy. He is the king of Epirus, a wild and untamed land on the northwest margin of the Greek world (roughly equivalent in modern terms to Albania and adjacent areas of Greece).

Pyrrhus is the most mature and fully developed character in *Andromache*. He is confident in his abilities and the rightness of his actions. He disregards Orestes as a threat because he is, in comparison, immature and inexperienced. Pyrrhus's death is brought about, however, by the one factor of his personality that is not controlled: his passion for Andromache. It is not a tragic flaw in the classic sense that it arose from circumstances (like Oedipus not knowing who his parents were). It is instead almost a force that seizes Pyrrhus from outside, like divine possession; this is how desire was commonly seen in ancient Greece. On the face of it, there is little reason for Pyrrhus to prefer Andromache to Hermione, since she is older (at a reasonable guess, Pyrrhus could hardly be as old as twenty, while Andromache might be thirty or older), foreign, of a different class and social level, and most likely less attractive than her rival—Hermione is the daughter of the legendary beauty Helen of Troy, after all. However, we can look to Pyrrhus's psychology for reasons why he might so desire Andromache. As the killer of her husband in single combat, Pyrrhus's father Achilles would have naturally have had the rights to Andromache as booty if he had lived to see the Greek victory. Because of the war, Pyrrhus never knew his father. It may be that Pyrrhus sees in Andromache some sort of connection to his father.

THEMES

Revenge

The official reason for Orestes's journey to the court of Pyrrhus in Epirus is to demand the surrender of the child Astyanax to a committee of Greek kings for execution. The ancient Greeks lived by a code of vendetta (a system of exchanges of violent, vengeful acts). Although he is a young child, Astyanax is at the center of a web of revenge. His uncle Paris abducted the famous Helen, betraying the hospitality of Menelaus and insulting the whole Greek nation. Every prince in Greece had hoped to marry the beautiful Helen and, to keep the peace among them, had sworn an oath to guarantee her marriage to Menelaus, the King of Sparta. The Trojan war was thereafter fought by them all to avenge Paris's insult.

Astyanax, the infant heir to the throne of Troy, was supposed to have been killed at the sack of the city to complete the Greek revenge but

TOPICS FOR FURTHER STUDY

- The second wife of Louis XIV founded a school at Saint-Cyr, the first secular high school for girls in France. As part of her patronage of the institution, she persuaded Racine to write two dramas specifically for the students there to perform. Research the performance practices of the day and then perform a brief scene from Racine's *Athalie* for your classmates.

- Vengeance is a major theme of historical legends from all over the world, like the Indian *Mahabharata* or the Japanese *Tale of the Heiki*. Write a brief one-act drama based on one of these in the style of Racine, emphasizing an act of revenge.

- Your school probably has procedures for peer mediation for conflict resolution. There are also a large number of Web sites and books devoted to that topic. Read *Coping through Conflict Resolution and Peer Mediation* by Carolyn Simpson (Hazelden, 1998) or another book on the subject written for young adults. Present an overview to your class on how the mediation process works, and then organize a class discussion of how these techniques could have been used to prevent the tragedy in *Andromache*.

- Racine presents the wedding of Pyrrhus and Andromache as happening more or less the way weddings were conducted in seventeenth-century France, except in a Greek temple rather than in a Catholic church. Greek wedding ceremonies were actually quite different than modern ones. The Web site *Diotima: Materials for the Study of Women and Gender in the Ancient World* (http://www.stoa.org/diotima) contains a wealth of information on weddings in ancient Greece and guides to further materials, both electronic and in print. Use this resource to research Greek weddings, and then revise the last act of *Andromache* employing a more authentic type of Greek wedding.

also to keep him from growing up to take revenge on the Greek kings. After it was discovered that there was a switching of babies and Odysseus killed an imposter instead of Astyanax, the Greeks want Astyanax dead. Pyrrhus, the son of Achilles who killed Astyanax's father Hector, has the most to fear from the future vengeance of the Trojan prince if he grows up, yet he is protecting the child because he has fallen in love with its mother, Andromache, the wife of Hector who was made Pyrrhus's slave when Troy was destroyed. Pyrrhus's love for Andromache is an insult to his fiancée, Hermione, because it attacks her honor, that is, her status: he is not treating her in the way she is entitled to be treated as the daughter of the king of Sparta. Her reaction to this is outrage and anger, growing as the insult is repeated: "It's my honour that's at stake.... Allow my anger time and room to grow." The pent up anger can only be released by revenge, violence that will redress the insult to status. Conversely, Hermione's love for Pyrrhus found its origin in the restoration of status he provided to her family's honor when he took revenge on their behalf by leading the final assault on Troy. Vengeance finally becomes tragedy when the violence it fuels grows larger than the original insult, leaving all the main characters of *Andromache* dead or mad.

Love

The true reason for Orestes's journey to the court of Pyrrhus in Epirus is his obsessive love for his cousin Hermione. She was given in marriage to Pyrrhus, the son of Achilles, by her father Menelaus, the king of Sparta (Orestes's uncle), in token of gratitude for Pyrrhus's role in the final destruction of Troy. Orestes is quite madly in love with her and, as her first cousin, might have expected to marry her in the normal course of aristocratic Greek society. Although Pyrrhus and Hermione are betrothed, Pyrrhus has not gone through with the marriage because he is in love with his slave Andromache, the former princess of Troy. Because he is the son of the man who killed her husband Hector, Andromache can do nothing but despise Pyrrhus. In the Greek conception, love is not a pleasant, constructive emotion. When Orestes describes his love to Hermione, it is in terms of the suffering and dishonor it has caused him:

> If I love...haven't I sworn and lied;
> Escaped and then come back; praised you and
>   spoken ill;
> Despaired and wept; indeed, am weeping still.

*Painting depicting Andromache mourning
Hector (Jacques Louis David)*

Love is like a spell cast by black magic that
tortures its victims until they yield. Pyrrhus tells
Andromache that because of his love for her, he
is "burnt by fiercer flames than any that I lit"
when burning Troy. The terrible pain and compulsion of love drives the plot of *Andromache* to
the same tragic end as revenge.

STYLE

Classical Drama
During the course of the fifth century BCE in
Athens, drama evolved from a simple song competition to a highly perfected theatrical form
with the qualities associated today with drama
in the broader sense (like Shakespeare's), opera,
and ballet. This was stimulated by an annual
dramatic festival in Athens, viewed by most of
the male population of the city, in the specially
built Theater of Dionysus. The victors gained
enormous prestige. Hundreds of plays were written in that century by dozens of playwrights.
Today fewer than forty complete plays exist,

the ones canonized by the critical taste of the
Byzantine Empire in the Middle Ages. More
than half of these are by Euripides, including
the *Trojan Women* and *Andromache*, the main
sources for Racine's *Andromache*.

Over the course of their competitive careers,
the Greek dramatists developed certain stylistic
constants that are called the dramatic unities.
After the period in which drama flourished, the
philosopher Aristotle wrote *Poetics*, in which he
codified the stylistic elements implicit in the plays
themselves. The action of a play is to take place in
no more than three physical locations in the same
city or even the same building (to accommodate
the sets and stage available in Athens). It is to take
place over the same time as that in which the play
is actually performed. No more than three principal characters are to be on stage at one time,
because that was the number of actors allowed
by the rules of the dramatic competition (each
actor played several different roles in various
scenes).

The Roman playwright Seneca, five hundred
years after the Greek dramatists, made a new creation based on their work. His plays had the same
subject matter as Greek drama, drawn from legendary history, and followed the dramatic unities,
but were not meant to be performed on a stage.
Rather they were read in an artistic salon, by a
group of like-minded friends interested in literature and theater. Racine drew on both Seneca and
the Greeks, more heavily favoring Seneca. Compared with his contemporary French playwrights,
who created a theater of baroque grandeur far
more elaborate than the Greek originals, Racine
had little interest in the theatrical art of staging his
plays, though they were indeed staged in full performances. He followed the dramatic unities even
more closely than did the Greek dramatists, but at
the same time, he followed Seneca in using rhetoric
to explore the psychology of his characters.

Baroque
The Renaissance was as much a change in attitude toward classical antiquity as it was a rediscovery of a forgotten past. This is least true of
drama, however, where the impact of the classical created something entirely new, especially in
France. The dramatic stage in Paris was still, at
about 1500, dominated by medieval genres and
works. Plays were either farce (slapstick comedy
with other purely ridiculous elements) or mysteries (reenactments of scenes from the Bible,

especially the execution of Jesus). The audience consisted of the common people of the city. In the early sixteenth century, the small body of surviving ancient Greek plays (newly reintroduced to western Europe) began to circulate among scholars and to be produced in the original Greek, which could only be understood by the most educated class. Gradually the plays began to be performed in French translations, and playwrights began to write highly derivative imitations of them in French.

After about 1600, new playwrights began to emerge who integrated Greek drama, the Latin drama of Seneca, and the theoretical criticism of Aristotle and Horace to create a mature artistic conception that resulted in new plays of great artistic importance. The evolution of French drama can be compared to the development of opera in Italy (also a reaction to the rediscovery of Greek drama) and to the emergence of Shakespeare and the other Elizabethan dramatists (though they were never so strictly classical as were playwrights of the French school). The entire cultural style of the seventeenth century is now called baroque. In drama, this meant a new emphasis on spectacular visual theatricality, something that did not interest Racine. However, Racine's work exhibits other baroque characteristics, such as in his language. Racine expresses the deep, possibly destroying, emotion that is the necessary element of drama in a precise and ordered structure of language and rhetoric more elegant than perhaps any other playwright. In all of his plays, Racine uses a vocabulary of only about eight hundred words (compare Shakespeare's vocabulary of about thirty thousand words, the largest of any English author). This limited vocabulary forced his plays to unfold with a pattern and a repetitiveness that find parallels in the repeated and elaborated forms of baroque music and architecture.

HISTORICAL CONTEXT

Classical Sources

In the introduction to the published edition of *Andromache*, Racine cites as his main sources Seneca's *Troades* (*Trojan Women*) and the second book of Vergil's *Aeneid*. This is odd, since at the most obvious level of plot, Racine's play follows, with some divergence, Euripides's *Andromache*. Most likely Racine meant that he aimed at the same

kinds of introspection and rhetorical structure that Seneca achieved. However, it is interesting to note the divergence of Racine's plot from that of Euripides. In the ancient version, Menelaus himself comes to take revenge on Andromache, perhaps because, as king of Sparta, he symbolizes Athens's rival in the then ongoing Peloponnesian war and makes a dramatic choice for the villain. Astyanax was truly killed at Troy, and now Menelaus wishes to kill Andromache and Molossus, her son by Neoptolemus (Pyrrhus). Andromache is tormented by Hermione, who is already married to Neoptolemus, with the accusation that the Trojan woman is making her sterile through witchcraft. Peleus, Neoptolemus's grandfather, intervenes to save Andromache and her son from Menelaus, but Orestes arrives (only at the end of the play) to announce that he has killed Neoptolemus (offstage) in Delphi. He then carries Hermione off. The goddess Thetis descends from heaven and decrees that the royal dynasty of Epirus will be founded by Molossus.

These differences are to be accounted for, not by Racine following any other source, but by his own invention. The legendary materials that the Greek dramatists worked with were considered by them to be essentially historical. The historiographical revolution that would remove the legendary Greek past from the realm of history belongs to the nineteenth century, but Racine felt the same freedom as his Greek and Roman predecessors to reshape the legendary material to fit his dramatic needs.

The Court of Louis XIV

Louis XIV recreated the early modern state as a system in which the king had absolute power, exercising more direct control over social institutions than at any time since the Roman Empire. It was characteristically baroque for the monarch to use art to support royal ideology. One part of this reform entailed the patronage, and therefore the control, of every form of artistic expression and especially in the creation of taste among the nobility and the populace at large. Louis XIV was responsible for the expansion of powers and influence of the Académie française, which to a large degree placed Racine, as its most influential member, as the leader of artistic development of France. Louis XIV's patronage of neoclassical drama over older medieval forms of drama that earlier French rulers had encouraged and even participated in fostered the development of the baroque style. His support for opera was even

COMPARE & CONTRAST

- **Bronze Age:** The aristocratic culture described in Greek drama is obsessed with honor; attacks against honor often flare up into violence.

  1660s: Aristocratic culture is still organized around concepts of personal honor; dueling is common.

  Today: Personal identity in Western culture is not based on honor, and insults do not routinely lead to murder as retaliation.

- **Bronze Age:** Citizens of defeated cities are routinely enslaved; Greeks even enslave other Greeks.

  1660s: Slavery is essentially limited to plantation agriculture as practiced in the Western and Arab worlds; slaves generally come from sub-Saharan Africa.

  Today: While slavery is officially outlawed throughout the world and does not exist in Western countries, slavery still exists, especially in Africa and Asia.

- **Bronze Age:** In aristocratic culture, marriages reflect alliances between families and have nothing to do with romantic feelings;

women in particular have little choice in their marriage partners.

1660s: Aristocrats in Western countries still practice arranged marriages for royal, political, and economic advancement.

Today: The ethos of Western culture is no longer aristocratic, and the most common reason for marriage is romantic love between individuals.

- **Bronze Age:** Marriage is a private affair between two families with no clergy involved. The wedding ceremony takes place in the bride's father's house between the father and his new son-in-law, after which the bride is given to the groom, and the new couple goes to his house.

  1660s: Weddings are solemnized by the marrying couple in church with a priest (an arrangement Racine projects back into the Greek era).

  Today: Many weddings are still conducted in churches, but a secular alternative exists with a judge or magistrate acting to marry the couple.

---

more important, especially in encouraging its spread outside of Italy. Louis XIV's patronage created a truly French baroque drama and opera and resulted in the invention of the modern form of ballet (based on the ancient mime in the same way opera was based on ancient drama).

CRITICAL OVERVIEW

Long neglected as a mannerist (with an exaggerated or artificial style) dramatist of historical interest only in the English-speaking world, Racine was rediscovered in the twentieth century as his depiction of intense emotion came to be perceived as realist drama. Along these lines, Roland Racevskis, in *Tragic Passages*, suggests that the empty shadow

of the generation of the Trojan War that the characters of *Andromache* try and fail to fill suggests Racine's own understanding of himself as an imitator, both of older French dramatists of his generation as well as of the ancients. Roland Barthes, in *On Racine*, sees this same gap between the old and new generation as space in which individual identify can be created. John Campbell, in *Questioning Racinian Tragedy*, uses *Andromache* to attack the old favorite contention of French scholarship that Racine's tragedy is particularly related to the Jansenist sect to which Racine's teachers belonged, but which he repudiated as an adult.

The remarkable depth of biographical information available about Racine with respect to his writings is demonstrated by a series of recent works concentrating on his annotation in his

Engraving of Orestes, son of Agamemnon (Philippe Chery)

WHAT DO I READ NEXT?

- Racine's plays suitable for high school students, *Esther* and *Athalie*, are not as often read today as some of his others but are available, among other places, in the second volume of the Bohn's Library translation of Racine from 1897, available online at Google Books.

- The play generally considered Racine's masterpiece, *Phèdre*, has been often translated, notably in 1998 by prominent English poet Ted Hughes.

- The four volumes of *The Actor's Molière* (1987–1992) present an anthology of the most popular plays by Molière, one of Racine's most important contemporary French dramatists.

- Ronald W. Tobin's 1999 *Jean Racine Revisited*, Volume 878 in Twayne's "World Authors" series, provides a general introduction to Racine and his work.

- Ronald W. Tobin's 1971 study *Racine and Seneca* traces the thematic and verbal similarities between Racine and his Roman model Seneca.

- The Japanese novelist Yukio Mishima's *Five Modern Nō Plays*, translated by Donald Keene in 1957, combine extreme emotional realism with the eruption of violent dramatic impulses to achieve an effect similar to Racine's tragedies.

own copies of Greek literature, for example, Susanna Phillippo's 1996 article in *L'Antiquité classique*, as well as her later monograph *Silent Witness*. In the latter she confirms Racine's express discounting of Euripides's *Andromache* as an important source for his own *Andromache* and finds hints that Racine widely looted Greek literature for inspiration for his own play, including Euripides's *Medea* and *Children of Hercules*.

CRITICISM

Bradley A. Skeen

Skeen is a classics professor. In the following essay, he analyzes Andromache *in the light of Freudian literary theory.*

That there is a deeper meaning in Racine's *Andromache* that can be revealed by holding the text up the mirror of Freudian psychoanalysis has been suggested by critics, including Roland Barthes and Mitchell Greenberg. Sigmund Freud is a very misunderstood student of human psychology. Many people reject, for example, his theory of the Oedipus complex out of a sense of moral outrage. Who, indeed, would not be outraged if he were baldly told that he wanted to murder his father and sleep with his mother? But is it so shocking to learn, with a more subtle understanding, that identity can only be formed first by using one's father (or better to say the parent of the same gender) as a model, and then by cutting oneself off from that model to develop as an individual being? That is the 'murder' that every child must commit. Is it too outrageous to

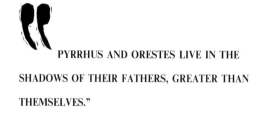

PYRRHUS AND ORESTES LIVE IN THE SHADOWS OF THEIR FATHERS, GREATER THAN THEMSELVES."

learn that the intense psychic energy that drives the personality in infancy must be used to form a bond with the mother who is the infant's source of food and life, and that later this same instinct is refashioned to ensure the continuity of life to form a bond with a lover? In short, there is a terrible confusion between the sometimes purposefully outrageous and revolutionary statements of Freud that form a popular conception, and his more subtle understanding of human psychology that can become a basis for understanding human art.

In "Totem and Taboo" Freud elaborates on the Oedipus complex. Freud imagines (based on what was then known of the lives of apes) the lives of the earliest human beings living in a band or horde consisting of a patriarchal leader, his wives, and their children. Once the male children approach adulthood, the patriarch kills them or drives them off: "One day the brothers who had been driven out came together, killed and devoured their father and so made an end to the patriarchal horde." Because the self-identities of the band of brothers were based on that of the father, they feel guilt at the murder they have committed. They punish themselves by refusing to take their sisters and mothers as wives. Freud told this rather fantastic tale in a effort to explain the origin of the universal taboo against incest and to historicize the Oedipal complex.

This story is so fantastic that it is hard to know how to approach it. It is certainly unrelated to the development of the human species as a historical fact, inasmuch as all animals scrupulously avoid incest for perfectly good genetic reasons (based on the genetics of Gregor Mendel, which by the time Freud was writing in 1913 were being integrated into the theory of evolution) with no need for an explanation in human psychology. Although it does rarely occur that a dominant male chimpanzee is killed by a group of younger apes (not necessarily his sons), the story is best considered a myth or "romance" that expresses an important idea in allegorical form. It tells, with all the force of literary art, the truth that children establish their identities through individuation, making a break with their parents to become their own beings. The Greeks too, as well as Racine, used myth to express truth in a manner more forceful and beautiful than plain statement. Barthes, in *On Racine*, says of the myth in "Totem and Taboo" that "such a history, even if it is only a 'romance' is the whole of Racine's theater" and, most of all, the whole of *Andromache*.

Pyrrhus and Orestes live in the shadows of their fathers, greater than themselves. Their fathers were the main protagonists of the Trojan War and died in it or because of it. For the sons, the Trojan War stands for the deaths of their fathers. Their own accomplishments are by no means meager, but they are dwarfed by what came before them. Pyrrhus may have led the final assault on Troy, but he is not the greatest warrior who ever lived: Achilles killed Hector in the climactic battle of the *Iliad*; Pyrrhus killed Priam, an old man—a man his father spared—cowering under the vain protection of the gods at an altar. Orestes tells Pyrrhus he is:

> Achilles's son, the conqueror of Troy.
> The father brought Prince Hector tumbling down
> His son with equal daring took his town.
> True son to a true Greek

This is courtier's flattery, Orestes telling his host what he wishes were true. No one could deny that Orestes's expedition to Tauris was noteworthy, but his father Agamemnon led the expedition to Troy, the greatest event in human history. As sons they are doomed to be mere ciphers compared with their fathers. With their fathers dead, all they can do is to struggle to take their place, a struggle to which they are terribly unequal.

Here the critic hears the objection that Oedipus killed his father; Orestes and Pyrrhus honored theirs. It is true that Orestes's father was killed by his mother, and then Orestes killed his mother and her lover, Aegisthus, in revenge. However, at the time of the vendetta, Aegisthus was the husband of Orestes's mother and reigning as king of Mycenae. How could there be a better substitute for Orestes's father? But Pyrrhus? Pyrrhus never met his father and surely completed his father's life's work, the destruction of Troy? Of course the younger men identify with their fathers after their murders. Orestes introduces himself to Pyrrhus by saying, "let me tell you first how proud I am to represent" the kings of Greece, his father's peers. But again, does Pyrrhus not identify with his father? In a very strange way, he admits to himself that he is going "against my father / Against myself." In fact he is driven by some strange force inside of himself, a force he calls love for Andromache, to become more and more his father's foe. His father worked to destroy Troy, but Pyrrhus labors to resurrect it. He

> does not recollect
> His father was Achilles; disavows
> His father's deeds; undoes them.

He struggles to become the husband of Andromache and the father of Astyanax. He struggles to become Hector, Achilles's hated enemy who fought a duel to the death with him. Pyrrhus is fighting to kill his father's memory. Loving Andromache is just one facet of the identity Pyrrhus is trying to mimic despite himself. He seems on the surface the most self-possessed and mature of all the characters in the play, but really is he more deeply controlled by his unconscious than any of them. His wavering back and forth in the decision to surrender Astyanax or not represents his inner struggle to forge his own identity, not to become merely his father's killer.

Andromache recognizes what Pyrrhus is doing. He weds her, adopts Hector's son, and, finally, he dies. To her mind, disturbed by grief, this last act is a vital one. Once Pyrrhus is dead, Andromache is able to accept Pyrrhus as her husband and is able to love him. Only when he has made the final step of identification with Hector, "Andromache ... now does for Pyrrhus / All a devoted widow ought to do." She sets out to avenge Pyrrhus as she never could Hector. For her, Pyrrhus became her husband in his mimicry of the dead generation.

Orestes also identifies himself with those who have died before him. At the moment when Hermione seems to have surrendered herself to him, when she swears to be his if he will avenge her against Pyrrhus's insult to her honor, Orestes responds to her very strangely:

> Then let's go
> And set all Greece ablazing, as before;
> You will be Helen, Agamemnon I;
> We'll put them through the sufferings of Troy,
> And be as famous as our fathers were.

In practice Orestes means to take Hermione as his wife, but his comparison makes no sense. Agamemnon did not wed Helen. What turmoil would follow a match between the younger pair? Pyrrhus snubbed the kings of Greece. They will

not be outraged that Orestes killed him; instead they will congratulate him. Orestes is Hermione's cousin, a powerful king in his own right, and now he has accomplished a heroic exploit in assassinating the traitor. He was practically engaged to Hermione before. The world would not be set ablaze by their marriage. It would not even raise an eyebrow. The thing that seems so thrilling and so forbidden to Pyrrhus is rather for him to become his father and Hermione to become her mother. To become them is to replace them. To kill them.

The Greeks felt guilt over the enormity of the crimes that were committed when Troy was sacked. As the god Poseidon says in the introduction to Euripides's *Trojan Women*, the Greeks destroyed sacred altars and ended a good deal of worship of the gods. They killed Priam, the patriarch of Troy, at an altar he sought out for sanctuary. How can they expect not to be punished? The murder of Agamemnon upon his return home and the wandering of Odysseus and the extinction of his entire contingent of soldiers and sailors were part of that punishment. Now the anxiety that the Greeks feel over their own crime is concentrated on the single object of Astyanax. To the Greeks nothing else is imaginable except that he will grow, rebuild Troy, and take revenge by destroying Greece, the only punishment appropriate for their crime in annihilating Troy. Pyrrhus dismisses the threat posed by a mere infant:

> Hector's son a danger?
> Might be the founder of a second Troy?
> Might take my life, because I let him live?
> You carry caution to extremes, my Lord.

Now that Pyrrhus and Hector have killed their fathers and struck off on their own, they find they are too weak to become their own men. Death and madness are the prices they pay for their failure. Their struggle is one that everyone has to go through and in which everyone, except the dead and the mad, must succeed in some way to become fully adult, fully human. That is the struggle that Racine puts before the audience in *Andromache*.

Source: Bradley Skeen, Critical Essay on *Andromache*, in *Drama for Students*, Gale, Cengage Learning, 2011.

Sarah Hemming

In the following review, Hemming reports on the recent spike in popularity of Racine's work.

Portrait of Pyrrhus, son of Achilles (© INTERFOTO/
Alamy)

While one could scarcely say that Racine was
all the rage on the London stage, there has certainly been more of the 17th-century French tra-
gedian around of late. Cheek by Jowl recently
brought a superb all-French production of *Andromaque* to the Barbican, the stripped-down staging
delivering the play as a psychological study of
obsession, grief and guilt. Now Nicholas Hytner
tackles Phedre in a lean and beautifully sculpted
production that relishes the awful inexorability of
the disaster, and again finds psychological truth in
the play's remorseless gaze. Ted Hughes' 1998
translation does not opt for Alexandrine couplets,
but renders the text in a sinewy, visceral verse of
his own. It's not pure Racine, but it works in its
way. But what holds the production back, as yet,
is that Helen Mirren, as the doomed queen besot-
ted with her stepson, doesn't quite fill the part.

From the moment the curtain rises on Bob
Crowley's austere set, it is clear that there will be
no escape. Theseus's palace here is configured
from great cracked slabs of honey-coloured rock:
the ceiling looms over the characters like the forces
that will crush them. To the side of the stage is the
brilliant blue of the Mediterranean sky, suggesting
a tantalising freedom. The characters—men in

military trousers; women in floor-length robes—
could be from any age and any hot country where
the moral parameters for the sexes are different.
One of the strengths of Hytner's staging is the
subtle contrast between the men, who stride, and
the women, who scurry. Dominic Cooper's Hippolytus has a proud, aloof beauty and when
Stanley Townsend's commanding, burly Theseus
walks in, everybody quakes.

Mirren's Phedre blows about this space like a
leaf. Pale and drawn, she vividly presents a proud,
clever woman, furious that she has been unhinged
by desire. She is excellent at the detail: at Phedre's
undignified scrabbling for scraps of hope, her
biting self-criticism and her ashen resolve at the
end. But the full scale of the role eludes her: she
hasn't yet found the immense presence required
to hold the stage, and keep holding it, with the
horror of her predicament or to convince you that
she cannot escape her demented state.

Still the production does grip, as each twist of
the plot tightens the knot. And there are some
tremendous performances in the supporting roles,
particularly Margaret Tyzack as Phedre's wily old
nurse and John Shrapnel as Hippolytus's counsel-
lor, who excels in the difficult task of reporting the
young man's gruesome death.

Source: Sarah Hemming, "A Queen without Command,"
in *Financial Times*, June 16, 2009, p. 15.

William A. Mould
*In the following excerpt, Mould examines the role
of maternal love in* Andromache.

Insofar as any person controls the destinies of
the characters of *Andromaque*, it is the title heroine. Every movement she makes is magnified as it
causes an ever greater reaction in Pyrrhus, Hermione and Oreste. The decision she must make, to
marry Pyrrhus or to see her child die, is the only
real decision in the tragedy; all the other characters
should say with Oreste, "Je me livre en aveugle au
destin qui m'entraîne" (I, 1). Andromaque's choice
must be based on her view of her role as mother of
Astyanax, so it is important to understand what
her view is. Piercing through the veil which would
cloak Andromaque in motherly sentimentality,
we shall examine her apparent indifference and
cruelty to her son. We will then see that the marriage-suicide plan she discloses as an "*innocent
stratagème*" marks her surrender to the ignoble
concept of maternity proned by Pyrrhus and
Céphise. It is at this moment, when she seems to
unite her duty to Hector and her love for

> THERE IS AN EVOLUTION IN THE CHARACTER OF ANDROMAQUE; WHAT SHE FIRST REJECTS SHE FINALLY ACCEPTS, BECAUSE SHE HAS ALLOWED HER VERY ELEVATED CONCEPT OF MATERNAL LOVE TO BE INFLUENCED BY PYRRHUS AND CÉPHISE."

Astyanax, that she strays farthest from her own heroic, generous ideal of maternal love.

Maternal Andromaque is generally considered from one of two points of view. The most obvious interpretation holds that Andromaque is a "good" mother: tender, loving, protective, concerned for her son's safety, entirely virtuous—"la tendre mère du petit Astyanax," in the words of Marcel Gutwirth in *Jean Racine: un itinéraire poétique* (Montréal: Presses de l'Université de Montréal, 1970, p. 50). An opposing view typified by Roland Barthes in *Sur Racine* (Paris: Seuil, 1963), emphasizes her love for Hector, her coquetry, certain of her violent remarks, to the exclusion of any maternal sentiment whatever: "Andromaque n'est pas une mère, mais une amante." Barthes' Andromaque is a "bad" mother, totally unconcerned for her son: "ce n'est nullement sa maternité qu'elle consulte (et si elle l'avait consultée, aurait-elle hésité un moment?)." Either attitude is based on a preconceived notion, more modern than classical, of what a mother should be.

We propose an interpretation which would reconcile these two apparently disparate views, while placing Andromaque's maternal conduct in the context of the classical ethic. Her concept of maternal love is quite consonant with the heroic ideal of the seventeenth century. The aristocracy, deprived in the interim 1637–1667 of any real function, may well have begun to lose the practice of feudal virtue, but certainly retained at least a nostalgia for the *générosité* of preceding generations. The heroic and generous ideal of maternity held by Andromaque would have been readily apparent to Racine's audience; we must ascertain how closely in practice she approaches her ideal. Andromaque is more than a grieving mother, full of tender affection and sweet embraces for her child; there is nothing maudlin in her love. Some

readers insist upon finding vulgar sentimentality in her; others find her cruel because she lacks it.

A few moments of reflection will convince the reader or spectator that Andromaque often appears to be a remarkably cruel mother. For example, in her first scene (I, 4) she appears indifferent to her son's fate. She seems to care little for him, to be primarily concerned with saving herself from Pyrrhus. When Pyrrhus informs her of the Greeks' desire for Astyanax, her first reaction is disbelieving sarcasm: "Digne objet de leur crainte!" When the king offers his aid to her and her son, she flatly rejects it, thus putting Astyanax in greater danger. She even implies that Pyrrhus would have to save Astyanax in spite of her: "Malgré moi, s'il le faut, lui donner un asile." She seems to abdicate all responsibility for her son, even to oppose his safety. She refuses all offers of royal honors for herself and Astyanax; she is willing to condemn him to servitude and possible death, from what appears to be a loathing for Pyrrhus. However, when the king offers himself as a second father to Astyanax ("Je vous rends votre fils, et je lui sers de père") she expresses no shock or horror. Indeed, she later accepts him willingly in this function: "Leur haine va donner un père au fils d'Hector" (IV, 1).

... Most modern critics agree with Lucien Goldmann's observation in *Le Dieu caché* (Paris: PUF, 1955, p. 362), that "son espoir est fallacieux. Le caractère de Pyrrhus *ne le justifie en rien*. Il peut aussi bien, probablement même, livrer Astyanax aux Grecs pour se venger d'avoir été trompé." Andromaque is able to hope because she has partially blinded herself to Pyrrhus' true nature. At the same time, she is quite aware that he is capable of breaking his promise, as the contradictions in the speech demonstrate. Despite her statement, "Je sais quel est Pyrrhus. Violent, mais sincère," she has had ample evidence of his faithlessness. Pyrrhus has shown himself to be not only violent, but weak, vacillating, angry, cruel and devoid of any true sense of honor. Sincerity, which implies both a sense of honor and consistency of thought and action, must be foreign to him. Andromaque has based her decision on the false hope that Pyrrhus will act as she herself would act, and she is deceiving herself, although not altogether on the conscious level. Her suicide plan is the final example of her cruelty to her son, for she has condemned him to death, or a living death, while saving her own honor; she can now say that she has done all in her power to save her son. All future responsibility is transferred to Céphise and Pyrrhus. Her suicide appears as a supremely egotistical act.

However, it is not a lack of concern for Astyanax which characterizes Andromaque so much as a refinement of ethical principle. Immersed in the past, she considers her son primarily as "le seul bien qui me reste et d'Hector et de Troie" (I, 4). For Andromaque, Hector lives on not only in Astyanax, but in Andromaque herself; he is "un époux qui croit revivre en elle" (IV, 1).

The past is tied up with Andromaque's conjugal loyalty and maternal instinct, and it evokes the dominant chord of grief which pervades her role. Her very first speech emphasizes her sorrow:

> Je passais jusqu'aux lieux où l'on garde mon fils.
> Puisqu'une fois le jour vous souffrez que je voie
> Le seul bien qui me reste et d'Hector et de Troie,
> J'allais, Seigneur, pleurer un moment avec lui:
> Je ne l'ai point encore embrassé d'aujourd'hui. [I, 4]

These verses are usually taken as demonstration of Andromaque's maternal love, but their tone is harsh; they are directed more against Pyrrhus than toward Astyanax. The emphasis is on Andromaque's mourning of Hector and Troy, with Astyanax mentioned only in order to exclude Pyrrhus.

Again, we must burrow beneath an apparent contradiction to find an underlying unity in Andromaque's character. One senses quickly that Andromaque would prefer reunion in death with Hector to survival in Pyrrhus' court; only the need to protect Astyanax keeps her alive. The boy would seem to be an obstacle to her happiness, to her real personal goal:

> Sa mort avancera la fin de mes ennuis.
> Je prolongeais pour lui ma vie et ma misère;
> Mais enfin sur ses pas j'irai revoir son père. [I, 4]

But she must save her son, although this salvation will be on a different level from what the other characters expect of her: "Ce fils, ma seule joie, et l'image d'Hector? / Ce fils, que de sa flamme il me laissa pour gage" (II, 8). That, in summary, is both the statement and the rationale of her attitude toward Astyanax. He is both the mother's reason for living and the reason for her martyrdom: "O mon fils, que tes jours coûtent cher à ta mère!" (III, 8). Here we must recognize Andromaque's evolution within the play, both as a mother and as a widow. The oft-noted conflict between those two sides of her character is only an illusion propagated by Pyrrhus and Céphise, to the advantage of their anti-heroic, sentimental view of Andromaque's maternity. In reality,

Andromaque's loyalty to the memory of Hector is the source of her maternal strength. Her recollection of Hector's farewell reminds Andromaque of her responsibility to preserve Astyanax's honor and to serve as an example to the child:

> "Je te laisse mon fils pour gage de ma foi:
> S'il me perd, je prétends qu'il me retrouve en toi.
> Si d'un heureux hymen la mémoire t'est chère,
> Montre au fils à quel point tu chérissais le père."
> [III, 8]

The apparent struggle between the widow and the mother provides the opportunity for a sophisticated development within the character herself, culminating in an attempt to resolve the conflict in a highly personal concept of maternal love and duty. As Goldmann points out again and again in *Le Dieu caché*, Astyanax is not only "l'image d'Hector," he *is* Hector reborn. In Andromaque's mind, the son is a reincarnation of the father (see the description quoted above of her moments with Astyanax) who "m'aurait tenu lieu…d'un époux" (I, 4). Thus two apparently warring duties, of widow and of mother, are united. As long as she retains a clear perception of this convergence, Andromaque can resist the facile appeal to maternal sentimentality.

There are essentially two concepts of maternal love expressed in the play, one explicit, the other implicit. In his *Studies in French Classical Tragedy* (Nashville, Tennessee: Vanderbilt University Press, 1958, p. 299), Lacy Lockert comments: "The more Andromache loved Hector, the more precious should the life of their child have seemed to her, and the more readily should she have sacrificed any personal repugnances with the feeling that by the preservation of that child she could be most truly loyal to its father." Anti-heroic, sentimental, and counter to the prevalent generosity of the classical ideal, such is the explicit concept expressed by Pyrrhus and Céphise: a mother should be willing to sacrifice all for her child, including her virtue and her given word. A mother should be tender, loving, gentle, and protective. Pyrrhus' "blackmail" speech is an attempt to inspire this concept of maternal love in Andromaque; he feels that the interests of the child should overcome all obstacles: "nos ennemis communs devraient nous réunir" (I, 4). Céphise offers essentially the same arguments as Pyrrhus:

> Il suffit que sa vue
> Désormais à vos yeux ne soit plus défendue.
> Vous lui pourrez bientôt prodiguer vos bontés,
> Et vos embrassements ne seront plus comptés.
> Quel plaisir d'élever un enfant qu'on voit naître…
> [IV, 1]

This is basically a sentimental view of motherhood; it is certain to appeal to Andromaque, but is quite contrary to the maternal ideal she has set for herself. Pyrrhus, of royal birth but base character, expresses a concept of maternal love which is, in contrast to Andromaque's, vulgar and sentimental. Céphise, a mere confidante, echoes this commonplace attitude. These two characters assume that their view is the only viable one, and they simply do not understand Andromaque's *générosité*.

What is Andromaque's concept of maternal love? She considers her son an extension of herself and her husband, and is consequently trying to act for him as if she were the two parents. She must choose for Astyanax the generous action that she and Hector would choose for themselves. In Andromaque's eyes, she is not dragging Astyanax down into ruin with her when she refuses Pyrrhus' help, but rather pulling him up into a heroic universe where life and death are of little importance. This is why, in the first part of the play, she seems cold and cruel to her son; in reality, it is at those moments that she most nearly approaches her ideal of motherhood. This ideal is rooted in *générosité*; it is because she must be an example that Andromaque may not weaken, may not succumb to Pyrrhus. She equates herself with Hector; she must then show herself as noble and heroic as he. By this token, a generous deed is an example to Astyanax; a vulgar action is a negation of Andromaque's concept of motherhood. Like Rodrigue's, Andromaque's choice between duty and love is apparent, not real; the mother of Astyanax must choose honor above life, for herself and for her son.

This choice may appear horrible, but it is consistent with the concept of maternal love. Where Andromaque is not consistent is in compromising—at the very moment when she superficially appears most swayed by maternal love. Surrounded by Pyrrhus and Céphise, and influenced by her own normal affection for her son, she vacillates. Her marriage-suicide plan is a compromise not with Pyrrhus, but with her own heroic concept of motherhood. Had her plan succeeded, she would have placed Astyanax in precisely that equivocal position which she wished to avoid for both of them. For eventually, Astyanax, even if he survived, would realize "Que Pyrrhus est son maître, et qu'il est fils d'Hector" (I, 4). It is here that egotism is strongest in Andromaque, who says: "J'irai seule rejoindre Hector et mes

aïeux" (IV, 1). Saving herself, she has truly abandoned Astyanax and acted contrary to her principles.

There is an evolution in the character of Andromaque; what she first rejects she finally accepts, because she has allowed her very elevated concept of maternal love to be influenced by Pyrrhus and Céphise. She slowly lowers herself to their plane, and then chooses to die in order to escape the compromise. Although Andromaque is spared the necessity of carrying her plan to completion, the moral compromise has taken place. Despite the fate of Hermione, Oreste and Pyrrhus, *Andromaque* ends happily for the title character and her son. One might then say that the play is dubiously called a tragedy. But Andromaque does not survive unscathed; her tragedy is perhaps greater than mere death. It is the mother's sacrifice of her ideal, her debasement, her compromise which may be viewed as the moral tragedy of *Andromaque*.

Source: William A. Mould, "The 'Innocent Strategème' of Racine's *Andromaque*," in *French Review*, Vol. 48, No. 3, February 1975, pp. 557–65.

SOURCES

Aristotle, *Poetics*, translated by I. Bywater, in *The Complete Works of Aristotle: The Revised Oxford Translation*, Vol. 3, Bollingen Series LXXI, edited by Jonathan Barnes, Princeton University Press, 1995, pp. 2315–20.

Barthes, Roland, *On Racine*, translated by Richard Howard, University of California Press, 1992.

Campbell, John, *Questioning Racinian Tragedy*, University of North Carolina Department of Romance Languages, 2005, pp. 151–76.

Euripides, *Orestes, Iphigeneia in Taurica, Andromache, Cyclops*, translated by Arthur Sanders Way, William Heinemann, 1912, pp. 411–513, http://books.google.com/books?id=ti5JAAAAYAAJ&source=gbs_navlinks_s (accessed August 31, 2010).

Freud, Sigmund, "Totem and Taboo," in *The Standard Edition of the Complete Psychological Works of Sigmund Freud*, Vol. 12, translated by James Strachey, Hogarth, 1958, pp. ix –161.

Greenberg, Mitchell, *Racine: From Ancient Myth to Tragic Modernity*, University of Minneapolis Press, 2010, pp. 53–88.

Phillippo, Susanna, "The Legacy of Homer: The *Iliad* Annotations of Jean Racine," in *L'Antiquité classique*, Vol. 65, 1996, pp. 1–29.

———, *Silent Witness: Racine's Non-Verbal Annotations of Euripides*, European Humanities Research Centre, 2003, pp. 70–75.

Racevskis, Roland, *Tragic Passages: Jean Racine's Art of the Threshold*, Bucknell University Press, 2008, pp. 73–90.

Racine, Jean, *Andromache*, translated by Eric Korn, Applause Theatre, 1988.

Vickers, Brian, *Towards Greek Tragedy: Drama, Myth, Society*, Longman, 1973.

Maskell describes the circumstances of production of Racine's plays and provides an especially useful collection of contemporary illustrations of theatrical performance and the theatrical experience.

Vossler, Karl, *Jean Racine*, translated by Isabel and Florence McHugh, Frederick Ungar, 1972.
    Vossler provides a window into the world of traditional French Racine criticism.

FURTHER READING

Bushnell, Rebecca, ed., *A Companion to Tragedy*, Blackwell, 2005.
    The essays in this volume deal with ancient tragedy as well as its renaissance and modern reception.

Ciavolella, Massimo, and Patrick Coleman, eds., *Culture and Authority in the Baroque*, University of Toronto Press, 2005.
    This collection of essays explores the ways in which the arts interacted with political power in baroque Europe.

Maskell, David, *Racine: A Theatrical Reading*, Clarendon Press, 1991.

SUGGESTED SEARCH TERMS

Jean Racine

Jean Racine AND Andromache

Jean Racine AND drama

Andromaque OR Andromache

French baroque

Astyanax

Racine AND Corneille

Andromache AND Euripides

Trojan War

Totem AND Taboo

Doubt

2008 John Patrick Shanley wrote and directed the 2008 Goodspeed Productions film *Doubt*, which he adapted from his own award-winning 2004 Broadway play of the same name. The story centers on news stories concerning sexual relations between Catholic priests and boys under their care. Instead of repeating the events reported in the news, however, the film, as its title implies, focuses on the suspicions that such a horror is happening.

The story takes place in the 1960s, when such impropriety was not discussed openly. The main characters are nuns: the young, idealistic Sister James is eager to dismiss the circumstantial evidence against Father Flynn, but her superior, the cold, authoritarian Sister Aloysius, feels certain that Father Flynn is guilty. The film does not give any definitive evidence of Father Flynn's guilt or innocence, leaving viewers to consider the facts, to watch the characters' behavior carefully, and to decide for themselves whether abuse is being systematically ignored by the church and community or whether one nun's rigid moral code has driven her to make unfounded accusations.

The play, starring Broadway stalwarts Cherry Jones and Brian F. O'Byrne as Sister Aloysius and Father Flynn, was a whirlwind success, winning Pulitzer, Drama Desk, and Tony awards for the play and numerous prestigious awards for its actors. The film, with Meryl Streep and Philip Seymour Hoffman in the leads, was just as revered, with five Academy Award nominations

and nominations in all the major film competitions. Also noted by critics were the performances by Amy Adams as Sister James and by Viola Davis, who came to international prominence with a career-making performance, as the mother of the boy who may have been abused.

PLOT SUMMARY

Doubt begins with establishing shots, introducing viewers to the mood of the Bronx, New York, in 1964, and in particular to the serene atmosphere on the grounds of St. Nicholas Church. A man plays a zither, an ancient instrument, on the street corner, and Jimmy Hurley is awakened by his mother to go to church, where he will serve as an altar boy during mass. Interior shots show St. Nicholas to be ancient and imposing.

Jimmy is joined at the church by Donald Miller, who asks if Jimmy thinks he is fat, a question that leaves the boy perplexed. Together they prepare the wine and incense for the service.

The credits end with a sermon given by Father Brendan Flynn on the topic of doubt, the same sermon that begins the play on which this film is based. The sermon touches on issues of hidden shame. As Father Flynn speaks, Sister Aloysius patrols the aisle, casually giving a boy who is talking during the mass a smack on the head. As the priest finishes his sermon, Sister Aloysius has a thoughtful look on her face.

In the sacristy (a room where the church's sacred objects are stored) after the mass, Donald approaches the priest and says that he would like to be a priest. Father Flynn entertains the boy with a toy ballerina and then tells him the toy is for him to keep.

As the children line up outside the school, the camera follows young Sister James. She says hello to Father Flynn, who jokes with some of the children. Her admiration for him is clear, though the camera quickly shows Sister Aloysius looking on sternly. When one boy, William London, touches Sister James on the shoulder while talking to her, Sister Aloysius calls him out of line across a courtyard of children. Father Flynn jokes about her sternness to Sister James, calling her a dragon.

While Sister James teaches a class about civics, Sister Aloysius walks in, silencing the children's laughter. Sister Aloysius finds a boy listening to a transistor radio and takes him down to the office, leaving Sister James with a bemused look.

At dinner in the convent, Sister James witnesses Sister Aloysius stealthily helping Sister Veronica find her fork. She later explains that Sister Veronica will be retired by the parish if her blindness is discovered. Sister James is surprised by this act of kindness from the stern old nun. At the same dinner, Sister Aloysius raises the question of why Father Flynn chose to talk about doubt in his sermon. She tells the other nuns to be alert, but she refuses to say what she suspects.

Sister Aloysius looks around Sister James's room and gives her advice about how to handle misbehavior. She observes Father Flynn out in the courtyard, talking with Monsignor Benedict, which flusters her momentarily. Her concern is lost, however, as she goes on giving Sister James tricks for catching misbehaving children.

During basketball practice, Father Flynn gives the boys tips on the game. He then goes into a discussion about keeping one's fingernails clean, even if, like his, they are worn long. He walks around the circle to make each boy look at his long, groomed nails.

Dinner at the rectory, among the priests, is shown in contrast to dinner in the convent. The nuns eat in silence, but the priests' dinner is raucous, with smoking, drinking, joking, and background music.

While teaching a class, Sister James receives a phone call, telling her to send Donald Miller to the rectory. Later, while her students are receiving a dance lesson, she sees Father Flynn put Donald's T-shirt into his locker, and she becomes suspicious. She goes to talk to Sister Aloysius about Donald, uncomfortably describing Father Flynn as Donald's "protector." Sister Aloysius pauses. She is certain that something terrible has happened between the priest and the boy and demands to know everything that Sister James has seen between them. Sister James denies any certainty of improper behavior, even though Sister Aloysius tells her that she seems to know something. Sister James describes a time when Donald returned from the rectory with alcohol on his breath, which makes Sister Aloysius certain that a sexual relationship has begun between Father Flynn and the boy. With no priest to turn to for help, Sister Aloysius determines that they will have to stop Father Flynn themselves.

FILM TECHNIQUE

Dutch Angle

A Dutch angle, or canted angle, occurs when the camera films a scene slightly askew from the normal horizontal perspective. Because this angle became a popular device in mystery and crime films, its use is often associated with evil and menace. The Dutch angle is used in two notable scenes in *Doubt*. The first time is at the start of the courtyard meeting between Father Flynn and Sister James. He is smoking a cigarette and looking suspicious, and she asks him directly whether Sister Aloysius's accusations are true. They are filmed at angles away from each other. The angle gradually straightens as he convinces her of his honesty. The Dutch angle is used again when Sister Aloysius returns to the school after meeting with Mrs. Miller, as she walks up the hall to her office. In her office, she will meet Father Flynn and have a heated argument about the issue at the heart of this story, and the camera angle prepares viewers for the danger to come.

Low-Key Lighting

Most of this film takes place in shadowy interiors, lit by candles, desk lamps, and light through venetian blinds. Some of this is because the original Broadway play set most of its action within the somber offices of the St. Nicholas school or in the church. The low-key lighting is appropriate for this story, in which guilt may or may not be hiding in the shadows. Shanley draws attention to this during the discussion about the coming Christmas pageant: when Father Flynn suggests that one of the boys can dress like Frosty the Snowman and dance, Sister Aloysius yanks open the shade, blinding him with sunlight as she asks whether he favors one of the boys over the others.

This film also has outdoor scenes, such as discussions in the courtyard and establishing shots of the neighborhood. Still, the lighting is dimmed by a persistently cloudy sky, giving the film a muted feeling, a reminder that it takes place in the past, when expectations of behavior were different.

Two Shot

A two shot is a camera angle that frames two actors on the screen at one time. Films that are adapted from stage plays often tend toward heavy use of the two shot, since many plays concern the interplay of dialogue between two characters. In adapting *Doubt* to the screen, however, Shanley and his director of photography, Roger Deakins, thoroughly reworked the stage play. There are still many two shots, as this is a commonly accepted way of showing two characters conversing, but the camera moves fluidly while people talk, following the speaking character or the listening character without the other person in sight, so that the film does not feel like a stage production.

High Angle

Shanley films his characters from high angles several times in *Doubt*. A few times, the high angle is used to show characters looking down on others, such as when Sister Aloysius observes the friendly relationship between Father Flynn and Monsignor Benedict, or when she sees William London recoil from the priest's touch. The high angle takes in all of the action below and gives viewers the feel of having a bird's-eye view. Later in the film, when Sister Aloysius is changing the light bulb over her desk, Shanley uses a high angle again, showing the action from the point of view of the light fixture. This draws attention to the recurring symbolism of the light that burns out and sputters on periodically throughout the film.

Father Flynn is called to meet with Sister Aloysius. While waiting to see her, he sits on the bench outside her office with Tommy Conroy, a boy who talked in class, as if they are both naughty students. Sister Aloysius sends Conroy off with a punishment, but she has to wait for Sister James to arrive before formally meeting with the priest.

© *Photos 12 | Alamy*

Inside her office, Father Flynn sits at Sister Aloysius's desk and has tea served to him. She is amazed at his long fingernails and at the amount of sugar he takes in his tea. In their meeting, which is supposed to be about the upcoming Christmas pageant, Father Flynn upsets Sister Aloysius by suggesting that they might include some secular songs, to create a stronger bond with the parishioners. His friendly approach to the children is contrasted by her stiff, formal approach. Sister Aloysius raises the issue of how Donald, the school's only black student, will be used in the pageant, which allows her to mention the strange behavior Sister James observed after Donald came back from the rectory. Asked directly, she tells Father Flynn that Donald's behavior is the purpose of the meeting. As he prepares to leave, Sister Aloysius mentions the alcohol that Sister James smelled on the boy's breath. Father Flynn thinks for a moment and then explains that Donald had been caught by the school's handyman, Mr. McGuinn, drinking the altar wine. Out of embarrassment for the boy, he told no one about their meeting. When he is gone, Sister James says that she believes him, but Sister Aloysius does not.

Sister James thinks that her suspicions are based on personal dislike. Insisting that Sister James sit down, Sister Aloysius phones Donald's mother.

Father Flynn's next sermon in the church is a thinly veiled response to Sister Aloysius. He talks about an old woman who gossiped and then went to her parish priest because she felt guilty. The priest, a character he calls "Father O'Rourke," speaking for him with a broad Irish accent, tells her outright that she has been wrong for bearing false witness. In Father Flynn's story, the priest tells the woman to cut open a pillow and let the feathers scatter in the breeze. He then tells her to gather all of the scattered feathers up. When she says she cannot, he makes his point: the feathers that cannot be called back are like gossip.

Father Flynn meets Sister James in the church courtyard and chats casually with her. She says that her brother is sick, but she is not willing to leave her class to visit him. She asks directly whether "it" is true: she does not mention the accusation of child molestation, but she tells him that he knows what she is talking about. He pointedly denies it, but she is skeptical. Father

Flynn warns her that there are people who wish to kill kindness. She has been won over; as she walks away, she tells him that she does not believe the accusations against him.

Standing in the crowded school hall, Father Flynn is approached by a girl who says that she has to tell someone about the boy she is in love with. He smiles and tells her to tell the boy. Donald looks at the priest, but instead of approaching him, Father Flynn goes into an office. As he walks away, William London knocks Donald's books from his hands, and another child callously steps on the ballerina figurine Father Flynn had given him. The priest shows up. He helps Donald to his feet and hugs him as Sister James looks on. In her classroom, Sister James in uncharacteristically stern with her pupils, in particular with Donald. She sends one boy, Jimmy Hurley, to the principal's office for trying to answer a question she asked Donald.

Donald's mother arrives at Sister Aloysius's office, where the nun is listening to the radio she confiscated earlier. Mrs. Miller says that Donald was upset about being removed from altar boy duty; however, she feels that the punishment was just, since he was drinking altar wine. She tells Sister Aloysius that Donald's father beats him and has expected the boy to have more trouble as the first black child at St. Nicholas. Trouble has not occurred, she says, since Father Flynn is watching out for him. They are interrupted by a knock at the door: as Sister Aloysius sends Jimmy away, Father Flynn passes by and sees Donald's mother in the nun's office. He is clearly upset.

Sister Aloysius walks Mrs. Miller to work. When she suggests a problem with Donald, Mrs. Miller states that her only concern is with getting Donald through the school year at St. Nicholas so that he can go on to a good high school. Even as Sister Aloysius becomes more direct about her fears concerning the relationship between the boy and the priest, stating outright that Father Flynn may have made sexual advances, Mrs. Miller refuses to worry. She understands the issue, but she does not want any trouble, and she does not want Donald blamed for whatever happened. He is gay, she explains. He is in the Catholic school because the boys at the public school were so hateful to him that they would have killed him if he stayed. She is actually pleased that Donald has a man like Father Flynn to care about him.

When Sister Aloysius returns to her office, Father Flynn walks in behind her. She reminds him that there should be at least one more person in the room, for propriety, but he is upset and wants to know why Donald's mother was there. They have a loud, frank discussion about their troubles with one another. She thinks he is not fit to be a priest, while he thinks she is blocking the school's progress. When he asks why she has mistrusted him all along, she tells him that she understands people like him. Pressed for evidence, she explains seeing William pull away when Father Flynn touched him. This is what gave her the certainty she feels about Father Flynn's improper relations with the boys.

Father Flynn discusses having her removed, but Sister Aloysius tells him that she phoned his last parish. She did not speak to the pastor there, who would stand behind Father Flynn, but instead spoke to a nun. He points out that she has broken the correct chain of command, but she insists that she will not stop her inquiry, even if it means going against church orthodoxy. As Father Flynn insists that he has done nothing wrong and that he cares about Donald, she demands that he transfer out of the parish. She does not believe that he could ever truly regret his sins. As she leaves she tells him over her shoulder that he should cut his fingernails. Father Flynn, left alone, sits at her desk, opens his bible and takes out the flowers pressed in it, which he arranges carefully on the book's cover.

At a mass, Father Flynn gives his farewell sermon. He moves through the congregation, saying his good-byes to the church members. William looks knowingly at him, and Donald is near tears.

In the school, Sister Veronica decorates a manger scene for Christmas. Sister James, who had gone to Baltimore to visit her brother, returns to find Sister Aloysius on a bench in the snow-covered courtyard. Father Flynn has been moved to a higher position, Sister Aloysius explains, as pastor of a different church and its affiliated school, regardless of what she explained about the priest's behavior. She tells Sister James that Father Flynn left because she lied about someone at his old school: his resignation was his confession, in her view. Her certainty wavers, though. She cries and tells Sister James that she has doubts. Sister James moves forward to take her hands, as the camera backs away.

CHARACTERS

Sister Aloysius Beauvier

Sister Aloysius is played by Meryl Streep, in a performance that garnered nominations for several awards, including the Academy Award for Best Performance by a Leading Actress, the Best Leading Actress award from the British Academy of Television and Film Arts, and a Golden Globe Award. She won awards for best actress from the Screen Actors Guild and the Broadcast Film Critics Association.

Sister Aloysius is a complex character. As the principal of St. Nicholas School, she struggles to maintain discipline, forcing her pupils to pay attention to the rules. She is not shy about striking a student she thinks is misbehaving. Although she is merciless in her discipline of the young students, she is kind to old Sister Veronica, covertly doing what she can to help Sister Veronica keep her failing eyesight a secret.

Sister Aloysius can see the old ways she follows slipping away. She tries to teach young Sister James tricks for keeping her students in line, such as hanging a picture with a glass cover above the blackboard so she can watch students in its reflection as she writes. She disagrees with the young nun's intention to be more of a friend than a frightening oppressor to the children in her care. Viewers of the film cannot clearly see whether the disdain Sister Aloysius shows toward the idea of a modern, friendly church might be driving her to suspect Father Flynn, since her worldview is based on suspicion rather than acceptance.

Late in the film, viewers learn that Sister Aloysius was once married, during World War II, and became a nun after her husband died in Italy. Her difficult life might explain her bitter and suspicious nature. The same scene, though, shows a lighthearted side to her, as she finds herself hooked on listening to a transistor radio she has confiscated from a student: she is still able to feel a sense of wonder at technology, and she does not feel that using a radio that is forbidden to a student is hypocritical.

The plot of this film is driven by Sister Aloysius's certainty that Father Flynn is a sexual predator. Her certainty stems from having seen one boy pull away when touched on the arm by the priest. Reasonable explanations are given for Father Flynn's actions, and the mother of the boy he might be abusing says that the boy might be better off with the priest's attention. Still,

Sister Aloysius proclaims her certainty of the wrongdoing and her dedication to exposing it. It is only in the end, after Father Flynn is gone, that she privately and tearfully admits to Sister James that she has doubts.

Tommy Conroy

Tommy, played by Paulie Litt, is the boy who is caught listening to a transistor radio during class. He later waits on the bench outside Sister Aloysius's office, sitting next to Father Flynn as if they are both bad boys waiting for their punishment.

Father Brendan Flynn

Philip Seymour Hoffman's performance as Father Flynn also garnered nominations for an Academy Award, a British Academy of Film and Television Arts Award, a Golden Globe Award, and a Critics' Choice Award. Father Flynn is seen as a hearty and jovial soul. The children of St. Nicholas like him because he talks to them as a peer, joking around with them, but he is also willing to offer them advice. He coaches the basketball team, and, over juice and cookies, he fields the children's questions about love and sex. The other priests like him because he can be boisterous with them, smoking and drinking and telling funny stories. Sister James, the young nun, is inclined to like Father Flynn because he shares her progressive views about education, as implied in the discussion about the upcoming Christmas pageant, in which they both support the inclusion of a secular song such as "Frosty the Snowman" to give the show a lighthearted mood.

The film never definitively settles whether Father Flynn is sexually involved with any of the students. He is adamant in his denial of improper behavior, but Sister Aloysius merely waves away his denials as a sign that he has no conscience. In the end, he does not confess to having a sexual relationship with Donald Miller. Sister Aloysius takes his agreement to transfer out of the parish as a form of confession, but viewers learn that his move is a promotion, putting him in charge of an entire parish and school, where he will be accountable to no priest or nun.

James "Jimmy" Hurley

This film opens with Jimmy Hurley, played by Lloyd Clay Brown, being awakened by his mother. Behind the opening credits, viewers see the setting through the eyes of an average boy. He rises early and dresses, buys a newspaper, greets people in the neighborhood, and arrives at church early to put on his vestments and serve as an altar boy beside Donald Miller, who is really the story's focus.

Later, when Donald is unable to answer Sister James's question about Patrick Henry, Jimmy cannot contain his enthusiasm and blurts out the answer. He is immediately sent to the principal's office. This proves to be an important plot point, because his arrival causes Sister Aloysius to open her office door, allowing Father Flynn to look in and see Donald's mother holding a conference with the nun.

Sister James

Sister James is played by Amy Adams in a performance that was nominated for several supporting actress awards, including the Academy Award, the Screen Actors Guild Award, and the Golden Globe Award. Sister James represents a younger person's view of religious education. She is hesitant to take advice from Sister Aloysius, who would like her to put a barrier between herself and her students; Sister James feels that the students should trust her, not fear her. As suspicions mount about Father Flynn, however, she finds herself being more distrustful of her students, slowly adopting Sister Aloysius's methods.

Sister James does not want to believe that Father Flynn is a sexual predator. She shares with him a progressive view of education and would like to see the methods of education at the school, which is staffed by nuns who are all much older than her, change to reflect the growing youth culture of the 1960s. She also is somewhat charmed by Father Flynn. She jumps at a chance to believe his explanations. When they talk to each other alone, and he tells her directly that he is not behaving improperly, Sister James expresses her relief and her confidence in him.

Sister James is absent during the final confrontation between Sister Aloysius and Father Flynn. She is out of town, visiting her sick brother in Baltimore, when Father Flynn leaves the St. Nicholas parish. When she hears that Sister Aloysius has driven him out, she is angry, feeling that he has been wrongly persecuted. She is aghast to hear that Sister Aloysius has lied to trap him, losing a bit of her innocence and her faith in the sanctity of the sisterhood. She is not as practically minded or as cynical as Sister Aloysius at the film's end, but the story clearly implies that she might become so as she ages.

William London

William London, played by Mike Roukis, is one of the boys in Sister James's class. He has a rebellious streak. When Father Flynn asks to see his nails, London pulls his hands away from the priest, who deflects the awkwardness of the situation by making the boy the butt of a joke. It is an important moment because Sister Aloysius later explains that William's discomfort with the priest, witnessed from a window above, was what confirmed for her the idea that Father Flynn was a pedophile. Soon after, when questioning Sister James about an upcoming test, William puts a hand on her shoulder, a familiarity that earns him a punishment by Sister Aloysius. He is sent home from school with a bloody nose on the day of the test, and Sister Aloysius suspects that William, being tricky, may have caused it himself to be excused.

Donald Miller

Donald is played by Joseph Foster II. In Shanley's stage play, Donald is talked about but never actually appears. His name is also different, changed from Muller in the original play to Miller in the film.

Donald is presented as a quiet, sensitive child. As the film progresses, viewers can see why he is withdrawn. He is abused by his father, as his mother explains to Sister Aloysius. At his previous school, a public school, his life was at stake when his classmates found out about his homosexual tendencies. He is picked on by boys in his class when Father Flynn is not around to protect and encourage him. As the first black student to attend the St. Nicholas school, he is an open target for bullies.

Donald's bond with Father Flynn is shown in the scene where another student knocks his books from his hands and crushes the toy ballerina given to him by the priest. When Father Flynn comes to help Donald back to his feet, he puts his arms around Donald, who buries his face in the priest's chest. He may be victimized by a sexual predator, but Donald is also in desperate need of the attention he gets from Father Flynn.

Mrs. Miller

With just one extended scene, Viola Davis's performance as Mrs. Miller gained worldwide attention for the previously unknown actress, earning her nominations for best supporting actress in the

Academy Awards, Critics' Choice Awards, and Golden Globe Awards, among others, and winning her awards from National Board of Review (for Best Breakthrough Performance) and Black Reel Awards.

Mrs. Miller is in a difficult emotional situation. She is a hardworking woman with an abusive home life. She knows that her son Donald is in a bad situation, not only because he is the first black student at St. Nicholas but also because she understands his homosexuality, though she cannot bring herself to discuss it directly with Sister Aloysius. Her one small beacon of hope is to get Donald through the eighth grade, so that he can enter a good high school and possibly move on to college from there. She has come to expect, though, that any trouble that occurs anywhere near Donald will be blamed on him, because of the racial standards of all-white schools of the day.

Sister Aloysius tells Mrs. Miller directly that her son is probably the victim of a pedophile and is aghast to see that the woman is not moved to have the perpetrator brought to justice. For her part, Mrs. Miller knows that bringing attention to the situation will only make Donald's situation worse with his father, with the other students, and with the school. She is actually glad that Donald, who is inclined to have a same-sex relationship anyway, is involved with someone as kind and intelligent as Father Flynn, and she is willing to let their relationship continue for the rest of the school year.

Sister Veronica

Sister Veronica, played by Alice Drummond, is an elderly nun at St. Nicholas. She is losing her eyesight. Sister Aloysius looks after her, covering up her blindness because she knows that the archdiocese will force her to retire if they find out about her weakness. When Sister Veronica trips over a branch in the courtyard, Sister Aloysius lies to a direct question from Father Flynn, telling the priest that her sight is fine.

THEMES

Race Relations

This film touches upon race relations going on at the time in which it is set, though race is not the main subject. The story takes place in 1964. The civil rights movement in the United States had

one of its most significant gains that year with the passage of the first Civil Rights Act, a piece of legislation that had been started by recently assassinated President Kennedy. One point of this law was desegregated schools. This led to a backlash in schools that had been historically attended by whites, as parents and students felt forced to accept students of other races.

Donald Miller's presence at St. Nicholas is not attributed to required integration of schools, but the hostility between races in the mid-1960s is still assumed. Sister Aloysius speaks of violence against Donald as an inevitable fact in a parish of Italian and Irish families. In one scene, just after Father Flynn has walked out of sight, a bully knocks Donald's books from his hand and laughs. The vulnerability of being the only black student at St. Nicholas makes a relationship with Father Flynn necessary for Donald. Sister Aloysius sees Donald's racial isolation as giving the priest his opportunity to take advantage of Donald.

Evil

For viewers who see the events of this movie through Sister Aloysius's eyes, Father Flynn represents the worst kind of evil because he is taking advantage of a child and cannot admit, even to himself, that what he is doing is wrong. For viewers who accept Father Flynn's perspective, Sister Aloysius is evil for having such a dark worldview that she would believe the worst about a good man based on circumstantial evidence. Sister James, whose perspective falls between those of the other two, is in an uneasy position because she is not entirely certain who is telling the truth. She vacillates. When talking with Father Flynn in the courtyard, for instance, she says honestly that she believes that he has done nothing wrong, but soon after, after seeing him hug Donald Miller in the hall, she loses her temper and shouts at her class, obviously disturbed. Viewers sense the stakes involved in this film through their identification with Sister James, who hopes for some moral clarity, but the film offers no definitive answer by the end.

Female Identity

It is Sister Aloysius who identifies her struggle to stop Father Flynn from taking advantage of Donald as a gender struggle within the church. She recalls a similar situation at another parish, St. Boniface, when she had to stop a pedophile, but in that case she had a priest who was willing to support her. At her present assignment, St.

READ, WATCH, WRITE

- Some Catholics have compared the charges made against priests to the charges that were later debunked about day-care workers in California who allegedly involved preschoolers in sexual assault and Satanic rituals. Use print and online resources to research the trial concerning the McMartin preschool scandal in the 1990s, which introduced the theory of "repressed memories" to the public. Then write a paper explaining whether the events of that trial altered your feelings about Father Flynn's guilt and Sister Aloysius's conviction about his guilt.

- Shanley has spoken about how his plays often reflect the thin line between dreams and real life. Find three to five scenes in this film that you think could be read as occurring in a dream, and present them to the class with your explanation of what is so dream-like about them.

- Alice Walker's novel *The Color Purple* focuses on a young woman who goes from abuse at the hands of her father to life with an abusive husband. In 1985, it was adapted as a film, starring Whoopi Goldberg, Danny Glover, and Oprah Winfrey and directed by Stephen Spielberg. Watch that film and take notes about its portrayal of child abuse. Think about whether its portrayal is the same as or different from the way *Doubt* treats the subject. Discuss the two films with a school counselor or child psychologist and report on which film they say is more realistic.

- In the film, Sister James accuses Sister Aloysius of pursuing charges against Father Flynn because of her dislike for him, based on the amount of sugar he takes in his tea, his use of a ballpoint pen, and his fondness for secular songs such as "Frosty the Snowman." Research body language in print and online sources. Using clips from television, movies, and the Internet, create a montage slide show or poster of gestures that might be interpreted as evidence of some hidden psychological trait.

- In the film, Father Flynn makes up a sermon about a woman who learns her lesson about gossip when her priest tells her to scatter pillow feathers to the wind. Choose some character trait that you dislike and write a story that illustrates its dangers. Present your story to the class in the form of a sermon either in person or in a video posted to YouTube.

- Shanley shows some ways in which Sister James is becoming hardened, like Sister Aloysius, such as when she adapts the method of using a reflection to frighten her students into thinking that she is all-seeing. He also shows her standing up to Sister Aloysius. Write a scene between Sister James and her brother taking place in modern times (fifty years after the events of this film), showing what kind of nun she has become.

Nicholas, she does not have the support of the men. "Here there's no man I can go to," she laments to Sister James. "Men run everything. We are going to have to stop him ourselves."

The film graphically supports her view of the gender inequity in a Catholic parish at the time by intercutting two dinner scenes. In the rectory, where the priests live, dinner is a lively event, with laughter, drinking, and smoking; when the

scene cuts to the convent, where the nuns dine, the sound stops abruptly. The nuns dine in silence, surrounded by bare walls, speaking to each other in muted tones.

In the end, Sister Aloysius is able to shake Father Flynn's composure by telling him that she broke the protocol when she phoned his last parish. If she had talked to the male priest there, as protocol requires, she would have heard

© *Moviestore collection Ltd | Alamy*

the official story of his dismissal. Instead, she says that she talked to a nun and was able to find out the real story. Father Flynn's anger about this tells her that he is hiding something that the male-dominated social order is willing to hide for him.

Religion

This film presents a conflict between two views of religion. Sister Aloysius represents the view that the church is to be blindly trusted and followed. She is not interested in being liked by the children under her control and instead insists that they must follow her orders without question. For Sister James, however, a part of her faith is to bond with her students, to treat with them with compassion. In their discussion in the courtyard, Father Flynn speaks about the philosophy of kindness that he sees in Sister James's face, at the same time accusing Sister Aloysius of killing kindness in the name of virtue.

Sister Aloysius stands for the church's sense of moral supremacy, but she is also willing to take an independent view of right and wrong.

Sister James is flabbergasted to hear that Sister Aloysius lied to trap the priest. Lying is a cardinal sin, but Sister Aloysius casually admits to it because she is certain that it is necessary to pursue a more important good. Sister James represents a modern religious view of compassion and love, and Sister Aloysius represents a traditional view of service to the Catholic hierarchy. Both of them must reconcile their views with the realities of the church and the school.

STYLE

Period Drama

This film takes place during the early 1960s. Great care was put into reproducing exact details of the period—the clothing, such as school uniforms and proper religious vestments; cars on the street; and the right kinds of office furnishings for a lower-class parish of the time. Clothes are of heavy wool, and the sets are trimmed with wood and iron. The accuracy of these details is important for convincing viewers that the events of the film are true to the period. The limitations of the stage required the original play to be stylized, with small, movable props used to merely suggest an office, a courtyard, and other locations, but the care that has been given to every little detail here gives the film a realistic, convincing feel.

Makeup

The actors in this film are major movie stars, but, unlike the aesthetic of many big-budget movies, their skin tone has been made to look pale and soft. The lead actors are playing people whose concern is religion, not looks, while Viola Davis (Mrs. Miller) and the other actors are playing people from a lower-class Bronx neighborhood. The makeup they are given makes them look drawn and tired: eyes and lips are not highlighted with mascara or lipstick, and wrinkles have not been erased with powder. The young actors playing the students at St. Nicholas are also pale, though their cheeks show a tinge of blush that conveys a liveliness that is absent from the adult characters.

CULTURAL CONTEXT

When Shanley wrote the play on which this film is based, the Catholic Church in the United States was in the midst of a growing scandal concerning priests who were alleged to have been sexually involved with children in their parishes. The scandal spread across the country and then across the globe. It continued on for years, reaching to the heights of the church hierarchy.

There were numerous charges made against clerics in many different areas of the country over the years, including the high-profile cases of Father Donald Roemer in Los Angeles in 1981, Father Gilbert Gauthe in Louisiana in 1984, and Father James Porter of Fall River, Massachusetts, in 1993. However, the problem of pedophile priests seemed isolated and sporadic. On January 6, 2002, however, the *Boston Globe* published a front-page story about the 1984 reassignment of Father John Geoghan, from St. Brendan's parish to St. Julia's. Geoghan was the subject of a criminal investigation at the time of the *Globe*'s story, and the facts it revealed about the church's treatment of Geoghan unleashed national, then international, outrage.

Geoghan, who had already been removed from the priesthood by the time of the newspaper article, was accused in more than eighty civil suits charging him with child molestation between 1962 and 1995. That was in addition to the more than thirty lawsuits against him that the church had already settled, for ten million dollars. Until the early years of the twenty-first century, however, the people in Boston and the other areas where Geoghan had worked were not aware of the charges against him. When the news came out, anger grew against Cardinal Bernard Law, who was Geoghan's superior in his later years with the church and, many felt, the key figure in keeping a child molester in direct contact with the children that were his prey. As facts of the case came out, Cardinal Law explained that he tried to keep the Geoghan case out of the public eye and to control it through internal disciplinary actions within the church. Later documents, however, showed that he kept a friendly tone with Geoghan. When parishioners saw the glowing notes of praise that Law sent to Geoghan, even as the priest was being forced to resign after psychological tests found him unfit for the priesthood, and found out about the money being spent to keep the Geoghan lawsuits out of the public eye, they were infuriated.

The Boston case brought worldwide attention to the problem of sexual abuse among the clergy, and it revealed what seemed to be a pattern of cover-up that was repeated around the globe. After seeing the damage done within the church community, the United States Conference of Catholic Bishops commissioned a complete report by the John Jay College of Criminal Justice to determine what had been done well and poorly in handling abusive priests in the past and to chart a course for the future. Their report, issued in 2004, provided a comprehensive approach for dealing with the problem. In the meantime, similar cases came to light across the globe, following the same pattern, with church officials found to have dealt with sexual abuse cases by focusing more on public image than on the needs of the victims. The most comprehensive of these was the Murphy Report on abuse in Ireland, which found that the church struggled "obsessively" to hide claims of sexual abuse between 1975 and 2004. Even more scandalous was the evidence released the same year that the Pope himself, Benedict XVI, when he was the Archbishop of Munich in 1980, was involved in reassigning a priest instead of punishing him for sexual abuse of a boy.

© *Moviestore collection Ltd | Alamy*

CRITICAL OVERVIEW

When it premiered on Broadway in 2005, John Patrick Shanley's play *Doubt* was an instant success. It won awards for best new play from several sources, including the New York Drama Critics Circle, the Drama Desk, and the Outer Critics Circle. It also won the Pulitzer Prize for Drama and received four Tony awards. Though a film version of the play was considered inevitable, many critics were surprised that it was directed by Shanley, who had not directed a film since *Joe Versus the Volcano*, which was released in 1990 to tepid reviews. Many critics felt that he did an admirable job directing, though there were some detractors, such as *Entertainment Weekly*'s Lisa Schwarzbaum, who felt that Meryl Streep and Philip Seymour Hoffman, both fine actors, "are also vulnerable actors in need of guidance from a director with a strong vision," which she felt Shanley lacked. "Streep," she says later, "apparently left to her own devices, lugs a load of mannerisms under the pruny nun's severe black habit, encouraged by the movie's literal-minded director."

Manohla Dargis, writing in the *New York Times*, thought that Shanley's "work with the actors is generally fine, though it's a mystery what he thought Ms. Streep . . . was doing." Dargis notes that Streep's "outsized performance has a whiff of burlesque, but she's really just operating in a different register from the other actors." By contrast, Michael V. Tueth of *America* wrapped up his review with the opinion that "not enough praise can be given to the performances of Meryl Streep as Sister Aloysius and Philip Seymour Hoffman as Father Flynn." It is an opinion echoed by the many film boards that nominated this film and its actors for major awards: the four major actors (Streep, Hoffman, Adams, and Davis) were nominated for Academy Awards, as was Shanley, for his adapted screenplay; Streep won Screen Actors Guild and Critics' Choice awards, and Davis won awards from Black Reel and the National Board of Review. Across the country, dozens of nominations and awards were chalked up at regional film festivals.

Though the film was widely acclaimed and ended up on many critics' lists of the best films of 2008, it still had its detractors. One example is

Stuart Diwell, whose review in the *Sunday Tasmanian* of Australia finds it "a disappointing piece of work by Shanley. It is heavy-handed and all his twists and turns to try to achieve moral ambiguity and emotional resonance are just too obvious." In *Commonweal*, Richard Alleva shares similar disappointment in a long dissection of the film that determined that the questions that it raises were less about philosophy and more about information that was left out. "But is *Doubt*'s doubt truly disturbing emotion communicated by a probing work of art," Alleva asks, "or is it just the uncertainty we have to feel whenever we don't have the facts of a case?" Like other critics, he did recognize the film's strengths, noting that "within the limits of the script, *Doubt* is well executed," but he and a few others did see weakness in a script that many critics singled out for praise.

CRITICISM

David Kelly

Kelly is a college instructor of creative writing and literature. In the following essay, he looks at how having the same author create the stage and film versions of Doubt *can give insight into the inherent differences between plays and movies.*

It is interesting and useful that John Patrick Shanley, the author of the hit Broadway drama *Doubt*, was able to write and direct the film version of his play. Like the psychological studies that examine the behaviors of twins separated at birth, to see what traits are constant and which are the residue of circumstances, Shanley's control over the film of his play allows us to consider the changes that should and must occur when a play is brought to the screen. Authors of original works often complain about how their work was "ruined" by Hollywood, but Shanley has no complaint. *Doubt* was successful as a stage play and then as a movie, indicating that the choices made for the film were apparently the right ones.

On stage, *Doubt* focused on the intellectual conundrum of what happens in a community based in faith if evidence arises that a good person, an important person, might be doing bad. Shanley created four distinct characters—an experienced nun, a novice, a mother, and the dubious priest. They all had reasonable personalities, but they mainly served as representatives of their types.

> O'BYRNE'S PRIEST WAS EERIE BECAUSE HE SEEMED ENTIRELY COMFORTABLE WITH HIMSELF, DESPITE THE MOUNTING EVIDENCE OF HIS GUILT. HOFFMAN HAS FATHER FLYNN LAUGH A LITTLE TOO JOVIALLY AND SMILE A LITTLE TOO SWEETLY TO ACHIEVE THE SAME EFFECT."

The characters rang true, though not as people so much as philosophical positions.

The physical spaces that the characters lived in were suggested, not rendered, in keeping with the limitations of the stage. Audiences were taken from one place to another, from the church to the courtyard to the principal's office, with shifts in lighting and the barest of sets. The stage play did not need to be convincing: people do not lose themselves in the world of a play so much as in the ideas it stands for. When brought to film, though, the story takes on another level of reality, one that is responsible for creating the feeling of a particular time and place. The fluidity of camera movements takes audiences beyond the fixed distance that holds steadily between a theater patron's seat and the stage. Film audiences are within the action, and they expect to feel themselves living within the world of the story.

The film version of *Doubt* takes viewers to the Bronx of the early 1960s. This involves more than just "opening up" the script, a process that unimaginative writers achieve by showing a few street scenes under the opening credits and moving a conversation or two to outdoor locations. Shanley did a little of this, particularly in the conversation between Sister Aloysius and Mrs. Miller, which occurs in the film during a walk up the block. However, Shanley also moves the camera around in a naturalistic way. He weaves long shots of the neighborhood in between scenes, creating a sense of a closed community even beyond the churchyard walls, and he uses close-ups to accent a character's look or gesture. He and his cinematographer use the camera to draw attention to particular objects, such as the rosary Father Flynn has wrapped around his hands or the transistor radio that Sister

WHAT DO I SEE NEXT?

- The 1987 made-for-television movie *The Father Clements Story* concerns a Chicago priest, played by Louis Gossett, Jr., who upset the church hierarchy when he adopted an at-risk teenager, played by Malcolm-Jamal Warner. Based on actual events, this film, written by Arthur Heinemann and Ted Tally, is an inspiring story of courage, often recommended for young-adult viewers. It was released on VHS by Live/Artisan in 1999 and is also available for download through online sources.

- Norman Jewison directed John Pielmeier's adaptation of his own stage play, *Agnes of God*. Set in a convent in Montreal, the script involves a psychologist (played by Jane Fonda) brought in to do an evaluation on a novice nun (played by Meg Tilly) who has given birth to an infant and then killed it. The film also stars Anne Bancroft as the order's Mother Superior. The film was released in theaters in 1985 and released on DVD by Sony Pictures in 2002.

- Before this film, Shanley's last outing as a writer and director was the 1990 comic fantasy *Joe Versus the Volcano*. The film, panned by critics upon its 1990 release, has come to be a cult favorite. It stars Tom Hanks as a man who agrees to jump into a volcano to appease tribal gods and Meg Ryan playing three roles. Warner Home Video released the film in 2002.

- Clint Eastwood's 2008 film *Changeling* is similar to this film in its treatment of mystery: set in Los Angeles in the 1920s, it concerns a young mother (Angelina Jolie) whose abducted son is returned to her, but she doubts, despite what the police and other authorities tell her, that the boy given to her actually is her son. The script, written by J. Michael Straczynski, won a British Academy of Television and Film Arts Award. The film is available on DVD from Universal Studios.

- Audrey Hepburn portrayed the complex struggle facing a young nun like Sister James who finds her new profession more trying than she had imagined in the 1959 film *The Nun's Story*. This epic, directed by Fred Zinnemann and also starring Peter Finch and Dame Peggy Ashcroft, follows Hepburn's Sister Luke to her assignment in the African Congo. It was released on DVD by Warner Home Video in 1998.

- The scandal about pedophilia in the priesthood was examined in the 2006 Academy Award–nominated documentary *Deliver Us from Evil*. Filmmaker Amy Berg interviewed defrocked Father Oliver O'Grady and several of his now-grown victims, following the trail of how such crimes could be allowed within the church. Lions Gate released the film on DVD in 2007.

- Greg Akari's film *Mysterious Skin*, starring Joseph Gordon-Levitt, Elisabeth Shue, and Brad Corbett, deals with the long-term effects of sexual abuse, following two boys who were abused by a stranger as they grow up to be young adults. The film is not rated, but it contains explicit imagery. It was released into theaters in 2004 and released on DVD by Strand Releasing in 2006.

Aloysius confiscates. These are all emblems of their time, and they serve to help audiences feel what it was like to be there and then.

Conspicuously, Shanley added some elements to the film version that seem to water his story down. These might be questioned, but the successful film that resulted indicates that they were the right choices for a film. It would be an exaggeration to call theatergoers more sophisticated than the general population, but the theater experience is certainly more thought-engaging than watching a movie. A film can be experienced in any number of venues these days: not just theaters, but in theaters or classrooms and on computer screens or mobile devices. The film audience is a thousand times broader, and it is good writing on Shanley's part to reach out to a broader audience.

Among the more controversial things he has added to the film is blatant symbolism that lacks even the barest pretense of subtlety. For instance, the wind picks up several times in the film, throwing windows open and driving rain across the screen, and audiences can feel confident that each time the wind draws attention to itself the emotions of the stony-faced characters are on the rise. The wind is easy to interpret symbolically, and so are the petals that Father Flynn has crushed in his bible, a sign of his love of life. The petals, like everything about Father Flynn, first seem joyful but end up as symbols of his resentment.

The oddest addition is the light over Sister Aloysius's desk. It seems to be connected directly to the nun's psyche, flickering off and on as her mood changes. At one point she even draws attention to its symbolic weight in a way that is almost comical. "Look at that. You blew out my light," she tells Sister James, after the younger nun has screwed up her courage to timidly but forcefully tell Sister Aloysius what she really thinks. The symbolism is so obvious that careful viewers might cringe, but, like the wind and the petals, it helps to keep viewers on track if their attention is prone to wandering.

One last addition worth noting is that the film version actually includes Donald, the young boy at the center of the sex scandal. On stage, Donald's behavior was mentioned, but audiences could not see him to help make their own judgments about Sister Aloysius's suspicions. There was no way to leave him out of the heightened reality of the film, though. The result adds little: Joseph Foster II does as much as he can with a role that calls for him to play confused, sad, and inscrutable, but the whole point of the role of Donald Miller is that audiences, like the nuns, cannot get a clear understanding of him. Still, his presence gives the potential molestation a reality that the stage play lacked. The play was about what would happen if Father Flynn was kind to an isolated boy but then sexually abused him; the film is about the effect of the priest's behavior on *this* particular boy.

Film requires different performances from the actors, and Shanley shaped his adaptation to achieve maximum effect. The most obvious example of this is often-lauded breakout performance by Viola Davis, playing Donald's mother, Mrs. Miller ("Muller" in the theatrical version). It is a terrific performance, but one that is centered around her face, which manages to give readers the sorrow, anger, and defiance wrapped up in a woman who needs to protect her son from his own father while trying to determine how much compromise will be needed for the boy to survive. On stage, that face would not register with audiences. In the Broadway production, Adriane Lenox conveyed Mrs. Muller's burden through its weight on her and its effect on her posture, with little chance for complexity. Similarly, Amy Adams's Sister James shows her hopes rising and falling through her doe eyes, which express either sorrow or relief at any moment. For Heather Goldenhersh in the stage version, the way to show Sister James's growth was in the hardening of her meek voice, which was definitely appropriate for the theater, but the eyes are more convincing portals to the soul. For subtlety, film has a distinct advantage.

One consistent criticism of the film was that it was "Oscar bait": by having such frequently lauded actors as Meryl Streep and Philip Seymour Hoffman star in a story about a serious subject, it seemed to be begging for awards. The backlash to this was that some critics went after Streep's performance, finding her Bronx-Irish accent a bit too thick and her puckered sternness too cartoonish. For such critics, Cherry Jones's aloofness as Sister Aloysius on stage would probably have been just as impersonal as the character needed to be. There is no way of telling whether Jones, a great actress who played the president on the television show *24* for two seasons, could have rendered a moving Sister Aloysius with a more sublime performance in the film, but it is worth noting that the accent and the facial expressions make Streep's version of the nun a person: when she sighs as she mentions her dead husband, it is clear that she is fully aware of her past life at that moment and is not just mentioning it as an idea she once had. When she promises to fight Father Flynn and win, there can be no question that she will. Some of Streep's choices may be a little over the top, but she earns that by filling in her portrayal with little touches that ring true. Hoffman, for his part, makes a more sinister Father Flynn than Brian F. O'Byrne did on Broadway. O'Byrne's priest was eerie because he seemed entirely comfortable with himself, despite the mounting evidence of his guilt. Hoffman has Father Flynn laugh a little too jovially and smile a little too sweetly to achieve the same effect. In this case, the difference is not so much the differences between the two media as the differences between the two men's acting styles. Even with the differences made for the

DOUBT IS A PIECE IN WHICH THE REACTIONARY MESSAGES ARE CARRIED BY WOMEN."

adaptation, the role would work for either actor on stage or on film.

Theater requires its audiences to suspend disbelief to a greater degree than film does. When watching a film that takes place in a small urban parish in the 1960s, viewers will not believe that they are there. They are, however, more likely to believe at some gut level that the characters on the screen are who they say they are. Theatergoers focus more on the ideas the story represents, seeing characters as representations of various social positions. Moviegoers, on the other hand, are more inclined to feel that they are in the room with the characters, just as the camera is in the room. John Patrick Shanley has offered up two versions of his story *Doubt*, each one tailored to a different medium. Each is successful in its unique way, which is a testament to the author's flexible imagination.

Source: David Kelly, Critical Essay on *Doubt*, in *Drama for Students*, Gale, Cengage Learning, 2011.

Ruth Riddick

In the following review, Riddick argues that the film does not live up to theatrical performances of the work, as the film does not provide a complete resolution.

"Lord, I believe; help my unbelief." Mark 9:24

Audiences come to *Doubt* expecting great things, maybe even a measure of catharsis for one of the most painful episodes in Catholic history. "A movie that's actually about something," touts pre-eminent industry news source *Variety*. The movie of *Doubt* is transposed by writer-director John Patrick Shanley from his hugely successful Pulitzer and Tony-winning play of the same name. It stars two of the most important American actors of our time.

But audiences will be disappointed. They may be especially disappointed if they've previously enjoyed *Doubt* in the theater. How is this possible? Variously described by significant critics as having "exact and merciless writing, powerful performances and timeless relevance," (Roger Ebert) and "two particularly well-matched antagonists,"

(Kenneth Turan), the movie is surely required—and pleasurable—viewing.

Doubt presents itself as a chamber piece; a duel of cello and guitar. In the overt story, Reverend Mother Meryl Streep suspects trendy-wannabe Father Philip Seymour Hoffman of "interfering with little boys" (in the language of the period). A heavily signposted parallel invites us to see the ferocious Streep as representing archaic intolerance, with Hoffman embodying the fun-church that awaits post-Vatican II.

Doubts entertained in this text are not about gender roles, of course. It wouldn't be a stretch for the viewer to conflate Streep's Sister Aloysius with the fabled Nurse Ratched, while who can resist a darlin' broth of a priest. "As a kid, I was confirmed and I went to church, but I was bored. Now, I feel the opposite," Hoffman has said of his role as Father Flynn, adding: "I wouldn't ever say whether the priest is innocent or guilty because I saw *Doubt* as being about something larger."

At the hidden level, it may well be. It's hardly too fanciful to view *Doubt* as recapitulating, in miniature and in semi-modern dress, the overthrow of female-centric religions. All patriarchal cultures have some version of this mythic story, which may help explain the appeal of the present rift. Aloysius scores in the local battle, but as surely as Father is promoted within the dominant male hierarchy, she has lost herself. Victory is so complete that, unlike Father, she comes to doubt her values and competencies. For this dramatic arc to work, we cannot be certain that Father is guilty. Nor can we be allowed to agree that Aloysius is entirely legitimate.

Meanwhile back in the Bronx, Sister Amy Adams, who appears to have had no exposure to the seven deadly sins or the wickedness of the world, is gradually corrupted by her superior in the way of those witches covens conjured by their costuming. We care only because, in her simpleton way, this little nun is the instigator of the suspicions that spur the overt plot; yet one of the children would have done as well, as in *The Crucible*.

Sister Amy's real function is to serve as a contrast with Aloysius to the latter's disadvantage; her fragile innocence being a more appropriate feminine persona than that of her masculinzed, embittered, manipulative boss. (*Doubt* is a piece in which the reactionary messages are carried by women.)

Anyone with a history of Catholic schooling will recognize the territory. In my own childhood, convent school girls were fiercely guarded from visiting priests, trendy or otherwise. There were no "private" conversations and, whether we liked it or not, our guardians were in sisterly agreement with Aloysius: "She's twelve years old, what could be 'private?'" (The oily retreat-leader, with—yes!—a guitar, was later discovered to have harbored a longterm mistress and child. But better that infraction than the other.) In the tacit power understanding of nuns everywhere, priests were accorded the necessary semblance of patriarchal deference.

But not at the expense of duty. As Aloysius, alert to the responsibilities of her position, promises her suspect: "I will go to your last parish, and the one before that if necessary. I'll find a parent [to accuse you]." Thanks to the vigilance of nuns, priestly molestation is not among the crimes of my childhood. Others, perhaps the fictional Donald Muller, were not so well protected.

Much has been made—rightly—of Viola Davis' cameo as the putative victim's mother. Perhaps we're relieved to shift focus, however briefly, from the emotional claustrophobia of St. Nicholas indoors. But what is the purpose of this entr'acte? Set ten years after *Brown v. Board of Education* mandated integration of public schools, there's little apparent reason why this mother and son need to be African-American. (In Shanley's world, do you have to be an outsider to be a victim of clerical sexual abuse? Surely not. But Father is not suspected of molesting within his own tribe.)

True, Mrs. Muller introduces uncomfortable realities from the crypto-colonial world beyond, but just as soon as she has her say, she's packed off to work, her challenging perspective tucked into a very proper period purse. The dreadful compromises of oppressed people are now surplus to dramatic requirements. So, why bother with her at all? In her own way, she's as expendable as Sister Amy Adams.

Except, of course, that it is left to Mrs. Muller to deliver the most pernicious message of all: don't rock the boat; however painful and compromised it may be, however much you suspect grave sin, whatever you believe your responsibility, or expect the consequences of your silence, to be. With all the authority of her oppression, Mrs. Muller is the serpent in Aloysius' grass: "Sister, I don't know if you and me are on the same side. I'll be standing with my son and those who are good with my son. It'd be nice to see you there."

What politically correct activist, never mind retro headmistress, could resist such an appeal? Does John Patrick Shanley really mean us to be this morally dense? And this in a drama ostentatiously invoking a mortal sin unremedied for suffering generations, a moral crisis yet to be fully resolved?

Thus the struggling conscience of the piece is abandoned.

What are we to make of the betrayal not only of Aloysius but of Meryl Streep? It's a truism to observe that there is nothing this actress can't transcend in her work: ethnicity, age, character, physical appearance, her own beauty. Yet, encumbered by a bonnet more reminiscent of Dutch Pennsylvania, Streep in full funerary suggests not gravitas but the lurking presence of a polygamous husband. (Would Shanley prefer this uppity bride of Christ in the gendered role of submissive wife?)

Yes, there are considerations of period, not otherwise scrupulously observed here, and no doubt nuns of Shanley's memory dressed in this manner, but in an artwork there are concerns larger than literal reality, as Philip Seymour Hoffman noted of this very piece. At the distance imposed by a proscenium arch, Broadway star Cherry Jones just about managed to overcome this handicap of dress, but the intimacy of the moving camera imposes a harsher standard.

By the time Reverend Mother Streep voices her doubt, she has been comprehensively abandoned by her writer-director and his artistic choices. It's hard to imagine her curtain line, the capitulating cri d'ame—"I have doubts!" falling flat in the hands of such an accomplished actress, but fall it does.

And with it the stated purpose of the piece, exposed now not as a fine play about ambiguity-under-pressure but as a "shell game" (Manohla Dargis, *New York Times*). Was there really less to *Doubt* than met the beguiled eye?

Surely we've all been duped enough. The sexual abuse of children and the betrayal of generations of dutiful Catholics are matters of real experience and history. There's no doubt about them at all.

Just as there's no doubt about the elemental debasement of women down through the Catholic years.

FINALLY, THE FILM EXPOSES A DEEPER
LAYER OF INSTITUTIONAL INJUSTICE THAT MAY
ACCOUNT FOR SISTER ALOYSIUS' NEED TO
DOMINATE THE ONLY REALM UNDER HER CONTROL."

But wait. There is one authentically chilling moment in this false film, accurate to its time in flavor and delivery. With faux frivolity, Fr. Hoffman, arriving to school as the children assemble for the morning, asks the boys: "And how are the little criminals today?" Talk about projection. Talk about self-fulfilling prophecies. No doubt about that either.

Source: Ruth Riddick, "Do We Care About *Doubt?*" in *Conscience*, Vol. 30, No. 1, Spring 2009, pp. 49–50.

Michael V. Tueth

In the following review, Tueth claims that the film investigates the psychological implications of the play on a deeper level.

The sun does not shine much in the Bronx neighborhood where John Patrick Shanley's powerful film, *Doubt*, is set. The atmosphere is gray and cold; its melancholy mood is disturbed only once in the film by a fierce windstorm that blows down many of the bare limbs of the convent trees. The winds of change are blowing in the Catholic Church in 1964, and Sister Aloysius Beauvier, the principal of the St. Nicholas parish school, seems determined to protect her domain from any corrupting influences in the air.

Catholics of a certain age might be tempted toward nostalgia by the film's opening shots, showing a quiet Sunday morning in this Irish-American neighborhood. The altar boys prepare the cruets of water and wine and negotiate which one of them will light the charcoal for the incense and which will ring the altar chimes for this pre-Vatican II Sunday Mass. The working-class parishioners, smartly dressed, with the women wearing the prescribed head-coverings, gently greet each other as they walk to church. Maybe Sister Aloysius has a point. Catholic life seemed simpler and more reliable then, with none of the questions and changes that the Second Vatican

Council and all the other forces of the 1960s would bring to the church.

But things are not as solid and certain as they seem. The first hint comes from a sermon given by a young priest, Father Brendan Flynn: "What do you do when you're not sure?" he asks the congregation. He reminds them of the bond of despair and uncertainty they shared a year earlier, when their beloved president John F. Kennedy was assassinated. He compares this, however, to a lonelier situation, offering as a parable the story of a sailor alone on a lifeboat who cannot see the stars to guide him. The priest proposes this as an image of the loneliness many in the congregation might feel because of some secret fear or pain in their lives that no one knows about. He suggests someone might be thinking, "No one knows that I've done something wrong."

Before long, Sister Aloysius suspects that someone has been doing something wrong: Father Flynn himself. She already clearly has a fundamental distrust of the young assistant pastor. He is too jovial for her tastes; he suggests that the school Christmas play should include a secular song like "Frosty the Snowman," which Sister Aloysius considers a heretical message about magic. As for his personal habits, he likes too much sugar in his tea, wears his fingernails too long, uses a ballpoint pen and possesses other hints of sensuality and adaptation to the modern world.

Father Flynn harbors a similar disapproval of Sister Aloysius' strict attitudes and demeanor, which he considers to be holding the school and the parish back from the newer vision of "a welcoming church." Sister Aloysius is more than ready to suspect him when a naive young nun suggests that he might be engaging in an inappropriate relationship with one of the eighth-grade boys. Sister Aloysius determines to get to the truth of this matter, while Father Flynn responds to her accusations with ferocious self-righteousness.

To tell here how the question is resolved would be more than a disservice to our readers, because as the story develops, the audience learns that there is much more than the possibility of sexual scandal lurking in the world of St. Nicholas Parish. Shanley's screenplay reveals layers of evil that reach to a heart of darkness worthy of Joseph Conrad or Graham Greene. Sister Aloysius has her own demons, many of which are revealed in the several scenes that Shanley has added to his Broadway script, not only "opening up" the setting but providing opportunities to see both Sister

Aloysius and Father Flynn interact with other members of their community. While the original play was set in only three locations—the parish church, Sister Aloysius' office and the convent cloister garden—and employed a cast of only four actors, the film makes excellent use of other locales and characters.

Sister Aloysius, for example, is shown tyrannizing the grade school children in the church, the classroom and the playground. When the young Sister James tells her that the students are "all uniformly terrified of you," she responds, "Yes. That's how it works." With little respect for anyone's agenda but her own, she invades Sister James's classroom in the midst of a lesson, and she feels free to wander up and down the pews of the church to monitor children's behavior during Father Flynn's homily. She presides over the convent meals with a mixture of gloom and sarcasm. The nuns eat their dinner in silence until Sister Aloysius rings her bell and begins the conversation; when the other nuns speak, she counters their comments with ridicule. And she certainly disapproves of Father Flynn's comfort with and affection for the students, especially Donald Muller, who, incidentally, is the first African-American student admitted into the school.

Meanwhile, Father Flynn's behavior gives Sister Aloysius further motive to suspect him. He embraces Donald after he is bullied by another student; the priest is spotted mysteriously returning Donald's undershirt to the boy's locker; and he calls Donald out of a class for a private conversation in the rectory, after which the boy returns to the classroom with the smell of alcohol on his breath. Father has several of the boys over to the rectory for soft drinks and "shooting the breeze." In one awkward scene, after a basketball practice, he encourages the boys to keep their fingernails clean and well manicured, letting them grow longer than Sister Aloysius would want. And, as Sister discovers, he has been assigned to three different parishes in the last five years.

The conflict between the priest and the nun, however, is more than personal; it signifies a more universal moral divide. When Sister James attempts to defend Father Flynn from any suspicion of misbehavior, Sister Aloysius responds, "You just want simplicity back." There is something admirable in her relentless determination not to let the issue lie unresolved but to pursue the truth, to "do what needs to be done," no matter how complicated or unpleasant the truth

may be. On the other hand, Father Flynn analyzes Sister Aloysius's search for "the truth" as a dangerous consequence of her generally joyless approach to life. As he tells Sister James: "There are people who go after your humanity... who tell you that the light in your heart is a weakness. Don't believe it. It's an old tactic of cruel people to kill kindness in the name of virtue." The drama pulls us between our admiration of Sister Aloysius's uncompromising search for the truth and Father Flynn's promotion of tolerance and compassion, or, as he puts it, Christ's message of "love. Not suspicion, disapproval and judgment."

Yet another level of evil operative in the parish neighborhood is revealed when Sister Aloysius holds a private conference with Donald's mother, who works as a cleaning woman in a nearby apartment complex. In one electrifying conversation, Mrs. Muller reveals other facts about the boy's home life and his personal confusion as well as her own attitude toward the accusations, exposing some even darker truths about race, class and the desperate search for upward mobility that private education promises to inner-city children. All these revelations seem to take Sister Aloysius by surprise.

Finally, the film exposes a deeper layer of institutional injustice that may account for Sister Aloysius' need to dominate the only realm under her control. As she remarks at one point, in the Catholic Church, "men run everything." Even she must admit that in the church's patriarchal system, Father Flynn is technically her superior. Her only recourse to any higher authority is to talk to the pastor, who, she is convinced, will side with Father Flynn. She is not allowed to appeal to the bishop of the archdiocese. Indeed, when Father Flynn later upbraids her for speaking to someone else about the matter, saying: "The church is very clear. You're supposed to go through the pastor," she responds: "Why? Do you have an understanding, you and he?" This portrayal of a clerical boys' club, especially in the U.S. church of the 1960s, might be even easier for today's film audiences to visualize after the many reports of official mishandling of sexual abuse cases among the clergy in recent years.

Not enough praise can be given to the performances of Meryl Streep as Sister Aloysius and Philip Seymour Hoffman as Father Flynn. How much more evidence do we need of their versatility? Just last year, Hoffman appeared onscreen as a depressed but articulate English professor in

"*The Savages*," as a sleek executive-turned-murderer in "*Before the Devil Knows You're Dead*" and as a fast-talking alpha male C.I.A. agent in "*Charlie Wilson's War*." His portrayal in "*Doubt*" of this likeable and eloquent young priest who may be hiding a secret draws on all of those characterizations to add complexity to the battle of wills in this drama. Ms. Streep has been even busier and more adventurous in the 10 films she has made in the last three years. While her recent roles have displayed a vast range of emotions, her portrayal of the conscientious and humorless Sister Aloysius requires instead a grim intensity and a willingness to forgo any audience sympathy or even approval. In every closeup and every debate with Hoffman or Amy Adams, as the innocent but ultimately confident Sister James, and particularly with Viola Davis (whose ten minutes on screen are a knockout) as Donald's worldly-wise mother, Streep employs the subtlest of expressions and body language to create the most chilling effects.

Only a few of Broadway's most acclaimed dramas in recent years ("*Closer*," "*Proof*" and "*The History Boys*," for example) have made it to the screen, and none was very successful in either financial or critical terms. "*Doubt*," the Tony Award winner for Best Play in 2005, might well have been destined for the same fate. However, as both director and screen-writer, John Patrick Shanley may beat the odds this year with a film that is sure to garner many nominations and perhaps some awards at Oscar time. By expanding his narrative with more scenes and characters, Shanley demonstrates how a film can improve on a play's psychological tensions. It can also deepen our awareness of the darkness to be encountered even within the most sacred locales of human faith and doubt.

Source: Michael V. Tueth, "Uncertain Sympathies: John Patrick Shanley's *Doubt*," in *America*, Vol. 200, No. 2, January 19, 2009, pp. 27–30.

John Petrakis

In the following review, Petrakis commends the film's script and performances, yet comments that the direction should be more subtle.

It is commonly assumed, and regularly taught, that the key difference between playwriting and screenwriting is that the former tells the bulk of its story with words (it is dialogue-driven), while the latter relies more heavily on images (it is camera-driven). This may be true, but a less obvious difference is that onstage one needs words and

performance to draw the audience's attention to a certain spot or action ("Hey, look here!"), while onscreen all you need is a close-up or a camera move—the viewer can't look anywhere else, no matter how much they might wish they could. It is a technique that served such visually teasing directors as Hitchcock and Polanski quite well, and it is at the heart of the film adaptation of *Doubt*, a 2004 Pulitzer Prize-winning play by John Patrick Shanley.

Doubt is a mystery story embracing a morality play concerning the things we know and those we only suspect. The tale takes place at St. Nicholas Catholic parish in the Bronx in 1964, where the old ways are gradually changing. President Kennedy, the patron saint of Catholic schoolboys in the 1960s, has been assassinated, leading to a new national sense of vulnerability. The reforms of Vatican II have begun to trickle down to the priests and nuns. The young and energetic priest, Father Brendan Flynn (Philip Seymour Hoffman), represents the future, and the strict and stern school principal, Sister Aloysius Beauvier (Meryl Streep), personifies tradition. This is made clear during Sister Aloysius's initial entrance, where she whacks a misbehaving kid across the back of the head to get his attention. The character in the midst of this ecclesiastical struggle, the one the viewer identifies with, is the sweet and dedicated Sister James (Amy Adams), who admires the compassion of Father Flynn while respecting the dedication of Sister Aloysius.

She is also the character who opens up the story's Pandora's box, turning a growing hostility between Sister Aloysius and the priest into an all-out war. She is concerned about the amount of personal attention that Father Flynn is paying to Donald Muller (Joseph Foster II), who is the school's first and only black student. It could just be that Father Flynn is reaching out to help a young boy in need, which is what she wants to believe, or it could be that Father Flynn is engaged in an unhealthy relationship with the boy, which is what she fears. When she takes those fears to Sister Aloysius, who has her own concerns about the forward-thinking priest, hell breaks loose—a bit at a time.

The question at the film's core is whether Sister Aloysius's judgment is colored by her disdain for Father Flynn, not to mention her long-simmering resentment at the subservient role the nuns must play in the church, even though they are the ones who keep things going on a daily basis, making the tough decisions about right, wrong and the gray areas in between.

The movie has two significant strengths, starting with the mesmerizing performances. Streep is hypnotic as a woman who must trust her instincts, despite knowing that she is dealing with a man's life and career, while Hoffman is nearly as good as a man who is trying desperately to navigate the choppy waters between two dangerous worlds. The film's most remarkable performance, however, is by Viola Davis as Mrs. Muller, Donald's mother. She has only one scene, in which Sister Aloysius reveals the fears about her son, but the way Davis deals with the news, showing in her face and bitter delivery that this is just another in a long line of indignities her people have suffered over the centuries, is the stuff that Academy Awards are made of.

Also impressive is the script itself, which Shanley has expanded a bit from the stage production. Of special note are the parable-like sermons that Father Flynn preaches to his lower-middle-class congregation and the electric confrontations between the priest and the nun in which nagging thoughts turn into direct accusations.

Where the film loses its footing is in the direction. Shanley chose to direct it himself, his first film directing assignment since 1990's *Joe Versus the Volcano*, and the 18-year layoff shows. The direction is heavy-handed, lacking the subtlety that the film demands. It's bad enough that he keeps having leaves blow around and windows rattle to remind us that the "winds of change" are blowing, but instead of relying on faces and gestures to suggest the way that confused people respond to confusing information, Shanley cuts away to a meaningless image or allows his camera to sort of drift. How much stronger the film would have been in the hands of someone whose visual sense was acute enough to make shot choices that would capture the underlying tragedy.

Source: John Petrakis, Review of *Doubt*, in *Christian Century*, Vol. 125, No. 26, December 30, 2008, p. 37.

SOURCES

Alleva, Richard, "Trick, No Treat," in *Commonweal*, January 20, 2009, pp. 20–21.

Belluck, Pam, "Papers in Pedophile Case Show Church Effort to Avert Scandal," in *New York Times*, January 25, 2002, p. A12.

Dargis, Manohla, "Between Heaven and Earth, Room for Ambiguity," in *New York Times*, December 12, 2008, p. O1.

Diwell, Stuart, "Shanley's Sermon Is Lost in Translation," in *Sunday Tasmanian* (Australia), February 1, 2009, p. 4.

Ferdinand, Pamela, "In Boston, Catholics React to Scandal: Evidence Grows of Sex Abuse Among Clergy," in *Washington Post*, February 18, 2002, http://www.washington post.com/ (accessed July 29, 2010).

Israely, Jeff, and Howard Chua-Eoan, "The Trial of Benedict XVI," in *Time*, Vol. 176, No. 22, June 7, 2010, pp. 36–43.

Miller, Lisa, and David France, "Sins of the Father," in *Newsweek*, March 4, 2002, http://www.newsweek.com/2002/03/03/sins-of-the-father.html (accessed August 19, 2010).

Schwarzbaum, Lisa, Review of *Doubt*, in *Entertainment Weekly*, December 12, 2008, pp. 48–49.

Shanley, John Patrick, *Doubt* (film), Goodspeed Productions, 2008.

———, *Doubt: A Parable* (play), Theater Communications Group, 2005.

Squires, Nick, "Vatican: Irish Sex Abuse Scandal 'Humiliating' for Catholic Church," in *Telegraph* (London, England), February 15, 2010, http://www.telegraph.co.uk/news/newstopics/religion/7242036/Vatican-Irish-sex-abuse-scandal- humiliating-for-Catholic-Church.html (accessed August 19, 2010).

Tueth, Michael V., "Uncertain Sympathies," in *America*, January 19–26, 2009, p. 29.

FURTHER READING

Allen, John L., Jr., "The Catholic Church," in *Foreign Policy*, November/December 2008, pp. 32–38.
    This article dispels commonly held myths about the Catholic Church, including misconceptions about the church's hierarchical structure and its attitudes toward sex. The article also includes a list of recommended readings at the end.

Hammel-Zabin, Amy, *Conversations with a Pedophile: In the Interest of Our Children*, Barricade Books, 2003.
    Hammel-Zabin, a therapist, recorded hours of conversation with a child molester who will be in prison for the rest of his life, examining the workings of the mind of such a person.

Irvine, Jacqueline Jordan, and Michele Foster, eds., *Growing Up African American in Catholic Schools*, Teachers College Press, 1996.
    This short book weaves together sociological perspectives with personal narratives to give insight into the situation Donald Miller faces in this film.

Jackowski, Karol, *The Silence We Keep: A Nun's View of the Catholic Priest Scandal*, Three Rivers Press, 2005.
> Sister Karol, who was ordained in 1964, published earlier books on lighter subjects. Here she writes from a purely personal perspective about the problems in her church that would allow a situation like the sex scandal to grow.

McChesney, Kathleen, "Pledges, Promises and Actions: The Road to Resolution of the Crisis of Abuse of Children by Catholic Clergy," in *Sin against the Innocents: Sexual Abuse by Priests and the Role of the Catholic Church*, edited by Thomas G. Plante, Praeger, 2004, pp. 39–46.
> McChesney's essay offers an examination of the difficult position the church found itself in as the twenty-first century began, and she offers some solutions for overcoming the problem.

SUGGESTED SEARCH TERMS

John Patrick Shanley

priest sex scandal

Shanley AND Doubt

Shanley AND priest

Doubt AND Meryl Streep

Streep AND Shanley

Catholic Church AND scandal

nun AND church hierarchy

Catholic Church AND desegregation

nuns AND sex scandal

Doubt AND Catholic Church

scandal AND Shanley

The Family Reunion

T. S. ELIOT

1939

Although T. S. Eliot's literary reputation largely rests on his poetry, he was also a well-known and respected playwright. Eliot's *The Family Reunion*, which is centered on the character of Henry Monchensey and his strained relationships with his family, is on one level a mystery play, as family members attempt to uncover the secrets related to the death of Henry's wife. At the same time, the play operates as a psychological drama, as Eliot explores what appears to be Henry's insanity. Eliot further incorporates supernatural elements that may be regarded either as signifiers of madness, or as actual spirits haunting various family members. These elements include ghosts, as well as the Eumenides, or the Greek deities associated with vengeance. The event around which the play is centered is Henry's homecoming, timed to correspond with his ailing, elderly mother's birthday. As family secrets are revealed, Henry's own emotional pain is exposed and examined by some family members, and disregarded by others. At the play's end, Henry resolves to leave his family and confront his personal demons. His mother dies after his departure. Through the course of the drama, Eliot explores the intertwining nature of isolation, madness, and guilt, and offers philosophical explorations on the nature of existence and reality. Although the title of the play suggests unity, the family is fractured as a group, and the individual members are isolated.

T.S. Eliot

Originally published in 1939, *The Family Reunion* is available in a 1964 edition published by Harcourt Brace.

AUTHOR BIOGRAPHY

Eliot was born on September 26, 1888, in St. Louis, Missouri, the seventh child of Charlotte Champe Stearns Eliot and Henry Ware Eliot. His mother was a schoolteacher and poet, his father a merchant. An early interest in writing led to the 1905 publication of his first poetry in his school magazine. Eliot earned his bachelor's and master's degrees from Harvard in 1909 and 1911. He traveled in Europe and then returned to Harvard to pursue a doctoral degree.

In 1914, Eliot was studying at Oxford University when World War I began. The following year he married his first wife, Vivienne Haigh-Wood. In 1915, Eliot published his first major poem, "The Love Song of J. Alfred Prufrock," which was followed two years later by his first poetry collection, *Prufrock and Other Observations.*

Eliot worked as a teacher and later, for Lloyds Bank. He left the bank in 1921 after suffering a nervous breakdown. In 1925, Eliot became the director of the publishing house Faber and Faber, establishing himself as a poet, critic, dramatist, and literary editor. Firmly rooted now in England, Eliot became a British subject, as well as a member of the Church of England, in 1927. His troubled marriage ended in 1932.

Though Eliot continued to write poetry, he also pursued a career as a dramatist during the 1930s. *The Family Reunion* was published and produced in 1939. His plays were produced in England, as well as New York. *The Cocktail Party* opened on Broadway in 1950. Eliot received the Nobel Prize in Literature in 1948.

In 1957, Eliot married Valerie Fletcher, his secretary. He continued to write throughout the 1950s. His last play, *The Elder Statesman*, was produced in London in 1958, and in New York in 1963. The following year, Eliot received the American Medal of Freedom at the U.S. Embassy in London. He died of emphysema on January 4, 1965, at his home in London.

PLOT SUMMARY

Part 1

SCENE 1

The Family Reunion is divided into two parts, rather than the more conventional acts. Part 1 is subtitled, "The Drawing Room, After Tea. An Afternoon in Late March." Scene 1 opens with Amy, the widowed Lady Monchensey, sitting in the drawing room with her three sisters (Ivy, Violet, and Agatha), her two brothers-in-law (Gerald and Charles), and the distant cousin Mary, who is much younger than the others in the group. The discussion is superficial: they speak of the weather and the capriciousness of youth.

After Mary exits, talk turns to the impending homecoming of Amy's son Harry. References are made to how difficult Harry's life has been for the past eight years, since he has been estranged from his family. The group wonders how changed Harry will be, and if he will find the family estate Wishwood to be much different after having been gone so long. As the conversation progresses it is revealed that Harry's wife died about a year prior. Ivy recounts how the unnamed wife was on board a ship with Harry

MEDIA ADAPTATIONS

- *The Family Reunion* was published as an audiocassette by Harper Audio in 1989.

and was "swept off the deck in the middle of a storm," her body was never found.

Harry arrives, and is alarmed to find his family sitting in a brightly lit room at night with the curtains open. He expresses his horror at the thought of being in a position where one could be watched by unseen watchers. The others attempt to reassure him, but Harry goes on about the "the eyes" that stared at him throughout his travels. Despite the attempt of his aunts and uncles to reassure him, Harry continues to rant about what he can see and the others cannot, about how he cannot explain himself, and how they cannot understand him. As Agatha pushes Harry to tell them what is troubling him, he eventually admits to having pushed his wife overboard to her death. The group immediately assumes it was an accident, and that Harry's grief has clouded his memory.

Harry exits, and the others discuss Harry's bizarre behavior. They resolve to discover what really happened. Amy decides to call the doctor, and exits. The others question Harry's servant about the incident on the ship. Meanwhile, the gathered family members have been waiting for Harry's brothers Arthur and John to arrive. Everyone exits the room, except Agatha.

SCENE 2

The scene opens with Mary entering the room and initiating a conversation with Agatha. Mary confesses to Agatha that she would like to leave Wishwood, and asks for Agatha's advice on the matter "because there's no one else to ask, / And because you are strong, and because you don't belong here / Any more than I do." These two women speak plainly to one another about Amy and her power over the family, and about

Harry. Mary reveals that Amy had originally intended her to be Harry's wife. As Mary continues to express her desire to escape Wishwood and asks for Agatha's help, Agatha discourages her, and exits.

Harry enters. Mary and Harry discuss their childhood at Wishwood, agreeing that the only time they felt happy or free was when they lost themselves to their imaginations as they played in the woods. Mary voices her experience of feeling like an outsider while at Wishwood. Harry attempts to explain to Mary his own confused feelings regarding his fractured sense of self. He admits to feeling haunted, watched, and he opens the curtains. When they part, as the stage directions indicate, the Eumenides appear. He speaks to these figures, but Mary assures him there is no one there, and she closes the curtains again. Harry, frustrated, insists they exist, and reopens the curtains, but no he longer can see the spirits.

SCENE 3

Violet, Ivy, Gerald, and Charles have joined Mary and Harry. Mary quietly excuses herself from the room. Amy enters, with Dr. Warburton, who attempts to engage Harry in conversation in order to discreetly evaluate him. Harry's aunts and uncles attempt to redirect the conversation whenever Harry begins to sound peculiar. Amy announces that they will have dinner without waiting for Arthur and John. The doctor, Amy, and Harry exit, leaving the Chorus on stage. As a group, the members of the chorus express a fear of the past and the future, and a sense of shame. These individuals exit the scene, and Agatha enters. Her soliloquy expresses an urgency concerned with the untangling of knots, perhaps referring to the fates of various characters, or the past and the future from the present.

Part 2

SCENE 1

Part 2, which is subtitled "The Library, After Dinner," opens with a conversation between Harry and Dr. Warburton. They discuss Harry's mother, and Harry asks Warburton about his father, who died long ago and whom Harry scarcely remembers. Warburton hints that some scandal surrounded Harry's parents, and cautions Harry against pursuing the matter. Warburton then tells Harry that Amy is in very poor health.

The police sergeant, Winchell, arrives to inform the family that John has been in an accident and has suffered a concussion. Amy, Violet, Ivy, Gerald, Agatha, and Charles enter the room and John's condition is discussed. Harry and Amy exit. The others discuss Harry's continued odd behavior. Harry reenters and informs them that Amy has gone to sleep. Ivy receives a phone call, and then informs the group that Arthur has been in an accident; he appears to have been drunk. The Chorus ends the scene by commenting on the past and the future, and the sense of waiting and impending doom.

SCENE 2

In this pivotal scene, Harry and Agatha discuss the family and Harry's role in it. Agatha presses Harry to try and express what he feels no one will understand. He alludes to the spirits, the eyes, the Eumenides he believes are watching him, and presses Agatha to reveal what she knows about his parents. According to Agatha, when Amy and her husband first came to Wishwood, Amy felt isolated from her husband, and asked her sister Agatha to join her there as a companion. Agatha tells Harry that his father wanted to murder Amy, and that Agatha opposed the idea, as Amy was pregnant with Harry and Agatha felt instinctively that Harry should have been hers. Although Agatha does not specifically acknowledge an affair with Harry's father, her position as a confidant of the father, and her role in the rift between Amy and her husband is revealed.

Knowing all this, Harry admits now that it is possible that he only dreamt he pushed his own wife off the ship. The two then discuss their mutual feelings of isolation, and their sense that they see more of reality than the others in the family, or than people in general. Agatha advises Harry to leave Wishwood forever. The Eumenides again appear, and Harry speaks to them, telling them he will follow them. Agatha, in a trance-like state, speaks of curses and the birth of a child, but seems to shake herself out of this state, and once again tells Harry he must leave. As Harry resolves more firmly to go, Amy enters and confronts Agatha and Harry, insisting that Harry remain. Harry attempts to explain briefly to his mother his reasoning, and departs.

SCENE 3

Amy expresses her bitter feelings toward Agatha and reveals what Agatha alluded to in her conversation with Harry, that Agatha and Amy's husband had an affair. As Amy accuses Agatha of taking her son from her, just as she took her husband from her, Mary enters, and wonders why Harry is leaving. Amy responds by denouncing Agatha. Mary is certain that Harry will be in danger if he leaves Wishwood, but Agatha contradicts her. The two women furthermore come to realize that they both have seen something otherworldly, although what these things are is not made plain. Mary resolves to leave Wishwood as well.

Harry reenters to bid farewell. Violet, Gerald and Charles have also entered the room, and Harry must once again attempt to explain himself. He is finally able to say goodbye and leave. Amy, Violet, and Gerald depart. Mary asks Harry's servant, Downing, who appears briefly, to remain always with Harry. Downing reveals that he too has seen what he describes as ghosts; he sees little out of the ordinary in this. The servant leaves as Ivy enters. She is soon followed by Gerald and Violet. The gathered group hears Amy call out from the other room, asking for Agatha and Mary, who exit to go to her aid. Warburton appears, only to be called away quickly by Mary. The members of the Chorus then begin a lament in which they express confusion, sadness, and despair. When they resume speaking in their individual characters, it is revealed that Amy has died. Agatha ends the play by observing that the curse has been ended.

CHARACTERS

Agatha
Agatha is one of Amy Monchensey's younger sisters. She is markedly different from Ivy and Violet, who in many ways simply mirror one another rather than revealing any depth. Agatha shares a unique bond with Harry; she alone seems sensitive to the emotional, psychological, and philosophical struggles with which Harry is dealing in the aftermath of his wife's death. She encourages him to explain what he thinks no one can understand, and she helps him to put his struggle within the context of the larger framework of family truths that have previously been hidden from him. Specifically, she reveals that after she came to stay with Amy and her husband Lord Monchensey when they were young, Harry's father wanted to kill Harry's mother, and Agatha further hints of a romantic relationship between Harry's father and herself.

In the time since she left Wishwood, presumably after Harry's birth—although she has returned for visits—Agatha has gone on to become the principal of a women's college. Agatha strenuously suggests to Harry that he permanently leave Wishwood if he is to survive and maintain his sanity. Agatha is at odds with almost every other member of the family, often disagreeing with them, and always defending Harry. She furthermore demonstrates, in her encouragement of Harry, that she values honesty and truth, and always pushes him toward self-examination. She is disapproving and dismissive of the other family members' attempts to overlook or disguise Harry's odd behavior, and cares little for their desire for propriety or discretion. Describing Harry's conception and birth as a curse, Agatha declares that the curse has ended with Amy's death.

Amy, the Dowager Lady Monchensey

Amy is a widow and the owner of the Wishwood estate. She is older than her three sisters—Agatha, Ivy, and Violet—and the mother of Harry, Arthur, and John. Amy has engineered a reunion of her family, centered around her birthday, in order, as she states, to mend the ruptures of the past, and ensure the future transition of the estate from her care into Harry's. Her protective attitude toward Harry is made clear when the others discuss his long absence and his wife's death.

The other characters remember her from their youth as a controlling, powerful woman. She knows of Agatha's affair with her husband and accuses Agatha of using her influence to steal Harry away. Amy cannot understand Agatha's influence over or relationship with Harry. Amy's reaction to Harry's disturbing behavior is first surprise, then dismissal. She next seeks medical attention, calling in Dr. Warburton to discreetly assess him. Jealous of Agatha's obvious connection with Harry, Amy becomes angry and emotional when she learns that Agatha has apparently encouraged Harry to leave Wishwood. Her bitterness regarding Agatha's affair with her husband comes to the forefront. After Harry's departure, Amy dies.

Arthur

Arthur is Harry's brother, and the son of Amy. He never appears in the play, although he is en route to the family reunion at Amy's home during the course of the play. He is in a car accident, and the family presumes that he was drunk at the time he was pursued by police and ran his car into a shop window.

Chorus

In the first part and scene of the play, the Chorus is identified as the following individuals: Ivy, Violet, Gerald, and Charles. As a group, the Chorus comments on the action of the play. Eliot's use of a Chorus in a modern play reflects his interest in classicism, that is, Greek literary models.

Downing

Downing is Harry's servant and chauffeur. He admits to having seen ghosts accompanying Harry; he does not seem to fear them, as they are concerned with Harry, and not him.

The Eumenides

Listed in the Dramatis Personae (the listing of characters at the beginning of the play), the Eumenides are also identified in the stage directions. They appear apparently only to Harry, although Agatha, Mary, and Downing all seem to be aware of some sort of spiritual presence in the home as well. According to Greek mythology, the Eumenides are another name for the Furies, three goddesses associated with vengeance.

Ivy

Ivy is one of Amy younger sisters, and Harry's aunt. She and her sister Violet are almost indistinguishable from one another in the play.

John

John is Harry's brother and Amy's son. John does not appear in the play. He suffers an accident on the way to the Monchensey home and is diagnosed, the family learns, with a concussion. Harry feels that it is John who should take over the management of the estate of Wishwood, rather than himself, as his mother intends.

Mary

Mary is the daughter of one of Amy Monchensey's cousins. Amy at one time intended Mary to be Harry's wife, but Harry instead married another woman. Nevertheless, Mary, apparently with few other prospects, remained on at Wishwood. She suspects that Amy intended her to be a wife who would remain in the shadows and allow Amy as much space and influence in Harry's life as she wished. Instead, Harry traveled with his wife throughout Europe for seven years, and he continued to travel for one additional year after his wife's death. Upon Harry's return, Mary begins to feel the need to leave Wishwood; she asks Agatha for help. Her discussion with Agatha reveals that she was once a student at the college where Agatha serves as principal.

Mary speaks often of her sense of isolation at Wishwood. To Agatha she confesses that she feels trapped at Wishwood by Amy and her manipulations. Mary further reveals to Agatha that she sees things others cannot—she alludes to both visions and ghosts—a trait or ability that aligns her with both Agatha and Harry. Mary recognizes that Agatha is as out of place at Wishwood as she is, although she does not elaborate on this perception. Along with Agatha, Mary speaks the haunting words at the play's end about the power of curses.

Harry, Lord Monchensey

Harry is the protagonist of the play. He arrives at Wishwood in a disturbed state of mind, a year after his wife's death, and after an eight-year absence from the family estate. In discussing his recent past, Harry reveals his belief that he pushed his wife overboard to her death during a storm at sea. The others assure him that this could not have been what happened, but after he leaves the room, their curiosity and suspicions on the matter are aired.

Throughout the course of the play, Harry expresses his conviction that the others cannot understand his frame of mind, cannot even understand reality in the same way that he does. He speaks of living in two worlds at the same time, of trying to explain things in a language the others do not speak. He believes he sees spirits of some kind, and that they have been pursuing him, watching him, and judging him for his actions. As he discusses these matters with Agatha, Harry is relieved to learn that she finds coherence in his words that the others do not recognize. He is tortured by guilt over his wife's death, but also feels that upon his return to Wishwood, he is cognizant of an even older pain, "A misery long forgotten." Agatha reveals to Harry truths that have been hidden, and urges him, for the sake of his health, sanity, and survival, to leave Wishwood. It is only through Agatha's intervention that Harry is able grasp the possibility of the future.

More gently than before, but still as urgently, Harry attempts to explain to his mother in particular and to the rest of his family in general, the reasons for his decisions. He insists that John is the rightful master of the Wishwood estate, and he leaves the family to pursue their own futures, vowing at the same time to face his own troubles, his sense of guilt, and his need for atonement.

Charles Piper

Charles is Harry's uncle and the brother of the deceased Lord Monchensey, Amy's late husband. Charles appears eager to disregard Harry's bizarre behavior in order to maintain the appearance of normalcy. He decides, despite the objection of his sisters, to discreetly question Harry's servant regarding the death of Harry's wife.

Gerald Piper

Gerald is Harry's uncle and the brother of the deceased Lord Monchensey, Amy's late husband. He is somewhat disengaged from the turmoil in the family, although he supports Charles in his decision to question Harry's servant about Harry's wife's death.

Violet

Violet is one of Amy's younger sisters, and Harry's aunt. She and her sister Ivy are almost interchangeable characters; neither stands out as a fully developed character. Violet observes that the family does not always welcome her observations. In reality, it is only Agatha who suggests that Violet judges Harry's behavior too harshly.

Dr. Warburton

Dr. Warburton is summoned by Amy to talk to Harry. She hopes that the doctor will be able to assess Harry discreetly and treat him if possible. During the extended conversation between Warburton and Harry, Harry assumes the doctor is there to speak with him about his unusual behavior and attempts to avoid this direction in the discussion, instead questioning Warburton about his parents. Warburton confirms that there are things that Harry does not know about his parents, and he urges Harry to not question Agatha about the matter. Warburton then proceeds to tell Harry that his mother's health is quite fragile. The doctor is also present when Amy dies.

Winchell

Winchell is the police sergeant who appears in the second part of the play, in the first scene. He informs the family that John has been in a car accident and has suffered a concussion.

THEMES

Isolation

A recurring theme in *The Family Reunion* is that of isolation, specifically, that particular sense of isolation one feels only within a family group. Many of the primary players in this drama—Harry, Mary, Agatha—either express this sense of isolation or are viewed by others in terms of isolation. Even marginal characters such as Violet seem to feel shades of this angst. At the opening of the play, Amy expresses her desire to keep the family together, yet during the course of the play, "together" becomes the opposite of what many characters in the play feel.

From the moment he returns home, Harry's sense of emotional isolation from his family is made clear. Agitated, he speaks of the eyes that watch him, and notices that the others cannot see these spirit figures. Returning to the family after an eight-year absence, Harry is told by his mother that the Wishwood estate is now his to manage. Harry feels isolated from everyone else by the differences in what and how they see, but also by virtue of the fact that the others cannot comprehend him. He feels that they are all "people to whom nothing has ever happened," and who therefore are unable to perceive "the unimportance of events." Harry feels that there is a vast difference between what has happened to him and the events that have occurred at Wishwood. The others are clearly mystified by his statements. Later, when Harry and Agatha speak privately, he begins to realize that Agatha is capable of grasping his meaning in a way the others cannot, and his sense of isolation begins to dissipate. He states that somehow, he feels "happy for a moment, as if I had come home."

Meanwhile, Mary expresses her own sense of isolation from the family. In fact, for Mary, this sense of isolation extends beyond the borders of her family. She states early on in the play that she does not "belong to any generation." She feels that her youth has passed her by, as she waited with Amy for Harry, but at the same time, she does not belong to the more elderly group of Amy's siblings. In her conversation with Agatha, Mary states that neither she nor Agatha truly belong at Wishwood. Speaking with Harry, Mary expresses her sense of always having felt she did not belong at Wishwood; she describes herself as a "misfit" and as "superfluous."

Agatha's isolation is recognized by herself and others, but she tends to dwell less on her feelings of isolation than Mary. However, Agatha does not contradict Mary when Mary tells her "you don't belong here / Any more than I do." Agatha soon acknowledges their mutual isolation by defining her role and Mary's within the family: "You and I, Mary, / Are only watchers and waiters."

Time

Time and its passage, along with the related notion of change, are primary themes in *The Family Reunion*. Amy insists from the beginning of the play that nothing has changed at Wishwood, that she has wanted everything to remain the same since Harry's departure so that he will feel welcome, comfortable, and at home when he returns to Wishwood. She states repeatedly, "Nothing has been changed." Harry is astounded by the statement, even after only being home a few moments. Upon viewing his family members, he tells them, "You all look so withered and young." The peculiar statement points to Harry's personal sense of hopelessness. He observes that everyone has aged, in terms of their being withered, but at the same time, they possess youthfulness in the sense of having a future. Harry sees his own future as bleak because he is haunted by his past. The blindness his family possesses—this inability to see things as they are that he repeatedly points out to them—also gives them the freedom to hope, the ability to believe in the future. Harry reasserts later how unsettling it has been to walk into a home in which Amy has insisted upon halting time's passage. He describes the situation as "unnatural" and states further that "It only makes the changing of people / All the more manifest."

In her discussion with Harry, Agatha tells him that she is able to guess what Harry thinks about his past, and even what his thoughts on the future—for himself and for Wishwood—might be, "But a present is missing, needed to connect them." Her statement is actually true, not just for Harry, but for many of the characters in the play. They live in a state of suspension between the past they remember and the future that Amy has tried to prepare for them (a future in which Harry has married Mary and taken over Wishwood). Yet no one seems to be living in the present. While they wait for Amy's desires to unfold, they talk, but no one acts. They wait for John and Arthur to arrive; these men never

TOPICS FOR FURTHER STUDY

- *The Family Reunion* is a play that creates a number of problems in its production for the stage. Directors often struggle with a means of portraying the Eumenides and the Chorus. Using print and online sources, examine criticism of modern stage productions of the play. Write an essay in which you analyze reviews of late twentieth- and early twenty-first-century productions of the play.

- The verse form of *The Family Reunion* was the feature of the work Eliot admits to being most focused on; he was first and foremost a poet. Individually or with a small group, write a one-act play in blank or free verse, or a combination of the two. Consider using family conflict, as Eliot did, as the subject matter. As a group—a small theater troupe—present your play to the class as a live production. Alternatively, film the play for your class to view either online or on DVD.

- African American poet and playwright Langston Hughes wrote during the same time period as Eliot. His play *Mulatto: A Play of the Deep South* was written during the Great Depression and performed on Broadway in 1935, although it was not published until 1963. The work explores a father-son relationship as well as racial prejudice in the American South of the 1930s. Read Hughes's play and conduct a formal analysis of the work. That is, analyze the play's form and study the ways in which the language and style of the play work in support of, or detract from, the play's themes. Examine other elements of Hughes's dramatic form, such as characterization and plot. Summarize your findings in a critical essay on the play.

- The ideas explored in *The Family Reunion* include the notion of a family's shame, as well as the despair and hope of the protagonist. Although set in a different time and place (Japan in the 1970s), Kyoko Mori's 1993 young-adult novel *Shizuko's Daughter* touches on similar themes. With a book group, read Mori's novel. Examine the elements of the work that are similar to Eliot's play. In what ways do the authors handle the family conflicts that occur in their story? Like Harry in Eliot's play, Yuki turns her despair over her family's particular issues into hope. How does she accomplish this? Set up an online blog or discussion group in which members of your book group post their thoughts and responses to the story, and make the discussion accessible to the rest of the class.

- Eliot's play was written during a time of great economic difficulty in Great Britain, yet the characters in the play are wealthy aristocrats. Study the issues related to social class differences in Great Britain during the 1930s. At this point in history, did the working and middle classes outnumber the upper classes? Were the upper classes—the land-owning gentry and the nobles—affected by the economic crises in Great Britain at the time? What types of conflicts existed among the various classes? Consider the government's role in perpetuating the class system in Great Britain during this time. Create a presentation, complete with charts and graphs, about the social-class population distribution to summarize your findings.

---

come. They wait for Harry to accept the management of the estate; he does not, but he lingers at Wishwood, agonizing over his past and his sense of guilt, until Agatha urges him forward. This act spurs the play into motion; Harry resolves to leave, as does Mary; Amy dies. The curse, as Agatha states, has ended, and time can once again move forward.

Wishwood was the family's country home in northern England. (St. Nick / Shutterstock.com)

STYLE

Modified Blank Verse Drama

Eliot used modified blank verse in *The Family Reunion*. Blank verse is poetry that is unrhymed, but written in iambic pentameter. Meter is a pattern of unaccented and accented syllables in a line of poetry. Each grouping of syllables is called a metrical foot. In an iambic foot, there is one unaccented syllable followed by one accented syllable. A line written in iambic pentameter contains five of these unaccented-accented feet. Eliot's dialogue in *The Family Reunion* contains a mix of blank verse lines with free verse poetry. Free verse poetry is unrhymed and unaccented. In the absence of rhyme and meter, the poet uses language and line breaks to shape the poem's meaning. In instances where verse rather than prose is utilized in a play (as opposed to a poem), the dramatist seeks to establish a more formal or serious rhythm to his characters' speeches than prose typically allows. Verse is often selected as the mode for dramatic tragedies, and Shakespearean and Greek tragedies were written in verse.

Classicism

Classicism refers to a respect for ancient Greek styles of art and literature. Eliot's works are often said to be influenced by his interest in Greek literature, and he was a self-described classicist, as observed by Patrick Deane in a 1992 essay for the *Journal of Modern Literature*. Eliot's use of verse as opposed to prose is one example of his nod to classicism in *The Family Reunion*. Additionally, he employs two other elements of Greek drama: the Chorus, and the Eumenides. The Chorus serves the same function in Eliot's drama as choruses did in the plays of the ancient Greeks. The character or characters that comprise the Chorus comment on the action of the play, are often used to divide the scenes of the play, and sometimes provide moral judgments on the other characters or events in the play. The Chorus was not a commonly used feature in modern drama by the time Eliot's play was written.

Finally, Eliot incorporates the Eumenides, the Greek deities also known as the Furies, into the play. Traditionally, in ancient Greek mythology,

COMPARE & CONTRAST

- **1930s:** Great Britain suffers from a severe economic crisis brought on by both the high cost of World War I and the global aftermath of the Great Depression in the United States. Unemployment rates are high, and war looms in Europe as Nazi Germany attacks Austria and Czechoslovakia. A cultural atmosphere of anxiety is prevalent.

  Today: The British economy is struggling to recover after the global economic crisis of the early twenty-first century and the high costs of Great Britain's involvement in the wars in Iraq and Afghanistan. By 2010, unemployment figures and economic indicators are showing some signs of improvement, yet public discontent remains high.

- **1930s:** British theater is thriving as playwrights explore a new, modern sense of freedom in literary forms. Audiences frequent theater performances to be diverted from their fears regarding the faltering economy. Mysteries, thrillers, and plays exploring sexuality and sexual taboos are popular.

  Today: British theater is undergoing what some have called a "new golden age." The industry is thriving on a combination of revivals of older dramas and new productions of original material.

- **1930s:** Class structures are rigid in Great Britain, with little mobility between the working class and the educated classes of the middle and upper ranks of society. The landed gentry, or owners of estates, and the noble, or titled, members of society comprise its upper classes. Such social structures often lend themselves to political conflict, as members of the lower classes fight for rights and privileges denied to them.

  Today: Great Britain seeks to de-emphasize its focus on class, yet the notion of class differences is still prevalent. A 2010 article by Will Hutton in the British newspaper the *Observer* discusses the class disparities in education, income, and opportunity.

---

the Eumenides are linked with the notion of vengeance. Harry sees the Eumenides at Wishwood, but states that they were with him before he arrived. He later comes to believe that they were leading him, rather than chasing him. Although their purpose is not entirely clear, Harry believes he must follow them, presumably as a means of atoning for his sense of guilt. As he comes to the certainty that they will lead him through his expiation, Harry now regards the specters as "bright angels" who will lead him "out of defilement" and toward "reconciliation." As Martin Scofield points out in his 1988 *T. S. Eliot: The Poems*, the transformation in the way the spirits are regarded mirrors the transformation that occurs in the Greek play *Orestes*, by Aeschylus, of the Eumenides from Furies to figures referred to as "the kindly ones."

HISTORICAL CONTEXT

Interwar Art and Literature

During the period of time between the end of World War I and the beginning of World War II, the modernist movement exploded in Great Britain. British writers and artists were influenced by the modernist movement already underway in the rest of Europe. In both art and literature, the rejection of traditional forms and structures was followed by experimentation with new modes of expression. Writers such as Eliot and his friend Ezra Pound, along with James Joyce, explored new literary forms. Pound advanced the use of free verse and imagism, or the emphasis on visual details and concrete images in writing. Eliot sought to create a new dramatic verse form, and Joyce experimented with language and was the innovator of a unique narrative style.

Also during this time, visual and literary arts were the battleground where the debate between form and function was held by artists and critics. Formalists maintained that a work's form was an intrinsic part of its content. They adhered to the view that the form of a work was more important than the social context within which it might be read, and also more important to an understanding of the work than biographical facts about the author. Functionalists, on the other hand, regarded art and literature as representative of a particular social context, and maintained that art and literature served a function within that context. Eliot is typically associated with a formalist viewpoint.

The Onset of World War II in Great Britain

Eliot was writing *The Family Reunion* just before the onset of World War II; the work was published in 1939, the same year Great Britain declared war on Germany. Although Eliot possessed dual citizenship—American and British— he had been living in London as a British subject since 1927. Never having fully recovered from the financial costs of World War I, Great Britain, like the rest of the world, was also impacted by the Great Depression during the 1930s. Unemployment was high. The monarchy was troubled. The recently crowned King Edward VIII abdicated in 1936 in order to marry his American mistress. His brother then became King George VI. In India, then a part of the British Empire, demonstrations were being staged in favor of Indian independence. Nazi Germany had taken over both Austria and Czechoslovakia by 1938, but in the late 1930s the British Prime Minister, Neville Chamberlain, was focused on the domestic economic crisis and consequently attempted to appease the Nazis through negotiations and concessions rather than face direct conflict. However, when Nazi leader Adolf Hitler invaded Poland on September 1, 1939, Britain and France both declared war on Germany within days. With Great Britain and France involved, World War II had begun. In 1940, after Hitler had launched attacks throughout Europe, Prime Minister Chamberlain resigned and was succeeded by Winston Churchill, who governed the nation over the course of the war.

The family is reunited to celebrate Amy's 60th birthday. (Cheryl E. Davis | Shutterstock.com)

CRITICAL OVERVIEW

The Family Reunion is commonly regarded as an innovative work in terms of its verse form, but its other features have been analyzed more harshly. Even Eliot faulted *The Family Reunion* as suffering in terms of plot and characterization, due to his intent focus on the play's verse form, according to Seán Lucy in *T. S. Eliot and the Idea of Tradition*. Nancy Duvall Hargrove, in a 1981 essay on Eliot for the *Dictionary of Literary Biography*, explains that although the play "was not well received when it opened at the Westminster Theatre in March 1939 and was not a great theatrical success in subsequent productions, it has nevertheless been the most often revived of Eliot's modern plays." Still, critics often find that beyond the aesthetics of Eliot's verse, the play is difficult to appreciate. Lucy describes the play as "an uneasy blend of formalism and realism." Lucy additionally finds the use of the Chorus in the play to have been a fascinating element, but ultimately this experiment "was a failure."

The use of the Eumenides, or Furies, is also the subject of some scholarly debate. Craig Raine, in his 2006 work *T. S. Eliot*, explores the way the Furies come to be viewed as harmless figures once Harry confronts them at Wishwood. Raine draws a parallel between this transformation and a form of treatment in psychoanalysis in which the subject releases repressed emotion by reliving, often through hypnosis, a traumatic event. Subhas Sarkar, in *T. S. Eliot: The Dramatist*, regards the Furies as emblematic of Harry's sense of sin. Observing the difficulty in staging a supernatural element such as the Furies, Sarkar states that depicting the Furies on stage "is bound to create a problem of representation and offer a direct challenge to realistic convention," but also notes that there is no other way to convey the "sense of original sin or inherited sin from which Harry intensely suffers." Sarkar reviews Eliot's own understanding of this difficulty in the production of the play, and traces the various methods by which Eliot attempted to stage the Eumenides. Similarly, Randy Malamud traces the difficulty directors face in staging the Furies. As Malamud writes in the 1994 *Where the Words Are Valid: T. S. Eliot's Communities of Drama*, "Based on this barrage of evidence from playwright, director, critics, and reviewers, it is safe to state that the Furies represent the single largest and most obvious dramaturgical blunder in the play."

CRITICISM

Catherine Dominic

Dominic is a novelist, freelance writer, and editor. In the following essay, she analyzes some of the philosophical concerns Eliot examines in The Family Reunion. *She maintains that while some critics, approaching the play's meaning through an analysis of its existential meaning, have found the play lacking, a study of its explorations of the nature of being and the nature of knowing reveals the value Eliot places on philosophical questioning for its own sake, rather than on resolution or context.*

The Family Reunion has been criticized as an unsuccessful play for many reasons. Eliot himself admitted, as critic Seán Lucy observes in the 1961 *T. S. Eliot and the Idea of Tradition*, that Eliot's plotting and characterization were neglected as he focused on the cultivation of

the play's dramatic verse. Given the shortcomings the dramatist himself acknowledged, readers, audiences, and critics have taken various paths to divine the meaning, purpose, message, or aesthetic value of the play. Some critics explore the play's existential nature as an avenue toward ascertaining meaning. (Existentialism is a branch of philosophy in which an individual's free will is emphasized as the only mechanism by which choices—moral or otherwise—can be made, in an existence devoid of any universal truths or guiding principles.) This path toward understanding the play has also been regarded as limited. Randy Malamud, in the 1994 *Where the Words Are Valid: T. S. Eliot's Communities of Drama*, finds that while there are existential elements to *The Family Reunion*, the play is deficient as an existential drama in that it lacks a context for comprehending the existential questions it asks. Malamud states, "The play is affected by all the malaise, uncertainty, and ambiguity that accompany the existential sensibility but without benefit of a consequent ameliorative (or instructive) aesthetic." Yet Eliot's philosophical concerns run deeper than the existential anxiety Harry exhibits, an angst that is further complicated by Christian notions of sin and guilt.

Another philosophical approach to the play delves not into Harry's torment over his choices and the judgment he inflicts upon himself, but into Harry's deeper ontological and epistemological concerns about the nature of being, and what it means to see truly, to know reality. (Ontology is the branch of philosophy that is concerned with the nature of being, of existence. Epistemology is the branch of philosophy dealing with the nature of knowledge and how it is acquired and understood.) By examining the ontological and epistemological issues in the play, the lack of resolution or context for understanding the play's existential questions becomes less pertinent. As Harry explores the philosophical questions about existence and knowledge, the only certainty the play offers is that the answers are ambiguous. Although Harry believes he is leaving Wishwood to pursue the only path "out of defilement— / Which leads in the end to reconciliation," Agatha remains convinced that there is no such certainty. Yet significantly, Agatha still encourages Harry in his quest. Through Harry, Eliot explores an individual tortured by his desire to understand the nature of his existence, to know what it means to know. Through

WHAT DO I READ NEXT?

- Eliot's long poem *The Waste Land* was originally published in 1922 and was edited by Eliot's friend, poet Ezra Pound. The poem's poetic and thematic experimentation and complexity have been heralded as exemplifying the modernist movement. The work was reissued by W. W. Norton in 2000.

- Lyndall Gordon's critical biography of Eliot, *T. S. Eliot: An Imperfect Life*, was published by W. W. Norton in 1999. Gordon explores the many dualities of Eliot's life and works, for example his American and British citizenship, and his Christian and secular philosophies. Additionally, Gordon explores Eliot's literary influences and accomplishments.

- *The Selected Poems of Ezra Pound* was originally published in 1926 and reprinted in 1957 by New Directions. This collection by Eliot's friend and peer reflects Pound's reputation as an innovator in modern English poetry.

- Jewish American playwright Lillian Hellman's play *The Little Foxes* was published in 1939, the same year as Eliot's *The Family Reunion*. It examines the conflict in an American family in the post-Civil War South. The work is available in a 1995 edition published by Dramatists Play Service.

- *The Migrant Farmworker's Son*, the 1996 young-adult drama by Silvia Gonzales, published by Dramatic Publishing, incorporates realism with the supernatural as the protagonist, Henry, struggles to live in two worlds: that of an American, and that of a Mexican immigrant. Gonzales incorporates poetry into her play, spoken by the ghost of an elderly farm worker, who encodes messages to Henry within his poems and aids in the family's reconciliation.

- *Modernism: Introduction to British Literature and Culture* by Leigh Willson offers a detailed analysis of the literary modernist movement in Great Britain and provides the historical and cultural context within which this movement is situated. The various subclassifications of the movement, including imagism and surrealism, are also discussed. The work was published by Continuum in 2007.

Agatha, Eliot emphasizes that the seeking of such knowledge is what is to be valued, rather than the unlikely attainment of resolution. Eliot is often described as a formalist, one who places value on form for its own sake, as its own meaning. The context in which meaning may be derived, in which answers or purpose may be found, is not the aim of the formalist. This formalist approach can help the reader appreciate the philosophical issues in *The Family Reunion*. It is in the form, that is, in the philosophical questioning itself, that Eliot finds value, rather than in cultural context; his purpose is not didacticism, but to explore the form of inquiry.

In examining the philosophical questions related to the nature being and knowing, Eliot uses the characters in his play for different purposes. The characters comprising the Chorus—Ivy, Violet, Charles, and Gerald—voice confusion and disinterest. Harry questions existence and meaning, deeply and desperately. While frustrated, he nevertheless continues to pursue clarity. The self-possessed Agatha appears to possess a sense of serenity. She is disengaged from the emotion in the play, in a manner characteristic of a sage and mystic, rather than similar to her more unenlightened kin. In the first scene in the play, the nature of knowing is called into question. Harry makes his first speech about understanding in the first scene of the play, shortly after he arrives home. He speaks of the significance of understanding as a thing unto itself, as well as

"THROUGH HARRY, ELIOT EXPLORES AN INDIVIDUAL TORTURED BY HIS DESIRE TO UNDERSTAND THE NATURE OF HIS EXISTENCE, TO KNOW WHAT IT MEANS TO KNOW. THROUGH AGATHA, ELIOT EMPHASIZES THAT THE SEEKING OF SUCH KNOWLEDGE IS WHAT IS TO BE VALUED, RATHER THAN THE UNLIKELY ATTAINMENT OF RESOLUTION."

his family's inability to truly understand. He suggests that his family is aware only of a surface reality, but that there is something deeper that he perceives. There is a world like a waking nightmare, one that has no comprehensible language. He struggles to communicate his perception that there is a world of external events, and a deeper, truer reality. While his family is largely dismissive of this strange talk, Agatha feels certain that Harry's meaning will become clearer to her, and that there is much that Harry himself does not grasp. She tells Harry, "There is more to understand: hold fast to that / As the way to freedom." This is the first indication of Agatha's level of spiritual, philosophical awareness. Not long after this exchange, the Chorus expresses their unwillingness to abandon their certainty concerning reality. "Hold tight," they declare, "we must insist that the world is what we have always taken it to be."

In the play's second scene, Harry and Mary discuss the nature of being. Harry has begun to discuss the distorted nature of his world, his perception that what he sees "May be one dream or another." Mary responds that he clearly hoped that by coming home, he would find his "real self." She is convinced that what Harry needs is to change something inside of himself. Harry denies this, and accuses Mary of being like the others, unable to understand. When he sees the Eumenides, Harry declares, speaking to the spirits, that when he knew her, presumably his dead wife, he was a different person. As he tries to pinpoint his identity in the past and in the present, he states, "I tell you, it is not me you are looking

at." He regards the nature of his being as fractured in time and this sense of the disunity of his being increases his frustration with Mary's inability to grasp his meaning.

In part 2, scene 2, a crucial conversation between Harry and Agatha occurs in which Harry's concerns with being and knowing are addressed by Agatha. First, she prods him to discuss his perceptions. Harry embarks on a lengthy speech in which he struggles with understanding the meaning of things he has seen. He goes on to discuss his feelings of existing in a state divided, of feeling "The degradation of being parted from my self, / From the self which persisted only as an eye, seeing." In this state of seeing, Harry witnessed himself, but without judgment. It was as if he had been watching himself in a dream. "When I was outside," he states, meaning outside of himself, "I could associate nothing of it with myself, / Though nothing else was real." Harry's ontological and epistemological struggles are united in this sentiment. He is expressing the way his fractured being perceived reality. Furthermore, Harry seems uncertain as to which self he really is—the self that is watching or the self that is being watched—and what reality is truly happening. Is what he is watching real? Or is reality the state of watching? Harry goes on to explain that he hoped everything would settle into the proper place in his mind once he returned to Wishwood, but what he found is a new sensation of something out of place, an old "misery" causing "a new torture." Agatha proceeds to tell him the secrets of his parents, of his father's desire to kill his mother, of her own tangled role. Harry finds this knowledge freeing, sensing that this old conflict impacted his own psyche more than he previously understood.

As Harry expresses his sense of freedom from his own mind, he and Agatha share a poetic exchange about what it is to exist in this dark, fractured state but still feel the compulsion toward wholeness and connection. Harry's relief at coming through this darkness and finding Agatha on the other side is tempered by her acknowledgment that this sense of relief is only the beginning of a long journey upon which Harry must now embark. Again she acts as advisor to Harry, coaching him along a path toward greater understanding. Harry still perceives that he exists in two realities and that he sees what others do not, but he accepts this as his role. He now views the spirits that have haunted him as guides. He no longer questions his sanity, but understands that others will continue to do so. Before Harry leaves, he accepts that there is much he does not understand, that the nature of his existence and his reality are clouded, unknowable, but that still he must go. Later, Agatha attempts to explain Harry's departure to Mary. She speaks of a multilayered reality to which Harry has access, but that others do not. Agatha insists that she would not "take the responsibility / of tempting them," meaning those who only live in this world, "over the border" between worlds. Harry, however, has already "been led across the frontier."

In his farewell speech, Harry appears lighthearted, despite all the uncertainty associated with his impending journey. He assures the others that if it were possible for them to understand, they would be happy about his leaving. Not long after, Amy dies. The Chorus begins a lengthy verse in which the understanding that reality may not be what it seems is expressed, but feared. The members of the Chorus state, "We do know what we are doing; / And even, when you think of it, / We do not know much about thinking." Referencing an earlier line concerned with the limitations of the "circle of our understanding," the Chorus wonders, "What is happening outside the circle? / And what is the meaning of happening?" They have become increasingly aware of Harry's ontological and epistemological struggles, but this awareness breeds terror rather than the acceptance that characterizes Harry's actions at the end of the play. "And what is being done to us?" they wonder, "And what are we, and what are we doing?" The agonized speech concludes with despair: "We have lost our way in the dark." Throughout this speech, the members of the Chorus have echoed precisely Harry's earlier sense of panic, his fearful recognition that who he is, how he exists, and the nature of reality itself are all unknown. Furthermore this void of knowledge, this confusion, is suddenly very relevant for the Chorus. It is as if they have become aware of all that they do not know, and it all suddenly matters very much. Yet as the speech ends, they step away into their individual characters, and address the particulars of Amy's funeral arrangements. Only Charles seems to wonder if some shift in his understanding has occurred, stating, "I fear that my mind is not what it was—or was it?—and yet I think that I might understand." In the end, they "adjust [themselves] to the moment" and "do the right thing."

Throughout the play, Harry sees the spirits, the Eumenides, who he is certain have been watching him. His terror of them turns to acceptance, particularly when Agatha admits to seeing them as well. Other characters—Mary and Harry's servant—also confess to having seen such spirits. Arguably Eliot's usage of the spirits undercuts the play's intriguing philosophical explorations. The play's examination of the nature of perception and reality, the nature of one's being and existence, could be successfully undertaken by Harry and Agatha without the element of spirits, ghosts, or Greek deities. If they are not viewed as supernatural elements, it is difficult to see them as anything but symbols of disturbed minds. Any intellectual engagement the reader has in these philosophical evaluations may, depending on his or her spiritual beliefs, be thwarted by the presence of the spirits. The intellectual value of Harry's and Agatha's examinations may be seen as diminished. Even without the claims of spirits, Harry's and Agatha's speeches are frequently fraught with unconventional ideas and attitudes. The spirits inject further ambiguity into how the characters, and their sanity, should be read.

The conclusion of the play underscores some of this ambiguity. Mary and Agatha speak of a curse, suggesting the way it connects the world of our perceptions and the world of reality. In this exchange, Harry's expanding understanding of such connections is underscored, and the earlier curse Agatha referred to as coming into being with Harry's conception is alluded to. Agatha's role in the play as wise advisor to Harry on matters of the two worlds he seems to inhabit and as mystic—she sees spirits and speaks mysteriously of curses—is further emphasized in her final speech about the ending of the curse.

Yet despite the presence of spirits in the play—either in the minds of the characters or as supernatural beings—Eliot offers a commentary on the nature of being and the nature of knowing in which questioning and uncertainty are embraced and the notions of absolutes and resolutions are dismissed. Agatha encourages Harry along a path toward accepting an understanding of reality and being that is ultimately unknowable but more complex and varied than most people are able to comprehend. There is no conclusion or context, for that is the nature of our knowledge—it is incomplete, and the journey itself is the only thing of value, for the

Amy's last words, "The clock has stopped,"
symbolized Harry's departure and her own death.

(pjmorley | Shutterstock.com)

resolution is unattainable. As Agatha tells Harry, "This is the next moment. This is the beginning."

Source: Catherine Dominic, Critical Essay on *The Family Reunion*, in *Drama for Students*, Gale, Cengage Learning, 2011.

Tim Walker

In the following review, Walker analyzes the problems he witnessed in a London production of The Family Reunion.

Over the years one gets into relationships with certain theatres—as one does certain friends—where one expects to be amused every time one visits them. The Donmar Warehouse is such a theatre.

I have been challenged, inspired, depressed and elated at this venue, but never, before I saw *The Family Reunion*, bored. I am not entirely sure what has gone wrong. One certainly can't fault the Nobel Prize-winning writer, T.S. Eliot, nor the cast, which includes William Gaunt, Penelope Wilton, Gemma Jones, Sam West, Anna Carteret and Una Stubbs, all of them, as ever, on splendid form.

Jeremy Herrin directs the proceedings with confidence and flair and achieves an interesting doom-laden atmosphere. There is a fine set of a dining-room in a country house designed by Bunny Christie and some exquisitely moody lighting courtesy of Rick Fisher.

It not only has good looks but also a lot to say about the timeless subject of a family and its problems. The return of Harry (West) to the family hearth after an absence of seven years to celebrate the birthday of his mother (Gemma Jones) is overshadowed by his admission that he may have killed his wife. His Aunt Agatha (Wilton) meanwhile seems to be a little too close to him for comfort, as indeed she once was to his father. It all goes to show Alan Bennett was spot on when he once noted that every family has a secret—and the secret is it isn't like any other family.

The rest of the chaps—Gaunt, Paul Shelley and Christopher Benjamin—all look on with suitably despairing looks, as indeed do the rest of the ladies. They even manage to make a success of the play's stagey preoccupation with occasional bursts of knowing dialogue which have to be spoken in unison directly to the audience.

Spectral infants walk across the stage, a ghost appears and a body falls from a window and there are some ferocious rows. But, for all that, this play never comes anywhere close to equalling the sum of its formidable parts. It lacks life—that indefinable quality which engages an audience. Maybe this production is simply too expertly handled for its own good: a Fabergé egg of a play, beautiful to behold and wonderfully executed, but sadly nothing more than that.

Over the years I have noticed a wearying consistency about the views of some of my fellow critics. It is as if early on they decide as a matter of policy to be, say, anti the *Globe*, pro musicals, anti Antony Sher or pro Bill Kenwright (most of them happen to be pro Bill, by the way, but then again the old charmer can always be relied upon to provide them with free interval drinks).

I reserve the right, by contrast, to be gloriously inconsistent at all times. I just don't believe that one can take a view about anything in the theatre and stick rigidly to it through thick and thin. Sometimes one just finds oneself enjoying or hating something despite oneself. Earlier this year I controversially observed that I didn't generally care for musicals, and then accorded *Marguerite* and *Gigi* five-star ratings. I also said when I saw *La Cage aux Folles* at the Menier Chocolate Factory in January that the show struck me as unpardonably dated.

Now, almost a year on, Terry Johnson's resilient production has transferred to the West End, and I found to my surprise that I loved every toe-tapping minute of it. I attribute this to a number of factors. Members of the cast, headed this time around by Denis Lawson as the nightclub owner Georges, do not seem to take themselves quite so seriously. A great big extrovert show like this was always going to look uncomfortable in a venue quite as cramped as the Menier and now it has the space to kick off its high heels and live a little.

The gay storyline, considered so terribly daring when the show was first seen in London in the 1980s, is now handled in a matter-of-fact, even post-gay sort of way that is in keeping with a more enlightened age. The emphasis this time around seems to be on doing justice to Jerry Herman's superb music and lyrics and getting the acting right—Lawson is a treat, as is Douglas Hodge as his drag star partner Albin.

Alistair Darling's name does not appear in the credits, but I ought also to acknowledge the Chancellor for putting me in the mood for a big, bold, brassy musical on Monday night. Still shellshocked by his pre-budget statement, I, along with the rest of the audience, rose in unison at the end to sing 'The best of times is now ... as for tomorrow, well, who knows?' I think, now that *Things Can Only Get Better* doesn't exactly ring true for Labour any more, the party could do worse than to adopt *La Cage's* showstopper as their new anthem.

Source: Tim Walker, "Dysfunctional Family: T. S. Eliot's Play Is Beautifully Acted, But Dull: Meanwhile Drag Queens Lighten Up Dark Times," in *London Sunday Telegraph*, November 30, 2008.

Keiko Saeki

In the following excerpt, Saeki discusses Eliot's use of poetic drama in The Family Reunion *and* The Cocktail Party.

A memorial plaque to Eliot mounted in 1998 on the sidewalk at the site of his birthplace, 2635 Locust Street in St. Louis, notes his titles: "Poet, Philosopher, Literary Critic, Dramatist, Nobel Laureate." In fact, Eliot did not get down to writing poetic drama until as late as his last masterpiece *Four Quartets* (1936–43), although he made an attempt to write his first poetic drama *Sweeney Agonistes* in 1923–25, but could not complete it. Nevertheless, he had been deeply interested in poetic drama and had

> IN FACT, ELIOT WRITES *THE COCKTAIL PARTY*, FIXING HIS EYES UPON EACH HUMAN RELATION UNDERMINED IN *THE FAMILY REUNION*."

written many essays on poetic dramas and poetic dramatists since the beginning.

1. THE DRAMATIST ELIOT'S ASPIRATIONS

Eliot used dramatic techniques in his early poems, while he was strongly conscious of poetic verse forms in his poetic dramas. Writing plays was always closely related to writing poems in his mind, as his interacting with the director E. Martin Browne during the writing of plays clearly shows. Eliot was convinced that a poetic drama was "more likely to come from poets learning how to write plays, than from skillful prose dramatists learning to write poetry" ("Poetry and Drama" *OPP* 86). In other words, Eliot's plays are definitely written by a poet. They have been often analyzed from such a point of view. However, it is not only the element of the poet who had been ambitious for a poetic drama that established the foundations of his poetic dramas.

In the early part of the 1930s, editing the *Criterion* made Eliot turn his eyes to the social world. He, as a Christian and a moralist, came to be concerned about the future of the modern world without God. He remarked in a lecture in 1933: "Every poet would like, I fancy, to be able to think that he had some direct social utility. He would like to convey the pleasures of poetry, not only to a larger audience, but to larger groups of people collectively; and the theatre is the best place in which to do it" (*UPUC* 147). Just after the lecture, he was asked to write ten choruses for a pageant play *The Rock* (1934) which had a social and religious purpose to provide funds for church-building in new housing areas. Next year, he wrote his first full-scale play *Murder in the Cathedral* (1935) and got a sense of an audience which reacted visibly and directly. These experiences made him think seriously about the theatre as a means of appealing to various people more directly. In those days, he became a Warden of a church and positively engaged in church works, which gave him more opportunities to relate to ordinary people. At the same time, he published the two major cultural studies, *The Idea of a Christian Society* (1939) and *Notes towards the Definition of Culture* (1948) on a parallel with writing his plays. It would seem, then, that the base of his poetic dramas was established from the points of view of a Christian and an intellectual person seeking to connect with more ordinary people as well as of a poet ambitious for a poetic drama.

Eliot's writing a poetic drama focusing on poetic verse forms had broken down in the mid-1920s. The dramatist Eliot's writing began to run smoothly after he became aware of a flesh-and-blood audience reacting directly and realized what he had to convey to them. He had expressed the lives of modern people and his own philosophy of life in his poems. They would be described in his plays more widely and deeply and changed by degrees. In this article, I won't attach importance to the development of poetic verse forms in his poetic dramas. Rather, I will pay attention to the view of life which he tried to describe and convey to his audience through his plays, especially focusing on *The Cocktail Party* (1949) which is said to have been most commercially successful.

2. THE FRONTIER BETWEEN THE TWO WORLDS

Eliot wrote the five poetic dramas for theatres. Speaking roughly, all he depicted in them were just the two worlds and the three kinds of people. Those two worlds are named variously by many critics—"the 'sainted' life" and "the common life" (Arrowsmith *The Critical Heritage* 639), "the 'spiritual' world" and "the 'normal' world" (G. Smith 197), "the Negative Way" and "the Way of Affirmation" (C.H. Smith 158, Hay 44), "the Negative Way" and "the Positive Way" (Kari 18), "the sacred" and "the profane" (McCarthy 37) or "the dimension of John of the Cross" and "the human dimension" (Yasuda 100). Eliot himself defines them as "our temporal (life)" and "(our) spiritual life," "a community of men and women" and "the higher forms of devotional life," or "the supernatural life" and "the natural life." (*The Idea of a Christian Society* 77, 79, 80). There exists the frontier between the two worlds. It is too difficult to cross it. His characters are divided into the three kinds on both sides of the frontier: (1) the characters who cross the frontier from the temporal ordinary world to the spiritual world, (2) those who lead and help them

to cross the frontier, and stay here by themselves, (3) those who can live just on this side of the frontier without noticing the meaning of crossing it. How these three kinds of people are connected with and influence each other—this is the most important theme common to all Eliot's plays. His five plays are in sequence but go through changes by degrees. I will note which world or characters Eliot puts more emphasis on or sympathizes with in each play.

To cross the frontier to the other side—Eliot had had this theme since the beginning. He depicted a state of mind of a man who killed his mistress in his fragmentary story "Eeldrop and Appleplex" (1917)—"The important fact is that for the man the act is eternal, and that for the brief space he has to live, he is already dead. He is already in a different world from ours. He has crossed the frontier" (Little Review 9). He had also been considerably interested in Kurtz who "had stepped over the edge" (Conrad 151). He had given up quoting a passage from *The Heart of Darkness* as an epigraph "The horror! the horror!" for *The Waste Land* (1922), obeying Pound's advice. It was the passage in which the narrator Marlow told about Kurtz on a death watch. Eliot quoted a passage from *The Heart of Darkness* as an epigraph "Mistah Kurtz—he dead." for "The Hollow Men" (1925) at last. In this poem, Eliot described a feeling of awe in the gaze of the hollow men who saw off "Those who have crossed / With direct eyes, to death's other Kingdom" (83). The hollow men are the same as Marlow who confesses "True, he [Kurtz] had made that last stride, he had stepped over the edge, while I had been permitted to draw back my hesitating foot" (Conrad 151). Here are the prototypes of those who cross the frontier and those who know the meaning and see them off with a feeling of awe. This theme, which has a sense of sin and an attitude of prayer behind, becomes more religious little by little and is integrated into his plays and evolves gradually. Eliot described in his plays the characters who could live just in the ordinary temporal world without noticing the meaning of crossing the frontier as well as those who crossed it and those who led, helped them to cross it and stay here by themselves, as mentioned above. In this sense, his drama is different from his poetry. It is also different from his early poems in which only the modern superficial sterile life is described. How are these two worlds between the frontier different and connected with each other? Where is Eliot fixing his eyes upon? These two are my main questions in this article.

After Eliot wrote of the martyr of Thomas Becket the Archbishop of Canterbury in his first poetic drama *Murder in the Cathedral*, he wrote the four contemporary dramas. Especially, his second drama *The Family Reunion* (1939) and the third *The Cocktail Party* (1949) exhibit a striking contrast in connection with the two questions above. *The Family Reunion* was originally the story of Harry who returned home obsessed with an idea that he had pushed his wife into the mid-Atlantic, became conscious of his sin and set out on a journey for expiation. Afterwards, it developed into "a story of sin and expiation" (333) of the Monchenseys, by adding Harry's mother Amy's death, a murderous feud between his parents and a love affair between Amy's husband and her sister Agatha. Harry recognizes that he just repeated the sin of his father who had an intention to kill his wife too, which brings a sigh of relief to Harry. He seems to make a triumphant departure for a journey for expiation at the end of the drama. He tramples down his ordinary family relation or affection. He leaves home following "the bright angels" without hesitation, even though he was warned that his cold attitudes might cause the death of his mother whose heart was very feeble. He seems neither to be penitent for his own intention to kill his wife nor to lament for her death. If anything, he seems relieved to know that he shares the intention to kill his wife with his father.

It is not shown where Harry has gone. When Eliot was asked about it by an actor who played the part of Harry, he just hinted "I think he and the chauffeur go off and get jobs in the East End" (Browne 136). However, the nature of his journey is suggested clearly by the words of Agatha who sees him off saying "You are the consciousness of your unhappy family, / Its bird sent flying through the purgatorial flame."

> . . . Family affection
> Was a kind of formal obligation, a duty
> Only noticed by its neglect. (Harry)

> . . . Love compels cruelty
> To those who do not understand love.
> What you have wished to know, what you have learned
> Mean the end of a relation, make it impossible
> (Agatha)

These words support Harry's way of life to break ordinary human relations and abandon all

earthly affection cruelly in the name of "love" which means divine love or "the negative way." In other words, Eliot gives his support to Harry's choice completely by these words. Eliot has crossed the frontier with Harry at the end of the drama—

> . . . Harry has crossed the frontier
> Beyond which safety and danger have a different meaning.
> And he cannot return. That is his privilege.
> (Agatha)

Amy's death is suggested only by her cry heard from behind the scenes. Agatha and Harry's cousin Mary, who supported his departure, are feeling tired and old at the moment of their second fresh start. Agatha and Mary blow out lighted candles on a cake for late Amy's birthday one by one with their transcendental last words, and the temporal ordinary world remains in the darkness at the very end of the drama.

It is possible to categorize the characters in *The Family Reunion* into the following three such groups as I mentioned above: (1) Harry, (2) Agatha, Mary and his chauffeur Downing, and (3) Amy and her brothers and sisters. It separates (2) from (3) whether they have eyes and ability to recognize the Eumenides—who have chased Harry as "specters" and are leading him now as "the bright angels!"—and their meaning or not. Agatha says to Mary—

> . . . You and I,
> My dear, may very likely meet again
> In our wanderings in the neutral territory
> Between two worlds. (Agatha)

In the same way, the characters in *The Cocktail Party* can be divided into (1) Celia, (2) Reilly, Julia and Alex, and (3) Edward, Lavinia and Peter. There exists the frontier between (1) and (2) (3), which is still extremely difficult to cross. It makes the greatest difference between *The Family Reunion* and *The Cocktail Party* how Eliot treats and describes the characters of (2) and (3) who stay in the temporal ordinary world.

After Eliot finished *The Family Reunion*, his writing another drama was interrupted by the World War II. He completed *Four Quartets* and wrote *Notes towards the Definition of Culture* during the years. Eliot's values changed crucially during the decade. For example, when he was writing *The Family Reunion*, he was openly critical of Amy—"Amy also understands nothing: she is merely a person of tremendous personality on one plane. . . . But Harry's departure is not a disaster for him, but a triumph. The tragedy is the tragedy of Amy, of a person living on Will alone." (Browne 107, Eliot's italics). Here is a strong theory from Harry's point of view that people who can understand nothing can't help being abandoned. This evaluation made a complete change after about ten years. Eliot confesses in "Poetry and Drama" which was written just after *The Cocktail Party*, "my sympathies now have come to be all with the mother, who seems to me, except perhaps for the chauffeur, the only complete human being in the play; and my hero now strikes me as an insufferable prig" (*OPP* 84). What does the change mean?

Amy has denied passage of time, refused any change, ignored even Harry's marriage and continued to dominate the family. However, at the very end of her life, she recognizes her faults and limitations—"At my age, I only just begin to apprehend the truth / About things too late to mend.... / ... / I always wanted too much for my children, / More than life can give. And now I am punished for it." Her words are full of anguish and resignation. But we can see some humility and humbleness there. Eliot demoted Harry from "a triumph" to "an insufferable prig," while he evaluated Amy's attitude to recognize her faults and limitations humbly still in the temporal ordinary world. These two changes are inextricably connected. We can see these reversed values in *The Cocktail Party*.

Eliot returned to the temporal ordinary world of *The Cocktail Party* ten years after he had crossed the frontier with Harry. *The Cocktail Party* draws up the curtain at a party scene with light laughter, which is quite different from the last scene in the darkness after Harry cut off any human relation and went forth to complete "a story of sin and expiation." "Eliot is not concerned with the person of exceptional spiritual awareness, or the saint, in isolation, but always with his relationship to the community, to ordinary men and women," as D. E. Jones clearly indicates (Jones 124). Eliot describes how the ordinary people as well as the exceptional person at the party will develop spiritually and choose their own life. He came back to remedy the temporal ordinary world discarded by Harry. It also means that Eliot reviews Harry's way of life. In fact, Eliot writes *The Cocktail Party*, fixing his eyes upon each human relation undermined in *The Family Reunion*. In this meaning, *The*

Cocktail Party is an elaborately modified version of *The Family Reunion*. . . .

Source: Keiko Saeki, "Return to the Ordinary World: From *The Family Reunion* to *The Cocktail Party*," in *Yeats Eliot Review*, Vol. 23, No. 4, Fall/Winter 2006, pp. 27–40.

John Peter

In the following review, Peter compares The Cocktail Party *to* The Family Reunion *and finds* The Cocktail Party *to be lacking.*

Though the play seems very much closer to *Sejanus* than to *Every Man In His Humour* one cannot feel that it was strange of Jonson to call *Volpone* a comedy. Some such description was usual on the title-pages of his times and of the two chief he chose the least misleading. But when Mr. Eliot calls his new play a comedy he seems to me to be closer to the position of a Shakespeare calling *Macbeth* a comedy on the strength of the Porter Scene. Only the incidentals in the play are, in fact, comic and, though on the stage they should be much more effective, on paper they barely deserve the adjective. I suppose that the more perspicacious readers will think of Dante and accept the description in the very limited sense in which it seems intended; the rest are likely, however, to yield to the general chorus of the dramatic critics, to accept the play as 'witty' and 'delightful', and to get little further into it than the title might seem to tempt them to get. If they find it unsatisfactory it will be on the grounds that parts of it are dull and not because—what is surely the real criterion for judgment—it is unsuccessful on the terms that it prescribes for itself.

A good deal of the play, and particularly that part of it that relates to Celia Coplestone, is a development of the ideas handled in *The Family Reunion*, and the reader will be well advised to discard any presuppositions which the use of the term 'Comedy' may raise and to treat the play with the same sobriety that he would bring to its predecessor. Like *The Family Reunion* it is an attempt to discuss religious topics in theatrical terms and, again like that play, it essays this discussion by using situations from modern life. Both plays, that is, attempt something much more difficult than is attempted in *Murder In The Cathedral*, where the remote historical setting allows even the sceptical among the audience to concur in the argument without, as it were, feeling themselves too personally or immediately implicated in it. The difficulty in

> 'ANYONE WHO TRIES TO WRITE POETIC
> DRAMA, EVEN TODAY,' ELIOT HAS WRITTEN,
> 'SHOULD KNOW THAT HALF OF HIS ENERGY MUST
> BE EXHAUSTED IN THE EFFORT TO ESCAPE FROM
> THE CONSTRICTING TOILS OF SHAKESPEARE.'"

both the later plays is to effect the necessary emotional synthesis between the world of ideas, of belief, in which the topics discussed may be said to exist, and the mundane world of taxis and boiled eggs which is the *milieu* of the characters. This is not to suggest that there is an inveterate hostility between these two worlds, but rather to indicate how comparatively easily a dramatist seeking to fuse them may be betrayed into, on the one hand, bathos and, on the other, seemingly gratuitous lurches towards sublimity. I think that it is significant that the single (fairly long) quotation in *The Cocktail Party* should be a neo-Platonic passage from *Prometheus Unbound*:

> For know there are two worlds of life and death:
> One that which thou beholdest; but the other
> Is underneath the grave....

That we should be given such lines seems to indicate that the playwright is aware of the dichotomy in his material and apprised of the difficulties inherent in his task. We begin, then, by looking at the play to see whether it has improved upon its predecessor in the handling of these difficulties.

Two improvements can be at once perceived. In the first place, because Sir Henry Harcourt-Reilly is made a professional consultant his analytical probings, comments and advice are given a more than individual authority, and seem far less queerly oracular than do the rather similar speeches of Agatha in the earlier play. This is so. I think, even when he ceases to speak as a doctor and reveals himself as a 'Guardian', intent upon the health of the soul rather than that of the body. His authority tends to pass over with him from the one rôle to the other, and if we are responding naturally we shall tend not to question it. In the second place the development

of Celia Coplestone (we might call her Harry Monchensey in the guise of a young woman) is really only half the play, the other half being concerned with the marital difficulties between Edward and Lavinia Chamberlayne. If not the most important part of the play this other half is at least the most prominent and this has the effect, not only of making the martyr seem more exceptional, more of a departure from the average (as she surely should seem), but also of giving a more balanced picture of religious experience than that given in *The Family Reunion*. The Chamberlaynes are shown as following a religious development of their own which, while quite different from it, is yet supplementary to that of Celia. As Reilly says:

> Neither way is better.
> Both ways are necessary. It is also necessary
> To make a choice between them.

The impression is thus quite different from that given by *The Family Reunion*. There we are left with the sense that virtue is somehow the prerogative of a limited class of 'sufferers', an esoteric quality to which more normal persons cannot hope to attain; here on the other hand martyrdom is only one of several varieties of religious experience, and that one of the less common. To an audience composed (let us hope) of non-'sufferers' the latter view is much more likely to recommend itself.

Another difference between the two plays is that there are evidently intended to be no fundamentally bad or trivial characters in *The Cocktail Party*. This may seem so slight a point as hardly to be worth noticing but in fact I think it is crucial. In life, I suppose, we are only aware of virtue negatively, and through knowing the virtuous party for some time. Sobriety is consistent but unaggressive, abstaining from drunkenness, charity from malice or unkindness, humility from arrogance or condescension, and so on. As soon as these qualities become too positive or overt, as soon as we have a man who ostentatiously refuses a drink or sententiously refuses to criticize his neighbour, we have, not virtue, but hypocrisy or priggishness. It is by their works that we know the virtuous and not by their professions, and it usually takes time before our knowledge ripens into any sort of assurance. Now where a dramatist means to present a virtuous character he has obviously to work in firmer and more immediate stuff than this and it is understandable that he usually employs his own sort of negative approach, by playing the character off against a number of others who are palpably less virtuous. At times, indeed, as in some of the Elizabethan and Jacobean plays, he is content to work almost entirely in negative terms—that is, through a cast of villains—and to allow his moral positives to present themselves merely as implications or inferences. Dramatically speaking, either of these approaches has obvious advantages over the direct approach, where the good characters have to be positively established *as* good, because they do not involve the characters in description or suggestion of one another's goodness, and so give rise to something more convincing than a dull assortment of eulogies. 'Damn braces, bless relaxes', said Blake: the relevance of this to drama should be self-evident.

In this play Eliot is trying to present virtue directly, without the traditional advantage of a contrast with its opposite, and it seems to me that he is often perilously close to relaxation of the kind I take Blake to have meant. At the end of the play Edward is clearly on the way to regeneration, his relations with Lavinia clearly more unselfish, yet how is this presented? Partly, to be sure, it is a matter of contrast with their previous relationship. But the dramatist does not leave it there. He goes on to give Edward a string of compliments and 'thoughtful' remarks that are as monotonous as they are unconvincing—'I hope you've not been worrying'. 'It's you who should be tired'. 'I like the dress you're wearing'. 'You have a very practical mind'. 'You lie down now, Lavinia'. Even if this is meant to suggest that Lavinia is pregnant it is surely an unhappy way of drawing attention to domestic harmony. Happiness in marriage would inhere in far less definite particulars—a glance, a touch, a tone of voice. Edward is, in fact, in a position analogous to the ostentatious professor of virtue: he has himself to *show* how virtuous he is, and we accordingly at once suspect that he is only mimicking the real thing. This is not charity but solicitude. Yet how else, granted the chosen approach, could the point be made? Celia is another focus for this sort of weakness, though she is at least removed off-stage when her decision is complete. It is true that Alex's laconic narration of her martyrdom is effective, true also that the reactions of the other characters are at first simple and convincing enough. But very soon they begin to magnify her image into portentousness so that it cracks and allows her validity as a symbol to drain away:

> I've only been interested in myself:
> And that isn't good enough for Celia.
> Do try to come to see us.
> You know, I think it would do us all good—
> You and me and Edward . . . to talk about Celia.
> I cannot help the feeling
> That, in some way, my responsibility
> Is greater than that of a band of half-crazed savages.

It seems to me that the unprejudiced reader will find this insistence almost as tiresome as the muscular Christianity of the foreman in *The Rock*, and will react away from rather than towards the values sought to be embodied in the martyr. His recollections of her pleasantly sensitive normality at the opening of the play will hinder him from seeing her in these large and cloudy terms, and he may even feel that she would have merited more sympathetic attention had she remained the woman she at first sight appears. Skilful acting could doubtless conceal some of these weaknesses but the play is not to be called successful because that is so.

It is not only to Celia, however, that this sort of jar, between an initial and a later character, is confined. Julia and Alex, who with Reilly make up the group of 'Guardians', have an even more striking metamorphosis from their initial selves. This is so palpable that it must be intentional, a sort of deliberate convention, and we are no doubt intended to take Edward's remark about 'the guardian' as a clue showing how to accept the convention:

> The self that wills—he is a feeble creature;
> He has to come to terms in the end
> With the obstinate, the tougher self; who does not
>   speak,
> Who never talks, who cannot argue;
> And who in some men may be the *guardian*. . . .

In the light of this the Julia and Alex of Acts Two and Three are presumably the inner selves of their analogues in Act One, and not real people at all. Yet the contrast between the selves in each case is almost wantonly exaggerated, and most readers or members of an audience must surely find it impossible to accept. Alex is at first vain ('I'm rather a famous cook') and suspicious ('Ah, so the aunt Really exists') and it would appear that he is also not above drinking half a bottle of Edward's champagne. As for Julia, she is vapid ('Lady Klootz'), avaricious ('Are there any prospects?'), featherbrained and inquisitive, and vain enough to take umbrage when Reilly sings his song. To transform this figure into a 'Guardian' of such potency that she can condescend ('You must accept your limitations') even to her fellow-Guardian, the perspicacious Reilly, seems to me preposterous. Are we to infer that no matter how stupidly vicious people may be on the surface they can be spotless within? The human Julia's flippant mention of St. Anthony is scarcely sufficient to bridge the yawning void between herself and her *alter ego*, and in fact it is difficult to see how, given two such different quantities, it could be bridged.

Obviously, it will be retorted, Eliot has not tried to bridge it: why impugn him for not doing what it was no part of his intention to do? This is easily said but I do not think that in this instance it is a valid defence. The fact is, as I have pointed out, that there is already something of a tension between the two worlds handled in the play, and to make the contrast between the Julia of the real world and the Julia of the spiritual world so gross is only to increase that tension to a point at which the play begins to tear apart. Where the play should be forcing us to see the interdependence of the two worlds, forcing us to admit that the spiritual underlies and informs the actual, we get instead the impression that they are so distinct, so little related, that to move from one to the other is like putting on an impenetrable disguise. What, after all, besides the name, have these Julias in common? Could we identify the one after being acquainted only with the other? That the deliberate convention of 'inner selves' should at first sight give an impression of simple ineptitude is thus not its chief defect. What is serious is that in another way it is itself inept, and draws attention to a material dichotomy which it was part of the business of the dramatist to dissolve or remove. I have not seen the play and I am aware that it might be argued that this contrast, between the earlier and the later Julia, is less serious on the stage. With a book one can turn back to the early pages and make comparisons; but on the stage there is a temporal progression which leaves us dependent on memory and for this reason we may tend to accept the changed figure more readily. The play's popularity may be evidence that the convention works better in the theatre than the study, and I should be happy to believe that it does. On the other hand there may be other reasons for its popularity, reasons more properly the province of the sociologist than of the critic. Even in the study do we, after all, *need* to turn back to the early pages for the contrast to be felt, and felt disturbingly?

These might be called structural criticisms. I should like to conclude by observing that the flaccidity of the verse does little to compensate for them. Some of Celia's speeches to Reilly in Act Two are so inexplicit that one is tempted to call them Eliotese. They seem to rely on certain concepts such as 'love' and 'shame' and 'aloneness' (I use this barbarism because the state is clearly neither loneliness nor solitude) yet they do nothing to make these concepts real. This is at all events what seems to me to be taking place in such a speech as Celia's. Again, at other times the verse is so obviously *not* verse that to have printed it as such gives one much the same pause as does the 'Comedy' of the title-page:

> Well, Peter, I'm awfully glad, for your sake,
> Though of course we . . . I shall miss you;
> You know how I depended on you for concerts,
> And picture exhibitions—more than you realized.
> It *was* fun, wasn't it! But now you'll have a chance,
> I hope, to realize your ambitions.
> I shall miss you.

'Anyone who tries to write poetic drama, even today', Eliot has written, 'should know that half of his energy must be exhausted in the effort to escape from the constricting toils of Shakespeare'. This was well said, and it is to his credit that in *The Family Reunion* and, more particularly, *Murder In The Cathedral* Eliot has written dramatic verse that is both verse and underivative. The impression left by *The Cocktail Party*, however, is rather that the 'constricting toils' have been, if that is possible, too thoroughly cast off. It is not that the dramatist here eschews Shakespeareanisms—no sane reader would throw that in his teeth—but that the verse is of so poor a quality as to make them unthinkable. Even a quotation from Shakespeare rather than Shelley would throw up its context in all too harsh a light. One seems to see the shade of William Archer smile ironically.

Source: John Peter, "Sin and Soda," in *Scrutiny*, Vol. 17, No. 1, Spring 1950, pp. 61–66.

SOURCES

Cannadine, David, "The Twentieth Century: Social Identities and Political Identities," and "Conclusion: Toward a 'Classless Society?,'" in *The Rise and Fall of Class in Britain*, Columbia University Press, 1999, pp. 109–94.

"Cost of Wars in Iraq and Afghanistan Tops £20bn," in *BBC News*, June 20, 2010, http://www.bbc.co.uk/news/10359548 (accessed August 15, 2010).

Deane, Patrick, "Rhetoric and Affect: Eliot's Classicism, Pound's Symbolism, and the Drafts of *The Waste Land*," in *Journal of Modern Literature*, Vol. 18, No. 1, Winter 1992, pp. 77–93.

Deeney, John, "When Men Were Men and Women Were Women," in *British Theatre between the Wars, 1918–1939*, edited by Clive Barker and Maggie Barbara Gale, Cambridge University Press, 2000, pp. 63–87.

Eliot, T. S., *The Family Reunion*, Harcourt Brace, 1967.

"Formalism and New Criticism," in *Internet Encyclopedia of Philosophy: A Peer-Reviewed Academic Resource*, http://www.iep.utm.edu/literary/#H (accessed August 15, 2010).

Fraser, Rebecca, "Overview: Britain, 1818–1945," in *BBC: British History In-Depth*, http://www.bbc.co.uk/history/british/britain_wwtwo/overview_britain_1918_1945_01.shtml (accessed August 15, 2010).

Hargrove, Nancy Duvall, "T. S. Eliot," in *Dictionary of Literary Biography*, Vol. 7, *Twentieth-Century American Dramatists, First Series*, edited by John MacNicholas, Gale Research, 1981, pp. 151–72.

Hutton, Will, "Of Course Class Still Matters—It Influences Everything That We Do," in *Observer* (London, England), January 10, 2010, http://www.guardian.co.uk/commentisfree/2010/jan/10/will-hutton-class-unfair-society (accessed August 15, 2010).

Lawson, Mark, "Is This a New Golden Age for British Theatre?," in *Guardian* (London, England), December 2, 2009, http://www.guardian.co.uk/stage/2009/dec/02/theatre-golden-age (accessed August 15, 2010).

Lucy, Seán, "The Realist Drama," in *T. S. Eliot and the Idea of Tradition*, Cohen West, 1961, pp. 193–209.

Malamud, Randy, "The Family Reunion: 'The Particular Has No Language,'" in *Where the Words Are Valid: T. S. Eliot's Communities of Drama*, Greenwood Press, 1994, pp. 93–116.

"Modernist Experiment: Overview," in *The Norton Anthology of English Literature: Norton Topics Online*, http://www.wwnorton.com/college/english/nael/20century/topic_2_05/welcome.htm (accessed August 15, 2010).

Peacock, Louisa, "Mass Strikes Loom in a 'Winter of Discontent' for UK Government," in *Telegraph* (London, England), August 6, 2010, http://www.telegraph.co.uk/finance/jobs/7928933/Mass-strikes-loom-in-a-winter-of-discontent-f or-UK-Government.html (accessed August 15, 2010).

Raine, Craig, "The Drama," in *T. S. Eliot*, Oxford University Press, 2006, pp. 115–26.

Saler, Michael T., "Framing the Picture," in *The Avant-Garde in Interwar England: Medieval Modernism and the London Underground*, Oxford University Press, 1999, pp. 3–24.

Sarkar, Subhas, "The Family Reunion," in *T. S. Eliot: The Dramatist*, Atlantic, 2006, pp. 126–75.

Scofield, Martin, "Notes," in *T. S. Eliot: The Poems*, Cambridge University Press, 1988 pp. 243–56.

Stokes, John, "Body Parts: The Success of the Thriller in the Inter-War Years," in *British Theatre between the Wars, 1918–1939*, edited by Clive Barker and Maggie Barbara Gale, Cambridge University Press, 2000, pp. 38–62.

Thackery, Frank W., and John E. Findling, eds., "World War II, 1939–1945," in *Events That Changed Great Britain Since 1689*, Greenwood Press, 2002, pp. 153–72.

"UK 'Close to Leaving Recession,'" in *BBC News*, January 12, 2010, http://news.bbc.co.uk/2/hi/business/8453136.stm (accessed August 15, 2010).

"UK Unemployment Falls to 2.46 Million," in *BBC News: Business*, http://www.bbc.co.uk/news/business-10936574 (accessed August 15, 2010).

FURTHER READING

Batchelor, David, Briony Fer, and Paul Wood, *Realism, Rationalism, Surrealism: Art between the Wars*, Yale University Press, 1993.

In this work, which includes a section on the realism of the 1930s, the authors explore the development of artistic movements in the time period between the world wars. Students of Eliot's *The Family Reunion* will have the opportunity to explore the artistic movements that paralleled and influenced developments in modern literature.

Conlon, John J., "T. S. Eliot," in *Great American Writers: Twentieth Century*, edited by R. Baird Shuman, Marshall Cavendish, 2002, pp. 437–58.

Conlon offers an overview of Eliot's life and works. Included in his analysis is a discussion of Eliot's dramas and their stage productions.

Marshik, Celia, *British Modernism and Censorship*, Cambridge University Press, 2006.

Marshik traces the history of British censorship of modernist literature, studying the way writers responded to and were shaped by the censorship of their works.

Stapleton, Julia, "Political Thought and National Identity in Britain, 1850–1950," in *History, Religion, and Culture: British Intellectual History 1750–1900*, edited by Stefan Collini, Richard Whatmore, and Brian Young, Cambridge University Press, 2000, pp. 245–69.

Stapleton explores the transformation of English nationalism and politics within the context of a society forced to re-examine its values during times of crisis and world war. Her discussion of the interwar years studies the interplay between the political developments of the time period and the English character.

SUGGESTED SEARCH TERMS

T. S. Eliot AND Family Reunion

T. S. Eliot AND drama

T. S. Eliot AND modernism

T. S. Eliot AND existentialism

T. S. Eliot AND Anglicanism

T. S. Eliot AND poetry

T. S. Eliot AND interwar literature

T. S. Eliot AND British citizenship

T. S. Eliot AND Ezra Pound

T. S. Eliot AND British theater

The Frozen Deep

WILKIE COLLINS

1857

The Frozen Deep was written by nineteenth-century English writer Wilkie Collins in collaboration with novelist Charles Dickens. First performed at London's Tavistock House in January 1857, the play was staged by a cast of amateur actors, including Collins and Dickens. It was revised and performed at the Olympic Theatre, London, in 1866.

The play was inspired by several attempts made by British seamen to navigate the Northwest Passage, a sea route through the Arctic Ocean. One of these expeditions was led by Sir John Franklin in 1845, but his expedition got ice-locked about halfway through the passage. Franklin died in 1847. In 1848, the ships were abandoned and the men tried to escape by land but none survived. This provided Collins and Dickens with their material for a heroic melodrama, into which they wove the themes of revenge, forgiveness, and love.

The text of the 1857 version of the play was first published in *Under the Management of Mr. Charles Dickens: His Production of "The Frozen Deep,"* edited by Robert Louis Brannan, in 1966. Although this book is out of print, it can be found in academic libraries, and inexpensive used copies can be found at used or online booksellers. No other published edition of the play exists. The play is not to be confused with the novella of the same name, which Collins published in 1874, based on the play.

Wilkie Collins (The Library of Congress)

AUTHOR BIOGRAPHY

Collins was born on January 8, 1824, in London, England, to William and Harriet Collins. His father was an artist. The young Collins attended a private school and toured Europe with his family. In 1841, he began working at a tea-importing firm in London. However, Collins had no interest in a business career, and he soon started writing fiction. His first story was published in *Illuminated* magazine in 1843. His first novel was *Antonina; or, The Fall of Rome* (1850).

Collins began to study law in 1846 and qualified as a lawyer in 1851, although he never practiced his profession. He met Charles Dickens in 1851, and five years later Collins became an editor of Dickens's magazine, *Household Words*. In 1856, he collaborated with Dickens in writing the play *The Frozen Deep*, which was first produced in 1857. Collins continued to write plays, including *The Lighthouse* (1857), *The Red Vial* (1858) and, with Dickens, *No Thoroughfare* (1867). Collins adapted many of his plays from his own novels or stories, such as *The Woman in White* (1871), which had earlier appeared as a

serialized novel and then as a book (1860). *No Name* appeared as a novel in 1862 and as a play in 1871.

In the 1860s, the novels *Armadale* (1866) and *The Moonstone* (1868) were among Collins's major achievements. The latter, a detective novel, remains the work for which he is best known. Other novels from later in his life include *Man and Wife* (1870), *Poor Miss Finch* (1872), and *Jezebel's Daughter* (1880). *The Frozen Deep and Other Tales* was published in 1874. The title story was adapted from the earlier play. In all, Collins wrote over thirty books, twelve plays, and many short stories, articles, and essays.

Collins had three children with Martha Rudd, whom he met in 1864, although the couple never married. In fact, from 1858 and continuing for nearly thirty years, Collins lived with another woman, Caroline Graves; they never married either. Collins was often in poor health, and in 1889 he suffered bronchitis and then a stroke. He died on September 23, 1889, in London.

PLOT SUMMARY

Act 1

The Frozen Deep begins in a room in a country house in Devonshire, England, in which Mrs. Steventon and Rose Ebsworth sit. Mrs. Steventon has just been handed a newspaper by the maid, and she scans it for any news of her husband, who has been away for three years on an expedition to the Arctic. Rose's father is the commander of the same expedition. Both women are staying at the house of Lucy Crayford, whose brother is on the expedition. As they talk they reveal that there is a fourth woman staying at the house, Clara Burnham, whose fiancé is on the expedition. The women are anxious because they have heard no news about the expedition for over a year. Rose says that without her father, she no longer enjoys going out and socializing. However, she is optimistic that he will return.

The talk turns to Nurse Esther, a Scottish nurse who is looking after Clara. Rose and Mrs. Steventon consider Nurse Esther a bad influence on Clara, because she claims to be psychic, having the gift of what she calls second sight. Nurse Esther enters, and when she is told it is the maid, not her, who is wanted, she says they will want her when they want news of their men folk.

MEDIA ADAPTATIONS

- A newly interpreted performance of *The Frozen Deep* was performed by the Ironduke company at the Edinburgh Festival in 2005. This performance was considered a world premiere, given the revisions to the original script.

- An audio CD version of *The Frozen Deep* was produced by The Again Shop in 2010.

She says she will speak about the men before the night is over.

After Nurse Esther exits, Lucy enters. She says she is worried about Clara's health, since she is a very sensitive girl and has become depressed and irritable. She suspects that Clara may have some hidden sorrow. Clara enters and Rose and Mrs. Steventon decide it is better if she is left alone with Lucy. Lucy tells the despondent Clara there is reason for optimism about the fate of the Arctic expedition. She says if they hear no news over the next year, a rescue expedition will be sent. She counsels Clara to be patient and to hope.

With some prodding from Lucy, Clara confesses that she does indeed have a secret sorrow. Hoping to draw her out, Lucy says that she has one, too. The man to whom she was engaged to marry fell in love with someone else, and Lucy broke off the engagement. Clara then tells her story. Her childhood playmate, a boy named Richard Wardour, grew up to love her. Clara could return only feelings of friendship, however. When Richard joined the navy, he made it clear to her that when he returned he would expect to marry her. She did not have the presence of mind to tell him not to have such hopes. Within two years, Clara was engaged to another man, Frank Aldersley, but Wardour returned and wanted Clara as his wife. When she told him her situation, he said the man who had won her affections would regret the day he met her. Clara later found out that Wardour is on the same Arctic expedition as Frank, although they are in different ships. On

Lucy's questioning, Clara reveals that Wardour does not know Frank's name, and that their engagement was not generally known either. However, she fears for what might happen if Wardour discovers who Frank is.

Nurse Esther is heard saying that the men on the expedition will never be found. Clara asks Nurse Esther whether she sees Frank. Esther replies that she sees two men, and says that the lamb is in the grip of the lion. There is blood, and everyone around is crying.

Act 2

The setting is a hut in the Arctic. Lieutenant Crayford calls for John Want, the cook, who wakes up reluctantly. He is freezing cold. Crayford tells him to continue his work of grinding bones to be used with water to make soup. Want thinks they will all be dead within ten days. Bateson brings a message that Captain Ebsworth wants to see Crayford, and Crayford exits.

Want makes the soup and talks with Frank Aldersley. Want tells a long story about why he first went to sea and how he got over seasickness, on the advice of his captain, by continuing to eat a lot.

Want exits into an inner hut, and Crayford returns. He tells Lieutenant Steventon that the captain has ordered the men from the two different ships to all gather together in this hut. Crayford gets some dice, which he says he needs for casting lots. It is clear that an exploring party is to be sent out. Frank, who has been seriously ill, falls asleep.

Crayford reports to Steventon that one of the men on the other ship, the *Wanderer*, is Richard Wardour, whom he knows well. He is fond of him, despite Wardour's reputation for being sullen and bad-tempered. Steventon says that Frank shares his poor opinion of Wardour. He adds that Frank is probably dreaming of Clara, his fiancée.

The men from the *Wanderer* enter, led by Captain Helding and Wardour. Frank wakes. Wardour shakes hands only with Crayford. Crayford addresses all the men and passes on the captain's instructions. He says there is little chance of being rescued, and they must take some action, since provisions are low, more men are getting sick, and winter is coming on. The plan is to send out a group to see if they can reach the nearest fur settlement. All the men want to volunteer for the expedition, but some must stay to look after the sick. Crayford says the officers will throw dice to decide. Those who throw under six will stay; those who throw over six go. The non-officers say they will choose by drawing folded papers from a hat that have written on them either "stay" or "go."

The men draw lots while the officers throw dice. Helding is to stay; Crayford is to go. Wardour, who professes not to care whether he goes or stays, throws a six and must throw again. Uninterested, he tells Frank to throw for him, and Frank throws a two, which means Wardour will stay. Frank throws an eight; he will go.

The meeting breaks up and preparations begin. Crayford orders that Frank's berth, since he no longer needs it, should be demolished and the wood used for fuel. Crayford and Wardour are left alone together, and Wardour explains why he did not care whether he stayed in the hut or went on the expedition. He relates his bitter disappointment over losing Clara, and repeats his threat to the unknown man who took her from him. He knows that at some time he will meet this man. It is all he lives for. Crayford is shocked and urges Wardour to set aside his desire for revenge. Wardour does not want to talk any more about it and says they should forget it. He takes an axe from Bateson which he says he will use to demolish Frank's berth.

Wardour is left alone to demolish the berth. As he chops with the axe he discovers the word Clara carved in the wood, and then the initials F. A. and C. B. He thinks immediately of Clara Burnham and wonders if Frank is the man he has been looking for.

Lieutenant Crayford enters, followed by Aldersley. Wardour engages Frank in conversation and finds they are both from the county of Kent, and also that Frank is a friend of the Burnham family, whom Wardour also knows. Wardour asks about Clara, and Frank says they are engaged. Wardour controls his reaction but within a moment or two, in an aside, makes it clear that he plans to kill Frank.

Captain Helding tells Crayford that one of his men who was to have gone on the expedition has fallen and broken his leg. Wardour volunteers to take his place, Helding supports him, and Crayford reluctantly agrees. Crayford tries to persuade Frank not to go, arguing that he is too weak following his illness. Frank is not to be persuaded, however. Wardour loads his gun, while a worried Crayford tells Frank to stick close to the other men.

Act 3

Some time has passed, and this act takes place in a cavern on the coast of Newfoundland. The men have been rescued, and John Want grumbles about having to keep company with Nurse Esther. Nurse Esther insults him, and in an aside he derides her claims to second sight.

Bateson enters and tells Want that Lucy, Clara, Rose, and Mrs. Steventon are nearby, having followed the rescue expedition from England. Lieutenant Steventon and his wife enter, with Captain Ebsworth and his daughter Rose. Nurse Esther complains to the women that she is being kept apart from Clara. Mrs. Steventon explains to her husband that this is because Frank is one of a number of men who are missing, and Nurse Esther's gloomy predictions about his fate could only upset Clara. Nurse Esther protests that she has always been right, and Rose hustles her away.

Clara, Lieutenant Crayford, and Lucy enter. They are soon to return to England but have not given up all hope for Frank. Clara retells the story she has been told about how brave Frank was when he left the hut to set off on the expedition. When Clara goes to rest for a while, Crayford admits to Lucy that he has no hope that Frank has survived. He tells her that all the men from the exploring party returned to the hut exhausted, except for Frank and Wardour, who continued to press on. Crayford is nervous that at any moment, Clara may find out the truth. Crayford exits while the others sit down for dinner.

They are interrupted by the appearance of Wardour. He is dressed in rags and looks almost insane as well as exhausted. No one recognizes him. They give him some food and drink, and he saves some of it in a bag. He tells them he is looking for a woman. Crayford enters and recognizes Wardour. He is angry because he assumes Wardour has murdered Frank. Clara enters; Wardour sees her and rushes out of the cavern. He returns carrying Frank and tells Clara that he saved Frank for her. Crayford apologizes to him, and Wardour explains how he overcame the temptation to kill Frank. Frank says he would never have made it back had it not been for Wardour. Clara speaks affectionately to Wardour, who embraces Crayford and then looks at Clara, calling her his sister and asking her to kiss him before he dies.

CHARACTERS

Frank Aldersley

Frank Aldersley is engaged to marry Clara Burnham. He has been away on the Arctic expedition for three years as an officer on the *Sea Mew*. Unbeknownst to him, Richard Wardour, who is on the other ship, the *Wanderer*, would kill him if he knew Frank was engaged to Clara, since Wardour, in love, had sworn to kill Clara's fiancé. Frank and Clara have kept the engagement secret because Frank needed to win promotion in the navy before they could marry. Frank has met Wardour and does not like him. In act 2 it is revealed that Frank has been seriously ill, but he wants to go on the expedition to the fur settlement. He throws an eight with the dice, which permits him to go. In the expedition, he and Wardour press on farther than all the others because, in Frank's case, he longs to see Clara again. By this time, Wardour knows who he is and has the opportunity to kill him but does not, choosing instead to save his life. Frank is thus reunited with Clara, and he acknowledges his debt to Wardour.

Bateson

Bateson is a member of the *Sea Mew* crew. He helps out with various tasks.

Clara Burnham

Clara Burnham is engaged to marry Frank Aldersley. She and Richard Wardour were neighbors growing up, and their fathers were friends. Wardour fell in love with her, but she could not reciprocate his feelings. Instead, she fell in love with Frank. Now that Frank is missing on the Arctic expedition, she is depressed because she fears that she may never see him again. Clara's father is dead, and her mother remarried and lives abroad, so Clara is alone in the world, except for her friends Lucy, Rose, and Mrs. Steventon. Clara's health and mental condition are delicate, and she has a Scottish nurse to look after her. Clara is fond of the nurse, although the other women think she is a bad influence on her. Mrs. Steventon comments that Clara has been "nervous and fanciful" since she was a child.

Lieutenant Crayford

Lieutenant Crayford is one of the officers aboard the *Sea Mew* and appears to be second in command. He is the brother of Lucy Crayford, of whom he is very fond. Lieutenant Crayford is an honorable man who is determined to do his duty even in the most adverse circumstances. He supervises the throwing of the dice and the drawing of lots for deciding who should go on the expedition to the fur settlement, and he makes sure everything is done fairly. He has known Richard Wardour for a long time and likes and respects him. When Wardour confesses to him his desire for revenge against Clara's fiancé, whoever that man might be, Crayford is shocked and tries to persuade him to abandon his desire for revenge. When Crayford discovers that the man Wardour seeks is Frank, Crayford does everything he can to keep the two men apart. When Wardour finally returns from the expedition, apparently alone, Crayford is quick to accuse him of murder, but then asks for forgiveness when he discovers Wardour's heroic acts.

Lucy Crayford

Lucy Crayford is the sister of Lieutenant Crayford. She is fond of Clara and does everything she can to look after her and cheer her up. Sensing that Clara has a secret sorrow, Lucy tells Clara about her own tormented past. She was once engaged to marry, but her fiancé fell in love with another woman. Lucy broke off the engagement, thus releasing the man from his obligation to her. She feels that she could never love anyone else as much, so she has resolved to remain single the rest of her life. This story encourages Clara to confide in Lucy the story of her former friendship with Richard Wardour.

Darker

Darker is one of the men on the *Sea Mew*. In act 2, he takes over the watch from Bateson.

Captain Ebsworth

Captain Ebsworth is the commander of the *Sea Mew*. He is Rose's father. In act 2 he is very ill but he still manages to issue the instructions to mount one last expedition to save their lives. He gives the instructions to Lieutenant Crayford, who carries them out. Captain Ebsworth appears to recover from his illness since he is once again in full command in act 3.

Rose Ebsworth

Rose Ebsworth is the daughter of Captain Ebsworth. She greatly misses her father and, although she likes music and dancing, she no longer has a desire to go out and socialize, since he is not there to protect her. Her mother is dead. Rose's best friend is Lucy Crayford, whom she has known for a long time. Rose is determined to be optimistic about the fate of the men.

Nurse Esther

Nurse Esther is the old Scottish nurse who has looked after Clara since her childhood. Clara is fond of her, but the other women think she is a bad influence on Clara. Nurse Esther is a strange woman who is given to trance-like fits in which she makes predictions about the future. She believes that she possesses what she calls second sight, and she repeatedly says that if the women want news of their men, they should listen to her. Clara believes Esther, but the others think she is a nuisance and should be sent away. At the end of act 1 Nurse Esther says she sees, using second sight, Frank and another man who is ready to harm him. She says she sees blood. In act 3, she believes that Frank is lost for good.

Captain Helding

Captain Helding is the commander of the *Wanderer*. He throws a seven at dice, and so goes on the expedition to the fur settlement. The main part he plays in the action is to support Wardour's desire to replace the injured man and go on the expedition.

Lieutenant Steventon

Lieutenant Steventon is the husband of Mrs. Steventon. He knows Wardour but does not like him, saying he is sullen and has a violent temper.

Mrs. Steventon

Mrs. Steventon is the wife of Lieutenant Steventon. She enjoys staying at the country house in Devonshire with Lucy, Rose, and Clara because in her home town people look down on her and reject her because she married a poor man. Mrs. Steventon is particularly forceful in her negative view of Nurse Esther.

John Want

John Want is the cook on the Arctic expedition. He has the thankless task of preparing food when there is almost none available. He grinds up bone so he can mix it with hot water to make soup. He likes to insist that he never grumbles about the bad conditions, but in fact he grumbles all the time and takes the most pessimistic view of the men's situation, saying they will all be dead within ten days. In act 3, he complains at length about the damp and the fog as he and the others stay at the cavern off the coast of Newfoundland, and he cannot stand the company of the nurse.

Richard Wardour

Richard Wardour is the man on whose actions the outcome of the play depends. He is the enemy of Frank Aldersley as soon as he finds out—by chance—that Frank is Clara's fiancé. Wardour and Clara had been friends since they were children because their fathers were friends and the two families lived next door to each other. Clara tells Lucy that as a boy Wardour was "headstrong and passionate" but also "generous" and "affectionate." He went to sea, indicating to her that when he returned he would expect to marry her. Clara did not return his love, and in the meantime, she met Frank, with whom she did fall in love. When Wardour returned, he was angry and made it clear he would kill her fiancé if they were ever to meet. On the expedition to the Arctic, Wardour has only one friend, Lieutenant Crayford, who thinks he has a generous heart. When Wardour finds out that Frank is Clara's fiancé, at first he wants to kill him. But when they are separated from the group he has a change of heart. He overcomes his desire for revenge and takes care of Frank, even placing Frank's welfare above his own. The result is that Frank survives, but Wardour, exhausted, dies.

THEMES

Courage

Almost everyone in the play displays courage in one form or another. The women show courage in maintaining their spirits in spite of the lack of news about the Arctic expedition. The officers on the ships think only of their duty, even though their situation seems hopeless, and they plan a final excursion that they hope will succeed. No one sinks into despair. Frank in particular sets off on the last expedition with courage in his heart, as Clara reveals in act 3. She has heard "how brave he was when he left the Hut, and went out with the best of them to battle his way through the Snow....He slung his snow-shoes over his shoulder with a smile."

TOPICS FOR FURTHER STUDY

- Read the novella *The Frozen Deep* that Collins developed from the play, and write an essay in which you compare it to the play. Does the novella contain the same themes as the play? As a work of literature, which do you think is more effective: play or novella?

- Research the history of the search for the Northwest Passage. Why was it considered so important? Who first discovered it? Who first navigated it? Develop a slide show, including maps and routes of various explorers, that shows where the Franklin expedition might have gotten ice-locked, and any escape routes by land that might have been open to the men. Insert appropriate text and captions. Use PowerPoint or a similar program and share your presentation with your classmates via slideshare.net. *Exploring the Polar Regions*, a book for young adults by Harry S. Anderson (Facts on File, 2004), will be useful in your research.

- With the exception of the 2005 performance at the Edinburgh Festival, *The Frozen Deep* has not been staged since the nineteenth century. With some classmates or the entire class, discuss why this might be. Is it good play? Could it be successfully staged today? What problems might be encountered? With some classmates, choose a short scene or two in the play and act it out, each person reading a part. Then discuss whether speaking the lines out loud altered your perceptions of what the possibilities might be for actual performance.

- Imagine that *The Frozen Deep* has been made into a film. Go to glogster.com and create a "glog," a kind of poster that you design yourself, advertising the film.

Love

Love is an ever-present theme. As befits a melodrama, all the women love their men dearly, with pure hearts. The men are equally pure-minded in how they regard the women in their lives. Men and women alike long to see each other again. Several different types of relationships are portrayed: brother and sister (Lucy Crayford and Lieutenant Crayford); husband and wife (Mr. and Mrs. Steventon), father and daughter (Captain Ebsworth and Rose); and betrothed couple (Frank and Clara). Frank and Clara are presented as the perfect couple, deeply in love. Steventon reports that Frank dreams a lot and always about Clara. He even calls out her name in his sleep. For her part, Clara keeps Frank's last letter to her close to her bosom. It contains withered flowers, which he gave to her the last time they met.

The play also presents the less rosy side of romantic love, and its power to wound people and alter their lives for the worse. For example, Lucy relates the story of how the man she was engaged to fell in love with another woman. Heartbroken, she decided she would never marry.

The emotional complications that romantic love can produce also provide the engine of the plot. Richard Wardour's basic decency as a man has been warped by his experience of love. His deep love for Clara was not returned, and this led him to indulge in the desire for revenge against the man who had claimed her heart. He also professes to despise women. However, Wardour's better nature wins out in the end. He is tempted to exact his revenge, and he has the perfect opportunity when he and Frank are separated from the group, but he chooses the better path.

The battle that goes in within Wardour's mind is not dramatized directly. The audience hears of it from Wardour only after the fact, when Wardour has already made his choice and seen it out almost to its tragic conclusion. The reason he decides to save Frank and put Frank's welfare above his own is because he hears Frank calling to Clara in his sleep to "Love him [Wardour], Clara, for helping me! love him for my sake!" His heart is touched by Frank's words, and the implication, since Wardour still loves Clara, is that to love someone truly, one must act in the interests of the loved one rather than in one's own narrow interest. Love and goodness therefore triumph over selfishness and revenge.

Superstition

The theme of superstition is associated with Nurse Esther, in her belief that she has psychic powers (what she calls second sight), that enable her to see into distant places and to predict the

The ships were entombed in ice, stranding the explorers. (*lfstewart | Shutterstock.com*)

future. Nurse Esther has an influence on Clara, who takes her pronouncements seriously, but the other women—Mrs. Steventon, Rose, and Lucy—dismiss her dire warnings as nonsense, as does John Want at the beginning of act 3. This is not surprising, since Nurse Esther's predictions turn out to be wrong. She says in act 1, for example, that the lost men will never be found. Her pessimistic superstition is contrasted with the Christian hope that the other characters express, as stated, for example, by Clara in act 3, who says that she sees "so much of the Mercy and Goodness of the Great Creator all around me—such brightness and beauty to delight us in the Earth and Heaven" that she cannot lose hope.

STYLE

Melodrama

A melodrama is a play or prose fiction that depends on sensational or violent action and often unlikely coincidences in the plot. It appeals to the emotions of the audience and may be sentimental. Melodramas feature characters that are either extremely good or extremely evil, and good always prevails in the end. (*The Frozen Deep* is almost an exception in that there is no very evil character, since Wardour, although capable of evil, in the end chooses the good.) Originally, a melodrama used songs and musical accompaniment to heighten the emotional response of the audience. *The Frozen Deep* makes much use of music, such as the Scottish music that accompanies the appearances of Nurse Esther, and the piano music that accompanies Lucy and Clara as they reveal their secrets to each other in act 1. Melodramas were extremely popular in mid-nineteenth-century England.

Dramatic Irony

In its broadest sense, dramatic irony occurs when the audience, and one or more characters in the play, are aware of some key fact or piece of information of which another character is ignorant. The audience is thus "in the know,"

COMPARE
&
CONTRAST

- **1850s:** Melodrama is a popular form of theatrical entertainment in England.

   Today: Melodrama flourishes in film and on television in Britain and the United States. Melodramas are sometimes also called soap operas or "weepies," meaning that they appeal strongly to the emotions, dramatizing situations in which virtuous characters work through a series of challenging or difficult life situations.

- **1850s:** The British Empire is expanding its realm of power, and the British are prominent in global exploration, including not only the Arctic, but Africa and Asia.

   Today: Britain's role in the world is more modest than it was in the nineteenth century. In terms of exploration, Britain has a space program overseen by the U.K. Space

Agency. Its mission is to explore and benefit from space. The U.K. Space Agency claims to have a six percent share of the global space market and to be second only to the United States in space science.

- **1850s:** Women have low status and few rights in Britain. If they are not provided for by a man they have to work in low-status jobs such as domestic service or factory hands. Women are not allowed to study at universities or enter the professions.

   Today: According to a 2009 report by Cambridge University, women in Britain outnumber men in high-status professions such as law, medicine, and architecture. However, they earn less than men in these professions and are less likely to be in senior positions.

---

which tends to heighten the interest of the spectators as to how the plot is going to unfold. Dramatic irony occurs in act 2 when Lieutenant Crayford realizes that Frank Aldersley is the man that Richard Wardour has vowed to kill. The audience is also aware of this fact, but Frank is ignorant of it, so he senses no danger when he goes off with Wardour on the last-ditch expedition. The audience, however, understands why Crayford is so concerned and tries to get Frank to stay behind.

HISTORICAL CONTEXT

The Franklin Expedition

During the 1850s, the tragic fate of the Arctic expedition led by Sir John Franklin (1776–1847), was still making news in England. The expedition had set off from England on May 19, 1845. The purpose was to chart the Northwest Passage, a sea route through the Arctic Ocean

that connected the Pacific and the Atlantic Ocean.

The expedition consisted of two ships, HMS *Terror* and HMS *Erebus*. On board were 129 men and officers. The ships contained much of the best technology of the day, including steam engines and a steam-based heating system. The expedition took on board three years' supply of food, including canned food.

The expedition was seen by two whaling ships on Baffin Bay, near Greenland, on July 26, but that was the last recorded sighting. Two years went by. For people waiting in England for news of how the expedition was faring (like the women in act 1 of *The Frozen Deep*), it was as if Franklin and his men had vanished from the face of the earth. In 1847, Franklin's wife, Lady Jane Franklin, urged the British government to search for her husband's expedition, and by 1852, three such expeditions had been sent out, with nothing to show for their efforts.

They cast dice to determine who would go for help, and who would stay behind. (*Pablo H Canidad /*
Shutterstock.com)

In 1854, Scottish explorer John Rae, also in search of what happened to the Franklin expedition, talked to Eskimos on King William Island who possessed items that were unmistakably from the two ships and who claimed to have seen the bodies of up to forty white men. The Eskimos also said they had seen evidence of cannibalism among the members of the ill-fated expedition. Rae returned to England and reported his findings, including the allegations of cannibalism. When published in newspapers, his report about cannibalism was met by indignation and disbelief. Charles Dickens took an interest in the controversy and tried to disprove the allegations by casting doubt on the words of the Eskimo witnesses. Dickens argued in his magazine *Household Words* (as reported by Robert Louis Brannan in the introduction to his book *Under the Management of Mr. Charles Dickens: His Production of "The Frozen Deep"*) that the Eskimos were untrustworthy and that Franklin and his men simply would not resort to such acts, even in the most dire circumstances.

Dickens published Rae's response, in which Rae defended his report, and there was further back-and-forth between them in the December 1854 issues of *Household Words*.

Interest in the expedition was further stimulated after the end of the Crimean War in 1856, when Lady Franklin appealed for another search expedition to be sent. It was a result of this continuing interest in the Franklin expedition that Dickens had the idea for a play based on an Arctic expedition that had encountered severe difficulties. He passed the idea on to Collins, who wrote the original version of the script, which Dickens then heavily edited.

The facts about the Franklin expedition gradually emerged in the years after the play was first performed. The ships became trapped in ice off King William Island in September 1846. Franklin died in June of the following year, and in 1848 the survivors, numbering just over one hundred, abandoned the ships and trekked over land to try to reach safety, but no one survived.

CRITICAL OVERVIEW

Although *The Frozen Deep* was first performed in an amateur production at Tavistock House, London, in 1857, professional reviewers were invited to the performance, and the play received extremely favorable reviews. What most impressed audience and reviewers alike was the performance of Charles Dickens as Richard Wardour, which moved many people to tears. The play was performed again in July, and then several times, with a professional cast, at the New Free Trade Hall in Manchester, England, in August. All these performances were highly successful. However, when the play was revised and performed again in 1866 at London's Royal Olympic Theatre, it was a failure, even being jeered by the audience. After this Collins decided that it should not be performed again. He rewrote the play in the form of a novella, which was published in 1874. For most readers since then, any acquaintance with *The Frozen Deep* has been through the novella, not the play.

In 1966, Robert Louis Brannan published the 1857 version of the play for the first time, with the text based on Dickens's own Prompt Book for the performance. Brannan calls the play an "unconventional melodrama," but does not rate it very highly. "Neither of the dramatic versions is a good play," he writes. He regards the play as interesting mostly because the 1857 version was very successful, and because Dickens helped to write it, was responsible for staging it, and even acted in the principal role.

CRITICISM

Bryan Aubrey

Aubrey holds a Ph.D. in English. In the following essay, he discusses the nature of Victorian melodrama and analyzes the character development of Richard Wardour, the hero of The Frozen Deep.

History has not been kind to the melodramas of Wilkie Collins. They are not performed today and are, for the most part, not even available in printed form. This is in contrast to at least a few of his novels and short stories, which remain in print even if they are not widely read. The neglect of Collins's plays is in part due to the low esteem in which drama of the Victorian period is held. The British are justifiably proud of their theatrical history from the Elizabethan and Jacobean age

> IN PARTICULAR, THE CARE WITH WHICH THE AUTHORS, DICKENS ESPECIALLY, DEVELOPED THE CHARACTER OF WARDOUR MAKES THIS MELODRAMA ONE OF THE MORE UNUSUAL EXAMPLES OF ITS TYPE ON THE VICTORIAN STAGE."

to the drama of the Restoration and of the Augustan Age. The Victorian period, however, is sometimes known as the "age of melodrama," and as Lillian Nayder notes in her book *Wilkie Collins*, "twentieth-century audiences have lost their taste for the extravagant emotionalism and the stark moral polarities that characterize the genre."

However, during Collins's day, some of his twelve melodramas, written between 1855 and 1882, and including *The Frozen Deep*, met with success, so it might be interesting to probe more deeply into why that should have been. Why might that have been? One reason was that melodrama satisfied the moral temper of the age, providing people with a simple entertainment that did not challenge their basic assumptions about life or give them anything difficult to think about. As distinguished literary critic Northrop Frye wrote in *Anatomy of Criticism*, "In melodrama two themes are important: the triumph of moral virtue over villainy, and the consequent idealizing of the moral views assumed to be held by the audience." For Robert W. Corrigan, in his essay, "Melodrama and the Popular Tradition in Nineteenth-Century British Theatre," the popularity of melodrama was in part a reflection of "the sturdy Victorian morality," that continued in spite of the rapid social changes of the era, and the fact that melodrama is a "simplification and an idealization of human experience in dramatic terms, and thus for Victorian audiences it was both an escape from an often harsh reality and also a projection of reality as it ought to be."

The Frozen Deep fits both these definitions nicely. Contemporary accounts and reviews of its performance in 1857 suggest that audiences were deeply moved by the noble self-sacrifice of the hero Richard Wardour, who overcomes the darker side of his nature the way a Victorian

WHAT DO I READ NEXT?

- *Woman in White* is Collins's most successful novel, originally published in book form in 1860. Based on a real-life criminal case, the complex plot is about a villain's attempt to steal the inheritance of a wealthy young heiress. A modern edition was published by Oxford University Press in 2008.

- *The Moonstone* (1868) is a much-admired detective novel by Collins, noted for keeping the reader in suspense. A precious yellow diamond is stolen, but who is the culprit? Different characters, including suspects and detectives, narrate their own versions of the story. A modern edition is available from Signet Classics (2009).

- *In the Land of White Death: An Epic Story of Survival in the Siberian Arctic* (2000) by Valerian Albanov is a gripping real-life account of Arctic peril. In 1912, Russian seaman Albanov was second in command of a ship that got locked in the Arctic ice. For eighteen months the crew endured hardship, but then Albanov and thirteen crew members decided to abandon the ship. Over the next three months they made an extremely hazardous 235-mile journey to safety. Albanov kept a diary of those perilous months, first published in Russia in 1917, and it appeared in English translation for the first time in the edition published by the Modern Library in 2000.

- *To Build a Fire and Other Stories* (1986) is a collection of adventure stories by American writer Jack London (1876–1916). London is known for his stories that pit man against nature, and the title story in this collection is a famous example. In the Klondike area in Canada during the Gold Rush days, a man must try to survive extreme cold after falling into a creek. There are twenty-five stories in this collection.

- Langston Hughes, a famous poet of the Harlem Renaissance, was also a playwright. Like Collins's works, Hughes's plays are less well known, and far less appreciated, than his other writings. *The Political Plays of Langston Hughes* (2000) brings some of those dramatic works to a modern audience.

- *The Frozen Deep* drew heavily on current events to shape its narrative. *With Their Eyes: September 11th—The View from a High School at Ground Zero*, edited by Annie Thomas and published in 2002, features monologues written by teens who witnessed the fall of the World Trade Center in 2001. The work is designed to be performed as reader's theater.

English officer and gentleman should do, even though it costs him his life. Despite being tested under extreme conditions, almost all the characters come out of their harrowing experience with flying colors; hope, courage, steadfastness, patience, and love are all rewarded. In the production at Tavistock House, the Union Jack (the British flag), was clearly visible in both acts 2 and 3—a little patriotic flourish that no doubt reinforced feelings of national pride in the audience.

But what is the reader in the twenty-first century to make of such a production? Does *The Frozen Deep* hold anything other than historical interest? At first blush the play may well strike the modern reader, as Nayder's comment quoted above suggests, as rather over the top in its sentimentality, particularly in the final death scene. The coincidences that first allow Wardour to learn of Frank's relationship to Clara and then place the two men alone together, apart from the group, strain credulity. The modern reader might also be acutely conscious of the rigid gender roles presented. While the men go off to perform feats of derring-do, the women sit around at home talking about how they miss the men and cheering one another up. It appears that they have nothing much else to do, although later they do muster the gumption to follow the rescue expedition all the way to Newfoundland.

If the modern reader notices things about the play that would not have occurred to a Victorian audience, and perhaps finds some aspects of it hard to take seriously, there is no doubt that Collins and Charles Dickens, who extensively revised Collins's script for the 1857 performance, took their task very seriously indeed. By all accounts their collaboration produced a deeply moving experience for the audience, and a close examination of the drama suggests that it is not without its interest or subtleties. In particular, the care with which the authors, Dickens especially, developed the character of Wardour makes this melodrama one of the more unusual examples of its type on the Victorian stage.

From the point of view of effective drama, much of the interest in act 1 rests on the sense of foreboding instilled by the presence of the Scottish nurse. Although the women, except for Clara, dismiss her pronouncements and her claim to possess second sight as nonsense, it is Nurse Esther's warnings makes them uneasy nonetheless. The predictions also leaves the audience wondering whether Nurse Esther's claim to supernatural precognition is based on some sliver of truth or is mere superstition. Collins and Dickens keep this dual possibility in the forefront because it maintains the dramatic interest. When the nurse says she will speak her prophecy when the moon comes up, it creates a sense of anticipation and even fear. The impact on the audience of her prediction, in which she sees "the lamb i' the grasp o' the lion," depends on the possibility that it may be true. In this way, act 1 reaches an effective climax.

The nurse's vision also adds weight to the sense of danger that has been present in act 1 since Clara told her story to Lucy. This is the first the audience hears about Richard Wardour, and being told about him in some detail before seeing him in person makes effective drama. Wardour is presented as a man of strong passions who reacts violently to being disappointed in love. When he returns from the navy, expecting Lucy to marry him, his fierce reaction to her rejection frightens her. She tells Clara, "I tremble when I think of his face. It comes across me in my dreams and makes me as frightened in the darkness as a

child." She then mentions Wardour's "awful look of fury and despair," his vow to gain revenge, and the revelation that Frank Aldersley, Clara's fiancé, has met up with this "moody silent stranger" on the Arctic expedition. This makes it clear that the melodrama is to develop beyond the element of "man versus nature" to include that of "man versus man," and the stage is appropriately darkened at this point. Is Wardour, the reader wonders, going to turn out to be the villain of the piece?

The first part of act 2 only increases the uneasiness with which the audience or reader contemplates the still unseen Wardour. Steventon and Crayford discuss him, and while Crayford refers to him as "one of the best officers and one of the hardiest men in the Queen's Navy," Steventon is puzzled by such a description, since he dislikes Wardour and regards him as possessing a violent temperament. When Wardour finally does appear he does little to change the mostly negative impression created by the earlier comments about him. He is largely silent, except for his remark that he likes the Arctic because there are no women there.

At this point there is no indication that Wardour will become the hero of the play, and this was exactly what Wilkie and Dickens intended. Wardour was not to be the typical hero of melodrama, all good and without internal conflict or complexity. Brannan points out in his introduction to his edition of the play, *Under the Management of Mr. Charles Dickens: His Production of "The Frozen Deep"* that Dickens—for this aspect of the drama appears to have been mostly his work—was dissatisfied with the heroes in his own novels because they were too good to be true. He wanted to create a better-rounded hero who is able to face and overcome the conflicts and turbulence inherent in his nature. As Brannan puts it, Dickens believed that for his hero, "Being made a 'man' would mean enduring severe inner trials and remaining faithful to a personal ideal of conduct."

With this in mind, the dramatists created yet another layer for the play. Going beyond the external conflicts implied in "man versus nature" and "man versus man," they developed a hero who must struggle with an internal conflict—"man against himself." It is in this that the success of the play lies and is the reason Victorian audiences found it so moving. Contrary to all expectations—the predictions of the nurse and

Setting off across the frozen Arctic in search of help (*Alexander Gorbunov / Shutterstock.com*)

the fears of Crayford and Clara—Wardour overcomes his lower instincts and acts in a way that commands admiration and respect. He manages to do this in the most extreme conditions when it would have been so easy to have done the opposite. Even the sophisticated modern reader, uncomfortable with the extremes of sensationalism and emotion that are part and parcel of Victorian melodrama, may discover something very touching about the transformation in this proud and passionate man who, drawing on great inner resources, achieves humility, simplicity, and selfless love, even at the expense of his own life. It was the belief of the dramatists that the depiction of such a man would hold up for others an ideal to which they might aspire.

Source: Bryan Aubrey, Critical Essay on *The Frozen Deep*, in *Drama for Students*, Gale, Cengage Learning, 2011.

Alexandra Neel

In the following review, Neel states that plays like The Frozen Deep *reveal a British tradition of using the distant Arctic as a proving ground for male national identity.*

A welcome addition to Francis Spufford's encyclopedic book *I May Be Some Time: Ice and the English Imagination* (1997), Jen Hill's *White Horizon: The Arctic in the Nineteenth-Century British Imagination* argues for the inclusion of the Arctic within postcolonial and imperial studies. Moreover, Hill claims that *because* the Arctic was considered peripheral and "conveniently removed . . . from colonial locations," it is the ideal space in which to examine the formation of the British national subject and the contours of British imperialism. As she succinctly puts it, "In articles, novels, plays, and poetry, the Arctic was a landscape on which assertions and critiques of nation and empire could unroll at a literal 'safe distance.'" While studies such as Lisa Bloom's seminal *Gender on Ice: American Ideologies of Polar Expeditions* (1993) and Robert G. David's *The Arctic in the British Imagination, 1818–1914* (2000) have made similar claims about the intimate connection between polar exploration narratives and nationalist discourse, Hill brings new material to the field as well as offers original readings of well-mapped territory, such as Mary Shelley's *Frankenstein* and Charlotte Brontë's *Jane Eyre*.

Indeed, Hill contends that rereading these canonical texts in light of their Arctic content not only yields fresh interpretive paths but also underscores how embedded the novels are within their socio-historical context, namely Romantic and Victorian imperialism and the making of the nationalist imperial subject.

After establishing the Arctic as a crucial space in which a nationalist British male identity is constituted, revealed, and challenged in various genres, Hill summarizes the stakes of her subsequent five chapters, which include an examination of "how exploration accounts construct one form of a foundational, nationalistic heroic masculinity"; an interpretation of "Jane [Eyre]'s 'Arctic' sufferings and her eventual rescue of Rochester," which, in Hill's estimation, "reveals the centrality of women to the spatial practices of empire"; an exploration of the origins of sensation fiction through an analysis of Charles Dickens and Wilkie Collins's fascination with cannibalism and their co-authored Arctic melodrama *The Frozen Deep* (1857); and a consideration of "the participation in empire by boys' adventure novels," which in R. M. Ballantyne's work, "foreshadows the exhaustion of Arctic space in imperial narrative and questions the very logic of boys' adventure and empire itself."

By far the most compelling and original contribution of *White Horizon* is "introducing Arctic space to larger discussions of the sensation genre," which, according to Hill, "complicates existing critical discussions of sensation and its relation to domestic space, nationalism, and colonialism." This is such an intriguing theory of the origins of sensation fiction that I would have liked an even lengthier exposition of it. As the argument stands, Hill asserts that plays like Collins and Dickens's *The Frozen Deep* reveal that "the profoundly domestic sensation genre has an unlikely genealogy that includes a tradition of using the distant Arctic as a proving ground for male national identity." In part, Hill can make this assertion by "[t]racing one influence on the sensation novel back to Dickens's *Household Words* articles on cannibalism and stable national identities through his transformation and extension of the same concerns in his contributions to and performance of *The Frozen Deep*." Just as Dickens's articles and melodrama incite a visceral response in his audience through their detailing of inconceivable horrors, so too sensation fiction, which, despite its transgressive tendencies, serves a politically

conservative end: the consolidation of national identity.

In a way, these broad-stroke claims are precisely the stakes of Hill's entire book: that is, seemingly insignificant references to the Arctic are crucial in understanding the discourse surrounding national identities in the wake of Britain's expanding empire. To her credit, Hill does not shy away from answering the question of why the Arctic in particular; she contends that the stark environment reveals the "hidden operations" behind imperial formations: "in the Arctic relationships between the geographic and the corporeal existed in stark relief and thus made legible and articulate invisible spaces of ideology and national subjectivity." While nuanced readings abound in *White Horizon,* at times, it takes a defensive posture in explaining why the Arctic matters, which can lead to some repetitiveness.

That said, the book is rigorously researched, and well organized, and it offers exciting comparisons between unlikely authors and genres, such as Eleanor Anne Porden's nationalist poem *The Arctic Expeditions* (1818) and Mary Shelley's *Frankenstein* (1818). In this chapter, Hill makes the important though often overlooked claim that *writing* is part and parcel of nationalist enterprise, especially in the case of women. This is particularly evident in Porden's case, who, according to Hill, self-consciously and proudly declares as much in all forms of written address—from her personal correspondence with her husband Sir John Franklin (a famous polar explorer who disappeared during his ill-fated 1848 Arctic expedition) to her poems, where "Porden equates the work of Arctic explorers with authorship." While the Arctic becomes the means for Porden to assert women's powerful role in empire building, it serves a different end for Mary Shelley. In Hill's words, "In *Frankenstein*'s gothic excesses and its ultimately destabilizing Arctic frame, Shelley rejects any reinscription of female presence in British imperial endeavor and by extension calls into question women's accepted role in the nation."

Hill is at her best in her reading of *Jane Eyre* (1847), which is a beautiful supplement to Gayatri Spivak's postcolonial intervention on the subject of *Jane Eyre*'s feminism. In Hill's analysis, the form Jane Eyre's feminism takes is based on heroic polar narratives, hence, masculinist and imperialist to the core. Hill tracks this polar genre not only in the more obvious moments of hardship in the novel—Lowood, Jane's trek across the moors—but also in those more opaque instances, namely, in Jane's Arctic sketches. For Hill, Jane's three sketches "are self-portraits . . . of a projected interior" and her "affinity with desolate polar expanses is more than symbolic, but is, rather, her primary mode of representing and understanding herself in the world." However, if the Arctic becomes the ground of Jane's self-expression, her self-expression of suffering is not innocent. Hill argues that "Jane's flight across the moors and her experience of bodily hardship can be seen as an effort to retrieve and save Britain from the perceived taint of colonial spaces"; in other words, Jane expiates and purifies Rochester of his colonial sins through a kind of Arctic whitewashing.

Just as Hill's use of an Arctic lens allows for new perspectives on canonical texts, so too it sheds light on more obscure texts, like Wilkie Collins's *Poor Miss Finch* (1871) with its chilling Arctic finale and Porden's *The Veils* (1815), which, in turn, better reveal the ideological work that informs literary and poetic production. In sum, Hill's book extends the geographical scope of postcolonial and imperial studies to the far north and enhances the ever-expanding field of polar studies with its broad range of genres.

Source: Alexandra Neel, "White Horizon: The Arctic in the Nineteenth-Century British Imagination," in *Studies in the Novel*, Vol. 41, No. 3, Winter 2009, pp. 497–99.

Michael Hollington

In the following essay, Hollington critiques Lillian Najder's book, which offers an account of the professional working relationship between Charles Dickens and Wilkie Collins as collaborative writers.

This is a work of exemplary scholarship which offers an admirably full account of the professional working relationship between Charles Dickens and Wilkie Collins as collaborative writers, to which all future students of either author will want to return over and again, as an indispensible framework for thinking about this subject. At the same time, I believe that it rides the thesis it develops about the materials so painstakingly assembled in a manner that is too hard, too black-and-white, and too drastically corrective of conventional notions of the stature of the respective authors. But the book is impressive and fascinating, even in its flaws, for it is the

CERTAINLY SOME OF HER CHARGES AGAINST DICKENS'S RACISM STICK—MOST NOTABLY, PERHAPS, IN THE CASE OF HIS SHOCKING IF COMMONPLACE REACTIONS TO THE INDIAN MUTINY."

scrupulousness of Najder's scholarship that regularly provides the material that raises most of the question marks about the conclusions she draws.

But if my own reservations about this study are to be properly evaluated and understood, I need to start by coming clean about the angle from which I approach it. I am a specialist of Dickens rather than of Collins, and although I have studied and written about Dickens's relationship with Collins, I have done so, I freely admit, from a largely Dickensian perspective, which is rather different from that adopted here. I have no difficulty in agreeing with Najder that there were tensions in their relationship, on both sides, which grew more severe as Collins became more and more of a rival to the elder man, and in finding her discussion of these for the most part illuminating. But I have more difficulty than Najder, on the one hand, in dismissing questions of relative and often differing artistic methods and aims, if not of artistic merit, between the two writers, and on the other, in reaching the conclusion that questions of the "correctness" or otherwise of their respective attitudes to such matters as gender and race are to be considered as the yardstick of their essential divergences.

Collins, Najder is essentially telling us in this book, was a much more enlightened and liberal man than the later Dickens, and the study of their collaborative fiction and journalism reveals how regularly their attitudes on gender and race clash, and how frequently, in the course of their collaborations, Dickens sought to suppress the younger author's voice. That is to say, her mission is not just to overturn J. W. T. Ley's 1924 judgment that "the Wilkie Collins influence . . . from an artistic point of view, has always seemed to me the most unfortunate happening in Dickens's life," but to challenge, from what she describes as a "materialist" perspective, the very notion that "artistic" judgments have any bearing on the fundamental issues at all, which, I conclude from her persistent emphases, are for her primarily political and ideological.

This gives her book throughout a welcome polemical and controversial edge, and arresting novelty of approach. But the problems that her tactics involve are apparent in her opening paragraph, which concerns Collins's attitude toward Dickens's death. She notes, evenhandedly enough, that Collins wrote to Catherine Beard to say how "shocked and grieved" he is by Dickens's death. But her attention is essentially drawn, not by this testimony in a letter to a mutual friend, but by that in another, to his agent, which describes the day of the funeral as "a lost day to me," because he could not spend any time reading the proofs of his new book. It would be possible to downplay this latter remark at the expense of the former, and to treat it as little more than routine griping between professionals about the pressure of work. Later, without noting the connection, Najder will offer evidence, in a letter to his mother, of Collins griping similarly to his mother in 1867 that "his very minutes are counted." But here she takes the opposite view—she dismisses the letter to Beard, and takes that to William Tindell very seriously as compelling evidence of an accumulated coolness of regard. She proceeds, without registering much shock, or even too much surprise (for surely Collins's professional career owed at least something to Dickens!), to explain and justify the cynicism she detects in it as resentment at the treatment Dickens had meted out to Collins during the course of the latter's career.

In her introductory chapter Najder continues, in an admirably clear way, with a summarized laying bare of the skeleton of argument of her book. But here, too, although there is obviously less of the rich, open, copious scholarly detail that later tends to place checks on some of her interpretative positions, statements are made that might raise quizzical eyebrows. She claims, for instance, that (to crudely paraphrase her views) *The Moonstone* (1868) is an antiracist book, and *Edwin Drood* (1870) a racist one. But the assertion that Dickens treats the Landlesses in a condescending, colonialist way—he "foregrounds their innate ferocity and displaces criminality from West to East"—already seems on the face of it a trifle odd, and will seem even more so later, at least if we follow the traditional view that the chief source of "criminality" in the novel is to be found in John Jasper. It is he,

rather than Dickens himself, who would seem to "displace" his guilt eastwards by trying to frame Neville as Edwin's murderer—at least if we take it (as Najder, as we shall see, does not!) that he is an Englishman. Similarly, the view that "Dickens associates opium consumption with eastern 'contagion' rather than British drug trafficking," might again seem puzzling in the light of clear evidence of a contrary position in the previous novel, *Our Mutual Friend* (1865), where Veneering is clearly pretty fiercely attacked as a capitalist drug-pusher (Bella, out for the day on the Thames with her father, imagines Reginald Wilfer "going to China in that handsome three-masted ship, to bring home opium, with which he would for ever cut out Chicksey, Veneering and Stubbles"—*OMF* II, viii, 318).

Chapter 1 then offers a stimulating overview, with material drawn from very wide sources, of Collins's work for Dickens as a contributor to *Household Words* (1850–1859). But the line it takes—treating Collins as an honorary woman, suffering from Dickens's controlling hand in much the same way as the female contributors to the magazine—seems to me questionable. There can be no question, of course, but that Dickens was a very hands-on editor who actively censored many of his contributors' works in strongly intrusive ways, and that this took a particularly regrettable form with women writers such as Eliza Lynn Lynton who "gets so near the sexual side of things as to be a little dangerous to us." But whether his jokes in correspondence with Collins about Dinah Mulock (Mrs. Craik), whom he does not in fact censor ("she shall have her own way. But after it's published show her this Proof, and ask her to consider whether her story would have been the better or worse for it") particularly deserve Najder's scorn—"promoting his superior, masculine knowledge, he makes her the subject of a private joke between men"—is moot. It might seem evidence of bias that she allows Collins by contrast to get away with pretty light reprimand for strongly derogatory remarks about the heroines of modern novels by women writers, in which he describes them as "Eve's daughters," "impudent young women," "Man-Haters" and the like. His apparent prejudice is more tolerable, because his subservient role in relation to Dickens is merged and elided with that of the women he writes about. Moreover, though one is indebted to Najder's valuable assembly of sarcastic views about the header "Conducted by Charles Dickens," on every page of *Household Words* and *All the Year Round* (1859–1895), it seems a rather sweeping move to conclude as she often tends to that therefore everything in the two journals is to be attributed to Dickens's views, and not to those of their individual author.

The fascinating thing, though, is that, throughout her book, Najder often asks hard questions of herself, at the risk of undermining her thesis. So she asks here, appropriately, whether Dickens might have been right to spot that Mulock was not much good, and would be more or less forgotten by the beginning of the twenty-first century (she is much concerned throughout with reputation in our time). But her answer, for me, veers off in what I take to be the wrong direction. Instead of ascertaining, logically, whether gender distinctions clouded his judgment in the case of women writers that are still revered—which would indeed tend to suggest a sexist slant in him—she finds a smoking gun in the fact that he did not spot the fact that Edward Bulwer Lytton (a man) would also decline in popularity. I do not see that this proves anything, whereas the eloquent testimony of George Eliot, reacting to his immediate praise of her work—"there can hardly be any climax of approbation for me after this, and I am so deeply moved by the finely felt and finely expressed sympathy that my incognito seems quite painful in forbidding me to tell Dickens how thoroughly his generous impulse has been appreciated"— might indeed have thrown some kind of spanner into the works of her argument (*The Letters of Charles Dickens*, ed. Graham Storey and Kathleen Tillotson, vol. 8 [Oxford: Clarendon P, 1995], 506n).

Chapters 2 through 5 then proceed to offer easily the most detailed, stimulating, but again controversial available accounts of their literary collaborations, chiefly on the Christmas numbers of the two journals, between 1856 and 1867. Certainly some of her charges against Dickens's racism stick—most notably, perhaps, in the case of his shocking if commonplace reactions to the Indian Mutiny. But elsewhere, they can be taken or left—and my reaction, on several occasions, leans toward leaving them. A Scottish legal "not proven," for instance, might be the verdict on her assertion that Dickens's work shows clear signs of a prejudice against Scots as inferior savages—to which Collins, of course, is immune, as their respective attitudes

toward the Highland nurse in *The Frozen Deep* (1866) are said to show. She uses the frictions caused in the Dickens household by the Hogarths as part of her evidence—but whether their being Scottish or their being in-laws was the greater irritant is not clear. She simply omits Dickens's triumphant visits to Scotland, his relations with many warm Edinburgh friends, and his many public and private expressions of esteem for Edinburgh and Scotland. She quotes Sir Walter Scott, comparing Highlanders to Eskimos in *Waverley* (1814), as the originator of a tradition of derogatory representation of that "race," but if she thinks that this is all there is to say about Scott's view of Highlanders in that text, one cannot be sure that she has actually read the book. Nor can one be absolutely certain of her command of Scottish geography and history, for she seems to ignore distinctions between Lowlands and Highlands, by simply conflating the two, in discussions of texts that are clearly specifically about the latter.

But for Najder, in her discussion of *The Perils of Certain English Prisoners* (1857) for instance, "Dickens's narrative naturalizes Victorian gender norms as well as imperial relations." She is too scrupulous a scholar, again, to suppress evidence that goes against her view, but she does tend once more to minimize it in favor of how she sees the case as a whole. Thus, although she concedes Dickens's aim of showing here "the bravery of our ladies in India," and admits that his writing emphasizes Miss Maryon's capacity to "handle the guns, hammer the flints, and look to the locks during the siege," she claims, perhaps rather arbitrarily, that her bravery "consists largely of endurance," citing as evidence her "dressing" and "soothing" the children, and offering "encouragement, and praise" of the men, when these are arguably signs of active rather than passive engagement.

Returning to race, and to the discussion of her interpretation of *Edwin Drood* begun above, I am frankly surprised that Najder, for all her concern with the contemporary, can in 2002 take seriously Howard Duffield's 1930 proposal that Jasper is a member of the Indian Thuggee cult. At any rate, in doing so, she goes against the views of most contemporary Droodians—Wendy Jacobson in 1977 and 1986, David Paroissien in 2002, or Jerome Meckier in 1987, with whose view (underlining a familiar Dickensian dialectic, that savagery is to be found in full flower on domestic doorsteps) that Jasper is "a thoroughly English murderer" I personally concur. She seems driven to accept much less reliable speculation from theorists of the novel's unwritten ending—Charles Forsyte's proposal that Jasper is half-Egyptian, or Felix Aylmer's that he is the son of a Muslim woman—in order to support her view that Dickens's novel is racist. For once her arguments in support of it seem to consist in a less than scrupulous process of "guilt by association"—"despite the variations among these solutions, and regardless of their plausibility, each one reflects and extends a single strategy on Dickens's part: the displacement of crime and criminality from West to East," she writes—when it seems more rational to conclude that whatever racism there is to be detected here belongs first and foremost with Duffield, Aylmer, and Forsyte.

And although I have given praise here to the range and comprehensiveness of the treatment of the literary relations of Dickens and Collins, there are in fact one or two areas in which I think she might have done more. Thus, for instance, although I can see the wisdom and distinctive novelty of focus in leaving biography largely in abeyance, I wonder whether at least some of the professional tensions she uncovers might not have been further illuminated by more frequent discussion of biographical issues (where she does do this, a little hesitantly at times, as when she discusses Dickens's negative feelings about other members of the Collins clan, the results are in fact useful). I wonder, too, whether it might not have been interesting to link, in a closer and more detailed way, both Collins's increasingly complex use of the method of multiple narration in his fictions, as well as Dickens's criticisms of it, particularly at the time of *The Moonstone*, to their own extended experience of the practice of writing in tandem or as part of a team.

Yet that would have been to take a more determinedly aesthetic and literary approach to the partnership than Najder is prepared to adopt. Her book's strengths and weaknesses, it seems to me, have to do with its relation, however distant, to some strands of the American Puritan tradition—on the one hand its scruple, scholarly thoroughness and honesty, and on the other, its apparent view that there are more important matters than art, and that we can and must judge and morally reprehend the

past from the perspective of the present. For although one cannot simply apply to her Gillian Beer's remarks (in the new introduction to *Darwin's Plots* [Cambridge: Cambridge UP, 2002]) about "the condescension of history towards Victorian terms," with its "dangerous capacity to let the present off the hook and to suggest that we are now free of prejudices we can so readily symptomise when we recognise them set back one hundred years or so" (for one thing, it is difficult to imagine Najder letting contemporary offenders against her standards off the hook), there is at times, for all its professed "materialism," a somewhat ahistorical feel to this book as it relentlessly uncovers Dickensian transgression. Beer, ironically, is thinking in part here of a great nineteenth-century woman writer, George Eliot, in whose works one may find scattered remarks whose apparent sexism and racism—her "scientific" contrast between "the small brain and vivacious temperament" of women "of the Gallic race" and the "larger brain and slower temperament of the English and Germans," whose women are therefore "dreamy and passive" (George Eliot, "Woman in France: Madame de Sable," in *The Essays of George Eliot*, ed. Thomas Pinney [London: Routledge and Kegan Paul, 1963], 55), for instance—might make most of the Dickensian indiscretions paraded here seem rather tame. But are we to proscribe George Eliot, and T. S. Eliot, and Dickens and D. H. Lawrence—not to mention Richard Wagner—because of their supposedly "tarnished" records in matters of "political correctness," and prefer "clean" writers like Wilkie Collins (leaving aside the question of whether he in fact was so or not)? Some of us, at least, could be out of a job were this view to be any more widespread than it already is.

Source: Michael Hollington, "Unequal Partners: Charles Dickens, Wilkie Collins, and Victorian Authorship," in *Clio*, Vol. 32, No. 4, 2003, p. 496.

William H. Marshall

In the following excerpt, Marshall critiques later works of Collins, including the adaptation of The Frozen Deep *as a novella.*

III. OTHER WORKS, 1870–89

. . . Of the six novelettes which Collins published during his final years, four can lay some claim to literary merit, and then unevenly. Of these probably the weakest is *The Frozen Deep* (1874), an adaptation of the drama of 1857 and

IF COLLINS ESSENTIALLY MISINTERPRETED
HIS AMERICAN MATERIALS, HE USED THEM WITH
EXTRAORDINARY SKILL TO CREATE AN ATMOSPHERE
THAT PERMEATES AND SUSTAINS THE NARRATIVE."

1866. The story is strikingly simple: Richard Wardour, replaced in the affections of Clara Burnham by an unknown man, vows revenge; on an Arctic expedition, Wardour learns that Clara's fiancé is one of his peers, Francis Aldersley, with whom, by accident, Wardour is separated from the rest of the group. He now has the power to attain revenge, but, undergoing a spiritual transformation, he leads Aldersley back to civilization—and to Clara—where, his expiation fulfilled, Wardour dies in exhaustion. One of Collins' most melodramatic accomplishments, *The Frozen Deep* is also one of his most celebrated—a fact which impinges upon any attempt to make a literary judgment of it. By any standard the work is deficient: the plot is hopelessly contrived, resting entirely upon a major coincidence, and the central character's principal decision, on which the only significant action turns, is incredibly motivated. Yet these conclusions may be obscured, or at least assimilated, by the image handed down through book and tradition of the play's production at Tavistock House in 1857, with Dickens' performance as Richard Wardour, passionate but exhausted, to Wilkie Collins' Francis Aldersley.

Miss or Mrs? (1873) has no tradition of dramatic performance either to confuse judgments of its literary merits or to emphasize its absurdities. At the center of the story stands Richard Turlington, a highly successful merchant of early middle age and, it is firmly suggested, of dubious past. As suitor to Natalie Graybrooke, daughter of the incredibly wealthy Sir Joseph, Turlington hesitates at nothing to bring the girl, with her wealth, to an early marriage; when he realizes that his schemes have been checked, he becomes savage in a way that is unparalleled in Collins' work, firing a pistol through a door in an effort to kill Sir Joseph. Unlike most of Collins' villains, Richard Turlington has in his past life only darkness, nothing to explain or mitigate the evil

that is his. He becomes totally sinister, and with his absolute villainy binds together the elements of what in all other respects is an extraordinarily weak piece of fiction.

In *John Jago's Ghost* (1873–74) the achievement is somewhat more remarkable, resting upon a greater variety of characters, generally well motivated and integrated with their stark rural American background. Based upon a legal episode which had occurred in Vermont in 1819, Collins' novelette uses the theme of the presumed dead returning to life. Found in earlier works, most strikingly in *Sister Rose* and "The Dead Hand," it was here put to credible use in the case of John Jago, for whose supposed murder the Meadowcroft brothers are convicted on the basis of massive circumstantial evidence. Only after the young men have been sentenced to death is Jago, who has fled the Meadowcroft farm in bitterness and anger, induced to return and then captured.

Aiding credibility and imposing a cohesiveness upon the narrative elements is the very mood permeating the farmhouse and all its world, from which only two beings are exempt, and they are the least compelling characters in the novelette: Philip Lefrank, a visiting Englishman, the narrator trying to impose a somewhat objective order on what he relates; Naomi Colebrook, the orphaned cousin of the Meadowcrofts, bright amidst their darkness. All else is the stark Puritan American setting, with its social suppression and personal frustration, in which brother betrays brother and the living are committed to the endurance until death of life's work and pain.

Miss Meadowcroft, the daughter of the invalid farmer Isaac Meadowcroft, though clearly an extreme instance, is representative of the spirit creating the atmosphere at the farm: "She was a melancholy, middle-aged woman, without visible attractions of any sort—one of those persons who appear to accept the obligation of living under protest, as a burden which they never would have consented to bear if they had only been consulted first" (Chapter II). If Collins essentially misinterpreted his American materials, he used them with extraordinary skill to create an atmosphere that permeates and sustains the narrative.

Countering those who insist upon a steady decline in Collins' abilities is the fact that for its kind *The Haunted Hotel: A Mystery of Modern*

Venice (1879) was one of his most successful undertakings. The question may arise about the worth of the *kind* itself, the sensation narrative, of which this is an almost pure example. With a highly complex and to no purpose plot—contrived around mysterious experiments, secrets from the past, the substitution of one man for another in death, and the shadowy barrier between sanity and madness—*The Haunted Hotel* moves toward one climactic scene, in which all the possibilities of sensation are realized. Agnes Lockwood, the female protagonist, awakens in the haunted room to find the evil Countess Narona sitting in a stupor beside her; "midway between her [own] face and the ceiling" hovers "a human head—severed at the neck, like a head struck from the body by a guillotine." Agnes, captured by the terror of the apparition, sees nothing else:

> The flesh of the face was gone. The shriveled skin was darkened in hue, like the skin of an Egyptian mummy—except at the neck. There it was of a lighter color; there it showed spots and splashes of the hue of that brown spot on the ceiling, which the child's fanciful terror had distorted into the likeness of a spot of blood. Thin remains of a discolored mustache and whiskers, hanging over the upper lip, and over the hollows where the cheeks had once been, made the head just recognizable as the head of a man. Over all the features death and time had done their obliterating work. The eyelids were closed. The hair on the skull, discolored like the hair on the face, had been burned away in places. The bluish lips, parted in a fixed grin, showed the double row of teeth. By slow degrees, the hovering head (perfectly still when she first saw it) began to descend toward Agnes as she lay beneath. By slow degrees, that strange doubly-blended odor, which the Commissioners had discovered in the vaults of the old palace—which had sickened Francis Westwick in the bed-chamber of the new hotel—spread its fetid exhalations over the room. Downward and downward the hideous apparition made its slow progress, until it stopped close over Agnes—stopped, and turned slowly, so that the face of it confronted the upturned face of the woman in the chair.

(Chapter XXII)

Mitigating the purity of this novelette as sensation fiction is the moral conflict that is taking place in the mind of Countess Narona, who sees herself compelled by fate to commit acts of evil and thereby bring on her own destruction. Thus she assimilates the fatality of the story into her own motivation, causing the incidents that would

otherwise be considered fatal; as T. S. Eliot emphasized, the melodramatic therefore becomes a quality of her character rather than of the work itself in which that character occurs.

In the last years Collins wrote some short stories, but few of significance. "The Fatal Fortune" (1874) is a more pointed attack upon the system of private asylums and their abuse by the unscrupulous than Collins had made in *The Woman in White*; here, painfully illustrating the most striking fault others were to find with his fiction of social criticism, he concluded with a frank statement of the "moral" of his story: "Assisted by a doctor, whose honesty and capacity must be taken on trust, these interested persons [the covetous relatives of a wealthy Englishman], in this nineteenth century of progress, can lawfully imprison their relative for life, in a country which calls itself free, and which declares that its justice is equally administered to all alike."

In 1887 Chatto and Windus published fourteen short stories in three volumes under the title *Little Novels*. Collected from Collins' periodical publication during the 1870's and the first half of the 1880's, these were retitled so that each bears the name of two characters, such as "Mrs. Zant and the Ghost" or "Miss Mina and the Groom." Contrived in their plots and in their happy conclusions, they illustrate nothing so much as the degree to which Collins was unevenly losing control of his materials; in each story there are perhaps several of the characteristics marking the earlier and finer work, but in none of these was the informing spirit active. . . .

Source: William H. Marshall, "The Shorter Works through 1870," in *Wilkie Collins*, Twayne Publishers, 1970, pp. 40–50, 108–112.

SOURCES

"About Us," in *UK Space Agency*, http://www.ukspaceagency.bis.gov.uk/Default.aspx (accessed July 14, 2010).

Beckford, Martin, "More British Women in 'High Status' Professions Than Men, Finds Study," in *Telegraph* (London, England), August 11, 2009, http://www.telegraph.co.uk/news/uknews/6005222/More-British-women-in-high-status-professio ns-than-men-finds-study.html (accessed July 14, 2010).

Brannan, Robert Louis, "Introduction," in *Under the Management of Mr. Charles Dickens: His Production of "The Frozen Deep,"* edited by Robert Louis Brannan, Cornell University Press, 1966, pp. 2, 4, 11, 13–17.

Collins, Wilkie, *The Frozen Deep*, in *Under the Management of Mr. Charles Dickens: His Production of "The Frozen Deep,"* edited by Robert Louis Brannan, Cornell University Press, 1966, pp. 101–160.

Cookman, Scott, *Ice Blink: The Tragic Fate of Sir John Franklin's Lost Polar Expedition*, Wiley, 2000.

Corrigan, Robert W., "Melodrama and the Popular Tradition in Nineteenth-Century British Theatre," in *Laurel British Drama: The Nineteenth Century*, edited by Robert W. Corrigan, Dell, 1967, p. 13.

Frye, Northrop, *Anatomy of Criticism: Four Essays*, Princeton University Press, 1957, p. 47.

Nayder, Lillian, *Wilkie Collins*, Twayne's English Author Series, No. 544, Twayne Publishers, 1997, p. 133.

Wojtczak, Helena, "Women's Status in Mid-19th Century England," in *Women of Victorian Hastings*, http://www.hastingspress.co.uk/history/19/overview.htm (accessed July 14, 2010).

FURTHER READING

Beattie, Owen, and John Geiger, *Frozen in Time: The Fate of the Franklin Expedition*, 3rd ed., Greystone Books, 2004.

> This is a thorough account of the Arctic expedition of Sir John Franklin. It incorporates the most up-to-date forensic evidence about what went wrong and also places the expedition in the context of other polar expeditions of the nineteenth century.

Marshall, William H., *Wilkie Collins*, Twayne's English Author Series, No. 94, Twayne Publishers, 1970.

> This is a concise survey of the work of Collins

and how he contributed to the development of the English novel.

Nayder, Lillian, "Chapter 3: The Cannibal, the Nurse, and the Cook: Variants of 'The Frozen Deep,'" in *Unequal Partners: Charles Dickens, Wilkie Collins and Victorian Authorship*, Cornell University Press, 2002, pp. 60–99.

> This book contains a detailed account of the several versions of *The Frozen Deep* and the different roles played by Collins and Dickens in writing and producing them.

Slater, Michael, *Charles Dickens: A Life Defined by Writing*, Yale University Press, 2009.

> This biography of Dickens contains an account of his involvement with the writing and production of *The Frozen Deep*.

SUGGESTED SEARCH TERMS

Wilkie Collins

Wilkie Collins AND Charles Dickens

Wilkie Collins AND The Frozen Deep

Charles Dickens AND The Frozen Deep

John Rae

second sight

Tavistock House

melodrama

Victorian melodrama

Northwest Passage

Sir John Franklin

Having Our Say: The Delany Sisters' First 100 Years

EMILY MANN

1995

Emily Mann's drama *Having Our Say: The Delany Sisters' First 100 Years* opened at the McCarter Theater in Princeton, New Jersey, on February 7, 1995. Mann's play is an adaptation of the 1991 book of the same name, written by sisters Sadie and Bessie Delany. After a month of preview performances, *Having Our Say* opened on Broadway at the Booth Theatre on April 6, 1995, where the play continued a successful run until closing December 31, 1995.

Having Our Say is a three-act play. The play consists of dialogue between the two African American sisters, recalling their lives over the previous 100-plus years. The play is constructed as a testimony, in which the two sisters give evidence about their lives, crediting their father and mother for the inspiration that led to their individual successes in life. The sisters welcome the audience into their home, where they proceed to speak to and entertain the audience with stories, photographs, and other memorabilia. Significant themes include racism, Jim Crow laws, strength of character, and determination. Mann received 1995 Tony Award nominations for best play and best director for *Having Our Say*. Mary Alice, who played the role of Dr. Bessie Delany in *Having Our Say*, was nominated for best actress. Mann's play was also nominated for an Outer Critics Circle Award and a Drama Desk Award in 1995 and received a Hull-Warriner Award, given by the Dramatists Guild of America, for the 1995 production.

AUTHOR BIOGRAPHY

Mann was born on April 12, 1952, to Arthur and Sylvia Mann. Mann and her sister, Carol, were raised in Northampton, Massachusetts, where their father was a history professor at Smith College. Mann graduated from Radcliffe College in 1974, with a bachelor of arts degree in literature. In 1976, she earned a master of fine arts degree at the University of Minnesota. Mann's first play, *Annulla: An Autobiography*, was produced at the Guthrie Theatre in Minneapolis in 1977. The following year, Mann was named associate director at the Guthrie, a position that she held until 1979. Her second play, *Still Life: A Documentary* (1980), won several Obie Awards. Mann married Gerry Bamman, a playwright, in 1981 and briefly became the artistic director at the Brooklyn Academy of Music from 1981 to 1982. In 1983, Mann was awarded a Guggenheim Fellowship. She briefly worked as a stage director at the Actors Theater in Louisville, Kentucky, before becoming the director for play development at New Dramatists in New York City, a position she held from 1984 to 1991. Mann's third play, *Execution of Justice*, debuted at the Actors Theater in 1984. During the next few years, Mann adapted several different works from previously published works, including *Nights and Days* (1984), *Betsey Brown* (1989), and *Miss Julia* (1993).

In 1990, Mann was also appointed the artistic director of the McCarter Theater in Princeton, New Jersey, where *Having Our Say* was first staged in 1995. Also in 1995, Mann announced that she had been diagnosed with multiple sclerosis. Her play, *Greensboro: A Requiem*, was first staged at the McCarter Theater in 1996. An anthology of Mann's work, *Testimonies: Four Plays*, was published in 1997. This anthology includes *Annulla: An Autobiography*, *Still Life*, *Execution of Justice*, and *Greensboro: A Requiem*. Mann wrote the screenplay for *Having Our Say*, which was filmed as a television movie for CBS in 1999. This film won a Peabody Award and was nominated for an Emmy Award. Two additional plays have followed, including *The House of Bernarda Alba: A Drama about Women in Villages of Spain* (1997) and *Meshugah* (1998), which is based on an Isaac Bashevis Singer story. *Execution of Justice*, for which Mann wrote the screenplay, was filmed for Showtime in 1999. Mann received an honorary doctorate in fine arts from Princeton University in 2002. She has one son, Nicholas, and is divorced.

PLOT SUMMARY

Act 1

Act 1 of *Having Our Say* introduces the two elderly sisters, Bessie and Sadie Delany. They speak directly to the audience, who are welcomed as guests into the sisters' home. The older sister, Sadie, stands alone on stage and introduces herself and her sister, Bessie, who soon joins her on stage. Sadie and Bessie have lived together most of their lives. Bessie welcomes the audience. She says that she never thought there would be a day when people would care what "two old Negro women have to say." The sisters claim they are not wealthy, but they did save their money, as their father had instructed. They donated 10 percent of their wages to the church, put 10 percent in savings, and lived off the remainder.

The sisters grew up in Raleigh, North Carolina, where their parents met and married. In act 1, they describe their parents' courtship and their early life. The sisters also talk about racism, especially the "rebby boys," who are white racist men. The sisters mention the contributions of blacks who helped to build the United States with their hard labor. They condemn racists, who have treated blacks badly. The sisters joke that the reason they have lived so long is that they never married.

Act 1 provides the background information about Bessie and Sadie Delany that the audience needs to fully understand and enter the sisters' lives. They hate telephones and had one only briefly when Bessie was still practicing dentistry. They have not had a telephone since 1957. The sisters are survivors, who learned to laugh as a way to escape oppression. Although they have lived in New York for seventy-five years, they consider themselves to be citizens of Raleigh. They are two diverse personalities, in many way opposites, but they balance one another. The sisters often finish one another's sentences, gesture in the same way, and speak in unison.

In the final section of this act, a projector casts images of old family photos on the wall, while the sisters discuss the photos and introduce the audience to each member of their family, as their photo appears. Bessie and Sadie talk about their father, who was a seven-year-old slave at the end of the Civil War, when slavery ended. They also talk about their mother, who met their father at college and who was every bit as smart as their father. Bessie and Sadie's parents, Henry Delany and Nanny Logan, were married as soon

MEDIA ADAPTATIONS

- *Having Our Say* was filmed as a made-for-television movie for CBS in 1999. The film starred Diahann Carroll and Ruby Dee as the Delany sisters. Mann wrote the screenplay, which was directed by Lynne Littman. The VHS recording of this film, released in 2001, is 100 minutes long.

as they finished college. The sisters explain that their maternal grandparents lived in separate homes on the same property for fifty years but never married because it was illegal for a white man to marry a black woman, even though the woman was only one quarter black. The sisters continue their discussion of family with photos of their siblings, as each new baby arrived and the family began to grow. The family home was also a refuge for people who needed a meal or a place to stay. The sisters recount a joyous and happy life, with parents who nurtured them and taught them to live honest and virtuous lives.

Act 2

In act 2, the sisters talk about Jim Crow laws and the oppression under which they lived for many years. They explain that Jim Crow laws were designed to keep black people from achieving what white people had. They also note that black women were even more oppressed than black men. The sisters' first experience with the new laws occurred when they were small children. One Sunday they were told to sit in the back of the trolley car instead of the front where they always sat. A park where they had often played suddenly had signs separating black from white. On the campus at St. Augustine's School, where they lived, black teachers lived separately from white teachers, but not all white teachers followed segregation rules that closely.

The sisters briefly mention that this day is their father's birthday, and they always cook his favorite meal on his birthday—chicken and gravy, rice and sweet potatoes, macaroni and cheese, cabbage,

cauliflower, broccoli, turnips, carrots, and birthday cake. They believe in celebrating their father every day of the year.

Sadie tells a story about how she ignored Jim Crow laws, refusing to sit in the back of a shoe store, but Bessie was more easily upset by the laws. When she was refused service at a store because she was black, Bessie would go home and weep. Bessie talks about the words used to describe her. These include "colored, Negro, black, and nigger," as well as "jiggerboo, pickaninny, coon." After mentioning these words, Bessie also talks about how she describes herself, but in the end, she thinks of herself as an American. Bessie says she never thought of herself as inferior, in spite of Jim Crow laws, which tried to convince her that she was less because she was black. Sadie notes that their parents tried to protect their children from the violence of racism, especially the lynching of black people. Nevertheless, the sisters heard stories of atrocities committed by white people against blacks. Bessie is still angry and states that if it were not for a few kind white people that she has known, she would hate all white people.

After graduating from school, the sisters were told they needed to make their own way and not accept scholarships, since that would make them obligated to someone. They got jobs teaching, and they had beaus. They also had run-ins with white people who treated them badly. Eventually, though, the two sisters made their way to New York City, where they entered college. Bessie wanted to go to medical school, but when she could not afford medical school, she settled on dental school. She was the only black woman out of 170 students. When she opened her dental practice, Bessie charged two dollars for an extraction. When she retired many years later, she was still charging two dollars. She did not raise her rates because she did not need the money. Sadie got a job teaching in Harlem, but she wanted to teach in the high school, where she would be paid more. Since black teachers were not hired for the high school, she used a bit of subterfuge to win a transfer to the high school. The sisters end act 2 with a discussion about the efforts to secure greater rights for blacks. While this was an important issue, for the sisters, equal rights for black women was just as important. The sisters find that women's rights and civil rights are equally important.

Act 3

Act 3 opens with the sisters describing the death of their father. When Bessie was thirty-seven and Sadie was thirty-nine, their father died suddenly. The death of their father was particularly difficult for Mama Delany, who moved from her home in Raleigh to New York City to live with Bessie and Sadie.

Sadie describes a trip to London, to see Paul Robeson in *Othello*. After the performance, Sadie and her mother were invited backstage to meet the actor. The sisters took Mama on many other trips, as well, including to see singer Marian Anderson perform in Washington, DC, and to meet former first lady Eleanor Roosevelt. Eventually Mama needed full-time care at home, and so one of the sisters needed to quit work and stay home. Although she enjoyed her dental practice, Bessie willingly agreed to quit work and stay home to care for their mother. Sadie was close to retiring with a pension, and Bessie had no pension. The sisters made their decision in an entirely pragmatic manner and after careful thought, as they did with everything else.

The sisters also describe the country during the Great Depression following the stock market crash of 1929. Bessie ran a government-sponsored dental clinic for the poor and was emphatic about the fact that this was not a government handout. She worked hard to earn the money the government paid to have her run this clinic. Although the depression was a tragedy for many, the sisters explain that they always knew that life was about more than money.

In this act, the sisters also recount the story of their young nephew, who was born with health problems that required constant medical care. When he died, it was the first time that the sisters realized that they could not control the world with prayer and hard work. They thought they "could do anything, fix any problem." After the death of their nephew, Bessie and Sadie "realized you can't always get what you want in life." In quick succession, two of their brothers died and then Mama Delany died. Sadie was devastated by the death of her mother and learned that she needed to look at the world differently because she was now the oldest surviving member of the family. As such, Sadie became the person who was to be consulted about important decisions.

After Mama Delany's death, the sisters moved to Mount Vernon, a predominantly white neighborhood. The discussion of this neighborhood

leads the sisters to a discussion of the civil rights movement, which was eclipsed by the war in Vietnam. The sisters express clear views about politicians, including those they feel were interested in helping further civil rights and equality for blacks. Both Sadie and Bessie are concerned about maintaining their health. They do yoga, although sometimes Bessie cheats at the exercises, and they eat lots of fresh vegetables and fruits each day. The neighborhood has changed, but Sadie is still strong enough and brave enough to confront gang activity in front of their home. The sisters feel they have lived so long because they stay alive for one another. They also celebrate the fact that they are still alive while the rebby boys, who hated them so much, are long dead. As the play ends, the sisters thank the audience for joining them to celebrate their Papa's birthday.

CHARACTERS

Bessie Delany

At the time the play takes place, Bessie is 101 years old. She was born on September 3, 1891. She is a retired dentist. Bessie's real name is Annie Elizabeth, but she has never been called by this name. She has, however, occasionally been called Queen Bess. She is emotional, quick to anger, outspoken, but also intuitive or even psychic. Bessie is also a busybody who watches everyone in the neighborhood. Bessie says she might not get to heaven, since she has probably offended God many times, although by the end of the play she is slightly more optimistic and thinks she might be able to get to heaven if she holds on to Sadie as she goes. Bessie has the darker complexion of the two sisters and is referred to as being more vinegar or spice than her sister, Sadie, who is sugar and molasses. Bessie remembers slights and injuries and holds a grudge, even though she acknowledges that God expects people to forget, as well as to forgive. Bessie is devoted to her sister and to her family, praying for each member of the family each morning and night.

Henry Delany
See Papa

Nanny Logan Delany
See Mama

Sadie Delany

At the time the play takes place, Sadie is 103 years old. She was born on September 19, 1889. Sadie was a "mama's child," but she describes feeling that the world was a safer place while her father was still alive. Sadie is calm and agreeable, described as sugar or molasses, whereas Bessie is more often described as vinegar and spice. Sadie's real name is Sarah Louise, but she has always been called Sadie or sweet sister Sadie. Her complexion is lighter than that of her younger sister, Bessie. Sadie has spent a lifetime of letting Bessie stand up for her; Sadie's protests were quieter, although just as active. After Mama dies, Sadie decides that she must think differently about her role in the family. As a result, she is the one to confront a group of gang members who are loitering in front of their home.

Mama

Mama Delany never appears on stage and has been dead many years, but the two sisters discuss her at length. Mama was an issue-free black woman. To be issue-free, means she has some black blood but was born to a free person who was not a slave. She was also very light skinned and could pass for white, although she did not choose to do so. Mama was embarrassed that because of miscegenation laws (those that banned interracial marriage), her parents were never married. She was also determined that she would marry legally. After marriage, she was a matron and teacher at the school where her husband was employed. The sisters describe Mama as a good woman who fed strangers and who always made sure her children were clean and well cared for. While her husband was still living, Mama never traveled, but after her husband's death, she moved to New York City and was always willing to go anywhere that was suggested to her. Even when quite elderly, she was eager for any adventure.

Papa

Papa Delany is never on stage, having died a long time ago, but the sisters speak of him as if he were still alive, often quoting their father's wisdom. He was educated but began life as a slave in Georgia. The family that owned him taught him to read, which was a violation of Georgia slave laws. He was encouraged to attend college by an Episcopalian priest and attended St. Augustine's School in Raleigh, North Carolina. After graduation, he was given a job at the school and eventually became vice-principal at St. Augustine. Papa edited the bible as he read verses to his children, leaving out any details he thought not suitable for children's ears. He also played the organ, and the sisters describe him as musical. Papa was the first elected black bishop of the Episcopal Church in the United States.

THEMES

Family

In *Having Our Say*, Bessie and Sadie relate the experiences of a lifetime of sibling and family love. The love the sisters feel for their family is very clear. As they talk about family, they show photos of the family, but it is the warmth of their descriptions of family and the way they cherish the photos that reveal how much family means to each sister. The sisters discuss their Mama and Papa more than any other family members. The parents' courtship and love for one another is one topic of discussion, but the sisters also discuss their parents' values, including the importance of being educated, of not being beholden to anyone else, and of fiscal responsibility. Bessie and Sadie discuss several of their brothers and their love for one nephew, who was born with health problems and who died at age ten. After the nephew's death, Bessie slept with the nephew's blanket on her bed and continued to do so for the next fifty years.

Sadie describes how, after the death of Papa, she felt like the world was less safe. There was no question about leaving the widowed Mama alone in Raleigh. The sisters devoted themselves to caring for their mother, traveling with her, and when she was in her nineties, helping her walk around the neighborhood, so that she would not be confined to the house. Bessie willingly gave up her career to stay home with her mother and care for her at the end of her life. Both sisters credit the companionship of the other sister for enabling them to live for so long. In fact, Bessie admits to some depression and is emphatic that it is Sadie that keeps her alive. Their love for one another provides a reason to continue living. Together they exercise and watch their diet, and each sister supports the other. Together they also pray for each member of their family and describe their prayers as taking a long time, since they must mention each member of the family by name.

TOPICS FOR FURTHER STUDY

- *The Face of Our Past: Images of Black Women From Colonial America to the Present* (2000) is a collection of photographic essays that relates the history of black women in the United States that is easily accessible for young adults. Choose two of the photographs from either the chapter "Work" or the chapter "Education," and write a comparative analysis in which you compare what the women in the photographs are experiencing with the experiences of the Delany sisters, in either work or education.

- Watch *Diary of a Tired Black Man* (2008), a film documentary that explores the experiences of African American men. Write an essay in which you discuss the different experiences of black men and women, based on a comparison of this film and *Having Our Say*.

- Drama is meant to be heard and seen and not just read. With one other student from your class, choose a section of dialogue from *Having Our Say* to memorize and then present to your classmates. After you and your partner have completed your performance, ask each of your classmates to write down at least one thing that they learned from hearing and seeing the play that they did not know just from reading it. Lead a class discussion based on what your classmates have written.

- Imagine for a moment that you are a producer and you plan to stage this play on Broadway. Prepare an oral report in which you explain which contemporary actors you would choose to play the two sisters in this play and why you would choose them. Pay special attention to the characterizations that Mann created and how these actors would portray these characters. Your analysis of these characters and the two actors to play these roles should include enough information to support your choices.

- *Having Our Say* recounts many of the life experiences that two African American women experienced during the twentieth century. To write the play, Mann interviewed the two Delany sisters. Interview someone who is at least eighty years old. Before the interview, prepare some questions to ask. You might think about changes in technology, travel, media, or a career field in which you have interest. Write down or record his or her story, being careful to note the details about the life your interviewee has experienced. Then write a paper in which you recount what you have learned and what you found was most important. You should also discuss any problems that you experienced in conducting your interview.

- Mann's play is a reminder of the changes that the civil rights movement brought to African Americans in the United States. With a group of classmates, create a group presentation in which you report on the civil rights movement of the second half of the twentieth century. Divide the work by assigning different chores to each member of the group. Good group presentations involve multimedia, so take the time to prepare a PowerPoint presentation that includes graphs, photos, and timelines. Be sure to prepare handouts for your classmates, which should include a bibliography of your sources.

Racism

Because they have lived more than a hundred years, Bessie and Sadie have experienced many different kinds of racism. They describe only a few instances in *Having Our Say*, but it is clear that the experiences have had a significant impact on their life. As small children, Bessie and Sadie learned to live under Jim Crow laws, and Sadie says that the effect of these laws cannot ever be undone. Even though they were small children when they were told they could not sit in the front of the trolley, both sisters remember the

Bessie Delany, age 102 (top) and Sadie Delany, age 104 (Time & Life Pictures | Getty Images)

affront vividly more than ninety years later. In their experience, Jim Crow meant that blacks and whites were separated, but it also meant that black women were even lower in the hierarchy than black men. Bessie explains in act 2 that black women had less power than every other group—white men, white women, and black men.

In act 1 of *Having Our Say*, Bessie and Sadie tell the audience about the "rebby boys," racist white men determined to torment blacks and keep them from being successful. It was the rebby boys who lynched men in front of their families or who lynched entire families for entertainment. Sadie handled racism better than Bessie. Sadie simply pretended Jim Crow did not exist, or she tried to pretend ignorance of the law, especially when told to keep separate from whites. Bessie describes the pain caused by racism and going home and crying. It is Bessie who explains that if it had not been for her white grandfather and his family and white missionaries, she might have grown up hating all white people.

Because of racism, Mama's parents could not marry because her father was white. Her mother was only a quarter black, but racial laws prevented the marriage of black and white couples in Virginia until 1967. Because Mama's parents were of two different races, they could not even live in the same home, even though they loved one another for fifty years. The sisters are equally proud that their father, who began life as a slave, was college educated and became the vice-principal of St. Augustine's School. He also became first elected black bishop of the Episcopal Church in the United States. As far as the Delany sisters are concerned, Papa proves that blacks can achieve as much as whites.

STYLE

Audience

Ordinarily an audience simply watches and listens to the actors on the stage. The audience experiences the drama on stage but does not participate in it. *Having Our Say* is different, however. The play opens with Sadie acknowledging the audience and inviting the audience to stay for dinner. She introduces herself to the audience as if they were guests. Bessie also introduces herself to the audience. Throughout the play, the sisters rarely address one another; instead, they recount the experiences of their lives to the audience. They pull out a photo album and show the audience family photos, just as they might do for any guest in their home. *Having Our Say* concludes with Sadie telling the audience how much she has enjoyed their visit and asking them to stay longer.

Dialogue

Traditionally, dialogue is conversation between people. Rules for dialogue require that it serve a purpose in the text, that it advance the plot, and that it not be in conflict with what the audience knows about the characters' personalities. In Mann's play, Sadie is described as "a mama's child," and her dialogue reinforces this statement. For instance, as the sisters are setting the table, it is Sadie who lovingly exclaims over her mother's cherished table linens and crystal dishes. Another example of how well the dialogue fits the characters can be found when Bessie speaks of Jim Crow laws and is emphatic that she is "just as good as anyone." This fits with Bessie's personality, which is stronger and more confrontational than Sadie's.

Having Our Say consists of a dialogue between two actors and the audience, but in this case, the audience is only presumed to have responded. At the beginning of the play, Sadie appears to respond to an audience request to speak with the sisters. The dialogue is one-sided, since the audience has no audible dialogue. This also occurs at the conclusion of the play, when Sadie says how much the sisters have enjoyed speaking with the audience, whom they invite to stay for dinner. Sadie uses the word "with" rather than "to." The implication is that there was a two-way conversation between the sisters and the audience.

Setting

The setting is the backdrop against which the play is taking place. The setting can be the location or the time of day or month or year. In a play, this is often described as the *mise en scéne* and includes the way the stage is set and how items are arranged on the stage. In *Having Our Say*, the setting is the Delany sisters' home, as well as the items the sisters handle as they speak to the audience. Bessie and Sadie are preparing a meal, and as they do so, they handle food, dishes, linens, and many other items commonly found in a kitchen or dining room that might reasonably be used to prepare and serve a meal. The setting supports Mann's premise that the audience is an invited guest at a birthday celebration dinner.

Theater of Testimony

The term "theater of testimony" originated with Barney Simon, who cofounded the Market Theatre of Johannesburg. Theater of testimony is used to describe works that combine documentary and testimony with theater. This term is applied to several of Mann's works in which testimony about an event or a history is being given by characters. These plays include *Annulla: An Autobiography*, *Still Life*, *Execution of Justice*, and *Greensboro: A Requiem*. The staging of *Having Our Say* allows the actresses playing Bessie and Sadie Delany the opportunity to speak directly to the audience, as if they were giving testimony about their lives. In a sense, they were witnesses to history, which the two sisters recount for the theater audience.

HISTORICAL CONTEXT

Jim Crow Laws

Although the Delany sisters first experienced Jim Crow laws in North Carolina, the laws themselves originated in the early part of the nineteenth century in the northern United States. Most northern whites agreed with their southern neighbors that whites were superior to blacks. In the north, only five New England states allowed blacks to vote. Schools and public transportation were segregated, and blacks were allowed to live in only the worst areas. Two states—Oregon and Illinois—banned blacks from entering the state. After the Civil War, the laws in most northern states were changed, and many areas were desegregated. One exception was in schools, where segregation remained in effect, often because neighborhoods remained segregated. In contrast, after Reconstruction ended, the southern states became even more oppressive for black citizens. Blacks were segregated at virtually all public facilities, including parks, swimming pools, water fountains, bathrooms, restaurants, theaters, libraries, buses and trains, and even in cemeteries. Blacks could not marry whites, and they were required to address white people using a title such as Mr. or Mrs. White people were free to enter a black person's house without knocking or asking permission. There was very little interaction between whites and blacks, and any infringement of the rules could result in violence.

Civil Rights Movement

In the closing minutes of *Having Our Say*, the sisters talk about having outlived the rebby boys, who tormented so many black people. In a way, they see having outlived the white racists as a sort of victory, and they briefly mention Dr. Martin Luther King, Jr., whom they admire for his efforts to secure freedom and equality for blacks. King pushed an agenda of civil disobedience that he hoped would focus the public's attention on the inequities that black citizens faced. Television coverage of the police response to his peaceful demonstrations, which included water cannons, police batons, and attacks by police dogs, helped to highlight what blacks were enduring and ultimately swayed public opinion against Jim Crow laws and racism. However, although people were often outraged at what they saw on television, change occurred very slowly and only with federal government assistance. In 1964, President Lyndon Johnson succeeded in getting Congress to pass a Civil Rights Act that outlawed discrimination in all public accommodations. This new law also had the authority to withhold government funds to communities that maintained segregated schools. In 1965, the Voting Rights Act prohibited many of

Sadie Delany was the first African American woman to teach Domestic Science in New York. (Monkey *Business Images / Shutterstock.com)*

the rules that southern states had used to prevent blacks from voting.

None of these changes occurred without turmoil and in many cases, violence and murder. Even with increased awareness of the inequities of segregation, many blacks still lived in segregated ghetto-like slums, and as a result, some became more militant in their demands for equality. In the mid-1960s, lack of jobs, overwhelming poverty, and episodes of police brutality finally led to race riots in more than 125 U.S. cities. The rage that caused these race riots evolved into a demand for Black Power, which some African Americans saw as a necessary violent response to injustice. Other people envisioned the movement as a way to embrace racial self-reliance and racial dignity and pride. Black Power also called upon blacks to take pride in their heritage. Ultimately, however, it was the Voting Rights Act and not violence that helped blacks emerge from segregation. Millions of black citizens registered to vote, which gave them a voice in local and national governments. In addition, a growing awareness of the destructive powers of racial intolerance helped to create

change. Jim Crow and segregation did not end simply because the rebby boys died; it was the death of the rebby boys' world that helped to bring about change.

CRITICAL OVERVIEW

When *Having Our Say* premiered on Broadway in 1995, Mann and the Delany sisters received positive critical reviews. In his review for the *New York Times*, Mel Gussow calls the story of the Delany sisters "inspirational." Gussow spends considerable time in his review discussing Mann's adaptation of the Delany sisters' book. He clearly prepared for the play and understood the history of the book upon which it is based and the lives of the Delany sisters. Because of this preparation, Gussow recognized what Mann had done in adapting the book for the theater and claims that "she has increased the intimacy of the storytelling." Gussow refers to Mann's technique as giving a "dramatic dimension to oral history." The end result, claims this critic, is "resolutely uplifting."

The review by Frank Scheck for the *Christian Science Monitor* was also generally positive, although Scheck questioned the staging of the play. In discussing the depiction by the actresses, he was especially complimentary of Gloria Foster, who plays the role of Sadie "with a quiet dignity that is wonderfully moving." Scheck's one complaint is that he wishes that Mann "had actually written a play about them," rather than use the dated technique "in which the audience is treated as a houseguest." Scheck criticizes this use of what he labels a "tired theatrical concept," because at times, he finds the actresses appear to be lecturing to the audience. In spite of this criticism, though, Scheck finds that *Having Our Say* presents a story and lives that are "tremendously moving and life-affirming."

In the years since *Having Our Say* was first produced on Broadway, the play has gone on national tours and has been produced in many locales. In 2009, *Having Our Say* returned to the McCarter Theater, where Mann first premiered the play in 1995. In Anita Gates's review for the *New York Times*, she begins by noting the timeliness of this performance, just as the country is discussing race and the recent election of President Obama. After noting the interaction between audience and actors, Gates writes that the sisters' memories are a reminder that in discussing race, "we're all in this together" and that the play itself is "as fresh as ever."

This same production of *Having Our Say* was also the subject of Simon Saltzman's review for the online magazine *CurtainUp*. Saltzman also notes the timeliness of this production, only months after President Barack Obama took office in 2009. This was also the year in which Mann celebrated twenty years as the McCarter Theater's artistic director. Although Saltzman clearly prefers the book to the staged drama, he still finds much to compliment. He notes that Mann "has a keen ear and eye for the truthful moment, and it never fails her or her actors." The closeness of the sisters is "irresistible" and reveals that the they were "two uncommon and remarkable women." Saltzman finds that *Having Our Say* "reveals the power of the positive spirit even as it revels in the personalities of two of the most courageous, extraordinary and inspiring women to come down the pike." Although several of the reviewers had minor complaints about *Having Our Say*, each also finds that Mann captured the lives of two interesting and compelling life stories, well worth the time spent at the theater.

CRITICISM

Sheri Metzger Karmiol

Karmiol teaches literature and drama at the University of New Mexico, where she is a lecturer in the University Honors Program. In the following essay, she discusses the racial implications involved in the authorship of Having Our Say.

In *Having Our Say*, Mann creates a play in which two black centenarians tell the story of their lives. The Delany sisters lived through Jim Crow. They experienced segregation and discrimination and lived through both the women's suffrage and women's equal rights movements. They also lived through the time of Rosa Parks and Martin Luther King, Jr., and they heard Marian Anderson sing after the Daughters of the American Revolution prevented her from performing in Washington, DC's Constitutional Hall. Bessie and Sadie Delany knew W. E. B. Du Bois and E. Franklin Frazier, and they lived through every black triumph and tragedy that occurred during the twentieth century. Their story has lessons worth learning and reminders of racial division and pain worth hearing.

In writing *Having Our Say*, Mann gives voice to two women who traditionally had no voice, but in doing so, she is also usurping their voices, or so some critics would like to argue. The issue in question is who can best tell a black woman's story. Both Amy Hill Hearth, the journalist who first wrote about the Delany sisters in the *New York Times* and later in the book that became the basis of the stage play *Having Our Say*, and Mann have experienced criticism that, as white authors, they were not well suited to write about the experiences of black women.

The argument that white women writers, such as Hearth and Mann, do not understand the experiences and struggles of black women and that in fact they lack sufficient knowledge of black history and racism appeared in several reviews of both Hearth's book and Mann's drama. In a 1993 interview, black playwright Alice Childress expressed concern that white women do not understand that the struggle for equality is more complex and more difficult for black women. Coincidentally the Childress interview takes place the same year that Hearth's book, *Having Our Say*, was published. In her interview with Shirley M. Jordan in *Broken Silences: Interviews with Black and White Women Writers*, Childress claims that for black

WHAT DO I READ NEXT?

- Mann's collection of four plays, *Testimonies: Four Plays* (1996), includes plays about the Holocaust (*Annulla*), the Vietnam War (*Still Life*), the assassination of San Francisco's mayor and supervisor (*Execution of Justice*), and an anti-Ku Klux Klan rally that turned into a killing spree (*Greensboro: A Requiem*).

- *My Name Is Number 4: A True Story From the Cultural Revolution* (2008), by Ting-xing Ye, is a memoir about the experiences of a young Chinese woman during the Chinese Cultural Revolution. This young-adult book captures the oppression and violence that the author faced during a period of political and social upheaval.

- *Beauty in Performance: Plays for African American Youth* (2006), by Carolyn Nur Wistrand, is a collection of four plays for young adults that portrays major events in the history of African Americans.

- *Dreaming in Color; Living in Black and White: Our Own Stories of Growing Up Black in America* (2000), by Laurel Holliday, is a collection of stories suitable for young adults. These stories were written by seventeen African Americans who recount their experiences dealing with prejudice, affirmative action, racism, and black pride.

- Nikki Giovanni's *Racism 101* (1985) is a collection of essays in which Giovanni writes about what it means to be an African American and how she feels about her experiences with race and racism.

- Alice Childress's play *Wine in the Wilderness* (1969) examines what it means to be an African American in a segregated and racist society. The play examines several of the issues touched upon in *Having Our Say*, including the lack of opportunities available to African Americans.

- *A Raisin in the Sun*, by Lorraine Hansberry (1959), is a play that explores segregation, racism, and the lack of economic opportunities that African Americans have faced.

- The collection *Black Theatre, USA: Plays by African Americans: The Recent Period, 1935–Today* (1996), by Ted Shine and edited by James V. Hatch, includes plays by Alice Childress, Langston Hughes, Lorraine Hansberry, Abram Hill, and James Baldwin, as well as many plays by less well-known playwrights.

- *African American Lives* is a two-part PBS film about the lives of several notable African Americans. In the film, the participants learn about their genetic pasts and discuss what it means to know their history.

---

women it is not enough to have the same opportunities as black men; black women want to have the same opportunities as white women. In other words, if white women want equality with white men, they should also be fighting for equality for all women. In this interview, Childress also argues that race is an insurmountable barrier that separates white and black women because white women have not experienced racism and thus cannot understand the struggle of black women. The Childress interview appears in a book that probes whether white and black authors can depict honest renderings of one another's lives. This concern about a white author's ability to interpret and

depict black lives is a fundamental issue for several reviewers of *Having Our Say*.

In his essay "The Crisis in Black Theatre Identity," Paul Carter Harrison writes of the need for black theater to be a forum for black writers, black directors, and black actors, as the only way to create legitimate black theater. In specifically addressing the writing of *Having Our Say*, Harrison refers to Mann's "good-natured intentions" in writing the play. His chief complaint is that Mann is not, herself, a black woman. Because she is white, she has never experienced the kind of life that black women experience, and

MANN GIVES VOICE TO TWO WOMEN WHO TRADITIONALLY HAD NO VOICE, BUT IN DOING SO, SHE IS ALSO USURPING THEIR VOICES, OR SO SOME CRITICS WOULD LIKE TO ARGUE."

thus, this lack of commonality has "limited her ability to discern the aspects of the storytelling that are dramatically different." In other words, according to Harrison, Mann cannot understand the nuances of the Delany sisters' experiences because she is not black. This limitation results in *Having Our Say* becoming "a 'feel good' exercise that allows black participation in the mainstream without the benefit of illuminating our particular story." Harrison uses the personal pronoun "our," but of course, *Having Our Say* is the Delany sisters' story, not Harrison's. In fact, in *Having Our Say*, Bessie says that while it might have been hard for black men, "colored women were on the *bottom*." Harrison has not experienced the life of a black woman, any more than Mann has.

Harrison laments that *Having Our Say* lacks the "African American oral tradition," although he never acknowledges that, in fact, the Delany sisters are giving voice to just that tradition. Mann uses the Delany sisters' own words, drawn from interviews with the sisters. In an interview with Alexis Greene in *Journal of Dramatic Theory and Criticism*, Mann suggests that "there is a history lesson there, for blacks as well as whites." Mann says this is taking authentic lived history "into the public arena and saying, 'Yeah, have a great time, but talk about it, because it's the real thing.'" Harrison misses the opportunity to engage in *Having Our Say* because he is so focused on Mann's race that he misses the Delany sisters' story.

Lest it seem that only Mann was singled out for her role in bringing *Having Our Say* to the public, it is worth noting that Hearth was also criticized for her role in bringing the book of the same title to publication. Hearth writes in the preface to *Having Our Say* that although she arranged and organized the book, the words are those of the Delany sisters. Although Bessie and Sadie initially declined to participate in writing a book, Hearth notes that "they came to see that by recording their

story, they were participating in a tradition as old as time": the telling of stories, passed from one generation to the next. In other words, the sisters were embracing that very African American oral tradition that Harrison worries is missing from the play. Hearth also claims that the story of the Delany sisters is, as they like to say, "not meant as 'black' or 'women's' history, but American history." If Hearth thought that the remarks in her preface would prevent criticism of a white writer telling a black story, she was wrong.

In her review of the Delany sisters' memoir, *Having Our Say*, Olive A. Taylor writes in the *Journal of Southern History* that she commends Hearth for getting the Delany sisters' story printed but at the same time finds it regrettable that "Hearth is insufficiently versed in the history of African Americans in general, and African American women in particular, to capture the historical significance of the Delany sisters." Taylor's basic concern is that Hearth fails to supply the necessary historical context that she deems necessary for this story. However, it is worth pointing out that *Having Our Say* is not a history text; it is essentially a memoir, and as such, the book not required to provide explanations of either historical events or personages.

The idea that white women are unqualified to engage in a public discourse about race contradicts the notion that all women share a common bond and a shared community. Iris Marion Young suggests in her essay "The Ideal of Community and the Politics of Difference" that "The ideal of community...privileges unity over difference, immediacy over mediation, sympathy over recognition of the limits of one's understanding of others from their point of view." Those individuals who are motivated by a desire for a community of black writers, directors, and actors are expressing their hope for what they envision as the ideal community, but this is not an inclusionary community. Clearly there are some problems with this kind of exclusionary community. Hearth writes in the foreword to *Having Our Say* that the Delany sisters did not want to write a book, yet when finally convinced to do so, they chose Hearth—a white woman writer. They might have chosen a black writer, and it is not unreasonable to suppose that the publisher could have just as easily chosen a black writer, if the Delany sisters had wanted one. Young fears that the quest for the ideal community will "tend to suppress differences among themselves or implicitly to exclude from their political

Bessie Delany was the second African American woman to be granted a dentistry license in New York.
(Paul B. Moore | Shutterstock.com)

groups persons with whom they do not identify." Rather than unity of purpose, the result is a community of difference.

Mann's own personal experience in staging *Having Our Say* suggests that there can be a community of inclusion, in which there is agreement about the need to discuss racism and a desire to heal from the wounds it inflicts. As Young states, "the ideal of community presumes subjects can understand one another as they understand themselves." Embracing this ideal community "denies the difference between subjects." Mann discovered this in South Africa. In a July 1999 interview, titled "In Conversation," in which Mann answered questions posed by an audience of conference members of the Association for Theatre in Higher Education, Mann describes taking *Having Our Say* to the Market Theatre in South Africa. After a serious question-and-answer dialogue at the end of the play, Mann was told of the South African hope that "our young people will listen to their elders and get their stories out of them." There was a desire to make sure that the stories of the South Africans would get told, but there was no concern

expressed that Mann—a white woman—was telling the story of two black women. *Having Our Say* was intended for a multiracial audience and as a way for people from diverse backgrounds and experiences to come together. Mann says that the play is "a healing piece about how we're all Americans, or we're all human beings." As Mann tells Greene, the function of the theater is "to entertain, to teach, and to inspire." *Having Our Say* accomplishes all of those goals.

Source: Sheri Metzger Karmiol, Critical Essay on *Having Our Say: The Delany Sisters' First 100 Years*, in *Drama for Students*, Gale, Cengage Learning, 2011.

Nelson Pressley

In the following article, Pressley argues that although Mann is not African American, her interpretation of the Delany sisters' story is realistic and successful.

Conventional wisdom in late 20th-century America holds that white directors need to tread carefully, if they dare to tread at all, on material that deals with the lives of African-Americans.

Emily Mann, the writer-director who adapted the 1991 book, *Having Our Say: The Delaney Sisters' First 100 Years* for the stage, is familiar with the issue. The play is based on the memoir of Sarah L. (Sadie) and A. Elizabeth (Bessie) Delany, two centenarian sisters whose father was born into slavery—a situation skeptics might say can be fully appreciated only by a black writer-director.

"I know all about it, believe me," says the 44-year-old Mann with a wry laugh. "I know what I'm up against—that white people are exploiting black people's stories. And at a certain point I thought, 'I could not do this, or I will do it—and if other people have a problem with it, they have a problem with it.'"

Not many people have a problem with *Having Our Say*. The play is a charming portrait of two fascinating women who, in the face of early 20th-century racism, become a high-school teacher and a dentist. The Delanys' story also is a journey across a large, rocky patch of American history.

As adapted and directed by Mann and performed by Mary Alice and Gloria Foster, *Having Our Say* became one of the surprise hits of the 1994–95 Broadway season. The national touring company, starring Lizan Mitchell and Micki Grant, has taken the show on the road, and the single-set, two-character drama will be the fifth most-produced play in the country's regional theaters this year.

Stylistically, *Having Our Say* is right up Mann's alley. Her method is to bring dramatic shape and theatrical energy to real-life material she pulls from archives or gathers in interviews. Her first play was *Annulla, An Autobiography*, based on an interview she conducted with a friend's aunt, a Jewish woman who survived World War II. *Still Life*, also culled from interviews, features straightforward testimony from a frighteningly violent Vietnam War veteran, his terrorized wife and his lover, who seems to view the vet's dark side with an assassin's calm. *Execution of Justice* deals with the murder of George Moscone (then mayor of San Francisco) and Harvey Milk (a city supervisor) at the hands of former City Councilman Dan White. And Mann's most recent work, *Greensboro: A Requiem*, revisits the 1979 incident in which members of the Ku Klux Klan and the American Nazis shot 13 people at an anti-Klan rally, killing five.

"I learned about the Holocaust in my grandmother's kitchen," recalls Mann. "And how most of us learn about great wisdom in the world and

what happens to people is literally in our aunts' or our mothers' or our grandmothers' kitchens. That's a very secure, safe, warm, familiar place." All of which explains why Emily Mann can say of *Having Our Say*, a kind of landscape of America told in intimate terms, "Its totally what I do. Its documentary. Its in their own words."

Mann grew up with a solid understanding of the civil-rights movement. Her father, a historian, was good friends with John Hope Franklin. They make a cameo appearance in *Having Our Say*, which uses a photograph of the two men, a white man and a black man, marching side by side through Alabama from Selma to Montgomery.

Her father's occupation helped push Mann's theatrical career in its unique direction. As a literature major at Harvard, she was interested in writing fiction and directing plays. Home on break from school, she came across an interview that her father had gathered in which a daughter talked with her mother about her experience in the Treblinka camp. The poignancy of the survivor's tale, coupled with the mother-daughter dynamic of the conversation, fired Mann's imagination. That encounter, she believed, would be powerful stuff in the theater.

After Harvard, Mann was the first female director accepted into a training program run by the University of Minnesota and the Guthrie Theater in Minneapolis. It was there that she turned the *Annulla Allen* transcript into a play. Since then, her career has taken her to theaters across the country as she has earned Obies and even an award from the National Association for the Advancement of Colored People. Mann is beginning her seventh season at the helm of the Kennedy Center's McCarter Theater in Washington, which won a Tony Award as the country's outstanding regional theater two years ago.

Mann talks about the Delany sisters, whom she met in their home in Mount Vernon, N.Y., with bubbly fondness. She recalls that at the end of their session together, Sadie told her, "Child, I feel like I've known you all my life"—a line that worked itself into the play. The warmth and charisma of the Delanys has a lot to do with their story's popularity. But the social angle matters, too; Mann calls the play "covertly political."

According to Mann, there is more political writing in the theater than many people realize, but she dislikes agitprop and tries to avoid it in her own work: "I think I'm talking about plays that have something to say. Is there enough of that? There's never enough of that, you know? In any society."

Says Mann, "Of course *Having Our Say* deals with the history of the African-American struggle in this country and of women's struggle in his country," Mann says. "But at base it talks about survival through family and love and education, and for them, faith in God and spirituality."

Source: Nelson Pressley, "Ars Longa, Vita Brevis," in *Insight on the News*, Vol. 12, No. 46, December 9, 1996, p. 36.

Larry S. Ledford

In the following review, Ledford details the way the play's production has evolved since its inception.

The book, *Having Our Say: The Delany Sisters' First 100 years*, sold more than 350,000 copies in hard cover and remained on the *New York Times* best-seller list for over six months in 1994. Written by Sadie and Bessie Delany with Amy Hill Hearth, the book has been adapted for the stage by Emily Mann, actress-playwright and artistic director of the McCarter Theatre in Princeton, New Jersey. Mann has directed the world premiere production, which opens at McCarter on Sat., Feb. 11, to run through Feb. 26.

Mann made her Broadway debut as both playwright and director of *Execution of Justice* in 1986. Since 1990, she has led McCarter Theatre into prominence among regional companies, this past June accepting the 1994 Tony Award for Outstanding Regional Theatre.

Actress Mary Alice, who won the Tony Award for her starring role opposite James Earl Jones in *Fences*, portrays 103-year-old Bessie Delany. One-hundred-five-year-old Sadie is played by Gloria Foster, whose New York credits include *Blood Wedding*, *Medea*, and *The Trojan Women*.

Produced by Camille Crosby and Judith Rutherford James, *Having Our Say* has been structured to be what Mann calls "theatre of testimony." In a recent interview, the playwright discussed the process of adapting into a three-act play the story of the two Delanys, which sprawls over 100 years of American history—including Jim Crow laws, near-lynchings, "colored only" train cars and water fountains, and the fight for civil rights.

Making It Work on Stage

"I chose to have the play remain in the present and 'story-tell,'" Mann says, "because I felt that was the form most appropriate for the theatre and for the source material—to meet these women as they are now, as you do in the book.

The audience, in essence, is like the interviewer, getting to know these characters and building a relationship with them as they reveal more and more of themselves through the events in their lives."

The next decision, continues Mann, was to select a central occasion that would tie these events together and make it a special day. She "decided it would be Papa's birthday"—when, as they have every year (even after his death)—the sisters are preparing his favorite dinner. The playwright explains that she chose the birthday in part because that is the day when Amy Hill Hearth had her own first interview with the Delanys. The situation also attracted Mann, "because it has been my experience that many of us have had older women in our lives in whose kitchens we sat as they were cooking and as they told us some of the important things about who we are."

Keeping the characters of the two sisters actively engaged throughout the course of the play was a key to dramatic development, which Mann found as a result of meeting with the real Delanys twice at their home in Mount Vernon, New York, last winter. "They have lived together so long," she says, "that each almost knows what the other is thinking or is about to say. And that was the key for me; the fact that they sometimes talk at once and often finish each other's sentences.

"The play becomes more than the stories they tell. It's really a portrait of two remarkable individuals, but is also almost a portrait of a marriage. It is an extraordinary study in relationships, in how two nearly opposite personalities can live in true harmony." That relationship was the key to Mann's finding both the rhythm and the velocity of the play.

We first meet the sisters in a more formal setting, "for tea," and then are invited to stay as they prepare dinner. In the course of three acts, the action moves from parlor to dining room to kitchen (designed by Tom Lynch). Asked about the development of production values for the play, Mann described another important element, the use of projections (by projections designers Wendall K. Harrington and Sage Carter).

"The sisters have an amazing family archive, an entire wall of photographs of their family with which they almost illustrate their stories as you talk to them. Obviously the audience couldn't see necessary details, so projections are used and it opens up the play so that it is not just in their home. Those rooms also become a 'memory space.'"

Almost from the beginning, says Mann, she had Mary Alice and Gloria Foster in mind for the cast. "They have been working with me for many months. Every time I would finish a draft they would get together and read it to me. So I have had their voices in my ear for quite some time."

Summing up, Mann notes that she likens writing "theatre of testimony" to working like a sculptor. "In most writing," she observes, "you work like a painter. The more you build, the higher the stack of pages, the closer you come to the finished piece. But in this form, you are more like a sculptor. The more you chip away, the smaller the stack becomes, the closer you are to finding the shape underneath."

The shape of *Having Our Say* has evolved in just over one year—a relatively short time for the development of a new play. And already its future is set beyond its world premiere in Princeton: the show moves to Broadway in April.

Source: Larry S. Ledford, "Emily Mann Has Her Say—and the Delanys Premiere," in *Back Stage*, Vol. 36, No. 6, February 10, 1995, pp. 5–6.

Stefan Kanfer

In the following review, Kanfer opines that Mann's adaptation stays true to the spirit of the Delanys' story.

Elderly people often complain that they remember their childhood precisely, but can't for the life of them tell you what they had for dinner yesterday. Although this is called the curse of old age, it ought to be counted as a blessing. When we listen to a veteran of World War I, a survivor of the Holocaust, the children of slaves, what we want is an eyewitness account of the distant past. Who cares about last night's entree?

The elderly siblings in *Having Our Say* are wise enough to separate the trivial from the significant. They spend about one tenth of the play cataloging the plaints of old age, and nine tenths summoning up their extraordinarily productive careers. Both of the self-styled "maiden ladies" are skilled at the business of remembering. And why not? They have been at it since the 19th century. Sadie Delany (Gloria Foster) is 103; her kid sister Bessie (Mary Alice) is 101.

The world first learned about these very real people in their double autobiography, a surprise bestseller in 1993. The Delanys' father, born into slavery, had one exceptional break. His master dared to teach Negro children how to read and write, despite the laws in the Confederate South

making the transmission of such knowledge illegal. Freed, Henry Beard Delany went on to college and divinity school and eventually became the first Bishop of his race in the Episcopal Church. For many years he taught at St. Augustine's College in Raleigh, North Carolina, a segregated institution where his wife, the daughter of a black slave and her white common-law husband, served as an administrator. The Delanys' 10 children grew up in a high moral atmosphere, and every one of them rose to a position of prominence.

The humorist Josh Billings once said that he never knew a centenarian to be remarkable for anything else. A pity he never met the Delany sisters. Sadie was the first black teacher of domestic science in New York City. Bessie went her one better. She attended Columbia University, and against incalculable odds graduated from its Dental School. Only one other black woman could display a similar diploma in the 1920s.

These were women born to challenge injustice and to lead by example. Affirmative action was not a buzz term to them, it was a way of life. And yet the Delany militance had a civil tone and temper that has all but vanished from current political debate. Act One opens with the sisters addressing the audience as if it were an honored guest in their modest home in Mt. Vernon, just outside New York City. Sadie, the first to speak, never loses her lofty dignity. Her manner is lenient and reasonable, no matter how bitter the memories of racism. Bessie will have no truck with accommodation. She is the curator of her grievances, forever taking them out, dusting them off, and retelling a story about their acquisition.

Nevertheless, she rarely raises her voice. The anecdotes do the shouting for her. The briefer they are, the louder their message. Take, for example, the incident of the large water fountain in downtown Raleigh. Like all public facilities it was forbiddingly marked "Colored" and "White." On an afternoon when no one was looking, Bessie recollects, "I sneaked over and had a taste of that White water." Pause. "It tasted just the same." Age has slowed her down to a hobble, but her speech is marked by impatience. She is disgruntled with the slow pace of the civil rights struggle, and the lack of leadership since the death of Martin Luther King Jr. She is even impatient with her sister's cadences—if Sadie takes too long coming to the point, Bessie rushes in to complete the sentence. A century of bias has left her undiminished, anxious to get on with things. "I'm just as good as anyone else," she asserts. "That's the way I was brought up." Pause. "I'll tell you the truth. I think I'm better."

She may be. Certainly she is better than the notes in the Playbill, apparently prepared by the show's producers, Camille O. Cosby and Judith Rutherford James. Those connoisseurs wishing to sample political correctness in extremis have only to turn to page 35. There they will find a unique chronicle of historical events occurring within the Delany sisters' lifetimes. A few entries should suffice. "1918: Spanish-American actress Rita Hayworth is born in Brooklyn. 1930: Anglo-American Grant Wood paints 'American Gothic' and African-American painter William H. Johnson receives the Harmon Award. 1955: White-American Jonas Salk develops polio vaccine. 1978: I. M. Pei, a Chinese-American, designs the National Gallery of Art." It all reminded me of last year's *New Yorker* cartoon, in which a dog frantically pursues a cat. The caption reads "Canine-American chasing Feline-American."

The irony is that the sisters want nothing to do with such labels. They go out of their way to refer to themselves as "Negroes" or "colored." Bessie declares, "I'm not black, I'm brown." This is not to diminish her sensitivity or activism (she was one of the protesters at the Capitol Theater in 1925, when it showed *Birth of a Nation*). Comparing the shade of her skin with Sadie's, Bessie goes on, "I'm darker than she is. And the darker you are, the harder it is." Her remarks amplify the tragedy of racial discrimination. Conversely, the laundry list of hyphenated Americans diminishes everyone it touches.

Happily, the actresses who impersonate the Delanys stick to the script and not the screed. As Sadie, Gloria Foster has an elegance of speech and a way of moving that records the years but defies the gravity pulling at her body and soul. As the skeletal Bessie, Mary Alice steals the evening. In addition to an exquisite sense of timing, she folds her face like a fine leather purse every time she delivers a good line—and she has a festival of them.

Thomas Lynch's revolving set creates islands of serenity within the stately Booth Theater, and Judy Dearing's costumes are true to the spirit of the aged. So is the work of adapter/director Emily Mann. When she first began the project, the Delany sisters told her the secret of longevity.

"You have to love your wounds," they stated. Mann has honored and returned that affection.

Source: Stefan Kanfer, "Review of *Having Our Say*," in *New Leader*, Vol. 78, No. 4, May 8, 1995, pp. 22–24.

SOURCES

Bigsby, Christopher, "Emily Mann," in *Contemporary American Playwrights*, Cambridge, 1999, pp. 132–64.

Davis, Ronald, "From Terror to Triumph: Historical Overview," in *Foothill College Web site*, http://www.foothill.edu/attach/bss/22_Jim%20Crow_EC.pdf (accessed Oct. 12, 2010).

Delany, Sara, and A. Elizabeth Delany, with Amy Hill Hearth, "Preface," in *Having Our Say: The Delany Sisters' First 100 Years*, Kodansha, 1993, pp. xii–xiii.

Gates, Anita, "Still Having Their Say," Review of *Having Our Say*, in *New York Times*, September 27, 2009, p. NJ12.

Greene, Alexis, "Interview with Emily Mann," in *Journal of Dramatic Theory and Criticism*, Vol. 14, No. 2, Spring 2000, pp. 77–97.

Gussow, Mel, "A Good Listener Who Writes Plays on Social Justice," Review of *Having Our Say*, in *New York Times*, April 18, 1995, p. C13.

Harmon, William, and Hugh Holman, *A Handbook to Literature*, 11th ed., Pearson Prentice Hall, 2009, pp. 50, 159, 348–49, 508.

Harrison, Paul Carter, "The Crisis in Black Theatre Identity," in *African American Review*, Vol. 31, No. 4, Winter 1997, pp. 567–78.

Hearth, Amy Hill, Sarah Louise Delany, and Annie Elizabeth Delany, *Having Our Say: The Delany Sisters' First 100 Years*, Delta, 1993.

Hobson, Katherine, "A Creature of the Theater: The Many Roles of Emily Mann," in *Princeton Alumni Weekly*, March 26, 2003, http://www.princeton.edu/paw/archive_new/PAW02-03/12-0326/features1.html (accessed July 6, 2010).

Humphrey, Paul, ed., "In the Wake of the Sixties—What Now?," in *America in the 20th Century*, 2nd ed., Vol. 12, Marshall Cavendish, 2003, pp. 1017–18.

Jordan, Shirley M., "Alice Childress," in *Broken Silences: Interviews with Black and White Women Writers*, edited by Shirley M. Jordan, Rutgers University Press, 1993, pp. 28–37.

LoBiondo, Maria, "Profile: Emily Mann, Artistic Director of McCarter Theatre," in *Princeton Patron Magazine*, 1995, http://www.princetonol.com/patron/emann/ (accessed June 21, 2010).

Mann, Emily, *Having Our Say: The Delany Sisters' First 100 Years*, Dramatists Play Service, 1996.

———, "In Conversation," in *Theatre Topics*, Vol. 1, No. 1, March 2000, pp. 1–16.

Saltzman, Simon, "Having Our Say," Review of *Having Our Say*, in *CurtainUp*, September 17, 2009, http://www.curtainup.com/havingoursaynj.html (accessed July 6, 2010).

Scheck, Frank, "The Venerable Delany Sisters Have Their Say on Broadway," Review of *Having Our Say*, in *Christian Science Monitor*, April 18, 1995, p. 13.

Taylor, Olive A., Review of *Having Our Say: The Delany Sisters' First 100 Years*, in *Journal of Southern History*, Vol. 62, No. 2, May 1996, pp. 432–34.

Wormser, Richard, "Introduction," in *The Rise and Fall of Jim Crow*, St. Martin's Griffin, 2004, pp. xi–xii.

Young, Iris Marion, "The Ideal of Community and the Politics of Difference," in *Social Theory and Practice*, Vol. 12, No. 1, Spring 1986, pp. 1–26; reprinted in *Feminism/Postmodernism*, edited by Linda Nicholson, Routledge, 1990, pp. 300–26.

FURTHER READING

Aronson, Marc, *Race: A History beyond Black and White*, Ginee Seo Books, 2007.
> This young-adult book is a history of racial and ethnic prejudice that traces prejudice back to the Sumerians. This history of racism compels readers to ask serious questions about how societies define race and what color or ethnicity means to people. The author discusses religious and ethnic prejudice, as well.

Bolden, Tonya, *The Book of African American Women: 150 Crusaders, Creators, and Uplifters*, Adams Media, 2004.
> This book is a collection of brief biographies, beginning with a 1619 biography of a slave brought to the Jamestown colony. Bolden includes biographies of famous women, but she also includes biographies of women who made significant contributions to African American history and culture without ever becoming famous.

Franklin, John Hope, and Alfred A. Moss, Jr., *From Slavery to Freedom: A History of African Americans*, Knopf, 2000.
> Franklin and Moss present a history of African American life in the United States. The authors recount African American history, beginning with slavery's origins and exploring the kidnapping of men and women in Africa and leading up to the civil rights movement of the last half of the twentieth century. The authors have included maps, charts, and many illustrations.

Packard, Jerrold M., *American Nightmare: The History of Jim Crow*, St. Martin's Press, 2003.
> Packard traces the origin of slavery as a legal institution and of Jim Crow laws, which were common throughout the United States. He also provides a detailed look at segregation and the court cases that brought an end to Jim Crow.

Sniderman, Paul M., and Thomas Piazza, *Black Pride and Black Prejudice*, Princeton University Press, 2004.
> The authors provides an often provocative look at race relations in the United States. The focus is on how African Americans view themselves and how they perceive they are viewed by other groups. Some of the topics covered include black pride and black intolerance and racism.

SUGGESTED SEARCH TERMS

Having Our Say AND Mann

Having Our Say AND Hearth

Delany sisters

Jim Crow laws

African American AND segregation

Having our Say AND St. Augustine school

Emily Mann AND testimony drama

Bessie AND Sadie Delany AND civil rights

Amy Hill Hearth AND Emily Mann

The Madwoman of Chaillot

JEAN GIRAUDOUX

1948

The play *The Madwoman of Chaillot* is a satire, dealing with a classic struggle between good and evil and filled with absurd dialogue and humorous word play. It opens at a sidewalk café in the Chaillot neighborhood of Paris, where a group of corrupt and heartless businessmen frankly discuss their plans to destroy Paris to get at the oil that lies beneath the city. When the eccentric Countess Aurelia, the Madwoman of Chaillot, learns of their plans, she takes it upon herself to try them in a mock court and eliminate them.

The play is a translation of the French play *La Folle de Chaillot* written by Jean Giraudoux in 1943 and first produced in Paris on December 19, 1945. The English version, translated and adapted by Maurice J. Valency, opened on Broadway in the Belasco Theater on December 27, 1948, and starred Martita Hunt as the Countess Aurelia. Hunt won the Tony Award for Best Leading Actress in a Play in 1949. Valency's adaptation follows Giraudoux's play closely but removes several references to localities and people in Paris with which American audiences would not be familiar. *The Madwoman of Chaillot* has been revived often in New York and London and is a staple of regional, college, and high school theater.

AUTHOR BIOGRAPHY

Giraudoux was born Hippolyte Jean Giraudoux in Bellac, France, on October 29, 1882, the younger of

Jean Giraudoux (© akg-images / Alamy)

with dysentery. He never fully regained his health. After the war, he began writing in earnest, publishing some twenty novels, literary and political studies, and travel books in ten years. He did not turn to drama until the 1920s; his first play, *Siegfried* (1928), was an adaptation of his 1922 novel *Siegfried et le Limousin*. The play starred and was directed by Louis Jouvet, who collaborated with Giraudoux on most of his plays from that time on.

During the 1930s, Giraudoux wrote nine more plays and more than a dozen other books and became a major literary figure. When war again loomed, he was named the head of wartime propaganda for France, but he retained his affection for Germany and did not recognize the Nazi threat as quickly as many of his peers. The occupation of France by Germany in 1940 ended all doubt, and Giraudoux's writing became less optimistic. Giraudoux completed *The Madwoman of Chaillot* in 1943, during the occupation but knew it could not be produced until the occupation was over. He died in Paris on January 31, 1944, of sudden kidney failure. The exact cause was never determined, and there was speculation (apparently unfounded) that he was the victim of a political murder.

two sons of a civil servant and his wife. Giraudoux was athletic and did well in school; in his teens he received a scholarship to attend a boarding school in Châteauroux, where he studied literature, philosophy, Greek, and Latin. After completing secondary school he completed two more years of pre-college study at a school near Paris and took full advantage of the opportunity to visit the theaters and cafés of the city. In 1903, after completing compulsory military service, he began university study at the Sorbonne and then the École Normale Supérieure in Paris. He focused on German literature and spent a year studying in Munich and traveling throughout Europe. He taught French at Harvard for one semester in 1907. During his university years, Giraudoux published his first stories in literary and popular magazines.

Giraudoux left the academic life in 1909, entering the foreign service. He served in the Foreign Ministry for the next thirty-five years. His work required him to travel extensively but left him time to work on his own writing. Giraudoux served in the military during World War I, was wounded twice, and made seriously ill

PLOT SUMMARY

Act 1

The action of *The Madwoman of Chaillot* occurs on a single day soon after World War II. As the play opens, the Waiter is seating two well-dressed men at a sidewalk café in Paris. According to the stage directions, the café is Chez Francis on the Place de l'Alma in the Chaillot district, a real café that was frequented by Giraudoux and other intellectuals and that is still open for business. As will be true for most of the characters, these two men are not given names in the play's list of characters, but are known by their titles: the President and the Baron. The President tells the Baron a bit about his past, from his childhood spent in poverty, through his early career dealing in counterfeit money and then drugs, to the present as the head of dozens of businesses. He has recently given the Baron a position on the board of directors of his newest corporation and is surprised to hear that the Baron wants to know what the corporation does. The President, it is revealed, does not know anything about the new company, including its

MEDIA ADAPTATIONS

- *The Madwoman of Chaillot* was adapted as a film in 1969, starring Katharine Hepburn, Yul Brynner, Danny Kaye, and Donald Pleasence. Directed by Bryan Forbes, the film retains the eccentricity and satire of the play but is set in the 1960s and adds references to the cold war, atomic weapons, and corrupt evangelical preachers. Not released on DVD, it can be found on VHS from Warner Home Video and as a download.

- The play was adapted as a Broadway musical titled *Dear World*, directed and choreographed by Joe Layton and opening on February 6, 1969. It starred Angela Lansbury, whose performance as the Countess was honored with the 1969 Tony Award for Best Leading Actress in a Musical, but the show received mostly negative reviews. Revised versions were produced in 2000 and 2002. A recording of the music performed by the original Broadway cast is available from Sony on CD or as a download.

name—nor does anyone else. Nevertheless, he reports, the company's stock is doing very well.

As the men talk, they are approached by a few of the common people of the Parisian streets: the Street Singer, the Flower Girl, the Juggler, and the Ragpicker. The President is rude to all of them, irritated that they do not respect their lowly place in his world. One character, referred to simply as the "Little Man," eavesdrops on the men's conversation and then rushes to their table and excitedly gives the President his life savings, gives the President a receipt for it, and exits. The men are joined by the Prospector, who, for a fee of "Fifty thousand. Cash," comes up with a name for the new corporation: "International Substrate of Paris, Inc." The Prospector also reveals the purpose of the business: it will drill for oil beneath Chaillot, destroying the entire neighborhood if necessary to gain access. He has, he reveals, a plan.

Their talk is interrupted by the entrance of the Countess Aurelia, the Madwoman of Chaillot, who has come to the café looking for bones and gizzards for the stray cats she feeds. Strangely dressed in mismatched clothing "in the grand fashion of 1885" and speaking seeming nonsense, she is also looking for a feather boa that has been missing for years. The President rises to complain about the Countess and the other eccentric characters, whom he sees as offenses against "order and discipline." Returning to his plan, the Prospector explains that he has already hired Pierre to bomb the city architect's office in order to get at the oil and promises his companions that at noon they will see the explosion. However, the Policeman rushes in carrying an unconscious man; Pierre, unable to go ahead with the bombing, has tried to kill himself by jumping off a bridge. The Policeman has prevented Pierre from jumping and then, following the instructions for saving a drowning man, has knocked Pierre unconscious to prevent the victim from dragging him underwater. A nonsensical argument follows, as the men encourage the Policeman to throw Pierre in the water and pull him out again to avoid trouble.

As Pierre regains consciousness, he sees the waitress, Irma, among those attending him, and the two fall instantly in love. Irma is called back into the café, but the Countess holds Pierre's hand until he is well enough to get up. She urges him to embrace life and all its delights. Pierre explains the men's quest for the oil beneath Paris, and when the Countess laughs at the idea that anyone would destroy beauty to obtain oil, the Ragpicker explains that the world has changed while the Countess has been "hiding," living "in a dream." In the past, the people of Paris were a community of empathetic souls, but they have been gradually replaced by empty, uncaring people who contribute nothing and value nothing but money. Businessmen whom the Ragpicker calls "pimps" have inserted themselves into the simplest transactions, whether for cabbages or for flowers; "little by little," he says, "the pimps have taken over the world."

The Countess decides instantly to rid the world of these pimps. She asks Irma to fetch her a little bottle of kerosene and dirt, sends a message asking three of her friends—Constance, Josephine, and Gabrielle—to come to her home that afternoon, and sends another message with the little bottle to the President and the Prospector, claiming that oil has been found beneath the cellar of her home. She reasons that she need invite only two of the businessmen, and the rest, sensing an opportunity for profit, will follow. As she and Pierre head to her home to get ready for the guests, Irma watches Pierre's back and whispers "I love you."

Act 2

Act 2 takes place in the cellar of the Countess's house. As the scene opens, she is talking with the Sewer Man. On a previous visit, he has promised to show the Countess the secret of her cellar, and now he does: there is a hidden door that conceals a circular staircase that descends down and down to nowhere. As the Sewer Man leaves, Irma announces the arrival of the Countess's friends. The script's list of characters identifies them as Madame Constance, the Madwoman of Passy (another neighborhood in Paris); Mademoiselle Gabrielle, the Madwoman of St. Sulpice; and Mademoiselle Josephine, the Madwoman of La Concorde. The Countess calls them simply by their first names, and they call her by hers, Aurelia. The four women sit down for tea, and the Countess tries to explain that they have important matters to discuss. Their conversation, however, is humorously disjointed. Constance has brought along her invisible dog, Dickie, and her friends indulge this way of grieving for her dead companion. Gabrielle, who has two imaginary friends and who often consults "her voices," is a virgin and is shocked at the vaguest mention of sex. Josephine arrives late because she was waiting to talk with U.S. President Woodrow Wilson, although when the play occurs he has been dead for twenty years.

Amid the women's chatter, the Countess explains that men intend to destroy the city to find oil. She proposes gathering all of the evil men into one room and getting rid of them. Josephine agrees that they have a legal right to get rid of the men, but only if there is a trial first. Because time is short, they decide to try the wicked men *in absentia* (without their being present), and they appoint the Ragpicker to represent them. With Josephine as judge, the Ragpicker speaks on behalf of the wealthy and corrupt men, while the rest of the commoners look on. He explains the difficulties of being rich and powerful, of having money fall out of the sky with no effort, of trying to think of ways to spend it. Giving a poor man a *sou* (a small French coin) would be a waste of time, he argues, because it would not help him get rid of his millions quickly enough. No matter what he does, he claims, money comes to him and

sticks to him. It is not his fault. Josephine and the gathered witnesses declare him guilty of worshipping money and give the Countess permission to execute all the pimps.

Most of the crowd exits, leaving the Countess alone with Pierre. She closes her eyes for a rest and imagines that Pierre is her long-lost lover, Adolphe Bertaut, who tells her that he has always loved her, although he left her many years before. Irma rushes in to announce that a procession of taxis and limousines, carrying a procession of presidents, has arrived. Led by the President from act 1, they dress and act alike. They give the Countess a contract, which they declare in whispers to be completely in their favor, and a bar of gold as down payment for the oil under her cellar. Setting the gold aside, she shows them to the secret staircase, and they go down. Now a group of prospectors arrives; they give the Countess another false document and head down the staircase. Next, members of the press arrive, promising to improve the Countess's profits by writing favorably about her oil. Although they boast that they do not need to see the oil to write about it, they steal the gold bar and follow the others down. Finally, a group of ladies arrive and follow the men down the stairs. The Countess closes the secret door, sealing the pimps underground, and all agree with Irma that "life is beautiful again." Disembodied voices of the newly freed people thank the Countess for saving them, Pierre and Irma declare their love, and the Countess turns her attention back to her cats.

CHARACTERS

Aurelia
See The Countess

The Baron
The Baron is an impressive man who arrives at Chez Francis with the President as the play opens. Although he has the air of money, in fact he has spent his life squandering inherited wealth. He has nothing left but his name, but that is all that is required of him when he is asked to be on the board of directors of the President's new company. The Baron surprises the President by asking the purpose of the company; apparently, men of business do not typically discuss such things, and since neither man has any skills

or ideas to contribute to the enterprise, it hardly matters what the company does.

Adolphe Bertaut

Adolphe Bertaut was the Countess's lover long ago. Although he has been gone for years, the Countess still talks about him frequently and carries on imaginary conversations with him. After the pimps have been destroyed, a group of Adolphe Bertauts appears onstage, thanking the Countess for purifying the world, promising to be bold and strong in the future, and asking for her hand in marriage, but she declares that it is too late.

The Broker

The Broker spouts numerical nonsense to the President and the Baron, not explaining anything of use.

Constance

The Countess's friend Madame Constance is identified in the script's list of characters and in the stage directions as the Madwoman of Passy, though within the play she is referred to only as "Constance." Dressed in white and wearing a big hat, she arrives at the Countess's cellar in act 2, accompanied by her imaginary dog, Dickie; the real Dickie died years before. Her husband is also dead, and because she lives in fear of being attacked by murderous men, friends must knock on her door and then yowl like cats before she will open it. As a widow, Constance knows more about men than the other women; she agrees that the wicked ones should be done away with but refuses to discuss the matter in front of Gabrielle's imaginary voices.

The Countess

The Countess Aurelia, Madwoman of Chaillot, is the elderly, dignified, and eccentric protagonist. She walks through the streets of Paris enjoying its people, its plants and animals, its beauty. The Countess dresses "in the grand fashion of 1885," with a full taffeta skirt and train, a hat and cameo pin, extravagant jewelry, and button shoes. She enters the stage calling for Irma, asking for bones and gizzards for the stray cats she feeds; the President is irritated by her loud eccentricity, and the Waiter explains that although she is the Madwoman of Chaillot, she is not mad. As if to contradict the Waiter, the Countess inquires after a feather boa that she misplaced five years before and fusses about a yellow scarf upsetting her mismatched color scheme.

When Pierre reveals that he was instructed to place a bomb, the common folk gently explain to the Countess that the pleasant and cheerful world she inhabits is a dream world; in fact, they explain, the world is filled with greedy and destructive men, or "pimps." The Countess has had little contact with men, and her one love affair ended sadly years ago when her lover, Adolphe Bertaut, left her for another woman. She determines on the spot to rid the world of these men, to restore the world to peace and beauty that very day. She invites her friends Constance, Gabrielle, and Josephine to tea at two o'clock and lures the President to her home at three o'clock to examine a supposed oil supply under her cellar.

In act 2, which takes place in the Countess's cellar, she explains to her three friends, who all refer to her by her first name, "Aurelia," that wicked men are trying to destroy the world. She asks them to agree that eliminating these men is just and then arranges a mock trial with her friend Josephine as judge and the Ragpicker as speaker for the defense. When the men are found guilty, the Countess proceeds with her plan. A swarm of presidents, prospectors, and press agents arrive at her home, lured by a fake sample of oil, and she allows them to treat her as though she can be easily tricked. In fact, she tricks them, urging them down the staircase to see the oil for themselves. When the last one has gone, she closes the trap door, ridding the world of them forever. "Nothing is ever so wrong in this world," she says, "that a sensible woman can't set it right in the course of an afternoon."

The Flower Girl

The Flower Girl is one of the common people whose presence annoys the President.

Gabrielle

The Countess's friend Mademoiselle Gabrielle, another guest at the tea party in act 2, is identified in the list of characters and in the stage directions as the Madwoman of St. Sulpice, though within the play she is referred to only as "Gabrielle." Although well into old age, Gabrielle dresses like a coquettish young French woman of the 1880s; she is a virgin and is shocked and embarrassed when the Countess says that the male sex is destroying the world. When Gabrielle is worried, she consults voices that used to come out of her sewing machine but now come out of her hot water bottle. She is hesitant at first about the idea of killing all of the wicked men, but she is willing to bow to Josephine's judgment.

Irma

Irma is a waitress at Chez Francis and is fond of the Countess and kind to all of the down-and-out commoners who pass by. She sets aside bones and other scraps for the Countess's stray cats and acts as a sort of lady-in-waiting at the Countess's tea party. Irma falls in love with Pierre the first time she sees him, attracted by his beauty. In a monologue that closes act 1, she states openheartedly that she loves beauty and kindness and loves being a waitress because of all of the people she meets; when she whispers "I love you" to Pierre, who has gone, it is the first time she has said it to a man. By the end of act 2, at the urging of the Countess, Pierre and Irma are in each other's arms.

Josephine

Josephine, the last to arrive at the Countess's cellar for tea, is identified in the script's list of characters and in the stage directions as the Madwoman of La Concorde. She arrives late because she has been waiting for President Woodrow Wilson, and has to be reminded by the Countess that Wilson died in 1924. Josephine is the sister-in-law of a lawyer, and so the others defer to her judgment on the wisdom and legality of executing the pimps. She speaks a few Latin phrases to show her education and decrees that the Countess's plan to kill all of the men at once is legal and practical—but only after a trial. She outlines a nonsensical plan for conducting a trial without the presence or the knowledge of the defendants, explains that in an emergency the court may appoint "the first passerby" to represent them, and ultimately allows the Ragpicker to speak, not as an attorney, but directly as the men on trial. She finds the pimps guilty of worshipping money.

The Juggler

The Juggler is another of the common people whose presence annoys the President. He performs as the Broker tries to explain economics, providing a satirical background for everything the Broker says.

The Ladies

After the press agents have gone down the staircase, a group of ladies arrives unexpectedly. The Countess admits them, and they identify themselves as "the most powerful pressure group in the world": the women behind the men of industry. They enter, walk through the cellar, and descend the staircase in a span of about one minute.

Little Man

The Little Man is seated at the next table when the President and the Baron discuss their new phantom corporation. Excited by the rising stock numbers he overhears, he "dumps a sackful of money" in front of the President, begging him to take it.

Madwoman of Chaillot

See The Countess

Madwoman of La Concorde

See Josephine

Madwoman of Passy

See Constance

Madwoman of St. Sulpice

See Gabrielle

Pierre

Pierre is a handsome young man who is being blackmailed by the Prospector and ordered to place a bomb at the city architect's office. He cannot go through with the bombing; instead he tries to throw himself into the Seine (the river that runs through Paris) and is rescued by the Policeman. When he is brought to the café, he meets the Countess and falls in love with Irma. In act 1, the Countess holds his hand until he regains full consciousness; in act 2, he holds the Countess's hand while she rests and, pretending to be her former lover, Adolphe Bertaut, assures her of her beauty and intelligence. As the play ends, the Countess urges Pierre to take Irma in his arms and kiss her.

The Policeman

The Policeman, seeing that Pierre is about to jump into the river, knocks him unconscious to stop him. This is his first day on the job and he does not know what to do next, so he refers to his training in saving a drowning man and performs artificial respiration. The Prospector tries to convince the Policeman that the only way to stay out of trouble is to throw Pierre into the water and rescue him properly, but before he can puzzle through this advice he is called away on another case.

The President

The President, the most prominent of the men the Ragpicker calls "pimps," arrives with the Baron at Chez Francis as the play opens. The President makes a show of his wealth and power: he smokes a private brand of cigar, he is rude to the café staff and to the common folk on the sidewalk, and he takes for granted that a hundred-franc note found on the sidewalk belongs to him. The President values order and discipline and is repulsed by the eccentric characters hanging around the café. Although he was born the son of a poor washerwoman and was frequently expelled from school, he found that he could make a lot of money passing counterfeit money and selling drugs. He has continued to make money and expand his empire and runs dozens of corporations and companies, but it is unclear what he contributes to these enterprises. His newest company, for example, is already making large profits on the stock exchange, even though the President does not yet know the name of the firm or what it does.

When the Prospector arrives, he reveals his plan for extracting oil from beneath Chaillot. The President is excited by the idea, and his only concern about the proposed bombing is that he might be sitting too close. When the Policeman comes in with the rescued Pierre, the President sneaks off to stay out of trouble. The President reappears at the end of the play, leading a company of interchangeable presidents who look and act alike. They give the Countess a phony contract for her oil rights and descend the unending staircase.

The Press Agents

Several press agents appear near the end of act 2, but only three of them speak. They have heard of the Countess's supposed discovery of oil and arrived at her cellar to get in on the story. They do not intend to do research but simply to write whatever kind of story will create the most profit for the oil holders. The Countess has to urge them to descend the staircase and see the oil for themselves.

The Prospector

The Prospector has discovered, by tasting the water, that oil lurks beneath the surface of Paris. With the backing of the President and his board of directors, he creates International Substrate of Paris, Inc., to drill for the oil. Because the city architect has refused to allow him to drill in the city, the Prospector hires Pierre to bomb the architect's office, eliminating the roadblock and

creating space for drilling. The Countess overhears his plan, setting the trial and punishment in motion, but the bombing plan fails. The Prospector returns in the final scene, looking for oil and profit, and eagerly descends the endless staircase with several other nameless prospectors.

The Ragpicker

The Ragpicker is one of the common people who hang around Chez Francis. He is something of a spokesman for the others, and he is the one who explains to the Countess that the world has changed. Instead of people enjoying beauty and each other, Paris is a city of strangers, and "little by little, the pimps have taken over the world." In act 2, the Countess chooses the Ragpicker to be the lawyer for the millionaires, but it is his suggestion that he speak directly in their words instead. The trial begins, and he promises "to lie, conceal and distort everything." He explains that he cannot help being rich, that money comes to him unbidden, that he owns everything and everyone.

The Sewer Man

The Sewer Man reveals to the Countess the secret of her cellar: the moving stone and the never-ending staircase it conceals.

The Street Singer

The Street Singer is another of the common people whose presence annoys the President.

The Waiter

The Waiter at Chez Francis seats the President and his party. The President orders the Waiter about rudely and expects the Waiter to shield him from the commoners. Irma uses the Waiter's name, Martial, but the script refers to him only by his title.

THEMES

Capitalism

One of the central themes of *The Madwoman of Chaillot* is the matter of who has money and who does not, where the money comes from, and what those who have money do with it. In the neighborhood of Chaillot near Chez Francis, there is a clear divide between the "haves" (such as the President, the Baron, and the Prospector, who have more money than they can possible spend but who are greedy for more) and the "have-nots" (the

TOPICS FOR FURTHER STUDY

- First, with a partner, study the speeches by the Broker in act 1 to get a sense of the Broker's deliberately obscure language. Second, using the Internet, learn what you can about the credit default swaps, derivatives, and other financial instruments that were part of the economic downturn that began in 2008. Finally, rewrite the conversation between the Broker and the President as though it were set today, and perform the scene for your class or create a video for class viewing or for posting online.

- In *The Madwoman of Chaillot*, first published in French in 1945, Giraudoux's Countess cannot understand why the men are willing to damage a city just to bring oil to the surface. Today, some people are worried that drilling for oil in the Alaskan National Wildlife Refuge (ANWR) or in the oceans could cause different kinds of damage. Research the arguments for and against drilling in ANWR or another location, and write an essay in which you explain how the situation in *The Madwoman of Chaillot* compares with the need for and the risks of drilling for oil today.

- Like many characters in fiction, the Countess seems to speak randomly at times, yet in the end she reveals a deeper understanding of the world around her than some of the characters whose thinking is more linear. Using the tools available on the Internet at MindMeister.com or other tools available to you, create a mind map showing the connectedness—or disjointedness—of the Countess's thoughts as the play progresses. For an extra challenge, use the site's brainstorming mode and create your map with a small team of classmates. Choose a different character, if you wish.

- Read several entries on the Web site *Stuff White People Like*, and ask classmates to read and share different entries. After students share their entries and the group has time to discuss the site, have each member of the class respond to the following questions: Is the site satire? Which elements are exaggerated, and which are not? Is the list offensive? Does it matter whether or not the author is white? How might similar lists for different cultures or groups be received? Create charts or tables tallying the responses to each question (several examples of such tables are available at pewresearch.org). You may wish to go further and write an essay analyzing the answers to one question or more.

- Read Virginia Hamilton's young-adult, Newbery Award-winning novel *M. C. Higgins, the Great* (1975), or watch the 1987 film version. Consider Hamilton's ideas about the effects of industrialization and capitalism on the poor, alongside Giraudoux's ideas on the same subject. Write a brief essay in which you describe the points on which the two authors agree, and explain why Giraudoux may have chosen to use satire to explore his ideas while Hamilton chose a more realistic approach.

Ragpicker, the Juggler, the Flower Girl, the Street Singer, and the other common people, who seem content with their ragged clothing and simple lives). According to the Ragpicker, the men with money, whom he calls "pimps," "have taken over the world." The President, for example, controls dozens of companies and corporations, and he has become wealthy through these businesses. He is so influential that the value of the stock in his new company goes up rapidly before he even has a name for it or knows what it will do. He disdains the street vendors and entertainers with their "raffish individualism."

Clearly, the play condemns this economic system, which places such value on money or capital and which produces such large gaps between the wealthy and the poor. In the mock trial, the Ragpicker-as-Pimp stands accused of "the crime

A scene from a production of La Folle de Chaillot, *performed in Paris in 1945* (*Roger Viollet | Getty Images*)

of worshipping money." In his defense, the Rag-picker declares, "Everyone knows that the poor are alone to blame for their poverty," and explains that it would be a waste of time to share his wealth with the poor: if he were to give away a few coins at a time he could not make a dent in what he has quickly enough to be worth the trouble. To have money, he declares, "is to be virtuous, honest, beautiful, and witty. And to be without it is to be ugly and boring and stupid and useless." Mocking these capitalist notions of money and its value is the heart of the play.

Environmentalism

While the greed and materialism of the evil men in *The Madwoman of Chaillot* have many harmful effects, the play focuses on their disregard for the environment. An important theme of the play is the Countess's successful attempt to protect the environment from industrialization. In

their quest for oil, the men of International Substrate of Paris, Inc., are willing to destroy the city of Paris, to cover it with "a forest of derricks and drills." These men love their machines, and "they are all connected like the works of a machine." "Is a park any better than a coal mine?" the Prospector asks. "What would you rather have in your garden—an almond tree or an oil well?"

By contrast, the Countess, the center of goodness in the play, appreciates the natural world; she feeds stray cats, pets dogs, and waters plants. She loves flowers, calling attention to the iris in her buttonhole and to the flowers along the streets. When she hears of the plan to drill for oil, she says, "I never heard of anything so silly!" When the Countess has done away with the pimps, she is thanked by the disembodied voices of "the friends of people . . . the friends of animals . . . the friends of friendship." She has succeeded in stopping the threat to the environment posed by the promise of oil.

Manichaeism

The world of the Countess in *The Madwoman of Chaillot* is a world of polarities: light and darkness, beauty and ugliness, good and evil. The President, the Baron, the Prospector, and the other "pimps" are comically, exaggeratedly evil: bad-tempered, rude, and greedy. The President despises the colorful, eccentric commoners and wishes he could simply "get rid of these people." When he speaks of beauty it is in describing the image of a manager and an interchangeable worker. The Prospector and his colleagues are willing to fill the streets of Paris with oil derricks. The pimps consume and are consumed by the material world; all of their talk is of money, possessions, and commodities. By contrast, the Countess and her friends are comically, exaggeratedly good: Irma and Pierre are as beautiful as angels; the Countess feels that "everything is pure delight"; and Constance and Gabrielle communicate with dogs and voices from the spirit world. The instant that the Countess closes the door to the staircase, the world changes: "Little by little, the scene is suffused with light, faint at first but increasing as if the very walls were glowing with quiet radiance of universal joy."

This type of duality is often described as "Manichean," a reference to the ancient Persian religion of Manichaeism, established in the third century by the prophet Mani. According to this faith, the world is constantly engaged in a struggle between light and darkness, good and evil. Within individual humans, light and dark battle for supremacy, light being associated with spirituality and darkness with materialism. Manichaeism was one of the most-practiced religions in the world until the end of the seventh century, and its influence is still felt. Although the belief system of Manichaeism is much more complex than this simple dichotomy, the term "Manichean" is often used to describe art that deals with a strict duality between good and evil.

STYLE

Satire

Satire is a literary form that uses humor or ridicule to point out human weaknesses, typically for the purpose of working toward justice. *The Madwoman of Chaillot* satirizes the ways that financial interests have worked against social harmony by exploiting or ignoring poor people and by risking the health of the environment. The exaggerated characters are one element that makes this play satirical: the President and his colleagues, for example, are drawn much larger than life. When money is found on the sidewalk, everyone assumes it belongs to the President, because all big bills belong to him; the Little Man is so excited about the possibility of riches that he hands his life savings over without knowing a single detail about the new company. The Broker speaks long paragraphs of numerical nonsense, and the others pretend to understand. The Prospector proposes blowing up a building full of workers and the others accept the plan as "modern methods." Everything the men say and do is so outrageous that it becomes funny—and scary. The height of the satire comes in act 2 when the Ragpicker pretends to speak in the words of the evil men. He promises to "lie, conceal and distort everything," and delivers a testimony that is heartless and self-absorbed and not far different from what the President and the Baron have said themselves. Giraudoux's satire points out the evil in these men by exaggerating it, forcing the audience to examine and reject that evil.

Stage Directions

The text or script of *The Madwoman of Chaillot* includes italicized material in parentheses, typically descriptions of actors entering or exiting or instructions about how particular lines should be uttered. Giraudoux uses an unusually large number of these insertions, called stage directions, to help readers, directors, and actors understand his vision for the play. One group of these stage directions describes in detail what the café and the Countess's cellar look like, and what the Countess and her friends are wearing. (Interestingly, the stage directions do not describe the clothing worn by the President and his colleagues.) Another set of directions simply tells the actors when to sit, stand, offer a cigar, or kiss. Occasionally, this stage business is intended to add humor or irony to a scene: when the Juggler juggles only while the Broker is giving his convoluted explanations for the actions of the stock market, the playwright subtly compares the Broker's work to a circus act. A third set of directions describes the emotions that should accompany a line, as when the Prospector, asked to name the new firm, "Nods, with complete comprehension." Without that stage direction, an actor might

COMPARE
&
CONTRAST

- **1940s:** No women hold important executive positions in major corporations in the United States or Europe.

  Today: Women head some of the largest corporations in the United States, including Kraft Foods, PepsiCo, and Xerox. Fifteen corporations on the 2010 Fortune 500 list of the nation's largest public companies are run by women.

- **1940s:** In the aftermath of World War II, which ends in 1945, the cold war begins. The cost of living increases in the United States and Europe, and the gap between rich and poor also increases.

  Today: In 2010, the United States, with a United Nations coalition of military forces, is fighting wars in Iraq and Afghanistan, and a worldwide economic crisis affects many lower- and middle-class families.

- **1940s:** Plays in translation are popular on Broadway. Productions include *The Madwoman of Chaillot* (opening in 1948), Jean Anouilh's *Antigone* (1946), and Jean-Paul Sartre's *No Exit* (1946).

  Today: Plays in translation are rare on Broadway, with the exception of productions staged by the Classic Stage Company, whose 2010–2011 season includes plays by Anton Chekhov and Molière.

---

not understand what the nod should look like, and readers would not know that a nod had occurred.

Some of the stage directions seem unimportant at first glance. Before the first line is spoken, for example, the directions call for the doorman to walk across the stage from right to left and leave, and for a blonde woman named Therese to enter the café from the left and sit down at the right side. The doorman, who crosses the stage three times in act 1, has only a few brief lines, and Therese never speaks or participates in the action in any way. However, creating the right atmosphere was important for the playwright, and the actions of these very minor characters help Chez Francis seem like a real, vibrant place. Many directors and actors believe that stage directions are unimportant and may be ignored, but most playwrights consider their stage directions to be an essential part of their artistic creation.

HISTORICAL CONTEXT

The Nazi Occupation of France
Between May 1940 and December 1944, during World War II, German forces occupied most of France. German leader Adolph Hitler had invited France to surrender in 1939, but France refused, and Germany invaded France on May 10, 1940, conquering it easily. An armistice agreement signed on June 22 ceded control of about half the country, but Germany seized the rest in 1942. During the occupation, life in France was difficult: money was tight, food shortages were common, tens of thousands of men were off fighting or being held as prisoners of war, and Allied bombs devastated the country. A thriving black market smuggled scarce goods to those who could pay premium prices and made great profits for some. The German government controlled the news media and the arts, censoring anything that challenged their authority. To say the least, many French people were demoralized, seeing little reason for hope. The occupation ended in 1944, after the famous D-day invasion and the battle of Normandy. The German forces finally surrendered in April and May of 1945.

During the 1930s and through the war, Giraudoux thought a great deal about what France would need to do when the war was over to recover and to build a just community for all its citizens. As John H. Reilly, in part of the Twayne's World Author Series, and other biographers report, Giraudoux was concerned about the growing influence of financiers and believed that preserving

In the play's cockeyed world, the pigeons don't fly anymore, they walk. (fpolat69 | Shutterstock.com)

historical sites and open spaces while engaging in intelligent growth and modernizing was essential for maintaining functional cities. He worried that government officials had forgotten about individual, common people. At the time of his death in 1945, Giraudoux was working on a book in which he warned France not to rush too quickly to industrialization or to financial manipulation to speed its recovery. This book, *Sans pouvoirs* (Without Powers), was published in 1946.

The Madwoman of Chaillot reflects the oppression felt by the French during occupation and a degree of optimism for the future. The play was written during the occupation, completed in 1943, but not performed until the war was over. As critic Robert Cohen points out in *Contemporary Literature*, although the play's common people fear the pimps, their language is the language of an occupied people, as when the Ragpicker says, "The people are different. There's been an invasion." The Countess wonders how her friends can tolerate a world "Where a man is not his own master," and she states simply and directly the wishes of all oppressed people: "If these men are the cause of the trouble, all we have to do is get rid

of them." While ending a war is easier said than done, Giraudoux knew that after occupation the French would face questions about finance, industry, social justice, and the environment, and this play expresses the choices he hoped his country would make.

CRITICAL OVERVIEW

The Madwoman of Chaillot was well received by both critics and the public when it opened on Broadway in 1948. Brooks Atkinson of the *New York Times* observed, soon after the opening, that while the tone is "gay and some of the scenes are hilarious, the impression it leaves is strangely moving." A contributor to *Newsweek* called the play "a stimulating and rewarding production in every department," while Euphemia Van Rensselaer Wyatt, writing in *Catholic World*, found it "so unusual in its conception, so mellow in its clarity, so superbly full of wit and yet so deeply cutting in its warning." The only negative comments in the major reviews concerned matters out of the playwright's control: Kappo Phelan of *Commonweal* found Maurice Valency's translation stilted, and Harold Clurman of the *New Republic* disliked the production while declaring the play itself "a little masterpiece."

Many books and articles have been written in French about Giraudoux's work and about this play in particular, but the body of critical work in English is relatively small. The 1950s and 1960s saw the largest number of publications about the playwright in English, as well as Broadway productions of seven more Giraudoux plays after *The Madwoman of Chaillot*. This wave of criticism typically attempted to reconcile Giraudoux's biography and place in history with his work. Marcel Reboussin, in a 1961 article in *Educational Theatre Journal*, discusses Giraudoux's work in the Ministry of Foreign Affairs before and during World War II, and describes *The Madwoman of Chaillot* as "a meditation on French problems of that time." Agnes D. Raymond, in *Jean Giraudoux: The Theatre of Victory and Defeat*, calls the play "militant literature" and "a work of propaganda" in which the playwright warns the French against war and "presents what he considers to be the only effective preventative: revolution."

However, in his 1959 biography *Jean Giraudoux: His Life and Works*, Laurent LeSage concludes the opposite, arguing that in his plays Giraudoux was not concerned with the "topical, the specific"; *The Madwoman of Chaillot*, he writes, "is only very incidentally an indictment of capitalism. It is . . . a hymn to a life of generosity and lovely make-believe." Germaine Brée, the same year, celebrates the play as "Unhampered by hidden meanings—symbolic or ideological."

Little criticism has been published in English since the early 1970s. In 2001, Victoria Korzeniowska explored the role of gender in *The Madwoman of Chaillot* in *The Heroine as Social Redeemer in the Plays of Jean Giraudoux*. "It is significant" in the play, she writes, "that those responsible for humanity's despair are all men." The play, she argues at length, "portrays a binary division between the masculine gender role with its inherent aggression and destruction, and the feminine gender role with its cooperative ethos and desire for social harmony."

CRITICISM

Cynthia A. Bily

Bily is an instructor in literature and writing. In the following essay, she demonstrates how Giraudoux

> THE COUNTESS BELIEVES, AS GIRAUDOUX DOES, THAT THE WORLD IS NOT HOPELESS, THAT THERE ARE CHOICES TO BE MADE AND ACTIONS TO BE TAKEN."

uses satirical exaggeration in The Madwoman of Chaillot *to highlight the choices society faces.*

Although *The Madwoman of Chaillot* has an unusually large number of characters (the first Broadway production at the Belasco Theatre on December 27, 1948, had forty actors in the cast), they can be easily divided into two groups: the satisfied and the greedy, the common folk and the financiers, the good and the evil. In this humorous and satirical play, the characters are caricatures, and for the most part, no one is complex enough to be good but flawed or torn between good and evil. The businessmen and the commoners live in completely different worlds, rarely communicating with each other, and each group is unable to understand the other. By establishing the two kinds of people as vastly different, Giraudoux is able to highlight the possibility of choosing which kind of person to be—or which kind of society to work toward.

The businessmen (they are all men) include the President, the Baron, the Prospector, the Broker, and their colleagues. These men live privileged lives but are always greedy for more. The President is already "president of eleven corporations, director of fifty-two companies" and is about to start a new corporation. He makes a show of his wealth, bragging about his private brand of cigars and the special bottle of port (a kind of wine) that is kept for him at the café. When the Ragpicker finds a hundred-franc note, the President immediately claims it, saying, "All hundred-franc notes . . . are mine," although the money, which would be a big help to the Ragpicker, could not possibly mean anything to a man worth millions.

It becomes clear in the first scene that the President's success has not come as a result of his own efforts. His early education was paid for through his mother's hard work bent over a washtub, and although he claims now that he is

WHAT DO I READ NEXT?

- The play *Tiger at the Gates* (1955) is Christopher Fry's translation of Giraudoux's *La guerre de Troie n'aura pas lieu* (1935; The Trojan War Will Not Take Place). Set within the gates of Troy the day before the war begins, the play features Hector and the women of Troy arguing for peace but unable to stop the war.

- One of the few Giraudoux novels available in English translation is *Choice of the Elect* (2002), translated by Henry B. Russell from the original *Choix des élues* (1939). The novel tells the story of Edme, a young mother who leaves her husband and son behind in California and sets off with her daughter to find her own place in the world.

- Joseph Heller's *Catch-22* (1961), set at the end of World War II, is considered one of the greatest English satirical novels. Often read in high schools, it focuses on the bombardier Yossarian. The novel mocks bureaucracy and its implications for individuals.

- Philip Reeve's award-winning *Mortal Engines* (2001), along with the other three novels in the author's "Hungry Cities Chronicles" series, is a critique of global capitalism and environmental destruction. The novel opens with the great Traction City of London chasing a smaller town over the dry bed that once was the North Sea.

- *Empty* (2010), by Suzanne Weyn, is a futuristic young-adult novel about decisions that must be made when the oil runs out.

- African American history and culture is satirized in George C. Wolfe's award-winning play *The Colored Museum* (1985), which includes eleven short scenes or "exhibits" including "Cookin' with Aunt Ethel," "Soldier with a Secret," and "The Last Mama-on-the-Couch Play."

- *Satire: From Horace to Yesterday's Comic Strips* (2005), by James Scott, explores how satire has been used by fiction writers, dramatists, poets, essayists, and cartoonists throughout history to mock the political and social events and characters of the day.

- *Our Dumb Century: The Onion Presents 100 Years of Headlines from America's Finest News Source* (1999), edited by Scott Dikkers, is a satire of news events during the twentieth century in the United States. Like other books published by the staff of the satirical newspaper the *Onion*, it presents itself as a collection of serious news stories and mocks historical, political, and social trends and ideas.

"eternally grateful to her, of course," he appreciated her gift so little that he was thrown out of school five times before quitting for good. He has earned his fortune through "passing a boxful of counterfeit notes" and then dealing drugs, never doing an honest day's work. He appears to contribute nothing to his current businesses— a point made startlingly clear by the fact that he knows neither the name nor the purpose of his newest company. Likewise, his newest member of the Board of Directors has no talents or ideas or funds to contribute. The Baron has not even done illegal work; he inherited his father's fortune and has spent his life squandering it. It is only his good name—or, to be more precise, his father's good name—that he can bring to his position on the board, but that is all the President needs to lend his business an atmosphere of respectability. Similarly, the President does not need a business plan or a product or an idea for his new business—he needs only a name for it: "A name that will stir the pulse, a trumpet call, set the brain awhirl, a movie star, inspire reverence, a cathedral."

Of the businessmen, the Prospector comes closest to doing actual work. He is the man who locates the "deposits of metal or liquid on which can be founded the only social unit of which our age is capable—the corporation." For three months he has been sampling water throughout Paris, looking for the source of the oil, and he has found it. At this point, his work is finished. He assumes, as the rest of the financiers do, that the oil is his for the taking and that any profits should go to the men who claim the oil. When the President says, "Just show us the point where you want to start digging. We'll do the rest," he does not, of course, mean that he and the Baron and their colleagues will actually do the physical labor. That will be done by, ideally, the "standardized worker with interchangeable parts," the "one composite drudge grunting and sweating." All of the hundred-franc notes, however, will still belong to the President.

These are the men the Ragpicker labels the "pimps." In normal usage, the word "pimp" refers to a man who is the boss of a prostitute and who takes a portion of everything she earns. The Ragpicker compares the financiers of the industrial age to pimps, indicating that, like the President and the others, "They don't do anything, they don't make anything—they just stand there and take their cut." Even though they do not produce anything of value, "They have all the power. And all the money. And they're greedy for more."

At the opposite end of the spectrum are the common people: the Waiter, the Street Singer, the Juggler, the Ragpicker, Irma the waitress, the Shoelace Peddler, and the rest. In direct contrast to the financiers, they work hard and earn little. It would be an easy and understandable thing for the Ragpicker to keep the hundred-franc note he found on the ground, but he is not instinctively greedy. Irma the waitress is the model of virtue, telling herself, "I hate ugliness. I love beauty. I hate meanness. I adore kindness." The pimps have blank faces, "The eyes—empty. The expression—not human," but Irma "has the face and figure of an angel." The common folk value friendship (forming another kind of social unit), they care about animals and flowers, they gather around to help the unconscious Pierre, and they protect the Countess from the knowledge that the world is changing and that they are "the last of the free people of the earth." Although the President was born poor, the son of a woman who did other people's laundry, he has no compassion for working people. "Get rid of that man," he orders the Waiter when the Street Singer approaches. He tells the Baron that "the first thing we have to do is get rid of

these people!" When the Countess has rid the world of the evil men and "Life is beautiful again," it is not because the commoners have gained wealth or power, but because "The air is pure, the sky is clear," and "on the street, utter strangers are shaking hands . . . and offering each other almond bars."

As the play begins, Pierre's fate hangs in the balance: he has allied himself with the financiers, but it is a reluctant alliance. It is no coincidence that the crime he is being blackmailed for is forging his father's signature to a note, echoing the way the President made his first thousand, "passing a boxful of counterfeit notes." Pierre is in exactly the same state that the President was in years before: he is poor but wants more, and he is willing to turn away from his parent to get it. The President seems to have had no qualms about escalating his crimes and finding "a nice berth in the narcotics business," but Pierre finds that he would rather die than place a bomb under the city architect's office. He does not know what there is to live for until the Countess shows him the beauty of her simple and natural world; his response to her lesson is immediate and comically overdramatic: "Oh, what a fool I've been!"

The Countess also learns something in act 1: she is shocked to hear that her friends have been unhappy and for so long. She asks, "Why are you complaining instead of doing something about it? . . . If these men are the cause of the trouble, all we have to do is get rid of them." The Countess believes, as Giraudoux does, that the world is not hopeless, that there are choices to be made and actions to be taken. In the world of the play, the choices seem obvious, because the playwright has satirically exaggerated the goodness of the good characters and the evil of the evil characters. The elimination of the evil men is also easy, without blood or fuss or consequences. As the Countess says, "Nothing is ever so wrong in this world that a sensible woman can't set it right in the course of an afternoon."

With further thought, it becomes clear that the financiers are not entirely to blame; they could not be so successful if others did not go along. The President has "personally organized eleven great corporations on the basis of eleven magnificent names." The stock of his newest company makes a profit of three and a half million francs in its first forty-five minutes, before the company has a name or a mission. Why are people investing in the President's companies without knowing

The three society ladies met for tea and talked to the invisible dog. (*Agphotographer | Shutterstock.com*)

anything about them? Why does the Little Man pour his life savings out onto the table, begging the President to take it? Why does everyone at the café accept without question that all hundred-franc notes belong to him? In the twentieth century, why do people buy larger homes than they can afford, or invest in financial products they do not understand? There is a great deal of humor in *The Madwoman of Chaillot*, but the play has a serious purpose: to encourage the audience to choose the park over the coal mine and the almond tree over the oil well, to forsake the world of pimps and of greed, to stop complaining and do something, and to "kiss each other . . . before it is too late."

Source: Cynthia A. Bily, Critical Essay on *The Madwoman of Chaillot*, in *Drama for Students*, Gale, Cengage Learning, 2011.

John Angell Grant

In the following review, Grant calls the play a lighthearted comedy about the human spirit which

allows the characters to not only survive but to look to the future with optimism.

Four businessmen decide to drill for oil in the sewers of Paris during World War II in French playwright Jean Giraudoux's strange and surreal 1945 comedy *The Madwoman of Chaillot*.

California Theater Center is currently running an exceptionally magical production of this unusual play in Sunnyvale, as part of their summer repertory season. If you want something a little different, but high quality, check this one out.

The Madwoman of Chaillot is a play about life turned upside down in wartime Paris. Profiteering and corporate skullduggery replace the explicit Nazi threat in a story that was written in a highly allegorical way, disguising the political realities of the Nazi occupation of Paris.

In this cockeyed world, the pigeons don't fly anymore. Instead, they walk. A ragpicker speaks in a schizophrenic coded language that is so poetical it makes sense.

Three society ladies meet for tea and talk to their invisible dog. A prospector tastes the water of Paris, and decides to drill for oil.

A mix of daily life and magical serendipitous moments, *The Madwoman of Chaillot* is more character-based than story-based. Some motifs are surprisingly contemporary, including hedge fund-like financial engineering, corporate name branding and a failed suicide bomber.

Here, a world in which money is king threatens to destroy the connected life of old Paris, and the difference between reality and illusion gets harder and harder to determine.

Maybe, wonders the Countess Aurelia (aka the Madwoman), the solution to all this difficulty lies in a woman with common sense taking the afternoon off to eliminate all the males who advocate war.

What's amazing about this play is the power one woman has to create an optimistic attitude in the world around her, and her power to change things. Of course, she's regarded as crazy. As the play gets more emotional, the dialogue becomes more cockeyed and abstract.

This surreal and lighthearted French comedy turns out to be about the human spirit, which allows the characters to not just survive, but to turn to the future with some plan for optimism.

Director Gayle Cornelison's Sunnyvale production is top-quality Peninsula theater that includes some surprisingly accomplished younger actors mixed in with the veterans.

In this richly textured cultural and political dance disguised as a vaudevillian pastiche, Cornelison has guided his performers to find a myriad of comic characters, moments, postures, attitudes and moves that still feel genuinely human and not shtick.

Chris Mahle stands out as a well-heeled street hustler turned corporate tycoon, sort of like a fast-talking Regis Philbin on crack. Kyle Payne twists his own facial expressions around enough to create a country western speechifying prospector who loves the flavor of petroleum in his drinking water.

Holly Cornelison is solid in her eccentric light-spirited performance as the Countess Aurelia/Madwoman. As a matter of routine, she changes the names of the men in her life every hour, and talks a suicidal man back to life.

Will Huddleston is stirring as the dark and inverted ragpicker who is increasingly pulled outward as the show's wise chorus character.

For set designer Will Lowry, the Eiffel Tower is an oil pump, the Arc de Triomphe has smokestacks coming out the top, and the Notre Dame cathedral features large advertising billboards across its facade.

For the play's businessmen, it all comes down to this: "What would you rather have in your backyard: an almond tree or an oil well?" I walked through the sewers of Paris myself a couple of months ago. Drilling for oil down there would be a nasty business.

The Madwoman, thankfully, gets the pigeons off their feet and flying once again.

Source: John Angell Grant, "Play's World of the Surreal Explores Power of Human Spirit," in *Palo Alto Daily News*, July 13, 2007.

John Moore

In the following review, Moore explains that the restrictions of the only approved English translation of the play make it sometimes hard to follow.

There is something audiences must understand going into *The Madwoman*, or they just might go a bit mad themselves.

The Denver Center Theatre Company's staging of Jean Giraudoux's 1942 French political satire *The Madwoman of Chaillot* is not a straightforward American adaptation. There is only one legally approved English translation, and Maurice

Valency penned it in 1948. And companies are allowed to update dialogue only on a strict, line-by-line basis—they are not permitted to make any larger revisions.

Language consultant Sylvie Drake oversaw a splendidly aggressive modernization of those lines, but it is doubtful anyone in the audience will understand the restrictions. That may explain an oft-overheard question upon exiting: How could something so urgently contemporary in content still come across as so oddly dated and simplistic in its execution?

But that explains how this wonderfully quirky play sounds so pointedly current in places and so tangential and dated in others. The result is a hybrid in form and in effect. It is fanciful and stilted at once, a fairy tale told within agitprop.

The Madwoman told of a comic revolution staged by four women against rich and powerful men who discover oil underneath the streets of German-occupied Paris. Retiring artistic director Donovan Marley rightly thought its huge, 30-person cast would make it the perfect parting gift to the company and city. And he rightly thought it easily would be seen as a modern metaphor.

So he and director Israel Hicks moved Giraudoux's untapped oil geyser to Manhattan, and the now 63-year-old villains morph with unnerving ease into the skin of America's most corrupt politicians and corporate chief executives of today.

It is daring to suggest that America's bottom (line)-feeders would stop at nothing, not even the demolition of the so recently decimated New York City, if the reward were oil. This suggests an act of corporate terrorism from within, which seems a far more terrible crime than the one done to us from without.

But the linguistic restrictions handcuff the script from hitting all of its targets, and so as a contemporary political satire, it pales in comparison to last fall's *Dirty Story*.

That said, anyone who has ever delighted in the DCTC's darkness over the past 21 years will be charmed by a wonderful parade of cameos. Marley has assembled 22 of his favorite actors as well as eight students. Knowing this may be the last time we see so many company giants onstage together makes the evening as nostalgic, sad and inevitable as a graduation.

The Madwoman opens busily in a New York park. We meet Bill Christ, John Hutton, Jamie

Horton and Randy Moore as men behaving very badly; Keith L. Hatten as the "rag picker" and Charles Weldon as a street singer; Mike Hartman as a drunk hippie foot doctor and Mark Rubald stealing the show (a significant accomplishment amid this company) as a sewer maintenance man. A mighty mistake, however, is an awkward company singalong to reggae great Bob Marley's "Get Up Stand Up."

Holding the piece together like a gigantic bear hug is Kathleen M. Brady as Aurelia, the formidable Madwoman of Tribeca. Of Brady's precious work one might only say how lovely, how lovely. She musters all her maternal whimsy to shepherd this band of poor into an action that will send the sleazeballs straight to hell, aided by secondary comic madwomen played by DCTC giants Annette Helde, Kim Staunton and Robin Moseley.

In the process Aurelia saves love itself as effectively as a midsummer night's spell, delivering despondent pawn Peter (a terrific turn by Christopher Kelly) from the brink of suicide and into the arms of the natural young Rachel Duvall, who makes a stunning DCTC debut in the midst of this cavalcade of probable farewells.

Beneath the whimsy are troubling moral questions. These politicos are not mere buffoons. They are fiends at the highest reaches of government, religion and public service, whose greed brings about destruction. So Aurelia's case against them comes with a disturbing suggeston:

> "If those who exploit the planet corrupt the young, rake in obscene commissions, achieve positions of power without the slightest qualifications and then wage war," she asks, "would we have the right to exterminate them?"

Though the play goes on too long, it culminates with a memorable curtain call: 29 actors clasping hands, circling Brady.

It is fascinating that Hicks has set this play not today but "in the spring of next year." It's a nice touch for a company currently steeped in its past, but with an eye on its future.

As this evening of transition ends, the line that resonates is Kelly's: "Life seems marvelous to me now," his Peter says. After 21 years, Marley has earned the right to depart enveloped in the same sentiment.

Source: John Moore, "Political Satire Bound Yet Determined," in *Denver Post*, April 8, 2005, p. FF4.

THE TRIAL SCENES IN GIRAUDOUX'S TWO PLAYS SERVE, THEN, TO POINT UP THE INADEQUACIES IN OUR SYSTEM OF JUSTICE AND, BY EXTENSION, THOSE IN OUR SOCIETY AS A WHOLE."

Mark C. Pilkinton

In the following essay, Pilkinton explains that Giraudoux's motivations for including trial scenes in Ondine *and* The Madwoman of Chaillot *include exploration of the questions of individual versus collective guilt and the role of jurisprudence in society.*

In two of his most famous plays, *Ondine* and *The Madwoman of Chaillot*, Jean Giraudoux makes use of a trial scene before he effects resolution. Playwrights often resort to a discussion or debate to make a point, but rarely do they put an actual trial scene into a play unless that trial scene is the overriding issue, e.g., *Inherit the Wind*. But in Giraudoux's two plays, trials materialize from nowhere. In *Ondine*, The Old One (disguised as The Second Fisherman) announces after capturing Ondine, "Prepare yourself. The judges are coming." In *The Madwoman of Chaillot*, Aurelia has not considered trying the evil men of the world until Josephine mentions it:

> Josephine: Your criminals have had a fair trial, I suppose?
> Countess: Trial?
> Josephine: Certainly. You can't kill anybody without a trial.

Giraudoux does little to prepare us for a trial, and this lack of preparation could be considered a fault, if the trials brought about reversals or discoveries that affected the outcomes of the plays. But the trials are fixed: the defendants, guilty from the outset, endure the machinations of the legal system to absolve their accusers of guilt. Giraudoux's trials serve two obvious purposes: to point up the absurdity of the system of jurisprudence and to move the focus of guilt from the individual to the society in general. They also play a less obvious but more important role: the trial scenes act as the chief destructive forces within the plays and, as such, elevate the plays to Poggioli's nihilistic/agonistic stages of the avant-garde.

To point out the inequities in our trial system, Giraudoux employs a theme of mendacity. Ondine's admitting that she is, indeed, an Ondine startles the judges. The First Judge says, "It is the first time we have tried an Ondine who does not deny being an Ondine." Ondine goes on to lie about her relationship with Bertram, a lie the judges uncover: "Why she wished to make us believe that she deceived you [Hans] with Bertram when in fact she did not, is a question beyond the scope of our inquiry." Uncovering the truth, however, does not change the guilty verdict; it only mollifies it by sparing Ondine "the humiliation of a public execution."

The importance of mendacity as a means of exposing absurdities in the trial system continues in *The Madwoman of Chaillot*:

> The Ragpicker: I swear to tell the truth, the whole truth, and nothing but the truth, so help me God.
> Josephine: Nonsense! You're not a witness. You're an attorney. It's your duty to lie, conceal and distort everything, and slander everybody.
> The Ragpicker: All right. I swear to lie, conceal and distort everything, and slander everybody.

Both trials, then, move steadily forward under the banner of prevarication to defeat the defendants.

The second obvious purpose in using trial scenes in these two plays, the dilution of guilt by making it impersonal, manifests itself in two distinctly different ways. Hans goes so far as to state that his complaint against Ondine holds true for all men:

> My complaint is the complaint of all mankind.
>
> Is it so much after all that God has granted us, these few yards of air between hell and heaven? Is it so attractive, after all, this bit of life we have, with these hands that get dirty, these teeth that fall out, this hair that turns gray? Why must these creatures trespass on our little world? Gentlemen, on the morning of my marriage, I claim the right to be left in peace in a world that is free of these intrusions, these threats, these seductions, alone with myself, with my bride, alone at last.

He wants to free himself of Ondine's ubiquity and sees the trial as a means of doing so. By letting the judges condemn her, he can, with a clear conscience, lead Bertha to the altar, ignorant, of course, of Ondine's pact with The Old One.

Josephine instigates the trial in *The Madwoman of Chaillot* and, in so doing, keeps consistently in character, for it is she who first brings up

the relationship between individual and group commitment. She views the murder of the world's criminals as highly impersonal: "The more there are, the more legal it is. It's impersonal. It's even military. It's the cardinal principle of battle—you get all your enemies in one place, and you kill them all together at one time." After introducing the idea of the trial, she goes on to assure the Countess that the trial, a mere formality, will not alter her plans: "Captain Dreyfus was not only innocent—he was defended by a marvelous orator. The result was precisely the same [guilty]. So you see, in having a trial, you run no risk whatever." The trial serves not to defend the millionaires of the world, but rather to get more persons to concur with the Countess. Without a trial, the consequence of action taken falls on only three individuals: Gabrielle, Josephine, and Aurelia. During the trial, Giraudoux's vagabonds move back onto the stage, providing an audience—a cross-section of downtrodden humanity—who agree, in unison, with the verdict of the court:

> Josephine: The trial is over.
> Countess: And the verdict?
> All: Guilty!
> Josephine: Guilty as charged.
> Countess: Then I have full authority to carry out the sentence?
> All: Yes!
> Countess: I can do what I like with them?
> All: Yes!
> Countess: I have the right to exterminate them?
> All: Yes!
> Josephine: Court adjourned!

When the criminals of the world descend into the bowels of the earth, one sees Aurelia acting not out of personal whim and prejudice, but as a servant of oppressed mankind. By sharing her guilt for the action, the audience also share her responsibility for seeing that conditions do not again degenerate so drastically.

The two points, a statement on the inequities of the trial system and the need for the dilution of guilt by making it collective, force other considerations within the plays. By showing the fatuity in the administration of the principles of the trial system, Giraudoux makes a statement about society as a whole. When the only non-violent means we have to defend ourselves fall prey to mendacity and absurdity, does it indicate the failure of our entire society, and not just its system of jurisprudence? In addition, does the collectivization of guilt make individual guilt any less intense? By looking at these two plays closely, we can answer these questions and, at the same time, see Giraudoux's third, less obvious, purpose: the destructive nature of the plays as exemplified in the trial scenes.

Certainly Hans does not succeed in his attempt to rid himself of the memory of Ondine. He goes mad soon after hearing the guilty verdict. The Old One (disguised as The Second Fisherman) attributes Hans's bizarre actions to his encountering of reality: "It's a way men have of escaping when they come up suddenly against a reality. They become what is called mad. All at once they are logical. They don't compromise. They don't marry the woman they don't love. They reason simply and clearly like the plants and the water. Like us." The trial brings not only Hans's death—because of Ondine's pact—but also the realization that he and she will never meet again: "We part for eternity, we go to different worlds. We must do this properly, Ondine. It is the first real farewell that has ever been said in this world."

His death, then, pays his debt to his actions. The trial precipitates his death, and his death brings about the destruction of relationships with Bertha and Ondine, as well as Ondine's disinvolvement with the human world. Giraudoux teaches no lesson, except perhaps that we are incapable of learning, incapable of understanding reality. Such a lesson affixes the destructive force of the play not on its characters, but on its audience.

The trial in *The Madwoman of Chaillot* gives Aurelia the verdict she wants and the consensus propriety demands. She sees the Presidents, Prospectors, and Press Agents as destructive creatures: "There are people in the world who want to destroy everything. They have the fever of destruction. Even when they pretend that they're building, it is only in order to destroy.... Humanity is now dedicated to the task of universal destruction." The trial expands their role somewhat when the Ragpicker, as defendant, states, "I am never guilty!... I am never quiet!... I am the law." When asked what he will do with the oil, he replies, "I propose to make war! I propose to conquer the world!" These propositions, together with the previous assertions, make these men not men at all, but the realistic aspirations of society. Money does the things the Ragpicker says it does: societies do wage war; they do try to conquer the world; they reject guilt; they are never quiet; they are, in fact, the law. Aurelia, then, marches all of society down into oblivion, not just the bad elements in it. She destroys society, not just evil society, with the prediction that her solution is less than final: "Only, the next time, don't wait until things begin

to look black. The minute you notice anything, tell me at once." At best, then, Giraudoux's Aurelia provides a respite from evil; she does not offer a lasting solution. Her means to attain this respite cast a dark shadow on the play as a whole.

To fight evil with evil, to counter destruction with destruction, to challenge murder with murder—these means to effect resolution, and we see resolution in both plays, become the victims of suicide, for they cannot perform their function without self-sacrifice.

Because of the destructive forces in *Ondine* and *The Madwoman of Chaillot*, forces made evident through the trial scenes, a liaison forms between the ideas of Giraudoux and those of Renato Poggioli. In his book *The Theory of the Avant-Garde*, Poggioli defines this form of action as nihilism: "The essence of nihilism lies in attaining non-action by acting, lies in destructive, not constructive, labor." Certainly, the Countess acts to attain non-action. She theorizes that if the evil men of the world no longer carry out their evil tasks, then conditions will improve. She achieves her goal through destructive, not constructive, labor.

Ondine poses more serious problems. Hans acts against Ondine "to be left in peace in a world that is free of these intrusions." The guilty verdict, a destructive force—"She shall have her throat cut without witnesses this day directly after sunset"—should free him to go to his non-active world. But Giraudoux does not free Hans so easily; rather, he makes the verdict against Ondine a verdict against Hans. The sadistic qualities of Hans's nihilistic effort expand rapidly into Poggioli's next stage of the avant-garde, agonism: "Agonism means tension.... In short, agonism means sacrifice and consecration: an hyperbolic passion, a bow bent toward the impossible, a paradoxical and positive form of spiritual defeatism." Agonism turns directed nihilism around to attack its progenitor. Poggioli continues, "So the agonistic tendency itself seems to represent the masochistic impulse in the avant-garde psychosis, just as the nihilistic seems to be the sadistic."

The Madwoman of Chaillot and *Ondine*, alike in their destructive natures, differ in the depths to which they fathom destruction. *The Madwoman of Chaillot*, a nihilistic play, never achieves the hyperbolic passion that *Ondine* does. The destructive forces never turn on the Countess as they do on Hans and Ondine.

The trial scenes in Giraudoux's two plays serve, then, to point up the inadequacies in our system of justice and, by extension, those in our society as a whole. They also serve to diffuse and dilute the guilt for the unavoidably guilty verdicts. Furthermore, the trial scenes nurture the growth of destruction and, in so doing, make the plays patently destructive in nature. As destructive plays, they possess characteristics inherent to Poggioli's concept of the nihilistic/agonistic stages of the avant-garde. The trials allow Giraudoux to expose the destructive forces of these two plays by legal means. By their very form, the trial scenes offer the audience credence and legality. They serve to reinforce the playwright's points and, by increasing the impact of Giraudoux's ideas, tend to make those ideas more catholic in intent and meaning.

Source: Mark C. Pilkinton, "The Significance of the Trial Scenes in *Ondine* and *The Madwoman of Chaillot*," in *Modern Drama*, Vol. 22, No. 2, June 1979, pp. 109–14.

Kappo Phelan

In the following review, Phelan admires the play but finds its translation into English choppy and lacking in rhythm.

All in all, I think it is just to say that a hopeless season has been saved by Alfred de Liagre's production of Jean Giraudoux's delightful Morality [*The Madwoman of Chaillot*]. It now remains to be seen whether the play itself can be saved for, and by, a *whole* audience; whether all those people whom Broadway no longer serves (has, in fact, never served), can somehow be reached and persuaded to attend. On the part of this column, I should like to convince both the old and the children, and even the merely grown-up, that here, at long last, is a sensible enchantment.

The story—mounted in wonderful soaring Christian Bérard settings, and lit with an accurate aqua-gold light—presents a large number of conflicting people. (It may be as well to explain here that *Chaillot* is a name for one of the most fashionable sections of Paris, and that Giraudoux's heroine is based on an authentic woman.) The Countess Aurelia, an ancient, ancient lady, inhabits a cellar below the Café Francis in the Place d'Alma. Here she lives, cherished by the small people of the district: her vagaries are protected, her visions are shared, and her goodness is returned by the Waiters, the Waitresses, the Peddlers, the Street Singers, the Flower Girls, the Entertainers, and the Ragpicker. When, however, she is at last confronted by the wickedness of the world, when she learns that a Prospector, a President, a Broker, and

a Director are planning to excavate the city in a search for oil to continue War, she feels forced to act. Summoning her sister Madwomen—of Passy, St. Sulpice, La Concorde—she holds a trial: a verdict is rendered, and by a simple ruse, and with the aid of the King of the Sewers, all of the Moneymen are skilfully introduced into her own secret sewer forever.

It is, unfortunately, impossible to describe all the charming details by which this fable is accomplished: the affair of the feather boa, the affair of the little dog, the affair of the Deaf Mute, the affair of President Wilson, the affair of Albert Bertaut. I imagine, for most sensitive people, it will be enough to say that this is a story of ultimate France. And of grace.

It is also unfortunate to have to admit that there are difficulties to be encountered in an American production. The first of these concerns translation. I have no doubt that Maurice Valency's adaptation is faithful to the words and to the spirit of the original. And certainly the spirit does shine through. But the problem is a technical one and has to do with *rhythm* rather than words. It is the same problem which has boxed every English translator of Pirandello from way back. These long speeches, which will flow in French or in Italian, simply do *not* flow in English; they jerk. And inevitably they are accompanied by jerking gesticulation. Mr. de Liagre has cast Martita Hunt—the fascinating British character-actress—in the lead, and it must be conceded that Miss Hunt's clipped enunciation adds even more unfamiliar staccato to the lines, and to her fellow-players' delivery. I think Mr. de Liagre's task was not to have sought a plain translator, but rather a librettist—a librettist of rhythms rather than notes, so that all could have been orchestrated correctly—actions and speeches—and the tempo of the whole varied and built toward the climax. That this process would involve considerable cutting and rearrangement is perfectly true. But I am convinced the result would thereby be paced in a manner more familiar and more dramatic to an American view.

For my part, the present arrangement is irresistible enough. The lovely Bérard costumes add as much point as does his set. There are entrancing musical interludes by Albert Hague and Alexander Haas. And (saving only the fact that they all appear too young), the Madwomen of Estelle Winwood, Nydia Westman, Doris Rich, and certainly Miss Hunt, are superb.

To conclude: this is necessarily, importantly, luckily, to be seen.

Source: Kappo Phelan, Review of *The Madwoman of Chaillot*, in *Commonweal*, Vol. 49, No. 14, January 14, 1949, pp. 351–52.

Harold Clurman

In the following review, Clurman admires the play itself, but finds that the staging lacks the lyricism of the original French production.

Paris went crazy over Giraudoux's *The Madwoman of Chaillot*, and so would I, were it not for the production given it at the Belasco Theatre. That made me mad. It was a case of love-hate at first sight.

In all fairness, however, it should be said that, regardless of its production, *The Madwoman of Chaillot* afforded me more pleasure than any other play produced this season. It is a little masterpiece, a model of what the theatre can still achieve in the way of poetic statement on contemporary material.

There are a number of approaches one might take to Giraudoux's gem. In another period, when the purely artistic or theatrical aspects of a play would in themselves suggest its total value, I should have been glad to confine my discussion of *The Madwoman* to its formal beauties. But today when a play is praised, it is usually spoken of as a delight, a hit, a thrill—terms that might just as appropriately be applied to a fashion show, a ball game or a ride on the shoot-the-chutes. For this reason I shall emphasize more than is customary, or perhaps even necessary, the meaning and sense of *The Madwoman.*

Balzac hated the bourgeoisie, because he was a royalist. His novels were at once an apocalyptic picture of the hell the bourgeoisie was in the process of creating and a testimony of the grandiose energy and magnificent scope that went into that creation. A romantic by temperament, Balzac was a realist in his art, because the hell he was describing was in fact a great new world being wrought before his very eyes, a world still destined to a long life. . . . Giraudoux, a witty impressionist and "realist" enough to serve as a minister in his country's government, wrote of the Paris of our day as a fantasist. For Giraudoux was a political conservative, and the conservative, who wants to see the ugliness of our times done away with, can only dream.

The Madwoman of Chaillot is the reverie of an honest, sensitive, wholly civilized Frenchman who at the end of his life (Giraudoux died in 1944) contemplates the world about him and sees that it is fast becoming a moral as well as a physical ruin. His alert eye and probing spirit tell him that the ideology of profit is the chief cause of the growing rottenness. He is a clever man, so he is amused, he is a good man, so he is saddened, he is a peaceful man, so he fancies, "If all the money-bags—the newly rich, the black marketeers, the sinister profiteers, the pimps of capital—were drowned in the sewers like rats . . . what then? Then the birds would sing again, love would flower, and Paris would once again become the poet's enchanted realm."

But who is to bring about this miracle? Not the government—which is merely the official face of the universal skulduggery; not the socialists, communists and anarchists, for they are either dry doctrinaires or indelicate fanatics. Who then? The old aristocrats, as indigent now and as lacking in standing as the disorganized proletariat of the streets. These aristocrats alone retain a sympathy for the adorable riff-raff of Paris—the ragpickers, the shoe-lace salesmen, the obsolete artists—who would be their natural allies in the annihilation of the filthy bourgeoisie. Giraudoux's play is a prank, a sophisticated Mother Goose tale. Yet, in spite of himself, Giraudoux is a revolutionary. For what his play ultimately says is: to be respectable in France even the conservatives must be revolutionary; and, if their conservatism prevents valid action, the least they can do is *wish*.

The Madwoman of Chaillot is iridescent with a fantasy that is compounded of sweet memories, ancient wisdom, a tradition that is still vibrant through the survival, amid the debris, of bright mental faculties and keen senses. "Paris is old, very old," says the Sewer-Man, and the romance of this play (like that of the Madwoman herself) is the romance of an old consciousness that seems derelict and grotesque in the linear and soulless new world of slot-machine efficiency. The young lovers have to learn the facts of life and take hope from the maxims of the mad.

Except for Christian Berard's sets (salvaged from the original production), which are on the creative level of the play itself, the current show is like a misguided reading of the script in the early stages of rehearsal. This does not mean that there are no gifted people at the Belasco, but acting talent in a play of this sort is only a first ingredient. It needs transformation into the lyric and modeled texture which the entire production should be.

I found James Westerfield, for example, well cast as the Sewer-Man; Estelle Winwood's mask and adeptness in the delivery of lines are excellent qualifications for the Madwoman of Passy, but her performance is still only a sketch. And while Martita Hunt in the title role is unquestionably an able actress, she plays it on the mistaken assumption (the director's or her own) that its essence lies in a picturesquely eccentric make-up and a stagily romantic "aristocracy," whereas it resides in the profound and almost gross earthiness of the woman's experience, its deep-delved decay. It is that decay which produces the character's and the play's wonderful glow.

Source: Harold Clurman, Review of *The Madwoman of Chaillot*, in *New Republic*, Vol. 120, No. 3, January 17, 1949, pp. 28–29.

SOURCES

Atkinson, Brooks, "Gallic Fantasy: Giraudoux's *The Madwoman of Chaillot* Brings Us a Civilized Mind," in *New York Times*, January 9, 1949, p. IX.

Brée, Germaine, "*The Madwoman of Chaillot*: A Modern Masque," in *Tulane Drama Review*, Vol. 3, No. 4, May 1959, p. 52.

Clurman, Harold, Review of *The Madwoman of Chaillot*, in *New Republic*, Vol. 120, No. 3, January 17, 1949, pp. 28–29; reprinted in *Drama Criticism*, edited by Thomas J. Schoenberg and Lawrence J. Trudeau, Vol. 36, Gale, Cengage Learning, 2010.

Cohen, Robert, "Some Political Implications of *The Madwoman of Chaillot*, in *Contemporary Literature*, Vol. 9, No. 2, Spring 1968, p. 211.

"Fortune 500," in *Fortune*, May 3, 2010, http://money.cnn.com/magazines/fortune/fortune500/2010/full_list/ (accessed July 22, 2010).

Gassner, John, *20 Best European Plays on the American Stage*, Crown, 1957.

Giraudoux, Jean, *The Madwoman of Chaillot*, translated and adapted by Maurice Valency, Dramatists Play Service, 1974.

"Jean Giraudoux," in *Internet Broadway Database*, http://www.ibdb.com/person.php?id = 6679 (accessed July 22, 2010).

Korzeniowska, Victoria B., *The Heroine as Social Redeemer in the Plays of Jean Giraudoux*, Peter Lang, 2001, p. 87.

LeSage, Laurent, *Jean Giraudoux: His Life and Works*, Pennsylvania State University Press, 1959, p. 106.

Phelan, Kappo, Review of *The Madwoman of Chaillot*, in *Commonweal*, Vol. 49, No. 14, January 14, 1949, pp. 351–52; reprinted in *Drama Criticism*, edited by Thomas J. Schoenberg and Lawrence J. Trudeau, Vol. 36, Gale, Cengage Learning, 2010.

Raymond, Agnes G., *Jean Giraudoux: The Theatre of Victory and Defeat*, University of Massachusetts Press, 1966, pp. 124, 127.

Reboussin, Marcel, "Giraudoux and *The Madwoman of Chaillot*," in *Educational Theatre Journal*, Vol. 13, No. 1, March 1961, pp. 11–17.

Review of *The Madwoman of Chaillot*, in *Newsweek*, January 10, 1949, p. 72; reprinted in *Drama Criticism*, edited by Thomas J. Schoenberg and Lawrence J. Trudeau, Vol. 36, Gale, Cengage Learning, 2010.

Reilly, John H., *Jean Giraudoux*, Twayne's World Author Series, No. 513, Twayne Publishers, 1978, pp. 15–25, 131–37.

Tardieu, Michel, *Manichaeism*, translated by M. B. DeBevoise, University of Illinois Press, 2009.

Wyatt, Euphemia Van Rensselaer, Review of *The Madwoman of Chaillot*, in *Catholic World*, February 1949, pp. 401–402; reprinted in *Drama Criticism*, edited by Thomas J. Schoenberg and Lawrence J. Trudeau, Vol. 36, Gale, Cengage Learning, 2010.

FURTHER READING

Bamber, Gascoigne, *Twentieth-Century Drama*, Hutchinson University Library, 1967.

This volume of literary criticism establishes a context for Giraudoux's work by studying him alongside eight of his contemporaries, including Luigi Pirandello, Bertolt Brecht, Jean-Paul Sartre, and Tennessee Williams.

Body, Jacques, *Jean Giraudoux: The Legend and the Secret*, translated by James Norwood, Fairleigh Dickinson University Press, 1991.

This is the most recent critical biography available in English and the one that delves most deeply into Giraudoux's political thought.

Lemaître, Georges, *Jean Giraudoux: The Writer and His Work*, Frederick Ungar, 1971.

Although somewhat dated, this volume is one of the most accessible introductions in English to Giraudoux's life and work, including solid analysis of the connections between the playwright's dramatic works and his essays and novels.

Spotts, Frederic, *The Shameful Peace: How French Artists and Intellectuals Survived the Nazi Occupation*, Yale University, 2008.

This book explores the period from 1940 to 1945, during which the Nazis occupied France and *The Madwoman of Chaillot* was written. Among other issues, Spotts looks at Hitler's plan to pacify the French through art.

SUGGESTED SEARCH TERMS

Madwoman of Chaillot

La Folle de Chaillot

Giraudoux AND madwoman

Giraudoux AND satire

Valency AND Chaillot

Giraudoux AND drama

Madwoman of Chaillot AND satire

Madwoman of Chaillot AND translation

Madwoman of Chaillot AND Broadway

The Miracle Worker

1962

By the time William Gibson's play *The Miracle Worker* was adapted to film in 1962 by director Arthur Penn, it had already been broadcast on television and then adapted as a long-running, acclaimed Broadway play, both also directed by Penn. Gibson, Penn, and Broadway producer Fred Coe did not trust the studio system to do justice by the play in adapting it to film, so they formed a new production company, Playfilm Productions, to keep control in their own hands.

The film is based on the true story of Helen Keller, who lost her ability to hear and see as an infant. Her family, at a loss over how to communicate with her, hired Annie Sullivan, a first-time teacher who had until recently been blind herself. The relationship between Helen and Annie was contentious and frequently violent, which the film captures with unblinking realism. The film's scenes of battle between the dedicated teacher and her uncomprehending student have become legendary. With Keller's skeptical family often working against her, Sullivan was able to a teach a girl who had been shut off from the outside world the value of communication. Keller graduated from Radcliffe College and became a writer and political activist known around the world.

Anne Bancroft, playing Sullivan, and Patty Duke, playing Keller, each won an Academy Award for her performance, reprising the roles they both played in the Broadway production. William Gibson was also nominated for his

adaptation of his own stage play. Arthur Penn was nominated but did not win for best director, but he became one of the most trusted and respected directors in Hollywood as a result of his work on this film.

PLOT SUMMARY

The Miracle Worker begins with Kate Keller backing away after putting her infant daughter into a crib. The child has been sick with acute congestion, but the doctor announces that she will be fine. As Captain Arthur Keller walks the doctor outside, Kate notices that the baby does not respond to her voice. Her horrified scream brings Captain Keller running, and he shouts and claps at the baby, but receives no response.

While the opening credits roll, the camera shows Helen Keller, now seven years old, stumbling to walk down a staircase, responding to the sensory input she can feel, such as the wind or a smooth glass ornament, which she then drops and breaks. After the credits end, there is immediate danger as Helen, with scissors in hand, wrestles with Martha, one of the servant children. This scene is shown in full in the play, with dialogue from Martha and her brother Percy, but in the film, the scene cuts immediately to the Keller family being summoned. A discussion ensues about what to do about the growing trouble Helen has become. Reluctantly, Captain Keller agrees to write to the Perkins Institution for the Blind in Boston and request a governess. James, the Captain's grown son from his first marriage, supports having Helen put in an asylum.

In Boston, Mr. Anagnos, Annie Sullivan's boss at the Perkins Institution, goes onto the train to see her off. He warns her to not be so proud that she will cause trouble, and then he gives her a gift, a ring, showing that she is loved in spite of her hardheadedness. As the train pulls away, the blind children from the school, gathered on the platform, wave goodbye. During the long train ride, Annie has flashbacks about her brother Jimmy, who was lame, and the time they were put into the charity orphanage.

Days later, she is met at the station in Tuscumbia, Alabama, by James Keller, and the two establish an argumentative relationship. At the house, Helen gets to know Annie by first feeling and then sniffing her fingertips. Nonverbally,

Annie tells her to take her suitcase upstairs, but when she tries to help the child carry it, Helen hits her. Annie is pleased with her spirit. Inside, she allows Helen to wear her hat and glasses and to unpack her suitcase. When Helen finds a doll that the children from the school sent for her as a present (a fact explained in the play but not the film), Annie tries to teach her to spell the word "doll" in sign language. James, passing the door, sarcastically expresses doubt that Helen can be taught.

Annie takes the doll away from Helen to give her an incentive to learn to spell, but Helen is resistant, keeping her hand clenched in a fist. She does spell the word, but when Annie gives her the doll she hits her in the face with it, knocking out a tooth, and runs away. She slams the door and locks Annie in the room. Annie calls for help from the window, and a great ruckus follows as James gets a ladder and Captain Keller climbs up to the window to carry Annie down, while neighbors and servants gather around to watch. Later, Annie sees Helen take the room key, which they had assumed she had lost, out of her mouth. She is delighted with the girl's cleverness, appreciating the challenge, as Helen drops the key down the well.

Later, Annie tries to teach Helen to write "bad girl" and "good girl" by having the girl feel her face as she frowns and then smiles, and Helen repeats her gestures. Just when Helen seems to understand how she should behave, she throws a vase to the floor, smashing it. Kate Keller enters and is intrigued with the sign language Annie is teaching her daughter. Kate agrees to help Annie teach Helen.

At breakfast, Annie is upset to see that Helen is allowed to wander around the table and eat from everyone's plates. Helen is upset when Annie will not let her eat from hers. They struggle, and when the family supports giving Helen whatever she wants in order to keep the peace, Annie asks them all to leave the room. What follows is nine minutes of mostly wordless battle between pupil and teacher. Helen acts out in any way possible, kicking her feet and smashing whatever she can get her hands on, while Annie fights for order, putting her into her chair and refusing to give her any food until she eats with her spoon. Helen throws food across the room and runs from the table, over the table and under the table. Each time, Annie strains to drag Helen back to her place, puts her food back on her

FILM TECHNIQUE

Double Exposure

Films usually capture one image at a time. Film technicians can, however, expose the same piece of film to a second image, which will appear in front of the first image, giving it a ghostly look. The effect is often used to link two visual ideas together. In *The Miracle Worker*, Penn uses this technique to imply flashbacks that are occurring in Annie Sullivan's head, called up by things that remind her of her traumatic childhood. Events from her past are superimposed over the image of how she looks now, creating the impression of past and present existing together. Penn also sometimes uses double exposures for overlapping when going from scene to scene, instead of fading out of the first scene before beginning the next.

Montage

A montage is a sequence of film images strung together to compress the passage of time. It was popularized in the early days of filmmaking by Russian director Sergei Eisenstein, who sought to expand on the conventions of film. By the time *The Miracle Worker* was released, audiences were familiar with the idea that a series of shots, each one showing a character with only slight changes, is meant to imply that much more has happened than the film shows. Penn uses this technique during Annie Sullivan's train ride from Massachusetts to Alabama to indicate her long, arduous ride without detracting too much from the film's main story, which begins in the Keller house. He also uses montage to imply how the two weeks when Helen and Annie spent alone together went by, showing such scenes as washing Helen's hair, touching a bird, and wading in a stream, all tied together with the general concept of Annie's

eagerness to make Helen understand that everything has a name.

Film Grain

While living in the boathouse with Helen, Annie has a traumatic dream about herself; she sees herself running down a hall and stepping into a room where a shrouded body is laid out on a table. There is no indication of whether this is an actual memory or just a dream. Penn has photographed this scene with a grainy texture, which makes it look unreal. That might be an indication of the way that the world seemed to Annie at that time, before her eyesight had been corrected, or it might be his way of showing that the entire event is fabricated in her imagination. The grainy photography helps the film blur the line between, on the one hand, the terrible, surreal experiences of living in the charity house and losing her brother and, on the other hand, the experience of being blind. It shows viewers that Annie's past is shrouded in uncertainty.

Voice-over

Besides remembering her childhood with unclear visual images, Annie frequently hears voices echoing her past. This technique is carried over from the stage version of the story, which presented her brother Jimmy's voice intermittently. On stage, the voice-over is efficient because it does not require new actors to appear before the audience, which could be confusing: audiences can tell that a sound to which only one person responds exists only in that one character's head. In the film, Penn uses the voices of Annie's past to distract her from her immediate surroundings when she is with people, and he uses them to take her into visual memories when she is alone.

---

plate, and sets it in front of her. When they finally emerge into the yard, Annie is able to report to Kate that Helen ate from her own plate and folded her own napkin. The maid announces that dinner will be served soon.

Back in her room, reading a report from the Perkins Institution, Annie remembers her brother Jimmy, recalling fleeting images of the terrible conditions they faced as children in the asylum. The report reminds her of the important

© *United Archives GmbH | Alamy*

connection between the body and the spirit when teaching the visually impaired. She leaves the house and runs to the boathouse on the Keller property.

That night, Captain Keller rages to his wife about Annie's methods, but Kate recognizes the importance of Helen folding her napkin. Annie arrives and says that she will continue to work with Helen only if she is given complete control of the child. Kate recalls how, before being stricken blind and deaf at nineteen months, Helen showed her intelligence by speaking the word "wah wah," meaning "water." They arrange to move Helen into the boathouse without telling her where they are going, to make her dependent solely on Annie. Captain Keller will only agree to allow this arrangement for two weeks.

Helen understands that she has been left alone with Annie, and she has a tantrum until she finds her doll. Annie again dreams of her young life, and she sees herself, a young blind girl, working her

way into the room where her brother Jimmy's lifeless body was laid out. She wakes shouting Jimmy's name, to find James Keller at the boathouse window. He talks to her about the futility of her task and tells her to consider having pity on Helen, but Annie does not see it as pity to leave Helen alone. "I will touch you," she says to the sleeping child. She calls the servant who was left with them, Percy, to spell to Helen in sign language, because the girl refuses to learn from Annie. Annie rewards Percy with cake and milk until Helen joins them.

In the next two weeks, Annie and Helen struggle against one another and learn to bond with each other. Helen becomes used to clean clothes and clean hair. Annie spells to her constantly, but Helen does not pick up the concept of language. At the end of their time together, the Kellers see an improvement in their daughter's hygiene, but they refuse to extend the time Annie has Helen to herself. Annie considers herself a failure.

Back at the Keller house, Annie is appalled to see Helen resorting to her old spoiled ways, throwing her napkin on the floor. When Annie tries to correct her, the Kellers intervene, feeling that Helen should be spoiled on the day of her return. Annie recognized her bad behavior as a test. When Helen splashes the water pitcher into Annie's face, Annie takes her out to the pump to make her refill it.

As water drips onto Helen's hand from the pump, her face shows the dawning of recognition. Suddenly, she understands that the word "water," which Annie has just spelled to her, represents the substance touching her. She says "wah wah," remembering the sound she made as an infant. After spelling the word into Annie's hand and finding that it is correct, Helen stumbles about, grabbing things and putting her hand out for Annie to give her the name of each. When she calms down, she asks about Annie herself, and is given the word "teacher." She finds the door keys in her mother's pocket and gives them to Annie.

That night, Annie sits on the porch by herself in the dark. Helen comes out and finds her. She kisses Annie on the cheek and nestles into her lap, and Annie spells the words "I love Helen" into her hand. The camera fades back, and the screen dims to black.

CHARACTERS

Mr. Anagnos
Mr. Anagnos, played by Jack Hollander, is Annie Sullivan's superior at the Perkins Institution for the Blind. When he puts her on the train to send her off from Boston to Tuscumbia, he implores her to control her temper and be humble. He is very fond of Annie, and he gives her a ring, presumably from all of the students at the Institution.

Aunt Ev
Aunt Ev, played by Kathleen Comegys, is a long-term visitor in the Keller household, though her relationship to the family is never explained. She is a southern woman who usually agrees with Colonel Keller's chivalrous, sexist worldview. The one notable exception is when she suggests applying to the Perkins Institution for help when Captain Keller is considering putting Helen into an asylum. Aunt Ev's interjection brings Annie Sullivan to the Keller home.

Captain Arthur Keller
Captain Keller is played by Victor Jory. He is a newspaper editor and a former Confederate army officer who has strong opinions about politics and about the roles of women. Helen is his daughter from his second marriage, to Kate. He also has a grown son, James, from his first marriage.

Captain Keller is constantly exasperated with Annie Sullivan. He initially opposes hiring a governess but gives in under his wife's insistence. When he meets Annie, he is disappointed to find out how young she is, and he is enraged that she has never taught before. After she spends a day fighting with Helen to get the child to fold her napkin, Captain Keller wants to fire her, but he agrees to give her a chance to work exclusively with Helen.

Though Captain Keller opposes Annie's plans for Helen, it is clear that he does so because he loves his child. After the two-week isolation in the boat house, Annie feels that she has been a failure, but the Captain looks at the improvements Helen has made and expresses his wish that Annie will stay with them for a long time. He and Annie have an earnest discussion, during which they find that they both have a shared desire to see Helen's life improve.

Helen Keller
Patty Duke played the role of Helen Keller to great acclaim on Broadway, and she won an Academy Award for Best Supporting Actress for her portrayal in this film. She was sixteen when the film was released, though Helen was seven when Annie Sullivan came to live with the Keller family.

In the film, Helen is a girl who lives among her loving family, but because she has been deprived of sight and hearing since infancy, she has little understanding of the world around her. She knows her family members as she knows much about the world, by smell and touch. She reaches out to her mother and father for comfort when upset. When her family members are not around, she panics.

Annie Sullivan arrives to be her governess and suspects that Helen is not as helpless as she pretends to be. She watches Helen cleverly hide a key in her mouth and then, after feeling around to determine that no one can observe her, drop the key down the well. Knowing that Helen is smart and capable, Annie calls her "spoiled" and "a tyrant." Her assumption is borne out in the dining room scene, during which Helen stubbornly fights Annie, throwing spoons and spitting food just because she is a petulant child who does not want to be given orders.

Helen's realization at the climax of the movie is that the letters Annie has spelled into her hand for the word "water" represent the fluid flowing from the pump. It is a realization that the real Helen Keller would later write about as a turning point in her life: understanding language, she was able to go on to control her world instead of being continually frightened by it. The film, and the play it was based on, have her saying the baby word "wah wah" that she learned before falling ill as a toddler, though this is just an external projection to show audiences what is going on in the child's mind at that crucial moment.

James Keller

James, or Jimmy, Keller is played by Andrew Prine. He is Colonel Keller's son by a previous marriage. Not much younger than the Colonel's new wife, James, in his twenties, is having trouble living up to the expectations of his strong-willed father. James and his father argue about politics at the dinner table, and his father barks out orders to him, often contradicting himself. As a result, James has cultivated an air of bemusement about the occurrences in the house.

James develops a peculiar bond with Annie Sullivan from the very first time he meets her at the train station. When she hears his name, she pauses with interest, finding it strange that Helen has a brother named James, just as she once did. He doubts that she can have any success teaching Helen to spell, and he tells her so, creating a tension between them. There is a flirtatious quality to their relationship, too, which becomes apparent when, speaking to her through the window of the boathouse, he compliments her, but he then makes her self-consciousness by saying that her eyes are what keeps her from being good-looking.

At the end, James drops his glib attitude and becomes serious in defying his father, directly telling him that he thinks Annie is doing the right thing for Helen. Gibson's stage play includes some dialogue about how James has felt forgotten by his father since the death of his mother. Even without this psychological background, the movie shows the breakthrough he feels in standing up to his father and speaking seriously for once.

Kate Keller

Kate is the second wife of Captain Keller and the mother of Helen. She is played in the film by Inga Swenson. Helen's strongest bond is with her mother, to whom she constantly reaches out, especially in times of distress.

When Annie Sullivan arrives at the house and begins teaching Helen sign language, Kate is the only one in the household to approve of her methods. She asks Annie to teach her sign language as well, hoping that she might be able to communicate with her child some day. It pains her to see Annie deprive Helen of things, and she worries about the battles that go on between teacher and student, but Kate is patient enough to trust Annie to do the right thing. Her patience is rewarded when she hears that Helen has folded her own napkin after the meal, although she is the only one among the Kellers to understand the groundbreaking significance of this.

Though she is hopeful enough to agree with Annie's methods, Kate also worries about her daughter and misses her when she is gone. When Captain Keller puts a two-week limit on Annie's time with Helen, Kate agrees. The film shows her giving in to her own interests at this point: she wants the best for her child, but she also wants her child near her. This idea is made clearer when Kate visits the boathouse where Annie and Helen are living and asks if she can take Helen out for a walk, which she knows would violate Annie's stated plan for education. Kate is conflicted, torn between what her mind knows is best and her love for her daughter.

Mildred Keller

Mildred is the baby child of the Kellers. She is not referred to by name in the film, though she is in the stage play. When Helen stumbles across her crib, knocking Mildred to the floor, the Kellers consider putting her into an asylum for the baby's safety.

Percy

Percy is the son of Viney, the Kellers' maid. He seldom speaks in the film, though the stage play had an early scene in which Percy and his sister Martha played with Helen until she turned violent. The same scene occurs in the film, without words. When Annie moves into the boathouse with Helen, they take along Percy, who sleeps in the next room. Annie wakes him from a sound sleep, to use him to communicate with Helen after the girl refuses to have anything to do with her teacher.

Annie Sullivan

Anne Bancroft won the Academy Award for Best Actress in a Leading Role for her portrayal of Annie Sullivan, having previously won the Tony Award for Best Actress in the Broadway stage version.

Viewers learn early on that Annie is a hard-headed young woman, when Mr. Anagnos, seeing her off on a train, advises her to be humble and patient. As the story develops, her difficult life comes into perspective, as she describes for the Kellers the horrors that she and her brother suffered at the charity house where they were raised, where disease and sexual predators were rampant. Because of her own difficult life as a blind child, she understands that Helen is capable of much more than her family expects of her.

The position as Helen's governess is Annie's first job and her first foray out into the open world. She is also new to sight: it is only with the most recent of many operations on her eyes that she is able to see. Though she is clearly out of her element in many ways, she has enough self-assurance to insist on organizing Helen's education in the way she sees fit, mostly in accordance with principles she learned at the Perkins Institution. She seems to the Kellers to be heartless in her treatment of Helen, but her lack of pity for the blind child is what enables Helen to grow.

Annie is haunted by memories of the past. She and her brother Jimmy were orphaned at approximately the same age that Helen is now. When she hears that Helen's brother is also named Jimmy, she pauses. The film shows her relationship with her brother graphically, with spectral images that float around in her imagination and echoing voices from her memory. The hardships that she cannot forget motivate Annie to work all the harder, so that Helen will not have to experience the horrors she has known.

Jimmy Sullivan

Jimmy is Annie Sullivan's dead brother. They were orphans, and lived in the charity home together as each other's only support. Annie was blind and Jimmy was lame. In Gibson's stage play, Jimmy is implied only by voices from offstage. The film shows Jimmy in flashback, indirectly, to indicate that he exists only in the memory of his visually impaired sister.

Viney

Viney is an African American maid in the Keller house. Her role in the film is so small that Beah Richards, who plays her, was not credited onscreen.

THEMES

Teacher-Student Relationship

A central theme of this story concerns the way that Annie Sullivan establishes a useful working relationship with her student. She arrives with enthusiasm to begin their working relationship, disappointed that Helen is not at the station when James meets her train. At the house, she lets Helen unpack her suitcase and try on her glasses and hat, watching her movements to assess the best course of action. Even after she has been locked in her room, Annie still looks at Helen with wonder, not anger, admiring the intelligence that the family members do not recognize.

The prolonged battle in the dining room is extreme, but it shows Annie's struggle to establish a working teacher-student relationship. This relationship is more physical than most, but that is because Helen's blindness and deafness limit the ways Annie has to teach her. She works to make Helen eat from her plate and fold her own napkin in order to establish a sense of order and respect in her student, so that Helen will pay attention to her and learn from her. Later, when her work is undone and Helen continually throws her napkin to the floor, she determines that they must be isolated together, so that Helen will learn that she has no choice but to listen to what her teacher says. This teaching technique works; in the end, Helen finally grasps the concept of language—the first step in a lifetime of education to come.

Family Relationships

The success that Helen Keller is able to achieve in this film is to some great extent due to the family surrounding her. The Kellers have arranged their family life around their neediest member. This is shown in the early scene when Percy, playing with Helen and his sister, knows to run and ring the bell on the porch when Helen unknowingly becomes dangerous. He has apparently been in similar situations before, and the family has created a system to work with it. Soon, she stumbles into the crib, and the family realizes how she might be a danger to the infant child. They discuss putting Helen in

READ, WATCH, WRITE

- Before there was Keller there was Laura Bridgman. Born fifty years before the events of this film, Bridgman became the first deaf and blind American to learn language. Read *The Imprisoned Guest: Samuel Howe and Laura Bridgman, The Original Deaf-Blind Girl* about Bridgman's relationship with Howe, then director of the Perkins Institution for the Blind, or research other Internet and print sources about their relationship. Create a chart that shows ways in which Bridgman's life was similar to Keller's and ways in which it was different.

- Alexander Graham Bell's relationship with Helen Keller arose from the interest that Bell, the inventor of the telephone, took in working with the hearing impaired. Research a device that is expected to be able to help the deaf or the blind in the near future, and prepare a display for your class that will explain the science of how it works.

- Talk to a teacher of special education who has not seen *The Miracle Worker*. Show them the nine-minute-long dining room scene in which Helen and Annie grapple over eating with a spoon. Ask them to comment on Annie's methods, pointing out what she does right and what she does wrong, and why. Show the scene to your class with explanations based on this interview with the teacher.

- The 2009 Home Box Office film *Temple Grandin* has the tagline: "Her gift to the world was being different." This movie gives a visual interpretation of what the world might look like to this gifted autistic thinker. Watch the film and, following its style, create a brief film or audio track that you think portrays what Keller saw or heard before working with Sullivan and then another showing how she had changed. Show it to your class and discuss the differences.

- Sarah Miller's 2007 book *Miss Spitfire*, written for young adults, tells the story of how Sullivan came to work with Keller from Sullivan's point of view. Read the book and compare its version of Sullivan to Anne Bancroft's portrayal. Gather scenes from recent movies that show actresses you think would be good in the role of Sullivan and explain what aspect of Sullivan each clip shows.

- Read Gibson's sequel, *Monday after the Miracle*, written in 1982 and published by Dramatists Play Service. This play closed almost immediately after it opened. Compare it with this film and write a review that explains why audiences rejected the sequel.

- Ask a large number of nonimpaired people, twenty-five or thirty, whether they think life would be more difficult being deaf or blind. Graph their answers, and create a presentation explaining what you learned about current attitudes toward disability. Use visual or audio aids in giving your presentation.

an asylum, which was one of the few ways of coping with people with special needs in the 1880s, but the family decides, at Aunt Ev's urging, to contact the Perkins Institution.

As the film progresses, the audience learns that it has been common for the Kellers to allow Helen to walk around the dinner table eating from their plates, because they feel that it would be cruel to her to deny her what she wants. Although Annie thinks they are spoiling her, the other family members see their permissiveness as giving Helen whatever little comfort they can.

When Annie moves Helen into the boathouse with her, the film shows how much the Kellers love the girl. Individually, Captain Keller, Kate, and James stop by to see her. Kate and the Captain miss Helen so much that they are unwilling to extend the experiment in the boathouse beyond two weeks, because they miss her and want her back with them.

Southern United States

The film mentions it only a few times, but the culture clash between the Kellers, living in Alabama, and Annie Sullivan, who came to them from Boston, is a significant part of this film's story. Annie is an independent woman with her own ideas, coming into an environment where women are valued as homemakers but not as independent thinkers. This is presented in the early scene in which Captain Keller, who was in the Confederate Army twenty years earlier and is still referred to by his military rank, insists on carrying Annie down the ladder. He is following a code of chivalry that was common before the war in the antebellum South.

Captain Keller's Southern heritage is expressed as a slightly sexist perspective that affects the events of the film. He is constantly frustrated with Annie because he expects her to be more demure and obedient, like Southern women. Audiences know from the warnings Mr. Anagnos gives her that

Annie is outspoken, but the film, along with Gibson's stage play, uses the culture clash between Southern and Northern views of men and women to magnify the personality clash between Annie and Captain Keller.

STYLE

Musical Theme

Late in the film, when she is living in the boathouse with Helen and feeling lonely, Annie picks up the baby doll that the children from the Perkins Institution sent with her. Rocking in a chair with the doll in her arms, she sings the traditional folk song "Hush, Little Baby," sometimes also referred to as "Mockingbird." The film continues to play her singing while showing Helen's parents, Kate and Arthur, at different places in the night, each looking forlorn. The song's lyrics concern gifts that a mother promises to give to her child. At the end of the film, when Helen has learned the significance of language, she comes to Annie and kisses her, and the soundtrack plays the song again. The film uses the song to draw attention to the gift that Annie has given to Helen.

Contrast

In most, though not all, of the scenes in which they appear together, Annie is wearing dark clothes and Helen is wearing clothes that are a few shades lighter. Much of Annie's costuming matches Anne Bancroft's dark hair and the dark glasses that her visually impaired character wears, while the costumes that Patty Duke, as Helen, wears are as light as her hair or lighter.

This visual scheme has nothing to do with the cliché about good characters wearing white and bad characters wearing black. It is simply a way of keeping the characters distinct from each other in a black-and-white film with much physical interaction. Audiences can tell Sullivan from Helen clearly as they move about the screen and can distinguish one character from the other even as they spend most of the film connected to each other by the hands.

CULTURAL CONTEXT

The fact that the Keller family has to send away to the Perkins Institution for the Blind in Boston for a tutor for Helen is consistent with the educational practices of the 1880s. At the time, the idea of education for people with special needs was relatively new and not very widespread, with most of the schools in America concentrated in the industrialized North.

Throughout most of history, people with vision or hearing problems were treated as a burden on society. It was not until the 1700s that education theorists began to promote the idea that people with physical disabilities could be taught, using methods that would be specific to their needs. Schools for the hearing impaired began in Europe: Braidwood's Academy for the Deaf and Dumb opened in Edinburgh, Scotland, in 1769, and the Royal Institution for Deaf Mutes in Paris, France, was established by Charles-Michel de l'Épée around the same time. In 1784, Valintin de Haüy began the National Institution for Young Blind Children in Paris. These schools were started by men who had worked with the

poor and had come to believe, in keeping with the general beliefs of the Enlightenment, that education could be the answer to the misery they encountered.

The United States lagged behind the European model by almost fifty years. The grandson of Thomas Braidwood tried to bring the methods that had been successful for him in Great Britain to North America, opening Braidwood's Academy in Virginia in 1812, but he could not maintain funding, and the school closed four years later. Schools for the deaf in New York and Pennsylvania, opened in 1818 and 1820, were more successful, with the New York school lasting more than a hundred years and the Pennsylvania School for the Deaf surviving to this day. The first school for the blind in America was the Perkins Institution, begun by Samuel Gridley Howe in 1829, based on the methods Haüy was using in Paris. It was followed soon by the New York Institute for the Blind, opened by Samuel Wood, Samuel Akerly, and John Dennison Russ in 1831.

Throughout the nineteenth century, support for education of the disabled grew along with faith in public education. Horace Mann, a Massachusetts legislator, made significant changes to the way education was viewed when he was appointed secretary of that state's board of education in 1837, pushing for government-provided education for all children, regardless of social class or religion. His ideas grew throughout the middle of the century with the growth of urbanization. As the Industrial Revolution took hold and factories brought families to cities looking for work, thousands upon thousands of children were left untended on the streets. Those who agreed with Mann's ideas about public education found growing support. The idea that deaf and blind children could be taught followed behind the idea of universal education, but the same moral justification moved it along.

In the rural South, the education movement did not capture the public imagination as powerfully as it did in the cities of the North. Most of the South was still agricultural. Children could be productive participants on farms, though the rising union movement in the cities fought to keep children from the dangers of working in factories. Farm children were less geographically concentrated, making the problem of education less urgent in rural areas. In the 1880s, when this story takes place, education was just becoming a

© *INTERFOTO | Alamy*

priority in the Kellers' home of Alabama, as it had become in the more populous northern states before the Civil War.

CRITICAL OVERVIEW

William Gibson's *The Miracle Worker* was originally broadcast on television in 1957, as a part of the CBS *Playhouse 90* anthology series. That production was directed by Arthur Penn and starred Teresa Wright, Patty McCormack, Burl Ives, and John Drew Barrymore. The show was a critical success, inspiring Gibson and Penn to work with Fred Coe, their producer, to bring the show to Broadway in 1959. The Broadway production, starring Anne Bancroft and Patty Duke, won critical praise and Tony awards for Best Play, Best Director (Penn), Best Actress (Bancroft), and Best Stage Technician (John Walters). It ran for 719 performances, with Suzanne Pleshette eventually

replacing Bancroft, and has been revived frequently in the ensuing fifty years.

Most critics were impressed with the way Gibson adapted Keller's story, explained in her autobiography, to the stage, though there were some dissenters. Claudia Cassidy, reviewing the traveling production for the *Chicago Tribune* when the show was in Chicago, blamed Gibson for a "flimsy" play loaded with "soap opera inventions" and claimed that he "cluttered the stage with stock characters, stock situations, and bad—well, let's be charitable and say frustrated—actors." The play was redeemed only, in Cassidy's view, by the biographical truth of Keller's life story.

The film version in 1962 was considered one of the year's most important releases. Bosley Crowther, writing in the *New York Times*, could hardly contain his enthusiasm as he wrote about "the absolutely tremendous and unforgettable display of physically powerful acting that Anne Bancroft and Patty Duke put on in William Gibson's stage play," which he declares, with awed admiration, made the translation to the screen. *Time* magazine, which had earlier published a cover story on the Broadway production, took a kind look at the parts Gibson created to make Keller's story come alive: "The pure drama at the center is enough to hold fast any audience capable of seeing and hearing," the *Time* critic wrote, "but writer Gibson nervously includes some fabricated tensions and artificial dramaturgy." The review praises Gibson for holding back the urge to include in the play any reference to Keller's future successes, and it determines that "Patty Duke is not so much Helen Keller in 1887 as language itself in an undiscovered state a hundred centuries ago." Forty-four years later, *Time*'s Richard Corliss included *The Miracle Worker* in an article titled "Seven Greatest Plays on Film." "It could be a soppy homily," Corliss wrote, noting the ways the film could have gone wrong, but instead found that Gibson "was true to the crusading ferocity of Helen's teacher." He concludes that "Arthur Penn's 1962 film captures this tutorial tug of wills in all its passion, defiance and tenderness."

Although many critics focused on the story that Gibson and Penn had to work with, a contributor to *Variety* took the time to recognize the film's other aspects, writing that "where the picture really excels, outside of its inherent story values, is in the realm of photographic technique." This review made readers aware of the ways Penn and his cameraman, Ernest Caparros, "have teamed to create artful, indelible strokes of visual storytelling and mood-molding. The measured dissolves, focal shifts and lighting and filtering enrich the production considerably." Over the years, as Penn's fame rose with films such as *Bonnie and Clyde* and *Little Big Man*, critics continued to look back on *The Miracle Worker* as a great start to a great career.

CRITICISM

David Kelly

Kelly is a college instructor in creative writing and literature. In the following essay, he examines the significance of the character of Helen's half-brother James in The Miracle Worker.

Andrew Prine's portrayal of James, Helen Keller's half-brother by her father's previous marriage, is one aspect of the film version of *The Miracle Worker* that seems lighter and less

> IF HELEN'S EDUCATION IS THE FILM'S A STORY, AND SULLIVAN'S MATURATION AS A FIRST-TIME TEACHER IS THE B STORY, THEN JAMES'S OEDIPAL RELATIONSHIP WITH HIS FATHER, COMPLETE WITH A STEPMOTHER YOUNG ENOUGH TO BE HIS OWN WIFE, SERVES AS A COMPLETE C STORY."

substantial than the rest of this award-heavy film. The movie is filled with serious issues, from Annie Sullivan's desperation to break through Helen's isolation to Sullivan's own need to come to grips with her horrifying childhood, to her struggle as a previously blind girl, dropped into a hostile culture hundreds of miles from the only life she has ever known. In the middle of this is Prine's James Keller, who stands on the side ready with smirks and sarcastic remarks. It is not a compelling performance, a fact made all the more conspicuous by being wedged between the Oscar-caliber performances of Patty Duke and Anne Bancroft; still, the film could never have been as successful if James had been left out.

James enters the film in a smiling, flirtatious way that makes him seem a possible romantic interest for Sullivan as she arrives in her new home. He jokes with her while picking her up at the railway station and offers to carry her suitcase. In the spirit of romantic comedies throughout the history of films, Sullivan wrests her bag away from him to show that she is his equal. They are well-matched in age, attractiveness, intelligence, and temperament. A few scenes later, though, any attraction between them becomes secondary to James's sarcasm. He scoffs at her teaching technique while she gives Helen her first taste of sign language. Sullivan is a teacher, but James feels free to interject his own theories about his half-sister's cognitive abilities. It is an unappealing moment that drops him from the status of romantic lead to buffoon in the audience's eyes. If there is anything less pleasant than watching someone underestimate a film's struggling hero, it is watching that person do so with a self-satisfied smirk.

WHAT DO I SEE NEXT?

- Patty Duke, who played young Helen Keller in *The Miracle Worker*, played Annie Sullivan in a remake for television seventeen years later. Duke won an Emmy Award for her performance. The film, directed by Paul Aaron, costars Melissa Gilbert as Helen. The 1979 film is available on DVD from Shout Factory, released in 2009.

- A more recent remake of *The Miracle Worker* was made for television and released by Disney Studios in 2000. Starring Hallie Kate Eisenberg, Alison Elliott, David Strathairn, and Lucas Black, this version credits Monte Merrick as well as Gibson for the script. It is available on DVD from Disney.

- The documentary *Unconquered: Helen Keller in Her Story* won the Academy Award for Best Documentary of 1955. Narrated by actress Katherine Cornwall, the film shows Keller, then in her seventies, going about a typical day in her life, and includes footage of her interacting with some of the famous people she has knows. This short film was released by Nobility Studios in 2009 on a DVD that also includes the film *Visions in Silent Darkness*, a more recent documentary about Keller.

- Director Sanjay Leela Bhansali's acclaimed 2005 film *Black* won Popular awards from the International Indian Film Academy for Best Picture, Best Director and Best Story. The film takes place in Simla, India, and mirrors the story of Helen Keller: a child born deaf and blind is on the verge of being admitted to an asylum before a talented young teacher arrives to introduce her to the concept of communication. The film stars Amitabh Bachchan and Rani Mukherjee. It is available on DVD with English subtitles from Yash Raj Films Home Entertainment.

- Of the many films made about characters with physical difficulties, one of the most acclaimed is the 1986 love story *Children of a Lesser God*, adapted by Mark Medoff from his stage play. One reason this film maintains its air of authenticity is that its lead, newcomer Marlee Matlin, who won the Oscar for Best Actress, is also deaf. The film also stars William Hurt and Piper Laurie. It was released on DVD by Paramount.

- The southern setting and the black-and-white photography link this film with another classic 1962 release, Robert Mulligan's *To Kill A Mockingbird*. This film tells a story of a single father, a lawyer who struggles to teach his children good values while racial turmoil ignites their small town. A special Collector's Edition was released in 1998 by Universal.

- The Who's rock opera *Tommy* is remembered for its songs by Pete Townshend and the visual stylings of acclaimed director Ken Russell, but the central plotline follows a pop-art version of Helen Keller's story: a child who is deaf, mute, and blind, shut off from the outside world, finds solace as a pinball phenomenon. The film, starring Who member Roger Daltrey along with a cast of notable 1970s rock stars, was released in 1975 and is available on DVD from Sony Pictures.

It is not until late in the film that James stands up for Sullivan's way of interacting with Helen. While he stands around on the periphery of the story, his attitude shifts from "it won't work" to "I have said all along that this is what we should do." His early flirtation becomes more solid, too. Standing outside her window on a moonlit night, he tells her, with his cocky bearing, that she would be a "handsome girl" if not for her eyes. These last few words make Sullivan turn away, self-conscious, and retaliate with a comment about his poor manners, bringing any idea of a romance between them to a close.

James Keller's relationship with Annie Sullivan is never made clear in the film. He does not become the companion that her brother once was, and he does not become a lover. Still, his presence helps define her, and given that she is the film's protagonist, that is exactly what he ought to be doing. Sullivan shows up at the Kellers' house under a cloud of suspicion from Helen's father. He does not trust her because of her youth and inexperience, but that fact is tempered by the audience's recognition that he has no faith in his own son, either, for the same reasons. Captain Keller is impatient with Sullivan because of her outspokenness, but then, he also silences James at every occasion, even when they agree. James is the skeptic whose questions about Sullivan's methods give the audience good reason to cheer her on. He is boastful when she is hesitant, and in the end their combined resilience is what is able to get Helen to the point of enlightenment, moments before her father would have called her education off.

If Helen's education is the film's A story, and Sullivan's maturation as a first-time teacher is the B story, then James's Oedipal relationship with his father, complete with a stepmother young enough to be his own wife, serves as a complete C story. Gibson mines the tensions inherent in their relationship to enrich the film's main stories.

James lives uncomfortably in his father's shadow and has been there for quite some time, apparently, when Sullivan shows up. His desire to have his voice heard has been a stealth campaign, so deeply submerged under wisecracks and irony that James does not even seem to understand what he is missing until given the chance to observe Sullivan assert herself. Some time before the movie starts, he became used to playing a dual role for his father: he is a fellow adult at times, offering, as the only other man in the picture, someone for the captain to argue politics with. However, he is easily dismissed as a child whenever his father does not feel like listening to him. Gibson could have left James, who is only a background character, straddling this fence, but instead he chose to bring James's story around to a conclusion. After he grouses about being ignored, his stepmother tells him specifically to stand up for himself; still, he might have been left without a voice in the Keller household if he were not moved to stand up for Sullivan.

Moving into the climactic scene at the pump, when Helen finally discovers the significance of communication, there is an argument. Captain Keller and his wife want Sullivan to quit hounding the girl for a moment, and Sullivan sees how easily Helen could slip back into her old spoiled ways. Helen splashes a pitcher of water on Sullivan, who drags her out to the pump to make her take responsibility for refilling it. Before Captain Keller can intervene on Helen's behalf, James intervenes on Sullivan's side, slamming a door in front of his father's face and blocking it with his body. There is nothing uncertain in this confrontation: "I'm right, and you're wrong," he shouts. These are the words he has waited his entire life to say. The high point of James Keller's life passes quickly, though, as the film moves immediately out to the pump, where audiences familiar with Helen Keller's story know the real breakthrough is about to take place. The shouting James adds a few degrees to the film's overall temperature coming into the pump scene, but as soon as he stands up to his domineering father, James fades into the background and is never heard from again.

Andrew Prine is a good enough actor to show James Keller's courageous stand, and he is perfect for showing James as the kind of young man who thinks he can never please his father and so pretends, with a smile, not to care. He does not have the range to show his character evolving from one personality to the other, but there is no need for him to do so. *The Miracle Worker* is not about him. If it were, James Keller could be considered underwritten and underperformed. As it is, though, his role is much more detailed than the plot requires.

Source: David Kelly, Critical Essay on *The Miracle Worker*, in *Drama for Students*, Gale, Cengage Learning, 2011.

Gary Crowdus and Richard Porton
In the following excerpted interview, Penn discusses the cinematic struggles of converting the play from the stage to film.

...Providing a succinct summary of Arthur Penn's career is not easy, since his films are not Hollywood escapist fare but, conversely, are certainly not examples of rarefied avant-garde cinema. Penn's films often blend frequently unsettling violence with contemplative sequences; stark aggression coexists with cerebral anguish. Nonetheless, when reviewing Penn's work, particular moments of visceral power tend to overshadow the calmer, introspective interludes. It is difficult to forget, even after many years have elapsed, the raw immediacy of Billy the Kid shooting [a] bystander out of his boots; a well-meaning sheriff's bloody assault by racist yahoos; the brutal lyricism of Bonnie and Clyde's bullet-riddled

© *Photos 12 | Alamy*

bodies; or a psychotic father's murder of his newly-wed daughter. These cathartic moments, culled from both the early and late phase of Penn's career, point to this director's determination to undermine his audience's complacency in a manner that is simultaneously shocking and thought-provoking. Unlike contemporary film school brats, Arthur Penn's apprenticeship began in the early days of broadcast television. Most memorably, he directed plays commissioned by Playhouse 90 and Philco Playhouse, two of the most oft-cited representatives of the medium's so-called "Golden Age." He subsequently achieved great success on Broadway, where he directed such distinguished productions as William Gibson's *The Miracle Worker* and *Two for the Seesaw*, Lillian Hellman's *Toys in the Attic*, and an *Evening with Nichols and May*. There are vital links between Penn's work in television and theater, and his film career. His experience as the floor manager at NBC's Colgate Comedy Hour influenced the jaundiced view of stand-up comedy that can be detected in *Mickey One* (1964), while something akin to Nichols and May's astringent satirical verve is evident in the darker humor of *Bonnie and Clyde* (1967) and *Little Big Man* (1970). Despite vast stylistic and thematic differences, Penn's early films are all coming of age stories

in which anguished protagonists undergo crucial, and frequently violent, transformations. *The Left-Handed Gun* (1957) featured a sensitive anti-hero (played with moody flair by Paul Newman), whose violent rage seemed primarily the result of adolescent confusion. Although this film was by no means the first Western to include Freudian motifs, Penn's audacious reinterpretation of the Billy the Kid legend went a long way toward subverting the stoic masculinity of traditional Western film heroes such as John Wayne and Jimmy Stewart. *The Miracle Worker* (1962), Penn's adaptation of William Gibson's much honored play, was an equally heterodox coming of age narrative that managed to avoid much of the sentimentality that usually plagues films devoted to the plight of handicapped protagonists. This account of the young Helen Keller's acquisition of language is harrowing, even a bit frightening at times, but never treacly. *Mickey One*, Penn's most experimental film, explores a young man's alienation (a word still very much in vogue during the early Sixties) in a convoluted manner that is reminiscent of European 'art cinema.' The paranoid comedian portrayed by Warren Beatty, however, is a quintessentially American figure whose quest for identity ends on a note of qualified affirmation. Although weighed down by Lillian Hellman's floridly melodramatic script (revised at the behest of a nervous studio by Horton Foote—the source material's original author—among others), *The Chase* (1965) remains one of the few American films to explore the complex social tapestry of a small southern town. Many films depict the provincial racism of the pre-Civil Rights era with varying degrees of success. This frequently over-the-top chronicle of avarice and hysteria placed an equal emphasis on the vicious divisions that were such an integral part of the old southern hierarchy . . . .

Cineaste: You've said about The Miracle Worker *that you were disappointed in your failure to fully adapt the stage play for the cinema. How would you have made it more cinematic?*

Penn: I think there should have been an almost silent film eloquence about the impact of Helen's affliction on the family so that we wouldn't have to have Captain Keller enunciate, "Two weeks, Miss Sullivan, two weeks, then the child comes back to us!" Those are lines that had to be said on the stage but that I didn't need on the screen. As a result of my lack of belief in the cinema at that time, I took the expository material from the stage, like that artificial time limitation, and kept it in.

I think I would have had the same physical actions, only done with a more searching camera than one that was relying on the dialog as well as the image. But there are parts of that film that I'm very proud of. The opening credits sequence, for example, probably more than anything else, illustrates what I mean—the danger to a child like that of a Christmas tree bail or of laundry hanging on a clothesline—because she had to be watched all the time.

Cineaste: Most of the action is anchored in this house, which becomes very ominous.

Penn: Yes, exactly. Years afterward, when I had my own children, I thought, gee, how that house must have resonated with the silence of that child, just moving as a presence, and people not being able to talk about her, even to each other, but just having to watch, with the child as the focus of all the behavior of the family. But we wouldn't need the words. We needed the words on the stage because there was no way to suggest how adversarial her malady was, beyond the fact that it was a demonstrated one. But you could do it in the cinema and you could do it very well. The big fight scene at the table, for instance, is a wonderful scene. It's a good piece of cinema because there was no dialog and no need for it.

Cineaste: Much of that scene was shot hand-held, wasn't it?

Penn: Yes.

Cineaste: And the shots are held for a fairly long time.

Penn: Yes, because I didn't see the need to cut until certain events needed to be punctuated or you needed another view on them. I thought the film should really resemble those early silent two- or three-reelers where they just kept the camera grinding. Those films were usually comedies, but there's also a basic humor underlying this scene which is really a little battle. You know, "You do that, I'll do this. You do this,

I'll do that." It was sort of a mano a mano, in that regard.

Cineaste: How did you achieve the visual effect used for Annie Sullivan's flashbacks?

Penn: It's quite technical, and I won't remember exactly, but we took the camera eyepiece and blocked out everything but a little square of the frame in the center with the intention that we would then optically blow that up to be the full frame. We did tests first to find the right ratio—I think it was something like fourteen times—and then we made that piece out of metal and put it into the camera. When we blew up that portion to fill the frame, it got very grainy and began to break down to the point where the emulsion could just hold an image. We wanted to get to that point where the image almost disappears to be the equivalent of Annie's inability to see. She was virtually blind herself, you know, so that was all she ever saw of the world. She had many eye operations before she was ever able to go to Alabama.

Cineaste: The lighting, especially in the interiors, often seems quite theatrical, with pools of light amidst surrounding darkness. Is that a carry-over from the stage presentation?

Penn: No, but that's a wonderful story. Ernie Caparros, the cinematographer, had never seen the play. He was a debonair fellow, a rather cynical Cuban, but a good cinematographer. When we began shooting, the film didn't seem to him to mean much of anything. About three weeks or so into the schedule, we shot the scene at the pump, the big defining scene, and Caparros saw the emotional power for the first time and he saw the effect of it on the crew. I mean, there were grown men standing there weeping. Suddenly, he got the idea—Academy Award!—and from that moment on it was, "Oh, I have to light the chadows."

Cineaste: Chadows?

Penn: Shadows.

Cineaste: Rembrandt lighting.

Penn: Exactly, we're talking chiaroscuro, and I'm saying, "Come on, Ernie. Let's go, Ernie, we've got to finish this movie," and he's saying, "No, no, I must light the chadows."

Cineaste: The sets seemed to be very sparsely decorated.

Penn: They were sparse at my request. I told George Jenkins, our art director, let's have no pictures on the wall. Let's have it be a sightless house in that respect, so that we don't ever see a picture or part of a picture at the edge of the frame. At first, he said, "Well, I don't know," but then he got the feel of it and leapt into it whole-heartedly. But it was a very strong intention about the film, to somehow convey the idea of a house that had lost its faith in sight and sound.

Cineaste: What's the story behind the casting of Patty Duke in that part?

Penn: We auditioned a lot of kids for the Broadway play, maybe a hundred or more. I'd say to them, "Show me how you'd walk if you were blind. OK, now show me how you'd do that if you were blind and couldn't hear." Well, they were all good, interesting kids, and then in came this little child and something just came out of her that was absolutely palpable, we all felt it. I had seen her in *The Goddess*, Paddy Chayefsky's film that Del Mann directed with Kim Stanley. She played a little part in it, but she was wonderful.

Cineaste: Whatever your dissatisfaction with The Miracle Worker—*and I think that's really a testament to your ambitions as a filmmaker—it is nevertheless an incredibly powerful piece of work and is also valuable for preserving your Broadway stage presentation.*

Penn: I have no regrets about it beyond the fact that I wasn't so mature in terms of my ideas about cinema then. It was only my second film and I was just putting my toe in the water, cinematically speaking, because I wasn't yet ready to plunge . . . .

Source: Gary Crowdus and Richard Porton, "The Importance of a Singular, Guiding Vision: An Interview with Arthur Penn," in *Cineaste*, Vol. 20, No. 2, Spring 1993, pp. 4–16.

Robert Brustein

In the following excerpt, Brustein praises Gibson's writing and dialogue in The Miracle Worker *as clever and compassionate, but considers the play's dramatic conflict to be subordinated to sociological ideology.*

Near the conclusion of *Two for the Seesaw*, the rambunctious street urchin, Gittel Mosca, is gently informed that "after the verb to love, to help is the sweetest in the tongue." William Gibson, setting aside more serious concerns to anatomize the sweeter, softer virtues, has thus far dedicated his dramatic career to the definition and conjugation of these two verbs.

For, like the play which preceded it, *The Miracle Worker*—written with the same wit . . . — is essentially a two-character work about the relationship of kindness to love. The time has been set back to the 1880's, the seesaw has been freighted from New York to Alabama, and precariously balanced upon it now are an afflicted child and a 20-year-old Irish girl from Boston; yet, the two plays are clearly lifted from the same trunk. In outline, both works are about the redemption and education of a helpless little ragamuffin by a more experienced, vaguely guilty mentor which results in mutual strengthening of character. Here the ragamuffin is not a Jewish dancer from the Bronx, but the child Helen Keller, while the helping hand belongs not to the disconsolate divorcé, Jerry Ryan, but to Helen's gifted teacher, Annie Sullivan. On the other hand, everybody's motivation remains constant. Annie's conscience-pangs over her desertion of her dying brother, for example, recall Jerry's uneasiness over his desertion of his wife, and both expiate their guilt through "help," unswerving dedication to the welfare of another. To press the parallel further, both plays rely excessively on extra-dramatic devices: *Two for the Seesaw* on a persistently clanging telephone, *The Miracle Worker* on a garrulous loudspeaker. And, despite the excellence of the writing, both plays impress me less as dramas of conflict than as socio-psychological essays on the subject of interpersonal relations.

The Miracle Worker documents a historical occurrence: Helen Keller's transformation from a hopelessly untidy, aggressive, isolated, willful animal, possessed only with a sense of touch, into a disciplined, well-groomed human being about to enter the world of languages. The factual story contains only two disclosures of a dramatic nature. Since one of them (that Helen has become deaf and blind from an infant disease) is expended in the opening moments, the bulk of the play consists of Gibson's filler. Some of this filler is purely theatrical: Helen and Annie engage in what are surely the most epic brawls ever staged. . . . Some filler is designed for edification: Annie lectures Helen's parents on the dangers of permissive child-rearing . . . , and, in an ill-defined subplot, a cowardly son learns at last to command the love and respect of his stern father by asserting himself. It is Gibson's penchant for instructing his characters in "mature" behavior which disturbs me most. In common with most playwrights of the modern school, love operates in his plays with all the intensity of an ideology, and the only development his people are permitted is a more accurate apprehension of the proper way to show affection.

In consequence, no event occurs in *The Miracle Worker* which is not somehow identified with love. Take the last scene, the other factual disclosure of the story and the "miracle" towards which everything moves. From history, we know that Helen Keller suddenly made the connection between words and things essential for learning language while pumping water from a well. On the stage, this discovery issues in a perfect orgy of embraces. The child pumps the water, grunts out the word, scurries back and forth along the length of the stage, rings a bell wildly, embraces her mother, kisses her once cold, now loving father, and finally offers her love to Annie whom she has hated throughout the action. As for Annie, finally permitted to express the affection she has purposely withheld, she spells out on the child's hand, "I love Helen…forever and ever," and the curtain descends.

What is one to say about this? Mr. Gibson's motives are undoubtedly impeccable, his heart is rooted in the proper place and, though he dances on the edge of Sentiment's soggy slough, he rarely falls in.… But I am afraid I am churlish enough not to respond very strongly to Human Documents, or Testaments to the Human Spirit, or even to Profound Convictions that Man will Endure and Prevail, unless they are accompanied by a good deal more grit, a good deal more mystery, and a great deal more information about the dark places of human motivation than we are given here.

I say this with regret because, although his craft is still a little shaky, Gibson possesses substantial literary and dramatic gifts, and an integrity of the highest order. In addition, he brings to his works authentic compassion, wit, bite, and humor, and a lively, literate prose style equalled by few American dramatists. (Annie's moving tribute to words, while appropriate for a character concerned with communication, is clearly a reflection of Gibson's own love affair with the English language). Since Gibson is one of a handful of theater writers who does not have to apologize for his dialogue, he can afford a faithful production which does not have to apologize for the play.

But his weakness for inspirational themes, if not suppressed, will inevitably doom him to the second rank. That Gibson has intelligence,

tough-mindedness, and a capacity for indignation, nobody who reads *The Seesaw Log* will deny, but his dramas persistently follow the safer, more familiar road of routine wisdom and spiritual uplift. Like most dramatists of his generation, Gibson confuses playwriting with psychological counseling; unlike most of them, he is capable of much more. His potential is large but it will never be fulfilled until he can find more compelling sources for his view of man than the cheery chapbooks of [Karen] Horney and [Erika] Fromm, until he can examine the more dangerous truths which lie beneath the comforting surface of the skin.…

Source: Robert Brustein, "Two for the Miracle," in *New Republic*, Vol. 141, No. 19, November 9, 1959, pp. 28–29.

Richard Hayes

In the following excerpt, Hayes describes Gibson's portrayal of Helen Keller as sincere and affecting.

Consider the image of the young Helen Keller that aches like a wound at the center of Mr. William Gibson's *The Miracle Worker*: the child locked in the body's cage against sight, speech, sound, her skin alone a raw key to the world, the very fact of her a majestic rebuke to all easy imaginations of justice and rationality. Mr. Gibson's account of the breaking of that cage—of Anne Sullivan's forceful entry into a demonic world of lawless, feral impulse—is scrupulously sincere and affecting always, what I should call an accomplishment in humane feeling. It touches on the mute, clawing Helen with distinguished pathos and on her resistance to Miss Sullivan with a tough-minded love. Everywhere, in these passages, the image is close and powerful, beyond analysis in its emotional purity. Elsewhere, the play has no more than a conventional aspect: busy details in realism too insignificant to bear examination. What comes about us finally with the shadow of radiance—in that moment when the broken circuit of speech and thought and sound is healed at last—is something of the fierce joy of expression, of that poet's glory in the power to name God's things in all their first being and beauty. It is the only point at which Mr. Gibson raises his substance to a pitch of impersonal exaltation, but it is overwhelming. Out of hideous darkness into light: the image is completed, and it is all.…

Mr. Gibson's play has taken the town, yet what will defeat the legitimate impulse and distinction of *The Miracle Worker* is, of course, to value it immoderately. I am most anxious to be understood on this point, not as a critical harpy, nor out of perversity, but in justice to those possibilities of theater which Mr. Gibson, quite honorably and doubtless with intent, does not even explore. The triumph of Miss Keller, the will and devotion of Miss Sullivan, are moral splendors of human history, very much on the order of Franklin Roosevelt's conquest of paralysis. They are intrinsically dramatic; they challenge that supine acquiescence by which we defend ourselves against the fact of ostensibly irremediable fatality. They are, if you will, "affirmations of the human spirit."

To attempt their translation into art, however—or something very like it—is rarely, indeed never, quite satisfying, because in no central way does it invoke the transfiguring power of the imagination. One recognizes the content of the moment, of the experience, but is released into nothing else: essentially it is a *fact* to which one has responded. That the fact may be a gratifying demonstration of human worth is, in itself, aesthetically irrelevant. Hence, while recording pleasure in *The Miracle Worker*, gratitude for the image of goodness with which it augments our moral life, in no sense can I think it a significant play, and its reception as such will add only further confusion to that wondrous babel of standards which is opinion in our theater.

Source: Richard Hayes, "Images," in *Commonweal*, Vol. 71, No. 10, December 4, 1959, p. 289.

SOURCES

Boers, David, *History of American Education*, Peter Lang Publishing, 2007, pp. 31–38.

Cassidy, Claudia, "On the Aisle," in *Chicago Tribune*, April 25, 1961, p. A1.

"Cinema: Performance Piece," in *Time*, May 25, 1962, http://www.time.com/time/magazine/article/0,9171,896264,00.html (accessed August 25, 2010).

Corliss, Richard, "Seven Greatest Plays on Film," in *Time*, May 1, 2006, http://www.time.com/time/magazine/article/0,9171,1186573,00.html (accessed August 25, 2010).

Crowther, Bosley, "Screen: *The Miracle Worker* Opens," in *New York Times*, May 23, 1962, p. 29.

Freeberg, Ernest, *The Education of Laura Bridgman*, Harvard University Press, 2001, pp. 10–13.

Gibson, William, *The Miracle Worker* (film), Playfilm Productions, 1962.

——, *The Miracle Worker* (play), Scribner, 2008.

Meyer, Adolphe E., *An Educational History of the American People*, 2nd ed., McGraw-Hill, 1957, pp. 159–71.

Nielsen, Kim E., "The Southern Ties of Helen Keller," in *Journal of Southern History*, November 1, 2007, http://www.highbeam.com/doc/1G1-171211802.html (accessed August 31, 2010).

Pinkerton, Nick, "Anthology Takes a Tour of the *Bonnie and Clyde* Director's America," in *Village Voice*, November 12, 2008.

Review of *The Miracle Worker*, in *Variety*, December 31, 1962, http://www.variety.com/review/VE1117793143.html?categoryid=31&cs=1&query=the+miracle+worker (accessed August 25, 2010).

Walker, Lou Ann, *Hand, Heart, & Mind: The Story of the Education of America's Deaf People*, Dial Books, 1994, pp. 26–39.

FURTHER READING

"The American Film Institute Interview with Arthur Penn," in *Arthur Penn: Interviews*, edited by Michael Chaiken and Paul Cronin, University of Mississippi Press, 2008, pp. 29–51.

In this interview, Penn describes the process of bringing *The Miracle Worker* to the screen and the sacrifices he and William Gibson and Fred Coe had to make to fulfill their vision. Penn also discusses his wish that he could remake the film.

"Helen Keller," in *American Foundation for the Blind*, http://www.afb.org/section.asp?sectionID=1 (accessed September 16, 2010).

The American Foundation for the Blind maintains a comprehensive page about Keller, with links to pictures of her, her writings (including her entire autobiography), and notes about other people in her life, including Sullivan, Mark Twain, Alexander Graham Bell, and more.

Keller, Helen, *The Story of My Life: The Restored Edition*, Modern Library, 2004.

Keller's autobiography, which was originally published in 1903, was the original source material for Gibson's play and screenplay.

Kleege, Georgina, *Blind Rage: Letters to Helen Keller*, Gallaudet University Press, 2006.

Kleege, who is blind, heard all of her life about Keller's personal triumph. Her book offers a reassessment of the Keller story, from her personal perspective as an activist for the blind, pointing out the negative aspects of the Keller model that are seldom discussed.

Nielsen, Kim E., "The Grown-Up Helen Keller," in *Alabama Heritage*, Spring 2009, pp. 20–29.

> The events portrayed in this film happened in the 1880s and her autobiography was published in 1903, but Keller lived until 1948. During those years, she was involved in the labor movement and the feminist movement. This article shows some of the results of the education Sullivan gave to her.

Sacks, Oliver, *Seeing Voices*, Vintage Press, 2000.

> Sacks, a clinical psychologist who is famous for writing popular, easy-to-understand books about complex subjects, wrote this book in 1989 to explain how the deaf perceive reality differently than the hearing. This book offers some insight into the isolated world of Helen Keller.

SUGGESTED SEARCH TERMS

Arthur Penn

Arthur Penn AND The Miracle Worker

Helen Keller AND newsreel

Helen Keller AND Perkins School for the Blind

Helen Keller AND Annie Sullivan

William Gibson AND Helen Keller

The Miracle Worker AND teleplay

The Miracle Worker AND theater

Perkins Institution AND film

Anne Sullivan Macy

Helen Keller AND Mark Twain

The Mystery of Edwin Drood

RUPERT HOLMES

1985

The Mystery of Edwin Drood, the musical theater adaptation of Charles Dickens's unfinished novel of the same name, premiered in 1985. Rupert Holmes wrote the original score and script for the play. At the time of the premiere, Holmes was best known for his pop music hit "Escape (The Piña Colada Song)" and had never written a musical, although he was an accomplished musician whose songs had been recorded by many well-known recording artists. Holmes was intrigued by the idea of adapting Dickens's unfinished novel for the stage but was daunted by the prospect of writing a satisfying conclusion for Dickens's mystery. He solved this problem by crafting several different endings and letting the audience vote on which one was to be performed on any given evening. The inventive musical won the Tony award for Best Musical in 1986.

The story of Edwin Drood is performed in the musical by a fictitious nineteenth-century theater company known as the Music Hall Royale. Edwin, betrothed to the lovely Rosa Bud, disappears after Christmas Eve dinner, and as with most mysteries, there are a host of characters that have reason to wish him gone, including his uncle John Jasper and the newly arrived Neville Landless, who both pine for the beautiful Rosa. The company members turn the mystery into an over-the-top melodrama, complete with ominous musical cues that follow any significant or suspicious remark. Like the novel, the musical

Rupert Holmes (Getty Images)

examines themes of madness, racial prejudice, and obsessive love, but the musical does so with a lighter touch, thanks to the humorous antics of the Music Hall Royale.

Despite the ironic, lighthearted tone of the musical, there are scenes of drug use (one character is an opium addict), and one of the main characters is the madam of a brothel; these elements may be undesirable for younger readers. The full script of the play, including all of the possible conclusions, was published as a book in 1986 as *The Mystery of Edwin Drood: A New Musical* but is currently out of print. However, it may be found in many public libraries, and used copies are available for purchase online.

AUTHOR BIOGRAPHY

Holmes was born David Goldstein on February 24, 1947, in Northwich, Cheshire, England, to Leonard and Gwendolyn Goldstein. His father, an American in the Air Force, met his British mother during his years in service. The family moved to the United States when Rupert was three years old.

Leonard Goldstein was a bandleader and classical clarinetist who became a public school music teacher. Hoping his son would become a classical clarinetist as well, Goldstein taught him to play the instrument. Holmes's musical training and talent earned him a scholarship to Syracuse University's music school, but he quickly abandoned the clarinet ("I hated the instrument," he said in an interview with Gregory Bossler in *Dramatist* magazine) for music theory and composition. After a year he transferred to the Manhattan School of Music; he eventually dropped out to concentrate on his career.

While in college Holmes wrote and arranged music for anyone who would hire him. He wrote and arranged songs for the Platters, the Drifters, marching bands, and a studio musician group called the Cuff Links. In 1974 he recorded his first solo album, *Widescreen*. Though his record label only pressed ten thousand copies of the album, somehow *Widescreen* came to the attention of Barbra Streisand, who loved it. She had Holmes contribute two songs to the soundtrack of her movie *A Star Is Born*, and then in 1975, Holmes arranged and coproduced her album *Lazy Afternoon* (he also wrote three of the songs). The collaboration with Streisand brought his music to the attention of other prominent recording artists, such as Barry Manilow and Dionne Warwick.

Holmes's biggest hit as a recording artist came in 1979, when "Escape (The Piña Colada Song)" became a number one hit. Holmes wrote the song at the last minute for his *Partners in Crime* album, because he felt the album needed an up-tempo song. Holmes was pleased with the success of the song but experienced some frustration at being labeled "the Piña Colada Guy" for years afterwards.

In 1983 Holmes was performing at a night club when he was approached by theater producer Joseph Papp, who asked if he had ever considered writing a musical. Holmes presented Papp with his idea of adapting Dickens's unfinished novel *The Mystery of Edwin Drood* as a musical. Holmes's musical, for which he wrote the book, score, lyrics, and orchestrations, premiered in August of 1985 and was an immediate hit. At the 1986 Tony Awards, *The Mystery of Edwin Drood* won Best Musical, Best Book, Best Score, Best Director (Wilford Leach), and Best Actor in a Musical (George Rose).

Holmes had little time to celebrate his triumph, however, before he was devastated by a personal tragedy: his ten-year-old daughter Wendy died suddenly of an undiagnosed brain tumor. After her death, Holmes found writing music too emotional to bear. He began writing comedy thrillers for the stage instead, first penning *Accomplice* in 1990, which won an Edgar award for Best Play from the Mystery Writers of America, and then *Solitary Confinement* in 1992. From 1995 to 1998, Holmes wrote and scored the television series *Remember WENN*, a comedy-drama about the travails of a Pittsburgh radio station in the 1930s.

The year 2002 was a busy one for Holmes; his play *Say Goodnight, Gracie*, a one-man show starring Frank Gorshin as George Burns, opened on Broadway, and his first musical since *The Mystery of Edwin Drood* opened as well: *Marty*, a musical adaptation of the Oscar-winning Paddy Chayefsky film.

Holmes's first mystery novel, *Where the Truth Lies*, was published in 2003; *Swing*, his second, was released in 2005. He also wrote the book for another musical, *Curtains*, for which he won a Drama Desk Award. In 2009, he began writing the book for a musical based on the 1964 Rat Pack movie *Robin and the 7 Hoods*.

Holmes and his wife, Liza, to whom he has been married since 1969, live in New York. They have two sons, Nick and Tim.

MEDIA ADAPTATIONS

- The original cast recording of the songs from *The Mystery of Edwin Drood* is available on CD from the Varese Sarabande label. The CD features Betty Buckley, Cleo Laine, George Rose, and Patti Cohenour and was released in 1995.

- The sheet music for twelve of the songs from the musical is available in a paperback compilation titled *The Mystery of Edwin Drood: Vocal Selections*, published by the Hal Leonard Corporation in 2004.

- MP3 downloads of *The Mystery of Edwin Drood*, from the album, *The Charles Dickens Radio Show*, each running thirty minutes, are available through Master Classics Records (2010).

PLOT SUMMARY

Before act 1 of *The Mystery of Edwin Drood*, the players of the Music Hall Royale, an 1873 theater company, appear in the house, jesting with the audience. Soon, the theater company's chairman, William Cartwright, takes the stage; the chairman serves as master of ceremonies and narrator. He brings the company to order.

Act 1
Act 1 opens with the song, "There You Are," in which the company expresses their gratitude to the audience for coming to their play. After the song concludes, the chairman introduces the Music Hall Royale's interpretation of Dickens's unfinished novel, *The Mystery of Edwin Drood*.

SCENE 1
The first scene takes place in the home of John Jasper, choirmaster of Cloisterham cathedral. As each new character enters the scene, the chairman flamboyantly introduces the actor

playing the character. Jasper begins with the song, "A Man Could Go Quite Mad," in which he sings of the "soul-stifling" boredom of his life as a choirmaster.

Jasper's nephew Edwin Drood arrives. Drood is played by a woman of the company, Miss Alice Nutting. Drood and Jasper drink a toast to Miss Rosa Bud, Drood's fiancée, to whom he has been betrothed since childhood. Drood informs Jasper that after their wedding, they will travel to Egypt, where Drood will seek his fortune as an engineer. He expresses his frustration at the arranged marriage (arranged by his and Rosa's late fathers). Jasper seems tormented by the mention of the wedding and staggers, appearing ill. He confesses to Drood that he has been taking "medicine for a pain" but forbids his nephew to speak of it to anyone. Drood promises, and the two sing a duet, "Two Kinsmen," in which they pledge their loyalty to each other.

SCENE 2
Scene 2 takes place in the conservatory of the Nun's House, a seminary for young ladies and the home of Miss Rosa Bud, Drood's fiancée. Rosa is in the conservatory with John Jasper, her music

teacher. Jasper tells Rosa he has composed a song especially for her. Reading over the intimate lyrics, Rosa protests that she cannot sing the song, but Jasper insists. Rosa sings "Moonfall" under the intense gaze of Jasper. After the song, Reverend Crisparkle enters the scene with Helena and Neville Landless. Jasper insists that Rosa sing the song again. She begins but cannot continue; she collapses and Helena consoles her.

Reverend Crisparkle introduces Helena and Neville, orphans from Ceylon (the country now called Sri Lanka). Neville is living with Crisparkle, and Helena will be living at the Nun's House with Rosa. Crisparkle has been charged with the task of calming Neville's "hot-tempered nature." Neville is immediately charmed by Rosa and is disappointed when Crisparkle informs him of her betrothal to Drood.

Helena befriends Rosa, and then asks if she is aware that Jasper is in love with her. Rosa is horrified at the suggestion and says that Jasper terrifies her. Rosa and Helena reprise (repeat the song) "Moonfall."

SCENE 3

The chairman introduces Nick Cricker, the actor playing Durdles, caretaker of the cathedral's tombs. Cricker introduces his son, young Nick, who will be playing the role of Deputy, Durdles's assistant. Next, the chairman sets the scene: Durdles and Deputy are outside the home of Mayor Thomas Sapsea, who is now returning home. However, the actor who is supposed to play Sapsea does not appear. The stage manager rushes onstage and whispers into the chairman's ear. The chairman then tells the audience that the actor who plays Sapsea is "once again Massively Indisposed." Instead, the role will be played by the chairman himself.

Now Durdles tells Sapsea (the chairman) that his late wife's tomb is finished and ready for the inscription. Durdles proudly brags about the size of the crypt and adds that Mr. Jasper has asked him if he will take him down to see it. In an aside to the audience, the chairman says, "Now that sounded suspiciously like a clue to me."

SCENE 4

Scene 4 takes place in the seedy London opium den and brothel of Princess Puffer, madam and proprietor. She sings "The Wages of Sin," in which she laments that a life of crime and debauchery is not very profitable.

The room is filled with shabby beds, on which lie various unconscious customers; in one of the beds is John Jasper. Jasper is seeing visions as a result of opium; he sees a vision of Rosa Bud and calls out her name. When Princess Puffer hears the name, she is startled and asks him, "Did you say Rosa Bud?" The question awakens Jasper from his trance, and he appears to have no knowledge of how he got to the opium den. After Jasper leaves, Princess Puffer asks aloud, "Who are you then? And *what* are you?" The chairman tells the audience to take note of this suspicious statement.

SCENE 5

Scene 5 takes place back in Cloisterham, on Cloisterham High Street. Reverend Crisparkle introduces Helena and Neville Landless to Edwin Drood and Rosa Bud. Neville and Edwin discuss Edwin's impending journey to Egypt, which is not far from where Helena and Neville are from. Edwin tells them that he is going to Egypt to construct a passage across the desert to Alexandria. The stones for paving this passage, Edwin tells them, will be taken from the pyramids. Neville is outraged at the suggestion and must be calmed by his sister. He apologizes for his temper and says that he is still not accustomed to the cool, restrained nature of England, after the "warm and uncivilized allure of our homeland." The three sing the song "Ceylon." John Jasper and Mayor Sapsea enter near the end of the song; when the others have exited, Jasper tells Sapsea of his fears that Neville is a dangerous man and will bring harm to his nephew Edwin. Sapsea accuses Jasper of exaggerating; Jasper insists that there are two sides of Neville, a civilized side and a murderous one, adding, "I myself suffer from this sort of duality on occasion." Jasper and Sapsea/chairman sing the song "Both Sides of the Coin." Sapsea agrees to keep a close eye on Neville.

SCENE 6

Deep in the crypts of Cloisterham cathedral, Jasper emerges from the mausoleum of Mrs. Sapsea. On the floor lies Durdles, asleep; Jasper removes a key from Durdles's key ring. Suddenly Deputy comes down the stairs, calling for Durdles; Jasper, enraged, grabs him and throttles him until he goes limp. Durdles wakes up, sees Deputy and accuses Jasper of murdering him. Jasper, feigning innocence, leans over to revive Deputy. Deputy, who has been faking, kicks him in the stomach. Durdles comments that the wine Jasper gave him was "more potent than I'm accustomed." Durdles and Jasper exit the crypt, and Durdles, suspicious, muses to the audience that Jasper is a mystery.

SCENE 7

It is Christmas Eve, and Edwin and Rosa are discussing their future. Rosa tells Edwin that she wishes to be like brother and sister, not husband and wife. Edwin confesses that he feels the same. They sing the duet "Perfect Strangers," in which they speculate that if they had met more naturally, rather than by arrangement, they may have fallen in love. After their song, Rosa asks Edwin to keep their change of plans a secret from Jasper. Edwin agrees.

SCENE 8

As Jasper's guests arrive at his home for Christmas Eve dinner, they all comment on the violent storm gathering outside. Crisparkle mentions that it was a night like this that Rosa's mother died, slipping from a cliff into the ocean and drowning. Crisparkle tells everyone that he was once engaged to Rosa's mother. After this revelation, Drood and Rosa arrive. Drood and Neville waste no time exchanging insults. Jasper distracts them from their quarrel with some mulled wine he has prepared. Edwin comments on how potent the wine is.

They all sit down to dinner; Edwin insults Neville again. Everyone at the party sings the song "No Good Can Come from Bad," in which Neville and Drood's quarrel escalates. Rosa, Crisparkle, and Helena sing of their fear that the argument will lead to violence; and Jasper repeatedly urges the diners to drink the wine.

After the song, Jasper begs Edwin and Neville to make peace with each other. They apologize and shake hands. Edwin says he wishes to walk by the river to see the storm; Neville joins him. Rosa, Helena, and Crisparkle exit. As Edwin and Neville set out for their walk, Jasper protests that Edwin's coat is too flimsy and insists that he take Jasper's own distinctive caped coat. The offer of the coat is followed by a portentous musical sting (short musical phrase used to punctuate the action in the play) from the orchestra.

SCENE 9

It is the next day—Christmas Day—and Edwin Drood has disappeared. Rosa meets Reverend Crisparkle near the cathedral and confesses her fear that something awful has happened to him. Bazzard, Crisparkle's assistant, arrives to

say there is still no news of Edwin. Jasper and Mayor Sapsea enter. Sapsea tells Jasper that he has convinced him of Neville's guilt and sends a party out to search for Neville and bring him to justice. Deputy enters shortly after and informs Jasper that Neville has been caught. Bazzard then enters with a grisly piece of evidence: the coat that Jasper lent to Edwin, torn and stained with blood.

At this point, the chairman tells the actor playing Bazzard, a Mr. Phillip Bax, that his part in the play is now finished. The chairman notes that Bax's roles in the Music Hall's productions have all been extremely small. Sadly, Bax concurs. Feeling sorry for the actor, the chairman offers to let him sing a song. Thrilled, Bax performs "Never the Luck," in which he bemoans his limited roles. After a rousing finish, the action of the play continues.

The townspeople who have hunted down Neville throw him roughly on stage. Mayor Sapsea accuses him of killing Drood, but Helena, who has just entered, points out that without Edwin's body, Sapsea cannot arrest anyone for his murder. Sapsea reluctantly releases Neville. Helena takes Neville upstage to comfort him, leaving Jasper and Rosa alone.

Jasper grabs Rosa's arm and confesses his desperate love for her; Rosa tells him he is mad. They sing the duet "The Name of Love," in which Jasper rages that Rosa will eventually submit to him, and Rosa tells him that his idea of love is twisted and evil. They segue into a reprise of the earlier song "Moonfall."

Act Two

SCENE 1

Six months have passed, and there is still no sign of Edwin Drood. The chairman directs the audience's attention to Cloisterham station, where John Jasper is stepping from the train, back from another visit to the opium den in London. He is followed off the train by two individuals: Princess Puffer and the mysterious Detective Dick Datchery, who wears a large coat and full beard. Both have arrived in Cloisterham to investigate the mystery of Edwin Drood's disappearance. They follow Jasper intently, each unaware of the other. They sing the duet "Settling Up the Score," in which they both vow to solve the mystery.

SCENE 2

Durdles, Deputy, Mayor Sapsea, Datchery, and Princess Puffer are on Cloisterham High

Street; Datchery asks if there are any available lodgings near the cathedral. Mayor Sapsea says the only lodgings are directly above John Jasper's. Datchery asks if this is the same John Jasper grieving the loss of his nephew, Edwin Drood; Princess Puffer hears this and asks after Jasper as well. Datchery exits; Puffer comments that he seems suspicious. Durdles cautions her not to jump to conclusions, which prompts the song "Off to the Races," the Music Hall Royale's signature number.

After this tune, Princess Puffer encounters Rosa Bud and gasps with shock; after Rosa exits, Puffer says that she now has one of the pieces of information she was seeking. Durdles asks if this means she will be leaving Cloisterham. Puffer replies that she will not; she is very close to solving the puzzle, and she is not going to quit so close to her goal. This leads to the song "Don't Quit While You're Ahead," sung by the entire company. As the company launches into an encore performance of the tune, suddenly the music stops. The chairman informs the audience sadly that this is the point where Dickens's novel stops, due to his death.

The chairman notes that most literary scholars believe that Dick Datchery was another character from the novel in disguise. Also, he points out that it is possible that Drood is still alive. He asks the cast to vote on the issue; they unanimously vote Drood dead. Alice Nutting, the actress who plays Drood, angrily storms off stage. The chairman and cast members then present the audience with the possible Datcheries: Helena, Bazzard, Neville, Crisparkle, or Rosa. The chairman asks the audience to vote on the true identity of Dick Datchery (by applause) and then announces the chosen Datchery.

Next, the chairman and cast present the audience with the candidates for Drood's killer: Jasper, Helena, Bazzard, Neville, Princess Puffer, Rosa Bud, or Reverend Crisparkle. The cast members then circulate throughout the audience and tally their votes by section.

Conclusion
It is dawn on the streets of Cloisterham. Princess Puffer is sleeping on the ground by the cathedral when Rosa passes by. Princess Puffer calls to her, and Rosa, puzzled, asks her how she knows her name. Princess Puffer reveals that she was Rosa's nanny until she was six years old. Rosa recognizes her and asks why she left. Princess Puffer sings

"The Garden Path to Hell," in which she relates the sad details of her downfall: she was seduced by a handsome man, who led her into prostitution and then left her. Later she turned to selling opium.

Next, Princess Puffer sings "Puffer's Confession," in which she reveals that she has been following John Jasper. Then, becoming suspicious of Datchery as well, she followed him to his lodgings and watched him undress, revealing that he was none other than . . . (here she announces the identity of Datchery chosen by the audience earlier). The chosen Datchery then sings his or her version of "Out on a Limerick," in which they reveal their motive for investigating the murder; all Datcheries come to the conclusion that John Jasper is the murderer and should be hung.

At this point, Jasper, careening between his two personalities (good and evil), maniacally sings "Jasper's Confession," in which he admits that he wanted Edwin Drood dead and imagined killing him many times while under the influence of opium. He also admits that the wine he gave Edwin and Neville on Christmas Eve was laudanum wine. After drinking some himself, he saw himself killing Edwin.

Now Durdles comes forward and claims that John Jasper did not kill Edwin. Durdles says he witnessed the murder and then afterwards saw Jasper come out, discover Edwin's body, carry it to Mrs. Sapsea's crypt and leave it there. Durdles then reveals the true identity of the murderer (selected earlier by the audience).

The character chosen as murderer then sings a confession revealing the motive. In the confessions of Crisparkle, Helena, Princess Puffer, and Rosa, it is revealed that Jasper was the intended victim, but Edwin was killed instead in error because he was wearing Jasper's coat. Bazzard commits the murder in his desire to be center stage; Neville admits to killing Edwin to win Rosa and get revenge. Each confession reprises a song sung earlier in the musical by the chosen character.

After the murderer has confessed, the chairman announces that, in order to give the story a happy ending, two of the characters should become lovers. The audience votes on which characters will fall in love, choosing from Rosa, Helena, and Princess Puffer for the first and from Sapsea, Neville, Bazzard, Crisparkle, Durdles, and Jasper for the other. The two chosen then confess their love to one another and sing a reprise of the duet "Perfect Strangers." The chairman then laments that Drood is not there to give his account of the whole affair. Suddenly there is a loud rumbling, and the crypt of Mrs. Sapsea rises through the floor of the stage. Edwin Drood emerges, alive, greeting one and all. He sings "The Writing on the Wall," in which he explains that he was only unconscious, not dead, when Jasper placed his body in the crypt. The musical then concludes with a rousing reprise of "Don't Quit While You're Ahead."

CHARACTERS

Mr. Phillip Bax

Mr. Phillip Bax is a long-standing member of the theater company who, unfortunately, seems doomed to play only the smallest roles. He is also the understudy for Clive Paget, who plays Jasper, but, as Bax gloomily points out, "Mr. Paget claims never to have missed a performance in his entire career." In sympathy, the chairman allows Bax a solo number near the end of the first act.

Bazzard

Bazzard is the eccentric assistant of Reverend Crisparkle, who has aspirations for the stage. He has written a play titled "The Thorn of Anxiety." Bazzard assists Crisparkle in investigating Drood's disappearance and also serves as the waiter for Jasper's Christmas Eve dinner.

Rosa Bud

Rosa is the innocent young woman engaged to Edwin Drood, a betrothal arranged by Rosa's and Edwin's fathers before their deaths. Rosa lives at the seminary called the Nun's House, where she is doted on by all. Like Edwin, Rosa is somewhat immature and lacks the fortitude of the formidable Helena, but she has a warm heart. Though she has no great passion for Edwin, she loves him dearly as she would a brother. She is terrified of Jasper and his attentions.

Chairman William Cartwright

William Cartwright is the jovial chairman of the Music Hall Royale theater company. He acts as master of ceremonies and narrator for the production. As each actor appears on stage for the first time, Cartwright introduces him or her with a flourish. The chairman also engages in comedic banter with the audience and the other

actors. When Mr. James Hitchens fails to appear to play the part of Mayor Sapsea, Cartwright takes over this role as well.

Miss Janet Conover

Miss Janet Conover is the Music Hall Royale player performing the role of Helena Landless. The chairman introduces her as "our own fiery spirit, the unpredictable Miss Janet Conover!"

Master Nick Cricker

Master Nick Cricker, the son of Nick Cricker, plays the part of Deputy. This is his first role with the company.

Mr. Nick Cricker

Mr. Nick Cricker is the actor performing the role of Durdles. He is described as "the Clown Prince of the Music Hall Royale."

The Reverend Mr. Crisparkle

Reverend Crisparkle is a kindly man and is the clergyman of Cloisterham cathedral. He takes responsibility for the orphaned Neville and Helena Landless after their abusive stepfather dies and is troubled by Neville's violent temper. Crisparkle was once in love with Rosa's mother and was briefly engaged to her, but she married another and later was drowned. If the audience votes Crisparkle as the murderer, he reveals that he killed Rosa's mother as well, believing her to be possessed by Satan.

Dick Datchery

Dick Datchery is a mysterious individual, sporting a heavy beard and large coat, who arrives in Cloisterham to investigate the disappearance of Edwin Drood. He is really one of the other characters in disguise; the identity of this character is determined by audience vote.

Deputy

Deputy is the boy who assists Durdles in his duties as caretaker of the cathedral crypts. Deputy is a feisty, street-wise urchin who discovers Jasper in the crypts after he has drugged Durdles with laudanum wine.

Edwin Drood

Edwin Drood (affectionately called Ned by Jasper and Rosa) is a careless young man whose life, until now, has been an easy one. Good-natured and fun loving, he is also occasionally immature and arrogant, as when he insults Neville. He is also not very observant, or he would probably notice that his uncle is in love with his fiancée, Rosa Bud (Helena deduces this the first time she meets Jasper). For the most part, however, he is a well-liked and well-intentioned young fellow who feels genuine affection for Rosa, though he does not love her in the romantic sense.

Durdles

Durdles is the caretaker of the Cloisterham cathedral crypts. Durdles is a plodding, irascible, and eccentric old man who spends more time drunk than sober, though he is more observant than some of the characters believe. It is Durdles who witnesses the murder and then reveals the identity of the murderer at the end of the play.

Mr. Victor Grinstead

Mr. Victor Grinstead is the actor playing Neville Landless. He is the newest member of the company.

Mr. James Hitchens

Mr. James Hitchens is the actor originally scheduled to play Mayor Sapsea. The audience never meets Mr. Hitchens, however, because he never arrives on stage. According to the chairman, the actor is "once again Massively Indisposed, due to injuries he received while fighting for a lady's honour . . . Apparently the lady wished to keep it." The chairman notes that regulars to the theater will not be surprised by Mr. Hitchens's absence, since he spends more time at the bar in the back of the theater than on the stage. The role of Mayor Sapsea is taken over by William Cartwright, the chairman of the Music Hall Royale.

John Jasper

John Jasper is one of the more complex characters of the play. Bored and uninspired by his career as choirmaster of Cloisterham cathedral, he has turned to opium for relief from the monotonous drudgery of his days and the torment of his unrequited love for Rosa Bud. His fondness for his nephew Edwin, Rosa's betrothed, prevents him from making his feelings known to Rosa.

Jasper has a split personality. When behaving normally, he is a good man, who truly loves his nephew and is troubled by his feelings for Rosa. When possessed by his evil side, he wishes his nephew dead and will stop at nothing to possess Edwin's beautiful bride-to-be.

Helena Landless

Helena is the twin sister of Neville Landless; the two siblings are orphans from Ceylon. They share a very close relationship. Helena is strong and forceful, and unlike Rosa, she is not afraid to stand up to the men of Cloisterham, including John Jasper. However, she has a more even temper than her excitable brother and is often called upon to calm him down. More than one mention is made of her mysterious, "geographically untraceable accent." When Helena was younger and being abused by her tyrannical stepfather, she would sometimes disguise herself as a boy in an effort to run away (without success). This fact makes her an excellent candidate for the character who masquerades as Datchery.

Neville Landless

Neville, twin brother of Helena, is a hot-blooded young man who gives way to his passions at the slightest provocation. Early in the play he tells Reverend Crisparkle that if his abusive stepfather had not died, he probably would have killed him, a confession that shocks the kindly clergyman. Neville is instantly smitten with Rosa the first time he meets her. Knowing she is betrothed to Drood makes Edwin's condescending treatment of him that much more aggravating. Neville's quick temper, dislike of Edwin, and desire for Rosa all make him a prime suspect in the murder.

Mr. Cedric Moncrieffe

Cedric Moncrieffe is the member of the company playing Reverend Crisparkle. He is a long-standing member, described as a "favourite fixture" of the Music Hall Royale.

Miss Alice Nutting

The character of Drood is played by Miss Alice Nutting of the Music Hall Royale. Her specialty is male impersonation. Miss Nutting is something of a diva; when the other cast members unanimously vote Drood dead at the end of the second act, Alice calls them names and storms off the stage, prompting the chairman to tell the audience, "You have no idea the week we've had with her. First her dressing room was too small, then her mustache was too bushy."

Clive Paget

Clive Paget is the member of the Music Hall Royale theater company who plays John Jasper. Paget, the principal male actor of the company, is a handsome rake and ladies' man. (In the opening song, "There You Are," he sings, "I've a lady down in front who's handed me her latch key—surely she must know that spells her doom!")

Miss Deidre Peregrine

Miss Deirdre Peregrine, described as "unspeakably lovely" by the chairman, is the actress performing the role of Rosa Bud. Though Deirdre plays the ingénue in this show, she does her share of flirting with the audience members in the house before the play commences.

Princess Puffer

Princess Puffer is the aging madam of the brothel and opium den in London frequented by John Jasper. She tells of her sad history in the song "The Garden Path to Hell"; she was seduced by a handsome man who introduced her to prostitution and then abandoned her, leaving her to make her own way in the world. Before this unfortunate event, she was the nanny of the lovely Rosa Bud. Princess Puffer is coarse, bawdy, and street-wise but harbors a sentimental nature, especially where Rosa is concerned.

Miss Angela Prysock

Company member Miss Angela Prysock plays Princess Puffer. Angela's specialty in the troupe is women of ill repute. The chairman introduces her as "the Grand Dame of the Music Hall Royale."

Mayor Thomas Sapsea

Mayor Sapsea is a pompous, self-important, but essentially harmless man who is easily manipulated by the more intelligent John Jasper. Jasper convinces Sapsea that Neville is a dangerous individual, though Sapsea's first opinion is that Neville is a "troubled but essentially well-meaning boy." Sapsea is recently widowed and has hired Durdles to construct an ostentatious monument for his late wife in the crypts of the cathedral. Sapsea is one of the few characters who is not a suspect in Edwin's murder.

Mr. James Throttle

Throttle is the stage manager and barkeep of the Music Hall Royale. He appears on stage from time to time to deliver messages to the chairman. At the beginning of the play, the chairman announces that Mr. Throttle can also arrange companionship for lonely audience members.

THEMES

Madness

The idea that Jasper's grasp on sanity is feeble is introduced when he first appears in act 1, scene 1, and sings "A Man Could Go Quite Mad." The song's lyrics also introduce the concept that despite his future conduct, Jasper is not inherently evil ("A man could go quite mad / And not be all that bad").

Jasper suffers from a split personality; one of his personas is evil, and the other is good. The clearest example of his condition comes at Princess Puffer's opium den. Suddenly roused from his opium vision by Puffer, Jasper has no memory of how he got there or who Puffer is. In the song "Both Sides of the Coin," Jasper sings, "There's more than room enough for two inside my mind." The lyrics of this song suggest that this condition is true, to a lesser degree, for all humans; everyone suppresses parts of themselves that they find undesirable. As Jasper says to Mayor Sapsea just before the song, "Do you not realize there is more than one side, one face to all things in nature?"

Jasper is not the only character who loses his sanity in the course of the musical. If Rosa Bud is chosen as the murderer of Edwin Drood, she too reveals that she has gone mad, singing, "A child can go quite mad / And not know good from bad / And calmly plan / To kill a man / And feel but only glad!" Rosa has been driven mad by the obsessive attentions of Jasper and plots to murder him, killing Edwin by mistake. Likewise, Reverend Crisparkle, if chosen as the murderer, reveals that he is mad, and apparently has been for many years, because he also murdered Rosa's mother. As he tells Rosa, "I'm sorry I had to kill your mother. After she married that—man—I detected clear signs of Satan within her and was forced to send her into the cleansing water." For Rosa and Crisparkle (unlike Jasper), madness is a convenient way to explain why two characters who have shown little inclination to violence and have every appearance of goodness should commit murder.

Colonialism

At the time of Dickens's death, the British Empire was continuing to grow through the colonization of countries all over the world (eventually inspiring the saying, "The sun never sets on the British Empire"). In act 1, scene 5, Edwin boasts of his upcoming journey to Egypt, where he plans to

TOPICS FOR FURTHER STUDY

- Read Dickens's unfinished novel *The Mystery of Edwin Drood*. Write your own ending. Find a classmate whose ending differs significantly from yours and have a debate in which you defend your conclusion, or post your ending on your Web page and invite comments from your classmates on the plausibility of your ending.

- The medical profession knows much more about mental illness and multiple personality disorders today than in Dickens's time. Research multiple personalities on the Internet and in print sources, and create a multimedia presentation in which you compare Dickens's John Jasper with a more realistic case of divided identity.

- One of the difficulties in adapting novels for the stage or for a film is condensing hundreds of pages into a two- to three-hour production. Holmes had to eliminate a number of Dickens's characters in order to tell the story of Edwin Drood on stage. Using a favorite novel of your own, go through the book chapter by chapter and list the main events and characters as they occur. Then determine which of the characters and scenes could be eliminated for a stage or film script and which are too important to the plot to remove. Write a rationale explaining your choices.

- Read Lewis Buzbee's young-adult novel *The Haunting of Charles Dickens*, in which a young girl meets Charles Dickens one night in London. If you could meet any author from the past, whom would you choose? Write an imaginary interview between yourself and the author. Then film a video of the interview starring you as the interviewer and a classmate as the author.

- Holmes's musical is staged by the fictional Music Hall Royale theater company. Using images found online or scanned into a computer, create a poster for the Music Hall Royale's production of *The Mystery of Edwin Drood*. Use illustrations and fonts consistent with the time period (1873).

---

perform the "miracle" of constructing a passage from Cairo to Alexandria. The paving stones for the passage, he says, will be taken from the pyramids.

This cavalier attitude towards other cultures is historically typical of Western colonizers. The British thought of themselves as benevolent conquerors, bringing civilization and culture to areas such as India and Ceylon. While the British did provide improvements in many areas, often raising the standards of living and education, many colonized countries resented the imposition of British culture and religion to the detriment of their own customs and traditions. Neville—a native of a colonized area—reacts angrily to Edwin's matter-of-fact suggestion of defacing the pyramids, calling it "English blasphemy." In the song that follows—"Ceylon"—Helena and Neville fondly recall their homeland,

while Edwin continues to boast of how he will make changes in Egypt. Edwin sings, "I will soon be /shaping, molding, / holding fortune / in my hand and / I'll improve and / shake and move and / change the lay and / nature of the land!"

The imposition of the Christian religion on other cultures is alluded to in the Christmas Eve dinner scene; when Neville comments on the severity of the storm outside by saying, "The gods must be angry," Reverend Crisparkle patiently corrects him, "*God* must be angry, Neville, not *gods*. We use the singular in England."

Love

The play gives us examples of many forms of love. Edwin and Rosa love each other, but it is a passionless love. Jasper loves and desires Rosa to the point of obsession, an obsession that accelerates his descent into madness. Neville's love for Rosa is an idealized, romantic love based on little knowledge of Rosa as a person (love at first sight). Jasper and Princess Puffer give us examples of a more parental type of love, Jasper for Edwin (when Jasper is in his more virtuous state) and Princess Puffer for Rosa.

The play offers no example of successful romantic love or marriage. The arranged betrothal of Edwin and Rosa not only fails to foster romantic love between them, it actually thwarts any that might have developed naturally. As Edwin and Rosa sing to each other in the duet "Perfect Strangers," "If we'd been perfect strangers, / I might have loved you perfectly." Likewise, Edwin laments to Jasper in the opening scene that because the marriage is prearranged, "our courtship suffers from an unavoidable flatness."

While the lack of passion is a problem for Rosa and Edwin, an excess of passion presents difficulties for Jasper and Neville. Jasper's obsession with Rosa contributes to his opium addiction and even leads him to treat her abusively (while possessed by the evil side of his personality). Neville's unrestrained passions, both for Rosa and in general, lead him to act impulsively and make him a prime suspect for murder. Because Dickens's novel was unfinished, neither Holmes nor the reader can know for sure if Dickens intended to present his audience with a more wholesome example of love, some happy medium between tedium and obsession, though Holmes gives the audience the opportunity to pair off two of the characters at the conclusion of the play.

Prejudice

The play presents some typical nineteenth-century biases towards people from Eastern nations. Neville exemplifies the stereotype of the hot-blooded, uncivilized, exotic native of the East. Jasper tells Mayor Sapsea that beneath Neville's English mannerisms, "There is a heathen Landless, a tribesman Landless, a half-blooded, half-bred half-caste who would kill as easily as he would comb his sleek hair!" Though more cool in temperament than Neville, Helena is presented as mysterious and exotic, with an "unplaceable" accent. While Holmes sometimes exaggerates these prejudices for theatrical and comic effect, they do represent real attitudes held by society in Dickens's time. In his landmark 1978 book *Orientalism*, Edward Said claimed that studies of the East by Western scholars and writers were skewed by assumptions about the Eastern personality; for example, the assumptions

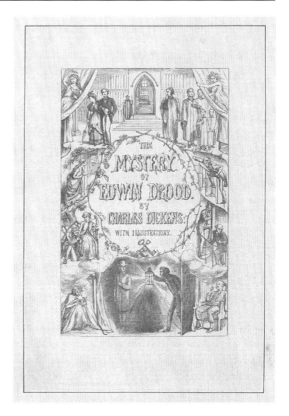

Cover of The Mystery of Edwin Drood *by Charles Dickens* (Getty Images)

that those from Eastern cultures had a more passionate, "hot-blooded" nature and that Eastern individuals had more emotional and less rational patterns of thought. In the play, Jasper cleverly exploits these attitudes in his attempt to frame Neville for the murder of Edwin.

STYLE

Metatheater

The term metatheater refers to techniques that call the audience's attention to the theatricality of the story presented; in other words, instead of permitting the audience to become lost in the world of the play, the playwright draws attention to the fact that the audience is watching a performance. The play-within-a-play technique used by Holmes in *The Mystery of Edwin Drood* is an example of metatheater. The chairman constantly reminds the audience that they are watching a play, through his frequent interruptions to introduce the company's actors (thus reminding the audience that they have other identities beyond their roles in the Drood story). Having the audience vote on the identities of Dick Datchery, the murderer, and the lovers is another metatheatrical device.

The device of the Music Hall Royale theater company and its antics serves an important purpose in the musical. The Dickens novel on which the play is based is one of his darkest works, featuring madness, drug addiction, obsession, and violence, none of which are usually ingredients for a lighthearted musical comedy. By inserting the comedic element of the actors' personal issues and temperaments—Clive Paget's womanizing nature, Phillip Bax's despair over his small roles, James Hitchens's failure to appear as Mayor Sapsea—Holmes lightens the mood of the play. Likewise, the musical stings that point out suspicious or prophetic statements also serve to transform a somber story into a melodramatic parody, as do self-conscious, stilted statements by the characters (such as Helena's comment to Reverend Crisparkle, "I only wish I could express my gratitude without this strange, somewhat geographically untraceable accent!").

Musical Theater

The Mystery of Edwin Drood is a musical. Music, in theater, can also be considered a form of metatheater, because when a character bursts into song in the middle of a scene, it reminds the audience that they are watching a performance (since in reality, most people do not burst unexpectedly into song in the middle of a conversation).

The style of much of the music is consistent with modern musical theater. Many of the songs are in a minor key, which adds to the dark, mysterious nature of the story ("Moonfall," a haunting melody first sung by Rosa, is a good example). Other songs pay tribute to the play's British roots; for instance, one can imagine "Off to the Races" being sung by the clientele of a rowdy English pub. When the murderer is selected, his confession reprises earlier songs from the musical, usually with altered lyrics.

Interactive Theater

The conclusion of *The Mystery of Edwin Drood* is determined by audience vote, which is the most unique element of the musical. The audience votes on three issues: the identity of Dick Datchery, the identity of the murderer, and which two characters should become lovers at the end of the play. Given the many possible combinations of these three

choices, a playgoer could attend the musical numerous times and never see the same show.

Other examples of interactive theater include *Tony n' Tina's Wedding*, in which audience members dance and dine as guests at an Italian couple's wedding; *The Boomerang Kid*, a 2007 play in which audience members vote on the direction of the plot via handheld electronic devices; and forms of improvisational theater (such as the Second City), in which the actors create scenes based on audience suggestions.

HISTORICAL CONTEXT

The Mystery of Edwin Drood first premiered in 1985. The 1980s were a time of uncertainty and unease for many. Ronald Reagan, in office less than three months, was the target of an assassination attempt in early 1981. Terrorist events, such as the hijacking of TWA flight 847 by the Hezbollah, an Islamic political group, and the hijacking of the cruise ship *Achille Lauro* by Palestinian terrorists (both in 1985); changes of leadership in the still-communist Soviet Union (called an "evil empire" by President Reagan in 1983); and the advent of AIDS, a frightening terminal disease, all made the world seem like a hostile and unstable place.

As a distraction from these events, many Americans enjoyed following the lives of the royal family in England. Two fairy-tale weddings (followed by far less idyllic marriages) took place in the 1980s: Charles and Diana in 1981, followed by Andrew and Sarah in 1986. Princess Diana also gave birth to two sons during this time, Prince William (heir to the throne of England) in 1982 and Prince Harry in 1984.

The 1980s produced some impressive musical theater, including Jerry Herman's *La Cage Aux Folles* in 1983 and Stephen Sondheim's *Sunday in the Park with George* in 1984. At the 1985 Tony Awards, the winner for Best Musical was *Big River*, a musical which had much in common with the next year's winner, *The Mystery of Edwin Drood*. The score for *Big River* was written by a popular songwriter who had never written for musical theater (country-western star Roger Miller), and the musical was based on a nineteenth-century novel by a literary giant, Mark Twain. In addition, the Broadway production of *Big River* featured Patti Cohenour in the role of Mary Jane Wilkes;

COMPARE & CONTRAST

- **1873:** Opium, besides being a recreational drug, is also used for medicinal purposes in the form of laudanum (an alcoholic dilution of opium) or morphine. Even some children's medicines contain opiates.

  1985: Heroin addiction is far more common in the twentieth century than opium addiction (though heroin is derived from opium). The sharing of needles by heroin addicts puts them at risk for a new disease, AIDS.

  Today: Heroin use has increased since 1985. This may be because the increased purity of the drug makes it possible to get its effects by sniffing or smoking rather than by injecting.

- **1873:** Audiences at a British theater performance feel free to shout out suggestions to the actors.

  1985: Audiences sit quietly through most theater performances, with the exception of improvisational theater.

  Today: While random shouting during most theater performances is still discouraged, the number of interactive shows is on the rise.

- **1873:** While arranged marriages have fallen out of favor in the West since the eighteenth century, they still take place, and one's choice of spouse is usually restricted to people in the same social and economic class.

  1985: In England and the United States, arranged marriages are virtually unheard of, though they still occur in some Asian and Middle Eastern countries.

  Today: Arranged marriages are very rare in Western countries. However, more and more people use online services to find compatible mates.

Cohenour would later play Rosa Bud in *The Mystery of Edwin Drood.*

British Theater

Holmes uses the device of a nineteenth-century theater company to add humor to Dickens's dark tale of obsession and madness. Like Holmes's musical, nineteenth-century British theater was far more interactive in nature than theater today. Repertory companies (such as the Music Hall Royale) were the norm, as opposed to hiring specific actors for roles in one particular play. Members of the company became well known to regular theatergoers and heckling by the audience (and reciprocation by the actors) was not uncommon.

British Colonization

After the British lost the American colonies in the late eighteenth century, they looked elsewhere to establish new colonies: Africa, Asia, and the Pacific. Though at the time of Dickens's death in 1870, the British Empire had yet to reach its peak (which occurred in the later nineteenth and early twentieth centuries), it already had a significant number of colonies throughout the world. Egypt was an area of great interest to Britain, especially after the opening of the Suez Canal in November of 1869, making Edwin Drood's proposed journey to Egypt a significant one, especially considering Dickens could not know the British would later occupy Egypt, from 1882 until 1922.

CRITICAL OVERVIEW

The Mystery of Edwin Drood premiered outdoors at the Delacorte Theater in Central Park as part of the New York Shakespeare Festival, and admission was free. While the show was extremely popular at the festival, some critics wondered if the show would fare as well when it moved indoor to the Imperial Theater, with

Edwin and Rosa under the trees (© *Lebrecht Music and Arts Photo Library | Alamy*)

tickets at forty-five dollars a seat. As reviewer Frank Rich of the *New York Times* writes, "The main mystery posed by the Broadway arrival of 'Edwin Drood' is whether the show's raucous, not to mention erratic, charms can retain their buoyancy indoors."

Fortunately, the musical was as big a hit indoors as out. The huge success of *Nicholas Nickleby* in 1981 had Broadway audiences in the mood for more Dickens, and the 1984 hit *Big River* had proved that a musical based on a nineteenth-century novel could be very entertaining. When *Drood* premiered at the Imperial theater, some critics had reservations about the script or the music, but few could deny that the show was great fun. In his review for the *Chicago Tribune*, Richard Christiansen calls the show "an irresistible invitation to happiness." Leo Savage, in the *New Leader*, describes it as an "enchanting evening." The source of all this merriment, according to some, is the audience participation in the second act, when playgoers get the chance to decide the outcome of the show. Rich also claims that once the voting begins, "the atmosphere in the theater becomes as merry as that of an unchaperoned auditorium of high-school kids," and in an earlier

review of the Central Park production, he calls the idea "delightful and ingenious." In a *Variety* review of a 2007 production of the musical by the Sacred Fools Theater Company, Terry Morgan claims that the voting "highlights the primal power of communal storytelling."

The voting, however, is not the only source of the musical's charms. The original cast, featuring Betty Buckley as Drood, George Rose as the chairman, and Cleo Laine as Princess Puffer, is often cited as another reason for the show's success. George Rose, in particular, is lauded for his "infectious high spirits and incomparable delivery" by Christiansen in his review. Rose won a Tony award for Best Actor for his performance.

Some critics qualify their praise with critical remarks regarding the music or the comedy gags; Rich, who was a fan of the voting, writes, "Too bad the audience can't vote along the way to decide which extraneous songs, scenes and gags might be weeded out." This need for editing is echoed by Savage, who claims that the show takes every opportunity for humor, including some which "might have been profitably passed up." Holmes's score is often described as uneven but entertaining on the whole. The overall joviality of the show and cast is enough to overrule any objections; as Savage writes, "At the Music Hall Royale any critical vacillation is quickly swept away by the upcoming big laugh."

CRITICISM

Laura Pryor

Pryor is a freelance writer with twenty-five years of experience in professional writing with an emphasis on fiction. In the following essay, she examines the changes Holmes made to Dickens's original story and the reasoning behind them.

In the acknowledgements of the published book for Rupert Holmes's musical *The Mystery of Edwin Drood*, Holmes freely admits that his play "was never intended to be a serious Dickensian adaptation" and that his goal, above all others, was "to amuse, divert, and entertain the patrons at almost any cost." How, and at what cost, did Holmes achieve his goal? How does a playwright take a novel (unfinished, at that) featuring opium addiction, obsession, violence, murder (possibly), and racial hatred and turn it into a musical that audiences and critics describe as jolly and irreverent?

The answer to this question is three-fold. First, Holmes used the metatheatrical device of a hammy, over-the-top nineteenth-century theater company to perform the story of Edwin Drood. Second, the structure of the play allows the audience to vote on the outcome of the tale, invariably leading to some preposterously implausible endings, such as Rosa Bud falling in love with Bazzard. Third, Holmes changed the events of Dickens's tale to make it lighter and less disturbing. Because most members of the audience, on any given night, have not read Dickens's unfinished novel, they are probably not fully aware just how preposterous these conclusions often are. In crafting his script, Holmes altered some significant details of the mystery, so that conclusions perfectly plausible in the musical would make little sense in the context of the novel.

Many of these details center around the fateful Christmas Eve dinner at John Jasper's house. This is a climactic scene in the first act of the musical, featuring Neville and Edwin in an escalating quarrel, urged on by Jasper with liberal helpings of drugged wine, all taking place within the song 'No Good Can Come from Bad." In the novel, Dickens describes, in great detail, the events leading up to the dinner, but no dinner scene is portrayed; the reader learns little of what transpired there. The wine-fueled row in which Neville and Edwin nearly come to blows occurs much earlier, shortly after Rosa collapses during her music lesson with Jasper. In this encounter at Jasper's home, Neville calls Edwin "a common boaster," and Edwin replies, "You may know a black common fellow, or a black common boaster, when you see him...but you are no judge of white men." After this insult, Neville hurls the contents of his wine glass at Edwin and then dashes the goblet into the fire. Later Jasper invites the two (not the entire cast of characters, as in the play) to Christmas Eve dinner to make peace with each other (or so he says). While clearly no such peace is achieved in the musical, in the novel Jasper tells Reverend Crisparkle after Edwin's disappearance, "all went smoothly and quietly when they were last together at my house."

Another significant alteration involves Jasper urging Edwin to wear his caped coat when he leaves to go on his walk with Neville (after which there is a "sinister and significant musical sting," according to the musical's script). This does not occur in the novel, and no such coat is found; only Edwin's watch and shirt pin are found in the river by Reverend Crisparkle. The addition of this detail by Holmes cleverly provides a bevy of additional suspects. Though only two characters have a clear motive for killing Edwin (Jasper and Neville), introducing the possibility of Edwin being mistaken for Jasper gives Rosa, Helena, and Princess Puffer motive for murder as well. This makes the voting aspect of the play more entertaining and encourages repeat visits to the playhouse as well, to see yet another character confess their guilt.

Holmes makes another alteration to engender sympathy for Princess Puffer; he reveals her to the be the past nanny of Rosa Bud (no such revelation occurs in the novel). When Puffer encounters Rosa on the street, and Rosa asks her why she left her position as governess, Puffer sings a sad story of seduction and abandonment. In the novel, Puffer encounters Edwin, not Rosa, on the fateful Christmas Eve. She asks his name, and when he tells her his name is Edwin, she replies, "You be thankful that your name ain't Ned." When Edwin asks why, she tells him it is "a threatened name. A dangerous name." Puffer has heard Jasper rant during his opium visions

WHAT DO I READ NEXT?

- The musical is loosely based on *The Mystery of Edwin Drood* (1870), an unfinished novel by Charles Dickens. It was Dickens's last work. Because he left no notes as to his intentions for the rest of the novel, there are many different theories as to how the story should end. The novel is considerably darker and more complex than the play.

- In *The Strange Case of Dr. Jekyll and Mr. Hyde*, Robert Louis Stevenson's famous 1886 novella of a man with a split personality, Dr. Jekyll suffers from a condition similar to that of John Jasper. Since Dickens's novel preceded Stevenson's story by sixteen years, it is possible that Stevenson was inspired in part by *The Mystery of Edwin Drood*. It is available in a 2010 edition published by CreateSpace.

- Like this musical, Holmes's 2005 mystery novel *Swing* features an interactive experience. The novel includes a CD of big band music, which is alluded to in the novel, and the songs include clues to solving the mystery. The story, set in the big band era, features Ray, a jazz musician who falls for a young composer; their love story is complicated by a murder mystery that Ray attempts to solve.

- The 2003 young-adult novel *Picture Perfect* features a teenage boy, Ian, whose best friend, Teddy, is murdered. Soon Ian is a suspect. Disturbing images and flashes of memory that Ian experiences reveal that he may be repressing facts about the day Teddy was murdered. As in *The Mystery of Edwin Drood*, the theme of multiple personalities is examined in this thriller by Elaine Marie Alphin.

- Japan's most famous mystery author, Akimitsu Takagi, wrote the 1965 novel *Honeymoon to Nowhere*, in which a young bride-to-be is determined to marry her fiancé despite some suspicious information unearthed by her father before the wedding. On their wedding night, her husband is called away by a colleague and never returns to their hotel; his body is found later, strangled. Besides being an entertaining mystery, the novel provides an interesting look at middle-class Japanese life circa 1965.

- Norrie Epstein's 1998 book *The Friendly Dickens* examines Dickens in a way that is accessible to the ordinary reader. She includes tips on how to read Dickens, which novels to try first, interviews with actors who have played Dickensian characters, and easy-to-read summaries of many of Dickens's works. Epstein wrote a similar book on Shakespeare (titled *The Friendly Shakespeare*).

- For those interested in Broadway musicals, the 1990 comprehensive guide *Broadway Musicals: Show by Show (Fifth Edition)* by Stanley and Kay Green, profiles over three hundred Broadway musicals, beginning with a play titled *The Black Crook* from 1866. Facts include the writers of the book and score, the original cast, producers, directors, and choreographers, plus the location and dates of the show's original run; these details are followed by a description of the play and its history.

and has taken it upon herself to warn the unfortunate "Ned" of whom he speaks. Unfortunately, the naïve Edwin finds it only "an odd coincidence" that Jasper (and only Jasper) calls him Ned.

One of the ironies of the musical, when compared to the novel, is the omission of Jasper as a candidate for the murderer (although he is presented as an option to the audience when voting begins, Jasper is never the chosen murderer, because in all possible versions of the musical he is cleared by Durdles, a witness). There is considerable evidence that Dickens intended to reveal Jasper as the murderer of Edwin Drood. Dickens consulted his good friend and biographer, John Forster, whenever he was working on a new

A typical English cemetery *(Adrian Zenz | Shutterstock.com)*

book; in the biography, *Life of Charles Dickens*, Forster claims that Dickens confided to him that Jasper murdered Drood and that at the conclusion of the book, Rosa would marry Tartar (an old friend of Crisparkle's, left out of the musical), Crisparkle would marry Helena, and Neville would die in the process of apprehending Jasper and revealing him as the culprit. Dickens's own children confirmed that if any changes were to be made to his intended story, he would consult first with Forster.

Just like the invention of the borrowed coat, however, the omission of Jasper as a candidate for murderer helps makes the outcome more entertaining. Anyone who has ever read or watched a mystery tale knows that having the most obvious suspect turn out to be the murderer is both boring and disappointing. The audience expects a twist. Dickens's daughter claimed that her father found the psychological aspect of Jasper's madness equally as important as the mystery theme of the novel; Holmes, on the other hand, is interested in entertainment, not exploring the human psyche. If Jasper was the murderer, this would lead to a boring and disappointing conclusion to the

musical—certainly something to be avoided at all costs.

Some conclusions to the novel written shortly after Dickens's death speculate that Edwin is still alive after his disappearance, though according to the aforementioned historical evidence, this would contradict Dickens's intentions. In his musical, Holmes has it both ways: first, Edwin is pronounced dead by a vote of the cast, and a murderer is selected; then, in the final scene, Edwin is resurrected, and the audience learns that he was never dead, only unconscious. This paves the way for a happy ending, complete with a rousing chorus of the upbeat "Don't Quit While You're Ahead."

The changes Holmes makes to the story allow his irreverent cast of nineteenth-century hams to turn a brooding psychological drama into a campy melodrama and enjoyable comedy. While Dickens might have taken issue with this, Holmes's desire to "amuse, divert, and entertain" is something Dickens surely would have understood.

Source: Laura Pryor, Critical Essay on *The Mystery of Edwin Drood*, in *Drama for Students*, Gale, Cengage Learning, 2011.

Elaine Liner

In the following review, Liner comments that her only complaint regarding the play is that it is too long.

When all elements come together, a night at the theater can be as refreshing as a three-day weekend. In WaterTower Theatre's production of the Rupert Holmes musical *The Mystery of Edwin Drood*, the cast is first-rate and the technical aspects are nearly flawless. Holmes' book and music offer a cleverly conceived play-within-a-play and more than 20 haunting and melodic songs. There's lively dancing, corny jokes and the tricky gimmick of allowing the audience to choose how to solve the "mystery" at the end. Only problem is, there's just about 45 minutes too much of a good thing. Pushing three hours, *Drood* at times feels like it's going to last the weekend long. But too much of a good show isn't such a bad deal. There's plenty to like about *Drood*. Based on an unfinished murder mystery by Charles Dickens, who dropped dead before writing down who the culprit was, *Drood* takes the form of an English music hall production. The troupe of actors playing actors playing Dickens' characters melodramatically present the story of the disappearance of Edwin Drood in song and dance. After Drood vanishes—at the place where Dickens stopped writing—audience votes decide who will take on the key roles of the investigating detective, the murderer and the pair of happy young lovers. Depending on how the voting winds up, the finale could veer off in hundreds of different directions. That kind of leeway is a lot to ask of a large cast, but the WaterTower bunch, ably directed by Terry Martin, is up to it.

In the leading role of the narrator, the "Chairman" of the troupe, is R. Bruce Elliott. Part Scrooge, part Puck, Elliott, thick gray hair parted in the middle and hanging to his shoulders, sets the mood for *Drood* by addressing the audience directly. "Let's all be as vulgar and uncivilized as legally possible," he says with a friendly growl. Elliott is an actor at a point in middle age where he is completely comfortable in his own skin and in his chosen profession. What a pleasure to watch this pro having such a good time and what fun to see him doing light comedy again. It's impossible not to like him.

In the title role is a WaterTower newcomer, Dara Whitehead. Young Edwin always is played by a woman, continuing an English music hall tradition of cross-gender impersonation, or so the Chairman tells us (Betty Buckley played Edwin on Broadway in the mid-'80s). Whitehead has a gorgeous, enormous voice and an androgynous physical silhouette that could carry her into big-voiced boy roles such as Victor/Victoria or Peter Pan. She's a pip.

As Edwin's love interest, the ingenue Rosa Bud, Arianna Movassagh wears a costume of pink confection that suits her sweet, bell-like soprano and kittenish face. Only Movassagh's wicked comic timing keeps the role from turning sickeningly sticky.

The cast doesn't lack for singing talent. Greg Allen lends his powerful baritone to the villainous role of John Jasper, the laudanum-chugging choirmaster who has the hots for Rosa's bud. M. Denise Lee, who might hold the title of Dallas' reigning musical diva, throws her thrilling voice into the torchy role of the prostitute, Princess Puffer, who runs an opium den frequented by the naughty choirmaster.

Michael Serrecchia, who overacts, oversings and over-everythings every musical role he ever gets (or at least the last two he had at Theatre Three), finally makes his hamminess work as the Reverend Chrisparkle. When he goes swanning off the stage with a flounce and a flourish, the audience falls out laughing.

For additional comic relief, there is David Stroh as the scrofulous gravedigger Durdles (and isn't that a rich old Dickensian name?). Teeth blacked out, one eye squinting, Stroh scuttles around the stage like a horny hermit crab. He's hilarious. Ditto Randy Pearlman as a bit player named Bazzard. He makes the most of an Act 1 showstopper, "Never the Luck," a tribute to small roles and unknown actors. Shades of Chicago's "Mr. Cellophane."

Even tarted up with the music hall silliness, the story that emerges from *The Mystery of Edwin Drood* offers a fascinating look at duality, the thin line separating good and evil in the human soul. This is a fine musical, more tuneful than most Webber-Rice shows and infinitely better lyrically than the screechfest known as *Les Miz*. It's just that there are about five or six too many numbers in Drood, including a ditty called "Off to the Races" that serves no purpose other than to delay the intermission after a first act that's more than 90 minutes long. At that point, the song could serve as the audience theme for the mad dash to the lavs. . . .

Source: Elaine Liner, "In a Drood Mood: Dickens Murder Mystery Satisfies at WaterTower; Fully Committed Fizzles at DTC," in *Dallas Observer*, April 17, 2003.

Bridget Kinsella

In the following interview, Kinsella questions Holmes about his diverse career as a novelist and a playwright.

Publishers Weekly: You've won a Grammy for your song writing, two Edgars for Broadway plays and multiple Tonys for your Broadway play The Mystery of Edwin Drood, *and you have just been nominated for a Tony in the Best Play category for your current show on Broadway,* Good Night, Gracie. *What made you decide to write a novel?*

Rupert Holmes: I like to do something new all the time. I like to change the medium I work in, and part of that is, it keeps me young. I'm always a novice. It's always my first time.

PW: How was writing a novel different from your other work?

RH: There are so many things you can do in a novel that you can't do in a stage play or a series. And what I longed for was to write for an audience of one. Now, when I worked in night-clubs sometimes, I played for an audience of one, but to write comedy that does not have to amuse 1,500 people all at the same time is a very different and intimate thing.

PW: Your central character is a female journalist with a big book deal to write about a Lewis and Martin kind of comic act caught up in a scandal involving "a dead girl in New Jersey." Where did the idea for the book come from?

RH: A comedy team requires the same degree of trust as a trapeze act. I thought about how vulnerable and dangerous that is, and I thought that might make an interesting backdrop for a tale of intrigue.

PW: How did your real dealings with Hollywood affect the story?

RH: I've been close to a number of famous people in my career and I am just so aware how hard it is for them to preserve their privacy and how difficult it would be for them to keep a secret.

PW: Why did you decide to place it in the '70s?

RH: It was a very luscious time and everyone thought you could get away with everything and that you'd never pay a price for it. The mores of the time were almost unforgivable, but it makes for a very interesting setting.

PW: One of the characters in the novel is a New Jersey mob boss. Was he really based on someone you knew?

RH: When I was first in the record business in the late '60s, there were still lots of little labels with lots of connections with people in the construction and murder business. They liked me, God help me, and it frightened me to death. Sally Santoro is based on two different fellows that I knew whose nails and shoes were equally well glossed. And they really talked the way you see gangsters talking in movies.

PW: With all of your accomplishments people still persist on calling you the pina colada guy for having written that overplayed hit from the late '70s. What do you say when people ask about that?

RH: I envision my tombstone and it's in the shape of a giant pineapple. Actually, I have a two-part answer: "Yes," and "I'm very, very sorry." But that song gave me the luxury of three years to write *The Mystery of Edwin Drood.*

PW: Random House is releasing a single written by you and performed by Melissa Manchester to promote the book. How did this come about?

RH: Movies get title songs—why shouldn't novels? Why wait until they make the movie? I think it's just that I don't know how to write a work—even if it's prose—without writing musical accompaniment to go with it.

PW: The protagonist is revealed only as K. O'Connor and the reader never learns her first name. What is it?

RH: You're the first to know that K is her middle initial. I've always loved that in the novel *Rebecca*, and in the movie, you never know the name of the heroine, because Rebecca is so overwhelming, and that the protagonist is Mrs. DeWinter, but you never know her [first] name. And *Rebecca* is one of several types of books that are role models and touchstones for *Where the Truth Lies.*

PW: Is your next novel a mystery?

RH: I think anything I write will have to have a mystery in it. Most stories have mysteries in them. Life is a mystery story where we don't necessarily get the answer.

Source: Bridget Kinsella, "Murder, with Music: Talks with Rupert Holmes," in *Publishers Weekly*, Vol. 250, No. 22, June 2, 2003, p. 33.

Leo Savage

In the following review, Savage comments that Holmes takes a modern approach to an age-old play with delightfully comedic results.

Willard Huntington Wright called it "a straightaway detective story which might almost be used as a model for this type of fiction." Better known as S. S. Van Dine, creator of the Philo Vance novels, he was giving his expert opinion of *The Mystery of Edwin Drood*, the last work started by Charles Dickens. It was published in installments during the spring of 1870, but Dickens died before writing the second half. Another expert, Dorothy L. Sayers, Agatha Christie's most famous rival, regretted that Edgar Allan Poe had died 21 years earlier, because in her eyes the man who wrote *The Murders in the Rue Morgue* was the only one who could have finished—and solved—*The Mystery of Edwin Drood*.

Several authors have tried to produce a conclusion that was as Dickensian as the first half, yet could pass for "a straightaway detective story." Dickens' whodunit, however, has remained a literary puzzle whose solution defies as well as tantalizes writers and even composers.

The latest, and perhaps most inventive, approach to the task is that of Rupert Holmes. He has done the book, music and lyrics for a new show bearing the title of the unfinished novel. Joseph Papp has brought it to Broadway's Imperial Theater after having had it blossom into a big success last summer at Central Park's open-air Delacorte Theater. The musical, though, does not attempt to provide any answer on its own. Rupert Holmes knows he is no Sherlock, let alone an Edgar Allan Poe. He further realizes how frustrating it would be to put oneself in Dickens' gumshoes after the great storyteller has accumulated the most sinister implications and multiplied the most divergent suspicions in order to make a really dark mystery out of the disappearance of a young man named Edwin Drood.

Thus the musical happily does not insist on its sleuthing, except for laughs. It merely wants to be funny, and much of the time it is. From the incomplete tale Holmes has picked up his somewhat modified characters and a few limited episodes of the complicated plot. What he gives us is a kind of neo-Dickensian show in the form of 19th-century threatrics fueled by 20th-century gimmicks. For while the boards of the Imperial Theater fictively belong to Mr. William Cartwright's second-rate repertory company at The Music Hall Royale in Victorian London, the New York audiences are invited to freely decide who the murderer might be on the basis of what they have just seen.

An extraordinarily vivid and winning Mr. William Cartwright (George Rose) eventually presides over the "dangerously democratic" voting as "Your Chairman." But being the actor-owner of The Music Hall Royale, he starts off playing the part of Thomas Sapsea, Mayor of the cathedral city of Cloisterham.

Next, we are introduced to The Reverend Mr. Crisparkle (George N. Martin). John Jasper (Howard McGillin), a church member, teaches piano to an orphan named Rosa Bud (Patti Cohenour) in his house at Minor Canon Corner and is supposed to take care of his nephew, another orphan named Edwin (played, Mr. Cartwright informs us, by the "male impersonator Alice Nutting"; here actually Betty Buckley). That Jasper is domineering and villainous we soon discover from the way he treats his charges and from his visits to the opium den run by bawdy Princess Puffer (Cleo Laine). Then there are two perfidious looking twins from Celon, Helena and Neville Landless (Jane Schneider and John Herrera), and the very Dickensian Durdles (Jerome Dempsey), an upgraded gravedigger who haunts the crypts of Cloisterham Cathedral. Finally, there is a non-Dickensian bit actor named Bazzard (Joe Griffasi) who will do anything to become somebody in The Music Hall Royale, and fully succeeds at the Imperial Theater.

The most amusing aspect of the enchanting evening is not the tongue-in-cheek treatment of what we have of the mystery Dickens concocted in his most Gothic vein. It comes from the opportunities for humor offered in showing a dyed-in-the-wool Victorian company performing a sinister melodrama with all the theatrical trimmings of the period. Thanks to the subtle wisdom Rose lavishes on Mr. William Cartwright, and to the entire company enthusiastically entering the game, the author and director Wilfred Leach do not miss any of these opportunities. Indeed, a few might have been profitably passed up. But at The Music Hall Royale any critical vacillation is quickly swept away by the upcoming big laugh.

The second half is equally entertaining. It begins with the unexpected appearance of a bearded, shaggy, unrecognizable sleuth whom they call Dick Datchery. As a result, we are not only faced with the question of what happened to Edwin Drood. We are asked to determine as well who is doing the sleuthing, and to resolve several other questions indirectly "suggested" by Charles Dickens that the Chairman now puts to us directly. Naturally, whatever our answers—as indicated by the votes recorded in the various electoral districts formed among the rows of seats we occupy—Holmes will manage to have the last word.

I generally am not favorably disposed toward what is sometimes forced on the public in the name of "audience participation." A theatrical piece should be able to retain attention without having the actors leave the stage to take hold of the spectators from the aisle. I remember a production at Joseph Papp's Public Theater where my wife and I refused to be dragged from one bench to another as part of the play. At the Imperial, though, Holmes and Leach and their emissaries avoid any trace of aggressivenes. Everybody seems happy, and you do not participate less if you abstain from raising an arm when the calls come for the votes.

The cast of *The Mystery of Edwin Drood* is perfect. Moreover, the production is wonderfully served by picturesque settings (Bob Shaw) and costumes (Lindsay W. Davis), ingenious lighting (Paul Gallo), and a mercifully tempered sound system (Tom Morse). I also like the way the choreographer (Graciela Daniele) handles John Jasper's pre-Freudian nightmare in Princess Puffer's opium den. It has mood, grace and sinuous acrobatics, with four sexy succubi coming out of Jasper's bed to undulate around his exploding complexes.

Source: Leo Savage, Review of *The Mystery of Edwin Drood*, in *New Leader*, Vol. 68, November 4, 1985, pp. 18–19.

SOURCES

Bossler, Gregory, "Rupert Holmes," in *Dramatist*, May/June 2003, pp. 18–29, http://www.rupertholmes.com/writings/dramatist/dramatist_0503.html (accessed July 25, 2010).

Christiansen, Richard, Review of *The Mystery of Edwin Drood*, in *Chicago Tribune*, December 17, 1985, http://articles.chicagotribune.com/1985-12-17/features/8503270275_1_edwin-drood-dickens-my stery-19th-century-english-music (accessed August 19, 2010).

Connor, Steven, ed., "Appendix B: The Evidence of Dickens's Contemporaries," in *The Mystery of Edwin Drood*, Everyman, 1996, pp. 281–85.

Daniel, Clifton, ed., *Chronicle of the 20th Century*, Chronicle Publications, 1988, pp. 1187, 1192, 1206, 1217, 1244, 1260, 1268, 1285.

Dickens, Charles, *The Mystery of Edwin Drood*, Everyman, 1996.

"Egypt: The Period of British Domination (1882–1952)," in *Britannica Online Encyclopedia*, http://www.britannica.com/EBchecked/topic/180382/Egypt/22393/The-period-of-British-domina tion-1882-1952 (accessed August 15, 2010).

Epstein, Joan F., and Joseph C. Gfroerer, "Heroin Abuse in the U.S.," in *Substance Abuse and Mental Health Services Administration*, http://www.oas.samhsa.gov/treatan/treana11.htm#E10E19 (accessed August 15, 2010).

Gordon, Meryl, "Escape from Piña Coladaville," in *New York Magazine*, August 11, 2003, http://www.rupertholmes.com/writings/new_york_mag_081103.html (accessed July 25, 2010).

Hanselman, Scott, "The Boomerang Kid: You'll Keep Coming Back," in *Splash*, http://www.lasplash.com/publish/Los_Angeles_Performances_116/The_Boomerang_Kid–You_1 l_Keep_Coming_Back.php (accessed August 15, 2010).

Holmes, Rupert, *The Mystery of Edwin Drood: A New Musical*, Nelson Doubleday, 1982.

Kenrick, John, "History of the Musical Stage: 1980s, Part II," in *Musicals101.com*, http://www.musicals101.com/1980bway2.htm (accessed August 19, 2010).

Morgan, Terry, Review of *The Mystery of Edwin Drood*, in *Variety*, September 25, 2007, http://www.variety.com/review/VE1117934875.html?categoryid = 33&cs = 1 (accessed August 19, 2010).

Parsons, Timothy, *The British Imperial Century, 1815–1914: A World History Perspective*, pp. 4–6, http://books.google.com/books?id = 81ZlzUsO8EYC&printsec = front cover#v = onepage&q&f = fals e (accessed August 15, 2010).

Rich, Frank, Review of *The Mystery of Edwin Drood*, in *New York Times*, August 23, 1985, http://theater.nytimes.com/mem/theater/treview.html?res = 9F02E2D6163BF930A1575BC0A963 948260 (accessed August 20, 2010).

———, Review of *The Mystery of Edwin Drood*, in *New York Times*, December 3, 1985, p. C21.

Rosen, Bruce, "Victorian History: Opium Dens and Opium Usage in Victorian England," in *Victorian History*, http://vichist.blogspot.com/2009/03/opium-dens-and-opium-usage-in-victorian.html (accessed August 15, 2010).

Said, Edward W., "The Scope of Orientalism," in *Orientalism*, Vintage Books, 1979, pp. 29–110.

Savage, Leo, Review of *The Mystery of Edwin Drood*, in *New Leader*, November 4, 1985, pp. 18–19.

"Suez Canal," in *Britannica Online Encyclopedia*, http://www.britannica.com/EBchecked/topic/571673/Suez-Canal/37107/History (accessed August 15, 2010).

Tony n' Tina's Wedding Web site, http://www.tonylovestina.com (August 25, 2010).

FURTHER READING

Ackroyd, Peter, *Dickens: Public Life and Private Passion*, Hylas Publishing, 2006.

This well-written biography of Dickens illustrates the contrast between the author's public and personal lives. While Dickens was tremendously popular and successful as an author, his personal life was often troubled, and he was haunted by his difficult childhood. Ackroyd, a noted Dickens scholar, gives the reader an insightful portrait of Dickens and also includes many historical illustrations and photos pertaining to his life and times.

Edgar, David, and Charles Dickens, *The Life and Adventures of Nicholas Nickleby, Parts One and Two*, Nelson Doubleday, 1982.

This is the complete script of the acclaimed stage adaptation of Dickens's novel, as performed in 1981 by the Royal Shakespeare Company. The book includes cast lists and eight pages of photos from the New York production. The stage production was over eight hours long and featured thirty-nine actors playing over one hundred and fifty parts. A film of the play was broadcast on the A&E network and is available as a DVD boxed set.

Kaminsky, Stuart, ed., *On a Raven's Wing: New Tales in Honor of Edgar Allan Poe*, Harper, 2009.

The Mystery Writers of America (of which Kaminsky is the Grand Master) sponsored this collection of twenty short stories inspired by the style of Poe. Rupert Holmes contributed the story "A Nomad of the Night"; other contributors include Mary Higgins Clark, Thomas H. Cook, and Paul Lovesey.

Pool, Daniel, *What Jane Austen Ate and Charles Dickens Knew*, Touchstone, 1994.

This guide to everyday life in the 1800s helps the reader understand the era and some of the archaic terms used by nineteenth-century authors. Pool offers a wealth of useful information on topics such as love and marriage, money, work, fashion, etiquette, and many other aspects of daily life.

Simmons, Dan, *Drood*, Little, Brown, 2009.

This psychological thriller is narrated by Wilkie Collins, fellow author and real-life friend of Charles Dickens. Collins (as portrayed by Simmons) proves to be an unreliable narrator, due to his opium addiction and his envy of Dickens's success. He tells of a mysterious and suspicious stranger named Drood whom Dickens encounters in a railway accident; together, Collins and Dickens pursue him into the sewers of London to discover his ghoulish secrets.

SUGGESTED SEARCH TERMS

Rupert Holmes

The Mystery of Edwin Drood

nineteenth-century British theater companies

The Mystery of Edwin Drood AND musical theater

Charles Dickens AND The Mystery of Edwin Drood

Charles Dickens AND musical theater

Tony awards AND The Mystery of Edwin Drood

interactive theater AND The Mystery of Edwin Drood

Rupert Holmes AND musical theater

Charles Dickens AND stage adaptations

Noises Off

MICHAEL FRAYN

1982

Noises Off is a popular 1982 play by the distinguished British playwright and novelist Michael
Frayn. Typical of Frayn's work, it is a farce
that combines elements of slapstick, absurdity,
clever puns, and other tricks of language.
Noises Off is set during the rehearsals and in
the backstage areas during performances of a
fictitious play: *Nothing On*. Frayn writes in an
interview with Denise Worrell in *Time* that he
had the idea while watching a performance of
one of his own plays from the wings: "It was
funnier from behind than in front, and I
thought 'One day I must write a farce from
behind.'" The phrase *noises off* is a stage direction that means sounds coming from off the set
are to heard on stage and by the audience. The
innovation in *Noises Off* is that in each of the
three acts, the audience sees the first act of
Nothing On performed over again. The first
act of *Noises Off* is a rehearsal seen more or
less as the audience for *Nothing On* would see
it. This play-within-a-play is a very inferior and
hackneyed farce, so bad that it is funny. The
second act takes place backstage during a performance of *Nothing On*, and the third act is a
later performance of *Nothing On*, seen again
from the front of its stage. Here, the endearing
eccentricities of the cast members are revealed
to be destructive failings that demolish the
world of the play.

Michael Frayn (© Gerry Walden | Alamy)

AUTHOR BIOGRAPHY

Frayn was born in an upper-middle-class British family in London on September 8, 1933. He attended Kensington Grammar School and earned a degree in philosophy at Emmanuel College of the University of Cambridge in 1967. He also did two years of compulsory military service, during which he learned Russian. He started work as a reporter for prominent English newspapers such as the *Guardian* and the *Observer*. He quickly became a columnist and was noted for the satirical style of his writing. After that, it was an easy transition to writing comic plays and novels. *Noises Off*, from 1982, is considered the most successful of his farces. *Copenhagen*, which deals with the Nazi nuclear bomb program during World War II, is considered to be a philosophical comedy and his most important play. It takes place during a historical meeting between the German physicist Werner Heisenberg and his Danish counterpart Niels Bohr. Frayn's novel *Headlong*, a farce set in the world of art history and art dealing, concerns the discovery of

a lost painting by Pieter Brueghel and was short-listed for the Booker Prize in 1999. Frayn is still an active writer. *Afterlife*, a play based on the life of Max Reinhardt (the longtime director of the Salzburg Festival), has been on the London stage since 2008. It concerns the production of a play, a German version of *Everyman*, a fifteenth-century play that is one of the first substantial texts to be written in modern English. Putting his cold war Russian to good use, Frayn is recognized as the greatest English translator of the works of the Russian playwright Anton Chekhov.

PLOT SUMMARY

Noises Off is divided into three acts. Each act revolves around a performance of the fictitious play-within-a-play *Nothing On*. The first act takes place during a rehearsal of *Nothing On*, the second act in the backstage area during a later performance, and the third act during the last performance, seen from the audience's perspective.

Act 1

The first act of *Noises Off* is set during a technical rehearsal of a fictitious play called *Nothing On* being staged at the Grand Theatre in Weston-super-Mare, a small town in southern England. A technical rehearsal is the first rehearsal of a play in which the cast does not simply read through their lines or concentrate on some other isolated aspect of the production but performs the play exactly as they hope to before their audiences.

The first thing that an audience sees at a performance of a play is the handbill, a small pamphlet that contains information such as the names and backgrounds of the cast members, a summary of the play, and advertisements. Frayn has provided a partial handbill for *Nothing On* to be circulated to audiences of *Noises Off* before the beginning of the play. It lists the characters of *Noises Off* as if they were real people and matches them with the characters and crew of *Nothing On*.

The plot of *Nothing On* involves a house that is being offered for rent. It is not occupied by its owners, the Brents, who have pretended to leave the country because they are attempting to defraud Inland Revenue (the British equivalent of the Internal Revenue Service). The services of a maid, Mrs. Clackett, who is employed by the Brents, come with the house. A real estate agent, Roger Tramplemain,

- *Noises Off* was adapted for film by Marty Kaplan, directed by Peter Bogdanovich, and released by Touchstone Pictures in 1992.

is in charge of finding a renter for the house, and he has brought his girlfriend there for a romantic meeting under the false pretense that he owns the house as a second home in the country. His girlfriend, Vicki, coincidentally works for Inland Revenue and has been assigned the Brents' file. Roger is under the impression that the housekeeper will be away since it is her afternoon off, but in fact they find her still on the premises, trying to eat a lunch of sardines while watching a television broadcast of some public event involving the British royal family. The Brents also return to the house, wishing to celebrate their wedding anniversary there. They are supposed to be living in Spain and hence are entitled to pay a lower income tax rate than they would if they spent even a single day in Britain during a given tax year. The two couples both think they are alone in the house, but they keep stumbling over traces (such as doors left open) of the other couple and being mystified by them. The effect is increased when a burglar (who turns out to be Vicki's long-lost father) breaks in. The tension builds as they all come closer and closer to running into each other. Finally, the two couples do confront each other, and in a last-ditch attempt to save the situation, Philip Brent ludicrously dresses up in bed sheets, trying to mimic traditional Arab dress. Just at that moment, a real Arab sheik who wants to rent the house makes his appearance. In a final absurdity, he happens to look just like Philip (they are both played by Frederick). This ends the first act of *Nothing On*, which is all that the audience of *Noises Off* ever sees.

The set on the stage for the first act of *Noises Off* is identical to that of *Nothing On*. When the curtain goes up, the audience sees the beginning of a theatrical production identical to *Nothing On* for about a page of the script. The action begins to reveal the circumstances of the plot to

the audience: Mrs. Clackett answers the phone and explains that her employers, the Brents, are in Spain, and if the caller wants to rent the house, he must call the real estate agent. She then proceeds to go into the television room to eat her lunch. As *Nothing On* unfolds, she is not supposed to go off and forget the plate of sardines she set down to answer the phone, but instead she takes them with her. At this point, a voice from the darkened theater floor begins to shout at the actress on the stage that she is doing it wrong: she is supposed to take the sardines. This is Lloyd Dallas, the character in *Noises Off* who is the director of *Nothing On*. The actress on the stage breaks out of the character she has been playing and begins to play Dotty Otley, who is portraying Mrs. Clackett in *Nothing On*. Dallas and Otley begin to discuss the stage directions from *Nothing On* that the actress ought to be performing. This is disorienting for the reader, though Frayn helps to keep things straight by printing the script for *Nothing On* inside text boxes, but it is far more disorienting for the viewer, for whom the illusion and space of the stage has just been obliterated.

As the rehearsal continues, the actors drift in and out of their roles in *Noises Off* and *Nothing On*. The action of *Noises Off* principally serves to establish character. All of the characters refer to each other with very affectionate (and often characteristically British) terms, such as "love" and "my precious." This is in accord with Frayn's belief that actors instinctively bond with each other because of the emotional effort required by the tremendously vulnerable and embarrassing nature of what they do. Dottie Otley (who is given top billing on the handbill for *Nothing On*) is revealed to be the primary investor in the show, betting her small life's savings on the success of the show.

The incidents of *Noises Off* often foreshadow what is to come in the later acts when the play breaks apart: fears about Selsdon's drunkenness or Brooke losing her contact lens in the middle of a scene. The disjointed, mistimed actions of the first act also form a counterpoint to the tightly paced, flawless timing of the second act.

Act 2

The second act is set a month later, backstage at a performance of *Nothing On*. Lloyd has not seen the company in the intervening time. He has been rehearsing a production of Shakespeare's *Richard III* for a festival in Wales. He imagines, at least, that this is much more important work than what he did with *Nothing On*. The company is on the verge of tearing itself apart over several romantic entanglements that have been developing since the rehearsal period. In fact, Lloyd has returned to visit Brooke, with whom he has been having an affair. He has a bottle of whiskey with him and, as though he were still the director, instructs Tim, the production manager, to get a bouquet of flowers for Brooke from a florist just outside the backstage door of the theater.

In the printed version, once the play begins, the text of the first act of *Nothing On* (which the actors fully perform) is printed in parallel columns with that of *Noises Off*. The latter describes what the actors and crew do backstage as they come offstage and wait to go back on. They cannot speak backstage since their voices would be heard through the thin set and interfere with the play being put on; the effect is like watching a silent film. The stage directions for *Noises Off* describe the rather optimistic hope of the cast and crew. They "express silent relief that the show has at last started, so all their problems are over." The action that follows is pure slapstick. It revolves around mutual misapprehensions and misunderstandings. As one female cast member after another thinks that the flowers Tim brings from the florist are for her, he has to bring in bouquet after bouquet. Everyone who sees Lloyd's bottle of whiskey thinks it belongs to Selsdon, who has a drinking problem, and tries to hide it, only to have another cast member think he or she has found Selsdon's hidden stash and transfer it to a new hiding place. Eventually, Selsdon gets hold of it, and one character after another has to take it away from him. Innocent actions such as searching for a lost contact lens or helping with a bloody nose are interpreted by various cast members as romantic betrayal. This leads to acts of revenge and physical attacks. Various noises of shouting and mayhem that are supposed to be made backstage as sound effects for *Nothing On* just happen to be made in earnest at precisely the right moment as cast members come close to killing each other. In this way, the two plays merge to produce comic effects that would have been impossible with one play alone.

Act 3

The third act takes place at the final performance, twelve weeks after the rehearsal in the first act. It simply shows a production of the play-within-the-play. *Noises Off* and *Nothing On* are eerily fused together. *Nothing On* becomes a vehicle for the hostilities and the fundamental incompetence of the characters of *Noises Off*. The actors now forget their lines and cues as they squabble on stage, short-circuiting the characters in *Nothing On*. Finally the entire structure of the play collapses: dramatically, as leads and understudies come on for the same role and a new plot must be devised to accommodate them, and literally, as the stage curtain falls over the cast, leaving them writhing like animals caught in a net.

CHARACTERS

Tim Allgood

Tim is the stage manager of the theater company producing *Nothing On*. His name is a pun alluding to his relative competence. Nevertheless, he is about to pass out with fatigue during the rehearsal in the first act because he spent the preceding seventy-two hours awake to finish the construction of the set. The problem is that he had initially built it backwards, facing away from the audience. This unlikely blunder is a foreshadowing of the transformation that is to take place in the second act. Later in the play, he is reduced to the position of Lloyd's servant, spending the whole of the second act running out to the florist to buy flowers on his orders. In the third act, he appears only as the burglar, mistakenly coming onstage as the whole structure of the play collapses.

Brooke Ashton

Brooke plays Vicki in *Nothing On*. Vicki is an Inland Revenue agent intent on having an affair with Roger Tramplemain, and she is investigating the Brents. Her appearance at their home for a liaison on the very night of their clandestine visit is a coincidence typical of a farce. Brooke's affair with Lloyd becomes the reason for his visit to the set three weeks after *Nothing On* begins its run, setting the second act in motion. Her tendency to lose her contact lenses is one of many premises that are established early in the play and later repeatedly exploited for jokes.

Belinda Blair

Belinda plays Flavia Brent in *Nothing On*. Flavia and her husband own the house where the play is set and are attempting to evade taxes. According to the handbill, Belinda started as a child actress and has been on the stage professionally her whole life. This gives her somewhat more professionalism than the other cast members, and she constantly tries to hold things together during the second act. Perhaps it is also her experience that enables her to expose Lloyd's incompetence as a director at the end of the third act.

Lloyd Dallas

Lloyd is the director of *Nothing On*. Like all the characters in *Noises Off*, he is a failure—in this case, an academic failure. The *Nothing On* handbill identifies him as a Cambridge graduate, and he is not above reminding the cast that he holds a formal degree while none of them do: "I'm just the one with the English degree. I don't know anything." Lloyd intends this last sentence ironically, because he truly believes that his degree gives him greater expertise about the theater than any of the cast or crew members. In fact, however, Lloyd knows far less about the theater than those he is nominally in charge of because he lacks the years of experience that they have. Further, the main thing that Lloyd "knows" is false. Lloyd spends much of the first act speaking in a parody of the Book of Genesis, as if the director is God and his directions give form to the world of the play: "And God said, Hold it. And they held it. And God saw that it was terrible." Lloyd had been indoctrinated at school with the auteur theory—that is, the view that the director alone is responsible for dramatic creativity. However, his experience is so limited that he is not yet able to acknowledge the real and vital roles played by every member of the collaborative endeavor of staging a play. In the third act, when Lloyd goes on stage in the burglar's costume, Belinda mocks him: "He's our social worker!... that nice man who comes in and tells us *what to do!*" He is forced to recognize that his own incompetence exceeds that of the cast as a whole and is ultimately responsible for the disaster that the play has become. At the end, even the structure of language disintegrates around him. No explanation is ever offered for his presence in the last performance of *Nothing On*, but since the absurdity of the farce requires it, it comes to pass.

Frederick Fellowes

Frederick plays two roles in *Nothing On*: Philip Brent and the sheik. Philip is one of the owners of the house where the play is set, and he is attempting to evade taxes. He has a habit of asking for rational explanations for the absurdities of the farcical plot of *Nothing On*. He also reacts hysterically (with a nose bleed) to witnessing the slightest act of personal violence, an irrational premise that is explained in the first act and then exploited for jokes in the second and third acts.

Robin Housemonger

Housemonger is the author of *Nothing On*, as indicated in the handbill. Though he does not appear as a character, his name suggests that Frayn equates the sort of play represented by *Nothing On* with pure commercial exploitation ("monger" means seller or vendor, and "house" refers to the audience in a theater performance), in contrast to his more serious work in *Noises Off*. Housemonger's name also has a connection with Roger Tramplemain, the real estate agent (a house seller) in *Nothing On*. By analogy, this may invite comparison between Lloyd Dallas, the main character of *Noises Off*, and Frayn himself.

Garry Lejeune

Garry plays Roger Tramplemain in *Nothing On*. Roger is the real estate agent in charge of renting the house where the play is set and is trying to seduce Vicki. Theater companies often include actors of various ages and of both sexes to accommodate the range of character types they are likely to encounter in their various productions. The actor who plays the dashing young male lead is, in British theater, traditionally called by the French term *jeune premier* (young lead). Garry's name is a pun on this term. Though his character is the lead in *Nothing On*, his role in *Noises Off* is comparatively insubstantial. Having appeared on television with Dotty, he doubtless owes his role to her influence. Toward the end of the third act, he trips over some props and falls down the stairs at the back of the set. It is unclear whether he lives or dies.

Selsdon Mowbray

Selsdon plays the burglar in *Nothing On*; he turns out to be Vicki's long-lost father. Selsdon was evidently once an actor in more legitimate theater, but he has fallen down to the level of *Nothing On* because of alcoholism. In the first act, Lloyd and the actors are constantly terrified he will get hold of a bottle of whiskey and drink until he passes out, an obvious parallel to the later collapse of the play. Much of the action in the second act revolves around keeping a bottle of whiskey away from him, while the unfounded fear that he is lying unconscious somewhere causes the absurdity of Tim and Lloyd both taking on the part of the burglar in the third act, heightening the onstage absurdity. In fact, however, he never succumbs to temptation.

Poppy Norton-Taylor

Poppy is the assistant stage manager in the company that is producing *Nothing On*. Poppy has an amateurish interest in the theater and has been given her job because she is the daughter of a sponsor of *Nothing On*. Although Lloyd's main romantic interest seems to have been Brooke, he nevertheless seems to have gotten Poppy pregnant during the period when the play was in rehearsal. This perhaps underlies the improvised ending of the third act, where Dotty proclaims Lloyd and Poppy (both on the stage as understudies) to be celebrating their wedding.

Dotty Otley

Dotty plays Mrs. Clackett, the maid, in *Nothing On*. Frayn derives considerable humor from the constant and varied mispronunciation of her name by the other actors onstage. In addition, she is listed in the handbill with the name of every character she has played on television that rhymes with Clackett. Despite her minor role in *Nothing On*, she has the highest billing of any cast member because she had a relatively successful career as a television actress when she was younger and because she has invested what little she managed to save in the production of *Nothing On*, making her the financial backer of the play. Her memory is deteriorating, and her inability to remember her lines established in the first act is an obvious fault line for the collapse of the play in the third act. She herself describes her failing memory in a highly fanciful way: "It's like a fruit machine in there. . . . I open my mouth and I never know if it's going to come out three oranges or two lemons and a banana." This does not, however, prevent her from having affairs with several male cast members. Despite her stake in the play, Dotty is the chief menace to its production, through both her incompetence as an actress and her genuine malice in taking out her jealous passions on the other cast members.

THEMES

Language and Languages

Language is part of the very fabric of human life and, as such, offers an unlimited scope for satire. Much of the most absurd language is commercial

TOPICS FOR FURTHER STUDY

- Although farce, as a genre, is deeply embedded in Western culture, the African American author Sterling Houston has adapted it to his own culture in his 2005 collection *Myth, Magic, and Farce: Four Multicultural Plays*. Write a short scene set during a rehearsal of one of Houston's farces.

- The animated television show *SpongeBob SquarePants*, especially in its later seasons, meets all the formal qualifications of farce. Episodes are posted online at the show's Web site: http://spongebob.nick.com/videos/browse/full-episodes/1/#browseVideos. Make a presentation to your class explaining some examples of the elements of farce in the show, illustrated by video clips.

- Frayn claims that for ten years before he happened to attend a performance in Prague, *Noises Off* was performed and read in the Czech Republic without the third act. What would be the effect of seeing the play in this shortened fashion? What reason is there for thinking this claim might be a joke by the author? Write a paper exploring the differences in meaning that would impress themselves on the audience between a full production of the play and a production with only the first two acts.

- Select a scene from one of William Shakespeare's comedies. Rewrite it, and even perform it, as the sort of satirical, broken-down farce that *Nothing On* is reduced to in the third act of *Noises Off*.

in nature, essentially used for advertising. Skillful advertising copywriters create a fantasy that their audiences believe will be attainable once they buy the product. The use of rhetoric for this kind of manipulation and deception leaves itself open to satire on many levels. Perhaps the most straightforward kind of satire of commercial language can be found, in an early example, in Jane Austen's *Mansfield Park*. In that novel, young Mr.

Rushworth comes into an inheritance of both property and money. He is not concerned with beautifying his country simply for the sake of beauty. He wants it to be redesigned by the landscape gardener Humphry Repton (a real individual who was an innovator in the use of advertising), not because he feels any aesthetic agreement with Repton but because then everyone will know how much money he was able to spend on it and that his taste is not his own but is shaped by popular opinion. At their base, those are the qualities that commercial speech cultivates, and Austen was able to find her humor merely by exposing those facts.

In Frayn's satires of commercial language (especially in the text of *Nothing On*, the play-within-a-play), he makes use of precisely the same technique as Austen but also goes quite a bit beyond it. Frayn's description of the set (an empty country house that is to be rented out) that serves for both *Noises Off* and *Nothing On* is described as being "from the estate agent's description of the property," that is, an ad written by a real-estate broker. The actual description makes it clear that what is being sold is an expensive fantasy meant to impress others: "Ideal for overseas company seeking English setting to house senior executive." The language of the description is inflated just a little more than in real advertising. No feature of the house is lacking an adjective: "notable," "mature," "delightful," "elegant," "light and airy," "modern," "luxurious," or "extensive." The satire becomes obvious when a closet is made a selling point and described as: "a small but well-proportioned linen cupboard." It could hardly be described simply as a closet; it must be praised as something extraordinary. The audience is being sold a fantasy puffed up with flattery.

This kind of joking subversion of advertising language is quite commonplace in English literature. In a way, that very ubiquity is what Frayn is calling attention to. Then, though, he reveals the real point of the satire at the end of the description of the house for rent: "All in all, a superb example of the traditional English set-builder's craft—a place where the discerning theatergoer will feel instantly at home." Commercial language is not the point of the satire at all; rather, the target is the language of the theater, which Frayn is proposing has become as hackneyed as advertising copy. Nevertheless, Frayn cannot resist restating his earlier theme in an even more exaggerated degree when the stage directions shift from the set to describe the first action of the play: "As the curtain

rises, the award-winning modern telephone is ringing." In this advertising language, the words may mean something quite different from their everyday uses, but at least the audience has come to understand what they mean. However, in farce, the words are suddenly revealed to mean something quite different again. The word *farce* comes from the Latin *farco*, which means to stuff. This may well have originally meant that the farce was something wedged into the program between serious or important dramas, but it could just as well refer to the heavily referential, overdetermined (that is, with multiple meanings or causes) use of language in farce.

Absurdity

One element of farce is the occurrence of extremely unlikely events: children separated at birth accidentally meeting their parents twenty years later, or the women of a nation forcing the men to end a war by going on a sex strike. In twentieth-century drama, like that of the surrealists or Samuel Beckett, this element of farce has been reinterpreted in a more serious manner to suggest larger concepts, such as the idea that existence is fundamentally absurd. Absurdity in *Noises Off* lies somewhere between the ridiculous and the profound. *Nothing On* certainly contains traditional elements of farce, such as Vicki and the burglar recognizing each other as long-lost daughter and father. However, the absurdities in *Noises Off* are treated reflexively. Frederick repeatedly asks for the absurd coincidences of *Nothing On* to be explained logically. For instance, he plays two roles, Philip Brent and the sheik, who resemble each other closely enough that the other characters in the play, including Frederick's wife, cannot tell them apart. Frederick wants to know how that can be. When he asks, he self-deprecatingly says, "You know how stupid I am about plot." Of course, it is the plot that does not make sense, not his question. When Lloyd answers him, he says: "All my studies in world drama lie at your disposal." His attitude, combining the condescension of a scholar helping a nonspecialist with the patronizing indulgence of an adult humoring a child, only heightens the absurdity. The answer that he gives, clearly fabricated as it is, is in fact drawn from numerous examples in world literature from Shakespeare to the Roman playwright Plautus. This reveals, if not the absurdity at the heart of existence, at least the absurdity at the heart of drama.

A scene from a 1992 production of Noises Off *(© Moviestore collection Ltd / Alamy)*

STYLE

Farce

A comedy that depends on improbable situations, physical humor, and wordplay is a farce. Farce is often considered a low type of humor, but it has its origins in the plays of the ancient Greek playwright Aristophanes, whose works would be described today as farces. Farce emerged in the eighteenth century from the background of popular comedic forms among street performers, such as the *commedia dell'arte*. The source of humor in a farce is unlimited and consists of anything that is ridiculous or laughable—puns, slapstick humor, mistaken identity, and outrageously improbable, contrived plots. The category is broad enough to encompass the comedies of Shakespeare and those of the Three Stooges. The plots in farces often revolve around social tensions, such as those surrounding sexual conquests or attempts to increase a character's wealth or status in an illegitimate manner. There is often an element of poetic justice in which a schemer is punished in some manner that pokes fun at the scheme. A typically farcical element of *Noises Off* is

the title of the play-within-a-play *Nothing On*. The title is a pun between the meaning of the phrase as theater jargon, being a theater that is not currently producing a play (suggesting that this particular play does not amount to very much), and the sexual meaning of the term referring to nudity. Sexual themes are very prevalent in farce because the humor allows the imagination of the viewer to bypass ordinary constraints. The characters express intensely felt emotions that are as universal as they are awkward and embarrassing, which people in real life must suppress and control. Seeing these feelings ridiculed in farce allows anxiety about them to be discharged.

Play-within-a-Play

A play-within-a-play usually takes place when the characters on stage are themselves viewing a play. Just as the audience is sitting in a theater viewing a stage, the actors on stage sit in a prop theater and view a stage set up on the stage. Perhaps the most famous play-within-a- play occurs in Shakespeare's *Hamlet*, when the title character produces a play for his uncle Claudius

COMPARE
&
CONTRAST

- **1980s:** When *Noises Off* is written in 1982, computerized word processing is still a relative novelty.

  Today: In 2000, speaking of a slight revision he made for a revival, Frayn says, "There's nothing like having to sit through a play twelve million times to make your fingers itch for the delete key." Today, all professional writing must be word processed (even if that represents a transcription from a handwritten draft), since typesetting is done electronically.

- **1980s:** The only phone in the play is a land line with a mechanical ringer and analog voice processing.

  Today: Cell phones are commonplace and doubtless would provide some opportunity for humor if the text of *Noises Off* were revised again.

- **1980s:** The Brents are attempting to become eligible to pay the lower nonresident income tax rate, but they must be absent from the country for an entire tax year.

  Today: Nonresident status with the Inland Revenue is easier to achieve, permitting a residency in Britain of as much as 182 days a year.

- **1980s:** The presence of wealthy Arabs from the Gulf states is a prominent feature of life in London, frequently commented on in the media and in literature of the period.

  Today: The most noticeable Arab presence in London featured in the media is impoverished Muslim fundamentalists from the Indian subcontinent, who are represented as frequently protesting in favor of the introduction of Sharia law into Britain and against the exercise of free speech they find offensive to Islam.

---

in which the characters act out crimes very similar to those that Hamlet suspects Claudius has committed, so that Hamlet can see whether or not he reacts in a guilty fashion. *Noises Off* takes the convention much farther, however. The play is set among a troupe of actors who are rehearsing a play called *Nothing On*, and the stage viewed by the audience consists of the play being used by the actors as they play other characters in their play, as well as the backstage areas of the theater represented in the play. At the beginning of *Noises Off*, the audience sees action that is identical to the beginning of *Nothing On*, but then the actors break out of their *Nothing On* roles and begin the performance of *Noises Off*, going over stage directions for the play they are rehearsing. This *reductio ad absurdum* (pushing something to such an extreme that it becomes absurd) is a farcical element of the play, leaving the reader and audience at first unable to tell what is going on, but it is meant to provoke a satisfying recognition once the realization is made. The confusing task of printing a text

with such complex stopping and starting of the play-within-a-play is handled in the published version of the script by printing the stage directions and dialogue of *Nothing On* in text boxes or parallel columns.

HISTORICAL CONTEXT

British Theater

Ornamented by Shakespeare, Great Britain is heir to one of the finest theater traditions in the world. The heart of the modern British theatrical world is in the West End theaters, the equivalent of the Broadway theater district in New York City. Although today the British theater scene is dominated by lavish and expensive productions typified by the works of Andrew Lloyd Weber, such as *The Phantom of the Opera*, in the early 1980s, more austere plays with less expensive production values were favored. This is the atmosphere that fostered the production of *Noises Off* in 1982. Farce was

One burglar at the beginning of the play turns into three burglars at the end. (Milan Vasicek | Shutterstock.com)

largely thought to be a dead art form by then because its quaint conventionality seemed old fashioned and fake compared with the revolutionary and realist dramas that had dominated the 1960s and 1970s. Frayn managed to revive farce not so much by transforming it as by showing its potential to a new generation. Farce is so topical (having to do with current events and items of interest) that works from the eighteenth or even nineteenth century are difficult to appreciate for modern audiences, even if they can easily adapt to ordinary comedies or dramas from then or even more remote periods. Nevertheless, the success of *Noises Off* quickly brought Frayn to prominence, and by 1985 he was a dominant writer for the British stage, with three plays running in the West End, and *Noises Off* continuing for almost ten years. Frayn's real-life success, however, is the opposite of the theatrical world represented in *Noises Off*. That is a very different reality of the British theater, a small touring company on the verge of financial, professional, and aesthetic

collapse, dependent not on art for success but on the titillation of farce, which, according to many critics, undermines the possibility of artistry. Peter Holland, in his 1992 review in the London *Times Literary Supplement*, describes a typical farce as a situation where "the men drop their trousers, the housekeeper drops her aitches, and the pretty ingénue runs on and off the stage in her underwear."

Feydeau

At the turn of the twentieth century Georges Feydeau was the most popular playwright in France, if not in the world. Despite his success, contemporary critics dismissed the importance of his plays because he wrote farces, although he is today considered to be an important forerunner of surrealism and other modern dramatic movements that rely on the absurd. Frayn first approached farce because he wanted to attack it as something old-fashioned, artless, and silly, but he soon found himself drawn into the linguistic and social complexity the form offers and was deeply influenced by his reading of Feydeau (who is still little known to modern English-speaking audiences). In his first conception of *Noises Off* Frayn had his theater company performing a Feydeau play in place of *Nothing On*, though he quickly abandoned the idea since his ramshackle regional theater company would hardly take on so obscure and difficult an author.

CRITICAL OVERVIEW

The initial reviews of *Noises Off* (together with the reviews of the film version) are collected in Michael Page's *File on Frayn.* They are surprisingly mixed in light of the play's popular and critical success. Page also collects a number of interviews Frayn gave for publicity purposes at the time of the play's original production, its American premiere, and its film adaptation.

Leslie Smith, in *Modern British Farce: A Selective Study of British Farce from Pinero to the Present Day*, draws comparisons between *Noises Off* and absurdist theatrical works such as Beckett's *Waiting for Godot.* Lines such as Frayn's "I'm just God.... I don't know anything" certainly suggest this could be a fruitful line of research, although very little secondary literature on *Noises Off* has yet been written.

Similarly, Merritt Moseley, in *Understanding Michael Frayn*, compares *Noises Off* to Tom Stoppard's 1967 *Rosencrantz and Guildenstern Are Dead*, in which the title characters helplessly try to live their own lives but are occasionally seized by a compulsion to go and act out their parts in *Hamlet.* One of the characters in that play observes, "We do on stage the things that are supposed to happen off. Which is a kind of integrity, if you look on every exit as being an entrance somewhere else." In both cases, the main point of the drama is to see a familiar play, as it were, from the other side.

CRITICISM

Bradley A. Skeen

Skeen is a classics professor. In the following essay, Skeen explores the intricacies of Frayn's farcical use of language in Noises Off.

WHAT DO I READ NEXT?

- David Dean's 2008 novel *The Defenestration of Bob T. Hash III* is a farce that concerns the writing and editing of a book-within-a-book.

- The 2007 collection of scholarly articles *Stoogeology: Essays on the Three Stooges*, edited by Peter Seeley and Gail W. Pieper, deals with a series of farcical films that often find a young-adult audience.

- Frayn claims that the inspiration for *Noises Off* came from his experiences being backstage at a production of his first performed play, *The Two of Us*, which was published as a monograph in 1970.

- Richard Sheridan's frequently reprinted 1779 farce *The Critic* (originally titled *The Critick Anticipated, or the Humours of the Green Room*) employs the device of being set backstage during a production of a play-within-a-play.

- Akira Kurosawa's 1949 Japanese film *Stray Dog* is partially set backstage at a theatrical production.

- Bi Feiyu's 2009 novel *The Moon Opera* is set backstage at the production of a Chinese opera and deals in part with the stress the traditional art form is put under by the impact of television and modernity.

- British teachers Steve Barlow and Steve Skidmore have written a parody of the famous *Star Wars* series called *Star Bores: May the Farce Be with You! The Original Parody.* It was published by HarperCollins UK in 2004.

Farce is often dismissed as a juvenile art form because of its reliance on devices such as slapstick comedy and themes such as sexual frustration. However, criticisms along these lines really reveal the critic's lack of appreciation of what is going on in farce. Slapstick, a type of physical comedy, in *Noises Off* requires the most intricate timing; when it is well executed, it can be described as balletic. Indeed, in this case,

> THE INTRICATE USE OF LANGUAGE
> REQUIRED BY THE HUMOR OF FARCE CAN BE SEEN
> IN THE FILM COMEDIES OF THE THREE STOOGES."

Frayn can do little more than suggest the complicated choreography of actions that the reader of the text can scarcely appreciate and that can only be created by the exertions of the director and the actors in a given production of the play. The very fact that such physical comedy can be appreciated only in action and not on the page may help to explain the accusation of the lack of sophistication. The theme of sexual frustration, which looms large in *Nothing On*, is also easily dismissed as a concern of the immature by those whose years have afforded them the wisdom to refrain from discussing such matters. However, it is an effective source of humor precisely because it is a common experience shared by all human beings and one whose pain is important in shaping almost everyone's emotional life, however well these truths may be hidden even from the self. That is precisely why it is "safe" to deal with the theme in farce: everyone can pretend that it is something trivial that does not apply them and that it can be easily dismissed by laughing at it.

Surely, though, the language in farce is nothing special. The bad puns and supposedly clever wordplay are so embarrassingly bad as to be nearly painful to hear, are they not? Isn't the language of farce truly sophomoric? Again, this attitude seems unexamined; it is difficult, sometimes, to make an honest examination of the source of the "pain," if something seems painfully bad. In fact, the audience members may be getting the pleasure of figuring out the wordplay, recognizing the mangled word or phrase that makes a pun or the two roots that have been freshly combined into a portmanteau. The simplicity and audacity of it may indeed provoke embarrassment, both on behalf of the playwright that he or she should do something so silly and on behalf of oneself for finding something so trivial to be so funny. But then again, is that not what the author intended all along? There is nothing immature about the language in farce. The humor often requires that the viewer immediately grasp a tremendous amount of knowledge to understand even the simplest joke, making for some of the most complicated use of language in literature. So much is compressed into a single phrase, so much is called for from the audience members in terms of their cultural understanding of every reference that the phrase evokes, that only a truly sophisticated viewer can grasp everything that is going on. This is why farce essentially cannot be translated. The density of reference cannot be achieved in the new language, and one is left with something very much simpler that does consist merely of slapstick and bad sex jokes. Even a slight cultural shift that does not require translation, such as that experienced by the modern American reader of Frayn's 1982 British work, can make much of the humor unintelligible.

The intricate use of language required by the humor of farce can be seen in the film comedies of the Three Stooges. In those farces, any characters that happen to be lawyers are invariable partners in the law firm Dewey, Cheatham, and Howe. To understand why that is funny, the viewer must first understand that the three names on the firm are in and of them themselves nothing exceptional or out of the ordinary. In fact, their distinctly British character lends them a certain aristocratic air, making them individually very appropriate names for a high-powered law firm. Next, the viewer must comprehend the bias against lawyers common in English literature, the stereotype that lawyers are all devious, twisting language and legislation for their own advantage; this bias is embodied in such terms as *shyster* and the frequent misquotations of Shakespeare about hanging all the lawyers, or the ubiquitous lawyer jokes on the order of "What do you call twelve dead lawyers at the bottom of the harbor? A good start." Only in this way does the name Cheatham begin to emerge as a homophone for the words "cheat 'em," referring to the supposedly common vice of lawyers. After this it starts to become apparent that the entire law firm name is a pun, a series of homophones that can be read as a sentence, or rather a brief but entire dialogue, with a wholly other meaning, describing the worst sort of lawyer imaginable: "Do we cheat 'em? And how!" It is a gleeful boast about the lawyers' hubris and powers of deception. To fully appreciate the meaning of that exchange, the audience must know that the cryptic phrase "And how!" was 1930s slang for agreement to a superlative degree: "thoroughly" or "yes, definitely." The expression thus reads

The plate of sardines was comically lost, found, trod on, and lost again. *(Paul Binet | Shutterstock.com)*

something like, "Of course we cheat everyone, and we do so very well too!" However, once one has spent a paragraph teasing out the meaning of the joke, all humor is lost. The audience member must be able to appreciate the joke instantly upon hearing it, and it is a very sophisticated skill to be able to know just how to evoke such an instant response in the audience.

Frayn is a literary genius whose use of language is comparable to that of the novelist Anthony Burgess, who is acknowledged as the greatest author of his generation. It is more difficult to untangle and understand the humor in his work than that in the Three Stooges. To see exactly the depth of reference that Frayn is capable of, and the rigor of the intellectual work he demands from his audience, let us play the same game we did a moment ago with the Three Stooges, with something from *Noises Off*. Choosing almost at random from the text, the eye falls upon the handbill for *Nothing On*, which mentions that Belinda Blair had previously acted in a play titled *Here Come les Girls!* The first

observation to be made is that the title is completely unintelligible and nonsensical, and yet quite familiar, even comfortable. The concept that language can be both things at once, and especially so in titles, headlines, and other phrases that are designed to hook an audience, is one that fascinated Frayn, and one which he had earlier explored in great depth in his novel *The Tin Men*.

The title *Here Comes les Girls!* achieves its simulation of familiarity through a simultaneous appeal to a number of types of title that were in common use in the 1970s and 1980s. Frayn purposefully makes reference to various clichéd formulas of titles for popular books and films, the kind of title that originated with one popular success and then was repeatedly copied to evoke the original success. A later example of this pattern was the gratuitous addition of the author's name before the title of a film adaptation of a literary work, as in *Bram Stoker's Dracula* or William Shakespeare's *Romeo and Juliet*, that was a fad in Hollywood in the 1990s. In regard to Frayn's farcical title, the first thing that stands out is the exclamation point. This comes from musicals and films such as *Oliver!* and *Oklahoma!* Anthony Burgess indulged in this particular fad also, in his unfilmed script based on the life of Shakespeare called *Will!* though he could not help but approach it as a sort of self-parody. This sort of title was very much in the air on the late 1970s and early 1980s. A timeless, trite Hollywood convention is the use of tiles that begin with the phrase "Here comes. . . ." The usage is perhaps derived from "Here comes the bride" and has predictably over the years given rise to a half-dozen film comedies called *Here Comes the Groom*, and one called *Here Comes the Bridesmaid*. An Internet search for books whose title begins with "Here Comes . . ." just in the five years before *Noises Off* was written returns more than five hundred unique results. One of them is Anthony Burgess's book on James Joyce, *Here Comes Everybody!* (a work that shares its title with a self-help book by William Schutz and a poetry anthology by Madeline Gleason). For Burgess, the title signifies the dense compression of reference and meaning Joyce achieves in almost every word of his writing, the same process seen here in Frayn. Another factor to consider is the entirely gratuitous use of the French definite article *les* with the English word *girls*. The use of French here suggests something racy and improper.

All of these references combine in the audience's imagination, first to form the impression of false familiarity, and then to suggest the hackneyed, tawdry nature of *Here Come les Girls!* Nothing with such a name could have the slightest artistic merit. Next comes the idea of the audacity of offering having acted in such a thing as a serious reference to recommend an actress's credentials. It is just that absurd daring that, if it comes quickly enough, will strike viewers as humorous but then will make them wonder what they are getting into by watching this play, a realization that is as unsettling as it is humorous.

It would be difficult to find a page of *Noises Off* that does not contain several phrases just as densely packed as *Here Come les Girls!* If anything, these phrases are more tightly packed than in much so-called serious literature, and they make greater demands on the audience to appreciate each joke in turn as they fall like a hailstorm. The idea that farce is not literature because it is sophomoric or lacking in art simply cannot be sustained under such a bombardment.

Source: Bradley Skeen, Critical Essay on *Noises Off*, in *Drama for Students*, Gale, Cengage Learning, 2011.

Jean Schiffman

In the following review, Schiffman discusses the tricks of the use of the farce in a modern entertainment environment.

Have the excesses of reality TV and the distractions of the digital age upped the ante for farce, a time-honored type of comedy usually characterized by slamming doors, mistaken identities, broad characterizations, and physical mayhem? Must the works of playwrights from Feydeau to Orton be rethought for the 21st century? Some directors might say so.

"I think in 2009 we need to have much more energy to hold an audience's attention," offers Robert Currier, artistic director of Matin Shakespeare Company, an outdoor summer theater in the San Francisco Bay Area. In his recent production of Oscar Wilde's *The Importance of Being Earnest* (which he calls a "verbal farce") was a Miss Prism so exceedingly fluttery that it seemed natural for her to engage in a variety of physical antics and pratfalls, and an Algernon who wandered cheerfully into the audience, grabbing sandwiches from people's picnic baskets and munching them (entirely justified by the fact that Wilde's Algie is a bit of a compulsive eater). Purists might say, "Aren't Wilde's witticisms enough?" But the audience, including me, loved seeing the comedy's farcical opportunities.

"In reality TV, you see people doing these ridiculous things—they'll do anything to become stars," says freelance director Mark Rucker. "Reality TV changes the way we see entertainment," raising the bar on what farcical behavior is.

But whether farce needs to be bigger than ever these days is for directors to decide. What actors need to know is that it does indeed need to be big and bold, as long as it's truthful within the context of the play's world. Actors also need to know what directors look for when casting a farce, what performers should bring to rehearsals, how much is too much, and how much is too little.

I recently saw a farce in which the central character, played by a reliably fine actor, remained an island of serenity amidst escalating chaos. A good choice in another context, perhaps—but not in farce. If all the characters don't get caught up in the spiraling action, the humor falls flat.

How do actors justify that kind of frazzled, exaggerated behavior (because justify it you must)? "You can always find a reason for somebody to do something," says Currier, "whether they're angry or frustrated or releasing long-held, pent-up emotion." Go see a Marx Brothers movie to see how it's done, he suggests.

Karl Kippola, a professor at American University in Washington, D.C., teaches his students how to justify "the magnitude of choices" required to play farce by pointing out moments in our everyday lives when our responses or actions seem out of proportion: "If the fast-food place gets our order wrong, if someone cuts us off in traffic, if we miss the bus, ordinarily normal people will freak out. If we can act in a larger-than-life manner about unimportant things, imagine what happens when the stakes truly are life and death."

The fact is, almost nothing is too much in farce, if it's justified and played truthfully. But that's a big if.

RAISING THE (MIS)STAKES

Don't start out trying to be funny, warn some of the directors I talked to. What you should bring to early rehearsals is what you'd bring to any rehearsal: a willingness to examine the given circumstances and look for your character's actions and objectives. As Kippola points out, it doesn't necessarily help actors to know they're in a comedy. Rarely is comedy per se taught; rather, actors are taught an acting technique that ought to serve them for any project.

"The key is never losing hold of the reality of the situation," Kippola says. "What the audience is going to find funny is when things spiral further and further out of control as these recognizable human beings' comfort zones keep shifting, moment to moment." The challenge is to be human while being big and broad. "Some actors have an instinctive feel for that," he says. "For others, their desire to embrace realism and honesty makes it feel false to them. The challenge in working with these actors is getting them to see they can make big choices while staying honest."

He adds, "I'm not interested in farces I can't relate to on a human level." Kippola concedes that audiences may well laugh at big, zany, unsubstantiated choices—but for the wrong reasons. Indeed, I've seen audiences guffaw when actors (and directors) pander to them, evoking cheap laughs. But that's not what you really want to do, right?

Kippola recently directed back-to-back productions of *Tartuffe*, one with students and one with professionals, and found that the students were more willing to do whatever he suggested, to dive in with big, strong choices, while the older, more-seasoned actors needed encouragement. In rehearsal, the professionals "brought their own interpretations," he says, "and making all those styles mesh was one of my biggest challenges, especially if one person is making big, bold choices and another less so. If everyone's not on the same page, you'll have an uneven production. Sometimes you have to pull back the more brilliant, interesting choices" for the sake of consistency.

"The hard thing about any comedy, but especially farce, is it has to be played truthfully," concurs Art Manke, who recently directed Michael Frayn's *Noises Off* at South Coast Rep in Costa Mesa, Calif. In farce, "a lot of people come to the material thinking, 'I have to do funny business, be broad.' The thing I discovered is that the obstacles are multiplied tenfold. They grow over the course of the play, forcing the actions and objectives to be stronger. That's what leads to the frenetic pace and heightened state.

"It's got to be played truthfully," he continues, "and I don't believe truth has a size. It can be the scale you play the Hollywood Bowl or the scale you play a film—you have to stilt the scale to the venue."

Rucker agrees: "You keep raising the stakes in farce so an actor discovers what his character's trying to do—then you make them do it 10 times more than in real life. That's, hopefully, hilarious and kind of moving because it's so human."

It's tempting for actors to go straight for the humor, Kippola says, but he didn't touch that until a week or two into rehearsals for *Tartuffe*: "If you try to make it funny first, it's difficult to make it rooted and honest." His early rehearsals were all about: Who are these characters? What are their relationships? What do you want? How are you going to get it? That's the time to establish the parameters of behavior in the world that's being created, he says, so actors can use them as guides in focusing their choices.

An instinct for comic timing, stamina for the demanding physical elements, a willingness to make—and the ability to justify—big choices, an understanding of how to raise the stakes for your character, emotional honesty, a spirit of cooperation (farce requires detailed ensemble work): All these are skills needed for farce. How does a director spot these qualities when casting? Rucker says he looks for a certain kind of fearlessness. But all things being equal, he adds, he'll choose the actor with the best access to truth over the one who makes superficial comic choices, because the truthful actor "I'd assume I could bring to bolder places."

On the other hand, Kippola says, "You have to show you're willing to dive in and commit. If I have an actor that can do that, then I can make sure their choices are rooted and honest." Two different directors, two different preferences.

"Audiences will laugh at something funny," says Rucker, "but laugh and be moved at something truthful." And as Kippola remarks, "The secret to success in farce is raising the stakes to a ridiculous level. Emotional investment will solve many acting problems."

Source: Jean Schiffman, "Playing Farce in the 21st Century: It's Even Louder, Faster, and Funnier—But Still Truthful," in *Back Stage*, Vol. 50, No. 35, August 27, 2009, p. 17.

Melinda Schupmann

In the following review, Schupmann praises the artful construction and fine ensemble work in a production of Noises Off.

Michael Frayn's delightfully complicated British farce could hardly have a better rendition than this. In dual roles as the real director of this production and playing the director of a play within a play, Geoff Elliott shows his comedic chops as he portrays the beleaguered director trying to cope with a less-than-stellar cast. Frayn's play requires split-second timing to pull off this production fraught with theatrical shenanigans, romantic complications, madcap physicality, and lots of slamming doors, and Elliott tackles all with surety.

The purported play is called "Nothing On." In Act 1, we watch a dress rehearsal of the play set in a country house owned by a tax evader and his wife (Stephen Rockwell and Jill Hill). They have arrived secretly to spend a weekend celebrating their anniversary. Unfortunately, their arrival coincides with a plan by their housekeeper (Deborah Strang) to stay late and watch the telly, as well as with a real estate agent's cozy weekend plans with his blond girlfriend (Mikael Salazar and Emily Kosloski).

Once the first act of "Nothing On" is established, our Act 2 takes place backstage, and Shaun Anthony, Lenne Klingaman, and Apollo Dukakis get their turns to add further complications to the mix. Adam Lillibridge's nearly hinged two-story set allows for seeing the zany mix-ups of the actors in the production. Finally,

> BUT THE VALUE IN *NOISES OFF* IS THAT IT HELPS TO DEFINE AND SOLIDIFY THROUGH EXAMPLE THE DIFFERENCE BETWEEN PARODY AND TRAVESTY."

in Act 3 we are treated to the often-hilarious mishaps as all cast members perform "Nothing On" with no holds barred.

This is a well-oiled ensemble production. Hill and Strang make the most of their slightly dotty Englishwomen. Kosloski's dim, wide-eyed blonde is an inspired performance aided by Salazar's gratifyingly inept lothario. Dukakis adds the old-pro touch to his bumbling burglar, and Rockwell's unassuming milquetoast is a choice bit of understated art.

Reviews cannot do Frayn justice. You have to see the play to appreciate its artful construction and to applaud the fine ensemble work.

Source: Melinda Schupmann, Review of *Noises Off*, in *Back Stage*, Vol. 50, No. 47, November 19, 2009, pp. 34–35.

Wade Harrell

In the following essay, Harrell evaluates Noises Off, *focusing on the third act and on the idea of a parody of a parody.*

After successful runs in London, New York, and other cities with a touring company across the U.S. in 1985, *Noises Off* probably has garnered a great deal more critical acclaim than it deserves. Jack Tinker of the *Daily Mail* calls it "Mr. Frayn's brilliant and best work" (Reprinted in *Noises Off*). To the theatre-goer, however, the play is very uneven comically, the first two acts being much funnier and more tantalizing than the third act. The first two acts satisfy our conventional notions of what good parody is, while the third act deteriorates into a muddle of confusion onstage. To the drama critic, the play raises an interesting set of problems concerning the quality of the play itself, and its placement within the genre. In short, it is hard to decide just exactly what kind of play it is— parody? travesty? improvisation?

An analysis of the play first requires a familiarity with some basic literary definitions. Hugh Holman, in *A Handbook of Literature*, offers the standard but perhaps obsolete definition of travesty. He says the travesty is "writing which by its incongruity of style or treatment ridicules a subject inherently noble or dignified." This definition is unsatisfying because it is too closely related to that of parody which he defines as "a composition burlesquing or imitating another, usually serious, piece of work. It is designed to ridicule. . . . " Enoch Brater, in an essay about parody in Tom Stoppard's plays, attempts a much needed distinction between parody and travesty. He says that "while both parody and travesty closely imitate the style of an author or work for comic effect or ridicule, only the former employs this strategy to make some critical commentary on the original. Travesty, on the other hand, makes no such evaluative claim and harbors no such analytical pretension" (Brater, 1981, 119). This distinction so far seems somewhat inadequate since ridiculing something is in fact making a critical commentary on it. But what Brater goes on to say is probably more important for differentiating the two: "A travesty is merely a burlesque whose tactics are gross distortion and incongruity for their own sake" (Brater, 1981, 119). Linda Hutcheon, (1985) in her exhaustive study of parody arrives at a broad but satisfying definition of parody as "repetition with difference." She goes on to assert that "any codified form, can, theoretically, be treated in terms of repetition with critical distance." It is clear from these definitions, that *Noises Off* is two-thirds well conceived parody which draws upon well-known codes, that is, props, plot twists, character types, etc., while the last act is clearly nonsensical travesty in which there are no readable codes for the audience and whose exaggerated action on stage is there for its own sake and as a way of compensating for other weaknesses in the plot.

Noises Off is not a well-made play, but the first two acts are made very well. Act I is exposition. Frayn teases us with a rehearsal for what we know will be a very funny parody of English comedy, with all the conventional codes: a fragile vase placed precariously on a small table, a box of important documents, a flight bag, telephones and newspapers, a plate of sardines, and a row of doors leading to various rooms in a deserted country estate. Add to this two couples who enter the house each thinking they will be alone. As the play opens we see the actors rehearsing *Nothing On,* a farce in one act. As the actors enter and attempt to rehearse, the

audience learns what is supposed to happen during the play. The rehearsal does not go smoothly, however. Lloyd, the director, keeps interrupting to reprimand the actors, one of the actresses disrupts the rehearsal by losing a contact lens, and one actor is nowhere to be found. All of this Frayn handles very well. Rather than presenting us with a complete version of *Nothing On*, he shows us only what we know to be the familiar props and a few of the events in a type of drama that we are already familiar with. What is funniest in Act One is what is left unsaid and undone, because the audience already knows what to expect. In short, Frayn has presented us a with clearly defined set of codes for the parody of a parody.

In Act Two, in the rising action, Frayn breaks those codes. In a clever twist, the audience is taken behind the stage during a production of *Nothing On* one month later and sees how the personal affairs, arguments, and actions of the crew and cast affect what happens on stage. The familiar props and situations that the audience expects in *Nothing On* never materialize. For example, we learn in the first act that at one point Belinda, who plays Flavia in *Nothing On*, is supposed to carry a dress on stage. What actually happens is that Lloyd, the director, sends Tim, the stage hand, to buy flowers for Brooke, who has the role of the dumb blonde in both plays and is his lover. Tim enters the backstage area with the flowers. Belinda enters and tells Tim that Selsdon, a fading and alcoholic star, has locked himself in his room. Tim gives the flowers to Belinda and goes in search of Selsdon. She in turn gives the flowers to Frederick, another actor, and grabs an axe in order to help Tim. Poppy enters to inform Belinda that she has an entrance; Belinda hands the axe to Brooke, another actress, so that she can make her entrance. Garry, a goodlooking but also dumb younger actor, enters and eyes Frederick's flowers suspiciously because the two men are both in love with Dotty, another actress. Frederick gives the flowers to Garry and exits the backstage area. Brooke comes down the stairs and Garry and Brooke exchange the flowers and axe, Garry intending to hit Frederick with the axe when he enters again. Belinda enters, grabs the flowers from Brooke, sends her after Selsdon, sees Garry, and runs to take the axe from him. Her cue comes, and she almost misses it, runs up the stairs, desperately grabs at a dress, misses, and enters the stage of

Nothing On with flowers instead of a dress. We hear her exclaim, "Darling, I never had a dress, or rather a bunch of flowers like this, did I?" Clearly, as its title suggests, much of the action of *Noises Off* happens offstage, as in the ancient Greek plays where much of the violence and bloodletting happens offstage. Again Frayn's understatement makes for a successful parody. The audience does not have to see every action on the stage of *Nothing On* because it can guess at the ramifications of what is happening backstage.

What the audience does see backstage are the codes of a serious parody being broken. The actors and actresses are misplacing props and nearly missing cues, throwing off the comic timing of the play within the play. Clearly, Frayn is breaking the codes of his parody of a parody, *Nothing On*, and is replacing them with new ones. That is, a dress becomes a bouquet of flowers. Certainly parody can parody itself, as long as the acceptable code is there and recognized by the audience. For example, Stoppard in *Travesties* parodies Joyce's *Ulysses*, which is of course itself a parody. Unfortunately, in Act Two, Frayn's new set of codes, the action that is now occurring on stage does not become familiar enough to us so that in the third act we will be able to realize, see, understand, or remember how the action is being modified. The problem may be that there is not enough time for what Hutcheon has described as the "critical distance," the time to decode and look at a work objectively.

In the third act, which is definitely the climax—there is no resolution to *Noises Off*—we become an audience to a production of *Nothing On* twelve weeks into its run. As the audience quickly guesses, the play has deteriorated. Unfortunately, as the play within the play has worsened, so has the quality of Frayn's own play. By this time the personal conflicts behind stage have to become so heated that they are not influencing what happens in *Nothing On*, rather they are dictating the action. And this action is chaos. As the title of the play within the play suggests, nothing of importance is happening onstage. The action has become far from what we know from the first act should be happening, and since all of our rules for what to expect have been broken, clearly anything could happen. It makes no difference whether Brooke enters with a dress, an axe, flowers, or even a dog. What is happening on stage is what Peter Kemp terms "an undermining" of the traditional formula for farce (Reprinted in *Noises Off*, np). I would argue that

this undermining has already occurred in Act Two. As Hutcheon writes, "The parodic text is granted a special license to transgress the limit of convention, but,...it can do so only temporarily and only within the controlled confines authorized by the text parodied—that is quite simply, within the confines dictated by 'recognizability'" (Hutcheon, 1985, 75). Clearly, in Act Three Frayn has lost that control and the audience no longer recognizes codes of what he is parodying. What we are left with in Act Three is simply travesty, where the actions are distorted and grotesque for no apparent reason. For example, *Nothing On* contains the conventional telephone, which of course will ring at the wrong time or be answered by the wrong people. In the third act, however, the phone is useless except to be torn to pieces. Consequently, the actors throw the phone to the floor, pull it by the cord, rip the receiver from it, and carry it all over the stage from room to room. Such an exaggerated emphasis on the phone as a prop, for no apparent reason, does not, I think, suggest that Act Three is very well-conceived drama. At another point a burglar is supposed to enter the villa, but in the final version of *Nothing On*, three burglars enter. This alone would be an acceptable variation on the familiar motif of having a masked intruder, except that one burglar is played by the director, another by the stage hand, and another by Selsdon, the actor who is supposed to play him. Again we have no information about why the director or the stage hand has gotten on stage. We only know they are not supposed to be there. As one might imagine, the third act resembles improvisation more than drama.

What is intriguing about the first two acts is what Frayn doesn't tell us or show us, but what we can speculate about. What makes Act Three less interesting is that while we can no longer see the actions backstage which are dictating the action on stage, we are also not in the least interested in speculating about them. The main reason for this is that there has been so little character development thus far. Somehow it seems important to know the backstage hijinks since the whole second act is devoted to them. However, we quickly forget about the actors and their personal affairs in Act Three, and they suddenly seem unimportant to Frayn, who separates us from them.

Robert Corrigan (1973) writes that often directors will seek to compensate for this lack of character development or lack of significance in the script with an exploitation of the action in an effort to achieve novelty and uniqueness. Corrigan says that "rapidity of pace is seen . . . as a means of compensating for the script's obvious insignificance." He goes on to warn that taken to the extreme, pacing can be detrimental because when everything is speeded up, what "has been created is not art at all, only confusion." It is clear that this is what has happened in Frayn's comedy in Act Three. Frayn has relied on stage directions calling for a rapid pace and much movement to compensate for a weak script and character development. The funniest parts of the play are in the first two acts when the action is centered on the comic action of only one person or on all the characters who are in turn concentrating on only one action, as when Brooke loses her contact lens and everyone must look for it. In Act Three there is so much divided action, with people entering and exiting and doors opening and closing, that the result is chaos for an audience who is probably looking for order. The disconcerting fact is that the order in Act Three is difficult to discern, and seems to be, in fact, non-existent.

Ironically, Frayn defended the weak second act of Chekhov's *The Cherry Orchard* in a 1978 essay by suggesting that the "difficulties with Act Two throw into even greater relief the sound structure of the rest of the play" (Frayn, 1978, xix). Clearly, this weak argument does not hold up for Frayn's own play or any other since certainly not all good plays must have weak spots for us to appreciate the rest of the structure. Rather, the best playwrights sustain a play's strengths throughout its duration, something that Frayn in *Noises Off* is unable to do.

But the value in *Noises Off* is that it helps to define and solidify through example the difference between parody and travesty. The first two acts, which are very clever and succeed well enough, illustrate that preconceived notions, rules, or codes are necessary to an understanding and appreciation of good parody, whose aim may be to ridicule. But the sheerly nonsensical third act just as clearly shows that when there is no preconceived idea of what to expect, drama may seem to lack order and turn into improvisation, while art itself turns into chaos.

Source: Wade Harrell, "When the Parody Parodies Itself: The Problem with Michael Frayn's *Noises Off*," in *From the Bard to Broadway*, edited by Karelisa V. Hartigan, University Press of America, 1987, pp. 87–93.

SOURCES

Austen, Jane, *Mansfield Park: A Novel in Three Volumes*, Oxford University Press, 1814, http://books.google.com/books?id=PwYUAAAAQAAJ&source=gbs_navlinks_s (accessed September 9, 2010).

Bermel, Albert, *Farce: A History from Aristophanes to Woody Allen*, Simon & Schuster, 1982.

Burgess, Anthony, *You've Had Your Time*, Heinemann, 1990, pp. 94–98.

Frayn, Michael, *Noises Off*, Metheun, 2000.

——, *The Tin Men*, Collins, 1965.

Holland, Peter, Review of *Noises Off*, in *Times Literary Supplement* (London, England); quoted in Michael Page, *File on Frayn*, Metheun, 1994, p. 33.

Moseley, Merritt, *Understanding Michael Frayn*, University of South Carolina Press, 2006, pp. 130–37.

Page, Michael, *File on Frayn*, Metheun, 1994, pp. 29–36.

Pronko, Leonard C., *Georges Feydeau*, Ungar, 1975.

Smith, Leslie, *Modern British Farce: A Selective Study of British Farce from Pinero to the Present Day*, Barnes & Noble, 1989, pp. 167–72.

Worrell, Denise, "Viewing a Farce from Behind," in *Time*, January 30, 1984, p. 70; quoted in Michael Page, *File on Frayn*, Metheun, 1994, p. 31.

FURTHER READING

Baker, Stuart, *Georges Feydeau and the Aesthetics of Farce*, UMI Research Press, 1981.
    This is one of the few English-language studies of the French comedian whom Frayn cites as his single most important influence as a writer of farce.

Frayn, Michael, *Stage Directions: Writing on Theatre, 1970–2008*, Faber & Faber, 2008.
    This volume collects Frayn's introductory essays from the published versions of his plays. It is especially useful for the later plays and the translations of Chekhov.

Freud, Sigmund, *Jokes and Their Relation to the Unconscious*, Routledge & Kegan Paul, 1960.
    Freud explores the psychological origins of humor as a means of venting desire through repression and other psychological defense mechanisms.

Hüsken, Wim, and Konrad Schoell, eds., *Farce and Farcical Elements*, Rodopi, 2002.
    The articles in this collection deal with the emergence of farce during the early modern period from earlier types of drama.

SUGGESTED SEARCH TERMS

Michael Frayn

Michael Frayn AND drama

Michael Frayn AND play

Michael Frayn AND Broadway

Michael Frayn AND farce

Noises Off AND Michael Frayn

farce

Feydeau AND farce

West End AND theater

play within a play

Once upon a Mattress

The musical comedy *Once upon a Mattress* is loosely based on the Hans Christian Andersen fairy tale "The Princess and the Pea." It tells the story of a queen who will do just about anything to keep her son, Prince Dauntless, from marrying, and she also decrees that no one in the court will marry anyone until her charming Prince Dauntless is wed. Thus, all of her subjects are under pressure to find a suitable wife for the prince. The queen successfully thwarts all measures to find a bride for her son until an unlikely candidate, in the form of Princess Winnifred, shows up.

Winnifred has none of the qualities the queen values. When Winnifred first appears in the royal court, her clothes are filthy and her hair is a mess—rather than crossing the moat bridge on horseback, she swam across and arrives at the castle soaking wet. Winnifred is outspoken, though she claims to be shy. She is nothing like the other princesses who have tried to win the queen's favor, but she is determined to outdo them, even if she has to stay up all night and study science and math, subjects that she hates. In the end—and with the help of the mute king, who applauds Winnifred's honest nature—she is victorious.

Once upon a Mattress opened on May 11, 1959, at the Phoenix Theatre in New York City and ran for 460 performances. The play has earned several Tony Award nominations, including Best Actress (Carol Burnett) and Best Musical in 1960. In 1997, the play received a Tony Award

MARY RODGERS, MARSHALL BARER, JAY THOMPSON, DEAN FULLER

1959

nomination for Best Revival of a Musical (a production that starred Sarah Jessica Parker as Princess Winnifred). The various television adaptations of this play (in 1964, 1972, and 2005) were nominated for Emmy Awards.

AUTHOR BIOGRAPHY

Once upon a Mattress had four different authors. Mary Rodgers created the musical compositions; Marshall Barer, who wrote the lyrics, also collaborated with Jay Thompson and Dean Fuller in writing the story.

Rodgers, who was born on January 11, 1931, is the daughter of music composer Richard Rodgers (of Rodgers and Hammerstein fame). She studied music at Wellesley College. Besides composing the music for *Once upon a Mattress*, she wrote the musical scores for several other plays, including *From A to Z* (1960), *Hot Spot* (1963), *The Mad Show* (1966), and *Working* (1978). However, she eventually gave up music composition and turned to writing children's books. Her most famous book was *Freaky Friday* (1972), which she adapted for the screen in 1977. Rodgers was married twice, the second time to Henry Guettel, with whom she had a son, Adam Guettel, an award-winning composer.

Barer, the lyricist for *Once upon a Mattress*, was born on February 19, 1923, in New York City. Barer began his career writing for magazines such as *Seventeen* and *Esquire*. Later, he composed children's songs for Golden Records and is best remembered in this category for the theme song for the *Mighty Mouse* cartoon show, "Here He Comes to Save the Day." Barer wrote music for various cabarets and, in 1957, for the Ziegfeld Follies, shortly before teaming up with Rodgers for *Once upon a Mattress*. Barer joined Rodgers again for the musical *The Mad Show* in 1966. Barer died of cancer in Santa Fe, New Mexico, on August 25, 1998.

Besides writing *Once upon a Mattress* with Fuller and Barer, Thompson wrote the music and lyrics for the opera *The Bible Salesman* (1961), which was a musical adaptation of an O. Henry short story. Thompson also wrote *The Oldest Trick in the World* (1961).

Fuller was born in Woodbury, New Hampshire, on December 12, 1911. He began his Broadway musical career in 1942 with the show *Once*

over Lightly. In the next decade, he was involved in three different shows, which included *Maggie* (1953), *New Faces of 1956* (1956), and the *Ziegfeld Follies of 1957* (1957). In 1955, he married Beverly Bozeman, a dancer and actress. He continued to write music for Broadway shows until the revival of *Once upon a Mattress* in 1997.

PLOT SUMMARY

Act 1

Once upon a Mattress is set in a fictitious British medieval castle in a fairy-tale time of knights on horseback and princesses dressed in long gowns. The play opens with a four-minute overture that is played right before the appearance of a minstrel (a singer and storyteller), who provides background for the story that is about to unfold on stage. In the song "Many Moons Ago," the minstrel relates how the prince has been waiting for a genuine princess, but a genuine princess has proven to be hard to find. When one young woman appears at the door of the castle and claims to be a princess, the queen insists on testing her, so the minstrel says. In essence, the minstrel is retelling the original Hans Christian Andersen story "The Princess and the Pea." When he finishes this account, the minstrel tells the audience that the real story did not happen that way. It is then that the other version of the story, as told through the musical *Once upon a Mattress*, begins.

According to this play, there was more than one princess who applied to woo the prince—there were thirteen. Though the prince saw some merit in each of the first twelve young women, each one eventually failed the queen's tests. In fact, those tests were designed to be so grueling that no one could pass, for the queen does not want her son to be married. The queen believes she is the only person on earth who knows how to take care of him, and she does not want to share this responsibility with anyone else. The audience also learns that the queen has decreed that no one in the kingdom may marry unless the prince finds a wife. This state of affairs leads to the next song, "An Opening for a Princess," in which the prince and an accompanying chorus of the court sing about their predicament of not being able to wed. The song, in part, sounds like a classified advertisement for a princess.

MEDIA ADAPTATIONS

- There are various adaptations of the original play *Once upon a Mattress*. In 1964, CBS produced a television version of the play, filmed in black and white. In 1972, CBS produced another version, this time in color. In 2005, ABC produced a third television adaptation, which has been released on DVD. An audio CD of the 1959 original production was made in 1993 and is available at Amazon.com.

Queen Aggravaine (the similarity in sound to *aggravate* is intentional) is very loud and annoying when she speaks. Not only is the sound of her voice aggravating, so too is what she says. She is rude to the princesses whom she tests, and she barely allows Prince Dauntless the Drab, her son, to get a word in. The queen's husband, King Sextimus, cannot get in a word either, not because the queen cuts him off but rather because he is mute. He has been cursed, and the curse cannot be broken until, as the saying goes, the mouse has eaten the hawk. The king and the jester sit to the side of the queen and make silent jokes, often mocking the queen through facial expressions and hand motions. However, at this point in the story, they do not interfere with the queen's plans.

Two more characters, Lady Larken and the chief knight Sir Harry, are introduced at this point. The two of them are in love and must get married, as Lady Larken has discovered that she is pregnant. Lady Larken tells Sir Harry that she does not want to disgrace him; she is willing to run away to save his reputation when it becomes obvious that she is pregnant. Sir Harry is the most honorable knight in the court, and he insists that they cannot get married, even in secret, because it would break the queen's law about not marrying until the prince finds a wife. Therefore, Harry commits to finding a suitable princess for Dauntless to marry. The twelfth princess has failed the queen's test, and the queen believes that she was the last princess available. However, Sir Harry convinces the queen to give him permission to go to the swamps, where he believes one more princess remains. After Lady Larken and Sir Harry sing the song "In a Little While," which tells of their future dreams of marrying (and also hints at the future birth of their child), Sir Harry sets off for the swamps.

Time passes as the kingdom anxiously awaits Sir Harry's return. The men and women of the court want to get on with their lives, marry their sweethearts, and raise families. Prince Dauntless is anxious to find out whether he will finally find a wife or will remain forever a bachelor. The queen does not want her precious son to wed and hopes Sir Harry is unsuccessful. After a long wait, everyone begins to believe that Harry has failed in his search.

Then there is a commotion. The sound of splashing water fills the courtyard. Suddenly, a drenched young woman appears at the top of the castle wall. She is a mess, with muddy clothes and dripping wet hair. She declares that she was so anxious to meet the prince that she swam the moat that surrounds the castle. She introduces herself as the princess from the swamps, Princess Winnifred. In a song, she claims to be shy, despite her current appearance and behavior. After Winnifred is finished singing, the queen tells her to leave. There is nothing about Winnifred that makes the queen believe she could possibly be a princess. However, Sir Harry says he has the papers to prove Winnifred's claim to royalty. The queen, however, insists that she leave; anyone could draw up false papers. Before the queen is able to enforce her wishes, though, Dauntless intervenes. He tells his mother that he likes this person. The fact that Dauntless speaks up worries the queen, as she is not used to having her son talk back to her.

Rather than insisting that Winnifred leave, then, the queen decides to come up with a test that no one could possibly pass. She confers with the wizard, and they come up with the most challenging test yet. She will challenge Winnifred in a new way: she will test her sensitivity, rather than her intelligence. Everyone knows, the queen assumes, that princesses are the most sensitive of all women. Through the song "Sensitivity," the queen details her plan of putting a tiny dried pea under a pile of twenty mattresses. If Winnifred sleeps through the night without being bothered by the pea, it will prove that she is not an authentic princess.

Winnifred is taken by some of the ladies-in-waiting to special quarters, where she finds new clothes. While she is getting ready for a dinner feast and dancing in the royal ballroom, the king comes in with the jester, who interprets the king's hand signals. By the end of their conversation, it is clear that the king approves of Winnifred, and she tells Dauntless that she likes his father. After the men leave, Winnifred sings "The Swamps of Home" to the women who are helping her dress. The song tells what it was like to live in the swamps all her life. After the ladies-in-waiting leave, Winnifred accidentally knocks over a vase filled with water. She is down on the floor cleaning up the mess when Lady Larken comes in and mistakes Winnifred for a maid. Sir Harry appears, recognizes the mistake Lady Larken has made, and the two of them begin to argue. Eventually Lady Larken leaves, angry with Sir Harry.

Later that night, the atmosphere around the castle is festive. Everyone appears to be having fun except for Lady Larken, who is busy planning to leave the kingdom. Lady Larken believes that Sir Harry no longer loves her, because they have had an argument. The king, the minstrel, and the jester empathize with Lady Larken and suggest that she go to Normandy; in a song, they describe this region of France as a vacation paradise.

The final scene of act 1 takes place in the ballroom. The queen announces that the dance of the evening will be the "Spanish Panic," which involves a fast-stepping routine. The queen hopes to wear out Princess Winnifred so that she will sleep through the night and not notice the pea, thus proving that she is not a legitimate princess. As the dance progresses, the queen orders the musicians to play faster and faster. In the end, Winnifred is the only person who remains standing—and she wants to dance more. No one else has the energy to keep up with her. The queen is frustrated because Winnifred acts as if she will never be tired.

Before going to bed, Winnifred tells Dauntless that she wants him to call her by her nickname. He calls her Winnie, but she tells him her nickname is Fred. This leads to "Song of Love," in which the prince declares that he thinks Fred is a beautiful name. The prince then states that he is in love with this princess who is named Fred. He sings about all her strange but wonderful characteristics, one of which is her physical strength.

Act 2

When act 2 opens, the queen is supervising the refurnishing of the room where Princess Winnifred will sleep. Twenty mattresses are being piled on top of one another, along with blankets and pillows. The king, the jester, and the minstrel are attempting to lead Lady Larken (who is disguised as a young boy) out of the castle, but when Lady Larken sneezes, the queen discovers the group. She sends the so-called young boy up to help Princess Winnifred get ready for bed. For some unexplained reason, the queen also demands that the minstrel leave the kingdom. This sets the scene for the chorus's song "Quiet." The song is intended to make everyone quiet so the princess can sleep, but the singers are actually very loud, as is the queen herself.

Prince Dauntless and Princess Winnifred, in the meantime, are studying amid piles of books, as Winifred prepares for the test she believes the queen will give her in the morning. Neither of them knows that the real test will not be a quiz, as has been the case for the other dozen princesses that preceded Winnifred. The test will be whether Winnifred is sensitive enough to be kept awake by a single pea under the pile of mattresses.

Winnifred is distressed. She says she has never been good at book knowledge. However, Dauntless encourages her, reminding her that if she passes the test, they can be married. Lady Larken enters the room, and Winnifred tells her that Sir Harry is a very fine gentleman who truly loves Lady Larken; therefore, Winnifred says, Lady Larken should make up with him. After Lady Larken leaves to find Sir Harry, Winnifred sends Dauntless away. Before he leaves, Winnifred vows she will study as hard as she is able. However, when she is alone she sings "Happily Ever After." Through this song, she recalls many famous fairy tales, all of them ending with the woman marrying the man of her dreams and the couple living happily ever after. Though none of the fairy tales mention having to study for a test, Winnifred concludes that she will return to her studies because she wants to live happily ever after too.

Sir Harry is then seen leading the minstrel to the castle's exit to banish him as the queen has insisted. The king and the jester plead with Harry to let the minstrel stay. The minstrel wants to talk to the wizard, because the wizard is the only one (other than the queen) who knows what the princess's test will be. If they find out what the test is, they will tell Winnifred. Sir Harry has been concerned about going against the queen and her laws, but he gives in and allows the minstrel to stay. Sir Harry is beginning to understand that love may be more powerful than the rules of the land. Dauntless comes in, and the others suggest that it is time for the king to explain to his son the relationships between men and women. Dauntless sings "Man to Man" as he asks his father questions and then interprets the hand motions that his father provides as answers. The king attempts to tell his son about the birds and the bees, but it is difficult to do this in sign language. Eventually the king gives up trying and merely suggests that babies come as gifts from the stork, once a common explanation given to children to explain where babies come from.

The jester and the minstrel make it to the wizard's room and try to cajole the wizard into giving up his secrets about the queen's test for Winnifred. The wizard does not want to give away any of the details in front of the jester, so the minstrel sends him away. Before the jester leaves the room, however, the wizard shows off some magic tricks and talks about the good old times when he used to perform. This stirs memories for the jester, whose father used to be a performer. In "Very Soft Shoes," the jester sings about his father.

After the jester sings his song, Lady Larken and Sir Harry bump into one another. Lady Larken apologizes for getting angry with Sir Harry. Believing that he no longer loves her, she tells him he has a right to change his mind about his feelings for her. In a song, Harry avows that he loved her yesterday, but today he loves her even more. Through this song, the couple reignite their love for one another.

The focus now shifts to Princess Winnifred and the pea. The queen has the small pea in her hand, and after counting all the mattresses, she slips the tiny pea under the bottom one. When the princess arrives, the queen gives her a sleeping potion and burns incense designed to ensure that Winnifred will sleep. However, Winnifred does not seem to be affected, and the queen orders that the Nightingale of Samarkand be brought into the room to sing her to sleep with the "Nightingale Lullaby." Try as she might, Winnifred cannot fall asleep. The mattresses are too lumpy and uncomfortable, and she tosses and turns and counts sheep all night.

The next morning, everyone awaits the test that they believe is about to begin. The queen confesses, however, that the test is already done. Dauntless wants to know the results, and his mother says that they have not yet been determined. Finally, Princess Winnifred appears. She is still counting in her attempt to fall asleep and tells them that she has counted up to thirty-seven thousand sheep or more. She moans that she has not been able to sleep all night. Even when Dauntless tells Winnifred that she has passed the test, she is not impressed. All she wants to do is sleep. Dauntless nearly faints in excitement, having finally found his bride, and he begins to lead Winnifred back to her room so she can sleep. However, the queen is upset, and she protests that Winnifred cannot become Dauntless's wife. Dauntless stops in his tracks, turns to his mother, and tells her to shut up. This fulfills the conditions for lifting the king's curse: the mouse (Dauntless) has eaten the hawk (the queen). At this moment, the queen loses her voice and the king is able to speak. As the finale (a big musical number at the end of a show) is sung by the chorus and Dauntless puts Winnifred to bed, the jester and minstrel remove several pointy pieces of equipment that they had hidden in the mattress to make sure that the princess would not sleep. However, Winnifred is still uncomfortable. Dauntless puts his hand under the last mattress and pulls out the pea, making the bed comfortable enough for Winnifred to fall sleep. This is the final proof that Winnifred is an authentic princess, indeed.

CHARACTERS

Queen Aggravaine

Queen Aggravaine rules the tiny kingdom of the play *Once upon a Mattress*. She is a dogmatic, egotistical monarch. Her rules are more important than any of her subjects' needs or desires, including those of her son. Though she insists that an all-important sign of female royalty is sensitivity, the queen exhibits not a morsel of this trait. She is rude, callous, and selfish. She treats her son as if he is a family pet rather than a human being. In addition, she is cunning and devious. She creates rules that work to her advantage and manipulates tests so that no one can pass them. She demands loyalty but exhibits none, except to herself.

Aggravaine is determined to be the only voice in the kingdom. Though it is never explained how it happened, the king has become mute through a curse, and the queen takes full advantage of his silence. She ignores the king throughout most of the play, and she dominates her son's life. When Dauntless shows signs that he is gaining enough courage to speak back to his mother, the queen becomes even more determined to make sure her son never marries. She sets up all-but-impossible tests for Winnifred and cheats to ensure that the young woman could never pass them. She attempts to drug Winnifred and to completely exhaust her so that she will sleep through the night. The queen remains smug until the last moment, almost assured that she has beaten the last candidate to try to become her son's bride. Even when Winnifred proves that she has passed the test, the queen is arrogant, stubbornly protesting that it is impossible that Winnifred could be good enough to marry Dauntless. However, once the spell is broken and the king is able to talk, Queen Aggravaine is finally put in her place. By the end of the play, it is the queen's turn to become unable to speak. Her loud voice quieted, she fades into the background.

Prince Dauntless the Drab

Prince Dauntless is the queen's son, who has never married. Dauntless is as quiet and reserved as his mother is loud and obnoxious. He wants to marry, but his mother insists that there is no one in the kingdom worthy of him. Dauntless allows his mother to direct his life. She tells him what to do, how to live, and even what to eat. He is awkward and shy, having been raised by an aggressive mother and a father who has lost his voice.

It is not until near the end of the play that Dauntless finally finds the courage to talk back to his mother and insist that she allow him to have what he wants. His heart has been opened by Princess Winnifred, and this gives him the strength of conviction and the clarity of thought to finally take control of his life. He experiences real love with Winnifred and does not want to lose her. Their relationship demonstrates that love is more powerful than royal declarations and imposed rules. Dauntless is able to defeat his mother and in the process win the hand of Princess Winnifred. By standing up to his mother, Prince Dauntless also frees all the other couples in the kingdom, giving them the right to marry.

Sir Harry

Sir Harry is the best knight in the kingdom. He is handsome and very loyal, both to the queen and to his love, Lady Larken. When he discovers that Lady Larken is pregnant, he becomes determined to find an eligible princess for Dauntless. If he is successful, then he too can marry. However, Harry does not come to this conclusion immediately. At first, he is torn, believing that his loyalty to the queen must supersede his love of and responsibility to Lady Larken. Eventually, though, Sir Harry sees the light and decides he must do what is necessary to marry Lady Larken, even if he has to scheme against the queen.

Jester

The jester is the close confidant of the king. He understands the king's hand gestures and often interprets what the king is trying to say. He also makes jokes with the king, often at the expense of the queen. The jester is involved in the plan to foil the queen so that Princess Winnifred can pass the queen's test. The jester's relationship with the king is similar to the role the wizard plays with the queen, one of secret complicity.

Lady Larken

Lady Larken is a beautiful lady-in-waiting in the queen's court. She is in love with Sir Harry, the most accomplished and respected knight in the queen's service. Lady Larken and Sir Harry are in the midst of a love affair, and Lady Larken announces to Sir Harry, early in the play, that she is pregnant. Since the queen has forbidden marriages until after her son, Prince Dauntless, is wed, Lady Larken is undecided about what she will do about the pregnancy. She does not want to shame Sir Harry, but she also wishes he could do something about the situation. She suggests that they get secretly married, but Sir Harry does not like the idea of breaking the queen's law.

Lady Larken represents the frustrations and problems that arise from the queen's strict laws. She is also the first person to ask whether or not love is more important than the law.

Minstrel

The minstrel acts as the narrator of this story. He opens the play with a song about the fairy tale upon which the play is based and then explains that the story that is about to unfold is really nothing like the fairy tale. The play—that is, reality—is much more complex. The minstrel's role is minimal, though he later is involved in prying the secret of Princess Winnifred's test from the wizard.

Nightingale of Samarkand

The Nightingale of Samarkand (played by a male actor in costume) attempts to sing Princess Winnifred to sleep. The queen has schemed to make the princess so sleepy she will not feel the pea under all the mattresses, thus proving that she is not royal enough for the prince. The Nightingale sings its best, but the princess eventually asks the bird to stop singing; it is only making her more annoyed about her inability to fall asleep.

King Sextimus the Silent

King Sextimus is the mute husband of the queen and the father of Prince Dauntless. Sextimus has lost his voice because of a curse. The story behind the curse is never explained, only how it can be broken.

For most of the play, the king is in the background. Not until he learns that Lady Larken is pregnant does he become involved in helping her flee the court. Once his son tells him that he likes Princess Winnifred, the king then takes on a greater role in finding a way to defy the queen and help Winnifred to pass the test. The king regains his speech when his son stands up to the queen and demands that she allow him to marry Princess Winnifred. The king regains not only his voice but also his courage to rebuke the queen. He claims his power as king, tells the queen to go away, and blesses the prince and his marriage to Princess Winnifred.

Princess Winnifred the Woebegone

Princess Winnifred is, according to this story, the last princess left in the kingdom who is eligible to marry Prince Dauntless. Princess Winnifred is unlike the other princesses who have previously attempted to win the prince's hand in that she is bold and anything but dainty. She speaks her mind and is not afraid of the queen. She even makes it known that she thinks the queen is loud and rather obnoxious.

Princess Winnifred was raised in the swamps and claims she is not well trained in book knowledge. She is physically strong and inclined to speak the truth as she sees it. These qualities attract the prince to her. She is concerned about passing the queen's test, but she is equally determined to win

the prize—marriage to Prince Dauntless and living happily ever after.

Wizard

The Wizard is the queen's assistant and confidant. He is constantly at the queen's side and helps her to concoct the strangest tests for the princesses who want to marry Dauntless. The wizard is as cunning as the queen, but only up to a point. He finally gives in toward the end of the play, when he is persuaded to help Sir Harry foil the queen's plan by ensuring that Winnifred sleeps through the night.

THEMES

Determination

At first Queen Aggravaine appears to be the most determined person in this play. She wants to keep her son unmarried, as she believes she is the best person to watch over him for the rest of her life. She is determined to do anything to that end, even cheat and lie.

However, as the play continues, it becomes apparent that both Prince Dauntless and Princess Winnifred are even more determined than the queen. They intend to be married, and much of the play is spent on their preparations to beat the queen at her all-but-impossible challenge.

Sir Harry also demonstrates determination in his quest to find a suitable princess for Prince Dauntless so that he and Lady Larken can be married. The king, once he meets Princess Winnifred, also becomes determined to undermine the queen because he discovers that his son is truly in love with Princess Winnifred.

Confidence

Prince Dauntless appears to doubt himself and lack confidence; he is constantly giving in to his mother's wishes. When Princess Winnifred appears on the scene, though, she seems to have enough confidence for both of them. Princess Winnifred's confidence inspires the prince, and he finally finds the courage to stand up to his mother. It is because of this newfound confidence that the curse on the prince's father, the king, is broken. The original curse stated that the king would remain mute until the mouse ate the hawk. The mouse, in this case, was the once-timid prince, who finally talks back to his mother, who represents the hawk. As soon as the prince exhibits his newfound confidence and

TOPICS FOR FURTHER STUDY

- Read the original Hans Christian Andersen story "The Princess and the Pea." What similarities exist between Andersen's story and the musical *Once upon a Mattress*? Besides the songs in the musical version, how do these two stories differ? What is the basic lesson in both stories? Do you think it is better told as a fairy tale or as a musical comedy? Write an essay about your conclusions that compares the two versions.

- Research the history of Broadway plays using online and print sources. Which plays bring in the most money for the producers, dramas or musicals? What do critics say about this phenomenon? Which type of play (drama or musical) is dominant today? What are some of the most financially successful plays in history? Create a multimedia documentary to present your findings. Provide video clips, posters, or music from some of the plays or musicals you discuss. Present the finished product to your class.

- Carol Burnett starred in the original production of *Once upon a Mattress* in 1959, which launched her acting career. Create a Web page showing Burnett's biography, including photos from the play in which she stars as Princess Winnifred and her later role in a television adaptation, in which she stars as the queen. List her awards, including her lifetime awards, such as her Kennedy Center Honor, the Presidential Medal of Freedom, and her star on the Hollywood Walk of Fame. Provide links to other related sites about Burnett on the Internet.

- Create a map that shows at least six contemporary royal families around the world. What roles do these kings and queens play in their countries? How are they financially and politically supported? Are they actively involved in governing their countries, or are they merely figureheads? Are there any active controversies concerning getting rid of these royal roles? Display your map as you tell the story of modern royal families.

- Watch Stephen Sondheim's Tony-winning musical *Into the Woods* (1987, for the original version; 1991, for the television adaptation). This play is also based on a mixture of fairy tales that were told by the Brothers Grimm. Sondheim's play is more serious than *Once upon a Mattress*. It starts off somewhat lightheartedly, but the second act delivers a special message. Take on the role of a drama critic and write a review that contrasts Sondheim's play with *Once upon a Mattress* and explains the strengths and weaknesses of these two plays. Include your personal assessment of why your classmates should or should not watch them. Be convincing in your judgments, giving full expression to your preferences and biases. Post your review online and invite your classmates to comment.

- Choose one of the scenes from *Once upon a Mattress* and create a miniature backdrop and props. Use any artistic medium (painted wood, clay, or other materials), but make the set large enough to display in your classroom while your class is reading the play. You may also create miniature replicas of the actors to go along with the set.

---

defeats his self-doubt, the king regains his voice and regains his power in the kingdom.

Although the princess lacks book knowledge, the source of many of the queen's perplexing quizzes, Winnifred has enough confidence in herself to do her best in beating the queen. She knows that the prince does indeed love her and that she loves him. She will try her hardest to become his bride. Princess Winnifred's confidence comes from knowing and understanding herself. She does not try to pretend to be anyone other than who she is. For instance, she does not try to be graceful or delicate, like the stereotypical fairy tale princess. She is loud and bold and is proud of herself. Her confidence is not something someone had to teach her. It comes to her naturally from merely being true to herself.

Silence

Until the very end of this play, the king is mute, allowing the queen full rule over the kingdom. She is the sole word of law and, with the wizard's help, she controls the fate of all the people of the court.

Although the prince retains his voice, he never talks back to his mother, so in essence, he too is relegated to a world of silence. The queen takes advantage of this silence and is often ridiculed, behind her back, for being so talkative. Not until the end of the play do the king and the prince regain their voices, silencing the queen.

Love

One of the questions that Lady Larken repeatedly asks her lover, Sir Harry, is whether love overrules law. Sir Harry has trouble answering this question for much of the play. He is adamant about never breaking a law, including the queen's law that no one may marry until the prince does. However, it is Sir Harry who heads out to the swamps to find the last princess who might be strong enough to pass the queen's test and be allowed to marry the prince. Harry does this out of his love of Lady Larken. Later, when he fears that the queen might outsmart Princess Winnifred, he admits that love is superior to the laws of the land.

It is also for love that Prince Dauntless finds the courage to stand up to his mother. He has fallen in love with Princess Winnifred and is determined to fulfill that love by marrying her. Another form of love that is expressed in this play is that between the gentle king and his son. Though the king cannot vocalize his love, he is very adept at expressing his love for his son through hand expressions and physical contact.

Royalty

This play raises questions about the nature of royalty. What is royalty? Can it be measured? The queen's definition of royalty is a high degree of physical sensitivity. She claims that a truly royal princess could be discomfited by the smallest pea placed under multiple mattresses. If a young woman cannot sleep because she is sensitive

Illustration from the 1911 fairytale classic The Princess and the Pea *(© Pictorial Press Ltd / Alamy)*

enough to feel and be disturbed by the pea, then she is truly of royal birth.

The story, however, describes royalty in another way. A truly royal person is one who sees the truth, in himself or herself and in others. Princess Winnifred sees the true worth of Prince Dauntless, for example. She sees his true strength and courage behind the façade of his shyness and fear. She also sees the love in the king's facial expressions. The irony in this story is that while the queen defines royalty in relation to sensitivity, of all the characters in this story, the queen lacks sensitivity the most. According to this play as a whole, there is no one special characteristic that defines royalty.

STYLE

Musical Theater

Once upon a Mattress is classified as a musical because the dialogue in the play is interspersed with songs and dancing. The songs further develop the story line by filling in background information, expressing inner emotions, or introducing a character to the audience.

There are different forms of musicals. One form, sometimes referred to as a book musical, has at its base a desire to tell a story. A musical revue, on the other hand, provides a stage to showcase the music or the musicians, singers, or dancers. The history of musicals can be traced back to ancient Greek theater, which often included music and dance. Ancient Roman theater also included music, sometimes whole orchestras.

Use of Irony

This play contains moments that are quietly ironic. Irony occurs when there is an incongruity between what might be expected and what actually happens. For instance, Queen Aggravaine puts Princess Winnifred through what the queen suggests is the ultimate test of sensitivity—the famed dried pea under a pile of mattresses. A true princess, the premise runs, is an extremely sensitive creature. For the queen to be a queen, however, she had to have been, at one time, a princess herself. The queen proves over and over again that she is the least sensitive person in the show.

In another ironic move, the king has been cursed and made mute, and yet, through his silent expressions, he conveys more sensitivity than the queen. Another example comes when Princess Winnifred sings a song that declares that she is shy, which the audience can tell is anything but the truth. The princess's language is very direct and to the point, which sometimes makes her appear somewhat inattentive to others' feelings, but like the king, the princess eventually proves that she is also more sensitive than the queen.

Fractured Fairy Tale

The Hans Christian Andersen fairy tale upon which the musical *Once upon a Mattress* is based is a very short story (less than four hundred words) with a serious theme. The original story was about how to distinguish an authentic and sensitive princess from a commoner; the musical instead makes it about a ruthless queen who is anything but sensitive. This twist makes the musical a fractured fairy tale, a parody of the original. A fractured fairy tale or parody is a purposeful misrepresentation of the original style or work. A fractured fairy tale often uses humor to make fun of the original work or the original topic.

In the original fairy tale, a princess is caught in a rainstorm and ends up at the front door of a prince who has searched the whole world in his attempts to find a bride. He has come home exhausted by his travels because no matter where he went, none of the women he encountered fit his definition of what a princess should be. Suddenly there is a young woman at his door. She is soaking wet and does not look very princess-like. In order to prove her royalty, the prince's mother suggests putting a dried pea under many mattresses to test the young woman's sensitivity.

The mother in the fairy tale plays a very minor role and has no motives other than helping her son find a true princess for a wife. The mother does not dominate her son, and the prince does not lose himself in his mother's shadow.

However, in the musical, many aspects of the original tale are turned on their head. This provides entertainment for the audience, as songs and dances make the story lively. Laughter, too, is a key ingredient; the audience is invited to laugh when the queen is overthrown by her meek son and husband. In another scene, instead of merely entering the castle drenched from a rainstorm, the princess in the staged adaptation of the fairy tale swims across the protective moat that surrounds the castle. This makes her appear somewhat ridiculous. She sings a song about how shy she is, but it is clear that she is anything but shy. She is loud and outgoing.

HISTORICAL CONTEXT

Rodgers and Hammerstein

Richard Rodgers (Mary's father) and Oscar Hammerstein II proved to be excellent inspirations for one another, and the musicals they wrote together have remained popular on Broadway for over fifty years. Rodgers wrote the music for which Hammerstein wrote the words.

Rodgers was born on June 28, 1902, on Long Island, New York. By the age of six, his gift for music had become apparent; he began playing the piano, mimicking music he heard. His parents put him in piano classes, and by the time he was fourteen, he had already written his own songs.

COMPARE
&
CONTRAST

- **1950s:** The famed partnership between Richard Rodgers (music composer) and Oscar Hammerstein II (lyricist) is at its peak. The pair have several Broadway musical hits, such as *Oklahoma!*, *Carousel*, *The King and I*, *The Sound of Music*, and *South Pacific*.

  Today: Though many of Rodgers and Hammerstein's musical have enjoyed revivals over the decades, the only one running on Broadway in 2010 is *South Pacific*.

- **1950s:** Broadway musicals are one source of popular music, but a new form is born. Rock and roll, through Elvis Presley and his hits such as "Don't Be Cruel," "Heartbreak Hotel," and "Blue Suede Shoes," makes its entry onto the music scene.

Today: Popular music is more likely to originate on the Internet than in Broadway musicals. Top-paid popular musicians include (according to *Forbes* magazine) Beyonce, who earns $87 million in 2010, making her the highest-paid female pop singer, and Lady Gaga, who earns over $62 million.

- **1950s:** In 1952, Princess Elizabeth Windsor becomes Queen Elizabeth II of England. She is only twenty-five years old and is married to Prince Philip, a member of the royal families of Greece and Denmark.

  Today: Princess Victoria of Sweden, who is the heiress to the Swedish throne, marries Daniel Westling, a commoner who is also the princess's personal trainer.

Rodgers met Lorenz "Larry" Hart, who wrote lyrics, and the two of them formed a songwriting partnership that lasted twenty-four years. With Hart, Rodgers wrote nine musicals, including *Babes in Arms* (1937) and *Pal Joey* (1940). The twosome also wrote the popular songs "My Funny Valentine" and "The Lady Is a Tramp."

Oscar Hammerstein II was born on July 12, 1895, in New York City, to a family well established in the theater. His father, William, managed a vaudeville theater; his uncle, Arthur, was a well-known producer; and his grandfather (for whom he was named) held a job as a promoter of operas.

Like Rodgers, Hammerstein began to study piano at an early age. Though his father encouraged a career in law, upon his father's death, Hammerstein came under the influence of family members who emphasized following a career in the theater. While studying at Columbia University, Hammerstein performed with and wrote for an acting troupe. It was also at Columbia that he met Rodgers, with whom he would later collaborate.

It was not until 1943 that Rodgers and Hammerstein began to work together. From that time until Hammerstein's death, the pair created some of the most memorable Broadway musicals of the twentieth century. Hammerstein wrote the lyrics and Rodgers composed the music. The first work that Rodgers and Hammerstein created was the musical *Oklahoma!* (1943), which ran for more than two thousand performances in its initial Broadway production. Musicals that followed included *Carousel* (1945), *South Pacific* (1949), *The King and I* (1951), *Flower Drum Song* (1958), and *The Sound of Music* (1960). The works of Rodgers and Hammerstein would go on to win Tony awards, Academy awards, Pulitzer prizes, Grammy awards, and Emmy awards.

Hammerstein died of cancer on August 23, 1960, after having completed the lyrics for his final play, *The Sound of Music*. Rodgers died nineteen years later at the age of seventy-seven.

Hans Christian Andersen and His Fairy Tales

The play *Once upon a Mattress* is based on a fairy tale written by Hans Christian Andersen (1805–1875). In "The Princess and the Pea" (first published in 1835), a young woman's claim to royalty is tested. She is told to sleep on a pile of mattresses, under which is concealed a single dried pea, and to

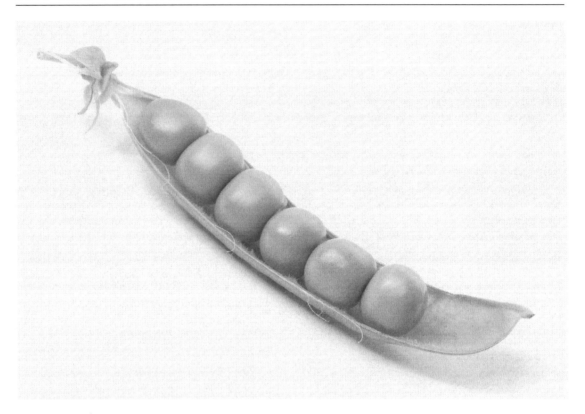

Peas in a pod (Yellowj | Shutterstock.com)

report in the morning whether she felt anything unusual. According to this story, if she detected the pea, that would be proof that she was sensitive enough to be a princess.

Andersen was born in the town of Odense, Denmark, but spent much of his adult life in Copenhagen, Denmark. He suffered humiliations early in life, from not fitting in well in school, being poor, and being physically frail and unattractive. Andersen's father encouraged the boy's imagination by reading to him and taking him to plays. Though he started school late, he eventually completed his education at Copenhagen University. At first he wrote books for adults, but Andersen is best remembered for his fairy tales. Some of his most famous stories are "The Emperor's New Clothes," "The Ugly Duckling," "The Little Mermaid," and "The Princess and the Pea." Though he had been poor in his youth, the popularity of his fiction provided him with money and influential friends in the later years of his life. He died of liver cancer in Copenhagen in 1875.

1950s U.S. Culture and Entertainment
The 1950s were marked by major changes in the culture of the United States. The long and harsh sacrifices of World War II were over, and the economy was booming. Peace and financial security seemed within the reach of a vast majority of the population.

The 1950s were a time of affordable suburban housing and other material comforts. Not all Americans enjoyed success, but the image portrayed of a typical U.S. family, such as those shown in new television programs, was one of accomplishment and affluence. The messages shown on television were that the American dream (prosperity) could be achieved by everyone.

With the advent of television, entertainment was changing. Broadway was doing well in the 1950s, with both musical hits, such as *My Fair Lady* (1950), *Guys and Dolls* (1951), and *The Music Man* (1958), and dramatic productions, such as *The Crucible* (1953) and *The Diary of Anne Frank* (1956). However, more and more people were staying home to watch television. Families gathered around the small sets (almost always black-and-white) every evening to tune in to their favorite shows. Many shows reflected the idealized situations of middle-class families that seldom quarreled, such as *Ozzie and Harriet*.

Music was also changing. Popular tunes, which had formerly been geared to adults, were now, with the new rock-and-roll music, focusing on teenagers. Those teenagers, for once, did not have to stay inside to hear their music. The innovation of transistor radios—small, battery-operated devices—allowed them to listen to the latest hits without being plugged in to an electrical outlet.

CRITICAL OVERVIEW

The musical *Once upon a Mattress* has been a perennial audience pleaser for several decades, sometimes to the surprise of critics. The play, in all its adaptations, has been nominated for several awards but has never won any. Despite this neglect, the play continues to enjoy revivals around the nation. Ben Brantley, writing a review of the 1996 revival of the musical, starring Sarah Jessica Parker, for the *New York Times*, refers to the popular musical as the "little-show-that-could of 1959," bringing to mind the children's story about the tiny train engine that mounted an impossible mountainside. According to Brantley, the play, though at times silly and "whimsy-laden," has become over the years "a favorite of stock and amateur theaters." Though Brantley praises the original 1959 production, he finds that the revival leaves a lot to be desired; he concludes, for example, that Parker is no match for Carol Burnett in the role of Princess Winnifred. The director of the revival, Gerald Gutierrez, Brantley believed, took out some of the best parts of the original play.

Reviewing a 2005 television production for the *New York Times*, Alessandra Stanley finds the musical to be "just as delightful as the original 1964 television musical that starred Carol Burnett." Stanley even suggests that the 2005 version might be better. Burnett, who had played Princess Winnifred in the original Broadway production, stars as the queen in the 2005 television adaptation and is, according to Stanley, "hilarious." In this production, Tracey Ullman plays the princess, and Stanley finds her "wonderful the minute she climbs out of the moat."

In a review for the *New Leader*, Stefan Kanfer describes the musical as a "modest little song-and-dance show," but points out that it "surprised everyone by becoming an overnight smash." Most of the credit, Kanfer writes, has to go to Carol Burnett,

who was then an unknown. Kanfer, in writing about the power of the play to excite audiences even several decades later, also gives the music of Mary Rodgers credit, remarking that it "remains inventive and fresh." Kanfer also praises lyricist Marshall Barer, who "always did know how to tell a joke in rhyme."

Brian Lowry, writing for *Variety*, was not as pleased with the 2005 television adaptation of *Once upon a Mattress*. He wrote, "This overly broad storybook project feels painfully dated." According to Lowry, even Burnett and Ullman were not strong enough to bring life back into the play.

CRITICISM

Joyce Hart

Hart is a published writer and teacher of creative writing. In the following essay, she examines the strengths and weaknesses of the female characters in Once upon a Mattress.

The three main female roles in the musical comedy *Once upon a Mattress*—the boisterous and self-serving queen, the determined Princess Winnifred, and the soft-spoken Lady Larken—have some interesting similarities, despite all their differences. Though many of their personal characteristics stand in opposition to one another, at the core they are all women who are well ahead of their time; they are strong, independent women who are not afraid of standing up for what they believe in. Their beliefs, however, vary, and very much affect the outcomes of their action. All three women want something, but their different approaches do not always help them achieve their goals.

Lady Larken has a minor role in this play, compared with the queen and the princess, but her situation is grave. She has found out that she is pregnant. Because of the queen's strict laws against weddings, Lady Larken is also unmarried. Lady Larken offers to go away so as not to embarrass Sir Harry or tarnish his excellent record of service to the queen. She suggests this unselfishly and without fear. She presents herself as a woman who is confident enough to figure out how to take care of herself and her child without becoming dependent on anyone. She makes the decision on her own and does not express negative feelings toward Sir Harry when he does not disagree with her. They do have an argument over other matters, which expresses the emotional tension they feel, but Lady Larken is willing to make this

WHAT DO I READ NEXT?

- Disney's stage musical *Lion King* features African-themed music, dances, and costumes. This Broadway musical was the winner of six Tony awards in 1998, including best musical of the year. It tells the story of Simba, a young lion who must learn how to rule his kingdom of African animals. This musical is an adaptation of a 1994 animated movie of the same name.

- Mary Rodgers, along with four other songwriters, composed the music for the 1978 production of *Working*. The story for this musical was based on a book written by Studs Terkel, the famed American historian who focused on the lives of ordinary working people. The play's characters include an ironworker, a delivery man, a teacher, an actor, and a waitress. The play's themes have remained contemporary, and it has therefore been revived several times.

- In 1957, two years before *Once upon a Mattress* was produced, the classic *West Side Story* was first staged. Drawing from William Shakespeare's *Romeo and Juliet*, it is a love story of star-crossed teens who are associated with rival gangs. Jerome Robbins won the 1958 Tony Award for best choreographer, and the music was written by Leonard Bernstein. This play was also adapted to film in 1961, and it has been revived on stage several times.

- Stephen Schwartz composed the music and lyrics for the 2003 musical *Wicked*, which uses characters and settings from L. Frank Baum's 1900 book *The Wonderful Wizard of Oz* and the 1938 movie, starring Judy Garland, that was an adaptation of it. The musical *Wicked* is itself an adaptation of a book by Gregory Maguire. In the musical, Glinda the Good Witch and the green-faced Elphaba,

Wicked Witch of the West, are at first the best of friends, but circumstances set them at odds with each other. *Wicked* was nominated for a 2004 Tony Award for best musical.

- *Mary Poppins*, by P. L. Travers, was published in 1934, the first in a series of eight books about an English nanny and her adventures with the Banks family. The stories of Mary Poppins were adapted for film in 1964 by Walt Disney Productions. Then in 2004, the story was adapted to the stage, with music and lyrics written by Richard M. Sherman and Robert B. Sherman. Two years later, the production moved to Broadway and was nominated for several Tony awards.

- *The Phantom of the Opera* was adapted from a 1911 French novel by Gaston Leroux. A silent film version starring Lon Chaney was produced in 1925 by Carl Laemmie. The first stage production, in 1988, was written by Andrew Lloyd Webber, and it continues to run at the Majestic Theatre in New York City. A recluse who lives in a grand theater falls in love with a young woman named Christine. He writes an opera for her and demands that those in charge produce his work with Christine in the lead. When Christine confesses that she is in love with someone else, the phantom threatens to kill the other man if Christine does not stay with him.

- *The Addams Family* is a lighthearted musical. This story actually began as a cartoon, created by Charles Addams in 1936, which continued until 1988. The cartoons were the basis of an ABC television series, which first aired in 1964, and a 1991 movie and its sequel. In 2009, Andrew Lippa wrote the lyrics and music for a staged production, which has earned two Tony Award nominations.

decision and leave the kingdom on her own. She is strong enough to take full responsibility for her circumstances.

The underlying question in Lady Larken's mind about Sir Harry is whether or not he truly loves her. She poses this question within the frame

"ALL THREE WOMEN WANT SOMETHING, BUT THEIR DIFFERENT APPROACHES DO NOT ALWAYS HELP THEM ACHIEVE THEIR GOALS."

of whether he believes love should be a stronger commitment than the laws of the land. She suggests that she and Sir Harry get married in secret so that their child will be considered legitimate— that is, born to married parents. Her questioning Sir Harry on this issue is done as a test of his love for her, but even when he falters in this test and comes up with an alternative possibility (finding another princess for Prince Dauntless to marry), Lady Larken does not fall into the trap of believing that only a man can save her. She begins to doubt Sir Harry's love, but she does not fall apart over the potential loss. Rather, she comes up with her own alternative plan—leaving the kingdom and finding a new life on her own in some distant land. It is not explained how she will do this or how this will make her life easier, but she follows through with her plan seemingly without fear or anger. In this manner, she exhibits her inner strength and her very modern view of life. She has put herself into a very uncomfortable position, but she is willing to face the consequences alone, if necessary. She will find some way to live her life independently. Lady Larken wants Sir Harry, but she knows that he has to want her too.

The queen also follows a path that she is willing to travel alone. She has made some choices that prove her strength. However, that strength comes from a different source than Lady Larken's. Whereas Lady Larken chooses to walk into an unknown world in which she will give birth to and raise her child, the queen attempts to control all the elements of her known world. Whereas Lady Larken demonstrates inner strength in her choices, the queen exhibits weakness. The queen is so strong in her convictions that she believes everyone should follow her path, but her beliefs are based on her need to have her son remain dependent on her. The queen has two men in her personal life, Prince Dauntless and the king. Both of them are in some way handicapped by the queen. The king has been cursed and cannot

speak, which allows the queen to take full authority over the kingdom. The prince seems unable to think for himself because of his mother's constant protective coddling. Because both men are somewhat debilitated, the queen's house is left completely in her rule.

Whereas Lady Larken is soft-spoken and emotionally available, the queen is obnoxiously loud and rude. She thinks of no one but herself. She is demeaning to everyone around her and works toward satisfying no one's emotional needs but her own. Her loud manner gives her a psychological edge of authority only because she frightens everyone around her. She is also egotistical and manipulative. She rules through terror, not respect. A feminist view shows that the queen has not evolved or fought for equal rights with men but rather has adopted the worst traits of a patriarchal (that is, males ruling simply because they are male) dictator. She uses fear and threats to gain what she alone wants. In addition, she is seen as having allowed her maternal instincts to grow out of control and to have made the worst use of feminine qualities. Because she is not strong enough in herself, she has not allowed her son the freedom to mature and become independent of her. Worse yet, the queen lives in fear of being replaced by her son's bringing a new woman into his life. The queen believes that she needs her son in order to define herself. If she loses him, who would she be?

The queen does not seem to need her husband, the king, at all. At most, he serves as a figurehead— someone who represents true power. She has pushed the king into the background and replaced her feelings for him with the twisted emotions she exhibits for her son. It is never revealed who the real ruling monarch is, the king or the queen. However, since the king has been made unable to speak by the curse, the queen has inherited the role of authority; in essence, the queen has earned her power by means of her husband's misfortune. She has not earned her authority on her own. Therefore, she is inauthentic, and it is only a matter of time before she loses the power that she has temporarily stolen.

The third female character, Princess Winnifred, in contrast to Lady Larken and the queen, is the strongest person in this play. She embodies some of the traits of the other two women, but she uses them to greater advantage and in a more balanced way. Right off the top, the audience becomes well aware that Princess Winnifred is her own person. She is going to do things her way, whether that way is acceptable to her social peers or not. She knows no other way to do things. She has a firm understanding of who she is, what she is capable of doing, and what she is not able to do. Though she can be as loud as the queen, she is not rude and obnoxious. Though she is fully capable of expressing her emotions, she is not as easily hurt as Lady Larken. When Princess Winnifred's path is blocked, she does whatever it takes to make her way around the obstacle.

Princess Winnifred is determined to marry Prince Dauntless. She is anxious to meet him, so she swims the moat to get inside the castle as quickly as possible. She finds that she likes him, so she is willing to stay up all night and study for the queen's test. She has read about other princesses who had it much easier. Sometimes a kiss from the prince was all it took for the two of them to be married. However, she does not become discouraged even after she has heard how difficult the queen has made it for every other young woman who wants to marry Dauntless. The queen does not scare her. Rather than being distracted by the queen, Princess Winnifred sinks all her energy into preparing herself. If she fails, it will not be for lack of trying. In the end, despite the fact that several men, including Sir Harry, have rigged the test in Princess Winnifred's favor, the princess wins—not because of her all-night studying but because of her authenticity. She proves that she is truly a princess because even the small pea under the mattresses makes her uncomfortable. She is sensitive, as the queen demanded, but Winnifred is also tough. She is strong but she is also vulnerable to falling in love.

Source: Joyce Hart, Critical Essay on *Once upon a Mattress*, in *Drama for Students*, Gale, Cengage Learning, 2011.

Terri Bryce Reeves

In the following review, Reeves remarks on the comedic nature of the play.

She can swim a castle moat, pump iron and gulp wine from a goblet, but is Winnifred a "real" princess?

Only her mattress knows for sure.

That's the foundation for *Once Upon a Mattress*, a musical comedy presented by City Players premiering tonight and running through Sunday at Ruth Eckerd Hall.

The musical, based on Hans Christian Andersen's fairy tale *The Princess and the Pea*,

Fairytale castle (© *International Photobank / Alamy*)

opened in 1959 with Carol Burnett playing the part of the irrepressible Princess Winnifred, or Fred, as friends call her.

In this version, the plucky part is played by Alexandra Gonzalez, a Tampa native and theater student at Roosevelt University in Chicago.

During the dress rehearsal, the mezzo-soprano scaled a 15-foot ladder running up the side of "20 soft, downy mattresses," plopped down and rolled around, dangling legs and arms.

"I don't need a harness. I'm fine," she was overheard saying later.

Gonzales, 19, said she has no fear of heights. In fact, being up there fulfills an ambition she has long had as a triplet.

"We had bunks, and I always wanted to be on the top," she said, displaying the same confidence and spunk as the character she plays.

Of more concern to her was that she do justice to the highly comedic role she plays.

"I was worried about doing comedy at first, but this musical has made me learn to trust my instincts," she said.

The cast is directed by Claud Smith, 48. He's a freelance creative consultant from Orlando who has masterminded theatrical productions for Disney, Busch Gardens and other theme parks. He was brought in by Betty Jane Pucci, who has been directing the group for decades.

"We had a chance to get this really great guy who's usually really busy," she said.

Smith designed the set to look like a pop-up storybook done in old-style pen and ink.

"The performers, on the other hand, are very colorful. It makes the story come alive," he said.

About half of the cast is new to City Players this year, he said. They've been rehearsing for six weeks and "are coming along very well," he said. "Because I travel a lot, it's taught me how to put together a show very quickly."

The classic-storybook look is enhanced by the skills of costume designer Marilyn Deighton of Youngstown, N.Y. She is an assistant professor at Niagara University, where she teaches costume technology.

She has previously worked in the area for various dinner and community theaters.

Deighton placed the 49 actors, ages 17 to 70-plus, in jewel tones, accented with gold and sparkles.

When Princess Winnifred emerges from the moat, she's supposed to look damp, so Deighton created a costume using sheer, multicolored tie-dyed fabric with tiny sequins "to look like water droplets from a distance."

Many of the men's costumes have been borrowed from Niagara University. One outfit came from a Broadway production.

About 25 were built from scratch, she said.

"I brought most of my shop down with me," she said.

For the uninitiated, *Once Upon a Mattress* tells the tale of mean Queen Aggravain, who has ruled that no one in the kingdom can marry until her son is wed.

The meddling mom really wants him by her side, so she keeps sabotaging the prospective brides.

Princess Winnifred, the 13th candidate for the prince's hand, arrives from the swamplands, refreshingly unrefined—and wet.

The queen devises a sensitivity test—a pea under 20 downy mattresses—to see if she can fall asleep.

"Any genuine princess would feel it," said the queen, played by Kate Gaudet.

But the test is not quite as foolproof as she imagines.

Source: Terri Bryce Reeves, "Funny 'Mattress' Springs to Life: Princess Winnifred Schleps into Town for a Weekend Show at Ruth Eckerd," in *St. Petersburg Times*, July 17, 2009, p. 6.

Elizabeth Miller

In the following review, Miller describes the play as an off-beat adaptation of a classic fairytale.

Jessie Grossman is the princess who charms the prince in this weekend's production of *Once Upon a Mattress* at the University Area Community Complex.

Grossman plays Princess Winnifred, the unlikely princess who steals the heart of Prince Dauntless in the musical comedy presented by the New Tampa Players.

"My character is the anti-princess, who by dumb luck makes all the right moves," said the 17-year-old Hillsborough High School student from Northdale.

Grossman seems to be a natural on stage. This is only her second theater performance and the second time she's scored a lead role. She played Prince Edward in the New Tampa Players' production of *The Prince and the Pauper* in 2005.

"I feel really proud because a lot of girls were trying out for the role," Grossman said.

Though she's taken dance her whole life, she recently began taking voice lessons and plans to pursue theater in college.

Her co-star Robby McNeel, 19, has been acting for most of his life. A director for Dearmon Creative Arts School of Theater, a home-school theater group, he currently directs a summer theater class at Idlewild Baptist Church.

McNeel said he had no trouble jumping into the role of Prince Dauntless since he played Sir Harry in the same show years ago with the Masque of Temple Terrace.

"Prince Dauntless is a complete mama's boy," said McNeel, a freelance photographer who lives in Lutz. "He wants to get married, but wants his mother's approval."

Based on the classic fairy tale *The Princess and the Pea*, the show, directed by Maria Brent, tells the story of Prince Dauntless, whose overprotective and conniving mother Queen Aggravain tries to keep him from marrying.

Since no one in the kingdom is allowed to marry until Dauntless finds a bride, the wacky cast of characters, including a wizard, a jester and a minstrel, set out to find a suitable princess and discover Winnifred of the swamp.

"All the characters really have a chance to shine," said Tom Pahl of Pebble Creek, a New Tampa Players member who finds himself cast in this production as King Sextimus.

Suzy Duic of Lutz plays the controlling Queen Aggravain. A newcomer to New Tampa Players, she is a stay-at-home mother returning to the stage after a long hiatus from acting.

With a minor in theater from the University of Vermont, Duic spent a year studying theater in London. She worked as an actor in New York City, landing spots on *One Life to Live* and *Guiding Light*, before going back to school for her master's degree and becoming a school psychologist.

"[Aggravain] is a fun role to play," she said, "I'm excited to be doing theater again. It's something I've missed."

Source: Elizabeth Miller, "Princess Story a Modern Spin: *Once Upon a Mattress* Updates a Classic Fairy Tale," in *St. Petersburg Times,* August 1, 2008, p. 16.

Stefan Kanfer

In the following review, Kanfer notes that the play easily lends itself to modern productions.

Long, Long ago, when dinosaurs roamed New York and people went to lavish musicals written by someone other than Andrew Lloyd Webber, a modest little song-and-dance show appeared Off Broadway. Its plot was about as complicated as a fairy tale—in fact, it was a fairy tale: about a comely but ill-dressed young woman who had to prove herself a princess by undergoing a severe test. Twenty mattresses were piled up, one upon the other, and underneath the bottom one a single pea was placed. Scores of other candidates had failed similar tests set up by the Wicked Queen. Would our heroine be sensitive enough to foil Her Majesty? Would she feel the object through all those strata?

That night, the Princess tossed and turned, unable to catch two winks, much less 40, because of the uncomfortable "lump" in her bed. Here, then, was irrefutable proof that the sleepless maiden possessed exquisite nerves, the kind that are found only in the bodies of aristocrats. The court, convinced beyond doubt that she was truly

a person of regal blood, allowed the Handsome Prince to take her hand in marriage. Because they were royalty, the couple walked off hand in hand into the sunset and lived happily ever after. Well, I told you it was long, long ago.

The show surprised everyone by becoming an overnight smash, not least because the person playing the Princess was a talented unknown named Carol Burnett. But more than three decades have passed since *Once Upon A Mattress* made its debut. This is the epoch of the ineffable Prince Charles and Diana, and the effable Sarah, Duchess of York ("Looks like an unemployed barmaid in search of a crown," said Mr. Blackwell recently, placing her on his 10 worst-dressed list.) The times would not seem propitious for an airy pageant about folks who live in castles. Yet the revival at the Broadhurst Theater boasts any number of unexpected assets.

Genes, like mattresses, will tell, and if Mary Rodgers' compositions are not quite up to those of her father, Richard, her work remains inventive and fresh after all these years. Lyricist Marshall Barer is a thoroughgoing professional who has set words to the music of Hoagy Carmichael, Kurt Weill, Duke Ellington, and Burton Lane among others. He always did know how to tell a joke in rhyme, and make exposition seem as graceful as a bow. I give you his scene-setter at the opening of the show:

> Many years ago in a far-off place
> Lived a handsome prince with a
> gloomy face
> For he did not have a bride.
> He sighed "alas" and he pined
> "alas,"
> But alas the prince couldn't find a lass
> Who would soothe his mother's pride. Or his send-
> up of nostalgia, when the Princess sings of her
> origins:
> Where'er I roam,
> The whips of fate may smart,
> But deep down in my heart
> One thought will abide
> And ne'er be forgotten.
> Though I search far and wide,
> There's no land as rotten
> As the swamps of home.

The Princess in this version is Sarah Jessica Parker, the centerpiece of *Once Upon a Mattress* and every other show she has appeared in, among them *How to Succeed, Sylvia* (in which she played a dog) and *The Heidi Chronicles.* Parker is one of those rare blondes who are endowed with knockout features, but who don't mind making fools of themselves in the pursuit of laughter. (Carole Lombard and Kay Kendall come to mind; so does the present-day Geena Davis.) The star can carry a tune around the stage, dance and whirl and pratfall without pausing to catch her breath, wring comedy out of a heart of stone, and the Queen (Mary Lou Rosato) certainly has one.

The supporting cast is a delight. The henpecked King (Heath Lamberts) is a mute who communicates with sign language—a role essayed by mimes as varied as Jack Gilford, who starred in the original production, and Buster Keaton, who played it on the road. What those skilled farceurs did with ease, Lamberts labors to achieve, but he gets his laughs. As Prince Dauntless, David Aaron Baker has the appropriate air of ingenuousness and eager curiosity about what boys and girls do when they're alone; Lawrence Clayton makes a splendid minstrel; the second leads, Jane Krakowski and Lewis Cleale, are funny and touching; and David Hibbard has some memorable moments as a Jester with memories of the time his old man played the Palace back in 1392.

Gerald Gutierrez handles the balmy proceedings with a firm hand, abetted by a lively book by Barer, Dean Fuller and Jay Thompson. Liza Gennaro's choreography is entry-level but diverting, Bruce Coughlin's deft orchestrations make the welkin ring, John Lee Beatty's sets have just the right mix of Camelot and Cloud-Cuckooland, and Jane Greenwood's costumes can be farcical or look smashing, depending of the need. Gifted as Parker is, this slender Mattress would not have been as endearing without all of these stalwarts. An old show business story recalls that Jerome Kern was standing in the wings when the curtain was about to rise on his latest show. "I hope it goes well," said a producer's assistant. Fourteen people replied, "Thanks." This is another of those occasions.

Source: Stefan Kanfer, Review of Once Upon A Mattress, in New Leader, Vol. 80, No. 1, January 13, 1997, pp. 22–23.

SOURCES

Brantley, Ben, "A Bride for the Prince? Stack Up the Bedding!," in New York Times, December 20, 1996, p. C1.

"Broadway, the American Musical," in Public Broadcasting Service, http://www.pbs.org/wnet/broadway/resources.html (accessed August 19, 2010).

"Dean Fuller: Biography," in The Rodgers and Hammerstein Organization, http://www.rnh.com/people_detail.asp?sub = bio&div = people&id = D_Fuller&s = 1 (accessed September 23, 2010).

"Lady Gaga Leads List of Celeb 100 Newcomers," in Forbes, http://www.forbes.com/2010/06/22/lady-gaga-kristin-stewart-business-entertainment-celeb-100-1 0-newcomers.html (accessed August 20, 2010).

Halliwell, Martin, American Culture in the 1950s, Edinburgh University Press, 2007.

"Jay Thompson: Biography," in The Rodgers and Hammerstein Organization, http://www.rnh.com/people_detail.asp?sub = bio&div = people&id = J_Thompson&s = 1 (accessed September 23, 2010).

Kanfer, Stefan, Review of Once upon a Mattress, in New Leader, January 13, 1997, Vol. 80, No. 1, pp. 22–23.

Lowry, Brian, Review of Once upon a Mattress, in Variety, December 14, 2005, http://variety.com/index.asp?layout = print_review&reviewid = VE1117929108&cate goryid = 32 (accessed August 19, 2010).

"Marshall Barer: Biography," in The Rodgers and Hammerstein Organization, http://www.rnh.com/people_detail.asp?sub = bio&div = people&id = M_Barer&s = 1 (accessed September 23, 2010).

"Mary Rodgers: Biography," in The Rodgers and Hammerstein Organization, http://www.rnh.com/people_detail.asp?sub = bio&div = people&id = M_Rodgers&s = 1 (accessed September 23, 2010).

Nolan, Frederick, The Sound of Their Music: The Story of Rodgers and Hammerstein, Applause Books, 2002.

Rodgers, Mary, Once upon a Mattress, Buena Vista Home Entertainment/Disney, 2005.

———, Once upon a Mattress (1959 Original Broadway Cast; soundtrack), Decca Records, 1993.

Stanley, Alessandra, "The Affable Princess Is Back as Queen," in New York Times, December 16, 2005, pp. E1, E32.

Wullschlager, Jackie, Hans Christian Andersen: The Life of a Storyteller, University of Chicago Press, 2002.

FURTHER READING

Bell, Mary Lou, Acting for Young Actors: The Ultimate Teen Guide, Back Stage Books, 2006.

Bell is an Emmy Award-winning director, as well as a teacher and professional actor. In this book, she helps teens who are interested in acting to learn the vocabulary of the theater and how to hone their skills and to develop their craft. Helpful exercises are included, as well as tip on auditioning, rehearsing, and improvisation.

Bloom, Ken, and Frank Vlastnik, Broadway Musicals: The 101 Greatest Shows of All Time, Black Dog & Leventhal Publishers, 2004.

Through photographs and narrative, these authors have put together a collection of their favorite Broadway shows and offer the reader a glimpse into the history of the productions. Plays include such classics as *Mame, Hello, Dolly!* and *Funny Girl.*

Jacobs, Leonard, *Historic Photos of Broadway: New York Theater: 1850–1970*, Turner Publishing, 2008.
   The 240 photographs in this collection offer students a historical view of the people who made Broadway. This book contains photographs rarely seen in any other publication of playwrights, such as Arthur Miller and Tennessee Williams, and composers, such as George and Ira Gershwin, Richard Rodgers, and Larry Hart.

Metzier, Bo, *What We Do—Working in the Theater*, Infinity Publishing, 2008.
   Metzier has worked in theater for over forty years. His experience includes educational theater, dinner theater, and off-Broadway productions. He has also been involved in television shows and rock concerts. Besides being an actor, Metzier has also helped to create sets, worked as a stage manager, and as a prop man. In this book, he offers students a glimpse into the backstage efforts that go into producing plays and musicals.

Rodgers, Richard, and others, *Broadway Greatest Hits*, Sony Audio CD, 1996.
   This collection of music offers the listener an audio journey through many of Broadway's best hits. The music includes songs from *Oklahoma!* (1943), *Annie Get Your Gun* (1946), *Fiddler on the Roof* (1964), *West Side Story* (1957), and many more. Songs are sung by the actors who were in the original casts.

Schumacher, Thomas, and Jeff Kurtti, *How Does the Show Go On: An Introduction to the Theater*, Disney Editions, 2007.
   Written to help young-adult readers better understand all the elements of theater production, this book takes students from the front of the theater, where the box office is located, to behind the curtains, where the props are located. Many exciting photographs and illustrations are provided.

Wienir, David, and Jodie Langel, *Making It on Broadway: Actors' Tales of Climbing to the Top*, Allworth Press, 2004.
   Wienir and Langel offer the reader insights into the struggles and the victories of performers who dreamed of making it on the stage. More than 150 stories are included in this collection, describing the challenges of performing seven nights a week, spending a lot of time away from families, as well as the exhilaration of winning a Tony Award. These stories are told candidly but also with a sense of humor.

SUGGESTED SEARCH TERMS

Mary Rodgers

Once upon a Mattress

Broadway musicals

Marshall Barer

Dean Fuller

Mary Rodgers and musical comedies

Once upon a Mattress AND history

Carol Burnett AND Once upon a Mattress

Broadway musicals AND twentieth century

Hans Christian Anderson AND fairy tales

Princess and the Pea

Princess and the Pea AND Once upon a Mattress

Sleep Deprivation Chamber

ADRIENNE KENNEDY, ADAM P. KENNEDY

1996

Adrienne Kennedy's play *Sleep Deprivation Chamber*, written with her son Adam P. Kennedy, is based on a true event. One night as Adam was driving home, a policeman stopped him for having a broken taillight on his car. In the play, a similar routine traffic stop escalates alarmingly, as the young man resists the police officer's aggressive approach and eventual brutal attack.

This confrontation is the focus of the play. Kennedy explores the event from various positions, all of them woven through surrealist dream sequences. Throughout the reenactment of this incident in the play, the young man (Teddy) and his mother (Suzanne) insist that he is innocent and that the police office is at fault. They insinuate that he was treated unfairly because he is black. The officer was white. They sense that they have little chance to win their case, but they are determined to be heard in a court of law. Although they are victorious in the end, the family suffers not only from the brutal beating but from the tension, fear, and frustration of having to defend themselves against the age-old racism they expect. They claim—the father, the mother, and the son— that they are psychologically tortured by the experience, as if they had been imprisoned in a sleep deprivation chamber.

Sleep Deprivation Chamber had its world premiere at the Joseph Papp Public Theater in New York in 1996. It was directed by Michael

Kahn and starred Trazana Beverley as Suzanne (the mother) and Kevin T. Carroll as Teddy (the son). According to critic Ben Brantley, writing for the *New York Times*, the play "is imperfect, but it has unsettling power." Though reviews were mixed, *Sleep Deprivation Chamber* won the 1996 Obie Award for best play of the year.

AUTHOR BIOGRAPHY

Adrienne Kennedy, the primary author of this play, was born on September 13, 1931, in Pittsburgh, Pennsylvania, to Cornell and Etta Wallace. Before Kennedy was old enough to go to school, her parents moved the family, which included her brother, Cornell, to Cleveland, Ohio, where Kennedy spent most of her childhood. She was a gifted child, learning to read before she started first grade. By the fifth grade, Kennedy had read all the books in her elementary school library. Although she was an avid reader, her interest in writing did not develop until she was in college, at the Ohio State University. Though she enjoyed her literature classes, she majored in education and graduated with a bachelor's degree in 1952.

She married Joseph Kennedy, a college boyfriend, in 1953. When he was drafted into the military and was sent to Korea, she, inspired by Tennessee Williams's works and his essays on script writing, began writing plays. After giving birth to her son Joseph, Jr., and upon her husband's return from the Korean War, Kennedy moved with her family to New York City in 1955. Searching for intellectual stimulation, Kennedy enrolled in the New School. While there, she wrote *Pale Blue Flowers*, a play influenced by Williams's *Glass Menagerie*, but this work was never produced on stage. Over the next decade, she continued to study writing, mostly at Columbia University, but she was unsuccessful in becoming a published writer. It was not until she took an extended trip through Europe and to Africa, giving her a different perspective on life, that Kennedy found her voice as a writer. She published her short story "Because of the King of France" in 1960. Two years later, her career as a playwright began with the off-Broadway production of her drama *Funnyhouse of a Negro*.

Since the 1960s, Kennedy has produced more than twenty plays, including *The Owl Answers*

(1963), *An Evening with Dead Essex* (1972), *Black Children's Day* (1980), *Diary of Lights* (1987), *The Ohio State Murders* (1992), *June and Jean in Concert* (1995), and *Mom, How Did You Meet the Beatles?* (2008). Her plays are often only one act long and deal with surrealistic themes such as nightmares and interior monologues. They reflect the lives of African Americans, with an emphasis on women, and are often autobiographical. Kennedy's approach to plays challenges traditional ideas about stage settings, linear timeframes, and plots, giving them an experimental appeal. Though she has been writing plays for more than forty years, Kennedy's name is not widely known. Her plays are appreciated not so much on the big theaters of New York but rather on smaller stages on college campuses and in Europe.

Besides being a playwright, Kennedy has also taught college courses at Yale University, Princeton University, Brown University, and the University of California, Berkeley. She has also written an autobiography, *People Who Led to My Plays* (1987). Kennedy is the winner of several awards, including two Obie awards, the first for *Funnyhouse of a Negro* (1964) and the second for *Sleep Deprivation Chamber* (1996). In 1994, she won the Academy Award in Literature from the American Academy of Arts and Letters. In 2003, she was presented with an honorary doctorate of literature from Ohio State University. Kennedy has two children, Joseph, Jr., and Adam. She and her husband were divorced in 1966. The playwright currently lives in New York City as of 2010.

PLOT SUMMARY

Scene 1
Sleep Deprivation Chamber opens during the winter at Antioch College in Yellow Springs, Ohio. The setting is in the theater department of the school, where a student cast is rehearsing William Shakespeare's play *Hamlet*. Suzanne, a middle-aged African American woman and a writer, is sitting at a desk. Her son, Teddy, joins the group; he is the director of the play. The student cast, focusing on an element in the Shakespeare play, says: "Ophelia, betrayal, disillusionment," setting the psychological tone of the Kennedy's play. As readers will soon discover, the main characters of *Sleep Deprivation Chamber* also feel betrayed and disillusioned.

While the rehearsal continues, Suzanne falls asleep, and her dreams are affected by lines from *Hamlet*. Suzanne imagines that Teddy has been accused of killing a French king and is sentenced to jail, where his body is dismembered. She shouts at those who have tortured her son. As Suzanne's dream continues, she pleads to some unseen authority figure, presumably begging for her son's life. She states that she is well read, her grandmother is religious, and her family is hard working. Then she writes a letter to an unnamed county manager, saying that another child of hers, Patrice, had telephoned her, crying. Something had happened involving the police and Teddy, while the children were staying with their father in Arlington, Virginia. This dream scene is a combination of what is happening around Suzanne (at the student rehearsal) and what has happened in her life in the recent past.

As the dream continues, Suzanne composes another letter, this one to Virginia governor Douglas Wilder. In the letter, she mentions the Arlington police department. This stimulates Teddy's memories (still in Suzanne's dream) as he recounts what happened the night he had an encounter with the police. Teddy sees the flashing lights of a patrol car; when the officer reaches Teddy's car, Teddy has already stepped out. The policeman tells him to return to his car, but Teddy does not do so. Instead, he continues to ask the policeman what he wants and what the problem is. He has pulled into the driveway of his father's house and tells the policeman that he lives there.

Suzanne continues her letter (still in her dream), telling Governor Wilder the merits of her family. Her former husband and father of her children, whose name is David, is an outstanding citizen and head of an organization called Africa/USA. Suzanne is a published writer and teacher. She tells the governor that she believes her son Teddy is being persecuted, a victim of racism, and mentions Emmett Till, a black youth who was murdered by white racists in the South during the civil rights movement. She then provides more details about the night of January 11: the officer's name was Holzer, and Teddy was stopped because of a broken taillight on his car. Teddy has never been in trouble before, she writes, and did not provoke the beating he was given. After Teddy was punched and kicked and dragged through the mud, Holzer arrested him, charging him with assault and battery.

Teddy, meanwhile, is being questioned by someone unseen on stage. The questioner wants to know how Teddy reacted when Officer Holzer hit him. He wants to know whether Teddy fell to the ground. Teddy confirms that he did fall and says that was when Holzer began kicking him, before dragging him through the mud. When the questioner asks what Teddy was saying to the officer at this time, Teddy points out that it is all but impossible to talk when someone is kicking you in the face. In any case, Teddy says, he was in a state of shock and could not speak.

Suzanne awakens and Teddy is at the table. Teddy asks her what else they should do to find his Uncle March, but Suzanne replies that she has done all she can. She has a friend in California who is writing stories about March for the newspaper that he works for, hoping to gain leads as to March's whereabouts. Patrice, who is living in California, has gone to stay at March's apartment, hoping he will return. March will come back, Suzanne believes. He has disappeared before. There is no further discussion about who March is at this time.

The unseen questioner returns with more inquiries. Teddy tells the questioner that the reason he pulled into his father's driveway that night was that there was nowhere else to pull off the road. The questioner wants to know how long it took Teddy to stop and how fast he was going.

Suzanne returns to dreaming. In this new dream, she encounters her brother-in-law, March. There is yellow tape across the door of March's cottage, marking the area as a crime scene. As it turns out, the cottage is marked because of the damage caused by an earthquake. According to signs left there, no one is to enter the cottage until it has been inspected for structural damage. Suzanne walks through the front door, though, and sees upturned furniture in March's living room. At the same time, in her dream, Teddy is being assaulted by the Virginia police officer. Teddy's face is swollen, and he cries out for his mother to help him. Suzanne offers the policeman a drink that has been poisoned.

There is a quick shift to Dr. David Alexander, Teddy's father, a sixty-something African American man. He is being questioned by an unseen lawyer for the prosecution. David is telling the lawyer what he saw the night of his son's beating. David claims that the police officer he saw was a black female named Summers; she had her gun drawn. The lawyer then questions

Alexander about his experience with weapons and whether he knows the shapes of various guns. Alexander responds that he was trained to use a weapon while he served in the Korean War as a medic, but he cannot describe the type of gun that Officer Summers was holding.

The play turns back to Suzanne and Teddy, who are still at the rehearsal of *Hamlet*. Teddy is thinking about his Uncle March, whom Teddy claims did "so much to help fight for racial equality." Where once his uncle wrote books and taught, now his memory is deteriorating and he often disappears. At the height of his career, March knew St. Clair Drake, a well-known and influential American sociologist. Teddy also mentions Fanon, which might refer to Frantz Omar Fanon, a black psychiatrist and philosopher from the island of Martinique, who focused his studies on the effects of decolonization. The third person Teddy mentions is Kwame Nkrumah, a leader of Ghana, who helped his country win independence from the United Kingdom and pushed for a united Africa. Mention of these men gives the audience a glimpse into the political attitude of the play's author and establishes the character and significance of Teddy's uncle March.

Once again, the unseen questioner asks Teddy for more information. The questioner wants to know why Teddy did not get back into his car when the policeman asked him to. Teddy responds that he wanted to talk to the officer; he wanted to know what the problem was. However, when he did try to open the car door, the policeman stopped him and told him to walk to the back of the car. When Teddy did this, the policeman grabbed Teddy's hand. Teddy pulled back and told the policeman not to touch him. At this, the policeman slapped him in the face, knocked him to the ground, and started kicking him.

Next, Teddy recalls a visit to a lawyer's office. The lawyer is an unnamed woman who tells Teddy that he will more than likely end up going to jail. She suggests that he plead guilty to all charges. He later visits a second lawyer and this time shows a video that his brother shot the night of the arrest.

Scene 2
Scene 2 takes place in Cleveland, Ohio, in a room of the Ohio Theatre. Another cast is rehearsing Suzanne's play, *The Ohio State Murders*. Meanwhile,

Suzanne is writing another letter to Governor Wilder. A voice from the cast interrupts. It is the heroine of the play, who has been asked to explain the violent imagery of the play. The heroine explains that the campus of Ohio State influences the imagery just as it had when she attended the school in 1949, her freshman year. Here, Kennedy is making a personal reference. In real life, Kennedy encountered what she has described as racial difficulties when she attended college.

The focus returns to Suzanne writing her letter. She explains that like Cleveland, New York City makes her nervous. People are mugged regularly. Then, a student working with Teddy reads sections from a police-training manual, which lays out the differences between white and black cultures. Statements are made about how police officers should treat blacks, such as not asking any personal information, as this is seen as being too intimate. However, the same questions can be asked of whites, as they see these types of questions not only as being appropriate but also as a sign of the police officer's attempt to be friendly. The manual also states that white people respect authority, while blacks do not.

Teddy is questioned again by an unseen person who wants to know how long Teddy thought he was unconscious after the officer hit him. The questioner also wants to know whether Teddy has a criminal record.

Suzanne reappears, writing a letter to Teddy's lawyer, a Mr. Edelstein. She wants to know whether Teddy might go to jail. Edelstein had previously stated that that was a possibility. Edelstein's voice is heard answering Suzanne's question. Edelstein believes he will be successful in winning, but he suggests that Suzanne constrain her emotions and prepare herself for a long, drawn-out process. Suzanne comes to the conclusion that if the trial goes to a jury, the chances are the jurors will all be white and prejudiced against her son.

With Teddy, the student cast reads more information from the police manual. It mentions the different dress styles of black people and white people, as well as the appropriateness, or lack thereof, of touching a white person versus touching a black person. In other words, according to the manual, there are two very different codes of conduct that the policemen are to follow, depending on the race of the person they are dealing with.

Next there is a discussion with Teddy's father, David, who is talking to a lawyer. The lawyer asks David to describe what happened on the night of Teddy's arrest. The lawyer wants to know whether the police officers had drawn their guns, what the officers looked like, what their names were, and what they were doing. David is unsure of what he saw that night because he was paying attention only to his son, who was calling out to him.

Suzanne has another dream. In this one, Teddy is sitting in attorney Edelstein's office in Washington, DC. He is telling Edelstein that he has come to Washington to finish some schoolwork because there is an outbreak of the plague going around campus, causing the atmosphere there to be very chaotic. Teddy is then transported to Cleveland. The year is 1943. He sees his maternal grandfather, who had been involved with the National Association for the Advancement of Colored People (NAACP), a major civil rights organization. This is done to demonstrate her father's involvement in a worthwhile cause: fighting discrimination.

Suzanne writes a letter to her daughter, Patrice. Their lawyer has insinuated that Suzanne might be irritating officials by writing so many letters, but Suzanne continues to write. Teddy's lawyer insists that Suzanne is emotionally out of control. Teddy tells his mother that the prosecuting lawyers want Teddy to say that he hit the police officer. That way, Teddy will receive only a minor sentencing, such as two months on probation, and his record will be wiped clean. Teddy tells his mother, though, that he is not going to confess to doing something he did not do. The prosecutors threaten to take the trial to a jury, which gives Teddy less of a chance of staying out of jail, as juries tend to side with the police.

Teddy and Mr. Edelstein meet with Mrs. Wagner, the lawyer for the police. Edelstein tries to make a deal with her, trying to avoid going to trial. He tells her there are two witnesses who will say that Teddy was a victim of police brutality. Wagner dismisses him, saying she is sure Teddy will be found guilty of assaulting a police officer, and then she tells them she is too busy and asks them to leave.

Scene 3

Scene 3 begins with another of Suzanne's dreams. Though she and Teddy (in the dream) are in London, Teddy continues to be questioned by an unknown person. The questions involve more details about the night Teddy was arrested.

Teddy explains that he had to go to the hospital that night because he was having trouble breathing. His face was badly bruised and he had cuts on his arms. He was also in a lot of pain.

Suzanne interrupts this part of the dream with a memory from the 1940s, when her father was attending another NAACP meeting. Suzanne hears him discussing how to make Cleveland a better place to live for black people.

The stage becomes a hotel room in Washington, DC. Suzanne is waiting for news about whether the judge will hear Teddy's case. Teddy calls to tell her that the District Attorney (Wagner) had asked to have Teddy's case tried before a jury, but the judge refuses to do so. The scene then fades to the courtroom, where Teddy is with his attorney, the judge, Wagner, and a court reporter. Wagner presents her case to the judge, telling the judge Officer Holzer's version of the story: Teddy was acting belligerently and therefore was a "hostile citizen."

Wagner continues to tell Holzer's side of the story, which includes Holzer's suspicions that Teddy was concealing a weapon inside his jacket. Holzer also claimed that Teddy struck him when he attempted to search him for a weapon. Holzer called for backup, and after the other officers arrived, they had to force Teddy to the ground and handcuff him. During this scuffle, Holzer had stated, Teddy might have been hurt. Next, Teddy's lawyer has a chance to tell Teddy's side of the story.

Later, Teddy tells his mother that he is afraid he might have to go to jail. He says police scare him and then tells his mother about an incident that happened to him in California when he was younger. He was with his cousins in a car and they got lost. When he saw a police car behind them, Teddy told his cousin to pull over so they could ask the police for directions. The Los Angeles police were belligerent and used racial slurs and profanity when they talked to the boys. Then they pushed the boys against a wall and placed a revolver next to Teddy's head. "Nigger, I'll blow your head off," one of the officers said. Then he asked where the boys got the car, implying that they must have stolen it. When Teddy said that the car belonged to a family member, the policeman doubted him.

The play then returns to the courtroom scene. Attorney Edelstein is interrogating Officer Holzer. Through the combination of Edelstein's questions and Holzer's answers, readers learn that the police officer had been trailing Teddy's car for much longer than Teddy had thought. Holzer had followed without turning on his lights, wanting to see what Teddy might do next. Holzer thought Teddy was acting suspiciously. After additional questions, Edelstein demonstrates that Holzer may have made mistakes in handling Teddy's case. For example, Holzer did not warn Teddy that he was going to frisk him to find out whether he had a gun. Holzer merely moved in on Teddy to do the search, which could have made Teddy assume that Holzer was going to hit him. Edelstein also reminds Holzer that he had made a statement to Teddy's father that Teddy had merely touched him; later, though, Holzer had amended his statement to that Teddy hit him. Edelstein also makes Officer Holzer confess that he hit and kicked Teddy several times. Holzer claims it was to subdue Teddy, but Edelstein makes Holzer confirm that Teddy was already on the ground, pinned by Holzer's full weight. This insinuates that Holzer was using excessive force. Holzer also admits that he never pulled out his gun or Taser, which might have been enough to subdue Teddy without the physical abuse.

In the end, the judge states that she did not hear any testimony from Holzer that would constitute an assault-and-battery charge against Teddy. The judge dismisses the case, and Teddy goes free.

CHARACTERS

David Alexander, Jr.
David Alexander, Jr., is Teddy's brother. David takes a video of the night of Teddy's arrest. The video records the sounds of the event, but the lighting was not good and the video is too dark to see clearly. However, on the night of Teddy's arrest, David, Jr., is more aggressive and more vocal in demanding Teddy's civil rights than his father is. David insists on recording Holzer's name and badge number and even threatens the police officer by telling him that he is going to be in trouble for what he has done in wrongfully arresting his brother.

Dr. David Alexander, Sr.
David is Suzanne's former husband and the father of her children Patrice, David, Jr., and Teddy. David plays a minor role in this play. He is mostly in the background, such as when

Teddy is assaulted by the police officer. David comes outside to ask the police what is happening, but he is not very active in attempting to stop the police or to protect his son. When questioned by the attorneys about what he saw that night, David tends to be vague and unsure.

March Alexander
March is the brother of Dr. David Alexander and brother-in-law of Suzanne. March's presence in this play is vague, more symbolic than real. March adds a depth of intelligence and community involvement in the Alexander family's history. He was a respected professor at a prestigious school, Stanford University, but he now suffers from dementia or some other ailment that makes him forgetful. He wanders off, not telling anyone where he is going. He disappears for days. His appearances in this play come mostly through Suzanne's dreams. His presence has only a slight bearing on the plot of this play.

Patrice Alexander
Patrice is the daughter of Suzanne and sister of Teddy. It was Patrice who made the phone call from her father's home in Arlington to her mother, telling of Teddy's arrest. Patrice is also involved in the search for her Uncle March. She goes to March's house when he disappears and stays there, waiting for him to return.

Suzanne Alexander
Suzanne is the mother of Teddy, Patrice, and David, Jr. She often appears in this play with Teddy. However, most of her appearances are made while she is asleep and dreaming. Her dreams provide background material about the Alexander family. In her dreams, she often sees her father, who was devoted to making Cleveland (where Suzanne lived as a child) a better place to live for African Americans. Suzanne's brother-in-law, March, also appears in her dreams.

When Suzanne is awake and talking to Teddy, she appears emotionally unstable. She is constantly worried about her son. She writes letters to everyone involved in Teddy's case, but then she also worries that her letters might not be doing Teddy any good. Teddy withholds information from his mother to keep her from writing more letters. Although she appears to be more involved in Teddy's case than Teddy's father, it is questionable whether she is doing Teddy any good.

Teddy Alexander

Teddy can be considered the protagonist of this play. Most of the action and focus of the play revolves around him, though he remains rather passive throughout. However, it is Teddy's arrest and subsequent trial that drives the play.

Teddy is a young African American man who is about to graduate from college. He has studied drama, and his thesis is the production of Shakespeare's play *Hamlet*. In the midst of preparing for this, Teddy has been arrested, and he is tried for an assault-and-battery charge against a police officer.

While visiting his father, Teddy was pulled over by a police officer, who dealt with him very aggressively. His only misdeed was driving with a broken taillight on his car. However, the incident became more complicated after the police officer knocked Teddy to the ground and kicked him. Adding to the complications was the fact that the officer was white and Teddy was black, creating suspicions that the traffic stop was the result of racial profiling and that the beating was a racist act on the part of the officer.

Teddy also suffers from fear. Even before this incident, he was afraid of the police, especially white officers, who had previously demonstrated racist attitudes toward him. Throughout the play, Teddy is concerned that he might end up going to jail, though he is innocent. He believes the court system is against him because he is black. Despite his fear, Teddy stands up for what he believes is right. He demands his rights and resists taking the easy way out of this mess by confessing to something he did not do—he contends that he did not hit the police officer.

Attorney Edelstein

Edelstein is the lawyer who helps the Alexander family prosecute the policeman who beat Teddy. In front of the judge, Edelstein asks the police officer Holzer specific questions that end up incriminating Holzer. Through Edelstein's careful and pointed inquiries, Holzer admits that he made mistakes in arresting Teddy. Edelstein convinces the judge that Teddy is not guilty of assault and battery.

Officer Thomas Holzer

Thomas Holzer is the police officer who beat Teddy. At first, Holzer claims that he merely stopped Teddy because of a broken taillight on his car. After he was stopped, Holzer states,

Teddy became hostile and assaulted him. Under interrogation in the courtroom, however, Holzer's story breaks down. Holzer admits that Teddy merely touched him, which Holzer admits he does not like. Holzer also refused to tell Teddy why he was being arrested and did not warn Teddy that he was moving toward him to frisk him to see whether Teddy was carrying a concealed weapon. In the end, the judge states that she believes police officers should perform their duties in a more professional manner than Holzer did; she sees no evidence that Holzer was in any way assaulted. Holzer, who had been a police officer for the Arlington police department for three years, had left this organization shortly before the trial. He had become a member of the U.S. Secret Service. There is no mention of the effects of the trial on Holzer or on his career. The play ends with a dismissal of the charge against Teddy.

Judge

The judge in Teddy's trial is specified as being female, but she is not named. She listens to the charges against Teddy and, in the end, dismisses them.

Summers

Police Officer Summers is the person whom Dr. David Alexander (Teddy's father) saw the night his son was beaten. Alexander tells a lawyer that Officer Summers, an African American woman, had her gun drawn. It is only in Dr. David Alexander's statement to the lawyer that Summers is mentioned. She does not appear in the play.

Mrs. Wagner

Mrs. Wagner is the district attorney who is in charge of prosecuting the case against Teddy. Teddy and Edelstein meet with Wagner to try and make a deal before the trial. Wagner insists that the trial will go to a jury. She believes she has a better chance of winning if the trial goes to a jury, because juries tend to support police officers. However, when both sides meet with the judge, the judge refuses to allow the case to go before a jury. In the end, Wagner loses the case.

THEMES

Racism

Kennedy's play *Sleep Deprivation Chamber* is well grounded in the theme of racism. Racism is the cause for the frustration and anger that the

TOPICS FOR FURTHER STUDY

- Go to the U.S. Department of Justice Web site and access the following page: http://www.cops.usdoj.gov/files/RIC/Publications/e04021486.pdf. The page contains a bulletin called *Mediating Citizen Complaints against Police Officers: A Guide for Police and Community Leaders*. Read the section on page 19 titled "Mediating Racial and Ethnic-Related Complaints." Prepare a presentation explaining this material and deliver it to your class. Then, lead a discussion of what your classmates think about the benefits and drawbacks of this community service. Take a final tally of who thinks it would work and who is against it.

- Read Richard Wormser's *The Rise and Fall of Jim Crow* (2004) or another book on the topic of segregation. Set up a Web site giving a brief history of segregation in the United States. List major issues, such as the organization of the Ku Klux Klan in the South, the policies that sent African American students to inferior schools, and the absence of the right to vote, and link to other sites that discuss the same issues. Provide a brief description of what you learned about segregation to your class and invite them to visit your Web site. Make sure that your Web site includes a place for students to leave comments about what they have learned.

- Read Lorraine Hansberry's play *A Raisin in the Sun*, which was first produced in 1959. What are some of the issues that her characters face in this play? Are they similar to the challenges that Teddy faces in Kennedy's drama? More than thirty years separate these two plays. Did you find that anything has changed in the U.S. society in terms of white attitudes toward African Americans as represented by these two plays? What are some of the more striking or disturbing similarities? Write an essay that analyzes and compares the two plays.

- Look up the term *racial profiling* in at least four different places and write a sentence or two with a clear, accurate explanation of the term. Then take a survey of students at your school. Ask them whether they know what racial profiling is (explain the term if needed) and whether they think they have ever been a victim of racial profiling. Ask the students to identify their ethnicity according to the categories used in the U.S. Census (http://www.census.gov/population/www/socdemo/race/racefactcb.html) or using their own self-identified group. Of the students you questioned, how many could correctly define racial profiling? How many had experienced it? Break down the percentages according to the various ethnicities. Report your findings in your social studies class in a multimedia presentation, using charts and graphs to represent the data.

- In the 2010 book *The New Jim Crow Mass Incarceration in the Age of Colorblindness*, legal scholar Michelle Alexander discusses the disproportionate number of black men who are in jail as evidence of the continuing existence of racism in the United States. According to the 2000 U.S. Census, although African Americans make up only 12 percent of the U.S. population, more than 40 percent of all prisoners are black. Using statistics from the U.S. Census Bureau (http://www.census.gov/) and the U.S. Department of Justice (http://www.justice.gov/), create a report on the prison system in the United States. Compare the number of prisons and prisoners with other countries, such as the United Kingdom and South Africa. How has the prison population changed in the past few decades? What percentage was black in the 1950s, the 1990s, and today? Create a Web site to display your findings and invite your class to visit your site.

A woman sleeping peacefully *(photomak / Shutterstock.com)*

main characters of this play experience. Kennedy alludes to the central actions of this play, the beating and arrest of her son, as having occurred because of racism. It is implied that the arrest would never have happened if her son was white or if the policeman had been black. The tension of racism and the characters' attempts to overcome it, dissolve it, or avoid it move this play forward.

Other reference to racism occurs when Teddy recalls an event from his past when he encountered white police officers who suspect that Teddy and his African American cousins have stolen the fancy car they are driving, insinuating that there was no way they could own such an expensive item. Those police officers address the boys with racist terminology, referring to them by derogatory names. The police are also reluctant to believe that the boys could live in a neighborhood as exclusive as Beverly Hills, a posh location in Los Angeles.

In addition, Mr. Edelstein, the attorney who defends Teddy, suggests that Officer Holzer, the policeman who arrested Teddy, did not stop Teddy for the broken taillight when he first encountered him, choosing instead to follow him and wait for him to get into more serious trouble. Edelstein insinuates that Holzer did so merely because Teddy was black. Edelstein also suggests that Officer Holzer may have been nervous once Teddy pulled into his father's driveway and had other African Americans around him, and that might have been why Holzer was so eager to assume that Teddy was acting aggressively against him.

Fear

Fear affects almost all the characters in Kennedy's play. Suzanne seems to be the most fearful, as most of her appearances in this play are consumed with worry about her son. Suzanne spends most of her time writing letters to prominent figures involved in Teddy's upcoming trial. When she is not writing letters, she is afraid that she has said the wrong things in those letters or has written too many or too few of them.

Although Teddy is also very much afraid, both during his encounter with Officer Holzer and while awaiting his trial, he carries on his normal life: he directs a play, attempts to finish a paper he is writing, and otherwise is involved with the world. His mother, on the other hand, is so consumed with her fear that she can barely stay awake.

Teddy, his mother, his father, and his lawyer are all fearful that Teddy will go to jail. They fear the power of white people over black people. They believe that a white jury will side with the police and will not believe Teddy's story.

Violence

The central action of this play is the brutal beating of Teddy by Officer Holzer. The scene of the violence is replayed several times as many of the characters are questioned about what happened on that critical night.

Teddy is questioned over and over again about the details of the beating. He must recount not only what happened but what he remembers of the pain he experienced. He must reenact the violence, at least in his mind, as he is forced to answer questions of how Officer Holzer hit him and how Teddy responded to the blows.

Teddy's father and his brother also are asked to detail what they witnessed that night. They each have their own renditions of the event, but both of them were shaken by the violence.

In addition to physical violence, the characters must endure emotional or psychological violence. The title of this play indicates the nature and depth of this violence. Sleep deprivation is a torture method that is often inflicted on political prisoners, and Kennedy portrays the emotional stress that Suzanne Alexander and her family experienced as akin to the psychological violence of sleep deprivation.

STYLE

Autobiographical Literature

Some critics argue that all fiction is derived from events in the author's life, which would therefore make all literature autobiographical. However, some authors lean more heavily than others on autobiographical material. Some writers use their personal experiences to color their stories, while others use their experiences as the very foundation of their works.

Most of the material in *Sleep Deprivation Chamber* comes directly from the experience of Kennedy's son, after a police officer in Arlington stopped him for a traffic violation, which was no more than a burned-out taillight. Though the author dramatizes the experience by adding dream sequences, flashbacks, and the repetition of various scenes, the overall expression of the play exemplifies her emotional stress caused by the details of this personal experience. In other words, the author uses the format of drama to vent her anger, sadness, and frustration. Although she changes the names of the characters and rearranges the sequence of events, she is, in essence, presenting her audience with her version of her son's arrest and the effect it had on the family. She emphasizes various points, such as her family's history of community involvement and fighting for the civil rights of African Americans, to highlight what she considers to be a prejudiced environment in which the system favors whites and does not give her family the respect they deserve. Though the events that occur in the play might have actually taken place, the concept of autobiographical fiction allows the author to make up or exaggerate some of the details. The fact that she is writing fiction, as opposed to pure autobiography, gives her a license to not completely tell the truth. This may be done to accentuate a point or to create a play that is more enticing for the audience.

Dream Sequences

Kennedy uses several dream sequences in this play. The dreams belong to Suzanne, who often falls asleep while something else is occurring. Kennedy uses these dream sequences to offer the audience additional background information. It is through the dream sequences that the audience learns about the history of the Alexander family, their involvement in the civil rights movement, and their educational training. These elements confirm the Alexander family as intelligent, well informed, and community oriented. Through her dreams, also, Suzanne discusses the letters she has written in her son's defense.

Kennedy could have offered this background information through dialogue between two characters or as flashbacks that are depicted in a separate scene. In using the dream sequences, however, the character of Suzanne merely narrates her dreams through monologue. The dream sequences offer a simple way for the author to fill in the gaps in the story line.

HISTORICAL CONTEXT

Rodney King

Rodney King became the icon of police brutality and racial profiling in the early 1990s when a bystander caught on videotape the beating that King endured from police while being arrested for a traffic violation. Riots and outrage followed the acquittal of the accused officers and the worldwide viewing of the videotape. As a result of the beating and the media attention that followed, the mere mention of Rodney King's name stirs memories of that day.

In the early morning hours of March 3, 1991, in Los Angeles, California, Rodney King drove down the Foothill Freeway on his way home. King had consumed alcohol earlier while watching a basketball game, and he was spotted by two Los Angeles police officers as he sped toward his home. A chase ensued, with both cars reportedly reaching speeds in excess of 100 mph. When King refused to stop, other police officers were called in to help with the pursuit. The policemen finally cornered King's car, forcing him to stop. King was attempting to get away, he later confessed, because driving under the influence of alcohol was a violation of his probation, the consequence of a previous offense.

There was a lot of confusion once King's car was stopped. First, King, who was a black man, refused to get out of his car. When he did come out, he acted strangely, according to the police and so they used their Taser guns (a nonlethal weapon that delivers an electric shock) on King. At first this subdued King, but he was soon up on his feet and was acting as if he was about to assault them or, at least, resist arrest. The police were not aware that a bystander, George Holliday, was making a video recording of the incident. The video shows what appears to be a brutal attack on King by the police. The video was later broadcast around the world, resulting in outcries of police brutality and racial profiling. The Los Angeles Police Department did not have a good reputation in the black community in Los Angeles before this incident, and this event fueled the antagonistic environment between the two groups. The video showed that King received fifty-six blows from the police batons and was kicked six times. King had to be treated at a local hospital.

The police officers involved in the beating were charged with use of excessive force but some were later acquitted in 1992. In reaction, riots broke out in parts of Los Angeles. The police and the U.S. Army, Marines, and National Guard were called in to stop the rioters. By the end, fifty-three people were dead and more than two thousand injured. When riots in other cities, such as Atlanta, Georgia, flared up, King went on television to beg for peace. The following year, the federal government issued its own investigation into the matter. A new trial followed, and two of the four officers involved were found guilty and sentenced to more than two years in jail.

The videotape of King's beating was played repeatedly on television, making the mention of King's name, ever since, synonymous with an example of the worst that can happen in cases of racial profiling.

Emmett Till

In her play, Kennedy mentions Emmett Till (1941–1955), who was an African American youth born in Chicago, Illinois. In 1955, when he was fourteen, Till was sent to spend part of the summer with his relatives in Mississippi. Though Till had experienced segregation in his Chicago neighborhood, he was not fully aware of the strict racial code of conduct in the Deep South, known as the Jim Crow laws. These unwritten laws demanded very specific behavior of black people, one of which declared that they should avert their eyes when encountering a white person. In addition, black men were not to flirt with white women.

Till had white friends in Chicago and was unaware of these social constrictions, so when some other youths dared him to talk to a white woman they encountered in a store, Till was bold enough to do so. A few days later, in the middle of the night, a group of white men showed up at Till's uncle's house and kidnapped Till. Three days after that, Till's body was found in the Tallahatchie River. He had been beaten so badly that his uncle could not recognize him. The only clue to Till's identity was an initialed ring he was wearing.

Till's mother, Mamie Till Bradley, insisted not only that her son's body be returned to Chicago but that the funeral would proceed with an open casket. She wanted the world to see how badly Till had been beaten. News stations

COMPARE
&
CONTRAST

- **1990s:** On March 3, 1991, a bystander video-tapes Los Angeles police brutally beating Rodney King, an African American man. The police officers are eventually tried and acquitted. In reaction, riots explode in Los Angeles neighborhoods.

  Today: In 2009, a San Francisco Bay Area Rapid Transit police officer is tried and convicted of involuntary manslaughter rather than second-degree murder after shooting and killing Oscar Grant, an African American youth, on the subway. The police officer claims Grant was resisting arrest. Looting, arson, and small riots break out in Oakland neighborhoods in protest.

- **1990s:** Racial profiling occurs when police use race in determining whether a person is considered likely to commit a crime. According to police records and a report by ABC News, during a three-month period in 1994, 94 percent of motorists stopped on the New Jersey Turnpike belong to a minority ethnic group.

  Today: Secretary of State Hillary Clinton condemns Arizona's 2010 immigration law, which requires Mexican Americans to prove their legal status by showing police officers their immigration documents. Clinton states that this is an invitation to racial profiling.

- **1990s:** Ida L. Castro, chairwoman of the U.S. Equal Employment Opportunity Commission, announces an increase in racial harassment, including incidents of displaying hangman's nooses. During the 1990s, these incidents increase tenfold compared with the previous decade.

  Today: James Clyburn, an African American U.S. Representative from South Carolina, receives racist messages, including pictures of nooses and racial slurs, from people protesting his vote in favor of U.S. health-care reform.

---

broadcast photographs of Till's body around the nation, stirring citizens, white and black, to more fully be aware of the cruelties endured in the South under the Jim Crow laws. When the white men who were accused of killing Till were found not guilty by an all-white jury, another surge of outrage stirred the country. Some believe that Till's murder helped to stimulate more activism in the fight for civil rights throughout the United States, but especially in the South.

St. Clair Drake and Kwame Nkrumah

Kennedy associates the names of St. Clair Drake and Kwame Nkrumah in her play as she attempts to classify Suzanne's brother-in-law, March Alexander, as a learned and well-respected intellectual in the movement to improve the lives of African Americans in the United States.

St. Clair Drake (1911–1990) was a pioneer in sociology, especially in terms of the lives of African American people. Drake created one of the first African Studies programs in an American college in 1946 while he taught at Roosevelt College in Chicago. Later, he became a professor at Stanford University in California and developed the Afro-American Studies Department there. One of his more famous books is *Black Metropolis: A Study of Negro Life in a Northern City* (1945), a study of segregation and discrimination.

Kwame Nkrumah (1909–1972), whom Kennedy also refers to in the play, is a historical figure who hailed from Africa. Nkrumah was first elected prime minister (from 1952–1960) of what was then a British colony called the Gold Coast. In 1960, he became the first president of the country, which was renamed Ghana. With Nkrumah's assistance, Ghana became the first European colony in Africa to gain independence

Sleepwalking through a dream (© *PHOTOTAKE Inc.* / *Alamy*)

---

with a majority rule. Nkrumah ruled Ghana until 1966, when he was deposed. While in office, Nkrumah promoted a Pan-African movement, whose goal it was to make all countries in Africa independent and to support unity among those countries. At one time, St. Clair Drake served as an advisor to Nkrumah.

CRITICAL OVERVIEW

Although Kennedy's play *Sleep Deprivation Chamber* won an Obie Award for best new play, critics have given the play mixed reviews. For example, writing for the publication *Backstage*, David Sheward begins his review by describing the play as having "arresting stage imagery" but lacking "cohesion." Sheward continues that the play has "fascinating collages," but "the pieces are more absorbing than the whole work."

Adam J. Davidson, writing for the *Chicago Tribune*, finds Kennedy's play true to life, though he admits that the play is sometimes confusing. It "reads like a troubled nightmare." The play is divided into scraps of "confusing dreams and memories," plunging the audience into the same confusion that the characters feel. Davidson says that this bewilderment is at the heart of "American racism," a major theme of the play.

Offering another explanation for the mixed reviews that Kennedy's plays have received, Caroline Jackson Smith, writing for *Black Masks*, contends that although critics have tended to recognize Kennedy's "bright new voice," the topics of her plays "shocked many people." After studying Kennedy's life work, Smith finds that the playwright is "a genius, a wise woman with a keen sense of humor, an innovator." Smith continues by defining Kennedy as "a woman who has turned her own pain into an entirely new vocabulary of dramatic langue, poetic images, and complex rhythmic structures." Smith adds: "She has the courage to write from the most nightmarish and revelatory places in herself."

In a review for the *Village Voice*, Alisa Solomon found clarity in Kennedy's *Sleep Deprivation Chamber*. "Though this play has a deceptively straightforward action...its power comes from the rippling effects of that action across memory and dreams." Solomon makes a reference to the Rodney King police brutality case that happened in the early 1990s in Los Angeles. She states that Kennedy's play is not about reminding the audience about that racial incident but rather is aimed at carrying the audience "into the frightful realm where such knowledge has emotional and political repercussions that can't be shaken off."

Ben Brantley, writing for the *New York Times*, also finds that Kennedy's play reflects reality, even though much of the play contained "the stuff of nightmares from which a person can never wake completely." Whereas Kennedy often writes about what often haunts her interior world, Brantley writes, this play is set in a "world that is crushingly real." However, Brantley adds, "This is not to say that 'Deprivation' is a naturalistic slice of life." The play drifts "between past and present, between the distortions of dreams and clinical courtroom detail." In the end, "fantasy and reality meld into a prison of the mind." Brantley commends Kennedy for creating an atmosphere of the "helplessness of the falsely accused."

Aileen Jacobson, writing for *Newsday*, is one of the reviewers who was less impressed by Kennedy's play. She begins her review by describing Kennedy as a playwright who "favors a style of writing that's poetic, fragmented and impressionistic." In this play, though, Jacobson finds that "the fragmented writing style, unfortunately, only serves to break apart instead of integrate various strands." In particular, Jacobson describes some of the characters as being too thin, mere stick figures, not fully developed. She also writes that Kennedy might have produced a stronger play if she had better "filtered" her anger, since the play is based on real events that her son suffered through. As it is written, the play is a "tense jumble of fury, shock and frustration."

CRITICISM

Joyce Hart

Hart is a published writer and teacher of creative writing. In the following essay, she dissects the character of March Alexander to better understand his presence in Sleep Deprivation Chamber.

The number of characters in Kennedy's play *Sleep Deprivation Chamber* is very limited, making the appearance of any one of them significant. Therefore, the inclusion of March Alexander, who at first appears to be very tangential to the plot, makes one wonder why he was created. After all, the man has developed some form of dementia and has wandered away from home for most of the play. For a long time, no one knows where he is. This is not the first time he has disappeared. He is an old man who does not seem to be involved in (and may not even know of) his nephew Teddy's recent difficulties with the police. If he truly suffers from dementia, it is questionable whether he would even understand the issues of police brutality against Teddy or have anything to offer in the form of advice. So why does the author incorporate him into this play?

The most obvious reason Kennedy might want to use such a character as March is to connect him to Suzanne's ceaseless concern of Teddy's history. Throughout the play, Suzanne has dreams about her family and writes letters to various Virginia officials who have influence

> WITHOUT A NEW GENERATION OF CIVIL RIGHTS ACTIVISTS WHO CARE ABOUT WHAT IS HAPPENING, MORE CASES SUCH AS TEDDY'S WILL GO UNNOTICED."

over the law case of her son, who has been accused of resisting arrest and in the process, attacking a police officer. Through these dreams and letters, in her attempts to prove that her son, Teddy, is innocent, Suzanne offers examples of Teddy's exemplary background, as well as that of his family. She writes about Teddy's being about to earn a college degree, which proves his intelligence and diligence. Teddy has never been in trouble with the police. He is a published writer who dreams of producing plays for a living. Everyone he has dealt with describes Teddy as being brilliant, Suzanne states. In case these statements are not enough, Suzanne also includes bits and pieces of history of Teddy's family.

Suzanne writes to one senator that she is a produced playwright and that Teddy's father is the head of a large project called Africa/USA. Suzanne writes that her daughter, Patrice, teaches at Stanford. Suzanne has a dream about her father that shows that he was active in the civil rights movement in Cleveland. Then she introduces her brother-in-law, March Alexander, and adds more family history and stature. March was a scholar who, like his niece, taught at Stanford University. March also fought for civil rights for blacks through his teaching as well as by defining his theories in his notable publications. At one time, March was friends with St. Clair Drake, and he counseled Kwame Nkrumah, Ghana's first president. In other words, March Alexander was once a very prominent and respected figure, especially in reference to black civil rights.

Thus, one purpose for the character of March is to showcase the Alexander family's reputation. Teddy comes from a well-established family, whose intelligence and community involvement are commendable. What about March's present status, though? At one time,

WHAT DO I READ NEXT?

- For an introduction to Kennedy's work, *Adrienne Kennedy in One Act* (1988) is a good place to start. This eight-play collection includes *The Owl Answers*, *A Lesson in Dead Language*, and *Sun*. An African American protagonist often leads these plays as the playwright explores such topics as failed marriages, segregation, and conflicts between light-skinned and dark-skinned African Americans.

- The first collection of Kennedy's works was published in 2001 in *The Adrienne Kennedy Reader*. Included in this book are her award-winning plays *Funnyhouse of a Negro*, *June and Jean in Concert*, and *Sleep Deprivation Chamber*. Many of Kennedy's plays deal with a similar theme: racism in the United States. Although Kennedy is best known as a playwright, she has also published short stories, which are included in this volume.

- *Understanding Adrienne Kennedy* (2005) by Philip C. Kolin is a comprehensive critical study of Kennedy's work and the effect of her life experiences on her dramas. Kolin also explores the meanings behind Kennedy's experimental creations, making them more accessible for her audiences.

- For a direct autobiographical view of the playwright, read Kennedy's *People Who Led to My Plays* (1996). In this book, Kennedy writes short entries, almost like a diary, about the people who influenced her writing. She includes prominent writers, such as Richard Wright; actors, such as Marlon Brando; artists, such as Jackson Pollock; and musicians, such as Chopin and Duke Ellington. Together, this collection of comments and reflections gives readers an insight into Kennedy's life and her inspirations.

- Young-adult readers may be interested in the set of authors showcased in *African American Women Writers* (1999). This volume contains female writers from the colonial period to the present. Included are passages from poet Phillis Wheatley, novelists Zora Neale Hurston and Terry McMillan, and playwright Lorraine Hansberry. Photographs and short biographies are provided for each author mentioned.

- LeRoi Jones (now Amiri Baraka), is a contemporary of Kennedy's. His works, like Kennedy's, focus on issues facing African Americans and are often presented in experimental form. *The LeRoi Jones/Amiri Baraka Reader* (1999) provides readers with an extensive coverage of his life's work. In this volume are selections of his poetry and essays and excerpts from his autobiography. The book is divided into four distinct periods in the author's life.

- Ntozake Shange is an African American playwright and poet. She is of the same generation as Kennedy and also an Obie Award–winning writer. Other similarities with Kennedy include her writing about African American issues with a feminist focus. Shange's most famous work is her *For Colored Girls Who Have Considered Suicide When the Rainbow Is Enuf* (1975), a play made up of twenty individual poems that deal with themes of love and abandonment. More recently, Shange has published several children's books, including her 2003 work *Ellington Was Not a Street*.

- Ama Ata Aidoo is a Ghanaian playwright and novelist who has focused much of her writing on the conflict between Western views of women's roles in society and those of her own African culture. Her 1992 novel *Changes* won the Commonwealth Writers Prize for best book of the year. The story revolves around Esi, a woman living in Accra, Ghana, who fights her husband and her traditional society for her independence. Though the book is set in Africa, critics have found that the feminist themes reflect women's issues around the globe.

March was the model for involvement in the black community, a scholar who presented his views of what blacks should embrace as their civil rights. He not only taught white and black students—the next generation of the civil rights movement—he also counseled heads of state in newly liberated African nations. He rubbed shoulders with other black intellectuals and was an important figure on the Stanford campus. Now, though, Teddy laments that March "seems forgotten by younger activists and educators." This statement by Teddy is a clue to one reason for March's inclusion in the play: as a symbol of the civil rights movement itself. Through March's history and Teddy's insights about him, Kennedy suggests that the civil rights movement, like March, has been forgotten.

Rather than teaching students and thus creating a new generation of activists, March now sits alone outside the university classrooms. One can imagine that students walk by March without recognizing who he is, without knowing his beliefs or what he has accomplished in his past. Today, March is ignored, much as Officer Holzer has ignored Teddy's civil rights.

However, it is not just the students and the future generations of activists who have forgotten March (and thus the civil rights movement). Kennedy implies that the civil rights movement has forgotten itself. If March represents the fight for civil rights and he has lost his memory—he often wanders off into the woods where no one can find him, vacating his home and not knowing how to get back—then the civil rights movement, Kennedy suggests, is likewise losing its way. Where are the civil rights leaders? Where are the Bobby Kennedys and the Dr. Martin Luther Kings and the Malcolm Xs who vocalized their concerns in the 1960s? Who is vocalizing civil rights concerns today? There is no public outcry when Teddy is beaten and falsely arrested, when his civil rights are threatened. Society's collective forgetting is as sad and frightening as March's dementia.

Suzanne, during one of her dream sequences, is sitting with March in front of his California cottage. She states that she sees men in the distance playing golf. This scene offers a graphic juxtaposition. While some men in the distance and are enjoying a frivolous sports game, totally unaware of any threat, March states there are

"great storms" coming. "This day there are great storms of wind, overturned trees, barns and houses, even forests," March says, and they "live near the epicenter." They will be, March implies, the victims of this storm. Then, Suzanne explains the setting: there has been a great earthquake. The Bay Bridge (linking San Francisco and Oakland) has been destroyed. Tapes that have the words "Crime Scene" printed on them cover the front of March's door, and there are signs that forbid anyone from entering his home. The destruction has already occurred, and there is more coming. Suzanne ignores all the signs telling her to stay away and walks into March's place and sees the destruction inside his house. Fallen furniture is everywhere, and in the midst of it is Teddy, being beaten by the police.

If March represents the civil rights movement and his home has been destroyed, Kennedy is saying that the foundation of the civil rights movement has been cracked. The police signs indicate that the foundation is so shaky that no one should attempt to enter. Upon entering the house, though, Suzanne sees her son being abused by a police officer. Are the warnings about entering the house being used by the police to hide their crimes? Or is the foundation in fact cracked and dangerous and the police are taking advantage of the situation? Kennedy suggests that the situation is indeed dangerous and the police know it; however, they are also using these conditions to keep people out of the house to conceal their own crime.

Through March, as the representative of the civil rights movement, Kennedy demonstrates what bad shape the movement is in. March, as one of the early advocates of the movement (in this play) has lost his mental capabilities and has wandered off into the woods. He no longer remembers the principles he once fought for. Because he can no longer remember, the next generation of youths no longer remembers him. They no longer remember the fight and ignore him as they pass by. Because the foundation of March's house has been cracked and condemned by the police, the police can act according to their own rules and disregard the Civil Rights Act by hiding behind misrepresentation and closed doors. Because of these conditions, March predicts that the earthquake they just suffered through is just the beginning. He believes a much bigger storm is on the way. Though he suffers from dementia, March senses

Hamlet and the Ghost (© *Mary Evans Picture Library |*
Alamy)

the complete breakdown of civil rights. Without
a new generation of civil rights activists who care
about what is happening, more cases such as
Teddy's will go unnoticed. Though Teddy was
lucky enough to win his case, others may not be
so fortunate.

Source: Joyce Hart, Critical Essay on *Sleep Deprivation
Chamber*, in *Drama for Students*, Gale, Cengage Learning, 2011.

Robert Vorlicky

*In the following review, Vorlicky notes that the
play is largely atypical of Kennedy's work.*

During 1995–96, the Signature Theatre
Company, which dedicates each season to a single playwright's work, for the first time focused
on the plays of an African American woman
playwright, Adrienne Kennedy. Kennedy's
seven plays produced for the Signature's season
included two world premieres, *June and Jean in
Concert* and *Sleep Deprivation Chamber*, which
eventually shared an Obie Award for best play.
It is the latter work, however, that is strikingly
unique in the author's body of work. In *Sleep*

Deprivation Chamber, Kennedy for the first time
shares authorship (her collaborator is her son,
Adam Kennedy), and atypically the play's inspiration is not drawn from the period between
1936 and 1961—a rich source of inspiration for
her earlier plays. Furthermore, *Sleep Deprivation Chamber* builds to an extended realistic
sequence in the form of a less than satisfying
courtroom trial, an approach rarely found in
Kennedy's previous writings.

Sleep Deprivation Chamber, whose action
resonates with the Rodney King case, is the fic-
tionalized account of Adam Kennedy's arrest
and beating by a white police officer in the driveway of his father's Arlington, Virginia, home in
1991. Adam had been signaled by the police to
stop several blocks from his home for a faulty
taillight. By continuing to drive until he reached
his father's property, Adam found himself
charged with resisting arrest and assaulting an
officer. Through the characters of Teddy
Alexander and his mother Suzanne, an author,
the Kennedys write themselves into the play's
thinly veiled mother-son relationship and
unfolding action; both the Kennedys and the
Alexanders face the trauma of police brutality
and the helplessness and uncertainty of the
struggles fostered by a deeply flawed legal system. This—and more—is written into the alter-
natingly fantastic and realistic landscapes of
Sleep Deprivation Chamber, set in a racist America that repeatedly prompts African-Americans
to ask: "What have I done? What's the charge?"
As revealed in monologues based upon her passionate letters to government officials about her
son's case, Suzanne is exhausted and suffocating
from her efforts to "fit into America."

Through the act of putting pen to paper,
however, Suzanne hopes to write her way to the
truth, despite the different versions of the story
of her son's arrest that circulate. Teddy, Adam's
alter ego (powerfully played by Kevin T. Carroll), has his version of the events that are captured in the play's realistic moments; Teddy's
father (Willie C. Carpenter) grippingly offers
his perspective in tense monologues that are con-
tested as they fluctuate between fact and conjec-
ture; and the arresting officer, Holzer (played
with cocky assuredness by Jonathan Fried) gets
his chance to narrate from the witness stand. In
her autobiography, Kennedy has written that
"contradictory voices" are essential to "penetrat-
ing to the truth of things" (*People Who Led to*

My Plays [New York: Theatre Communications Group, 1988], 86). For her own part in coming to terms with this nightmare, Adrienne Kennedy's strategy is finally to reengage art—to write a play—where she has the freedom to return to the life of the imagination in order to begin to unravel life's increasingly daunting, sinister realities.

As shaped by veteran Kennedy director Michael Kahn, *Sleep Deprivation Chamber* moves fluidly from the realistic scenes of Teddy's dealings with the police on the night of the arrest and his meetings with lawyers, to expressionist and surrealist scenes, often of Suzanne's nightmares involving her children: these range from Teddy's confinement to Yorick's gravesite (he is shown early in the play rehearsing *Hamlet* with classmates at Antioch College) to her daughter, Patrice, standing naked on the Stanford campus. Images of confinement, humiliation, deprivation, and death overwhelm Suzanne's dreamlife, as their stage manifestations are bathed in Jeffrey S. Koger's evocative lighting and mounted in E. David Cosier's efficient and flexible set design. What connects Suzanne's nightmares and waking hours, however, are her complex, deep feelings toward her children, which are captured in her language. As rendered by Trazana Beverley, Suzanne's outbursts of anguish are those of a woman who has given birth to a child, only to fear moment-to-moment for what injustices and pain will envelop it. The judge "judged a mother," concludes Suzanne, upon hearing the outcome of her child's initial courtroom hearing.

Suzanne's vivid coupling of her roles as experienced mother and as accomplished writer (both of which generate waves of pain and pleasure, terror and ecstasy) distinguishes her from Kennedy's earlier heroines. In *Sleep Deprivation Chamber*, the older Suzanne becomes the "writing mother," or the "mother writing," whereby self, role, and deed coexist. However tenuous, this fragile union (one which is noticeably absent in Kennedy's other work) is born out of an evolving present informed by the nightmares and fantasies of the past and future.

Through treating both her son's actual tragic experience (i.e., *his* story) and her wrenching reactions to it, the elder Kennedy finds the raw material to coauthor the family drama that in her autobiography she confesses she yearned

to write, yet rejected, as a younger woman. At its weakest moments—the lengthy realistic courtroom scene—*Sleep Deprivation Chamber* becomes unnecessarily melodramatic and redundant. At its strongest moments—the theatrically varied interplay between the distinct "realities" experienced by parent and child—the play strikes close to the heart of the tradition of American domestic family drama. More importantly, perhaps, Adrienne and Adam Kennedy have written a compelling contemporary story about African-American family life, one that joins the rich portraits already created by Lorraine Hansberry and August Wilson. Unlike Hansberry and Wilson, however, the Kennedys are voices of the 1990s. Their time is now, their experience is immediate—and their vision of America is uncompromising and disturbingly bleak. They challenge us, collectively and individually, to break out of our own sleep deprivation chambers.

Source: Robert Vorlicky, Review of *Sleep Deprivation Chamber*, in *Theater Journal*, Vol. 49, No. 1, March 1997, pp. 67–69.

David Sheward

In the following excerpted review, Sheward argues that the play's many different elements do not seem to come together to form a unified production.

Two productions currently running at the Joseph Papp Public Theater have arresting stage imagery, but lack cohesion. They're fascinating collages in which the pieces are more absorbing than the whole work.

At the Public's Susan Shiva Theater, the Signature Theatre Company continues its season-long exploration of the poetic work of Adrienne Kennedy. The latest offering is *Sleep Deprivation Chamber*, a collaboration between Kennedy and her son Adam. Based on a true incident, this rambling play details the horrors the Alexanders (read the Kennedys), an upper-middle-class, African-American family, encounter when the [son] Teddy is savagely beaten by the police without provocation. Gritty, ultra-realistic re-enactments of the event and subsequent legal proceedings are juxtaposed with dream scenes from *Hamlet* (the play Teddy is directing for his thesis) and the mother's nostalgic recollections of her childhood in the 1940s. The real-life segments are staged by Michael Kahn with the brutal directness of a *Cops* videotape, but they go on endlessly and are repeated ad nauseum. Most of the fantasies and the scenes involving the mother (played by an over-the-top Trazana Beverley) seem tangential and extraneous. Despite the timeliness and potential power of the story, Kahn and the authors fail to tie these disparate elements together into in an integrated production. . . .

Source: David Sheward, Review of *Sleep Deprivation Chamber*, in *Back Stage*, Vol. 37, No. 11, March 15, 1996, p. 60.

SOURCES

Alexander, Michelle, *The New Jim Crow: Mass Incarceration in the Age of Colorblindness*, New Press, 2010.

Brantley, Ben, "Righting a Wrong in a World Out of Joint," in *New York Times*, February 27, 1996, p. C11.

Davidson, Adam J., "Dreams, Escapes," in *Chicago Tribune*, September 7, 1997, Vol. 37, p. 8.

"EEOC Chairwoman Responds to Surge of Workplace Noose Incidents at NAACP Annual Convention," in *U.S. Equal Employment Opportunity Commission*, http:// www.eeoc.gov/eeoc/newsroom/release/7-13-00-b.cfm (accessed July 13, 2000).

Flint, Peter B., "St. Clair Drake, Pioneer in Study of Black Americans, Dies at 79," in *New York Times*, http://www.nytimes.com/1990/06/21/obituaries/st-clair-drake-pioneer-in-study-of-black-americans-dies-at-79.html (accessed June 21, 1990).

Gray, Madison, "The L.A. Riots: 15 Years after Rodney King," in *Time*, http://www.time.com/time/specials/ 2007/article/0,28804,1614117_1614084_1614831,00.html (accessed July 21, 2010).

Jacobson, Aileen, "Raw Anger over Injustice, Drama Decries Beating, Betrayal of Black Man," in *Newsday*, February 26, 1996, p. B2.

Kennedy, Adrienne, and Adam P. Kennedy, *Sleep Deprivation Chamber*, Dramatists Play Service, 1996.

Nelson, Marilyn, *A Wreath for Emmett Till*, Fraphia, 2009.

"N.J. Knew of Racial Profiling for Years," in *ABC News/ U.S.*, http://abcnews.go.com/US/story?id=95406&page=1 (accessed July 12, 2010).

Sheward, David, Review of *Sleep Deprivation Chamber*, in *Back Stage*, March 15, 1996, Vol. 37, No. 11, p. 60.

Smith, Caroline Jackson, "From Drama to Literature: The Unparalleled Vision of Adrienne Kennedy," in *Black Masks*, March 30, 1996, Vol. 12, p. 5.

Solomon, Alisa, "Middle of the Night," in *Village Voice*, March 5, 1996, Vol. 41, No. 10, p. 70.

Yergin, Daniel, and Joseph Stanislaw, *The Commanding Heights: The Battle for the World Economy*, Simon & Schuster, 1998, pp. 66–69.

FURTHER READING

Bradman, Tony, ed., *Skin Deep: A Collection of Stories about Racism*, Puffin Books, 2004.

> This book contains a collection of short stories by authors of young-adult works. The topics of these stories involve different aspects of racism, including bullying, exclusion, hatred, and war. The stories come from various cultural backgrounds, not only those of the United States but also those of the United Kingdom, Australia, India, and Europe. Overall, the stories are hopeful, and teens from all over the world should be able to relate to the experiences that these stories explore.

Fremon, David K., *The Jim Crow Laws and Racism in American History*, Enslow Publishers, 2000.

> The political and legal aspects of racism in the United States, from the end of the Civil War to the death of Martin Luther King, Jr., are covered in this young-adult book. As African Americans won their freedom from slavery and fought for their right to vote, they faced many life-threatening challenges. Topics such as segregation, the Great Migration of southern blacks to northern cities to search for work, and the Montgomery Bus Boycott are detailed in this book, as are the lives of prominent black leaders such as Booker T. Washington, W. E. B. DuBois, Thurgood Marshall, and Rosa Parks.

Juarez, Juan Antonio, *Brotherhood of Corruption: A Cop Breaks the Silence on Police Abuse, Brutality, and Racial Profiling*, Chicago Review Press, 2004.

> Juarez was a police officer in Chicago for seven years. In this book, he tells his side of the story of police brutality. Juarez was eager to join the police force, but once inside, he found that his idealistic ideas about how the police department was run were unrealistic. He witnessed many incidents of police brutality and corruption.

Meeks, Kenneth, *Driving while Black*, Broadway, 2000.

> This is a handbook geared toward a young-adult audience and filled with information about what to do should you find yourself a victim of racial profiling. This book explains your rights regarding legal searches and steps to take to reduce the risk of becoming a victim of racial profiling. Also included in the book are case histories of racial profiling incidents.

Seltzer, Richard, and Nicole E. Johnson, eds., *Experiencing Racism: Exploring Discrimination through the Eyes of College Students*, Lexington Books, 2009.

> Seltzer and Johnson have collected essays written by college students who comment on their own personal experiences with race and racism. The editors provide textual analysis to

illuminate common themes that run through these essays, helping readers explore the extent of racism in the United States.

Tatum, Beverly Daniel, *Why Are All the Black Kids Sitting Together in the Cafeteria? A Psychologist Explains the Development of Racial Identity*, Basic Books, 2003.

Referred to as an excellent starting point for a discussion about race, this book offers a look into how racial identity has developed in the United States. The author is a developmental psychologist and a consultant for multicultural groups. As an African American, she has studied the effects of blacks going to predominantly white schools and has developed a college course on the psychology of racism. Her book helps readers understand the roots of racism and why it is so hard to talk about it.

SUGGESTED SEARCH TERMS

Adrienne Kennedy

Adrienne Kennedy AND Sleep Deprivation Chamber

racial profiling

police brutality AND African Americans

Sleep Deprivation Chamber

Adrienne Kennedy

Adrienne Kennedy AND Adam P. Kennedy

African American dramatists

Adrienne Kennedy AND awards

Sleep Deprivation Chamber reviews

Adrienne Kennedy AND plays

Adrienne Kennedy AND CalArts

Sunday in the Park with George

STEPHEN SONDHEIM

1984

Sunday in the Park with George is a musical with music and lyrics by Stephen Sondheim and book by James Lapine. It was first produced at the Booth Theater in New York City in May 1984. The musical was inspired by a painting, *A Sunday Afternoon on the Island of La Grande Jatte*, by the nineteenth-century French painter Georges Seurat. Seurat is the principal character in act 1. He is shown in the park in Paris drawing the characters that will later appear in his painting. The emphasis is on how he neglects his personal life in favor of his art. Act 2 focuses on Seurat's great-grandson George, also an artist, who has been inspired by Seurat's work but is having difficulty expressing a new artistic vision. The musical explores the themes of art, creativity, and human relationships.

With a career that has spanned fifty years, Sondheim is considered the greatest living composer of musical theater in the United States, and *Sunday in the Park with George* is one of his best-known works. It was nominated for ten Tony Awards and won two, for Best Scene Design and Best Lighting. The musical also won the Pulitzer Prize for Drama in 1985.

The text of the play is available in *Four by Sondheim*, published by Applause Books in 2000.

AUTHOR BIOGRAPHY

Sondheim was born on March 22, 1930, in New York City. His father, Herbert, was a dress

Stephen Sondheim (Getty Images)

manufacturer, and his mother, Janet, was a dress designer. Sondheim's parents were divorced when he was ten, and Sondheim went with his mother to live on a farm in Pennsylvania. As a boy, Sondheim became friends with the son of Oscar Hammerstein II, the renowned playwright and lyricist, and he soon conceived a desire to write for the theater. The elder Hammerstein became his mentor. At Williams College, in Williamstown, Massachusetts, Sondheim wrote scripts and scores, and after graduating in 1950, he studied with composer Milton Babbitt.

His first work on Broadway was to write the lyrics for Leonard Bernstein's *West Side Story* (1957) and for Jule Styne's musical *Gypsy* (1959). The first show for which he wrote both music and lyrics was *A Funny Thing Happened on the Way to the Forum* (1962), followed by *Anyone Can Whistle* (1964). In 1970 he and playwright George Furth collaborated to create the landmark musical *Company* (1970), which established his reputation as an innovative voice in musical theater.

Since then, Sondheim has written many successful shows and won numerous awards. He is regarded as the greatest living composer and lyricist in American musical theater. His work in the 1970s and 1980s includes *Follies* (1971); *A Little Night Music* (1973), which won thirteen awards, including Tony Awards for Best Musical and Best Music and Lyrics; *Pacific Overtures* (1976); *Sweeney Todd* (1979), which won twenty-four awards and has been performed by several opera companies; *Merrily We Roll Along* (1981); *Sunday in the Park with George* (1984), which won twelve awards, including the Pulitzer Prize for Drama in 1985; and *Into the Woods* (1987), which won a Tony Award for Best Score. His later work includes *Dick Tracy* (1990), *Assassins* (1990), *Passion* (1994), which won the Tony Awards for Best Musical and Best Score, and *Bounce* (2003). A revised version of *Bounce*, titled *Road Show*, premiered in New York in 2008.

PLOT SUMMARY

Act 1

Sunday in the Park with George begins on a Sunday in 1884 in a park on an island in the River Seine in Paris. The artist George sits at an easel with a drawing pad and chalk. Dot enters, and he tells her to stand still while he draws. Unhappy, she grumbles about various things. An Old Lady (who is later revealed to be George's mother) enters, bickering with her Nurse. They discuss the tower that is being built in the city for the International Exposition. Dot tries to get George to interact with her, and when she fails she complains about how cold he is. She admits that she loves his painting, but she wishes he would give her more attention and not regard her merely as an artist's model.

The Old Lady observes the young boys swimming, while the Nurse engages the coachman, Franz, in conversation. The artist Jules and his wife Yvonne stroll by, commenting on how they do not like one of George's paintings. A *tableau vivant* (living picture) of the painting is created on stage. Jules and Yvonne exchange a few words with George and then call for Franz, interrupting his attempt to arrange a meeting with the Nurse.

The scene switches to George's studio, where Dot is powdering her face and George is

MEDIA ADAPTATIONS

- *Sunday in the Park with George* is available on audio CD, featuring the original Broadway cast, and released by RCA in 2007.

- A DVD of a live performance of the musical was released in 1999 by Image Entertainment, starring Mandy Patinkin as George and Bernadette Peters as Dot, his mistress.

painting. She is expecting George to take her to a show known as the Follies, but George cannot bring himself to stop painting. She exits, very disappointed, and George wonders how long her fit of pique will last.

On another Sunday afternoon on the island, George paints an argumentative Boatman, while two shop girls, Celeste 1 and Celeste 2, note that Dot has entered with her new companion, Louis the baker. After Dot and Louis exit, Jules and Yvonne enter with their child Louise, and they briefly discuss George's work in a critical way. All the characters, including the Old Lady and the Nurse, describe the nature of artists in disparaging terms, and then Jules and Yvonne remark that George's work should not be included in the next art show.

Dot sits on a park bench, and Louis exits. Using an instructional book, Dot practices her grammar; she is learning to read. The child Louise tries to pet the Boatman's dog but the Boatman shoos her away. When George reproaches him, he insults all artists and hurries off. George sketches the dog. He speaks to Dot, but Louis returns and George retreats. He continues to sketch the dog, then the Nurse, then Franz and his wife, Frieda. The two Celestes try to attract the attention of two soldiers. Jules returns and tells George there should be more in his life than work. After Jules exits, George goes back to sketching the Boatman, who again criticizes all artists. Dot explains why she has chosen Louis. The two Celestes meet two

soldiers, and each tries to win the more attractive of the two. (The second soldier is a cut-out, not an actual character.) Left alone on the stage, George laments losing Dot but says he knew that she would go because he gives too much attention to his art.

In George's studio, Dot asks George to give her the painting he made of her; she is pregnant and engaged to Louis, but she wants something to remember George by. George is reluctant to part with the painting. Jules and Yvonne enter and view George's painting. Dot and Yvonne discuss the problems of being with an artist; Dot thinks Jules does not like George's work but Yvonne claims that he respects it. Dot states that Jules is jealous of George. Meanwhile, George tries to explain his artistic technique to Jules, saying that he is trying to create something original. Jules thinks that the only reason George has invited him to the studio is to persuade Jules to get the painting George is working on exhibited in the next group show. Jules and Yvonne exit, and George reflects. He does not believe that Jules understands what he is trying to do. Dot tells George she and Louis are going to the United States. Dot and George argue about why their relationship did not work. He says she did not accept him for who he is, while she says they are not meant to be together.

Back in the park, George is drawing the Old Lady, who is his mother. They reminisce about when he was a child. Celeste 1 enters, arm-in-arm with one of the soldiers. They are pleased to have gotten free of their other companions, but the makings of a quarrel soon emerge. Dot enters carrying her baby. She asks George again for the painting, but George says he repainted it using another model. Dot is angered by George's refusal to acknowledge that the baby is his, not Louis's. The Old Lady says she worries about George, and she reminisces about him as a child. Jules and Frieda enter, looking for a private place so they can begin an amorous affair. Louise tells her mother, Yvonne, that she has seen her father and Frieda together, and Yvonne accuses Jules. Franz and Frieda are drawn into the argument. The two Celestes quarrel also, and soon everyone is fighting while George and the Old Lady watch. George calls for order, and the subjects of his painting start to sing in harmony and take up the poses they will have in the finished painting.

Act 2

A *tableau vivant* of *A Sunday Afternoon on the Island of La Grande Jatte* is shown, and all the characters in the tableau start complaining about one thing or another. They are not enjoying themselves in the painting in which they appear. George enters and stands in front of the tableau. He reflects on his childhood and how he always had an artist's eye. After he exits, the characters offer brief eulogies to George, who died at age thirty-one. As they exit, the painting is gradually dismantled, and the stage is left bare.

It is now 1984, and the scene is a museum where the painting hangs. George, the great-grandson of the artist, wheels in Marie, his ninety-eight-year-old grandmother (the daughter of the first George and Dot), in a wheelchair. A large white machine is brought on stage. George, an inventor-sculptor, has invented it and calls it a Chromolume. It is the seventh in a series. George says he was commissioned by the museum to commemorate Georges Seurat's famous painting. He has been invited to give a presentation about it, and Marie will help him with it. In what follows, George and Marie read from a prepared text, along with film projections of the images they talk about and emissions of light from the machine.

In their presentation, George and Marie give a brief biography of Georges Seurat and his artistic technique. He developed a new style, and his work was exhibited at the Eighth Impressionist Exhibition, where in general it was not well received.

George then starts up his Chromolume machine and the stage is filled with color and light and images from the famous painting. But then there is an electrical short circuit and the machine fails. The machine is repaired and the presentation continues.

At a reception afterward, the present-day George's work, "Sunday: Island of Light," is on display. Various people make complimentary remarks about the originality of George's work, while others are less convinced.

George enters with Marie and Elaine, his former wife. Bob Greenberg, the museum director introduces George to Harriet Pawling, a patron of the arts, and her friend Billy Webster. Harriet and Billy express appreciation for George's work, and Marie tells them that next month she and George are going to France to visit the island where Georges Seurat made the famous painting. George comments about the difficulty of being an artist and about how to produce a good work of art. George meets two people who can help his career. Charles Redmond, from a museum in Texas, hints that his museum would be interested in giving him a big commission, and Lee Randolph, the present museum's public relations man, talks about getting good press coverage about George's presentation. Then Dennis, George's technician, tells him he is quitting and returning to NASA.

George continues to talk about the difficulties of succeeding in the competitive modern art world, where artists need commissions from institutions and recognition from art critics. One such critic, Blair Daniels, engages George in conversation. Blair used to support George but now finds his work repetitive. George is upset by her criticism. Alex and Betty, both of whom are artists, disagree about the merits of his work.

After most of the people have gone, Marie tells Blair that the best legacy anyone can leave is children and art. She wants George to have a child. Looking up at the painting, she admires Dot, her mother, and tells George that he would have liked her.

Some weeks later, George and his technician Dennis are in Paris, on the island where Seurat made his painting. He has brought his Chromolume, although he intends to make no more of them. He also has with him the reading book that Dot wrote in, and he reflects on the ways in which his own life reflects that of his great-grandfather. Dot appears and tells George how much she learned from him. George says he no longer knows what to do in his artwork, and Dot tells him to keep moving on and not to worry what the critics say.

As George reads some words the elder George had spoken about order and design, as recorded by Dot, the characters from the painting enter and take up their positions and bow to George. Then they slowly leave, and a white canvas drop descends. George reads that a blank canvas was his great-grandfather's favorite, since it is full of possibilities.

CHARACTERS

Alex

Alex is a modern-day artist. He thinks George's work is outdated, no longer new, and that his success is just a matter of good marketing. Alex's friend Betty thinks he is jealous of George.

Betty

In act 2, Betty is an artist who likes George's work, disagreeing with her friend Alex.

Boatman

The Boatman is at the park and is drawn by Georges Seurat for inclusion in his painting. The Boatman dresses badly and speaks disparagingly of the people in the park. He prefers the company of his dog. He chases Louise away when she tries to pet the dog. He is argumentative and does not like artists.

Celeste #1

Celeste #1 appears in the park and is drawn by Georges Seurat for his painting. She and her friend, Celeste #2, are shop girls, although Celeste #1 says she hates the work. They go fishing, then compete for the attention of a soldier. Celeste #1 loses to her friend in their attempt to befriend the Soldier, and the two girls fall out over the incident.

Celeste #2

Celeste #2 is a friend of Celeste #1. She triumphs over her friend in winning the attention of a soldier. She ends up quarreling with him and insulting him.

Blair Daniels

Blair Daniels is an art critic who chats with George after George's presentation in act 2. She used to appreciate and support George's art but now thinks he is just repeating himself and that his work no longer has much value. She urges him to do something new.

Dennis

Dennis is the modern-day George's technical assistant who operates the Chromolume. He tells George he is going to quit and return to NASA. At first he says this is because there is too much pressure in the work, but later he admits that he wants to work on something new.

Dot

Dot is act 1 George's mistress and his artistic model. She has to stand still under the hot sun for long periods on the island while George draws her, and she complains about it. However, she also tries to convince herself that there are worse things to do than pose for an artist in a park on a Sunday. Dot is not an educated woman but is slowly teaching herself to read and write. She is very fond of George and admires his work as a painter, but she is exasperated by him as well because he gives more attention to his art than to her. For example, he promises to take her to the Follies but then is too engrossed in his art to fulfill his promise. Finally, she makes the decision to leave him. Even though she is pregnant by George, she agrees to marry Louis, the baker, who gives her the love and attention she needs. Had George been willing to do that, she would have remained with him. But she realizes that she and George do not belong together. Dot and Louis emigrate from Paris to Charleston, South Carolina. Marie, her baby, becomes the grandmother of George, the modern-day artist in act 2.

Naomi Eissen

Naomi Eissen is a composer. She has written the music that accompanies George's presentation in act 2.

Elaine

Elaine is George's ex-wife in act 2. She has remained close to Marie, George's grandmother, and helps to look after her.

Franz

Franz is the coachman who works for Jules and Yvonne. He wants to strike up a flirtatious relationship with the Nurse. He gets upset when Louise wants him to play with her because this is his day off. He has no respect for his employers, since he does not consider that creating art is real work. He thinks that he is the one who does all the work. Along with his wife, Frieda, he is fired by Jules, but not because of any fault of his own. Jules is simply attempting to cover up his attempted seduction of Frieda.

Frieda

Frieda is the wife of Franz and cook for Jules and Yvonne. She knows that Franz wants to sneak off with the Nurse and wonders whether she should just turn a blind eye. Frieda allows

Jules, her employer, to make amorous advances to her. When Yvonne hears about it there is a quarrel, and Jules, trying to save himself, fires Frieda and Franz.

George of Act 1
The George of act 1 is Georges Seurat, the famous nineteenth-century French painter, and he is shown drawing the characters who will later appear in his painting *A Sunday Afternoon on the Island of La Grande Jatte*. George is completely dedicated to his art. His mistress Dot says that sometimes he stays up all night painting. George uses an unusual and original painting technique, and he is not yet accepted by the art establishment, so he needs the support of a more senior artist, Jules, to ensure that his work gets exhibited. Jules, however, does not like George's work much and does not understand it.

George is better at art than he is at life. He neglects Dot because he always has his mind on his art. He is secretive and does not confide as much in Dot as she would like. She loves him but finds him exasperating. He cannot keep a promise to her, whether it is to take her out for the evening or to give her a painting for which she was the model. George well knows that he cannot pay full attention to any woman because of the demands of his art, so he is not surprised when Dot leaves him for Louis. After she has made her decision, George tells her that he needed her, but she would not accept who he was. George is the father of Dot's baby, Marie, who appears in act 2 as the grandmother of the present-day George.

George of Act 2
The George who appears in act 2 is a thirty-two-year-old artist who describes himself as an inventor/sculptor. George is Georges Seurat's great-grandson, although he does not really believe this, since he is skeptical of the story that Seurat rather than Louis was the father of Marie, George's grandmother. George has been invited by a museum to create a work that would commemorate Seurat's *A Sunday Afternoon on the Island of La Grande Jatte*, and the result is his seventh Chromolume, a machine that creates patterns of color and light. With Marie, he makes a presentation in the museum, speaking of Seurat and demonstrating his own work. He has also been invited by the French government to make a presentation on the island where Seurat made his famous painting. George has

had success as an artist because at first people thought his work original. But now that he has created his seventh Chromolume people are telling him it is time he did something new, and he knows this is true. He turns down a commission from a museum in Texas because he needs a new direction for his creativity. He does not know what that might be. At the very end, however, in his vision of Dot, he seems to be moving toward a new artistic vision.

Bob Greenberg
Bob Greenberg is the director of the museum where George exhibits his work in act 2. He has to keep up with rapidly changing tastes and fashions in the art world.

Jules
Jules is a middle-aged, well-established artist in nineteenth-century Paris. He is married to Yvonne. Jules does not like George's painting and thinks it should not be included in the next group show. He tells George not to keep changing his technique. According to Dot he is jealous of George, and Yvonne, Jules's wife, does not dispute this when Dot mentions it to her. When Jules visits George's studio, George explains his painting technique, but Jules is impatient and does not want to listen. He knows George has invited him there because he needs Jules's help in getting the painting included in the next group show. George is aware that Jules does not like him.

Jules tries to start an affair with Frieda, their cook. Yvonne finds out, and he makes a lame excuse. Yvonne hits him, and he claims that Frieda lured him into it.

Louis
Louis is a baker who marries Dot. Dot thinks he is kind and has a good heart, and unlike George he pays attention to her. She is just happy to have found someone after putting up with George's neglect of her for so long. Everyone likes Louis, and he and Dot emigrate from France to the United States. Louis is not given a single line of dialogue.

Louise
Louise is the young child of Jules and Yvonne. She runs around the park, annoying the Boatman and seeing things she should not.

Marie

Marie is George's ninety-eight-year-old grand-mother in act 2. She is the daughter of Dot and has fond memories of her. Marie is confined to a wheelchair, but she is able to assist George in his presentation at the museum. She thinks very highly of his work. Marie dies before she is able to accompany George to Paris for his presentation.

Mr. and Mrs.

Mr. and Mrs. are an American couple from the South. They do not like Paris and cannot wait to get back home. Although they have only just arrived, they decide to return home by the end of the week. Paris is just not as nice as it looks in the paintings.

Nurse

The Nurse looks after the Old Lady on Sundays. She looks after her own mother during the week but does not want to do so on Sundays, so with the money she is paid by the Old Lady she pays someone else to take care of her own mother. She finds the Old Lady tiresome, however, and is ready to sneak off for an encounter with Franz.

Old Lady

The Old Lady, the mother of George in act 1, is an irritable woman who is helped, rather unwillingly, by the Nurse. She does not think much of George's artistic calling; when she sees Dot with Louis she remarks that Dot has taken a step up, a reference to the fact that George does not earn much money. The Old Lady thinks artists are peculiar.

Harriet Pawling

Harriet Pawling is a patron of the arts who admires George's work in act 2. She is a friend of Billy Webster. She is also a member of the board at the museum where George's work is displayed. Her family has a foundation, and she hints to George that she might commission him for a new work.

Lee Randolph

Lee Randolph is the publicist at the museum where George's painting hangs in act 2.

Charles Redmond

Charles Redmond is a visiting curator of a museum in Texas. He is enthusiastic about George's work and hints that the museum may commission a new work from him.

The Soldier

The Soldier's name is Napoleon. The Soldier has spent the whole week indoors with other soldiers and is pleased to be out in the park on a sunny Sunday. Both Celestes try to befriend him, but Celeste #2 wins out over her friend.

Yvonne

Yvonne is married to Jules. Neither she nor her husband likes George's painting. She thinks it lacks life, although she may just be saying that to echo her husband's opinion. Yvonne tells Dot she does not like talking about art even though she is married to an artist. It appears that her marriage to Jules is not entirely happy because he does not give her much attention. She secretly likes George. Dot does not like her.

Billy Webster

Billy Webster is a friend of Harriet Pawling. He does not understand George's work.

THEMES

Art

Art, as revealed by George's work in making *A Sunday Afternoon on the Island of La Grande Jatte*, creates order and harmony out of all the disparate, discordant elements of life. All the lives of the characters who appear in the painting have their own tensions and dissatisfactions. No one is really satisfied with their lot. They quarrel, flirt, and complain, but the artist uses his sense of order and design to create something that is aesthetically pleasing. This is shown in particular in the climax to act 1. All the characters are on the stage, and the conflicts between them come to a head. There is chaos on the stage, with all the characters speaking at once. But then the characters suddenly freeze, the Old Lady says "Remember, George," and as George says, "Order. Design. Tension. Balance. Harmony," the characters start to sing in unison and take up the positions they will occupy in the painting. They sing of their "perfect" park (which they had earlier been complaining about) which they will pass through "forever." Art therefore creates beauty, perfection, and permanence out of the discordant and fleeting manifestations of life. As

TOPICS FOR FURTHER STUDY

- Some critics have argued that the musical is disjointed, that act 1 is complete in itself and act 2 is too separate from it for the complete work to form a satisfying whole. Discuss this with a small group of students. Here are some questions to consider: Is the George of act 2 as interesting a character as the George of act 1? Does the song "Move On" give a feeling of resolution to the whole play? Is the role Dot is playing at this point convincing? If so, does this come from the music or the lyrics, or both? Summarize the findings of your group in a short essay.

- Visit the Web site of the Art Institute of Chicago. It links to several Web pages about the exhibition "Seurat and the Making of *La Grande Jatte*," held in 2004. Also consult *Georges Seurat*, by Mike Venezia, which is a volume in the "Getting to Know the World's Greatest Artists" series (Children's Press, 2003). Using this and other research, prepare a short presentation for your class, with slides explaining Seurat's technique and the process by which he created this painting. Be sure to attempt to explain the universal appeal of this painting,

which is one of the most famous paintings in the world. Why should this be so? You can share your presentation with your classmates via Slideshare.net.

- Listen to or watch either Andrew Lloyd Webber's musical *Cats* or *The Phantom of the Opera*, both written in the 1980s, and compare one of them to Sondheim's *Sunday in the Park with George*. Which musical do you prefer, and why? Why is Lloyd Webber more popular at the box office than Sondheim? Write an essay in which you present your arguments.

- *Sunday in the Park with George* explores how art builds on and is inspired by other art. George of act 2 creates art that is inspired by the George of act 1. Sondheim created a musical inspired by the work of Georges Seurat. With this in mind, create your own original work that is inspired by another piece of visual art, music, or literature. You could write a poem inspired by Sondheim's musical, for example, or a short story. Or you could make a drawing or painting inspired by some other work—a poem, a play, or a song, for example.

George has sung to his mother a few minutes earlier, "You watch / While I revise the world," and she comments, "You make it beautiful."

Connectedness

An important theme is how the artist, who is dedicated to realizing his own distinct vision, relates to other people. The George of act 1 may be a fine artist but he is unable to connect with others on a human level. He is always wrapped up in his work, which is what he cares most about. Dot would be happy to be devoted to him if he would only show her some attention and love, rather than treating her just as an artist's model. She thinks he is hiding behind his work and that he cares only about

"Things—not people." It appears that George has always been somewhat self-absorbed, not fully present to those around him, and he knows that this is so. Toward the end of act 1, when his mother, the Old Lady, has pointed out, "You were always in some other place—seeing something no one else could see," George says mournfully to himself, "Connect, George." For although he is deeply connected to his art, he is disconnected from life. He does not even take any interest in his child, telling Dot that it is Louis's child now that she has decided to marry him. George is contrasted with Louis, who is friendly and fits in with everyone. "Louis makes a connection," Dot says. He feeds people with his delicious pastries, and that is enough to

Georges Seurat, the man who inspired the musical (© INTERFOTO | Alamy)

make him popular. Artists such as George, however, offer food for the soul, but this does not mean they fit in with other people or society as a whole. Indeed, many of the characters in act 1 (the Boatman for example) express a negative opinion either of George or of artists in general, since they are not like normal people.

Creativity

The essence of art is creativity, and this is bound up with the artist's originality and his technique. In preparing to create art, the George of act 1 closely observes his subjects and sees them in some unusual way that is peculiar to him. He explains his original technique to Jules, the complacent, establishment artist who does not understand new approaches, and Jules complains that George is "always changing!" But this is part of his enterprise. He must forge his own artistic self by experimenting with new methods. He tells Jules, "Why should I paint like you or anybody else? I am trying to get

through to something new. Something that is my own."

Creativity and originality are also themes of act 2. George has created an original piece of art through his Chromolumes, but he has just made his seventh Chromolume, and he is starting to repeat himself. Various people, from Dennis his technician, who quits to do something new, to the art critic Blair Daniels, tell him this. His problem is that he does not know where to go, artistically speaking. He must somehow forge an original creative vision. This finally happens at the end of the musical in his vision of Dot, in which he sees his environment in a way that he has not seen it before. He seems mystically united in spirit with his famous ancestor, and it is implied that this provides him with the creative renewal he desperately needs.

STYLE

Musical Theater

Musicals are dramatic stage works that feature many songs or "numbers," as well as some spoken dialogue, although some musicals are what is known as "through-composed," which means that the entire play is set to music. An example of a through-composed musical is Sondheim's *Sweeney Todd* (1979). In the twentieth century, musicals evolved from operetta and other musical entertainments such as burlesque and vaudeville. Musicals are sometimes classified as either musical comedy or musical play. The former are usually lighthearted, often featuring song- and-dance routines, and they have simple plots. The latter are more serious works, with demanding plots and subjects, and more complex integration between lyrics and music. Sondheim's works fall into the category of musical play. *Sunday in the Park with George* contains sophisticated ideas about creativity, art, and their relationship to life, with clever, thought-provoking lyrics that make the musical a serious work of art rather than mere escapist entertainment.

Word Play

Sondheim has been called the best lyricist on Broadway. In this musical, in addition to rhyme, he uses various forms of word play (the witty use of language, often involving puns) and figurative language to enrich his song lyrics. A pun occurs when a word is used that sounds exactly like, or very similar to, another word that has a different meaning, allowing more than one interpretation. In Dot's song about Louis the baker, for example, she puns on the word "kneads," which is something bakers do with bread, using it primarily as a reference to the way Louis massages her. But since "kneads" is pronounced the same as "needs," she manages with that one phrase, "he kneads me," to get in a little dig at George, who has failed to show Dot that he needs her.

Ambiguity of meaning similar to a pun occurs in George's song "Putting It Together" in act 2, about how a work of art is built up from small elements. He sings that "Every moment makes a contribution" and "first of all, you need a good foundation." The ambiguity is that both "contribution" and "foundation" refer not only to the work of art but also the financial structure (monetary contributions, foundations for the arts) that artists need to support their work. This type of pun is similar to a double entendre, in which a word or phrase can be understood in two different ways. Another example occurs later in the same song, in which George sings about the political skills the modern artist needs to get the funding he needs. While being a bit of a politician, the artist must also know "where to draw the line." The phrase refers both to how far the artist can permit himself to go in his political manipulations and also to the necessary skills of the artist in drawing the lines of his painting.

Metaphor

Sondheim also employs metaphor on at least two important occasions in the play. In "Finish the Hat," for example, that phrase refers to more than simply finishing his drawing of a hat. The hat comes to signify the artistic imagination through which the artist enters his creative space. The hat is a metaphor for the creative process. This is what he means by "entering the world of the hat."

The image of a tree is used metaphorically. This occurs when Marie talks about the importance of the family tree in the context of her mother, Dot. What matters in life, she thinks, is children and art. At the time, George is not interested. Immediately after that, however, the stage shows just one tree, behind many tall buildings. This is the island on the Seine that has changed so much since the time George in act 1

made his painting. Buildings have replaced the trees. This tree is one link to the original painting, just as the family tree is the human link between Dot, Marie, and the two Georges. George, struggling to regain his artistic vision, alludes to the presence of the tree and jokes about his grandmother's comment about the family tree. He does not yet understand. Then Dot appears and helps him to restore his creative vision, which shows him the importance of knowing and honoring the family tree, from which his art as well as his life is descended. Thus the tree, understood in its literal and metaphoric sense, is the vital connection between art and life that forms one of the play's themes.

HISTORICAL CONTEXT

Georges Seurat and Pointillism

Georges Seurat was an artist of great originality who had a significant influence on the art of his time. Seurat was born in Paris in 1859. He discovered his talent for drawing early, and in 1878 he was admitted to the École des Beaux-Arts. He fulfilled a year of military service in 1880 and returned to Paris to set up his studio and begin his experiments on an innovative way of painting. In 1884, he exhibited his *Bathing at Asnieres* (which is created as a *tableau vivant* in *Sunday in the Park with George*) and began work on a huge painting, *A Sunday Afternoon on the Island of La Grande Jatte*. La Grande Jatte was an island in the Seine and a popular place for people to go on Sundays to stroll or use their sailboats and canoes. Seurat exhibited this painting, which measured 81.25 inches by 120.25 inches, from May to June 1886 at the Eighth Impressionist Exhibition. His work was also exhibited for the first time in New York in the same year.

Seurat had a technical, scientific mind, and he was interested in theories about light and color. He read the work of the chemist Michel Eugene Chevereul (1786–1889), who theorized about color and how optical effects were achieved. The method Seurat developed became known as pointillism, although he preferred the term divisionism. In pointillism, the artist makes thousands of tiny brush strokes like dots that are of different colors but blend together when viewed from a distance. The points are made of primary colors but create the impression of a variety of secondary colors according to how

COMPARE & CONTRAST

- **1880s:** In France, the movement known as neo-impressionism is led by Georges Seurat. Seurat develops the technique known as pointillism.

  1980s: The French artistic movement known as "free figuration" (*figuration libre*) flourishes and includes artists such as Robert Combas and Remi Blanchard.

  Today: French artists tend not to identify with any particular movement but pursue their own personal artistic visions. One prominent French artist is Pierre Huyghe, who wins the Hugo Boss Prize from the Guggenheim Museum in 2002.

- **1880s:** The first musical comedies are produced on Broadway, with music composed by David Braham and lyrics by Edward (Ned) Harrigan. Harrigan also acts in the shows along with Tony Hart. The stories and characters are drawn from the lower classes in New York. One notable example is *Cordelia's Aspirations* (1883).

  1980s: Along with Sondheim, whose musical *Into the Woods* is produced on Broadway in 1987, the other big name in musical theater is British composer Andrew Lloyd Webber, whose plays *Cats* (British premiere, 1981) and *The Phantom of the Opera* (1986) are both big hits on Broadway, beginning in 1982 and 1988, respectively.

  Today: One of the most successful of Broadway musicals of the twenty-first century is Stephen Schwartz's *Wicked* (2003 and still running as of 2010), an adaptation of *The Wizard of Oz* told from the point of view of the Wicked Witch. Other successful shows include Monty Python's *Spamalot* (2005), which runs for 1,575 performances, and *Avenue Q* (2003–), which wins Tony Awards for Best Book, Score, and Musical.

- **1880s:** The artistic movement known as impressionism, which began in France in the 1860s, reaches the United States.

  1980s: The dominant artistic movement in the United States, as well as Germany and Italy, is neoexpressionism, which is a reaction to the popularity of minimalism in the 1970s. Leading American neoexpressionists include Julian Schnabel, Philip Guston, and David Salle.

  Today: American art exhibits a wide variety of techniques and subjects. There is no single dominant movement. Among the many prominent artists in the United States are Carrie Mae Weems, Mary Heilmann, Jeff Koons, Allan McCollum, and Cindy Sherman, all of whom are featured in the PBS series *Art21—Art in the Twenty-first Century*.

they are placed. In other words, is the color is created by the eye rather than by premixing on the part of the artist. This is shown in the musical when Jules says a color in George's painting is violet but George takes him closer to the canvas, points out that the colors are in fact red and blue, and says, "Your eye made the violet." At first the new technique was subject to some fierce criticism in the art world. There were accusations (as Jules makes in the play) that Seurat's figures were not lifelike, but as more people learned to

understand what he was doing, his stature as an artist grew.

As a man, Seurat appears to have had some of the personal qualities that Sondheim ascribes to him in his musical. John Rewald, in his book *Post-Impressionism from van Gogh to Gauguin*, offers this comment about the artist: "Georges Seurat was a strange man, proud and often almost haughty, whose secretiveness surprised even his closest friends." Rewald also points out that when Seurat was working intensely on

A Sunday Afternoon on the Island of La Grande Jatte *by Georges Seurat* *(© The Print Collector | Alamy)*

A Sunday Afternoon on the Island of La Grande Jatte and going to the island every day, he would refuse to have lunch with his friends because he feared it might distract him from his work. When he saw friend and fellow painter Charles Angrand on the island, he "greeted him without even putting his palette down, scarcely detaching his half-closed eyes from his motif." When he worked on the painting at his studio in the afternoons he would barely pause to eat.

Seurat died of a throat infection in 1891 at the age of thirty-one.

CRITICAL OVERVIEW

When *Sunday in the Park with George* was first produced in New York, reviews were mixed. Some reviewers felt that the characters were not compelling and that although the lyrics were sharp and interesting, the music did not have enough memorable melodies. This was not the first time Sondheim's work had been subjected to this kind of criticism. However, other critics saw great merit in the work. Among its champions was Frank Rich of the *New York Times*. Rich applauds the originality of the work, which demands that "an audience radically change its whole way of looking at the Broadway musical." He refers to the fact that there is little plot in the musical and that the individual characters are not the focus of interest. Rich adds that the musical is "an audacious, haunting and, in its own intensely personal way, touching work." Rich comments further about the "lovely, wildly inventive score that sometimes remakes the modern French composers whose revolution in music paralleled the post-impressionists' in art.... The accompanying lyrics can be brilliantly funny."

Since its first production in 1984, there have been a number of revivals of the show. In 1989, a production by the Forum Theater Group in New Jersey was praised by Alvin Klein in the *New York Times*, who comments that "the remarkable 1984 musical about the creative process in general and, in particular, about the process of creating a new way of painting, re-emerges resplendently." In 2008, a production at New York's Studio 54 prompted *Hollywood Reporter*'s Frank Scheck to comment that "the work beautifully illustrates both the exuberant and exhausting aspects of the creative process."

CRITICISM

Bryan Aubrey

Aubrey holds a Ph.D. in English. In the following essay, he discusses the relationship between art and life in Sunday in the Park with George.

When Stephen Sondheim decided to create a musical based on the artistic process of one man, Georges Seurat, as he created a particular work of art, *A Sunday Afternoon on the Island of La Grande Jatte*, he was posing a challenge to himself and also taking a substantial risk. The material he had in mind did not at first look promising for a dramatic work; there was little plot, and most of the characters were not developed to the point where they would become interesting to an audience. Somehow the esoteric material had to be made accessible to an audience on first hearing so that it could have a long run on Broadway, which was necessary for financial reasons. In his career up to that point, Sondheim had resisted giving audiences the sentimental fare that they might expect from a musical. He did not write soaring melodies or traditional choruses, and his detractors called his work too cerebral, lacking in emotion. When *Sunday in the Park with George* appeared in 1984, some of these criticisms resurfaced, but the show ran successfully for eighteen months on Broadway, was awarded the Pulitzer Prize for Drama in 1985, and won over many of its critics.

For the newcomer to Sondheim's work, *Sunday in the Park with George* is undoubtedly less immediately accessible than other 1980s Broadway hits such as Claude-Michel Schönberg's *Les Miserables* and Andrew Lloyd Webber's *Cats* and *The Phantom of the Opera*. It demands to be taken seriously as a work of art and is one of the musicals often cited in the claim that Sondheim raised the standard of the Broadway musical during the 1970s and 1980s. With an inventive score that often provides musical equivalents of Seurat's pointillist technique, the play provides insight into how this revolutionary artist went about his work (at least as Sondheim imagines it), the demands it placed on him, and what it cost him

> THE GEORGE OF ACT 2 WOULD BE ABLE TO CONTINUE BEING A SUCCESSFUL ARTIST, WINNING IMPORTANT COMMISSIONS, IF HE WERE PREPARED TO IGNORE THE FACT THAT HE HAS CEASED TO BE CREATIVE."

in terms of intimate human relationships. Act 2, criticized by some as being disconnected from the first act, offers something of a satire on the business of contemporary art while presenting (and resolving) the crisis of creativity faced by George, the great-grandson of the George of act 1.

Sunday in the Park with George begins where it ends, with the white canvas of the artist representing the blank field on which he can explore all the possibilities of his art. He announces his task: "bring order to the whole." George's intense concentration on his work is immediate from the outset, as is the restlessness and dissatisfaction of his model, his mistress Dot. The tension between the rigid demands of art and the need—felt by George as well as Dot—for human love is what drives the plot in act 1. George simply has to create art. He has no choice in the matter. His art is an expression of who he is. Dot, a more simple soul, finds that this is what draws her to him; she loves his painting, and something about the fierceness with which he pursues his art is very attractive to her: "Fixed. Cold. / That's you, George, you're bizarre. Fixed. Cold. / I like that in a man." At the same time, Dot frets because George never gives her the attention that she needs and longs for. Indeed, he seems hardly capable of such a thing, and several times during the first part of the show Dot expresses her own insight into how this rather odd man, set apart from others by the demands of his gift, sees the world and responds to it—both the objects and people he draws and the people he interacts with in his personal life. In the song "Color and Light," for example, in which the staccato musical accompaniment suggests the repeated tiny brush strokes of the artist, Dot muses that with George, it is "as if he sees you and he doesn't all at once." This highlights a characteristic of the lyrics of this show; they are

WHAT DO I READ NEXT?

- Sondheim's witty farce *A Funny Thing Happened on the Way to the Forum*, inspired by the plays of the ancient Roman dramatist Plautus, was first performed in 1962. Sondheim is often acclaimed as Broadway's finest lyricist, and the text of the play, available in an edition published by Applause Books in 2000, gives ample reason for such verdicts.

- *Stanley* (1996), by British playwright Pam Gems, is a play about the life of the British artist Sir Stanley Spencer (1891–1959). The play covers about thirty-five years in Spencer's life, from his initially happy marriage to fellow artist Hilda Carline to his last days spent in solitary pursuit of his art. Spencer is revealed as a complex figure, an inspired artist whose personal flaws created unhappiness for those close to him.

- *Vincent in Brixton* (2002) is a play by Nicholas Wright about the time the twenty-year-old Vincent van Gogh spent in Brixton, London, in 1873. Not much is known about this period in van Gogh's life, but in the play, he has a love affair with an older woman that changes his life. Having premiered in London, the play won the Olivier Award for Best New Play in 2003 and transferred to Broadway.

- *Seurat and the Making of "La Grande Jatte,"* by Robert L. Herbert and Neil Harris (2004), is a detailed examination of how Seurat conceived and created his masterpiece, *A Sunday Afternoon on the Island of La Grande Jatte*, and the influence the painting has had on later artists. Harris discusses how the painting achieved its iconic status in the United States. The book includes fifty-five preparatory studies, including drawings and oil sketches.

- Although primarily known as a novelist, Zora Neale Hurston also wrote a considerable number of plays, some of which were successfully produced in her lifetime. In *Zora Neale Hurston: Collected Plays* (2008), edited by Jean L. Cole and Charles Mitchell, these plays are brought out of the obscurity they had fallen into. They present a rich and varied portrait of African American life in the early twentieth century.

- *Great Songs from Musicals for Teens* (2001), compiled by Louise Lerch, is a collection of music from a variety of musicals, from *South Pacific* to *Guys and Dolls* and *Big River*. The book comes with a CD of recordings by young singers and an accompaniment track for each song. There is a Young Women's edition and a Young Men's edition.

---

sharp and convey much in a few words. Here, Dot captures in one sentence the dual nature of the consciousness and the perceptions of the man she is in love with. It is as if the artist overshadows the man; when George gazes at Dot he takes exact note of the play of color and light in her form, but the real person at the heart of all that swirl of color and light seems to escape him. If it is the gift of the artist to see in ways that others do not, in the case of this particular artist, that gift is also a curse, because it has adverse consequences in his personal life. It is as if art

swallows up life. Many great artists, including writers and composers as well as painters, have been willing to accept such a trade-off because they know they have a contribution to make to history and human culture that dwarfs the success or failure of their personal lives. What matters to such outstanding individuals—and George in the play is one of them—is to honor the gift, to bring the work of art to birth as an imperative from within.

For Dot, the situation is painful. In one of the more cruel paradoxes of romantic love,

George's lack of availability simply makes her want him even more. Eventually she makes the difficult decision to leave him in favor of Louis, the amiable but mediocre baker, who at least has the capacity to give affection. Dot is prepared to overlook one glaring defect in Louis, who gets along with everyone: "That's the trouble, nothing's wrong with him." That witty line again captures the paradox of the romantic attraction Dot feels for her brilliant but flawed George; by comparison, Louis is just not very interesting.

But if Dot suffers—her lighthearted song about Louis notwithstanding—George does not escape scot-free either, as is revealed in the song "Finish the Hat," which occupies a crucial position toward the end of the first act. It is a song that expresses great passion and emotional turmoil, and it certainly gives the lie to the notion that Sondheim's work lacks these qualities. The situation is that Dot has told George she is going to leave him; it appears that his declared need to "finish the hat" rather than take her to the Follies, as they had agreed, was the last straw. In this song, George expresses a range of emotions, including frustration, defiance, acceptance, and joy. He shows great self-awareness, not only of his own creative process but also of his relationships with women. While he is creating, nothing exists for him other than the object of his contemplation, whether he is "Mapping out the sky" or "Finishing a hat." He is lost in his art, and then, when the time comes to return to the flesh-and-blood world, he is always "turning back too late," and either the woman who has waited is the wrong woman for him, or the right one has departed. He says to himself that he gives all he can, all he is able to give, but at the same time he knows it is not enough, because his art has taken hold of him and will not let him go. His partner knows this, too. She knows, and George knows that she knows, that "however you live, / There's a part of you always standing by," carrying on the work of being an artist and shutting out everything else. The situation clearly causes him pain, but on the other hand, he cannot and has no wish to disguise the joy he feels through the act of creation. He has created through his art a hat, which before there never was, and this gives him a thrill and a satisfaction that he can know in no other way. The audience, however, is left to contemplate the irony of that last line when, alone on the stage, he shows the hat he has sketched not to Dot, who is not there, nor to any other

human, but to Fifi, a cardboard cut-out of a dog. The creation of art, one gets to feel, is a lonely business. For many listeners, this poignant song, in which George's gift and his tragedy coexist alongside each other, is the emotional highlight of the first act.

When that act closes, George is shown doing what he does best. In "Sunday," through his agency, the discordance of life gives way to the beauty and harmony of art. In that final tableau of "A Sunday Afternoon on the Island of La Grande Jatte," George is fulfilled. He has done what he was born to do—and yet he is alone and, in some deep sense that he would acknowledge only in rare moments to himself, he is incomplete.

Act 2 must at some point return to this George, while at the same time telling the story of another artist, another George. The George of act 2 is a contrast to the other George in several important respects. He is commercially successful. He knows how to play the game of modern art, competing for commissions, raising money, drumming up publicity, doing the social schmoozing, talking to all the right people. This George has mastered the art of self-promotion in a way that one cannot imagine the George of act 1 having much time for. In fact, the only time act 1 George tries such a thing is when he invites Jules to his studio to look at his painting, but Jules knows straightaway that George is trying to win his support in getting the painting exhibited, and he does not react favorably.

The George of act 2 would be able to continue being a successful artist, winning important commissions, if he were prepared to ignore the fact that he has ceased to be creative. In his work he is merely repeating what he has done before, and he knows this will not do. Again he is in sharp contrast to the earlier George. That George has not been accepted by his contemporaries, but he is a man who is fully in charge of his craft. He knows exactly what he is doing; he is confident, artistically speaking, and he does not falter; he brings the inner vision to fruition.

However, these two Georges do have one thing in common. Neither is good in intimate relationships (George number two is divorced) or has much understanding of the value of family. They cannot balance the competing demands of art and life. Marie tries to tell act 2 George of the importance of this in "Children and Art," but he listens to her only reluctantly. Like act 1 George, he is left saying to himself, "Connect, George. Connect,"

A garden version of the painting (*Jeffrey M. Frank | Shutterstock.com*)

like a man who knows that he cannot. Also lamenting his vanished creativity, George cuts a sad figure at this point. It is left to Dot, who suddenly appears to him in some kind of vision, to heal both Georges. For some in the audience, the return of a wiser Dot may seem too much like a *deus ex machina*, connecting act 2 with act 1 and miraculously creating a happy ending that cannot otherwise be achieved. Be that as it may, there is much to admire in "Move On," the pleasing duet she sings with George, in which she manages to address both Georges, both of whom discover what they need. Act 1 George finally acknowledges that he and Dot have always belonged together, and act 2 George rediscovers his ability to see the world in new ways and so recover his creativity. They have both learned, in different ways, to connect.

Source: Bryan Aubrey, Critical Essay on *Sunday in the Park with George*, in *Drama for Students*, Gale, Cengage Learning, 2011.

Leonard Jacobs

In the following review, Jacobs explains the techniques Sondheim used to make this biographical story suited for the stage.

"We feel like we're bringing it home," says British actor Daniel Evans of *Sunday in the Park With George*, the 1984 Stephen Sondheim James Lapine Pulitzer Prize winning musical that Round-about Theatre Company is reviving on Broadway, opening Feb. 21. Directed by Sam Buntrock, the production originated at London's intimate Menier Chocolate Factory in 2006 before moving to the West End. Evans, in the title role, and Jenna Russell, playing Dot in Act 1 and Marie in Act 2, won Olivier Awards—the equivalent of Tonys—for their work. Both grasp how profound the memories are of *Sunday*'s, original stars, Mandy Patinkin and Bernadette Peters. "We have great respect for it and them, but we have to throw it around," Evans says.

Sunday explores the life of Georges Seurat, the French neoimpressionist painter whose fascination with the ability of the eye, instead of the brush, to fuse color led to his creation of pointillism. Act 1 finds George developing his masterwork, *A Sunday Afternoon on the Island of La Grande Jatte*. To expedite the story, the authors devised a fictional character, the aforementioned Dot, as George's mistress. Act 1 climaxes with the characters forming a tableau replicating Seurat's finished painting. Act 2 leaps a century ahead as George's fictional great-grandson, also an artist named George, struggles to forge a style of his own. His 98-year-old grandmother, Marie—the illegitimate child of the earlier George and Dot—can help him if only he'll listen.

"We started in London at this tiny theatre with 150 seats," says Evans, who has acted in the U.K. since age 18 and been on Broadway once before, in the Royal Shakespeare Company's *A Mid-summer Night's Dream* in 1996, as Lysander. "It was sort of a—I don't want to say a joke, but a madcap idea of putting Sunday on with no money, no wing space, and a ceiling so low you couldn't fly anything." Buntrock, he says, "was an animator in a different life, and he came up with the idea that to recreate the painting you could use digital technology." Thus Evans has had the bizarre experience of acting and singing while a video of himself plays on a screen.

Distinguishing their performances from those of Patinkin, Peters, and the many other actors who have played George and Dot was essential, they say. "Initial rehearsals were difficult because I had to ban myself from hearing the original recording," says Evans. "I'd no interest in impersonating Mandy Patinkin. This is my response to these parts. It's Jenna's response. Hopefully, that's what people enjoy."

Adds Russell, who joined the *Sunday* cast midway through its London runs, "I suppose my fear of looking at the DVD is I might see some fabulous comedy business I have to steal or a moment I've not done. Also, we're still discovering stuff because we've been playing at this for a long time. Just today we did our first run-through, which was highly emotional. We're singing 'Move On,' and I thought, If this room was with the people we normally have in rehearsal—this time, the authors were there—I would have had a few tears."

CANVASSING CHARACTERS

Evans and Russell seem so intertwined, on and off stage, they often finish each other's sentences or offer gentle yet intuitive analyses of each other's thoughts. As Russell discusses her acting choices, Evans nods. At the appropriate moment, his hand on her arm, he says, "What's glorious about Jenna is all her naughtiness, her sense of fun, her emotional connection to the role, her seriousness—it all comes through." They giggle, and Russell nods in kind.

Then Russell continues: "Stephen Sondheim told me how his characters sing is how they speak, and I think *Sunday* is a really good illustration of someone's mental state of mind." In the opening (and title) number, for example, Dot, posing for George, resists being stationary. "There she is, still, yet her mind is racing," Russell says. "She feels her sweat; she has a cheeky, laughing-at-herself moment; she has these beautiful, lyrical bits on how wonderful George is, then her brain races to something else. There's a lot of the child in Dot. And I've always thought her role is to love George a hundred million billion percent. Marie's job is to love George for all his mistakes, to want what's best for him. I think Dot's like a firefly: She's all over the place. But when called upon, she's a great, strong, extraordinary woman. Like everyone, she wants someone to love her, to give her a hug, tell her she's gorgeous."

That is what the Act 1 George, obsessed with his work, cannot do. Thus, the actors say, their performances pivot at times on a tension they relish. Playing a distant figure, Evans says, is perhaps his hardest task. "George can be cold," he says. "One of my challenges is playing someone seemingly disconnected so that the audience can empathize, so they think, 'Oh, I understand George. I hate him for not giving Dot what she needs, but I understand him a little.' We all can understand obsession, addiction. I also think George can be warm and funny, generous, naughty, and dirt. I think he and Dot have an amazing private life together. I think they have a wonderful sexual relationship."

"When she can peel him away from his painting," Russell says.

"And once he starts," Evans continues, "what happens for me is the warmth gets transferred to the painting. It gets all the warmth and passion, which Dot thinks is cold. He doesn't think he's cold. I think he thinks it's hard for him to say, 'I love you; I need you.'"

"And that drives her mental," Russell says.

"It drives him mental," Evans adds. "When we were singing 'We Do Not Belong Together,' I agree with almost everything she sings. George and Dot should have belonged together, yet he can't bring himself to say, 'Don't go.' The painting is a sort of reparation. In the painting, she's in the shade; she has a hat and a parasol. He takes care of her in the painting, which becomes world-famous. I think of that when we perform. George can't express his love, but he can in his art."

MAKING THE CONNECTION

Russell has thought a lot about Act 2 of *Sunday* which [some] critics consider a slog. She agrees that the narrative is less linear: whereas Act 1 concerns Seurat's need to finish his masterwork, Act 2 concerns the latter-day George's inability to define his aesthetic voice. Introducing new, contemporary characters, she says, makes the actors' jobs harder.

"As at the end of Act 1, you have the lovely painting, all the people up there in their lovely outfits, and they go off suddenly, and it's all a bit cold," Russell says. "It's, Who are these new people? What about these characters we've spent all this time with, that we're in love with? It takes a good five minutes where you feel the audience going, 'No, stay in the 19th century.' But they warm up." After George sings "Putting It Together," she says, *Sunday* "starts to shrink, in a way; the writing becomes beautiful, honest, and moving. Soon it's really just George and Marie, then just George after she dies."

"Act 2 George is the other side of the coin," adds Evans. "James Lapine said that in Act 1, George knows himself, but no one else understands him. In Act 2, everyone understands George but himself. I think that's right. The modern George is a brilliant artist who sold out; he's repeating the same old shit. Marie says he has a connection with his great-grandfather, a great artist he's cynical about. Then he has an epiphany where he reconnects with his past. He realizes what he must do as artist, yes, but also what he must do as a person."

Source: Leonard Jacobs, "Twinkle and Shimmer and Buzz: The Stars of Roundabout's *Sunday in the Park with George* Talk Sondheim and Art," in *Back Stage West*, Vol. 15, No. 4, January 24, 2008, p. 8.

David Sheward

In the following review, Sheward comments that scaled-down music and production values allow for focus on the play's emotional component.

Less is becoming more for the musicals of Stephen Sondheim. Revivals of *Sweeney Todd, Company,* and now *Sunday in the Park With George* have stripped away the elaborate production values of the original mountings to better reveal the rich emotional life within the intricate rhymes and complex melodies. Like Georges Seurat, the driven NeoImpressionist painter at the center of *Sunday*, Sondheim has been accused of coldness and formality. But

thanks to Sam Buntrock's minimalist yet elegant staging and to passionate leading performances from Daniel Evans and Jenna Russell, who have been imported from the Olivier Award-winning Menier Chocolate Factory production in London, this dissertation on the creative process is also a moving human drama.

The 1984 Broadway version employed pop-up and flown-in pieces to create the 1880s Parisian park Seurat immortalized in his gigantic pointillist canvas *A Sunday Afternoon on the Island of La Grande Jatte* and a 1980s museum displaying a multimedia installation created by his descendant. For this production, designer David Farley has created an evocative, cream-colored set that could be either an art gallery before an exhibition is installed or a painter's studio. Buntrock illuminates this nearly blank canvas with subtly animated projections created by Timothy Bird and the Knifedge Creative Network. While these effects are impressive and clever, they never overshadow Sondheim and book writer James Lapine's main story: the painful yet rewarding relationship between an artist and his muse.

That connection is given electric life by Evans and Russell in dual roles. In Act 1, Evans is George, a painter, and Russell is Dot, his lover and model. In Act 2, Evans essays another George, a modern-day conceptual artist, and Russell is his grandmother Marie, who is the illegitimate daughter of George and Dot. As both artists, Evans' body seems to pulse with irresistible energy as he transmits his ideas either onto canvas or into electronic images. He also physicalizes the war between his artistic and emotional needs, almost tearing himself apart as he is pulled between completing his painting and tending to Dot. This battle carries over into his songs, making "Finishing the Hat" a wrenching declaration of artistic obsession. "Putting It Together," in which the 1980s George spreads himself too thinly among patrons and art critics, becomes a dance of frantic self-promotion.

Russell is equally emotive and versatile, playing Dot with a rough, working-class British dialect and making her need for George palpable in its desperation, then emphasizing in Marie the life-loving girl inside the aged, twisted figure confined to a wheelchair. Mary Beth Peil, Anne L. Nathan, and Alexander Gemignani are among the standouts in a tight ensemble expertly populating two eras.

In keeping with the scaled-down theme, the score is performed by an ensemble of five, yet the sweet and rich Sondheim sounds could be coming from a full orchestra. Hats off to musical supervisor Caroline Humphris, orchestrator Jason Carr, and music coordinator John Miller.

Source: David Sheward, "*Sunday in the Park with George*: The Menier Chocolate Factory and Roundabout Theatre Company at Studio 54," in *Back Stage East*, Vol. 49, No. 9, February 28, 2008, p. 2.

Jeremy McCarter

In the following review, McCarter describes how the play employs impressive and innovative pyrotechnics.

Gripped by an impulse familiar to stage folk through the ages, a wily showman once got the idea to punch up a production of Shakespeare's *Henry VIII* by firing an actual cannon onstage. The blast stopped the show, all right. It also started the fire that burned the original Globe Theatre to the ground.

The relationship between special effects and stagecraft is less incendiary now than it was in 1613, but that doesn't mean it's tranquil. From the drooping Phantom chandelier to the gee-whiz tricks of Disney's Imagineers, elaborate FX tend to dehumanize a story and short-circuit the audience's imagination—two developments disastrous to an art form that depends on its human connection and enticement to the imagination. Lucky, then, that two new shows offer some of the best reasons yet to think that 21st-century FX could do some good onstage.

The appeal of *Sunday in the Park With George* has always been the chance to hear one great artist (Stephen Sondheim) use another great artist (Georges Seurat) to help us understand the creation of great art. As the Seurat of Sondheim and librettist James Lapine's story struggles to complete his pointillist masterpiece *A Sunday Afternoon on the Island of the Grande Jatte*, director Sam Buntrock uses marvelously precise digital projections to make the painting come to life: Splotches of color appear on a translucent canvas under Seurat's brush; a steamer on the back wall glides along the Seine. It looks irresistibly cool, and the projections capture Seurat's fevered focus on his work. When George (Daniel Evans, who has a Daniel Day-Lewis-ish intensity) says he is "living in" the painting, we understand how disorienting that must have felt.

Yet technology is less kind to the ear than to the eye in Buntrock's revival (imported from London by the Roundabout). For all the dazzling visuals, the score has a synthesized quality that sounds like an artifact of the show's original staging in 1984. Nor, alas, can digital imagery do much for a story that loses steam. Once Seurat finishes his painting, at intermission, we spend all of Act Two with his less interesting great-grandson. As badass as young George's Chromolume looks here—all whirling lights—the evening inevitably feels like a visually sumptuous letdown.

If Buntrock shows how the inspired use of gadgetry offers a fresh way to evoke the heart of a story, Bob McGrath shows that FX can be a boon, not a detriment, to a play's humanity. In *The Slug Bearers of Kayrol Island* (Or, *The Friends of Dr. Rushower*) at the Vineyard, he sets cartoonist Ben Katchor and composer Mark Mulcahy's whimsical story in a comic book come to life. Katchor's drawings (familiar from strips like "Julius Knipl, Real Estate Photographer") are projected here on tilting screens, so the actors inhabit a world of hand-drawn color and light.

The attempts of a girl named GinGin to find love while liberating the slug bearers—laborers who transport the lead weights that give consumer electronics an illusion of substance—may not have much dramatic heft, but it's charming and never cloys. As Katchor's drawings whisk us from an apartment high atop New York to a distant tropical island, the show doesn't deaden the imagination, it piques it: So this is what it's like to live in a Fauvist dream.

At BAM, Rupert Goold is directing the first *Macbeth* that seems like it could be sponsored by a cutlery association. The long knives are always out in this production—the short ones, too. Patrick Stewart delivers the famous soliloquy "If it were done when 'tis done, then 'twere well it were done quickly" while cutting the cork on a wine bottle. Later he slices a sandwich for Banquo's murderers, a fitting gesture for his weirdly off-hand approach: Murder doesn't seem like a serious thing here, an odd choice for the greatest play about guilt ever written.

Otherwise Goold's production is notable mainly for its aggression. Loud and—at three hours—long, it wows you with the occasional cinematic twist (Banquo dies via cloak-and-dagger high jinks on a train), then resumes bullying you with its Stalinesque imagery, its dingy-hospital aesthetic, its witches who rap their way through "Double, double, toil and trouble." Hip-hop renders the chant indecipherable, which is, all in all, probably for the best.

Not long after *Sunday in the Park With George* opened on Broadway in 1984, the critic Robert Brustein called it "the first Broadway musical that is mainly about the set." Employing pop-up cardboard cutouts and laser beams that might come off as eighties kitsch today, the set was stunning enough to some that it upstaged the score ("An act of self-immolation for Sondheim," wrote another critic). Last-minute song swaps, prop problems, and visits from federal inspectors to make sure the lasers were safe led to premature rumors of disaster. But the musical went on to win the one prize that has nothing to do with staging—the Pulitzer.

Source: Jeremy McCarter, "The Digital Stage: *Sunday in the Park with George* and the Slug Bearers Prove that Disney Doesn't Have a Lock on Theatrical Pyrotechnics," in *New York*, Vol. 41, No. 8, March 3, 2008, pp. 64–65.

SOURCES

"Art:21—Art in the Twenty-first Century," in *PBS.org*, http://www.pbs.org/art21/ (accessed July 27, 2010).

Kenrick, John, "History of the Musical Stage, 1879–1880: The First Musical Comedies," in *Musicals101.com*, http://www.musicals101.com/1879to99.htm (accessed July 23, 2010).

———, "History of the Musical Stage, The 1980s," in *Musicals101.com*, http://www.musicals101.com/1980bway.htm (accessed July 23, 2010).

———, "History of the Musical Stage, 2000 to Today," in *Musicals101.com*, http://www.musicals101.com/2000bway.htm (accessed July 23, 2010).

Klein, Alvin, "Theater: An Enthralling 'Sunday in Park,'" in *New York Times*, December 24, 1989.

"New York–Paris, 1945–2005," in *Tajan*, http://www.tajan.com/en/news/cp-2005-05-25-5564.asp (accessed July 24, 2010).

Otten, Liam, "American Art of the 1980s," in *Washington University in St. Louis Web site*, December 8, 2003, http://news.wustl.edu/news/Pages/565.aspx (accessed July 25, 2010).

"Pierre Huyghe," in *PBS.org*, http://www.pbs.org/art21/artists/huyghe/ (accessed July 24, 2010).

Rewald, John, *Post-Impressionism from van Gogh to Gauguin*, rev. 3rd ed., The Museum of Modern Art, New York, 1978, pp. 73, 82.

Rich, Frank, "Stage: 'Sunday in the Park with George,'" in *New York Times*, May 3, 1984.

Scheck, Frank, Review of *Sunday in the Park with George*, in *Hollywood Reporter*, Vol. 403, No. 33, February 22, 2008, p. 18.

Sondheim, Stephen, *Sunday in the Park with George*, in *Four by Sondheim: Wheeler, Lapine, Shevelove and Gelbart*, Applause Books, 2000, pp. 561–708.

"Stephen Sondheim: Master of the Musical," in *Academy of Achievement*, http://www.achievement.org/autodoc/page/son0bio-1 (accessed July 24, 2010).

FURTHER READING

Gordon, Joanne, ed., *Stephen Sondheim: A Casebook*, Routledge, 1999.
This is a collection of fourteen essays on a range of Sondheim's works. Particularly interesting is "Portraits of the Artist: *Sunday in the Park with George* as 'Postmodern' Drama" by Edward T. Bonahue, Jr.

Horowitz, Mark Eden, *Sondheim on Music: Minor Details and Major Decisions*, Scarecrow Press, 2003.
This is a collection of interviews with Sondheim in which he talks about his work as a composer. It includes a fascinating chapter on *Sunday in the Park with George* in which he discusses what he was aiming for and the musical techniques he used to attain his goals.

Secrest, Meryl, *Stephen Sondheim: A Life*, Knopf, 1998.
This biography, written with Sondheim's cooperation, examines Sondheim's life and his work. The composer emerges as a complex figure, wholly dedicated to his art.

Wood, James N., *Impressionism and Post-Impressionism at the Art Institute of Chicago*, Hudson Hills Press, 2000.
This book presents 147 paintings, sculptures, prints, and drawings from the collection of the Art Institute of Chicago, tracing impressionism from its origins to the transformations it underwent in the early twentieth century. Seurat is represented by five paintings, including *A Sunday Afternoon on the Island of La Grande Jatte*.

SUGGESTED SEARCH TERMS

Stephen Sondheim

Stephen Sondheim AND Sunday in the Park with George

Georges Seurat

A Sunday Afternoon on the Island of La Grande Jatte

neo-impressionism

pointillism

post-impressionism

James Lapine

Broadway musical

Musical AND Sondheim

Musical Theatre AND Sondheim

This Is a Test

STEPHEN GREGG

1988

Published in 1988, *This Is a Test* is playwright Stephen Gregg's most popular play. According to its publisher, Dramatic Publishing Company, it continues to be one of the most widely produced one-act plays in high schools across America, even decades after its debut. The author himself indicates that according to *Dramatics*, an educational theater magazine, the play immediately shot to the number-one slot in performances and stayed there for fourteen years.

Like his other eight dramas, *This Is a Test* is about young adults with real-life issues. In this case, Gregg primarily explores test anxiety and self-image. Although these two themes are common to many works written about teens, Gregg's approach differs in that he takes his reader inside the head of his main character, Alan, through a dream sequence.

The play is popular among middle- and high-school drama clubs because it allows much room for interpretation and flexibility to cast actors according to who is available. For instance, most characters in the play can be played by males or females, so the play lends itself well to any mix of student actors. Gregg wrote the drama so that liberties could be taken with staging as well.

AUTHOR BIOGRAPHY

Gregg was born on May 19, 1963, in Sacramento, California. After spending his childhood

The teacher said "don't think of this as a test." (*Tony Wear / Shutterstock.com*)

in Albuquerque, New Mexico, Gregg returned to California, where he studied English literature and microbiology at Stanford University. By the time of his graduation in 1985, he had already begun writing plays.

Gregg received a 1990 Jerome Fellowship from the Playwrights Center of Minneapolis, and two years later earned a Heideman Award from the Actors Theatre of Louisville for best ten-minute play. That same year, he was awarded a Chesterfield Film Fellowship. In 1994, he was honored with the International Thespians Founders Award for his service to youth and theater.

The prolific author has written nine stage plays as well as six screenplays. Play titles include *Sex Lives of Superheroes* (1990); *The Largest Elizabeth in the World* (1991); *The Zero Sum Mind* (1991); *Small Actors*; *Wake-Up Call* (2002); *Poor Little Lambs* (2003); *S. P. A. R.* (2003); and *Sunday Night*, which is available in full text on the author's Web site but has yet to be officially published. His plays are consistently produced by school drama clubs across the country, the most popular being the 1988 one-act piece, *This Is a Test*. Directors

praise the play for its humorous look at a serious subject—teen anxiety—as much as they appreciate its ability to be acted out using improvisation and individual interpretation. Fellow playwright and Playscripts.com publishing company founder Doug Rand calls the play "genre-defining," as the brief play literally changed the field of high school drama with its ground-breaking structure: one act with a large, flexible cast and a script that was written to entertain rather than teach a lesson.

Gregg has had moderate success with his screenplays as well, which include *Seven Girlfriends*; *Weetzie Bat*; *Nuclear Family*; *X-Mas*; *Animal Instinct*; and *Ten Wishes*.

Gregg is married to photographer Todd Stern makes his home in California, where he continues to write scripts.

PLOT SUMMARY

The play opens with a distinct Voice announcing the test. The announcement mimics announcements made by a public service called the

Emergency Broadcast System during the cold war. High-school sophomores Alan and Lois are seated at their desks in a classroom with other students. Lois is tidy and seems ready to get to work, whereas Alan is a rumpled mess and clearly in panic mode after studying all night for an exam, only to feel unprepared and exhausted.

Alan begins to daydream, and in that dream a Chorus of voices takes him through an exercise he and Lois just participated in the day before. The purpose of the exercise is to focus on the object being passed among participants. As Alan complains that he cannot get the exercise out of his head, the Teacher walks in carrying the tests.

Teacher watches Alan a bit suspiciously, then reminds students that this test is of even greater importance than usual, though all answers could be found on the review sheets. Alan, of course, never saw the review sheets, which puts him into an even greater panic. As students begin the test, the Voice begins reading the first question as well as the multiple-choice answers, none of which Alan recognizes from his hours of studying. Meanwhile, as he struggles, the Chorus continues the redundant drama exercise of naming inanimate objects. As this is going on, fellow student Chris repeatedly asks how much time is left on the test. He annoys Alan.

Alan tries hard to concentrate, but soon he sees the other students in class cheating. They're either copying each others' papers or reading crib notes they wrote. Soon every student seems to be making signals that provide answers. As Alan realizes what is going on, he becomes agitated and raises his hand to inform the Teacher of what is going on.

He decides against tattling on his classmates and instead asks if the test will be graded on a curve. The cheating among his peers becomes more obvious as Pat, a stereotypical overachieving student, begins waving flags around as a way to send signals. Chris creates Morse code with flashlight signals, and even Lois gets in on the cheating action.

Alan accidentally asks the answer to question number six out loud and Teacher believes he is cheating (although he is the only one in class who is not cheating). Oblivious to what is really going on, Teacher turns his back to the class and warns Alan that he needs to behave honorably. As Alan tries to concentrate on section two of the test, the Voice begins reading true or false questions, and Alan answers them out loud.

Soon, the Chorus voices are back at it, naming objects again. Only this time, they are related to Alan's personal life, not his academic activities.

Unaware of what is happening, Alan gets sucked into the game with the Chorus and ends up yelling out loud. When Chris asks again how much time is left, Alan works himself into a frenzy as he hears there are only nine minutes left to work. At that point, football star Evan walks into the room. He is late because he was at practice, but Teacher does not have a problem with his student's tardiness. He has Evan look over the test, and it is clear Evan does not know any of the answers, but he lies and says the only one he is unsure of is the second-to-last one. Teacher answers the question for Evan and asks if he would have said it the same way. Evan assures him he would and the pleased Teacher gives the undeserving student an A+. Alan is incensed that Evan gets away with special treatment just because he is a gifted athlete and (the audience assumes) popular among his peers.

Teacher informs Alan that Evan's grades no longer matter because he has already been accepted to any college he wishes to attend, even though he is only a sophomore. When Alan doubts Evan's abilities, Teacher accuses him of jealousy. At this point, Pat asks for two more blue books, the small, bound books of paper that some schools have students use to record test answers.

Compared to Evan and even Pat, Alan feels pathetic as he lists his shortcomings. After his pity party has come to an end, Lois, Pat, and Chris each ask for yet another blue book, only they sing the request to the tune of the song *Hallelujah* from Handel's *Messiah*. As a reward, they each get ten points of extra credit.

Alan moves on to the next question, which is an opinion essay worth thirty points. He relaxes as he realizes he can ace an essay; Chorus voices begin the drama exercise again. Alan's relief is shattered when he tries to read the essay prompt and discovers it is written in Chinese. When he complains to Teacher, he learns that the class was taught Chinese on Tuesday, the day he was absent. Beaten, Alan throws his head down on his desk as he proclaims the test a nightmare.

Alan's mother enters from offstage and taps him on the shoulder, waking him as he slumbers at his desk. She informs him he's been studying all night and should take a break since he has the highest grade in class. Then she surprises him with the news that he was accepted into the college of his choice, Majestica University. Mother then leaves to bake cookies for her son.

Teacher warns Alan to stop daydreaming, but Alan already recognizes that it is too late. Time is almost up and he has not answered one question. The Voice begins reading the questions again, and question three of the section dissects Alan's less becoming traits and habits, asking students to pick that which is most annoying. After complaints from students because the question is too hard and the list incomplete, Teacher strikes it from the test and makes question nineteen worth twenty points as opposed to ten.

Alan knows the answer to question nineteen, and he is overjoyed at being able to write down what he is certain is correct information. Just then, Teacher announces that he has changed his mind, and whatever grade the students earn on this midterm test is the grade they will have for the rest of class. He does not feel like coming up with more assignments that he will have to grade, nor does he want to grade more tests. While he is speaking, the rest of the class begins to chatter in Chinese, bringing a sense of utter chaos to the scene.

The Voice returns, speaking above both Teacher and students, and lets readers and viewers know that the test is over.

CHARACTERS

Alan

Alan is the main character of the play and also the person whose dream makes up most of the story. Alan is a typical high-school student: academically average, not gifted in athletics, socially awkward, and prone to serious stress when it comes to taking tests.

Alan tries hard but manages to talk himself out of even the possibility of doing well. He studied all night for the test, but as he sits down to take it, he convinces himself he knows nothing. He hears voices in his head and lets his teenage angst take over as he fails to answer question after question. As he realizes he will surely fail the test, his thoughts turn to his personal life, which fares even worse than his breadth of knowledge. In his mind, Alan cannot live up to anyone's expectations, especially his own.

Alan's Mother

Alan's mother does what mothers often do: reassures her son of his abilities even as he sits worrying that he does not know anything. She wakes him at his desk, where he fell asleep studying. After informing him that he was accepted into Majestica University, she leaves to bake him cookies. Alan's mom is symbolic of comfort and encouragement; while he frets and wallows in angst, she reminds him of how proud she is of him, just for being himself.

Chorus

The Chorus is made up of several voices whose purpose is, as a whole, to be the voices Alan hears in his head as his anxiety deepens. They are a constant reminder of who Alan is and what he is not. As the play progresses, and Alan begins dissecting his personal life, the Chorus points out all the things wrong with Alan: his social life, his looks, and his lack of talent and skill.

Chris

Chris is that classmate other students find annoying. He continually asks how much time they have left to work on the test, and when the teacher asks who gets hurt the most when people cheat, Chris provides the answer all adults look for: the cheater. Chris is the kind of student his peers believe the teacher loves because he is diligent and conscientious.

Evan

Evan is a football player who comes to class late and faces no consequences for his actions. He represents the popular crowd: the students other students believe get preferential treatment by the teachers. Evan displays an air of entitlement as he takes full advantage of Teacher's admiration, accepting an A+ for a test he never takes. Evan is already accepted into the college of his choice simply because he is an athlete.

Lois

Lois helps Alan as the two study all night for a test. Unlike Alan, however, Lois is a strong student, confident in herself and her abilities. Her cool demeanor and attitude are in direct contrast to Alan's anxiety and certainty that he will fail. Lois spends the opening scene trying to convince Alan that he knows more than he thinks he does and that being anxious will serve only to make things worse. She is the voice of reason.

Pat

Pat is another classmate other students typically find annoying: the overachiever. Whereas other students might use one blue book to write their answers in for the test, Pat uses many and keeps asking for more. Pat is the kind of person who, if he could say something in five words, will use ten.

Teacher

Teacher is portrayed from a student's point of view rather than from an objective point of view. He is, at first, concerned about his students and their performance, and he confirms that if they studied the review sheets, they should do well. But Teacher becomes more unjust as the play progresses. He gives Evan an A+, even though he did not take the test or even show up to class on time. When everyone in class except Alan is cheating, Teacher overlooks the transgressions and accuses Alan of the bad behavior. The essay question on the test is written in Chinese script, and when Alan exclaims he cannot read it, Teacher tells him to take it up with the Attendance Committee. As the dream unfolds, Teacher gets decidedly worse until the test—and the play—are over.

The Voice

The Voice is the Official Voice of Life. It announces the beginning of the play, and as Alan wracks his brain trying to figure out answers, the Voice reads off the multiple choice answers. At the end of the play, as Alan realizes he knows the correct answers to question nineteen, which is now worth twice as many points as before, the Voice reappears to usher Alan back to real life.

THEMES

Anxiety

The entire play revolves around one student's anxiety over taking a test. Readers know that Alan is anxious, before he even utters one word. The author's description of his appearance gives him away: "His shirt is buttoned incorrectly, his socks do not match, and his hair sticks out at odd angles. His expression is both dazed and frantic."

Alan's anxiety is evident throughout the play by the way he behaves: banging his head on his desk, making faces, and hearing voices in his head that aren't really there. From the first scene through the last, anxiety is the theme around which the play revolves.

Self Image

Alan has a relatively low sense of self-esteem and sees himself as a loser, someone who passes through life unnoticed because he has no outstanding qualities. One of the questions on the multiple-choice test asks students which of Alan's shortcomings is most annoying. The choices include the way he shuffles instead of walking; poor posture; bad breath; an irritating laugh; his sloppy fashion sense; his whiny voice; his odd sense of humor; his poor performance on tests; and an embarrassing personal problem, the nature of which is never revealed. Clearly, Alan focuses on, and possibly exaggerates, his less-than-desirable qualities.

Midway through the play, Alan laments his role as a terrible student who faces a bleak and desolate future. He even considers himself an orphan. "Well, I have parents but they probably don't like me very much. I wouldn't either."

Evan, the football player, provides a contrast to Alan's low self-image. Evan saunters into class on test day, late. Although he apologizes for his tardiness, his only reason is that he was at football practice, and he says it in a way that indicates he trusts the teacher will not confront him. And the teacher does not. Instead, the teacher actually answers one test question for Evan, seeks Evan's agreement in the answer, and awards him with an A+—a higher-than-perfect grade. Evan has no reaction to this, which shows that he is accustomed to such treatment and feels entitled to it.

Teacher-Student Relationships

At first, the teacher in the play seems to be fair, someone with his students' best interests at heart. Stephen Gregg demonstrates this by having the teacher remind the students that if they studied the review sheets, they should feel confident that they will do well on the test.

On the other hand, Alan must feel his teacher is somewhat abusive of the power of his position, because he emphasizes the scope of the results of the test. After explaining that the test is a midterm that will impact each student's overall grade, he extrapolates further, saying grade point average is a major factor in determining where to go to college. He tells the students, "It might help if you

TOPICS FOR FURTHER STUDY

- John Hughes wrote and directed some of the most successful teen movies in the 1980s. Watch *The Breakfast Club*, a movie that brings together five students who have been sentenced to detention. Each student is a member of a different clique, much like the students in Gregg's play. Compare and contrast the characters in the play with those in the film. Using presentation manager software, such as Gliffy or another suitable application, prepare a presentation on the differences and similarities between the two casts of characters.

- Think about how the classroom and study resources have changed since the 1980s, when the play was written and published. Rewrite the one-act play, incorporating those changes. Be sure to take into consideration technology, classroom dynamics, and trends.

- Do you think *This Is a Test*, as it is written, is as effective today as it was during the 1980s? Craft your response in an essay or blog post, using portions of the text to support your viewpoint.

- Set up and design a blog on which you post a review of *This Is a Test*. Remember, it is not enough to say you like or do not like a piece of literature. Use specific evidence from the text to illustrate your point. Invite classmates to comment on your review.

- Read *Wake-Up Call*, another of Gregg's plays written about young adults. Compare the plot and characters to *This Is a Test*. Which seems more realistic? Which play do you prefer, and why? Write a short paper in response to these questions.

- Think about the play if Alan was a girl. What changes? Do any issues become more important or any less so? Write an essay that highlights the changes that you think would need to be made to the plot and dialogue.

didn't think of this as a test so much as you think of it as your future." Of course, this scene turns out to be part of a dream sequence, and so its accuracy as representative of reality is questionable. It does, however, reflect a general student perception of many teachers, which is that they can, and do, make up rules arbitrarily.

Another example of this is the teacher's relationship with Evan, the football star. Alan obviously feels that students like Evan receive special treatment, that there is a set of (more lenient) rules that apply just to them because they are talented in sports. The teacher does not make Evan take the test, but then tells him he did a great job. When Alan questions the teacher's integrity, the teacher turns on Evan: "Alan, are you doubting the word of one of your classmates?" When Alan hesitates to accuse Evan further, the teacher continues, "Evan always gets hundreds. You know that." This conversation would be highly unlikely, as would the scene that prompted it. Yet this is how Alan perceives the relationship between Evan and the teacher. By the end of the play, the teacher seems to prefer everyone else to Alan.

STYLE

One-Act Play

This Is a Test was appropriately written as a one-act play rather than a full-length drama. The point of this particular play—that some students suffer great angst when faced with taking a test—works well as a shorter production. Had the playwright written it as a longer piece, he would have had to incorporate more action, or perhaps added a few secondary story lines, which would have diluted the impact of the play.

As he tried to study, his mind wandered and he daydreamed. (*Andrey Shadrin / Shutterstock.com*)

There is a type of writing called flash fiction, generally a story that is written in about one thousand words. That the author tells an entire story in a very brief span, and the fact that it is so short and concise, helps emphasize the theme. *This Is a Test* is just like that. The form contributes to the play's impact.

The one-act form also contributes to the viewer's ability to stay focused from start to finish. Because the play is short, it does not run the risk of losing its audience as easily as a longer play might. And because the play was written for both a young-adult cast and audience, the short form makes sense.

Dream Sequence

It isn't until almost the end of the play that viewers understand that the classroom scene is part of Alan's dream. In making it a dream, Gregg makes all scenarios possible, even if they would not likely occur in reality. For example, it is almost certain that a teacher would never give a midterm test and then tell students he just does not feel like putting the time and effort into grading it, to then give more assignments and

tests, thus having to grade more papers. Yet that is what Alan's teacher does. In order to avoid having to go through the effort of that process, the teacher announces, "we'll just say that whatever grade you got here is the grade you get for the course."

As part of the dream, the Chorus voices work together to provide a sort of surreal feel to Alan's experience on test day. The Chorus performs a rote exercise traditionally used in drama classes to increase the participants' ability to pay attention. One voice calls out the name of an object and the others repeat that name. Alan, having studied all night in lieu of sleeping, is exhausted on test day. At first, the Chorus voices point out obvious objects—a desk, a phone, a book and so on—but toward the end, the voices become almost taunting, pointing out Alan's dull life, his hopeless future, his pathetic town.

First-Person Narrative

Although there is no official narrator for the play, the experience belongs to Alan. He is a member of the cast, a character on the stage, but he is also clearly the main character and the

COMPARE & CONTRAST

- **1980s:** Students have very limited methods with which to cheat in the classroom. They can write answers on their skin or clothing or show each other their papers, but there are limited options.

  Today: Students can cheat in class using traditional methods, but they now have the added alternatives provided by technology. Students are able to store audio answers to test questions in their MP3 players, or text each other answers using their cell phones. They can also use cell phones to access the Internet and find answers to questions that perplex them. Powerful, high-tech calculators can store equations students expect to need on tests, and students are even able to beam answers to each other using the latest infrared or Bluetooth transmission capabilities on Personal Digital Assistants.

- **1980s:** Experts and researchers are only just beginning to study self-esteem and self-image and how these relate to teen performance in school, peer interaction, and health.

  Today: Teen self-esteem is under assault from sources that did not exist even a decade ago. Social networking sites like Facebook, MySpace, and Twitter have led to a new phenomenon known as cyberbullying.

- **1980s:** Teen angst is a common topic with filmmakers, and many are the top-grossing films of the decade. Some of the more popular titles include *The Breakfast Club*, *Sixteen Candles*, *Fast Times at Ridgemont High*, *Risky Business*, and *Ferris Bueller's Day Off*.

  Today: Directors and producers continue to profit from the timeless theme of teen angst in movies such as *Sleepover*, *Mean Girls*, *She's the Man*, *Thirteen*, *What a Girl Wants*, *Friday Night Lights*, and *Youth in Revolt*.

---

one through whom the audience sees the plot unfold. This is called first-person narrative.

When it is revealed that the first sequence of events in the classroom is Alan's dream, the audience realizes they are being allowed into his mind; they are seeing the world from his point of view. This makes the story more immediate, more personal. Thus, the feelings of test anxiety and paranoia and low self-image are made with greater impact.

HISTORICAL CONTEXT

Educational Reform
In the 1980s, education was the biggest budget item in every single state budget in America. Governors pushed for reform in two ways: control education costs or make education spending more cost-effective. In many instances, they wanted to achieve both goals. To do that, they looked to business leaders as partners in reforming the labor-intensive educational system.

As a result, incentive structures that traditionally improved business performance were adapted to the public education system. Although theoretically this strategy was expected to work, in reality, it served only to divide educators and public officials. Educators became more focused on inputs, which included resources for teacher training, salary increases, and resources for reducing class size. Policy makers focused more on accountability. To that end, schools across America began emphasizing standardized testing.

Because government funding of schools—and in some cases, teacher salary increases—began to be directly correlated to testing results, teachers and students alike felt pressure to perform. Standardized, required testing reached new

It seemed everyone was writing except Alan. (© *Martin Sheilds | Alamy*)

levels with the advent of state tests that determined graduation and promotion, and many educators and parents began to believe the tests were more concerned with accountability than with measuring the students' knowledge.

Cheating

Although no one wants to believe it, academic cheating has been, and continues to be, rampant. More than two thousand California high school students were surveyed in 1986, and 96.7 percent admitted they had seen others cheat. At that time, cheating was limited to using notes, gaining access to test questions, using signals, and copying from peer papers. By the turn of the century, students had access to technology such as cell phones that made cheating easier and sneakier. Research papers could be bought online, and students could frequent Web sites designed specifically to help users cheat.

Classroom Dynamics

In the 1980s, classrooms were still quite traditional in terms of how they were arranged as well

as the resources they had at their disposal. Lessons were taught using overhead projectors, chalkboards, textbooks, worksheets and handouts, and sometimes filmstrips. Desks were still primarily placed in rows from front to back, facing the chalkboard. In addition, students were encouraged to work independently. Group work was not the norm, but more like an occasional exercise, an alternative way of learning.

As decades passed, classroom structure changed. In many of today's classrooms, desks have been replaced by tables, or arranged so that students face one another, in pods. Students are commonly assigned projects in which they are expected to pair off or team up with several peers, each being delegated a portion of the work. Although they may be graded on individual effort, the project often receives one final grade, and every student who worked on it, regardless of individual effort, receives that grade.

Modes of learning have changed a great deal since the 1980s as well. Teachers are expected to incorporate technology into their lessons, even in subjects like physical education. To that end, students are assigned projects like creating a blog to journal their academic and personal goals. They might be expected to follow a teacher's postings on Twitter, or listen to math lessons on podcasts. Textbooks are now more commonly used only as a reference, and even that is becoming outdated because current information can be found in an instant on the Internet.

CRITICAL OVERVIEW

This Is a Test has not been heavily reviewed or critiqued despite its continuous popularity as a high school play production. On his official Web site, author Stephen Gregg admits, "If you've heard of me, it's more than likely because of this play, which was written in 1987."

Gregg considers the play an enriching experience but wishes he could change some aspects of it. One of those is a cultural reference to a television sitcom that was popular in the 1980s, *Mork and Mindy*. There is a good chance modern, young readers will not understand that reference, and it dates the play, limiting it in a way. Gregg encourages directors and producers to change that reference if they so desire.

The author confesses that the brief lines of Chinese are not, in fact, authentic. He made them up and, in hindsight, finds that culturally offensive. Again, he encourages performers to make up their own translations.

Mistakes and regrets aside, *This Is a Test* has its fair share of champions. In the introduction to the published version of the play, Kem Forbus of Graham Junior High in Texas says, "My cast and crew received a '1' rating for their performance at the Junior High Festival. The audience loved it. Alan is a student we can all identify with."

CRITICISM

Rebecca Valentine

Valentine is a self-employed writer with an extensive background in literary analysis and theory. In the following essay, she posits that the strength of This Is a Test *resides more in its form than its content.*

Decades after it was written and initially published, Gregg's one-act play *This Is a Test* is still being regularly performed in high schools throughout America. The play's simplicity is deceptive, as it seems, on the surface, to be nothing more than a bare-bones story, and an age-old one at that: student panics on test day. But that simplicity is at the core of this play's strength. What makes *This Is a Test* work is not the content of the play, but its style. The play is nothing more than a framework on which to build an experience that virtually every person involved in the play—cast member or audience member—has survived.

The fact that *This Is a Test* continues to be interpreted and performed on a regular basis despite the passing of time signifies its value to both players and viewers alike. Yet that value does not lie in what Gregg is saying. Indeed, the work belongs to a rookie writer, someone a mere two years out of college. In many ways, when Gregg *does* say something, it imposes limitations on the work.

For example, by his own admission, the playwright wishes he had not included references that date the play. Mentioning the television sitcom *Mork and Mindy*, which aired on ABC from 1978 through 1982, puts the play in a very specific time frame. As it continues to be produced into the twenty-first century, only a select few will know what a Mork is. Likewise, Gregg includes the use of blue books, a testing tool in which students write their answers (often an essay) that is used primarily at colleges, universities, and other post-secondary institutions. Most teen actors and even most adult viewers probably would not understand the reference or what the use of multiple blue books for one test signifies about a student.

Another example of dated cultural references appears in the very opening of the play. Gregg sets the stage: "There is a high-pitched whine of the type that comes on the television during the emergency broadcast system tests." The Emergency Broadcast System (EBS) was developed as a means through which the President of the United States could communicate quickly with the public in the event of war or national crisis. Introduced in 1963, it was used until 1997, when it was replaced with the Emergency Alert System. Although the system was never used for national emergency, it did go off more than 20,000 times in a twenty-year period

WHAT DO I READ NEXT?

- Earl Hipp's 2008 book *Fighting Invisible Tigers: Stress Management for Teens* provides ten techniques proven to help teens reduce stress. In addition to introducing readers of this young-adult reference to relaxation exercises, Hipp discusses time management strategies and takes time to explain how stress pushes adolescents to the edge of their coping abilities.

- Nobuo K. Shimahara's 2001 reference volume *Teaching in Japan* gives firsthand accounts of the cultural differences and sociopolitical influences of Japan's educational system over the last two decades.

- *The Largest Elizabeth in the World* is Gregg's 1995 play about a girl who grows to be seventeen feet tall. He originally wrote two versions of the story, one significantly longer than the other. Although he chose to publish the shorter version, he later regretted his decision and now makes the longer version available on his Web site.

- Part of the "FAQ: Teen Life" series, Frances O'Connor's 2009 audiobook *Frequently Asked Questions about Academic Anxiety* examines the causes and warning signs of anxiety and how to manage them.

- In *Closing the Racial Academic Achievement Gap* (2006), Matthew Lynch explores the factors involved in the educational achievement gap between white and African American students. Lynch goes beyond pointing out the problems to offering possible solutions to this disparity.

- Sue Townsend investigates the serious topic of teen angst with a sense of humor in her 2003 young-adult novel *The Secret Diary of Adrian Mole, Aged 13 3/4*. The British teen has an opinion on every topic and is not afraid to voice it as he learns to navigate the tricky waters of adolescence.

- Ethicist Bruce Weinstein has written *Is It Still Cheating if I Don't Get Caught?* (2009), an exploration of the ethical ramifications of cheating. He draws his conclusions on other topics as well—social networking, drugs, bullying—based on five principles. Do no harm, be fair, love, respect others, and make things better when possible. This guide is written for a high-school audience.

- *Climb On! Dynamic Strategies for Teen Success* (2005) is John Beede's motivational guide for teens who want to reach their full potential but are not quite sure how to go about it. Beede provides practical advice, tips, and exercises for young people to take those first steps on the journey to self-fulfillment. Beede is a frequent speaker at Future Business Leaders of America dinners and conventions.

---

to announce severe weather conditions and to alert viewers to civil emergency messages.

The system was tested weekly. Each activation of the EBS test system began with a cacophonous attention signal that would interrupt any television program viewers might be watching. It was an ear-splitting sound, almost painful. It would immediately be followed by a deep male voice reciting a variation of this message: "This is a test. For the next sixty seconds, this station will conduct a test of the Emergency Broadcast

System. This is only a test." This is the message Gregg used to write the first speaking lines of his play, spoken by the Voice.

The problem with this, as in other examples, is that younger actors and audience members will not pick up on the humor Gregg uses because they may not understand the reference. Even the title of the play is based on the EBS tests, though it is quite possible, if not probable, that teens do not understand or realize that. So the nuance is lost.

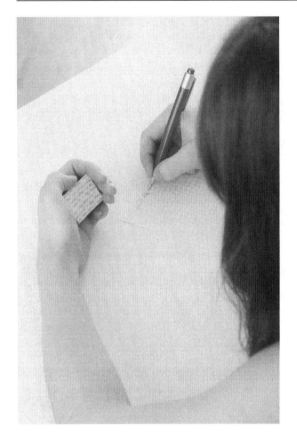

He could see she was cheating. *(Piotr Marcinski / Shutterstock.com)*

Where Gregg scores points with young actors and their frustrated directors is in the structure and style of his play. It is brief; one act is short enough that even the most easily distracted youth can focus through to the end. But Gregg goes a step further and encourages drama clubs and groups to improvise according to their own immediate needs, microculture, and desires.

One of the most obvious ways in which he does this is by creating characters that can be played as male or female. There is no language that cannot be adjusted, no gender stereotypes that must be addressed. Should Evan become Ava, she can carry a volleyball in her backpack instead of a football. If Alan becomes Alana, she can struggle even further with fashion issues. Every character is easily adaptable to fit any actor. And seeing as how this is not a physically challenging play production, actors with physical disabilities can easily play a role.

But the possibilities extend beyond casting. The scene in which everyone but Alan is cheating

is written to reflect traditional methods of cheating, such as copying off peer papers and holding up signs while making hand signals. A modern acting troupe could take that scene much further and have students cheating using text messages or PDAs that have tones or even a vibrating buzz that, when sent back and forth, sounds out a melody line popular with today's teens. Similarly, instead of having Lois, Chris, and Pat request blue books to the tune of "Hallelujah,"— a traditional classic that youth may be familiar with but which can't be counted on—they could make the request sung to the tune of a more current song teens would recognize.

By keeping his play simple, Gregg opened up a world of possibilities in terms of interpretation and improvisation of his play, *This Is a Test*.

Source: Rebecca Valentine, Critical Essay on *This Is a Test*, in *Drama for Students*, Gale, Cengage Learning, 2011.

Melinda Long

In the following review, Long discusses performances of three of Gregg's one-act plays.

This weekend, No Refund Theatre depicts the more disturbing events of everyday life.

NRT will be performing *Poor Little Lambs*, *Wake-Up Call*, and *Zero-Sum Mind*, three one-act plays by play writer Stephen Gregg.

Gregg, a native of Albuquerque, New Mexico, graduated from [Stanford] University in 1985. His one-act play *This is a Test* has been the most produced high school one-act play in the country for the last 12 years.

This weekend's first one-act, *Poor Little Lambs*, involves a grandmother and her five grandchildren sharing an afternoon at a baseball game. The grandchildren mock and tease the grandmother throughout the afternoon and create a game to keep points on who can make the grandmother give new details to the same stories she tells over and over again.

In the end, the grandmother proves that she is not as senile as the grandchildren seem to think.

"At first my character is used to being the grandmother, but in the end she comes out victorious," said Jessica Summers, who plays the role of the grandmother.

The second one-act, *Wake-Up Call*, is about a high school boy Joe, who cannot discern the difference between fantasy and reality. In the play, Joe's girlfriend, Rochelle, develops a plan to poison her father and asks for Joe's help. When Joe awakes, his mother comforts him before coming on to him and lewdly making passes toward him.

Joe is played by Jon Trump, a first time actor for the NRT. Trump auditioned for this particular character because he found the play-wright to be interesting.

"My character is pretty challenging," Trump said. "I have never been hit on by my mom."

As the night goes on, the acts get progressively more absurd, said Adam Kapp, director of the plays.

The third one-act, *Zero-Sum Mind*, is set in the future. In the play, every time the actors learn something, they forget something else. Throughout the play, the characters try to have conversations without learning anything new. One particular character learns so much that she forgets how to breathe.

Kapp received some helpful advice from the writer Gregg by keeping in contact with him throughout the rehearsals leading up to the play.

"He was very responsive and offered me advice and ideas that he has tried before," Kapp said. "I invited him to the play but I do not expect him to come."

This weekend's acts are all dark comedy, involving the theatre of the absurd. It should be good for a laugh, said Kapp. . . .

Source: Melinda Long, "Acts of Absurdity," in *Daily Collegian Online*, March 22, 2002.

Diana Spinrad

In the following excerpt, Spinrad describes The Largest Elizabeth in the World *as a hilarious absurdist fantasy.*

Playwright Stephen Gregg's *The Largest Elizabeth in the World* is a hilarious absurdist fantasy about a teenage girl who grows to be 50 feet tall. Gregg, who also penned Griffin's successful *Sex Lives of Superheroes*, produced last season, displays a remarkable talent for merging the ridiculous and the mundane. He creates characters with a wealth of quirks and puts them in bizarre situations, yet manages to ground his plays in a basic honesty about human nature. *The Largest Elizabeth in the World* is a kind of teen-oriented "Woody Allen meets Edward Scissorhands."

Gregg seems to have taken the idea for the show from the Roches song of the same name. In the song, "Elizabeth" refers to a prissy schmuck; the opening line is "Don't you sometimes feel like the largest Elizabeth in the world? / Usually at a time when the boy is indifferent to the girl." Gregg translates "largest Elizabeth" literally, and sticks with the song's major theme: "Wouldn't you like to feel like yourself after suffering so many years?"

It's a play about self-discovery and adolescent awkwardness, teen rebellion and the acceptance of people who are different. Its flaw is that it is about all those things and more—grief at the loss of a loved one, budding sexuality, possibly even eating disorders—but Gregg never clarifies the play's main point. Elizabeth's growth spurt seems a metaphor, but for what?

Still, Griffin Theatre's production makes the journey to the disappointing ending a delightful one, so much so that the play's final ambiguity almost doesn't matter. Christopher L. Sheley's set combines suburban reality with cartoon cutouts of strangely painted palm trees, creating a world in which the play's ludicrous and ordinary elements are equally at home. William J. Massolia's sound design emphasizes the silly. His combination of pop tunes ("Big Girls Don't Cry") and boppy instrumentals that sound like scene-change music for *My Three Sons* had me laughing throughout.

Director Neil Wilson has a flair for the absurd that shows in a myriad of ways. Elizabeth's growth is achieved with ingenious staging and some simple props. Wilson allows his talented young actors to flaunt their oddity but never to push it to the point of inanity. Somehow each strange character is a fully rounded human being.

Dawn-Christian Maxey is superb as Amanda, the nasty sister. A toned-down Sandra Bernhardt, she has a menacing voice and lust for torment that would make her right at home in the Addams family. Laurel Holloman as Elizabeth is a completely believable teenager, a good girl who's trying to discover her own voice. The nuances of her portrayal—more like film than stage acting—emphasize her otherness in a world of broadly played characters. G. Scott Thomas and Debra Rich turn in strong performances as the aggravating father and wacky neighbor, who strike up an oddly touching romance over candy corn. Wayne E. Pyle is a bit one-dimensional as Joseph, Elizabeth's nerdy love interest, but as the play gets wilder Pyle seems to find his place, and by his earnest final moments he's extremely winning. . . .

Source: Diana Spinrad, Reviews of *The Largest Elizabeth in the World/Sovietiquette: My Days in Russia*, in *Chicago Reader*, December 12, 1991.

B. Roland Lewis

In the following essay, Lewis maintains that one-act plays justify themselves as worthwhile studies of human life and character.

THE ONE-ACT PLAY AS A DRAMATIC TYPE

Students of literature and of life are quite agreed that both the subject-matter and the technique of any literary product are often very largely determined by the prevailing social conditions of the period during which it has been produced. There is frequently prevailing mode and convention in literary activity quite as much as there is in the current social decorum. To-day it is not the three-act play nor the five-act play that is the centre of interest in dramatic expression: it is the *One-act play*,—not a new form of course, but one that, despite unsympathetic animadversion, challenges attention.

Theatre managers, the general theatre-going public, actors, playwrights, and even the professors in the University, recognize its presence. It is to be observed, too, that no apology is being offered for the better sort of contemporary One-act plays, and indeed none is needed. They justify themselves as worthwhile studies of human life and character. Their effectiveness as a form of dramatic expression is their own justification for being. They cannot be written, any more than can the three-act form, without adequate first-hand acquaintance with life. A good many lack dramatic style and value—and so do many of the longer plays—but a surprisingly large number possess them. The One-act play can no longer be dismissed, with a lofty wave of the academic hand, as of no consequence. It is with us; and it warrants being taken seriously.

The One-act play is claiming recognition as a specific dramatic type. The short-story, and likewise the novel, was once an embryo and an experiment; but no enlightened person, nowadays, would care to hold that it has not developed into a worthy literary type. Its popularity is attested by the fact that most of the contemporary fiction writers have essayed it. This shorter form

> IN ITS FINISHED AND MORE SIGNIFICANT FORM IT IS NOT A 'PLAYLET,' NOR A 'SKETCH,' NOR A SO-CALLED 'SKIT,' NOR A PLAY THAT IS MERELY SHORT."

of fiction was once apologetic, and that not so many years ago; but it has come unto its own and now enjoys the recognition of being a distinctive type of prose narrative. What the One-act play asks is not an advocate or a defender. It asks opportunity for development! Its possibilities are as much greater than the short-story as the drama is greater than the novel. The One-act play is no longer wholly an experiment; it is succeeding in high places. And the signs of the times are that at a date not far distant, perhaps already arrived, this form of drama will stand erect and take its place among the significant types of literary expression.

It is either lack of acquaintance with the One-act play or lack of sympathy for the unconventional, though ever so worthy, in drama that some students of dramatic art have failed to appreciate the real nature and value of this shorter form. Five years ago the One-act play was not so conspicuous as it is now; hence there may have been reason for William Archer's saying, in his book on Play-Making where he discusses the routine of composition, "Go-as-you-please composition may be possible for the novelist, perhaps even for the writer of a one-act play, a mere piece of dialogue, etc." Nothing could be more unsympathetic and more from the point than this. If the One-act play, in its better form, is anything at all it is not "go-as-you-please composition" and is not "a mere piece of dialogue." "But the one-act play," says Walter Prichard Eaton, "has an obvious right to existence, as much as the short-story, and there are plentiful proofs that it can be terse, vivid and significant." Again, he holds, "It is the one-act play in our country to-day—which will bear the most watching for signs of imagination and for flashes of insight and interpretative significance." Sir James M. Barrie's "*The Twelve-Pound Look*," Marion Craig Wentworth's

"*War Brides*," Fenn and Price's "*'Op-o'-Me-Thumb*," William Butler Yeats's "*The Hour-Glass*," Zona Gale's "*Neighbors*," Paul Hervieu's "*Modesty*," August Strindberg's "*Facing Death*," Edward Goodman's "*Eugenically Speaking*," Lord Dunsany's "*The Glittering Gate*" and "*The Lost Silk Hat*," George Cram Cook and Susan Glaspell's "*Suppressed Desires*," Alice Gerstenberg's "*Overtones*," and many others that could well be listed, are not "go-as-you-please composition" and are not "a mere piece of dialogue."

The One-act play is not merely a thing of practice for the amateur and the novice. A critic of no mean value, in a current volume on play-writing, has asserted that the One-act play offers the amateur the easiest opportunity for testing his skill, and that the time and the labor involved in its composition is perhaps less than a fourth or a fifth of that demanded for a five-act drama. "Beginners," he says, "will do well to practise the various forms of composition in the brief sketch, before venturing upon the full fledged play." It is quite well known that some good plays have been written in a few days, others have required months and even years of arduous labor. Some novels have been quickly composed; whereas some short-stories have required the undivided attention of the author for weeks and months. The time element for composing a One-act play, or any other form of literature, is wholly relative; and comparisons of any kind are invidious. Those who have written One-act plays give ample testimony that their composition is not a matter of time but a matter as serious and important as the composition of any other form. And to recommend to amateurs that they try out their powers by practising with the One-act form with the view that the One-act piece is only a stepping-stone to the three-act form, is only to reveal one's ignorance of the constructive problem involved in the shorter type of dramatic composition. In individual cases, no doubt the advice is sound; but to urge it as a general recommendation is to relegate the One-act play into a category where it does not belong. There is not a writer of the short-story, with all its richness of subject-matter and technical excellence, but would resent any insistence that the prospective novelist would do well to begin on the short-story as a stepping-stone to novel-writing. The short-story is a distinctive type unto itself, and proficiency therein is no guarantee of a similar result in the novel if the one is to be used as apprenticeship for the

other. Here again comparisons are futile. Indeed, the One-act play, like the short-story, is a type unto itself; and to suggest that the prospective playwright use the One-act play only as a thing on which to practise before attempting the larger form, is, in but exceptional individual cases, almost an insult to the type.

Another writer of a recent volume on dramaturgy, in a chapter on the One-act play, says that as used in the theatre to-day such plays may roughly be divided "into curtain-raisers, vaudeville sketches, and a third class suitable for amateur theatricals." It is granted that "playlets" and "dramatic skits"—for several centuries too—have frequently been used thus, and that they are still being used in a number of places. But there has come into existence a number of One-act plays that are *not* curtain raisers, *not* vaudeville sketches, and *not* material merely for amateur theatricals. The mere fact that a good One-act play does appear in these capacities is in itself no evidence against the play of lack of value. Indeed, many contemporary first-class One-act plays do reach these places and some have their origin in these ways; but there is also a conspicuous group that have not had their origin in vaudeville as such and have not appeared in more or less untoward places. On the contrary, they have been presented in high-places successfully and have, again and again, received the plaudits of the multitude. The day when the One-act play is to be used only as a "curtain-raiser," an "after-piece," a "vaudeville skit," or "amateur theatricals," is rapidly coming to an end; not that they will never again appear there but that they are coming unto their own even as the short-story has come unto its own. Hermann Sudermann's "*Fritschen*," Fenn and Price's "*'Op-o'-Me-Thumb*," Paul Hervieu's "*Modesty*," Anton Tchekov's "*A Marriage Proposal*," Sir James M. Barrie's "*The Twelve-Pound Look*," John Millington Synge's "*Riders to the Sea*," are not necessarily conventional vaudeville material; they are fore-runners and examples of what gives promise of being a significant dramatic product of a not far-off future.

To-day, the greatest obstacles to the One-act play are the conventions of the stage and of the longer forms of dramatic writing. The conventional objection that an audience cannot easily adjust itself to the changing scenes of a bill of One-act plays for an evening's performance is ridiculous and not founded on psychological fact. One has yet to hear a music-lover report that he was unable to appreciate a concert of miscellaneous numbers because he could not adjust himself psychologically to the various parts of the programme. The auditor unconsciously adjusts himself, and that, too, without any loss of appreciation. Any theory to the contrary is not true to human experience. Again, so far as careful observation and detailed inquiry can determine, no vaudeville audience experiences any difficulty in adjusting itself to the various acts of a variety bill. A theatre audience has something of the characteristics of a crowd, and, as such, is always wholly receptive to any stimulus, varied and changing though it be. Vaudeville stunts are usually so complete in themselves and often constructed with such artistry that each part has the effect of completeness in itself; accordingly, the mind has no difficulty in adjusting itself to each one of the acts as it is presented. Whatever bit of shock there may be at the beginning of a following number, it is soon forgotten in the emotional response to the matter immediately in hand. Even in a long play of three or five acts, between which there are the respective intermissions and interruptions, one experiences little difficulty in re-adjusting oneself at the rise of each curtain; and this is true not only in plays in which the story is not told in direct sequence of events, but also in plays between the acts of which there are often long lapses of time. One-act plays, when well done, are masterpieces of technical construction; they are individual and complete units; and an audience, receptive in mind rather than reflective and active, makes adjustment to any change with little conscious effort. Indeed, the objection to an evening bill of One-act plays, on the ground that a theatre group is not able easily to adjust itself to the several plays, is a make-believe and conventional one. It is not true to the psychological facts in the case, and human experience disproves it, all pedantic theories to the contrary notwithstanding.

Another objection made to the One-act play is the conventional one that it is too small to be of any value. Too frequently literary critics have been almost obsessed with the idea that bigness or large complexity are the first criteria by which a given product shall be judged. Indeed, Milton is known by his "*Paradise Lost*," not by his "Comus" and minor poems; Dante, by his "*Divina Commedia*" and not by his supposedly minor products. The sympathetic student, however,

knows that in many cases the really superior values do not always lie in the large products of a man of letters but often in the smaller and more highly artistic bits of work. Largeness of conception or bigness of structure are in themselves no guarantee of literary excellence. A literary product is essentially a work of art; whether it be wrought out on a large scale or on a small one is quite another matter. The lyric is quite as much an art form as is the epic. The cameo is as much an art product and has as much claim to be recognized as has the statue; the etching is often superior in art values to the larger painting; the short-story is as much a literary type as is the larger novel; and the One-act play must not be lightly thrown aside just because it happens to be smaller than the three-act form. Art of any kind must not be judged in the light of the cult of mere bigness.

THE TECHNIQUE OF THE ONE-ACT PLAY

The One-act play, then, needs no apology for its being. In its finished and more significant form it is not a "playlet," nor a "sketch," nor a so-called "skit," nor a play that is merely short. These seldom or never aim at a definite and unmistakable unity either in purpose or in construction; they are not art. On the other hand, the One-act play has for its end a singleness of impression—a definite artistic effect. The One-act form is to the longer dramatic piece what the highly developed short-story is to the novel. In either case, the two forms have much in common, but the shorter types, because of their greater economy of means and material, are more intent upon producing the singleness of effect so characteristic of their function.

A One-act play is not necessarily short. Usually it is rather short because it presents but a single dramatic situation or crisis and because it aims at a singleness of effect in comparatively short compass. While economy of material and of time are always considerations, the length of the One-act piece depends very largely upon the nature of the dramatic situation with which it deals. To handle it most effectively may require fifteen pages or fifty, the performance thereof may require thirty minutes or the larger part of an hour. The length of the One-act form is wholly relative. If the playwright, in constructing his play, keeps in mind that with but a few characters and with but a single situation wrought out to a crucial moment and that with the greatest economy of material and means, he is to secure a definite and single dramatic effect, the length of the play will not go far wrong. The material and purpose of Sir James M. Barrie's "*The Twelve-Pound Look*" are somewhat different from those of Mary Aldis's "*Extreme Unction*"; the former requires some forty pages for its handling while the latter needs but a scarce fifteen; and, in the performance thereof, the one acts for the better part of an hour, whereas the other is complete within thirty or thirty-five minutes,—yet both are unmistakably good One-act plays. The One-act form, therefore, is not circumscribed by a more or less definite and conventional time limit as is the three-act form.

Technically considered, the One-act play is just as much a distinctive dramatic problem as is the longer form. In either case, the playwright aims so to handle his material as to provoke interest and emotional response from the audience. Since the one form is characteristically shorter than the other and since the one is, because of the shorter time and space at its disposal, obliged to exercise, to the highest degree, economy of material and of means, it follows that, while both may have much in common, the dramaturgy of the one is somewhat different from that of the other. The One-act form must, as it were, be presented in a "single sitting"; it must start at the beginning with certain definite elements and pass quickly and effectively to the end without a halt or a digression. In the three-act play there is often something of a break in the sequence. The longer form, composed as it is of three, four or five acts, is conceived in a series of units each one of which bears on the larger encompassing theme. Each act has its own dramatic value and likewise has its own dramatic relation to the whole play. In the case of the One-act piece, there is but one consideration—the material and method immediately in hand. To construct one building so as to procure a unified and artistic effect is one problem; and to construct several, each one of which is something of a problem in itself, and at the same time to arrange them in a group that will produce a unity of impression, is another and different consideration. The One-act play, like the short-story, has a technique characteristically its own.

Not only is the technical problem in the One-act form distinct from that of the three-act form, it is also, in many ways, more exacting and more difficult. The play must begin at once, and, with but a minimum of exposition, must get

under way and move rapidly and effectively to a crucial moment, and must terminate at the psychologically opportune time. Though the time and space are relatively limited, the dramatic picture and situation must be complete in itself; there must be a singleness of impression. Whatever is done must be done quickly, deftly, and with a master hand. The One-act play is, at its best, the most finished, the most artistic, and the most closely wrought of dramatic forms. It thus manifests a higher art and perfection of technique than the longer play and equals the best drama in constructive excellence. Technique, therefore, is one of its prime considerations; and therein lies one of its difficult problems.

The One-act play is well-made or it is nothing at all. Drama of any kind, when really effective, is usually well-made. A careful analysis of Sir James M. Barrie's "*The Twelve-Pound Look*," Lord Dunsany's "*The Lost Silk Hat*," Paul Hervieu's "*Modesty*," George Cram Cook and Susan Glaspell's "*Suppressed Desires*," and William Butler Yeats's "*The Hour-Glass*," will reveal that these representative One-act plays are not only well-made but are also genuine art. A good One-act play is not a mere mechanical *tour de force*: mechanics and artistry it has of course, but it is also a bit of real dramatic art. A finished cameo is quite as much a work of art as is the finished statue; yet both have mechanics and design in their structure; and probably those of the cameo are more deft and more highly specialized than those of the full-sized statue, because the work has been done under more restricted conditions. The One-act play is to the longer dramatic form what the delicately wrought cameo is to the statue; and just in proportion as the cameo requires much more delicate workmanship than does the statue, so the One-act play must be well-made or the chances are that it will not be a genuine art product.

Naturally the material of the One-act form is somewhat episodical. No whole life's story can be treated adequately, no complex plot can be entertained. Unlike the longer form, it shows not the whole man—except by passing hint—but a significant moment or experience, a significant character-trait. However vividly this chosen moment may be interpreted,—and the One-act play must be vivid,—much will still be left to the imagination. It is the aim of the One-act form to trace the causal relations of but one circumstance, so that this circumstance may be intensified and significant. The writer of the One-act play isolates so that he may throw the strong flash-light more searchingly on some one significant event, on some fundamental element of character, on some moving emotion. He deliberately presents in a vigorous, compressed, and suggestive way, a simplification and idealization of a particular part or aspect of life. He often opens but a momentary little vista of life, but it is so clear-cut and so significant that a whole life is often revealed thereby.

It must not be thought that because the One-act play deals with but one crisis or situation, it is weak and inconsequential; on the contrary, since only one event or situation can be emphasized, it follows that the writer is obliged to choose the one determining crisis which makes or mars the supreme struggle of a soul, the one great change or turning-point or end of a life-history. Such moments are the really vital material for drama; nothing affords more wonderful opportunity for striking analysis, for emotional stress, for the suggestion of a whole character sketched in the act of meeting its test. To segregate a bit of significant experience and to present a finished picture of its aspects and effects; to dissect a motive so searching and skilful that its very roots are laid bare; to detach a single figure from a dramatic sequence and portray a sketch of its character; to bring a series of actions into clear light in a sudden and brief human crisis; to tell a significant story briefly and with suggestion; to portray the humor of a person or an incident, or in a trice, to reveal the touch of tragedy resting like the finger of fate on an experience or on a character—these are some of the possibilities of the One-act play when handled by a master dramatist.

This shorter dramatic form, which is so effectively challenging attention, is cunningly wrought. In the hands of a novice it becomes weak and flabby; in the hands of a master workman it surpasses the short-story in value and possibilities. From first to last, it must be direct, concrete, highly concentrated, forceful, and closely wielded. Because of its strict technical requirements, it has developed a regularity and definiteness of constructive technique almost unknown to the other dramatic forms. Nowhere else must the literary artist be so conscious of his method of workmanship as in the One-act play. Even the sonnet in its most perfect form does not surpass it. Economy of material and method and

subtlety of treatment are essential to the singleness of effect sought. This constructive regularity of structure is, however, not a hindrance to beauty or to genuine power; all this but lends the charm of perfection. The sonnet and the cameo are admirable if for no other reason than their superior workmanship. The One-act play does not lose by any reason of its technical requirements; indeed this is one of its greatest assets and possibilities.

The One-act play is before us whether we will or no; it is presenting its claim for recognition as a specific dramatic form. Its possibilities are as much greater than those of the short-story as the drama is superior to the novel. At present the greatest obstacles to its full development and acceptance are the traditions and conventions of the longer dramatic form. Notwithstanding this, professional dramatists, actors, stage managers, and devotees of the drama have not hesitated to make use of the shorter form. Moreover, the zealous activities, in the One-act play, of high-class amateurs and semi-professionals in clubs, in Little Theatres, and in universities, are a most encouraging and healthful indication. The One-act play asks for but one thing,—opportunity for development!

Source: B. Roland Lewis, "The Case of the One-act Play: The One-act Play as a Dramatic Type," in *The Technique of the One-act Play*, John W. Luce, 1918, pp. 9–26.

SOURCES

Clabaugh, Gary K., and Edward G. Rozycki, "Cheating Trends," in *Preventing Cheating and Plagiarism*, 2nd ed., New Foundations Press, 2009, http://www.newfoundations.com/PREVPLAGWEB/CheatingTrends1.html (accessed September 5, 2010).

"Emergency Broadcast System Test (1981)," in *The Museum of Classic Chicago Television*, http://chicago.fuzzymemories.tv/screen.php?c=2970&m=xxwmaqxx&p=4 (accessed September 5, 2010).

Forbus, Kem, Review of *This Is a Test*, in *This Is a Test*, Dramatic Publishing, 1988, p. 4.

Gregg, Stephen, "About This Is a Test," on *Stephen Gregg Plays*, http://stephengreggplays.com/play_about_test.htm (accessed September 4, 2010).

———, *This Is a Test*, Dramatic Publishing, 1988.

Ravitch, Diane, "A Brief History of Testing and Accountability," in *Hoover Digest*, No. 4, 2002, http://www.hoover.org/publications/hoover-digest/article/7286 (accessed September 4, 2010).

FURTHER READING

Caldwell, Betty, *What's My Style? Test and Study Secrets for Procrastinating Teens*, Outskirts Press, 2009.

Caldwell translates research into accessible skills for the student who does well in class but tends to struggle on tests, who masters complex issues but cannot untangle the simple ones, and who may be a gifted learner.

Friedman, Lise, and Mary Dowdle, *Break a Leg! The Kid's Guide to Acting and Stagecraft*, Workman Publishing, 2002.

The authors provide a how-to guide for students in grades four through ten and cover topics such as acting techniques, overcoming stage fright, and how to analyze scripts. For those interested, they take readers backstage and discuss acting as a career.

Gallo, Donald R., ed., *Center Stage: One-Act Plays for Teenage Readers and Actors*, HarperCollins, 1991.

Gallo has pulled together ten short plays written for—and to be performed by—young-adult audiences. The plays range from humorous to dramatic and are written so that students of all reading levels can enjoy the story lines.

Robinson, Stearn, and Tom Corbett, *Dreamer's Dictionary*, Grand Central Publishing, 1986.

Considered by many to be the expert resource on dreams, this reference has sold more than one million copies since its original publication. The authors explain, in detail, the hidden meaning of symbols and events in dreams.

Rozakis, Laurie, *Test-Taking Strategies and Study Skills for the Utterly Confused*, McGraw-Hill, 2002.

Written for a high-school and beyond audience, this study guide provides strategies for taking specific standardized tests such as the ACT and SAT, but also covers more general test-related topics, including time management, study habits, and memory enhancement.

SUGGESTED SEARCH TERMS

Stephen Gregg

This Is a Test AND Stephen Gregg

Stephen Gregg AND criticism

This Is a Test AND reviews

teens AND test anxiety

teens AND cheating

Stephen Gregg AND playwright

Stephen Gregg AND one-act play

Stephen Gregg AND drama

This Is a Test AND one-act play

Tom Thumb

HENRY FIELDING

1730

Henry Fielding's famous eighteenth-century satirical play *Tom Thumb* was first produced on April 24, 1730, at the Little Theatre in the Haymarket, located in Westminster, England. It was an instant success, running almost continually until June 22. It was first produced as a coda (or afterpiece) to Fielding's 1730 play *The Author's Farce; and The Pleasures of the Town.* The version of *Tom Thumb* that readers will find today includes two scenes (as well as a prologue and an epilogue) that were added about two weeks after the play's first performance. In Fielding's day, the extended version often circulated in print under the pseudonym Scriblerus Secundus. The play was further revised and expanded as *The Tragedy of Tragedies*, premiering on March 24, 1731. Today, however, the longer version is discussed and studied by scholars as an entirely separate work.

Tom Thumb is a two-act play that, on its surface, portrays Tom as a conquering hero returning to King Arthur's court. The king rewards Tom with his daughter's hand in marriage, and jealousies, murders, and general hijinks follow. The play, however, is more accurately described as a biting literary and political satire. In it, Fielding steals flowery lines from his fellow playwrights and inserts them out of context to maximize their comic effect while poking fun at their authors. The farce also pokes fun at heroic drama and at Sir Robert Walpole, who was de facto prime minister of England from 1721 to 1742.

Henry Fielding (The Library of Congress)

AUTHOR BIOGRAPHY

Fielding was born in Sharpham, England, on April 22, 1707. He was the firstborn son of Lieutenant Edmund Fielding and Sarah Gould. Both of his parents were the descendants of English gentry. He had many siblings, and his sister Sarah would also become a respected writer. Fielding attended Eton College from 1719 to 1724 and then moved to London. He briefly attended Leiden University in the Netherlands around 1728 before returning to London after running out of funds. Fielding then began to earn his primary income from his satirical plays. His first, *Love in Several Masques: A Comedy*, premiered in 1728. His 1730 play *The Author's Farce; and The Pleasures of the Town* was published under the pseudonym Scriblerus Secundus. *Tom Thumb* was first produced April 24, 1730, at the Little Theatre in the Haymarket, and a slightly revised version was printed a couple of weeks later under the Secundus name. The play was further revised and expanded as *The Tragedy of Tragedies*, and it premiered on March 24, 1731. Fielding's other early plays include *Rape upon Rape* (1730) and *The Covent-Garden Tragedy* (1732).

On November 28, 1734, Fielding married Charlotte Cradock, and the couple had four daughters and a son. His plays produced and published around this time include *Don Quixote in England: A Comedy* (1734), *The Universal Gallant; or, The Different Husbands: A Comedy* (1735), and *Tumble-Down Dick; or, Phaeton in the Suds* (1736). By 1737, Fielding had so angered Sir Robert Walpole with his critical satires that the Theatrical Licensing Act was passed, severely limiting Fielding's ability to continue publishing and staging his work. For a time, he worked as a lawyer to supplement his income. He also began writing novels, including *The History of the Adventures of Joseph Andrews and of His Friend Mr. Abraham Adams, Written in Imitation of the Manner of Cervantes, Author of Don Quixote* (1742) and *The Female Husband* (1746). Fielding's most famous novel, both during his lifetime and today, is *The History of Tom Jones, a Foundling*. The book was published in six volumes in 1749.

After ten years of marriage, Fielding's wife died, and he remarried amidst a scandal on November 27, 1747. His second wife, Mary Daniel, was Charlotte's former maid. She was pregnant at the time of the marriage, and the couple ultimately had two sons and three daughters. Fielding was named chief magistrate of London in 1748, and many of his published works during this time were political tracts and legal studies. He also founded the infamous *Covent-Garden Journal* in 1752. The biweekly periodical incited the "Paper War" of 1752–1753, which pitted writers against literary critics. Two years later, Fielding's health failed rapidly, and he was plagued by gout and asthma. He headed to Portugal in the hopes that the warmer, drier climate would ease his suffering, but he died in Lisbon on October 8, 1754. He is entombed in Lisbon at the *Cimeterio Ingles* (English Cemetery).

PLOT SUMMARY

Prologue

Tom Thumb is written in blank verse, a type of poetry that is typically written in iambic pentameter (a particular pattern of stressed and unstressed syllables) and without rhyme. The prologue is addressed directly to the audience and is meant to be delivered by the actor who plays Lord Grizzle. The speech advises audiences that

MEDIA ADAPTATIONS

- Although no exact media adaptations of *Tom Thumb* exist, Fielding's play features a character common to English folklore and fairy tale, and is a media adaptation in its own right. The character of Tom Thumb appears in numerous iterations throughout history, including a 2002 feature-length Walt Disney Video cartoon film, *The Adventures of Tom Thumb & Thumbelina*, directed by Glenn Chaika.

while plays often focus on mythical Greek and Roman heroes, England should turn its attention to its own mythical figures, specifically Tom Thumb, a folkloric figure who dates back to the sixteenth century and is said to stand no taller than his father's thumb.

Act 1

SCENE 1

The first scene opens in King Arthur's palace. Mr. Doodle says to Mr. Noodle that it is a beautiful day, as if all of nature is smiling. Mr. Noodle agrees, commenting that the great hero Tom Thumb is on his way. With him are a horde of ugly giants; all of them have been conquered and are in chains. Doodle declares that when Tom Thumb was born, so was the hero of England. Noodle reports that he has heard rumors that Tom has no bones, only gristle (cartilage and other tough tissues). Doodle wishes that all of England's subjects were made the same way, the better to vanquish their enemies. They hear trumpets and announce that the king is approaching. They go to prepare for his arrival.

SCENE 2

King Arthur announces that it is a happy day and no one should be sad, yet Queen Dollalolla is crying. She claims that they are tears of joy. The king declares that all his subjects should cry in the same manner, until his kingdom becomes an ocean. Doodle appears, hoping to discuss a petition with the king. Arthur states that it is a day of celebration and no business shall be conducted on such a day. Trumpets herald the arrival of Tom Thumb.

SCENE 3

The king thanks Tom for his services and offers to reward him, but Tom is humble and modest, replying that doing his duty to King Arthur is reward enough. The queen is clearly smitten by Tom Thumb, calling him "a lovely creature" in an aside (a comment that is supposed to be heard only by the audience).

King Arthur praises Tom further, and they discuss the captive giants, who are stationed outside the gates because they are too big to enter the palace. Arthur then declares that he wants Tom to marry his daughter, Princess Huncamunca. Tom accepts with joy, waxing poetic on her many charms. The queen objects to the betrothal, noting that Tom is of low birth. The king, however, feels that Tom is a better man than all of the world's greatest rulers. The queen continues to object, angering King Arthur. He says he will put her on trial before he allows her to become the man and make him the woman.

Noodle applauds the king. Doodle and Lord Grizzle are also present in this scene, though they do not speak. Tom rejoices at the thought of becoming Princess Huncamunca's husband. The group exits, leaving Lord Grizzle behind.

SCENE 4

Grizzle ridicules Tom and the court's favor of him. Like the queen, he feels that Tom is a peasant not worthy of the honors bestowed upon him.

SCENE 5

Queen Dollalolla finds Lord Grizzle and they share their mutual dislike for Tom. Secretly, of course, the queen is upset because she wants Tom to be her lover. She notes that Tom is an illegitimate child who is not fit to inherit the throne. Grizzle and the queen plot against him. Grizzle wants to kill Tom, but the queen is hesitant. She does not know how they can conquer the man who conquered the giants. Grizzle thinks that the giants are a ruse; he observes that no one has even seen them.

The queen is shocked at Grizzle's audacity. She says he is a jealous traitor and a dog. She plots with him nevertheless, commenting as though he were a dog, "I use thee."

SCENE 6

The queen is alone, and she delivers a six-teen-line monologue (continuous speech given by one actor) in which she reveals her love for Tom but also her fear for her own virtue. She hopes that her husband will die so she can marry Tom Thumb and have both her love and her honor.

Act 2

SCENE 1

The bailiff and his follower wish that the law of harsh justice ruled the land in place of lawyers and reason. They step aside as Lord Noodle passes, and they indicate that they are plotting against him.

SCENE 2

Tom Thumb confides to Noodle that while he loves Huncamunca, he is afraid to get married. He says his grandmother warned him against marriage. Lord Noodle chides Tom, calling him a great warrior who is afraid of his own grandmother. He describes the pleasures and benefits of marriage and convinces Tom to wed. The bailiff appears (along with his follower) and arrests Noodle as a debtor. Tom is enraged and vows to take his revenge.

Tom Thumb kills the bailiff and his follower. He says all bailiffs should follow suit (that is, die) so that all debtors may go free.

SCENE 3

The scene takes place in Princess Huncamunca's rooms. She is lovesick over Tom, and she asks her maid Cleora to sing and distract her. Cleora does so, but Huncamunca continues to pine for Tom. Her maid Mustacha teases her for being in love with a commoner.

SCENE 4

The king enters and demands to be alone with his daughter. The maids leave, and King Arthur asks Princess Huncamunca why she has been so sad lately. The princess replies that she is in need of a husband, and the king tells her she has been promised to Tom Thumb. Huncamunca's joy is immediately apparent to the king, and she admits that she is indeed in love with Tom.

SCENE 5

Doodle enters and announces that Tom Thumb is dead. Huncamunca faints, and the men revive her with the rum she hides under her bed. In shock and disbelief, the king demands to see the doctors who tended to Tom.

SCENE 6

Two physicians are presented to the king by Doodle. They both attended to Tom, and the first says that Tom died of distemper. The other disagrees: "He complained of a Pain in his Arm, I would have immediately cut off his Arm, and have laid open his head." The king pokes holes in both of the doctors' arguments.

SCENE 7

Tom Thumb enters, searching for Huncamunca. He heard a rumor that she has died. The king is overjoyed to see him, and the physicians observe that their cures have apparently worked after all.

SCENE 8

Noodle appears and informs King Arthur that there are rumors of a plot to poison Tom. He says that a monkey dressed as Tom was mistakenly poisoned instead. This is the "Tom" that the doctors tended to, and the King derides them for not noticing the difference between a monkey and a tiny man.

The king wants to head to the temple so that Tom Thumb and Princess Huncamunca can be married right away. He hopes that they will have many children. The king desires his kingdom to be peopled by several generations of Tom Thumbs. He compares this process to that of a maggot in cheese, multiplying until the cheese is infested with maggots.

Tom is so overjoyed at the thought of marrying Huncamunca that he says, "I have lost myself." Huncamunca responds: "Forbid it, all the Stars; for you're so small, / That were you lost, you'd find your self no more."

SCENE 9

The doctors argue nonsensically over their respective diagnoses of "Tom."

SCENE 10

Queen Dollalolla laments her impending loss of Tom Thumb, but she mentions another hero who is worthy of her attentions. She hears a loud noise and wonders what it can be.

SCENE 11

The king, queen, and princess are gathered together with their court and Huncamunca's maids. King Arthur declares that all prisoners and debtors should be freed and their debts paid. He declares a celebration for Tom and Huncamunca's wedding day. A dance commences.

SCENE 12

Noodle and Grizzle enter, and Noodle tells the king he saw a cow swallow Tom Thumb whole. In an aside, Grizzle curses the cow for killing Tom; he wanted to take vengeance on Tom himself. The king announces that all the prisoners should be recaptured and all of their debts reinstated.

The ghost of Tom Thumb appears and confirms that he was indeed swallowed by the cow. Lord Grizzle is overjoyed at once again having his vengeance, and he promptly kills Tom's ghost. Enraged, Huncamunca kills Grizzle. Doodle is outraged that the princess has killed Lord Grizzle, so he kills her. The queen is maddened by the death of her daughter, and she murders Doodle. Noodle responds by killing the queen. Cleora steps forward and kills Noodle, but Mustacha cries that Cleora has killed her lover, and so Mustacha slays her. The king calls Mustacha a murderess and strikes her dead. He then takes his own life. As he dies, he says: "Kings, Queens, and Knaves throw one another down / . . . So all our Pack upon the Floor is cast, / And all I boast is, that I fall the last."

Epilogue

The epilogue is delivered by Tom Thumb, who declares that he has been revived from the dead once again. He says he fears critics more than cows or Lord Grizzle's dagger. Although he is small, he says, the world is peopled with little men (here, "little" means unimportant). He says that while women may think him too tiny to love, he has a large soul and would be a good companion.

CHARACTERS

King Arthur

King Arthur is the ruler of the court; he presides over the play's many characters. The reference to this mythic king (who appears throughout English literature and legend) places the play in the realm of myth and fairy tale.

The king loves Tom for conquering the giants and bringing honor to his kingdom. He compares Tom to the world's greatest rulers and

wants him to marry his daughter. In a striking image, the king wishes for his kingdom to be filled with Tom's offspring the same way a rind of cheese is infested by maggots.

The king appears to be a fair man, wishing to avoid the discussion of business on a day of celebration and desiring that all the kingdom celebrate with him. He also shows that he is concerned for his daughter's happiness when he worries over her apparent sadness. However, he also shows that he believes that men should be in charge of women, a common belief in the 1700s. He is angered at the queen's insistent objections to the marriage of Tom and Huncamunca and threatens to put her on trial if she continues to oppose him.

The king also shows a tendency to be changeable on several occasions. When he declares that everyone should be smiling and then learns that the queen is shedding tears of joy, he immediately changes his pronouncement and states that all his subjects should be crying with joy as well. He reverses another proclamation toward the end of the play, after decreeing that prisoners and debtors should be pardoned in celebration of Huncamunca's wedding. When he learns shortly afterward that Tom has died, the king demands that the prisoners be recaptured.

Bailiff

The bailiff wishes that lawyers and reason were abolished so he could dispense justice according to his own will. He arrests Noodle as a debtor but is immediately killed by Tom for doing so.

Bailiff's Follower

The bailiff's follower is exactly that. He assists the bailiff and parrots his opinions, even dying as the bailiff does.

Cleora

Cleora is one of Huncamunca's maids. She sings for the princess, to distract Huncamunca from her love for Tom. At the end of the play, Cleora kills Noodle because he has murdered the queen. Since Noodle is revealed to be Mustacha's lover, Cleora is in turn murdered by Mustacha.

Queen Dollalolla

The queen is King Arthur's wife and Princess Huncamunca's mother. She shows herself to be a conniving and jealous person. While she says she objects to Tom marrying Huncamunca because he is an illegitimate child and a peasant, she actually does so because she is in love with Tom. The queen commiserates with Grizzle over the betrothal and plots with him to put a stop to it. However, she does not want Grizzle to kill Tom. She is also shocked and angered by Grizzle's claims that Tom did not actually capture any giants. She is likely angry because this statement threatens the integrity and honor of her kingdom and its famed accomplishments. She calls Grizzle a dog and says she intends to use him like one.

When she is alone, the queen reveals that she loves Tom but also loves her own honor and will not cheat on her husband. Still, she hopes her husband will die so she can have both a lover and her honor. Queen Dollalolla also shows herself to be fickle (like her husband) when she sets her sights on another hero after learning that Tom and Huncamunca will indeed be wed. It appears that the queen loves famous heroes in general, not Tom or his personality specifically.

Mr. Doodle

Mr. Doodle is a member of King Arthur's court who sings the praises of Tom Thumb and wishes that all the subjects in the kingdom were like him. He attempts to discuss a petition with the king but is rebuffed because it is a day of celebration. Doodle also mistakenly announces that Tom is dead.

Doodle is upset that Huncamunca has killed Lord Grizzle, and he kills her for doing so. As retribution for killing her daughter, Doodle is immediately killed by the queen. There is little discernible difference between Doodle and Noodle, which may be why their names are so similar.

Lord Grizzle

Lord Grizzle does not like Tom. He believes Tom's claims of conquering the giants are false and he does not think that a peasant should be allowed to marry a princess. (In *The Tragedy of Tragedies*, Grizzle is in love with Huncamunca and Tom is his romantic rival as well.) Grizzle and the queen commiserate with one another over Huncamunca's betrothal to Tom, and they plot to prevent it. Grizzle wants to kill Tom despite the queen's protests, and he is angry at the cow who swallowed Tom for stealing his chance to do so.

When Tom's ghost appears, Grizzle succeeds in killing it, but he is immediately killed by Huncamunca for doing so.

Princess Huncamunca

Princess Huncamunca is the daughter of King Arthur and Queen Dollalolla. Unbeknownst to her parents, she is in love with Tom Thumb. She is overjoyed when the king unwittingly decides to betroth her to him. When the princess (falsely) learns that Tom Thumb is dead, she faints, yet she is comically able to tell her father and Doodle that her bottle of rum is hidden beneath the bed.

As she pines for Tom, she asks Cleora to sing for her. When Mustacha says that Tom is too common for her, Huncamunca says that she suspects Mustacha of hiding her own love for Tom by ridiculing him.

At the end of the play, Huncamunca kills Grizzle for murdering her beloved's ghost. She is murdered in turn by Doodle.

Mustacha

Mustacha is one of Huncamunca's two maids. She does not believe that Huncamunca should love or marry a peasant. Although Huncamunca threatens to accuse Mustacha of being in love with Tom, it is later revealed that Mustacha and Noodle are lovers. Indeed, Mustacha flies into a rage and kills Cleora for slaying Noodle. She is then murdered by the king.

Mr. Noodle

A subject in King Arthur's court (and Mustacha's secret lover), Mr. Noodle announces that Tom Thumb, the conquering hero, is returning to court. He reports that he has heard rumors that Tom has no bones and is made entirely of gristle. Noodle applauds the king for belittling his wife when she dares to defy him, and he is arrested by the bailiff as a debtor. He also teases Tom for being a great warrior who is afraid of his grandmother and her warnings about marriage. He ultimately convinces Tom to wed by describing the pleasures of married life.

When Doodle falsely reports that Tom has been killed, Noodle explains the mix-up, noting that a monkey dressed like Tom was poisoned in Tom's place. Later, Noodle reports Tom's actual death. He then kills the queen for murdering Doodle and is subsequently slain by Cleora.

Physician 1

The first physician speaks in prose, albeit non-sensically, and references several Latin terms, also nonsensically. He claims that "Tom" died of distemper and denies the second physician's objections, as well as the king's logical arguments, against this claim.

Physician 2

The second physician speaks in the same manner as his colleague, although he disagrees with the first physician's diagnosis and procedures. When he and the first physician are alone, he reveals that he is not familiar with distemper, the disease the other doctor described.

Tom Thumb

Tom Thumb is the tiny hero who conquered the giants, returning triumphant to King Arthur's court. He shows that he is modest and humble when he refuses to name a reward; he claims that doing his duty to the king is reward enough. However, Tom is in love with Princess Huncamunca, and he accepts the king's offer of her hand in marriage. Later, Tom reveals that although he does love the princess, he is afraid to get married. He is teased by Noodle for being able to kill giants while still being scared of his grandmother's advice.

When Tom is eaten by a cow, his ghost appears in court and is promptly killed by Lord Grizzle. This sets in motion a series of murders that end with the king's suicide and the death of all of the play's main characters. During the epilogue Tom is revived once again, and he reveals that he is not scared of death but of critics. He also describes the truly small men of the world and implores womankind to see through his size and into his heart.

THEMES

Ignorance (Theory of Knowledge)

Compared with modern advances and technologies in medicine, doctors in the eighteenth century were largely ignorant and ineffective. Fielding was known to dislike physicians and their craft, believing them to be frauds. This dislike is evident in *Tom Thumb*. The doctors are too ignorant to notice the difference between a tiny man and a monkey. They are also unable to agree on a diagnosis. They speak nonsensically and rely on Latin terms in order to appear intelligent. Although one doctor asserts that "Tom" died of distemper, it is later revealed that the monkey was poisoned. Although their patient has died, when the real Tom appears, the doctors claim that their cures have worked.

Fielding's distaste for medical practitioners is especially notable when one considers that two scenes in this short play are devoted to the inept physicians. These scenes do little to advance the plot. The only practical role that the doctors serve in the play is to alert the audience to the plot to poison Tom, a plot that is revealed not by the bumbling doctors but by Noodle. The physicians' odd place in the play is also underscored by their speaking manner: unlike the rest of the characters, the physicians speak in prose rather than in verse.

Love

One of the driving forces in the play is love. Tom Thumb is in love with Princess Huncamunca and is overjoyed at the thought of marrying her, even minutes after telling the king that he does not need or want a reward for his heroic accomplishments. Although Tom is afraid of marriage because of his grandmother's warnings, he is persuaded to wed after Noodle describes the benefits of a loving marriage. Tom's love for the princess is also apparent when he rushes to the palace after hearing a rumor that Huncamunca has died.

Princess Huncamunca's love for Tom initially causes her sadness; she believes they can never be together because of their different social standings. Her joy at learning of the betrothal is apparent to her father, the king. Her grief when she believes him to be dead is also obvious, as she faints upon hearing the news. Her love is demonstrated again when she kills Grizzle for murdering Tom's ghost.

Queen Dollalolla also reveals herself to be in love with Tom. To her, he is "a lovely creature," a tidbit that is shared in one of the play's two asides. Still, the queen is unable to act on her feelings, not because she thinks it is immoral to cheat on her husband but because she loves being perceived as virtuous (regardless of her utter lack of virtue). The affair between Mustacha and Noodle is another love revealed in the play's last lines. Even the play's epilogue is largely about love. The tiny Tom, resurrected once more, advises women to look past his

TOPICS FOR FURTHER STUDY

- Read T. H. White's classic young-adult novel *The Once and Future King* (1958), another rendition of the legend of King Arthur. Next, research different interpretations (literary, mythical, or historical) of the Arthurian legends. Compile and present your findings to the class in a multimedia presentation that incorporates pictures and quotations about the legends.

- Divide the scenes of *Tom Thumb* amongst your classmates. Perform your scene and digitally film the production. Use a video editing program, such as iMovie, to edit the scenes together and then post the results on a video sharing Web site, such as *YouTube*.

- Research the history and politics of England in the 1700s and create a fact-filled computerized or hand-created poster that displays your research. Find out about the goals and motivations of some of the major political groups, and investigate social conditions (education, income, and amount of freedom) for several groups, such as women,

landholders, clergy, the nobility, and the poor.

- *Tom Thumb* was originally performed as an afterpiece to Fielding's *The Author's Farce; and The Pleasures of the Town*, and was meant to underscore its themes and motifs. Read *The Author's Farce* and write an essay in which you analyze how the plays complement one another.

- Create a Web log post regarding the ways in which *Tom Thumb* appears to have been influenced by the works of William Shakespeare. Invite comments from your classmates about the influences they see.

- Conduct Internet and traditional book research about the Little Theatre in Haymarket where *Tom Thumb* first premiered. Based on your information, compose a set design for the play as it might have appeared in 1730. For extra credit, create a second design that would be more fitting in contemporary theaters. Create your set as a computerized three-dimensional design program, diorama, or a drawing.

stature and that of all men like him, and into their "mighty souls."

Revenge

Revenge is another of the themes that moves the plot forward. Lord Grizzle does not believe that a man of low birth should be allowed to marry a princess, and so he plots to assassinate Tom Thumb. In *The Tragedy of Tragedies*, Grizzle is in love with Huncamunca, and Tom becomes a romantic rival as well. In a way, the queen is also seeking revenge, both for her inability to have Tom for herself and for her husband's dismissal of her objections to the wedding of Tom and Huncamunca. By plotting with Grizzle to stop the marriage, the queen hopes to achieve her desires while subverting her husband's.

The best examples of revenge occur in the play's final scene. Grizzle feels that his vengeance has been stolen by the errant cow that swallows Tom, but he is able to recapture it when he slays Tom's ghost. This sets off a chain reaction of revenge. Huncamunca takes her revenge on Grizzle for killing Tom's ghost. Doodle avenges Grizzle's death by killing Huncamunca, and so the cycle of revenge continues until all of the main characters have killed one another. To extrapolate from early-twentieth-century Indian political leader Mohandas Gandhi's famous quote, "An eye for an eye makes the whole world blind," *Tom Thumb* demonstrates that revenge is a never-ending, destructive cycle. In the case of Fielding's play, a life for a life makes everyone dead.

17th-century engraving of Tom Thumb (Lebrecht Music and Arts Photo Library / Alamy)

STYLE

Satire

A satire is any work of art that ridicules something outside itself (such as an idea, value, or political figure). Satires are generally literary in form, and they use comedy and exaggeration to expose a deeper truth or moral, one generally directed toward the object of ridicule. Nearly all of Fielding's early plays were satires, and *Tom Thumb* is no exception. Through his portrayal of the bumbling physicians, Fielding satirizes doctors and the medical field. For the most part, however, the play's target is Sir Robert Walpole, the de

facto prime minister of England, who served from 1721 to 1742. L. J. Morrissey, in the critical introduction to the dual edition *"Tom Thumb" and the "Tragedy of Tragedies"*, points out that the play references fox hunting, Walpole's favorite sport, while quotes regarding peace relate to Walpole's stated political goals. Morrissey also finds that the king's description of Tom as the "preserver of my kingdom" is a reference to Walpole.

Most satires also rely on parody, a comic form of mimicry. This can be seen in Fielding's misappropriation of quotes from other playwrights. The play satirizes the overblown and flowery poetic verse popular in the plays of

COMPARE
&
CONTRAST

- **1700s:** Although the position of prime minister in England has not yet been created, Sir Robert Walpole serves in a prototype of the role as First Lord of the Treasury from 1721 to 1742. Today he is considered by historians to have been England's first prime minister.

  Today: England's prime minister is Conservative Party leader David Cameron. He was elected to the position by the House of Commons in 2010.

- **1700s:** The Enlightenment (or Age of Enlightenment) is in full swing. The era is typified by the rise of reason over superstition or religious belief. (Fielding references reason through the bailiff character in *Tom Thumb*.) The Enlightenment pervaded both science and art, and the role of the church and existing political hierarchies were also challenged at this time.

  Today: While it is difficult to describe an era while it is still taking place, today can be seen as part of a post-postmodernist age. This cultural era rejects the irony and lack of sincerity of postmodernism (which was itself a reaction to the self-consciousness and sense of separation from the past that characterized modernism) and seeks to find an acceptable balance between faith and reason.

- **1700s:** Plays are the predominant form of entertainment. Citizens of the lower classes are often illiterate, and books are seen as expensive luxuries.

  Today: While literacy and books are commonplace, television and movies (the technological descendants of plays) are the most common forms of entertainment.

Fielding's predecessors, such as John Fletcher, James Thomson, and John Dryden.

Farce

A farce is a type of comedic play that usually contains humorously overblown situations. They are characterized by cases of mistaken identity, puns, sexual innuendo, or slapstick (physical comedy). *Tom Thumb* features all but the last of these, although one could make a case that the play's last scene is, in fact, an example of slapstick (or at least could be performed as such). In Fielding's play, a monkey dressed in Tom's clothes is mistaken for Tom and poisoned. The doctors who attend to "Tom" also do not notice that their charge is an animal and not a small human. Puns and sexual innuendo abound as well, particularly in reference to Tom and Huncamunca's impending wedding night. The last scene, in which all of the characters kill one another, is a parody of the last scene in William Shakespeare's *Hamlet*.

HISTORICAL CONTEXT

Sir Robert Walpole

In much the same way that the president of the United States is parodied frequently on television shows such as *Saturday Night Live*, Fielding's plays satirized the leader of the day, de facto prime minister Sir Robert Walpole. Born August 26, 1676, Walpole was the first Earl of Orford, elected to parliament in 1701. The two-party political system of the day pitted Whigs against Tories, and Walpole was a Whig who served under King George I and King George II. Walpole became the first Lord of the Treasury in 1721, when he achieved enough political influence to be considered prime minister. This power was further secured in 1730, when Lord Charles Townshend retired, leaving Walpole as lone head of the Cabinet. He continued to serve in this capacity until 1742, following a major military defeat of Britain by Spain in the Battle of Cartagena. He holds the distinction of having

An engraving from 1869 showing Tom Thumb as a newborn baby (© *Pictorial Press Ltd / Alamy*)

been England's prime minister for the longest period of time.

Theatrical Licensing Act of 1737

The difference between today's satirization of the president and the mocking of the prime minister in the early eighteenth century hinges on the issue of free speech. Free speech was not a right granted to English citizens of that day. Fielding's plays, particularly *Tom Thumb* and *The Covent-Garden Tragedy*, openly satirized Walpole. These plays and others by Fielding's contemporaries so incensed the government that the Theatrical Licensing Act was passed on June 21, 1737. The act required all plays to be approved by the Lord Chamberlain before being staged. The act effectively allowed the government to control the theater. The act was so detrimental to the theater that Fielding was forced to become a lawyer to supplement his income. The act also was at least partly responsible for a theatrical turn away from satire and a

turn toward novel writing for some play-wrights, including Fielding.

The Folkloric Origins of Tom Thumb

The tale of Tom Thumb likely has its origins in English folklore passed down through the oral tradition. References to the character first began to appear in print in the early 1600s (as in a 1621 edition of *The History of Tom Thumb*), but those early references acknowledge that the tale was not new. The story of Tom Thumb begins during King Arthur's reign when the wizard Merlin visits a childless couple in disguise. They are kind to him and so he grants them a magical son, one who is born the size of his father's thumb and never grows any bigger. Tom's size makes him prone to many accidents, and throughout his adventures he is swallowed in turn by a cow, a giant, and a fish, though he survives to tell the tale. He is also seized by a raven, which flies away with him; another time, he is accidentally baked into a pudding by his mother. Tom's travels eventually bring him to King Arthur's court, where he wins the king's favor and is named an honorary knight of the Round Table.

Traditional folklore regarding Tom finds him traveling to fairyland. When he returns, all the people he once knew are long dead. The new king, Thunston, is pleased by the tiny man, and he rewards him with a carriage pulled by six mice. According to legend, Tom is ultimately killed by the bite of a poisonous spider.

CRITICAL OVERVIEW

Tom Thumb was an instant popular success. According to L. J. Morrissey, in the critical introduction to the dual edition *"Tom Thumb" and the "Tragedy of Tragedies,"* the play "was Fielding's first overnight success." It "ran nearly uninterrupted" for almost "forty nights." Morrissey writes that "this success can be accounted for in part by the vigour and gaiety of the farce." Nevertheless, "it is the satire and the burlesque [racy content] that must have pleased Fielding's audience most."

Assessing *Tom Thumb* in the *Dictionary of Literary Biography*, Paula R. Backscheider calls it "a hilarious play and one rich in original verbal effects." She also commends "Fielding's satire and verbal virtuosity." Offering a similar opinion, Morrissey finds that Fielding's "parody of the heroic drama . . . is delicious."

The play is "meticulously specific . . . in quarrying from more than forty tragedies," notes Maurice Johnson in *Fielding's Art of Fiction: Eleven Essays on "Shamela," "Joseph Andrews," "Tom Jones," and "Amelia."* It "maintains its strength of fascination because it has a good deal to say about all pretentiousness and inanity, not necessarily dramatic." Johnson also notes that "if the 'tragic' text . . . seems familiar, with its theme of Love-and-Honour, its blazing hero, its inflammable heroine, . . . these conventionally familiar elements are at once jerked into grotesque distortion." He explains that "the hero is a manikin, the heroine bears the preposterous name of Huncamunca, the hero is eaten (offstage) by a red cow, and at the end everyone kills everyone else." Johnson concludes, "Rhetoric murders rhetoric itself."

CRITICISM

Leah Tieger

Tieger is a freelance writer and editor. In the following essay, she discusses the quotes, allusions, and folklore that inform Tom Thumb.

Henry Fielding's two-act play *Tom Thumb* is something of an amalgam (a thing made of many elements). It draws upon English folklore, borrows (and changes) lines from other plays and playwrights, and satirizes the government. While the exact origin of the Tom Thumb folk figure is not known, it is attributed to England and was first referred to in print in 1621. Fielding's rendition stays true to its roots in Tom's size and the setting within King Arthur's court. As in the folktale, Tom successfully faces giants and is a favorite subject of King Arthur's. However, the folk tale describes Tom's birth as being brought about by magic. In Fielding's play, the queen says he is illegitimate (the child of parents who were unwed when he was born). In the original folk tale, Tom is swallowed whole by a cow, but he is digested whole and thus lives through the ordeal. (He dies from the same event in the play.) In the folk and fairy tale renditions, Tom's size draws him into much mischief that often results in grand adventures or reward. In Fielding's telling, Tom's size is predominantly a source of comedy. A monkey is mistaken for him, and

WHAT DO I READ NEXT?

- The final scene in *Tom Thumb* can be seen as an homage to, or parody of, William Shakespeare's *Hamlet* (circa 1600–1601 and available in various forms). A parallel between Tom's ghost and the ghost of Hamlet's father also exists.

- A modern example of satire can be found in Joseph Heller's 1961 novel *Catch-22*, which critiques the American military of the World War II era. It references Lewis Carroll's children's fantasy *Alice in Wonderland*.

- To gain further insight on Fielding's short play, read the expanded and heavily revised version *The Tragedy of Tragedies* (1731).

- For a cultural and social history of the century in which Fielding lived and wrote, read Jeremy Black's 2007 book *Culture in Eighteenth-Century England: A Subject for Taste*. The volume details the lives and work of the country's leading writers and artists, the popularity of satire, and the economy. It also explores the music and architectural styles of the day.

- *Tom Thumb* is based on a popular figure in English folklore, and Pleasant DeSpain's 2005 compilation *Thirty-three Multicultural Tales to Tell* will introduce readers to folk tales from around the world. Classics that are well known within their own culture are brought to an English-speaking audience in a format that is appropriate for children and young adults, as well as older readers. Stories from around the globe are included, with selections taken from countries as diverse as Japan, Africa, and Fiji.

- John Dryden is one of the playwrights whose work is misappropriated in *Tom Thumb*. A predecessor of Fielding's, Dryden is best known for his circa 1671 play *Marriage à la Mode*.

jokes about his size (especially regarding his ability to be a good husband to Huncamunca) abound. It is not known why Fielding chose the tale of Tom Thumb as the vehicle for his political

Russ Tamblin as Tom Thumb in the 1958 film (© *Moviestore collection Ltd / Alamy*)

and literary satire. One explanation lies in the play's actual text. In the prologue, the actor who plays Lord Grizzle advises the audience that English heroes should be the subjects of English plays. In this manner, Fielding pokes fun at the common English heroic drama, which often drew on Greek tragedies and Roman mythology for its subject matter.

As a political satire, Fielding attacks Sir Robert Walpole by referencing fox hunting, the then–prime minister's favorite sport. This correlation in mentioned by L. J. Morrissey in the critical introduction to the dual edition *Tom Thumb and the Tragedy of Tragedies.* Morrissey also writes that the quotes relating to peace reference Walpole's stated political goals. He also observes that the king's description of Tom as the "preserver of my kingdom" is a comment directed toward Walpole. Near the end of act 2, scene 8, the king compares the multiplying

offspring of Tom Thumb and Huncamunca to maggots infesting cheese. Morrissey writes that "the maggot simile might be a nasty new thrust at Walpole." The slightly revised version of *Tom Thumb* was published under the pseudonym Scriblerus Secundus, and even this relates to Walpole. At the time, there were two distinct political factions, the Whigs and the Tories. Walpole was a Whig, and Fielding's pseudonym references a group of Tory writers known as the Scriblerus Club. The group included such writers as Alexander Pope and Jonathan Swift. As Morrissey puts it, the pseudonym was "obviously Fielding's attempt to align himself with the group of Tory wits who had banded together in 1713." Another noteworthy observation regarding Fielding's relentless satire of Walpole can be seen in *The Tragedy of Tragedies,* Fielding's expanded version of *Tom Thumb.* Morrissey remarks that political pamphlets of the day described Walpole as "the Great man," while

Tom Thumb is referred to "the Great" throughout *The Tragedy of Tragedies*. Here, Fielding's choice of the Tom Thumb character becomes more apparent; he uses him to effectively describe Walpole as a tiny man.

As a parody of heroic drama, *Tom Thumb* opens with a prologue that pans plays featuring Roman and Greek characters. The ploy is a classic bait and switch—a tactic of promising one thing and delivering something different— as the introduction of an English hero does little to diminish the play's overblown, unrealistic circumstances. Although tiny, Tom Thumb serves as a classic dramatic hero; he has conquered the giant, won the king's and the people's admiration, won the hearts of the royal women, and become engaged to the princess. Certainly, Fielding's decision to give the princess the silly name Huncamunca emphasizes the ridiculousness of Tom's love for her. As in all such narratives, would-be lovers and jealous men plot the hero's downfall. A monkey is mistaken for Tom and poisoned. Tom is swallowed by a cow but returns to his love in the form of a ghost. Heightening the play's ridiculous nature, Tom's ghost is murdered. The event triggers a hilarious chain reaction in which each character kills the next, leaving the king to kill himself and brag with his last breath: "Kings, Queens, and Knaves throw one another down / . . . So all our Pack upon the Floor is cast, / And all I boast is, that I fall the last." The series of instantaneous murders that ends the play further underscores the nature of *Tom Thumb* as a dramatic parody; it directly references and lampoons the final scene in William Shakespeare's tragedy *Hamlet*.

Tom Thumb borrows lines from Shakespeare, John Fletcher, James Thomson, and John Dryden. However, as Paula R. Backscheider finds in the *Dictionary of Literary Biography*, "Fielding parodies the way Shakespeare's imitators have plundered the Bard's plays by transplanting lines, as his contemporaries often did, and putting them, as he saw the eighteenth-century writers doing, in thoroughly inappropriate places." Backscheider explains: "Thumb tells Noodle that he loves Huncamunca: 'Whole Days, and Nights, and Years shall be too short / For our Enjoyment; ev'ry Sun shall rise / Blushing, to see us in our Bed together'" (act 2, scene 2). This line, reminiscent of Shakespeare's work, appears in Dryden's rendition of *Antony and Cleopatra*.

Fielding's play is also written in blank verse and is both an homage to and a parody of the plays of Shakespeare and Fielding's other predecessors. Although he poked fun at the flowery language that often accompanied blank verse, Fielding was also instrumental in repopularizing the format.

Source: Leah Tieger, Critical Essay on *Tom Thumb*, in *Drama for Students*, Gale, Cengage Learning, 2011.

Richard Bevis

In the following excerpt, Bevis proposes that the successful novel technique of the "normative author" was developed via Fielding's use of the rehearsal format in his satirical plays.

One of the most venerable clichés in critical discussions of Fielding's fiction has been the novelist's "theatricality." Originally this was just a metaphor describing authorial tone and perspective: Fielding the showman, pulling his armchair up to the proscenium, and so on. (The explicit use of the puppeteer-author analogy by Fielding's admirer Thackeray in *Vanity Fair* probably helped to establish the image.) For a long time almost nothing specific was adduced, partly because few admirers of Fielding's novels were also students of his plays. Sir Walter Scott's remarks about *Tom Jones* in the "Introductory Epistle" to *The Fortunes of Nigel* (1822), however, occur during a conversation between "Author" and "Captain" that quotes Bayes in *The Rehearsal*, suggesting that Scott saw the connection I am tracing. And Leslie Stephen did observe that Fielding's tendency to serve as a chorus, commenting on the thoughts and actions of his characters, worked better in his fiction than in his drama.

The modern debate began in 1929 when F. W. Bateson cited Stephen's discussion and, while generally agreeing, asserted that Fielding's dramatic burlesques were superior to his comedies and ought to be distinguished from them. Bateson argued that each of the burlesques (except *Tom Thumb*) has a character or group that expresses Fielding's own views, and that his "comments and interpolations" in the novels seem to have "less justification" than in the plays. These latter points, however, have seldom received support. Irvin Ehrenpreis granted (1964) that the narrative method of *Tom Jones* recalls the format of *The Rehearsal* and Fielding's own "satirical farces," but he judged the novel's narrator more trustworthy than the Author-characters in frame-plays who "unintentionally" expose their own absurdities. J. Paul Hunter agreed (1975) that the rehearsal format anticipates the narrative strategy of the novels, where its reflexivity reaches fruition, and that the rehearsals' Authors are often obtuse and foolish characters. Claude Rawson has gone further (1985) in emphasizing the *contrast* between the novels' narrators and the plays' Authors, whom he finds weak, limited, and—specifically refuting Bateson—unrepresentative of Henry Fielding.

It seems, then, that the legitimate point which had been made about Fielding's use of the play-within-a-play format is now in danger of being lost in a debate among critics of fiction about narrators and Author-characters. The sharpness of the distinctions that Rawson in particular wants to make between Fielding's narrators and Authors all but severs the relation that has been pointed out between Fielding's modes of self-representation and self-expression in his plays and in his fiction. He employed the seventeenth-century idea of the satirical frame-play, with significant alterations, as the foundation of his own style in both genres.

The rehearsal format, although it has some Jacobean and French adumbrations, was defined by the Duke of Buckingham and other wits in *The Rehearsal* (1671), which, in addition to its own enduring popularity, begat numerous imitations, including Sheridan's *The Critic* (1779). Essentially, the form has two layers: some new drama is being rehearsed (or performed: for my purposes it makes little difference which), but it is observed and discussed by characters in the outer play. The Author is in attendance, perhaps with friends or a rival. The visitors are generally naive, or sceptical, or outraged; they may ask questions and challenge the action or dialogue; they need to be educated in the Author's rationale: in other words, they

serve as our surrogates. The actors' blunders or changes may evoke further interventions from the Author. We have the pleasure of a glimpse behind the scenes: more than a glimpse, really, since it involves not only the technical operations of the theatre, but the workings of the dramatist's mind.

Because the rehearsal format originated in satire of John Dryden and heroic drama, the Author was conventionally a dunce, infatuated with his new toy and oblivious to its absurdities, which are patent to his visitors and to us. The point is important because Fielding's use of the Author was so different. In *The Rehearsal* itself, Bayes is fatuously proud of precisely what makes him ridiculous:

> Now, Sir, because I'll do nothing here that ever was done before, instead of beginning with a Scene that discovers something of the Plot, I begin this Play with a whisper. . . . I despise your Johnson and Beaumont, that borrow'd all they writ from Nature: I am for fetching it purely out of my own fancy, I.

Novelty-mad and smugly self-assured, Bayes could have sat for Swift's Spider/Modern in *The Battle of the Books*. For sixty years his character was as definitive as the play itself, his name sometimes being used generically (*Bays's Opera; Bayes in Petticoats*). And though Fielding violated this tradition, a stupid or ridiculous or corrupt Author remained the norm: witness Puff in *The Critic*.

None of the obscure rehearsal plays between Buckingham and Fielding departed from Buckingham's lead in the matter of the Author's character. In John Lacy's *Sir Hercules Buffoon; or, the Poetical Squire* (1684), the Author is, obviously, "a farcical figure." *The Female Wits* (anonymous, 1697) is designed to satirize its principal Author, Marsilia (Mrs. Manley), whose foolish heroic play is rehearsed, and two other women writers. Elkanah Settle's *The World in the Moon* (1697) and *The City-Ramble; or a Playhouse Wedding* (1711) present rehearsals, but lack Authors (see Smith, pp. 66–71, 88). Charles Gildon attempted a sequel to Buckingham's work: *A New Rehearsal; or, Bays the Younger* (1714). And Thomas D'Urfey's *The Two Queens of Brentford* (1721, not performed) has a reasonable-sounding critic, but he is not the Author (Smith, pp. 122–23).

John Gay in some ways prepared the ground for Fielding. *The What D'Ye Call It* (1715) contains a deliberately silly, mock-tragic playlet, ostensibly by the Steward, acting on a hint from Sir Roger. Although the Steward shrewdly uses the playlet's performance (not rehearsal) as a device to obtain justice from Sir Roger and helps to establish the play's values, he is not the kind of "normative" Author that Fielding would provide as an omnipresent guide. He appears only briefly at the beginning and end (totalling about one-twelfth of the play's length), and his interests are moral and paternal, not critical. *Three Hours After Marriage* (1717, with Pope and Arbuthnot) presents only ridiculous Authors—Phoebe Clinket, Plotwell, and Sir Tremendous—who, whether read as particular caricatures or general types, represent the antitheses of the play's own values. The Beggar in *The Beggar's Opera* (1728), however, is a clear step towards using the Author as the playwright's spokesman, though he, like the Steward, appears only at the beginning and end.

Buckingham's convention further broke down amidst a rash of frame-plays in the spring of 1730. The most successful and important of these was Henry Fielding's *The Author's Farce*, which opened at the Little Theatre in the Haymarket on March 30th. It is important not only in marking Fielding's shift from regular comedy to play-within-a-play burlesque, but also, within the latter tradition, in the development of the normative Author who may instruct us and direct the satire instead of receiving it.

In *The Author's Farce*, Luckless is a penniless writer, besieged in his garret by his landlady, unable to sell his play to either Bookweight, a Grub Street hackmaster, or the theatrical managers Marplay and Sparkish (Cibber and Wilks). In act 3, though, he produces a puppet show ("The Author's Farce") at the Little Theatre and becomes Fielding's surrogate, at least to the extent that both men are using one mode and venue simultaneously to satirize theatrical and literary fashions. If his play is at times as nonsensical as Bayes's, Luckless knows it, but "Who would not then rather eat by his nonsense than starve by his wit?" His farce is designed for an age that "would allow Tom Durfey a better poet than Congreve or Wycherley." The burden of satire is shifted from the Author to the Town, and the theatres that cater to it. In Hades, Luckless parades the current theatrical charlatans before Charon: Sir Farcical (Cibber again) "understands no language at all"; Orator

Henley's oration "has a great deal of nonsense in it." Luckless begs us to "notice how Sir Farcical's song sets Nonsense asleep." Luckless's play is finally halted only on the dubious objection, "Shall you abuse Nonsense when the whole town supports it?" and he himself is finally proclaimed "Henry I, King of Bantam!" The parallels with Fielding's own career and views are too numerous to ignore.

A similar play opened on the same date over at Drury Lane: Gabriel Odingsells's *Bay's Opera*, which, with interruptions and revisions, managed to survive for three nights. The audience can be forgiven for feeling confused and offended. General Briton, who upholds Pantomime, they took as a satire on their own taste (and on a particular officer). Bays is also puzzling: Dane Smith describes him as satirical and farcical, yet also "the serious expositor" of Odingsells's views (Smith, pp. 150–51). If true, this would make Odingsells the co-founder with Fielding of the normative Author, but it is an extremely dubious proposition. Initially Bays hints that he prefers true dramatic poetry to pantomime and opera, and once he says, "I copy after Nature," but all of his other comments and actions indicate that he has gone over to what he takes to be the winning side ("the nearest way to Wit was to turn out of the Road of Common Sense"). Odingsells makes both Bays (whose name connoted stupidity) and Tragedo, the representative of Shakespeare, ridiculous. To top it off, the two characters were played by Colley Cibber's egregious offspring, Theophilus Cibber and Charlotte Charke.

A third rehearsal play of 1730, however, *The Fashionable Lady* (2 April, Goodman's Fields), by James Ralph, a friend of Fielding, does have a reasonable, sensible author-surrogate, one Drama. Again his play ("Harlequin's Opera") is senseless enough, but Drama claims that he is simply imitating modern opera, "the more absurd, the more fashionable." He and Meanwell, an intelligent visitor, agree that the success of such trivial pieces as his is shameful, possibly just a fad owing to the absence of legitimate drama (2.1). Like Bays and Luckless (and several of Fielding's later Authors), Drama has seen what audiences want and has decided to supply it. But Drama and Luckless have kept their minds free of cant; the awfulness of their plays does not reflect on them—as it does on Bayes/Bays—but on spectators.

. . . Strictly speaking, Fielding first used the rehearsal format in *Pasquin, A Dramatick Satire on the Times: being the Rehearsal of Two Plays* . . . (1736). There are two Authors: Trapwit presents a comedy—rather like Fielding's own *Don Quixote in England* (1734)—that shows how electors are suborned in country towns, while Fustian rehearses a *Dunciad*-like tragedy in which Queen Common Sense is attacked by Queen Ignorance, supported by the learned professions and the patent theatres. The treatment of the two Authors is different, and uneven: sometimes they are above the audiences and sometimes of them, sometimes a standard and sometimes absurd. Sheldon Sacks has shown that such role-shifting is also characteristic of Fielding's fictional narrators; what we need, perhaps, is an analysis as painstaking as Sacks' of the Authors' shifting roles, which confuse and divide readers. When Claude Rawson wants to show that Fielding's Authors are weak, foolish characters, unable to express their creator, he adduces Trapwit (Rawson, pp. 271, 303). But Rawson fails to distinguish between different Authors, and Trapwit is a bad—i.e., atypical—example. He is by far the weaker of the two here, almost "a conventional Bayes" (Smith, p. 206), whereas Fustian—despite his name—is at times nearly Fielding's mouthpiece.

. . . In *Eurydice* (1737), another rehearsal play, Fielding went back to the Hadean setting of Luckless's puppet show in *The Author's Farce*. Again the Author—here, for once, simply called that—is reasonable and sensible, voicing Fielding's (and usually the Scriblerians') views on theatrical and social matters (Smith, p. 218). The denizens of Hades closely resemble London's *beau monde*; Eurydice is the "fine lady" of a dozen Augustan satires. Author is hard on beaux who set up for critics: he points out that a farce *ought* to be "ridiculous" in order to satisfy decorum, and launches a serious attack on Italian opera, similar to Pope's in the fourth book of the *Dunciad*. But the play failed at Drury Lane, an event which became the subject of Fielding's last play, *Eurydice Hiss'd*.

In between, Fielding produced *The Historical Register for 1736* (1737), a play whose sharp attacks on Walpole helped bring on the Licensing Act of 1737. Fielding never went further in identifying with and speaking through the Author of a rehearsal play than in the case of Medley, the shrewd, serious satirist who directs and interprets the action of *The Historical Register* (Smith, pp. 220–21; Dudden 1:196, 200; Lewis, pp. 187, 188). Questioned about the moral of his piece, Medley replies straightforwardly:

> Why, Sir, my design is to ridicule the vicious and foolish customs of the age, and that in a fair manner, without fear, favor, or ill-nature, and without scurrility, ill manners, or commonplace. I hope to expose the reigning follies in such a manner that men shall laugh themselves out of them before they feel that they are touched.

This is, of course, the classic rationale for satire, worth comparing with the narrator's apologia in book 3, chapter 1 of *Joseph Andrews*: "I describe not Men, but Manners; not an Individual, but a Species . . . hold the Glass to thousands in their Closets, that they may contemplate their Deformity, and endeavour to reduce it," etc.

"But," asks the critic Sowrwit, "what thread or connection can you have in this history? For instance, how is your political connected with your theatrical?" Medley/Fielding is expecting this one:

> Oh, very easily. When my politics come to a farce, they very naturally lead to the playhouse where, let me tell you, there are some politicians too, where there is lying, flattering, dissembling, promising, deceiving and undermining, as well as in any court in Christendom.

This is a long way from Bayes, and very close to Scriblerus Secundus in *The Grub-Street Opera*, i.e. to Fielding, who is trying hard to bring his views on Robert Walpole and on Colley Cibber into a single focus. Fielding supplemented Medley's accusations about corrupt management in his Dedication to the first edition, and repeated the satire on auctions and levees in the novels (Dudden, 1:198, nn. 2, 3; 202, n. 2; 204–5).

Eurydice Hiss'd, a much slighter play, was soon added to *The Historical Register* as an afterpiece. Also in the rehearsal format, it boasts two Authors: Spatter, whose "tragedy" "the damnation of Eurydice" is being rehearsed, and Pillage, the Author (of *Pasquin* and *Eurydice*!) within this "tragedy." Pillage's *dicta* vacillate so wildly that William W. Appleton has proposed that he represents both Fielding and Walpole. It is very unlikely, however—or at least very seldom—that Pillage's words or actions can stand for Fielding's. Pillage, whose name connotes plagiary, manipulates his "friends" to achieve his ends, profits from them much as the diabolic Quidam does in *The Historical Register*, and looks forward to the time "When none shall dare to hiss within the house" (1.1). The critic Honestus sometimes speaks for Fielding, but the normative Author who affords perspective on both Pillage and Walpole is Spatter:

> Sir, I intend first to warn all future authors from depending solely on a party to support them against the judgment of the town. Secondly, showing that even the author of a farce may have his attendants and dependents, I hope greater persons may learn to despise them, which may be a more useful moral than you may apprehend; for perhaps the mean ambition of being worshipped, flattered and attended by such fellows as these may have led men into the worst of schemes. . . .

By this time, Fielding's audiences understood that for him playwrights and theatrical managers constituted legitimate parallels to Parliament's political managers, especially Walpole.

Throughout most of his career as a dramatist, then, from 1730 to 1737, Fielding showed a penchant for the rehearsal (or performance) format featuring an Author whose views at least partially overlap with his own: a type distinct from 'Bayes,' conventionally a satiric butt and the last person to understand what is wrong with his play or the system. Fielding's Authors were moreover original, insofar as he made them articulate the play's meaning and embody its values.

Source: Richard Bevis, "Fielding's Normative Authors: *Tom Jones* and the Rehearsal Play," in *Philological Quarterly*, Vol. 69, No. 1, Winter 1990, pp. 55–70.

Harry B. Weiss

In the following essay, Weiss traces the changes that have taken place in the versions of the Tom Thumb story over history.

At the outset, I may as well admit that I have no intention, in this account, of tracking the story of Tom Thumb to its lair. Although this has been attempted by various learned men, the results are not always satisfying. Dr. Johnson, it is said, once "withdrew his attention" from a great man who bored him and "thought about Tom Thumb." Without seeming to place myself in such distinguished company, perhaps I too may be permitted to say that my thoughts

> EVER SINCE THE STORY HAS BEEN CURRENT, TOM'S THRILLING ADVENTURES HAVE BEEN TOLD AND RETOLD, WITH MODIFICATIONS BY EACH GENERATION, AND MANY VARIATIONS OCCUR IN THE NUMEROUS EDITIONS WITHIN A GENERATION."

about Tom Thumb are the result of boredom, or if you prefer, idle curiosity.

Although I am concerned here mainly with the changes which have taken place in the version during the past three hundred years, it seems necessary to mention briefly a few facts and dates relating to early information about Tom Thumb. Reginald Scot, in his "*Discoverie of Witchcraft*," printed in 1584, speaking "Of vaine apparitions, how people have beene brought to feare bugges," mentions "Tom thombe" along with the giants, imps, fairies, satyrs, witches, goblins, etc., with which "in our childhood our mothers maids have so terrified us." And Thomas Nashe in "*Pierce Penilesse His Supplication to the Diuell*" (1592) grumbles that "eury grosse braind Idiot is suffered to come into print, who if hee set foorth a Pamphlet of the praise of Pudding-pricks, or write a Treatise of Tom Thumme, or the exploits of Vntruss; it is bought vp thicke and threefold, when better things lie dead."

In 1621 the tale appeared, in prose, in Richard Johnson's "*The History of Tom Thumbe the Little, for his small stature surnamed King Arthur's Dwarfe: Whose Life and aduentures containe many strange and wonderfull accidents, published for the delight of merry Time-spenders.*" Tom Thumb also appears in Drayton's "*Nymphidia*" (1627) and it would be possible to mention other notable instances where Tom Thumb has been utilized to advantage, such as Fielding's burlesque, "*Tom Thumb A Tragedy*" (1730) and Kane O'Hara's "*Tom Thumb; A Burletta, Altered from Henry Fielding*" (1830).

The earliest Tom Thumb in Europe appears to be the Thaumlin or Little Thumb of the Northmen, a dwarf of Scandinavian descent. The popular Danish history of Svend Tomling treats of "a man no bigger than a thumb, who would be married to a woman three ells and three quarters long." Then there is the "Daumerling," a little Thumb of the Germans, who is swallowed by a dun cow. It is said that the German and Danish "Thumb" stories contain much that is found in the northern versions. In India Tom Thumb has his counterpart in the Khodra Khan of the Mohammedans. In the Hindoo story, Vamuna is so tiny that he thinks the water-filled impression of a cow's hoof in the earth is a lake and he begs King Mahabali for a piece of ground over which he may walk in three strides.

Tom Thumb, a comic story, belongs to one of the groups or divisions of the so-called Swallow cycle. The hero is swallowed by a cow, a giant, a fish, a miller and a salmon, and escapes from all in safety. According to Macculloch, many swallow myths gradually change into stories which attempt to account for various natural events. The curiosity of man makes him invent stories explaining such events. Or an inventive story-teller might build upon an old myth. Many folk-tales of various countries have been changed and modified during the passage of centuries, yet they retain some common characteristics and enough of their antiquity to identify them as the remains of beliefs, customs and ideas of a forgotten age.

In this account, however, we shall not go back beyond the 1630 edition of *Tom Thumb*, which was bequeathed to the Bodleian Library by the author of the "*Anatomy of Melancholy.*" This small black letter edition bears the title "*Tom Thumbe, his life and death: wherein is declared many maruailous acts of manhood, full of wonder, and strange merriments. Which little knight lived in King Arthurs time, and famous in the court of Great Brittaine. London, printed for John Wright. 1630.*" The ballad, consisting of 135 lines, opens as follows:

> In Arthurs court Tom Thumbe did Liue,
> A man of mickle might,
> The best of all the table round,
> And eke a doughty knight:
>
> His stature but an inch in height,
> Or quarter of a span;
> Then thinke you not this little knight,
> Was prou'd a valiant man?
>
> His father was a plow-man plaine,
> His mother milkt the cow,
> But yet the way to get a sonne
> "This" couple knew not how,

> Until such time this good old man
> To learned Merlin goes,
> And there to him his deepe desires
> In secret manner showes,
>
> How in his heart he wisht to have
> A childe in time to come,
> To be his heire, though it might be
> No bigger than his Thumbe.

Merlin told the plowman that his wish would come true and Tom was eventually "begot and borne in halfe an houre" and in four minutes he grew as tall as the plowman's thumb. Of course he was under the protection of the fairies, and at his christening, which was attended by the "Fayry-Queene" with her "traine of Goblins grim," he was named Tom Thumb. Little is told of his early childhood. The fairy queen clothed him in garments which lasted many years, a hat made of an oak leaf, a shirt of a spider's web, his hose and doublet of thistle down, his garters, two little hairs pulled from "his mothers eye" and his boots and shoes from a mouse's skin. Thus attired he sallies forth to play with the neighboring children, losing his "cherry stones," stealing a fresh supply from his playmates, indulging in such tricks as hanging "Black pots, and glasses vpon a bright sunne-beame," and laughing at the whippings which the other boys received when their attempts to do the same ended in broken crockery. Because of the turmoil which Tom created when he went out to play, his mother kept him at home, and from then on his adventures commenced in earnest.

> He sate vpon the pudding-boule,
> The candle for to hold;
> Of which there is vnto this day
> A pretty pastime told:
>
> For Tom fell in, and could not be
> For euer after found,
> For in the blood and batter he
> Was strangely lost and drownd.

Although his mother searched long, it was in vain, and unknowingly she thrust her son into the pudding and the pudding into the kettle. But the pudding bounced around so violently that she thought the devil was inside and very charitably she bestowed it upon a passing tinker. Tom's voice issuing from the pudding scared the tinker so that he threw it down and ran. Tom then emerged and returned home, but only to get into fresh trouble. When Tom's mother went to milk her cows, she tied him fast to a thistle so that the blustery wind would not blow him away, but alas, a cow came by and ate the thistle, Tom and all, and Tom traveled the entire length of the cow's alimentary canal. His next escapade happened while he was helping his father plow. He fell into the furrow, was carried away, just like a grain of corn, by a raven and

> Unto a giants castle top,
> In which he let him fall,
> Where soone the giant swallowed vp
> His body, cloathes and all.
>
> But in his belly did Tom Thumbe
> So great a rumbling make,
> That neither day nor night he could
> The smallest quiet take,
>
> Until the gyant had him spewd
> Three miles into the sea,
> Whereas a fish soone tooke him vp
> And bore him thence away.

The fish was caught and sent to King Arthur. Tom was discovered and enjoyed high favor at court. He danced a "galliard braue vpon his queenes left hand," went on hunting trips with the king, paid a visit to his parents, who feasted him three days on a hazel nut, and returned to King Arthur's court where he engaged in tournaments, vanquishing all his opponents to the great amazement of the knights, but as a result of such strenuous exertions finally becoming sick, and dying, in spite of the skill and cunning of King Arthur's physician.

> And so with peace and quietnesse
> He left this earth below;
> And vp into the Fayry Land
> His ghost did fading goe.

He was received by the Fairy Queen "with musicke and sweet melody" and King Arthur, after mourning with his knights for forty days, built a "tomb of marble gray," "in remembrance of his name."

Thus ends what appears to be the original tale of Tom Thumb, but the story was amplified by the addition of a second and third part, both detailing fresh adventures but lacking the charm and quaintness of the original version. Hazlitt has stated that the author of these later parts was "not trammelled by rhythm, grammar or geography." The second part commences with Tom's return from fairyland and his fall "into a pan of firmity," in good King Edgar's court, causing the cook to drop the pan and mess things up generally. Tom was dragged over to the king's table, where

> With clubs and staves, forks and prongs,
> He guarded was, unpitied,
> To answer for the mighty Wrongs,
> Which he had there committed.

Just as they began to vote on what form his death should take, Tom escaped from such an unfriendly atmosphere by jumping down a miller's throat and in addition to whistling, singing and dancing,

> Tom often pinch'd him by the tripes,
> And made the Miller roar,
> Alas! alas! ten thousand stripes
> Could not have vex'd him more.

After calling in the doctor and twenty learned men and after confessing to various thefts, the miller jumped in a river "and turn'd Tom Thumb into the tide," where he was swallowed by a salmon which was caught and finally purchased by the king's steward. Tom was brought before the king, impaled on a fork, but the affairs of state were not to be interrupted then by such a slender cause and so the cook was instructed to keep Tom a prisoner, which he did by binding him hand and foot and placing him in a mouse trap. After an interval of a week, Tom was taken before the king, but he made such a good plea that he was pardoned and taken into favor.

His troubles, however, were not at an end. While riding on a mouse, a-hunting with the king, a farmer's cat captured both and ran to the top of a tree. After a sad and bloody fight during which the cat scratched and Tom ran his sword through her, the cat dropped him. From this encounter he did not recover. His injuries were too severe. And so the fairy queen sent "a mighty swarm of pretty Fairy Sprites" for him.

> They put him in a winding sheet,
> More white than Lillies fair,
> These Fairies all with music sweet
> Did mount the lofty air.

But "death's fatal arrows prov'd in vain," because "he was hurried back again down from the Fairy Land," and a third part of the tale deals with "his Marvellous Acts of Manhood, performed after his second return from Fairy Land." His first adventure, however, after reaching the earth was so undignified and so devoid of romanticism that only in a "limited and unexpurgated" edition would it be proper to mention it. In due course Tom finally appeared before King Thunston's court where he underwent another trial, coming through, as usual, with honors and ingratiating himself with the king. In fact the king thought so highly of Tom that he bought him a coach drawn by six mice and he lived in splendid ease. But horrors! the microscopic wretch attempted to ravish the queen and,

> The Queen, with rage and fury fir'd,
> To see herself abus'd,
> That of the King she then desir'd,
> Tom Thumb might be accus'd.

> That nothing would her wrath appease,
> To free her from all strife,
> Or set her mind at perfect ease,
> Until she had his life.

Tom escaped this time on a butterfly which after giving him an uncomfortable ride, unluckily flew back to the court where Tom was discovered and captured. He was brought to trial, a very sick man, and

> So the King his sentence he declar'd,
> How hanged he should be,
> And that a Gibbet should be rear'd,
> And none should set him free.

Tom was imprisoned in a mousetrap, but a cat, mistaking him for a mouse, broke his prison and in endeavoring to escape he fell into a spider's web.

> The spider, watching for his Prey,
> Tom took to be a fly,
> And seized him without delay,
> Regarding not his cry.

> The blood out of his body drains,
> He yielded up his breath;
> Thus he was freed from all Pains
> By his unlook'd for death.

> Thus you have heard his actions all,
> Likewise his actions great,
> His Rise, his Progress, and his fall,
> Thus ushered in by fate.

> Although he's dead, his Memory lives,
> Recorded ever sure;
> His very name some pleasure gives,
> And ever will endure.

This in brief is the story of Tom Thumb as told in three parts. During the reigns of James I, Charles I and Charles II, Tom Thumb enjoyed continued popularity, and he was frequently mentioned by contemporary authors. Ritson in 1791, when he reprinted the 1630 version of Tom Thumb in his "*Pieces of Ancient Popular Poetry*" (London), said that "every city, town, village, shop, stall, man, woman and child in the kingdom" was familiar with it. John Newbery published editions in 1768, 1786 and 1789. Various versions circulated as chap-books down to the beginning of the nineteenth century and even later. The tale was popular in this country, too. In the Boston, Massachusetts, *Chronicle* for August 29, 1768, John Mein advertised "*The Famous Tommy Thumb's Little Story Book: Containing His Life and Surprising Adventures,*" etc. "*London: Printed for S. Crowder.*" And in 1686, or some 80 years earlier, John Dunton sold "*The History of Tom Thumb*" in his Boston warehouse. Although these titles were imported, the tale was printed in this country. John Boyle, of Boston, in 1771 printed "*The Famous Tommy Thumb's Little Story-Book. Containing his Life and Adventures.*" And later, in 1813, N. Coverly, Jr., Milk Street, Boston, printed "*The Life and Death of Tom Thumb.*" However, English editions with their quaint woodcut illustrations continued to circulate in this country until the middle of the nineteenth century, some gaily colored in red, pink and green. McLoughlin Brothers in 1870 or 1871 published "*Tom Thumb*" in their "Cinderella Series" and at present various American publishers of children's books usually include a stray title of "*Tom Thumb*" in their lists. But all in all, Tom is not nearly so popular now as he was fifty or seventy-five years ago.

Ever since the story has been current, Tom's thrilling adventures have been told and retold, with modifications by each generation, and many variations occur in the numerous editions within a generation. Although the coarseness of the seventeenth century would not be permitted to circulate in the nurseries of to-day, it should be remembered that in the seventeenth century Tom Thumb was as popular with adults as with children, and no doubt some of the allusions in the early accounts were not intended particularly for childish understanding.

Some of the liberties taken with the text appear to be quite unnecessary. In present-day versions, no one will object to the deletion of expressions which are now highly unconventional and which are objectionable to those of squeamish sensibilities—at least not so long as the early versions are obtainable. However, nearly every one who has arranged the tale for publication has made changes, probably under the delusion that the original was being improved upon. And so in some present-day accounts we are told that Merlin, because the plowman's wife refused him admittance to her home, when he was cold, revenged himself by seeing to it that her baby boy grew no bigger than her thumb. The thistle which the cow ate in 1630 has now become a buttercup. Tom's hat is made, not of an oak leaf but of a rose leaf. And under no circumstances is Tom now allowed to get beyond the cow's mouth. His mother either saves him in time or the cow sneezes him to safety or the cow, hearing strange noises in her throat, simply opens her mouth without further ado and Tom falls out.

The real reason for the queen's displeasure with Tom is never even hinted at. That of course would be unthinkable, and so the queen is made to appear jealous because Tom gets a coach and six mice, or no reason is given at all. Kisses have been injected into modern versions also. Tom's mother kisses him after he escapes from the pudding and before she puts him to bed. Such an act of endearment seems strangely out of place in Tom Thumb's life. He is not at all kissable, and his adventures are not of the sort that admit expressions of affection. But when "adapters" and "arrangers" go so far as to have Tom place carpet tacks in the path of the cat—then something should be done about it.

Many years ago, Dr. Wagstaffe concluded that although Tom Thumb was looked upon merely as entertainment for children, it was "perhaps a performance not unworthy the perusal of the judicious." Dr. Wagstaffe believed that the design of the tale was to recommend virtue and to demonstrate that "however any one may labour under the disadvantages of stature and deformity, or the meanness of parentage, yet if his mind and actions are above the ordinary level, those very disadvantages that seem to depress him add a lustre to his character." Even now some of our "adapters" show a trace of Hannah More-ism at the ends of their adaptations, but for the most part Tom Thumb has been fortunate in escaping the clutches of the moralists.

According to tradition, Tom Thumb died at Lincoln, which was one of the five Danish towns of England, and according to the same tradition his tombstone was a little blue flagstone, in the cathedral, which has long since disappeared. Although the authenticity of this remains uncertain, there can be no doubt about Tom Thumb himself being very much alive to-day, which is my excuse for bringing him up, as Thomas Nashe has said, "thicke and threefold, when better things lie dead."

Source: Harry B. Weiss, "Three Hundred Years of Tom Thumb," in *Scientific Monthly*, Vol. 34, No. 2, February 1932, pp. 157–66.

SOURCES

Armintor, Deborah Needleman, "'Go, Get Your Husband Put into Commission': Fielding's *Tom Thumb* Plays and the Labor of Little Men," in *Eighteenth Century: Theory and Interpretation*, Vol. 44, No. 1, Spring 2003, p. 69.

Backscheider, Paula R., "Henry Fielding," in *Dictionary of Literary Biography*, Vol. 84, *Restoration and Eighteenth-Century Dramatists, Second Series*, edited by Paula R. Backscheider, Gale Research, 1989, pp. 117–45.

Fielding, Henry, *Tom Thumb*, in *"Tom Thumb" and the "Tragedy of Tragedies,"* University of California Press, 1970, pp. 20–38.

Jacob, Margaret, *The Enlightenment: A Brief History with Documents*, Bedford/St. Martin's, 2000.

Johnson, Maurice, "The Art of Parody: *Shamela*," in *Fielding's Art of Fiction: Eleven Essays on "Shamela," "Joseph Andrews," "Tom Jones," and "Amelia,"* University of Pennsylvania Press, 1961, pp. 19–45.

Kudlinski, Kathleen, "Gandhi's Famous Sayings," in *Gandhi: Young Nation Builder*, Fitzgerald Books, 2007, pp. 179–81.

Lyall, Sarah, "Man in the News: David Cameron: Cameron Faces Challenges beyond His Coalition," in *New York Times*, May 11, 2010.

Morrissey, L. J., "Critical Introduction," in *"Tom Thumb" and the "Tragedy of Tragedies,"* University of California Press, 1970, pp. 1–9.

Opie, Iona, and Peter Opie, "The History of Tom Thumb," in *The Classic Fairy Tales*, Oxford University Press, 1980, pp. 36–41.

Paulson, Ronald, *The Life of Henry Fielding: A Critical Biography*, Wiley-Blackwell, 2000.

Pearce, Edward, *The Great Man: Sir Robert Walpole: Scoundrel, Genius and Britain's First Prime Minister*, Random House, 2007.

Porter, Roy, *English Society in the Eighteenth Century*, 2nd ed., Penguin, 1990.

Sarup, Madan, *An Introductory Guide to Post-Structuralism and Postmodernism*, 2nd ed., University of Georgia Press, 1993.

FURTHER READING

Black, Jeremy, *Walpole in Power*, History Press, 2001.
This biography of Walpole explores the career of Britain's first prime minister and Fielding's favorite satirical target. Black explores Walpole's political achievements, noting that he established an unprecedented period of stability while growing and securing the power of the House of Commons.

Fielding, Henry, *Tom Jones*, edited by Simon Stern and John Bender, Oxford University Press, 2008.

First published as *The History of Tom Jones, a Foundling* in 1749, this novel is considered Fielding's best work and is still widely studied and read today. It is also viewed as a shining example of eighteenth-century English literature. It portrays protagonist Tom Jones, an abandoned orphan found on the land of the wealthy Squire Allworthy.

Fletcher, John, and Francis Beaumont, *Collected Works of Francis Beaumont and John Fletcher*, BiblioLife, 2008.
John Fletcher was another predecessor of Fielding's whose work is misappropriated in *Tom Thumb*. His most famous plays, collected in this volume, were written with Francis Beaumont.

Woloch, Isser, *Eighteenth-Century Europe: Tradition and Progress, 1715–1789*, W. W. Norton, 1981.
This volume widens the focus on the eighteenth century, encompassing all of Europe, placing England in a larger historical context. As Woloch demonstrates, the years in which Fielding was most prolific were part of a period in which Europe's population exploded amidst industrial and agricultural revolutions in the United Kingdom.

SUGGESTED SEARCH TERMS

Tom Thumb AND play

Tom Thumb AND Henry Fielding

Tom Thumb AND satire

Tom Thumb AND eighteenth-century England

Henry Fielding AND Sir Robert Walpole

Henry Fielding AND Theatrical Licensing Act of 1737

Tom Thumb AND Tragedies of Tragedies

Tom Thumb AND The Author's Farce

Tom Thumb AND folk tales

Tom Thumb AND Arthurian legends

Glossary of Literary Terms

A

Abstract: Used as a noun, the term refers to a short summary or outline of a longer work. As an adjective applied to writing or literary works, abstract refers to words or phrases that name things not knowable through the five senses. Examples of abstracts include the *Cliffs Notes* summaries of major literary works. Examples of abstract terms or concepts include "idea," "guilt" "honesty," and "loyalty."

Absurd, Theater of the: See *Theater of the Absurd*

Absurdism: See *Theater of the Absurd*

Act: A major section of a play. Acts are divided into varying numbers of shorter scenes. From ancient times to the nineteenth century plays were generally constructed of five acts, but modern works typically consist of one, two, or three acts. Examples of five-act plays include the works of Sophocles and Shakespeare, while the plays of Arthur Miller commonly have a three-act structure.

Acto: A one-act Chicano theater piece developed out of collective improvisation. *Actos* were performed by members of Luis Valdez's Teatro Campesino in California during the mid-1960s.

Aestheticism: A literary and artistic movement of the nineteenth century. Followers of the movement believed that art should not be mixed with social, political, or moral teaching. The statement "art for art's sake" is a good summary of aestheticism. The movement had its roots in France, but it gained widespread importance in England in the last half of the nineteenth century, where it helped change the Victorian practice of including moral lessons in literature. Oscar Wilde is one of the best-known "aesthetes" of the late nineteenth century.

Age of Johnson: The period in English literature between 1750 and 1798, named after the most prominent literary figure of the age, Samuel Johnson. Works written during this time are noted for their emphasis on "sensibility," or emotional quality. These works formed a transition between the rational works of the Age of Reason, or Neoclassical period, and the emphasis on individual feelings and responses of the Romantic period. Significant writers during the Age of Johnson included the novelists Ann Radcliffe and Henry Mackenzie, dramatists Richard Sheridan and Oliver Goldsmith, and poets William Collins and Thomas Gray. Also known as Age of Sensibility

Age of Reason: See *Neoclassicism*

Age of Sensibility: See *Age of Johnson*

Alexandrine Meter: See *Meter*

Allegory: A narrative technique in which characters representing things or abstract ideas are used to convey a message or teach a lesson.

Allegory is typically used to teach moral, ethical, or religious lessons but is sometimes used for satiric or political purposes. Examples of allegorical works include Edmund Spenser's *The Faerie Queene* and John Bunyan's *The Pilgrim's Progress*.

Allusion: A reference to a familiar literary or historical person or event, used to make an idea more easily understood. For example, describing someone as a "Romeo" makes an allusion to William Shakespeare's famous young lover in *Romeo and Juliet*.

Amerind Literature: The writing and oral traditions of Native Americans. Native American literature was originally passed on by word of mouth, so it consisted largely of stories and events that were easily memorized. Amerind prose is often rhythmic like poetry because it was recited to the beat of a ceremonial drum. Examples of Amerind literature include the autobiographical *Black Elk Speaks,* the works of N. Scott Momaday, James Welch, and Craig Lee Strete, and the poetry of Luci Tapahonso.

Analogy: A comparison of two things made to explain something unfamiliar through its similarities to something familiar, or to prove one point based on the acceptedness of another. Similes and metaphors are types of analogies. Analogies often take the form of an extended simile, as in William Blake's aphorism: "As the caterpillar chooses the fairest leaves to lay her eggs on, so the priest lays his curse on the fairest joys."

Angry Young Men: A group of British writers of the 1950s whose work expressed bitterness and disillusionment with society. Common to their work is an anti-hero who rebels against a corrupt social order and strives for personal integrity. The term has been used to describe Kingsley Amis, John Osborne, Colin Wilson, John Wain, and others.

Antagonist: The major character in a narrative or drama who works against the hero or protagonist. An example of an evil antagonist is Richard Lovelace in Samuel Richardson's *Clarissa,* while a virtuous antagonist is Macduff in William Shakespeare's *Macbeth.*

Anthropomorphism: The presentation of animals or objects in human shape or with human characteristics. The term is derived from the Greek word for "human form." The fables of Aesop, the animated films of Walt Disney, and Richard Adams's *Watership Down* feature anthropomorphic characters.

Anti-hero: A central character in a work of literature who lacks traditional heroic qualities such as courage, physical prowess, and fortitude. Anti-heros typically distrust conventional values and are unable to commit themselves to any ideals. They generally feel helpless in a world over which they have no control. Anti-heroes usually accept, and often celebrate, their positions as social outcasts. A well-known anti-hero is Yossarian in Joseph Heller's novel *Catch-22.*

Antimasque: See *Masque*

Antithesis: The antithesis of something is its direct opposite. In literature, the use of antithesis as a figure of speech results in two statements that show a contrast through the balancing of two opposite ideas. Technically, it is the second portion of the statement that is defined as the "antithesis"; the first portion is the "thesis." An example of antithesis is found in the following portion of Abraham Lincoln's "Gettysburg Address"; notice the opposition between the verbs "remember" and "forget" and the phrases "what we say" and "what they did": "The world will little note nor long remember what we say here, but it can never forget what they did here."

Apocrypha: Writings tentatively attributed to an author but not proven or universally accepted to be their works. The term was originally applied to certain books of the Bible that were not considered inspired and so were not included in the "sacred canon." Geoffrey Chaucer, William Shakespeare, Thomas Kyd, Thomas Middleton, and John Marston all have apocrypha. Apocryphal books of the Bible include the Old Testament's Book of Enoch and New Testament's Gospel of Peter.

Apollonian and Dionysian: The two impulses believed to guide authors of dramatic tragedy. The Apollonian impulse is named after Apollo, the Greek god of light and beauty and the symbol of intellectual order. The Dionysian impulse is named after Dionysus, the Greek god of wine and the symbol of the unrestrained forces of nature. The Apollonian impulse is to create a rational, harmonious world, while the Dionysian is to express the irrational forces of personality. Friedrich Nietzche uses these terms in *The*

Birth of Tragedy to designate contrasting elements in Greek tragedy.

Apostrophe: A statement, question, or request addressed to an inanimate object or concept or to a nonexistent or absent person. Requests for inspiration from the muses in poetry are examples of apostrophe, as is Marc Antony's address to Caesar's corpse in William Shakespeare's *Julius Caesar*: "O, pardon me, thou bleeding piece of earth, That I am meek and gentle with these butchers!... Woe to the hand that shed this costly blood!..."

Archetype: The word archetype is commonly used to describe an original pattern or model from which all other things of the same kind are made. This term was introduced to literary criticism from the psychology of Carl Jung. It expresses Jung's theory that behind every person's "unconscious," or repressed memories of the past, lies the "collective unconscious" of the human race: memories of the countless typical experiences of our ancestors. These memories are said to prompt illogical associations that trigger powerful emotions in the reader. Often, the emotional process is primitive, even primordial. Archetypes are the literary images that grow out of the "collective unconscious." They appear in literature as incidents and plots that repeat basic patterns of life. They may also appear as stereotyped characters. Examples of literary archetypes include themes such as birth and death and characters such as the Earth Mother.

Argument: The argument of a work is the author's subject matter or principal idea. Examples of defined "argument" portions of works include John Milton's *Arguments* to each of the books of *Paradise Lost* and the "Argument" to Robert Herrick's *Hesperides*.

Aristotelian Criticism: Specifically, the method of evaluating and analyzing tragedy formulated by the Greek philosopher Aristotle in his *Poetics*. More generally, the term indicates any form of criticism that follows Aristotle's views. Aristotelian criticism focuses on the form and logical structure of a work, apart from its historical or social context, in contrast to "Platonic Criticism," which stresses the usefulness of art. Adherents of New Criticism including John Crowe Ransom and Cleanth Brooks utilize and value the basic ideas of Aristotelian criticism for textual analysis.

Art for Art's Sake: See *Aestheticism*

Aside: A comment made by a stage performer that is intended to be heard by the audience but supposedly not by other characters. Eugene O'Neill's *Strange Interlude* is an extended use of the aside in modern theater.

Audience: The people for whom a piece of literature is written. Authors usually write with a certain audience in mind, for example, children, members of a religious or ethnic group, or colleagues in a professional field. The term "audience" also applies to the people who gather to see or hear any performance, including plays, poetry readings, speeches, and concerts. Jane Austen's parody of the gothic novel, *Northanger Abbey,* was originally intended for (and also pokes fun at) an audience of young and avid female gothic novel readers.

Avant-garde: A French term meaning "vanguard." It is used in literary criticism to describe new writing that rejects traditional approaches to literature in favor of innovations in style or content. Twentieth-century examples of the literary *avant-garde* include the Black Mountain School of poets, the Bloomsbury Group, and the Beat Movement.

B

Ballad: A short poem that tells a simple story and has a repeated refrain. Ballads were originally intended to be sung. Early ballads, known as folk ballads, were passed down through generations, so their authors are often unknown. Later ballads composed by known authors are called literary ballads. An example of an anonymous folk ballad is "Edward," which dates from the Middle Ages. Samuel Taylor Coleridge's "The Rime of the Ancient Mariner" and John Keats's "La Belle Dame sans Merci" are examples of literary ballads.

Baroque: A term used in literary criticism to describe literature that is complex or ornate in style or diction. Baroque works typically express tension, anxiety, and violent emotion. The term "Baroque Age" designates a period in Western European literature beginning in the late sixteenth century and ending about one hundred years later. Works of this period often mirror the qualities of works more generally associated with the label "baroque" and sometimes feature elaborate conceits. Examples of Baroque works include John Lyly's *Euphues: The Anatomy of Wit,* Luis de Gongora's *Soledads,* and William Shakespeare's *As You Like It.*

Baroque Age: See *Baroque*

Baroque Period: See *Baroque*

Beat Generation: See *Beat Movement*

Beat Movement: A period featuring a group of American poets and novelists of the 1950s and 1960s—including Jack Kerouac, Allen Ginsberg, Gregory Corso, William S. Burroughs, and Lawrence Ferlinghetti—who rejected established social and literary values. Using such techniques as stream of consciousness writing and jazz-influenced free verse and focusing on unusual or abnormal states of mind—generated by religious ecstasy or the use of drugs—the Beat writers aimed to create works that were unconventional in both form and subject matter. Kerouac's *On the Road* is perhaps the best-known example of a Beat Generation novel, and Ginsberg's *Howl* is a famous collection of Beat poetry.

Black Aesthetic Movement: A period of artistic and literary development among African Americans in the 1960s and early 1970s. This was the first major African-American artistic movement since the Harlem Renaissance and was closely paralleled by the civil rights and black power movements. The black aesthetic writers attempted to produce works of art that would be meaningful to the black masses. Key figures in black aesthetics included one of its founders, poet and playwright Amiri Baraka, formerly known as LeRoi Jones; poet and essayist Haki R. Madhubuti, formerly Don L. Lee; poet and playwright Sonia Sanchez; and dramatist Ed Bullins. Works representative of the Black Aesthetic Movement include Amiri Baraka's play *Dutchman,* a 1964 Obie award-winner; *Black Fire: An Anthology of Afro-American Writing,* edited by Baraka and playwright Larry Neal and published in 1968; and Sonia Sanchez's poetry collection *We a BaddDDD People,* published in 1970. Also known as Black Arts Movement.

Black Arts Movement: See *Black Aesthetic Movement*

Black Comedy: See *Black Humor*

Black Humor: Writing that places grotesque elements side by side with humorous ones in an attempt to shock the reader, forcing him or her to laugh at the horrifying reality of a disordered world. Joseph Heller's novel *Catch-22* is considered a superb example of the use of black humor. Other well-known authors who use black humor include Kurt Vonnegut, Edward Albee, Eugene Ionesco, and Harold Pinter. Also known as Black Comedy.

Blank Verse: Loosely, any unrhymed poetry, but more generally, unrhymed iambic pentameter verse (composed of lines of five two-syllable feet with the first syllable accented, the second unaccented). Blank verse has been used by poets since the Renaissance for its flexibility and its graceful, dignified tone. John Milton's *Paradise Lost* is in blank verse, as are most of William Shakespeare's plays.

Bloomsbury Group: A group of English writers, artists, and intellectuals who held informal artistic and philosophical discussions in Bloomsbury, a district of London, from around 1907 to the early 1930s. The Bloomsbury Group held no uniform philosophical beliefs but did commonly express an aversion to moral prudery and a desire for greater social tolerance. At various times the circle included Virginia Woolf, E. M. Forster, Clive Bell, Lytton Strachey, and John Maynard Keynes.

Bon Mot: A French term meaning "good word." A *bon mot* is a witty remark or clever observation. Charles Lamb and Oscar Wilde are celebrated for their witty *bon mots.* Two examples by Oscar Wilde stand out: (1) "All women become their mothers. That is their tragedy. No man does. That's his." (2) "A man cannot be too careful in the choice of his enemies."

Breath Verse: See *Projective Verse*

Burlesque: Any literary work that uses exaggeration to make its subject appear ridiculous, either by treating a trivial subject with profound seriousness or by treating a dignified subject frivolously. The word "burlesque" may also be used as an adjective, as in "burlesque show," to mean "striptease act." Examples of literary burlesque include the comedies of Aristophanes, Miguel de Cervantes's *Don Quixote*, Samuel Butler's poem "Hudibras," and John Gay's play *The Beggar's Opera*.

C

Cadence: The natural rhythm of language caused by the alternation of accented and unaccented syllables. Much modern poetry— notably free verse—deliberately manipulates cadence to create complex rhythmic effects. James Macpherson's "Ossian poems" are richly cadenced, as is the poetry of the Symbolists, Walt Whitman, and Amy Lowell.

Caesura: A pause in a line of poetry, usually occurring near the middle. It typically corresponds to a break in the natural rhythm or sense of the line but is sometimes shifted to create special meanings or rhythmic effects. The opening line of Edgar Allan Poe's "The Raven" contains a caesura following "dreary": "Once upon a midnight dreary, while I pondered weak and weary . . . ."

Canzone: A short Italian or Provencal lyric poem, commonly about love and often set to music. The *canzone* has no set form but typically contains five or six stanzas made up of seven to twenty lines of eleven syllables each. A shorter, five- to ten-line "envoy," or concluding stanza, completes the poem. Masters of the *canzone* form include Petrarch, Dante Alighieri, Torquato Tasso, and Guido Cavalcanti.

Carpe Diem: A Latin term meaning "seize the day." This is a traditional theme of poetry, especially lyrics. A *carpe diem* poem advises the reader or the person it addresses to live for today and enjoy the pleasures of the moment. Two celebrated *carpe diem* poems are Andrew Marvell's "To His Coy Mistress" and Robert Herrick's poem beginning "Gather ye rosebuds while ye may . . . ."

Catharsis: The release or purging of unwanted emotions—specifically fear and pity— brought about by exposure to art. The term was first used by the Greek philosopher Aristotle in his *Poetics* to refer to the desired effect of tragedy on spectators. A famous example of catharsis is realized in Sophocles' *Oedipus Rex,* when Oedipus discovers that

his wife, Jacosta, is his own mother and that the stranger he killed on the road was his own father.

Celtic Renaissance: A period of Irish literary and cultural history at the end of the nineteenth century. Followers of the movement aimed to create a romantic vision of Celtic myth and legend. The most significant works of the Celtic Renaissance typically present a dreamy, unreal world, usually in reaction against the reality of contemporary problems. William Butler Yeats's *The Wanderings of Oisin* is among the most significant works of the Celtic Renaissance. Also known as Celtic Twilight.

Celtic Twilight: See *Celtic Renaissance*

Character: Broadly speaking, a person in a literary work. The actions of characters are what constitute the plot of a story, novel, or poem. There are numerous types of characters, ranging from simple, stereotypical figures to intricate, multifaceted ones. In the techniques of anthropomorphism and personification, animals—and even places or things—can assume aspects of character. "Characterization" is the process by which an author creates vivid, believable characters in a work of art. This may be done in a variety of ways, including (1) direct description of the character by the narrator; (2) the direct presentation of the speech, thoughts, or actions of the character; and (3) the responses of other characters to the character. The term "character" also refers to a form originated by the ancient Greek writer Theophrastus that later became popular in the seventeenth and eighteenth centuries. It is a short essay or sketch of a person who prominently displays a specific attribute or quality, such as miserliness or ambition. Notable characters in literature include Oedipus Rex, Don Quixote de la Mancha, Macbeth, Candide, Hester Prynne, Ebenezer Scrooge, Huckleberry Finn, Jay Gatsby, Scarlett O'Hara, James Bond, and Kunta Kinte.

Characterization: See *Character*

Chorus: In ancient Greek drama, a group of actors who commented on and interpreted the unfolding action on the stage. Initially the chorus was a major component of the presentation, but over time it became less significant, with its numbers reduced and its role eventually limited to commentary between acts. By the sixteenth century the chorus—if employed at all—was typically a single person who provided a prologue and an epilogue and occasionally appeared between acts to introduce or underscore an important event. The chorus in William Shakespeare's *Henry V* functions in this way. Modern dramas rarely feature a chorus, but T. S. Eliot's *Murder in the Cathedral* and Arthur Miller's *A View from the Bridge* are notable exceptions. The Stage Manager in Thornton Wilder's *Our Town* performs a role similar to that of the chorus.

Chronicle: A record of events presented in chronological order. Although the scope and level of detail provided varies greatly among the chronicles surviving from ancient times, some, such as the *Anglo-Saxon Chronicle,* feature vivid descriptions and a lively recounting of events. During the Elizabethan Age, many dramas—appropriately called "chronicle plays"—were based on material from chronicles. Many of William Shakespeare's dramas of English history as well as Christopher Marlowe's *Edward II* are based in part on Raphael Holinshead's *Chronicles of England, Scotland, and Ireland.*

Classical: In its strictest definition in literary criticism, classicism refers to works of ancient Greek or Roman literature. The term may also be used to describe a literary work of recognized importance (a "classic") from any time period or literature that exhibits the traits of classicism. Classical authors from ancient Greek and Roman times include Juvenal and Homer. Examples of later works and authors now described as classical include French literature of the seventeenth century, Western novels of the nineteenth century, and American fiction of the mid-nineteenth century such as that written by James Fenimore Cooper and Mark Twain.

Classicism: A term used in literary criticism to describe critical doctrines that have their roots in ancient Greek and Roman literature, philosophy, and art. Works associated with classicism typically exhibit restraint on the part of the author, unity of design and purpose, clarity, simplicity, logical organization, and respect for tradition. Examples of literary classicism include Cicero's prose, the dramas of Pierre Corneille and Jean Racine, the poetry of John Dryden and

Alexander Pope, and the writings of J. W. von Goethe, G. E. Lessing, and T. S. Eliot.

Climax: The turning point in a narrative, the moment when the conflict is at its most intense. Typically, the structure of stories, novels, and plays is one of rising action, in which tension builds to the climax, followed by falling action, in which tension lessens as the story moves to its conclusion. The climax in James Fenimore Cooper's *The Last of the Mohicans* occurs when Magua and his captive Cora are pursued to the edge of a cliff by Uncas. Magua kills Uncas but is subsequently killed by Hawkeye.

Colloquialism: A word, phrase, or form of pronunciation that is acceptable in casual conversation but not in formal, written communication. It is considered more acceptable than slang. An example of colloquialism can be found in Rudyard Kipling's *Barrack-room Ballads:* When 'Omer smote 'is bloomin' lyre He'd 'eard men sing by land and sea; An' what he thought 'e might require 'E went an' took—the same as me!

Comedy: One of two major types of drama, the other being tragedy. Its aim is to amuse, and it typically ends happily. Comedy assumes many forms, such as farce and burlesque, and uses a variety of techniques, from parody to satire. In a restricted sense the term comedy refers only to dramatic presentations, but in general usage it is commonly applied to nondramatic works as well. Examples of comedies range from the plays of Aristophanes, Terrence, and Plautus, Dante Alighieri's *The Divine Comedy,* Francois Rabelais's *Pantagruel* and *Gargantua,* and some of Geoffrey Chaucer's tales and William Shakespeare's plays to Noel Coward's play *Private Lives* and James Thurber's short story "The Secret Life of Walter Mitty."

Comedy of Manners: A play about the manners and conventions of an aristocratic, highly sophisticated society. The characters are usually types rather than individualized personalities, and plot is less important than atmosphere. Such plays were an important aspect of late seventeenth-century English comedy. The comedy of manners was revived in the eighteenth century by Oliver Goldsmith and Richard Brinsley Sheridan, enjoyed a second revival in the late nineteenth century, and has endured into the twentieth century. Examples of comedies of manners include William Congreve's *The Way of the World* in the late seventeenth century, Oliver Goldsmith's *She Stoops to Conquer* and Richard Brinsley Sheridan's *The School for Scandal* in the eighteenth century, Oscar Wilde's *The Importance of Being Earnest* in the nineteenth century, and W. Somerset Maugham's *The Circle* in the twentieth century.

Comic Relief: The use of humor to lighten the mood of a serious or tragic story, especially in plays. The technique is very common in Elizabethan works, and can be an integral part of the plot or simply a brief event designed to break the tension of the scene. The Gravediggers' scene in William Shakespeare's *Hamlet* is a frequently cited example of comic relief.

Commedia dell'arte: An Italian term meaning "the comedy of guilds" or "the comedy of professional actors." This form of dramatic comedy was popular in Italy during the sixteenth century. Actors were assigned stock roles (such as Pulcinella, the stupid servant, or Pantalone, the old merchant) and given a basic plot to follow, but all dialogue was improvised. The roles were rigidly typed and the plots were formulaic, usually revolving around young lovers who thwarted their elders and attained wealth and happiness. A rigid convention of the *commedia dell'arte* is the periodic intrusion of Harlequin, who interrupts the play with low buffoonery. Peppino de Filippo's *Metamorphoses of a Wandering Minstrel* gave modern audiences an idea of what *commedia dell'arte* may have been like. Various scenarios for *commedia dell'arte* were compiled in Petraccone's *La commedia dell'arte, storia, technica, scenari,* published in 1927.

Complaint: A lyric poem, popular in the Renaissance, in which the speaker expresses sorrow about his or her condition. Typically, the speaker's sadness is caused by an unresponsive lover, but some complaints cite other sources of unhappiness, such as poverty or fate. A commonly cited example is "A Complaint by Night of the Lover Not Beloved" by Henry Howard, Earl of Surrey. Thomas Sackville's "Complaint of Henry, Duke of Buckingham" traces the duke's unhappiness to his ruthless ambition.

Conceit: A clever and fanciful metaphor, usually expressed through elaborate and extended comparison, that presents a striking parallel between two seemingly dissimilar things— for example, elaborately comparing a beautiful woman to an object like a garden or the sun. The conceit was a popular device throughout the Elizabethan Age and Baroque Age and was the principal technique of the seventeenth-century English metaphysical poets. This usage of the word conceit is unrelated to the best-known definition of conceit as an arrogant attitude or behavior. The conceit figures prominently in the works of John Donne, Emily Dickinson, and T. S. Eliot.

Concrete: Concrete is the opposite of abstract, and refers to a thing that actually exists or a description that allows the reader to experience an object or concept with the senses. Henry David Thoreau's *Walden* contains much concrete description of nature and wildlife.

Concrete Poetry: Poetry in which visual elements play a large part in the poetic effect. Punctuation marks, letters, or words are arranged on a page to form a visual design: a cross, for example, or a bumblebee. Max Bill and Eugene Gomringer were among the early practitioners of concrete poetry; Haroldo de Campos and Augusto de Campos are among contemporary authors of concrete poetry.

Confessional Poetry: A form of poetry in which the poet reveals very personal, intimate, sometimes shocking information about himself or herself. Anne Sexton, Sylvia Plath, Robert Lowell, and John Berryman wrote poetry in the confessional vein.

Conflict: The conflict in a work of fiction is the issue to be resolved in the story. It usually occurs between two characters, the protagonist and the antagonist, or between the protagonist and society or the protagonist and himself or herself. Conflict in Theodore Dreiser's novel *Sister Carrie* comes as a result of urban society, while Jack London's short story "To Build a Fire" concerns the protagonist's battle against the cold and himself.

Connotation: The impression that a word gives beyond its defined meaning. Connotations may be universally understood or may be significant only to a certain group. Both "horse" and "steed" denote the same animal, but "steed" has a different connotation, deriving from the chivalrous or romantic narratives in which the word was once often used.

Consonance: Consonance occurs in poetry when words appearing at the ends of two or more verses have similar final consonant sounds but have final vowel sounds that differ, as with "stuff" and "off." Consonance is found in "The curfew tolls the knells of parting day" from Thomas Grey's "An Elegy Written in a Country Church Yard." Also known as Half Rhyme or Slant Rhyme.

Convention: Any widely accepted literary device, style, or form. A soliloquy, in which a character reveals to the audience his or her private thoughts, is an example of a dramatic convention.

Corrido: A Mexican ballad. Examples of *corridos* include "Muerte del afamado Bilito," "La voz de mi conciencia," "Lucio Perez," "La juida," and "Los presos."

Couplet: Two lines of poetry with the same rhyme and meter, often expressing a complete and self-contained thought. The following couplet is from Alexander Pope's "Elegy to the Memory of an Unfortunate Lady": 'Tis Use alone that sanctifies Expense, And Splendour borrows all her rays from Sense.

Criticism: The systematic study and evaluation of literary works, usually based on a specific method or set of principles. An important part of literary studies since ancient times, the practice of criticism has given rise to numerous theories, methods, and "schools," sometimes producing conflicting, even contradictory, interpretations of literature in general as well as of individual works. Even such basic issues as what constitutes a poem or a novel have been the subject of much criticism over the centuries. Seminal texts of literary criticism include Plato's *Republic,* Aristotle's *Poetics,* Sir Philip Sidney's *The Defence of Poesie,* John Dryden's *Of Dramatic Poesie,* and William Wordsworth's "Preface" to the second edition of his *Lyrical Ballads.* Contemporary schools of criticism include deconstruction, feminist, psychoanalytic, poststructuralist, new historicist, postcolonialist, and reader-response.

D

Dactyl: See *Foot*

Dadaism: A protest movement in art and literature founded by Tristan Tzara in 1916. Followers of the movement expressed their outrage at the destruction brought about by World War I by revolting against numerous forms of social convention. The Dadaists presented works marked by calculated madness and flamboyant nonsense. They stressed total freedom of expression, commonly through primitive displays of emotion and illogical, often senseless, poetry. The movement ended shortly after the war, when it was replaced by surrealism. Proponents of Dadaism include Andre Breton, Louis Aragon, Philippe Soupault, and Paul Eluard.

Decadent: See *Decadents*

Decadents: The followers of a nineteenth-century literary movement that had its beginnings in French aestheticism. Decadent literature displays a fascination with perverse and morbid states; a search for novelty and sensation—the "new thrill"; a preoccupation with mysticism; and a belief in the senselessness of human existence. The movement is closely associated with the doctrine Art for Art's Sake. The term "decadence" is sometimes used to denote a decline in the quality of art or literature following a period of greatness. Major French decadents are Charles Baudelaire and Arthur Rimbaud. English decadents include Oscar Wilde, Ernest Dowson, and Frank Harris.

Deconstruction: A method of literary criticism developed by Jacques Derrida and characterized by multiple conflicting interpretations of a given work. Deconstructionists consider the impact of the language of a work and suggest that the true meaning of the work is not necessarily the meaning that the author intended. Jacques Derrida's *De la grammatologie* is the seminal text on deconstructive strategies; among American practitioners of this method of criticism are Paul de Man and J. Hillis Miller.

Deduction: The process of reaching a conclusion through reasoning from general premises to a specific premise. An example of deduction is present in the following syllogism: Premise: All mammals are animals. Premise: All whales are mammals. Conclusion: Therefore, all whales are animals.

Denotation: The definition of a word, apart from the impressions or feelings it creates in the reader. The word "apartheid" denotes a political and economic policy of segregation by race, but its connotations—oppression, slavery, inequality—are numerous.

Denouement: A French word meaning "the unknotting." In literary criticism, it denotes the resolution of conflict in fiction or drama. The *denouement* follows the climax and provides an outcome to the primary plot situation as well as an explanation of secondary plot complications. The *denouement* often involves a character's recognition of his or her state of mind or moral condition. A well-known example of *denouement* is the last scene of the play *As You Like It* by William Shakespeare, in which couples are married, an evildoer repents, the identities of two disguised characters are revealed, and a ruler is restored to power. Also known as Falling Action.

Description: Descriptive writing is intended to allow a reader to picture the scene or setting in which the action of a story takes place. The form this description takes often evokes an intended emotional response—a dark, spooky graveyard will evoke fear, and a peaceful, sunny meadow will evoke calmness. An example of a descriptive story is Edgar Allan Poe's *Landor's Cottage,* which offers a detailed depiction of a New York country estate.

Detective Story: A narrative about the solution of a mystery or the identification of a criminal. The conventions of the detective story include the detective's scrupulous use of logic in solving the mystery; incompetent or ineffectual police; a suspect who appears guilty at first but is later proved innocent; and the detective's friend or confidant—often the narrator—whose slowness in interpreting clues emphasizes by contrast the detective's brilliance. Edgar Allan Poe's "Murders in the Rue Morgue" is commonly regarded as the earliest example of this type of story. With this work, Poe established many of the conventions of the detective story genre, which are still in practice. Other practitioners of this vast and extremely popular genre include Arthur Conan Doyle, Dashiell Hammett, and Agatha Christie.

Deus ex machina: A Latin term meaning "god out of a machine." In Greek drama, a god was often lowered onto the stage by a mechanism of some kind to rescue the hero or untangle the plot. By extension, the term refers to any artificial device or coincidence used to bring about a convenient and simple solution to a plot. This is a common device in melodramas and includes such fortunate circumstances as the sudden receipt of a legacy to save the family farm or a last-minute stay of execution. The *deus ex machina* invariably rewards the virtuous and punishes evildoers. Examples of *deus ex machina* include King Louis XIV in Jean-Baptiste Moliere's *Tartuffe* and Queen Victoria in *The Pirates of Penzance* by William Gilbert and Arthur Sullivan. Bertolt Brecht parodies the abuse of such devices in the conclusion of his *Threepenny Opera.*

Dialogue: In its widest sense, dialogue is simply conversation between people in a literary work; in its most restricted sense, it refers specifically to the speech of characters in a drama. As a specific literary genre, a "dialogue" is a composition in which characters debate an issue or idea. The Greek philosopher Plato frequently expounded his theories in the form of dialogues.

Diction: The selection and arrangement of words in a literary work. Either or both may vary depending on the desired effect. There are four general types of diction: "formal," used in scholarly or lofty writing; "informal," used in relaxed but educated conversation; "colloquial," used in everyday speech; and "slang," containing newly coined words and other terms not accepted in formal usage.

Didactic: A term used to describe works of literature that aim to teach some moral, religious, political, or practical lesson. Although didactic elements are often found in artistically pleasing works, the term "didactic" usually refers to literature in which the message is more important than the form. The term may also be used to criticize a work that the critic finds "overly didactic," that is, heavy-handed in its delivery of a lesson. Examples of didactic literature include John Bunyan's *Pilgrim's Progress,* Alexander Pope's *Essay* *on Criticism,* Jean-Jacques Rousseau's *Emile,* and Elizabeth Inchbald's *Simple Story.*

Dimeter: See *Meter*

Dionysian: See *Apollonian and Dionysian*

Discordia concours: A Latin phrase meaning "discord in harmony." The term was coined by the eighteenth-century English writer Samuel Johnson to describe "a combination of dissimilar images or discovery of occult resemblances in things apparently unlike." Johnson created the expression by reversing a phrase by the Latin poet Horace. The metaphysical poetry of John Donne, Richard Crashaw, Abraham Cowley, George Herbert, and Edward Taylor among others, contains many examples of *discordia concours.* In Donne's "A Valediction: Forbidding Mourning," the poet compares the union of himself with his lover to a draftsman's compass: If they be two, they are two so, As stiff twin compasses are two: Thy soul, the fixed foot, makes no show To move, but doth, if the other do; And though it in the center sit, Yet when the other far doth roam, It leans, and hearkens after it, And grows erect, as that comes home.

Dissonance: A combination of harsh or jarring sounds, especially in poetry. Although such combinations may be accidental, poets sometimes intentionally make them to achieve particular effects. Dissonance is also sometimes used to refer to close but not identical rhymes. When this is the case, the word functions as a synonym for consonance. Robert Browning, Gerard Manley Hopkins, and many other poets have made deliberate use of dissonance.

Doppelganger: A literary technique by which a character is duplicated (usually in the form of an alter ego, though sometimes as a ghostly counterpart) or divided into two distinct, usually opposite personalities. The use of this character device is widespread in nineteenth- and twentieth- century literature, and indicates a growing awareness among authors that the "self" is really a composite of many "selves." A well-known story containing a *doppelganger* character is Robert Louis Stevenson's *Dr. Jekyll and Mr. Hyde,* which dramatizes an internal struggle between good and evil. Also known as The Double.

Double Entendre: A corruption of a French phrase meaning "double meaning." The term is used to indicate a word or phrase that is deliberately ambiguous, especially when one of the meanings is risque or improper. An example of a *double entendre* is the Elizabethan usage of the verb "die," which refers both to death and to orgasm.

Double, The: See *Doppelganger*

Draft: Any preliminary version of a written work. An author may write dozens of drafts which are revised to form the final work, or he or she may write only one, with few or no revisions. Dorothy Parker's observation that "I can't write five words but that I change seven" humorously indicates the purpose of the draft.

Drama: In its widest sense, a drama is any work designed to be presented by actors on a stage. Similarly, "drama" denotes a broad literary genre that includes a variety of forms, from pageant and spectacle to tragedy and comedy, as well as countless types and subtypes. More commonly in modern usage, however, a drama is a work that treats serious subjects and themes but does not aim at the grandeur of tragedy. This use of the term originated with the eighteenth-century French writer Denis Diderot, who used the word *drame* to designate his plays about middle- class life; thus "drama" typically features characters of a less exalted stature than those of tragedy. Examples of classical dramas include Menander's comedy *Dyscolus* and Sophocles' tragedy *Oedipus Rex.* Contemporary dramas include Eugene O'Neill's *The Iceman Cometh,* Lillian Hellman's *Little Foxes,* and August Wilson's *Ma Rainey's Black Bottom.*

Dramatic Irony: Occurs when the audience of a play or the reader of a work of literature knows something that a character in the work itself does not know. The irony is in the contrast between the intended meaning of the statements or actions of a character and the additional information understood by the audience. A celebrated example of dramatic irony is in Act V of William Shakespeare's *Romeo and Juliet,* where two young lovers meet their end as a result of a tragic misunderstanding. Here, the audience has full knowledge that Juliet's apparent "death" is merely temporary; she will regain her senses when the mysterious "sleeping potion" she has taken wears off. But Romeo, mistaking Juliet's drug-induced trance for true death, kills himself in grief. Upon awakening, Juliet discovers Romeo's corpse and, in despair, slays herself.

Dramatic Monologue: See *Monologue*

Dramatic Poetry: Any lyric work that employs elements of drama such as dialogue, conflict, or characterization, but excluding works that are intended for stage presentation. A monologue is a form of dramatic poetry.

Dramatis Personae: The characters in a work of literature, particularly a drama. The list of characters printed before the main text of a play or in the program is the *dramatis personae*.

Dream Allegory: See *Dream Vision*

Dream Vision: A literary convention, chiefly of the Middle Ages. In a dream vision a story is presented as a literal dream of the narrator. This device was commonly used to teach moral and religious lessons. Important works of this type are *The Divine Comedy* by Dante Alighieri, *Piers Plowman* by William Langland, and *The Pilgrim's Progress* by John Bunyan. Also known as Dream Allegory.

Dystopia: An imaginary place in a work of fiction where the characters lead dehumanized, fearful lives. Jack London's *The Iron Heel*, Yevgeny Zamyatin's *My*, Aldous Huxley's *Brave New World*, George Orwell's *Nineteen Eighty-four*, and Margaret Atwood's *Handmaid's Tale* portray versions of dystopia.

E

Eclogue: In classical literature, a poem featuring rural themes and structured as a dialogue among shepherds. Eclogues often took specific poetic forms, such as elegies or love poems. Some were written as the soliloquy of a shepherd. In later centuries, "eclogue" came to refer to any poem that was in the pastoral tradition or that had a dialogue or monologue structure. A classical example of an eclogue is Virgil's *Eclogues,* also known as *Bucolics.* Giovanni Boccaccio, Edmund Spenser, Andrew Marvell, Jonathan Swift, and Louis MacNeice also wrote eclogues.

Edwardian: Describes cultural conventions identified with the period of the reign of Edward VII of England (1901-1910). Writers of the Edwardian Age typically displayed a strong reaction against the propriety and conservatism of the Victorian Age. Their work often exhibits distrust of authority in religion, politics, and art and expresses strong doubts about the soundness of conventional values. Writers of this era include George Bernard Shaw, H. G. Wells, and Joseph Conrad.

Edwardian Age: See *Edwardian*

Electra Complex: A daughter's amorous obsession with her father. The term Electra complex comes from the plays of Euripides and Sophocles entitled *Electra,* in which the character Electra drives her brother Orestes to kill their mother and her lover in revenge for the murder of their father.

Elegy: A lyric poem that laments the death of a person or the eventual death of all people. In a conventional elegy, set in a classical world, the poet and subject are spoken of as shepherds. In modern criticism, the word elegy is often used to refer to a poem that is melancholy or mournfully contemplative. John Milton's "Lycidas" and Percy Bysshe Shelley's "Adonais" are two examples of this form.

Elizabethan Age: A period of great economic growth, religious controversy, and nationalism closely associated with the reign of Elizabeth I of England (1558-1603). The Elizabethan Age is considered a part of the general renaissance—that is, the flowering of arts and literature—that took place in Europe during the fourteenth through sixteenth centuries. The era is considered the golden age of English literature. The most important dramas in English and a great deal of lyric poetry were produced during this period, and modern English criticism began around this time. The notable authors of the period—Philip Sidney, Edmund Spenser, Christopher Marlowe, William Shakespeare, Ben Jonson, Francis Bacon, and John Donne—are among the best in all of English literature.

Elizabethan Drama: English comic and tragic plays produced during the Renaissance, or more narrowly, those plays written during the last years of and few years after Queen Elizabeth's reign. William Shakespeare is considered an Elizabethan dramatist in the broader sense, although most of his work was produced during the reign of James I. Examples of Elizabethan comedies include John Lyly's *The Woman in the Moone,* Thomas Dekker's *The Roaring Girl, or, Moll Cut Purse,* and William Shakespeare's *Twelfth Night.* Examples of Elizabethan tragedies include William Shakespeare's *Antony and Cleopatra,* Thomas Kyd's *The Spanish Tragedy,* and John Webster's *The Tragedy of the Duchess of Malfi.*

Empathy: A sense of shared experience, including emotional and physical feelings, with someone or something other than oneself. Empathy is often used to describe the response of a reader to a literary character. An example of an empathic passage is William Shakespeare's description in his narrative poem *Venus and Adonis* of: the snail, whose tender horns being hit, Shrinks backward in his shelly cave with pain. Readers of Gerard Manley Hopkins's *The Windhover* may experience some of the physical sensations evoked in the description of the movement of the falcon.

English Sonnet: See *Sonnet*

Enjambment: The running over of the sense and structure of a line of verse or a couplet into the following verse or couplet. Andrew Marvell's "To His Coy Mistress" is structured as a series of enjambments, as in lines 11-12: "My vegetable love should grow/Vaster than empires and more slow."

Enlightenment, The: An eighteenth-century philosophical movement. It began in France but had a wide impact throughout Europe and America. Thinkers of the Enlightenment valued reason and believed that both the individual and society could achieve a state of perfection. Corresponding to this essentially humanist vision was a resistance to religious authority. Important figures of the Enlightenment were Denis Diderot and Voltaire in France, Edward Gibbon and David Hume in England, and Thomas Paine and Thomas Jefferson in the United States.

Epic: A long narrative poem about the adventures of a hero of great historic or legendary importance. The setting is vast and the action is often given cosmic significance through the intervention of supernatural forces such as gods, angels, or demons. Epics are typically written in a classical style of grand simplicity with elaborate metaphors and allusions that

enhance the symbolic importance of a hero's adventures. Some well-known epics are Homer's *Iliad* and *Odyssey,* Virgil's *Aeneid,* and John Milton's *Paradise Lost.*

Epic Simile: See *Homeric Simile*

Epic Theater: A theory of theatrical presentation developed by twentieth-century German playwright Bertolt Brecht. Brecht created a type of drama that the audience could view with complete detachment. He used what he termed "alienation effects" to create an emotional distance between the audience and the action on stage. Among these effects are: short, self-contained scenes that keep the play from building to a cathartic climax; songs that comment on the action; and techniques of acting that prevent the actor from developing an emotional identity with his role. Besides the plays of Bertolt Brecht, other plays that utilize epic theater conventions include those of Georg Buchner, Frank Wedekind, Erwin Piscator, and Leopold Jessner.

Epigram: A saying that makes the speaker's point quickly and concisely. Samuel Taylor Coleridge wrote an epigram that neatly sums up the form: What is an Epigram? A Dwarfish whole, Its body brevity, and wit its soul.

Epilogue: A concluding statement or section of a literary work. In dramas, particularly those of the seventeenth and eighteenth centuries, the epilogue is a closing speech, often in verse, delivered by an actor at the end of a play and spoken directly to the audience. A famous epilogue is Puck's speech at the end of William Shakespeare's *A Midsummer Night's Dream.*

Epiphany: A sudden revelation of truth inspired by a seemingly trivial incident. The term was widely used by James Joyce in his critical writings, and the stories in Joyce's *Dubliners* are commonly called "epiphanies."

Episode: An incident that forms part of a story and is significantly related to it. Episodes may be either self-contained narratives or events that depend on a larger context for their sense and importance. Examples of episodes include the founding of Wilmington, Delaware in Charles Reade's *The Disinherited Heir* and the individual events comprising the picaresque novels and medieval romances.

Episodic Plot: See *Plot*

Epitaph: An inscription on a tomb or tombstone, or a verse written on the occasion of a person's death. Epitaphs may be serious or humorous. Dorothy Parker's epitaph reads, "I told you I was sick."

Epithalamion: A song or poem written to honor and commemorate a marriage ceremony. Famous examples include Edmund Spenser's "Epithalamion" and e. e. cummings's "Epithalamion." Also spelled Epithalamium.

Epithalamium: See *Epithalamion*

Epithet: A word or phrase, often disparaging or abusive, that expresses a character trait of someone or something. "The Napoleon of crime" is an epithet applied to Professor Moriarty, arch-rival of Sherlock Holmes in Arthur Conan Doyle's series of detective stories.

Exempla: See *Exemplum*

Exemplum: A tale with a moral message. This form of literary sermonizing flourished during the Middle Ages, when *exempla* appeared in collections known as "example-books." The works of Geoffrey Chaucer are full of *exempla*.

Existentialism: A predominantly twentieth-century philosophy concerned with the nature and perception of human existence. There are two major strains of existentialist thought: atheistic and Christian. Followers of atheistic existentialism believe that the individual is alone in a godless universe and that the basic human condition is one of suffering and loneliness. Nevertheless, because there are no fixed values, individuals can create their own characters—indeed, they can shape themselves—through the exercise of free will. The atheistic strain culminates in and is popularly associated with the works of Jean-Paul Sartre. The Christian existentialists, on the other hand, believe that only in God may people find freedom from life's anguish. The two strains hold certain beliefs in common: that existence cannot be fully understood or described through empirical effort; that anguish is a universal element of life; that individuals must bear responsibility for their actions; and that there is no common standard of behavior or perception for religious and ethical matters. Existentialist thought figures prominently in the works of such authors as Eugene Ionesco, Franz Kafka, Fyodor Dostoyevsky, Simone de Beauvoir, Samuel Beckett, and Albert Camus.

Expatriates: See *Expatriatism*

Expatriatism: The practice of leaving one's country to live for an extended period in another country. Literary expatriates include English poets Percy Bysshe Shelley and John Keats in Italy, Polish novelist Joseph Conrad in England, American writers Richard Wright, James Baldwin, Gertrude Stein, and Ernest Hemingway in France, and Trinidadian author Neil Bissondath in Canada.

Exposition: Writing intended to explain the nature of an idea, thing, or theme. Expository writing is often combined with description, narration, or argument. In dramatic writing, the exposition is the introductory material which presents the characters, setting, and tone of the play. An example of dramatic exposition occurs in many nineteenth-century drawing-room comedies in which the butler and the maid open the play with relevant talk about their master and mistress; in composition, exposition relays factual information, as in encyclopedia entries.

Expressionism: An indistinct literary term, originally used to describe an early twentieth-century school of German painting. The term applies to almost any mode of unconventional, highly subjective writing that distorts reality in some way. Advocates of Expressionism include dramatists George Kaiser, Ernst Toller, Luigi Pirandello, Federico Garcia Lorca, Eugene O'Neill, and Elmer Rice; poets George Heym, Ernst Stadler, August Stramm, Gottfried Benn, and Georg Trakl; and novelists Franz Kafka and James Joyce.

Extended Monologue: See *Monologue*

F

Fable: A prose or verse narrative intended to convey a moral. Animals or inanimate objects with human characteristics often serve as characters in fables. A famous fable is Aesop's "The Tortoise and the Hare."

Fairy Tales: Short narratives featuring mythical beings such as fairies, elves, and sprites. These tales originally belonged to the folklore of a particular nation or region, such as those collected in Germany by Jacob and Wilhelm Grimm. Two other celebrated writers of fairy tales are Hans Christian Andersen and Rudyard Kipling.

Falling Action: See *Denouement*

Fantasy: A literary form related to mythology and folklore. Fantasy literature is typically set in non-existent realms and features supernatural beings. Notable examples of fantasy literature are *The Lord of the Rings* by J. R. R. Tolkien and the Gormenghast trilogy by Mervyn Peake.

Farce: A type of comedy characterized by broad humor, outlandish incidents, and often vulgar subject matter. Much of the "comedy" in film and television could more accurately be described as farce.

Feet: See *Foot*

Feminine Rhyme: See *Rhyme*

Femme fatale: A French phrase with the literal translation "fatal woman." A *femme fatale* is a sensuous, alluring woman who often leads men into danger or trouble. A classic example of the *femme fatale* is the nameless character in Billy Wilder's *The Seven Year Itch,* portrayed by Marilyn Monroe in the film adaptation.

Fiction: Any story that is the product of imagination rather than a documentation of fact. characters and events in such narratives may be based in real life but their ultimate form and configuration is a creation of the author. Geoffrey Chaucer's *The Canterbury Tales,* Laurence Sterne's *Tristram Shandy,* and Margaret Mitchell's *Gone with the Wind* are examples of fiction.

Figurative Language: A technique in writing in which the author temporarily interrupts the order, construction, or meaning of the writing for a particular effect. This interruption takes the form of one or more figures of speech such as hyperbole, irony, or simile. Figurative language is the opposite of literal language, in which every word is truthful, accurate, and free of exaggeration or embellishment. Examples of figurative language are tropes such as metaphor and rhetorical figures such as apostrophe.

Figures of Speech: Writing that differs from customary conventions for construction, meaning, order, or significance for the purpose of a special meaning or effect. There are two major types of figures of speech: rhetorical figures, which do not make changes in the meaning of the words, and tropes, which do. Types of figures of speech include simile, hyperbole, alliteration, and pun, among many others.

Fin de siecle: A French term meaning "end of the century." The term is used to denote the last decade of the nineteenth century, a transition period when writers and other artists abandoned old conventions and looked for new techniques and objectives. Two writers commonly associated with the *fin de siecle* mindset are Oscar Wilde and George Bernard Shaw.

First Person: See *Point of View*

Flashback: A device used in literature to present action that occurred before the beginning of the story. Flashbacks are often introduced as the dreams or recollections of one or more characters. Flashback techniques are often used in films, where they are typically set off by a gradual changing of one picture to another.

Foil: A character in a work of literature whose physical or psychological qualities contrast strongly with, and therefore highlight, the corresponding qualities of another character. In his Sherlock Holmes stories, Arthur Conan Doyle portrayed Dr. Watson as a man of normal habits and intelligence, making him a foil for the eccentric and wonderfully perceptive Sherlock Holmes.

Folk Ballad: See *Ballad*

Folklore: Traditions and myths preserved in a culture or group of people. Typically, these are passed on by word of mouth in various forms—such as legends, songs, and proverbs—or preserved in customs and ceremonies. This term was first used by W. J. Thoms in 1846. Sir James Frazer's *The Golden Bough* is the record of English folklore; myths about the frontier and the Old South exemplify American folklore.

Folktale: A story originating in oral tradition. Folktales fall into a variety of categories, including legends, ghost stories, fairy tales, fables, and anecdotes based on historical figures and events. Examples of folktales include Giambattista Basile's *The Pentamerone,* which contains the tales of Puss in Boots, Rapunzel, Cinderella, and Beauty and the Beast, and Joel Chandler Harris's Uncle Remus stories, which represent transplanted African folktales and American tales about the characters Mike Fink, Johnny Appleseed, Paul Bunyan, and Pecos Bill.

Foot: The smallest unit of rhythm in a line of poetry. In English-language poetry, a foot is typically one accented syllable combined with one or two unaccented syllables. There are many different types of feet. When the accent is on the second syllable of a two syllable word (con-*tort*), the foot is an "iamb"; the reverse accentual pattern (*tor*-ture) is a "trochee." Other feet that commonly occur in poetry in English are "anapest," two unaccented syllables followed by an accented syllable as in inter-*cept*, and "dactyl," an accented syllable followed by two unaccented syllables as in *su*-i-cide.

Foreshadowing: A device used in literature to create expectation or to set up an explanation of later developments. In Charles Dickens's *Great Expectations,* the graveyard encounter at the beginning of the novel between Pip and the escaped convict Magwitch foreshadows the baleful atmosphere and events that comprise much of the narrative.

Form: The pattern or construction of a work which identifies its genre and distinguishes it from other genres. Examples of forms include the different genres, such as the lyric form or the short story form, and various patterns for poetry, such as the verse form or the stanza form.

Formalism: In literary criticism, the belief that literature should follow prescribed rules of construction, such as those that govern the sonnet form. Examples of formalism are found in the work of the New Critics and structuralists.

Fourteener Meter: See *Meter*

Free Verse: Poetry that lacks regular metrical and rhyme patterns but that tries to capture the cadences of everyday speech. The form allows a poet to exploit a variety of rhythmical effects within a single poem. Free-verse techniques have been widely used in the twentieth century by such writers as Ezra Pound, T. S. Eliot, Carl Sandburg, and William Carlos Williams. Also known as *Vers libre*.

Futurism: A flamboyant literary and artistic movement that developed in France, Italy,

and Russia from 1908 through the 1920s. Futurist theater and poetry abandoned traditional literary forms. In their place, followers of the movement attempted to achieve total freedom of expression through bizarre imagery and deformed or newly invented words. The Futurists were self-consciously modern artists who attempted to incorporate the appearances and sounds of modern life into their work. Futurist writers include Filippo Tommaso Marinetti, Wyndham Lewis, Guillaume Apollinaire, Velimir Khlebnikov, and Vladimir Mayakovsky.

G

Genre: A category of literary work. In critical theory, genre may refer to both the content of a given work—tragedy, comedy, pastoral— and to its form, such as poetry, novel, or drama. This term also refers to types of popular literature, as in the genres of science fiction or the detective story.

Genteel Tradition: A term coined by critic George Santayana to describe the literary practice of certain late nineteenth-century American writers, especially New Englanders. Followers of the Genteel Tradition emphasized conventionality in social, religious, moral, and literary standards. Some of the best-known writers of the Genteel Tradition are R. H. Stoddard and Bayard Taylor.

Gilded Age: A period in American history during the 1870s characterized by political corruption and materialism. A number of important novels of social and political criticism were written during this time. Examples of Gilded Age literature include Henry Adams's *Democracy* and F. Marion Crawford's *An American Politician.*

Gothic: See *Gothicism*

Gothicism: In literary criticism, works characterized by a taste for the medieval or morbidly attractive. A gothic novel prominently features elements of horror, the supernatural, gloom, and violence: clanking chains, terror, charnel houses, ghosts, medieval castles, and mysteriously slamming doors. The term "gothic novel" is also applied to novels that lack elements of the traditional Gothic setting but that create a similar atmosphere of terror or dread. Mary Shelley's *Frankenstein* is perhaps the best-known English work of this kind.

Gothic Novel: See *Gothicism*

Great Chain of Being: The belief that all things and creatures in nature are organized in a hierarchy from inanimate objects at the bottom to God at the top. This system of belief was popular in the seventeenth and eighteenth centuries. A summary of the concept of the great chain of being can be found in the first epistle of Alexander Pope's *An Essay on Man,* and more recently in Arthur O. Lovejoy's *The Great Chain of Being: A Study of the History of an Idea.*

Grotesque: In literary criticism, the subject matter of a work or a style of expression characterized by exaggeration, deformity, freakishness, and disorder. The grotesque often includes an element of comic absurdity. Early examples of literary grotesque include Francois Rabelais's *Pantagruel* and *Gargantua* and Thomas Nashe's *The Unfortunate Traveller,* while more recent examples can be found in the works of Edgar Allan Poe, Evelyn Waugh, Eudora Welty, Flannery O'Connor, Eugene Ionesco, Gunter Grass, Thomas Mann, Mervyn Peake, and Joseph Heller, among many others.

H

Haiku: The shortest form of Japanese poetry, constructed in three lines of five, seven, and five syllables respectively. The message of a *haiku* poem usually centers on some aspect of spirituality and provokes an emotional response in the reader. Early masters of *haiku* include Basho, Buson, Kobayashi Issa, and Masaoka Shiki. English writers of *haiku* include the Imagists, notably Ezra Pound, H. D., Amy Lowell, Carl Sandburg, and William Carlos Williams. Also known as *Hokku.*

Half Rhyme: See *Consonance*

Hamartia: In tragedy, the event or act that leads to the hero's or heroine's downfall. This term is often incorrectly used as a synonym for tragic flaw. In Richard Wright's *Native Son,* the act that seals Bigger Thomas's fate is his first impulsive murder.

Harlem Renaissance: The Harlem Renaissance of the 1920s is generally considered the first significant movement of black writers and artists in the United States. During this period, new and established black writers published more fiction and poetry than ever before, the first influential black literary journals were established, and black authors and artists received their first widespread recognition and serious critical appraisal. Among the major writers associated with this period are Claude McKay, Jean Toomer, Countee Cullen, Langston Hughes, Arna Bontemps, Nella Larsen, and Zora Neale Hurston. Works representative of the Harlem Renaissance include Arna Bontemps's poems "The Return" and "Golgotha Is a Mountain," Claude McKay's novel *Home to Harlem,* Nella Larsen's novel *Passing,* Langston Hughes's poem "The Negro Speaks of Rivers," and the journals *Crisis* and *Opportunity,* both founded during this period. Also known as Negro Renaissance and New Negro Movement.

Harlequin: A stock character of the *commedia dell'arte* who occasionally interrupted the action with silly antics. Harlequin first appeared on the English stage in John Day's *The Travailes of the Three English Brothers.* The San Francisco Mime Troupe is one of the few modern groups to adapt Harlequin to the needs of contemporary satire.

Hellenism: Imitation of ancient Greek thought or styles. Also, an approach to life that focuses on the growth and development of the intellect. "Hellenism" is sometimes used to refer to the belief that reason can be applied to examine all human experience. A cogent discussion of Hellenism can be found in Matthew Arnold's *Culture and Anarchy.*

Heptameter: See *Meter*

Hero/Heroine: The principal sympathetic character (male or female) in a literary work. Heroes and heroines typically exhibit admirable traits: idealism, courage, and integrity, for example. Famous heroes and heroines include Pip in Charles Dickens's *Great Expectations,* the anonymous narrator in Ralph Ellison's *Invisible Man,* and Sethe in Toni Morrison's *Beloved.*

Heroic Couplet: A rhyming couplet written in iambic pentameter (a verse with five iambic feet). The following lines by Alexander Pope are an example: "Truth guards the Poet, sanctifies the line,/ And makes Immortal, Verse as mean as mine."

Heroic Line: The meter and length of a line of verse in epic or heroic poetry. This varies by language and time period. For example, in English poetry, the heroic line is iambic pentameter (a verse with five iambic feet); in French, the alexandrine (a verse with six iambic feet); in classical literature, dactylic hexameter (a verse with six dactylic feet).

Heroine: See *Hero/Heroine*

Hexameter: See *Meter*

Historical Criticism: The study of a work based on its impact on the world of the time period in which it was written. Examples of post-modern historical criticism can be found in the work of Michel Foucault, Hayden White, Stephen Greenblatt, and Jonathan Goldberg.

Hokku: See *Haiku*

Holocaust: See *Holocaust Literature*

Holocaust Literature: Literature influenced by or written about the Holocaust of World War II. Such literature includes true stories of survival in concentration camps, escape, and life after the war, as well as fictional works and poetry. Representative works of Holocaust literature include Saul Bellow's *Mr. Sammler's Planet*, Anne Frank's *The Diary of a Young Girl*, Jerzy Kosinski's *The Painted Bird*, Arthur Miller's *Incident at Vichy*, Czeslaw Milosz's *Collected Poems*, William Styron's *Sophie's Choice*, and Art Spiegelman's *Maus*.

Homeric Simile: An elaborate, detailed comparison written as a simile many lines in length. An example of an epic simile from John Milton's *Paradise Lost* follows: Angel Forms, who lay entranced Thick as autumnal leaves that strow the brooks In Vallombrosa, where the Etrurian shades High over-arched embower; or scattered sedge Afloat, when with fierce winds Orion armed Hath vexed the Red-Sea coast, whose waves o'erthrew Busiris and his Memphian chivalry, While with perfidious hatred they pursued The sojourners of Goshen, who beheld From the safe shore their floating carcasses And broken chariot-wheels. Also known as Epic Simile.

Horatian Satire: See *Satire*

Humanism: A philosophy that places faith in the dignity of humankind and rejects the medieval perception of the individual as a weak, fallen creature. "Humanists" typically believe in the perfectibility of human nature and view reason and education as the means to that end. Humanist thought is represented in the works of Marsilio Ficino, Ludovico Castelvetro, Edmund Spenser, John Milton, Dean John Colet, Desiderius Erasmus, John Dryden, Alexander Pope, Matthew Arnold, and Irving Babbitt.

Humors: Mentions of the humors refer to the ancient Greek theory that a person's health and personality were determined by the balance of four basic fluids in the body: blood, phlegm, yellow bile, and black bile. A dominance of any fluid would cause extremes in behavior. An excess of blood created a sanguine person who was joyful, aggressive, and passionate; a phlegmatic person was shy, fearful, and sluggish; too much yellow bile led to a choleric temperament characterized by impatience, anger, bitterness, and stubbornness; and excessive black bile created melancholy, a state of laziness, gluttony, and lack of motivation. Literary treatment of the humors is exemplified by several characters in Ben Jonson's plays *Every Man in His Humour* and *Every Man out of His Humour*. Also spelled Humours.

Humours: See *Humors*

Hyperbole: In literary criticism, deliberate exaggeration used to achieve an effect. In William Shakespeare's *Macbeth*, Lady Macbeth hyperbolizes when she says, "All the perfumes of Arabia could not sweeten this little hand."

I

Iamb: See *Foot*

Idiom: A word construction or verbal expression closely associated with a given language. For example, in colloquial English the construction "how come" can be used instead of "why" to introduce a question. Similarly, "a piece of cake" is sometimes used to describe a task that is easily done.

Image: A concrete representation of an object or sensory experience. Typically, such a representation helps evoke the feelings associated with the object or experience itself. Images are either "literal" or "figurative." Literal images are especially concrete and involve little or no extension of the obvious meaning of the words used to express them. Figurative images do not follow the literal meaning of the words exactly. Images in literature are usually visual, but the term "image" can also refer to the representation of any sensory experience. In his poem "The Shepherd's Hour," Paul Verlaine presents the following image: "The Moon is red through horizon's fog;/ In a dancing mist the hazy meadow sleeps." The first line is broadly literal, while the second line involves turns of meaning associated with dancing and sleeping.

Imagery: The array of images in a literary work. Also, figurative language. William Butler Yeats's "The Second Coming" offers a powerful image of encroaching anarchy: Turning and turning in the widening gyre The falcon cannot hear the falconer; Things fall apart . . . .

Imagism: An English and American poetry movement that flourished between 1908 and 1917. The Imagists used precise, clearly presented images in their works. They also used common, everyday speech and aimed for conciseness, concrete imagery, and the creation of new rhythms. Participants in the Imagist movement included Ezra Pound, H. D. (Hilda Doolittle), and Amy Lowell, among others.

In medias res: A Latin term meaning "in the middle of things." It refers to the technique of beginning a story at its midpoint and then using various flashback devices to reveal previous action. This technique originated in such epics as Virgil's *Aeneid.*

Induction: The process of reaching a conclusion by reasoning from specific premises to form a general premise. Also, an introductory portion of a work of literature, especially a play. Geoffrey Chaucer's "Prologue" to the *Canterbury Tales,* Thomas Sackville's "Induction" to *The Mirror of Magistrates,* and the opening scene in William Shakespeare's *The Taming of the Shrew* are examples of inductions to literary works.

Intentional Fallacy: The belief that judgments of a literary work based solely on an author's stated or implied intentions are false and misleading. Critics who believe in the concept of the intentional fallacy typically argue that the work itself is sufficient matter for interpretation, even though they may concede that an author's statement of purpose can be useful. Analysis of William Wordsworth's *Lyrical Ballads* based on the observations about poetry he makes in his "Preface" to the second edition of that work is an example of the intentional fallacy.

Interior Monologue: A narrative technique in which characters' thoughts are revealed in a way that appears to be uncontrolled by the author. The interior monologue typically aims to reveal the inner self of a character. It portrays emotional experiences as they occur at both a conscious and unconscious level. images are often used to represent sensations or emotions. One of the best-known interior monologues in English is the Molly Bloom section at the close of James Joyce's *Ulysses.* The interior monologue is also common in the works of Virginia Woolf.

Internal Rhyme: Rhyme that occurs within a single line of verse. An example is in the opening line of Edgar Allan Poe's "The Raven": "Once upon a midnight dreary, while I pondered weak and weary." Here, "dreary" and "weary" make an internal rhyme.

Irish Literary Renaissance: A late nineteenth- and early twentieth-century movement in Irish literature. Members of the movement aimed to reduce the influence of British culture in Ireland and create an Irish national literature. William Butler Yeats, George Moore, and Sean O'Casey are three of the best-known figures of the movement.

Irony: In literary criticism, the effect of language in which the intended meaning is the opposite of what is stated. The title of Jonathan Swift's "A Modest Proposal" is ironic because what Swift proposes in this essay is cannibalism—hardly "modest."

Italian Sonnet: See *Sonnet*

J

Jacobean Age: The period of the reign of James I of England (1603-1625). The early literature of this period reflected the worldview of the Elizabethan Age, but a darker, more cynical attitude steadily grew in the art and literature of the Jacobean Age. This was an important time for English drama and poetry. Milestones include William Shakespeare's tragedies, tragicomedies, and sonnets; Ben Jonson's various dramas; and John Donne's metaphysical poetry.

Jargon: Language that is used or understood only by a select group of people. Jargon may refer to terminology used in a certain profession, such as computer jargon, or it may refer to any nonsensical language that is not understood by most people. Literary examples of jargon are Francois Villon's *Ballades en jargon,* which is composed in the secret language of the *coquillards,* and Anthony Burgess's *A Clockwork Orange,* narrated in the fictional characters' language of "Nadsat."

Juvenalian Satire: See *Satire*

K

Knickerbocker Group: A somewhat indistinct group of New York writers of the first half of the nineteenth century. Members of the group were linked only by location and a common theme: New York life. Two famous members of the Knickerbocker Group were Washington Irving and William Cullen Bryant. The group's name derives from Irving's *Knickerbocker's History of New York.*

L

Lais: See *Lay*

Lay: A song or simple narrative poem. The form originated in medieval France. Early French *lais* were often based on the Celtic legends and other tales sung by Breton minstrels— thus the name of the "Breton lay." In fourteenth-century England, the term "lay" was used to describe short narratives written in imitation of the Breton lays. The most notable of these is Geoffrey Chaucer's "The Minstrel's Tale."

Leitmotiv: See *Motif*

Literal Language: An author uses literal language when he or she writes without exaggerating or embellishing the subject matter and without any tools of figurative language. To say "He ran very quickly down the street" is to use literal language, whereas to say "He ran like a hare down the street" would be using figurative language.

Literary Ballad: See *Ballad*

Literature: Literature is broadly defined as any written or spoken material, but the term most often refers to creative works. Literature includes poetry, drama, fiction, and many kinds of nonfiction writing, as well as

oral, dramatic, and broadcast compositions not necessarily preserved in a written format, such as films and television programs.

Lost Generation: A term first used by Gertrude Stein to describe the post-World War I generation of American writers: men and women haunted by a sense of betrayal and emptiness brought about by the destructiveness of the war. The term is commonly applied to Hart Crane, Ernest Hemingway, F. Scott Fitzgerald, and others.

Lyric Poetry: A poem expressing the subjective feelings and personal emotions of the poet. Such poetry is melodic, since it was originally accompanied by a lyre in recitals. Most Western poetry in the twentieth century may be classified as lyrical. Examples of lyric poetry include A. E. Housman's elegy "To an Athlete Dying Young," the odes of Pindar and Horace, Thomas Gray and William Collins, the sonnets of Sir Thomas Wyatt and Sir Philip Sidney, Elizabeth Barrett Browning and Rainer Maria Rilke, and a host of other forms in the poetry of William Blake and Christina Rossetti, among many others.

M

Mannerism: Exaggerated, artificial adherence to a literary manner or style. Also, a popular style of the visual arts of late sixteenth-century Europe that was marked by elongation of the human form and by intentional spatial distortion. Literary works that are self-consciously high-toned and artistic are often said to be "mannered." Authors of such works include Henry James and Gertrude Stein.

Masculine Rhyme: See *Rhyme*

Masque: A lavish and elaborate form of entertainment, often performed in royal courts, that emphasizes song, dance, and costumery. The Renaissance form of the masque grew out of the spectacles of masked figures common in medieval England and Europe. The masque reached its peak of popularity and development in seventeenth-century England, during the reigns of James I and, especially, of Charles I. Ben Jonson, the most significant masque writer, also created the "antimasque," which incorporates elements of humor and the grotesque into the traditional masque and achieved greater dramatic quality. Masque-like interludes appear in

Edmund Spenser's *The Faerie Queene* and in William Shakespeare's *The Tempest*. One of the best-known English masques is John Milton's *Comus*.

Measure: The foot, verse, or time sequence used in a literary work, especially a poem. Measure is often used somewhat incorrectly as a synonym for meter.

Melodrama: A play in which the typical plot is a conflict between characters who personify extreme good and evil. Melodramas usually end happily and emphasize sensationalism. Other literary forms that use the same techniques are often labeled "melodramatic." The term was formerly used to describe a combination of drama and music; as such, it was synonymous with "opera." Augustin Daly's *Under the Gaslight* and Dion Boucicault's *The Octoroon, The Colleen Bawn,* and *The Poor of New York* are examples of melodramas. The most popular media for twentieth-century melodramas are motion pictures and television.

Metaphor: A figure of speech that expresses an idea through the image of another object. Metaphors suggest the essence of the first object by identifying it with certain qualities of the second object. An example is "But soft, what light through yonder window breaks?/ It is the east, and Juliet is the sun" in William Shakespeare's *Romeo and Juliet.* Here, Juliet, the first object, is identified with qualities of the second object, the sun.

Metaphysical Conceit: See *Conceit*

Metaphysical Poetry: The body of poetry produced by a group of seventeenth-century English writers called the "Metaphysical Poets." The group includes John Donne and Andrew Marvell. The Metaphysical Poets made use of everyday speech, intellectual analysis, and unique imagery. They aimed to portray the ordinary conflicts and contradictions of life. Their poems often took the form of an argument, and many of them emphasize physical and religious love as well as the fleeting nature of life. Elaborate conceits are typical in metaphysical poetry. Marvell's "To His Coy Mistress" is a well-known example of a metaphysical poem.

Metaphysical Poets: See *Metaphysical Poetry*

Meter: In literary criticism, the repetition of sound patterns that creates a rhythm in poetry. The patterns are based on the number of syllables and the presence and absence of accents. The unit of rhythm in a line is called a foot. Types of meter are classified according to the number of feet in a line. These are the standard English lines: Monometer, one foot; Dimeter, two feet; Trimeter, three feet; Tetrameter, four feet; Pentameter, five feet; Hexameter, six feet (also called the Alexandrine); Heptameter, seven feet (also called the "Fourteener" when the feet are iambic). The most common English meter is the iambic pentameter, in which each line contains ten syllables, or five iambic feet, which individually are composed of an unstressed syllable followed by an accented syllable. Both of the following lines from Alfred, Lord Tennyson's "Ulysses" are written in iambic pentameter: Made weak by time and fate, but strong in will To strive, to seek, to find, and not to yield.

Mise en scene: The costumes, scenery, and other properties of a drama. Herbert Beerbohm Tree was renowned for the elaborate *mises en scene* of his lavish Shakespearean productions at His Majesty's Theatre between 1897 and 1915.

Modernism: Modern literary practices. Also, the principles of a literary school that lasted from roughly the beginning of the twentieth century until the end of World War II. Modernism is defined by its rejection of the literary conventions of the nineteenth century and by its opposition to conventional morality, taste, traditions, and economic values. Many writers are associated with the concepts of Modernism, including Albert Camus, Marcel Proust, D. H. Lawrence, W. H. Auden, Ernest Hemingway, William Faulkner, William Butler Yeats, Thomas Mann, Tennessee Williams, Eugene O'Neill, and James Joyce.

Monologue: A composition, written or oral, by a single individual. More specifically, a speech given by a single individual in a drama or other public entertainment. It has no set length, although it is usually several or more lines long. An example of an "extended monologue"—that is, a monologue of great length and seriousness—occurs in the one-act, one-character play *The Stronger* by August Strindberg.

Monometer: See *Meter*

Mood: The prevailing emotions of a work or of the author in his or her creation of the work. The mood of a work is not always what might be expected based on its subject matter. The poem "Dover Beach" by Matthew Arnold offers examples of two different moods originating from the same experience: watching the ocean at night. The mood of the first three lines—The sea is calm tonight The tide is full, the moon lies fair Upon the straights . . . . is in sharp contrast to the mood of the last three lines—And we are here as on a darkling plain Swept with confused alarms of struggle and flight, Where ignorant armies clash by night.

Motif: A theme, character type, image, metaphor, or other verbal element that recurs throughout a single work of literature or occurs in a number of different works over a period of time. For example, the various manifestations of the color white in Herman Melville's *Moby Dick* is a "specific" *motif,* while the trials of star-crossed lovers is a "conventional" *motif* from the literature of all periods. Also known as *Motiv* or *Leitmotiv.*

Motiv: See *Motif*

Muckrakers: An early twentieth-century group of American writers. Typically, their works exposed the wrongdoings of big business and government in the United States. Upton Sinclair's *The Jungle* exemplifies the muckraking novel.

Muses: Nine Greek mythological goddesses, the daughters of Zeus and Mnemosyne (Memory). Each muse patronized a specific area of the liberal arts and sciences. Calliope presided over epic poetry, Clio over history, Erato over love poetry, Euterpe over music or lyric poetry, Melpomene over tragedy, Polyhymnia over hymns to the gods, Terpsichore over dance, Thalia over comedy, and Urania over astronomy. Poets and writers traditionally made appeals to the Muses for inspiration in their work. John Milton invokes the aid of a muse at the beginning of the first book of his *Paradise Lost:* Of Man's First disobedience, and the Fruit of the Forbidden Tree, whose mortal taste Brought Death into the World, and all our woe, With loss of Eden, till one greater Man Restore us, and regain the blissful Seat, Sing Heav'nly Muse, that on the secret top of Oreb, or of Sinai, didst inspire That Shepherd, who first taught the chosen Seed, In the Beginning how the Heav'ns and Earth Rose out of Chaos . . . .

Mystery: See *Suspense*

Myth: An anonymous tale emerging from the traditional beliefs of a culture or social unit. Myths use supernatural explanations for natural phenomena. They may also explain cosmic issues like creation and death. Collections of myths, known as mythologies, are common to all cultures and nations, but the best-known myths belong to the Norse, Roman, and Greek mythologies. A famous myth is the story of Arachne, an arrogant young girl who challenged a goddess, Athena, to a weaving contest; when the girl won, Athena was enraged and turned Arachne into a spider, thus explaining the existence of spiders.

N

Narration: The telling of a series of events, real or invented. A narration may be either a simple narrative, in which the events are recounted chronologically, or a narrative with a plot, in which the account is given in a style reflecting the author's artistic concept of the story. Narration is sometimes used as a synonym for "storyline." The recounting of scary stories around a campfire is a form of narration.

Narrative: A verse or prose accounting of an event or sequence of events, real or invented. The term is also used as an adjective in the sense "method of narration." For example, in literary criticism, the expression "narrative technique" usually refers to the way the author structures and presents his or her story. Narratives range from the shortest accounts of events, as in Julius Caesar's remark, "I came, I saw, I conquered," to the longest historical or biographical works, as in Edward Gibbon's *The Decline and Fall of the Roman Empire,* as well as diaries, travelogues, novels, ballads, epics, short stories, and other fictional forms.

Narrative Poetry: A nondramatic poem in which the author tells a story. Such poems may be of any length or level of complexity. Epics such as *Beowulf* and ballads are forms of narrative poetry.

Narrator: The teller of a story. The narrator may be the author or a character in the story through whom the author speaks. Huckleberry Finn is the narrator of Mark Twain's *The Adventures of Huckleberry Finn.*

Naturalism: A literary movement of the late nineteenth and early twentieth centuries. The movement's major theorist, French novelist Emile Zola, envisioned a type of fiction that would examine human life with the objectivity of scientific inquiry. The Naturalists typically viewed human beings as either the products of "biological determinism," ruled by hereditary instincts and engaged in an endless struggle for survival, or as the products of "socioeconomic determinism," ruled by social and economic forces beyond their control. In their works, the Naturalists generally ignored the highest levels of society and focused on degradation: poverty, alcoholism, prostitution, insanity, and disease. Naturalism influenced authors throughout the world, including Henrik Ibsen and Thomas Hardy. In the United States, in particular, Naturalism had a profound impact. Among the authors who embraced its principles are Theodore Dreiser, Eugene O'Neill, Stephen Crane, Jack London, and Frank Norris.

Negritude: A literary movement based on the concept of a shared cultural bond on the part of black Africans, wherever they may be in the world. It traces its origins to the former French colonies of Africa and the Caribbean. Negritude poets, novelists, and essayists generally stress four points in their writings: One, black alienation from traditional African culture can lead to feelings of inferiority. Two, European colonialism and Western education should be resisted. Three, black Africans should seek to affirm and define their own identity. Four, African culture can and should be reclaimed. Many Negritude writers also claim that blacks can make unique contributions to the world, based on a heightened appreciation of nature, rhythm, and human emotions—aspects of life they say are not so highly valued in the materialistic and rationalistic West. Examples of Negritude literature include the poetry of both Senegalese Leopold Senghor in *Hosties noires* and Martiniquais Aime-Fernand Cesaire in *Return to My Native Land.*

Negro Renaissance: See *Harlem Renaissance*

Neoclassical Period: See *Neoclassicism*

Neoclassicism: In literary criticism, this term refers to the revival of the attitudes and styles of expression of classical literature. It is generally used to describe a period in European history beginning in the late seventeenth century and lasting until about 1800. In its purest form, Neoclassicism marked a return to order, proportion, restraint, logic, accuracy, and decorum. In England, where Neoclassicism perhaps was most popular, it reflected the influence of seventeenth- century French writers, especially dramatists. Neoclassical writers typically reacted against the intensity and enthusiasm of the Renaissance period. They wrote works that appealed to the intellect, using elevated language and classical literary forms such as satire and the ode. Neoclassical works were often governed by the classical goal of instruction. English neoclassicists included Alexander Pope, Jonathan Swift, Joseph Addison, Sir Richard Steele, John Gay, and Matthew Prior; French neoclassicists included Pierre Corneille and Jean-Baptiste Moliere. Also known as Age of Reason.

Neoclassicists: See *Neoclassicism*

New Criticism: A movement in literary criticism, dating from the late 1920s, that stressed close textual analysis in the interpretation of works of literature. The New Critics saw little merit in historical and biographical analysis. Rather, they aimed to examine the text alone, free from the question of how external events—biographical or otherwise—may have helped shape it. This predominantly American school was named "New Criticism" by one of its practitioners, John Crowe Ransom. Other important New Critics included Allen Tate, R. P. Blackmur, Robert Penn Warren, and Cleanth Brooks.

New Negro Movement: See *Harlem Renaissance*

Noble Savage: The idea that primitive man is noble and good but becomes evil and corrupted as he becomes civilized. The concept of the noble savage originated in the Renaissance period but is more closely identified with such later writers as Jean-Jacques Rousseau and Aphra Behn. First described in John Dryden's play *The Conquest of Granada,* the noble savage is portrayed by the various Native Americans in James Fenimore Cooper's "Leatherstocking Tales," by Queequeg, Daggoo, and Tashtego in Herman Melville's *Moby Dick,* and by John the Savage in Aldous Huxley's *Brave New World.*

O

Objective Correlative: An outward set of objects, a situation, or a chain of events corresponding to an inward experience and evoking this experience in the reader. The term frequently appears in modern criticism in discussions of authors' intended effects on the emotional responses of readers. This term was originally used by T. S. Eliot in his 1919 essay "Hamlet."

Objectivity: A quality in writing characterized by the absence of the author's opinion or feeling about the subject matter. Objectivity is an important factor in criticism. The novels of Henry James and, to a certain extent, the poems of John Larkin demonstrate objectivity, and it is central to John Keats's concept of "negative capability." Critical and journalistic writing usually are or attempt to be objective.

Occasional Verse: poetry written on the occasion of a significant historical or personal event. *Vers de societe* is sometimes called occasional verse although it is of a less serious nature. Famous examples of occasional verse include Andrew Marvell's "Horatian Ode upon Cromwell's Return from England," Walt Whitman's "When Lilacs Last in the Dooryard Bloom'd"—written upon the death of Abraham Lincoln—and Edmund Spenser's commemoration of his wedding, "Epithalamion."

Octave: A poem or stanza composed of eight lines. The term octave most often represents the first eight lines of a Petrarchan sonnet. An example of an octave is taken from a translation of a Petrarchan sonnet by Sir Thomas Wyatt: The pillar perisht is whereto I leant, The strongest stay of mine unquiet mind; The like of it no man again can find, From East to West Still seeking though he went. To mind unhap! for hap away hath rent Of all my joy the very bark and rind; And I, alas, by chance am thus assigned Daily to mourn till death do it relent.

Ode: Name given to an extended lyric poem characterized by exalted emotion and dignified style. An ode usually concerns a single, serious theme. Most odes, but not all, are addressed to an object or individual. Odes are distinguished from other lyric poetic forms by their complex rhythmic and stanzaic patterns. An example of this form is John Keats's "Ode to a Nightingale."

Oedipus Complex: A son's amorous obsession with his mother. The phrase is derived from the story of the ancient Theban hero Oedipus, who unknowingly killed his father and married his mother. Literary occurrences of the Oedipus complex include Andre Gide's *Oedipe* and Jean Cocteau's *La Machine infernale,* as well as the most famous, Sophocles' *Oedipus Rex.*

Omniscience: See *Point of View*

Onomatopoeia: The use of words whose sounds express or suggest their meaning. In its simplest sense, onomatopoeia may be represented by words that mimic the sounds they denote such as "hiss" or "meow." At a more subtle level, the pattern and rhythm of sounds and rhymes of a line or poem may be onomatopoeic. A celebrated example of onomatopoeia is the repetition of the word "bells" in Edgar Allan Poe's poem "The Bells."

Opera: A type of stage performance, usually a drama, in which the dialogue is sung. Classic examples of opera include Giuseppi Verdi's *La traviata,* Giacomo Puccini's *La Boheme,* and Richard Wagner's *Tristan und Isolde.* Major twentieth- century contributors to the form include Richard Strauss and Alban Berg.

Operetta: A usually romantic comic opera. John Gay's *The Beggar's Opera,* Richard Sheridan's *The Duenna,* and numerous works by William Gilbert and Arthur Sullivan are examples of operettas.

Oral Tradition: See *Oral Transmission*

Oral Transmission: A process by which songs, ballads, folklore, and other material are transmitted by word of mouth. The tradition of oral transmission predates the written record systems of literate society. Oral transmission preserves material sometimes over generations, although often with variations. Memory plays a large part in the recitation and preservation of orally transmitted material. Breton lays, French *fabliaux,* national epics (including the Anglo-Saxon *Beowulf,* the Spanish *El Cid,* and the Finnish *Kalevala*), Native American myths and legends, and African folktales told by plantation slaves are examples of orally transmitted literature.

Oration: Formal speaking intended to motivate the listeners to some action or feeling. Such public speaking was much more common before the development of timely printed communication such as newspapers. Famous examples of oration include Abraham Lincoln's "Gettysburg Address" and Dr. Martin Luther King Jr.'s "I Have a Dream" speech.

Ottava Rima: An eight-line stanza of poetry composed in iambic pentameter (a five-foot line in which each foot consists of an unaccented syllable followed by an accented syllable), following the abababcc rhyme scheme. This form has been prominently used by such important English writers as Lord Byron, Henry Wadsworth Longfellow, and W. B. Yeats.

Oxymoron: A phrase combining two contradictory terms. Oxymorons may be intentional or unintentional. The following speech from William Shakespeare's *Romeo and Juliet* uses several oxymorons: Why, then, O brawling love! O loving hate! O anything, of nothing first create! O heavy lightness! serious vanity! Mis-shapen chaos of well-seeming forms! Feather of lead, bright smoke, cold fire, sick health! This love feel I, that feel no love in this.

P

Pantheism: The idea that all things are both a manifestation or revelation of God and a part of God at the same time. Pantheism was a common attitude in the early societies of Egypt, India, and Greece—the term derives from the Greek *pan* meaning "all" and *theos* meaning "deity." It later became a significant part of the Christian faith. William Wordsworth and Ralph Waldo Emerson are among the many writers who have expressed the pantheistic attitude in their works.

Parable: A story intended to teach a moral lesson or answer an ethical question. In the West, the best examples of parables are those of Jesus Christ in the New Testament, notably "The Prodigal Son," but parables also are used in Sufism, rabbinic literature, Hasidism, and Zen Buddhism.

Paradox: A statement that appears illogical or contradictory at first, but may actually point to an underlying truth. "Less is more" is an example of a paradox. Literary examples include Francis Bacon's statement, "The most corrected copies are commonly the least correct," and "All animals are equal, but some animals are more equal than others" from George Orwell's *Animal Farm.*

Parallelism: A method of comparison of two ideas in which each is developed in the same grammatical structure. Ralph Waldo Emerson's "Civilization" contains this example of parallelism: Raphael paints wisdom; Handel sings it, Phidias carves it, Shakespeare writes it, Wren builds it, Columbus sails it, Luther preaches it, Washington arms it, Watt mechanizes it.

Parnassianism: A mid nineteenth-century movement in French literature. Followers of the movement stressed adherence to well-defined artistic forms as a reaction against the often chaotic expression of the artist's ego that dominated the work of the Romantics. The Parnassians also rejected the moral, ethical, and social themes exhibited in the works of French Romantics such as Victor Hugo. The aesthetic doctrines of the Parnassians strongly influenced the later symbolist and decadent movements. Members of the Parnassian school include Leconte de Lisle, Sully Prudhomme, Albert Glatigny, Francois Coppee, and Theodore de Banville.

Parody: In literary criticism, this term refers to an imitation of a serious literary work or the signature style of a particular author in a ridiculous manner. A typical parody adopts the style of the original and applies it to an inappropriate subject for humorous effect. Parody is a form of satire and could be considered the literary equivalent of a caricature or cartoon. Henry Fielding's *Shamela* is a parody of Samuel Richardson's *Pamela.*

Pastoral: A term derived from the Latin word "pastor," meaning shepherd. A pastoral is a literary composition on a rural theme. The conventions of the pastoral were originated by the third-century Greek poet Theocritus, who wrote about the experiences, love affairs, and pastimes of Sicilian shepherds. In a pastoral, characters and language of a courtly nature are often placed in a simple setting. The term pastoral is also used to classify dramas, elegies, and lyrics that exhibit the use of country settings and shepherd characters. Percy Bysshe Shelley's "Adonais" and John Milton's "Lycidas" are two famous examples of pastorals.

Pastorela: The Spanish name for the shepherds play, a folk drama reenacted during the Christmas season. Examples of *pastorelas* include Gomez Manrique's *Representacion del nacimiento* and the dramas of Lucas Fernandez and Juan del Encina.

Pathetic Fallacy: A term coined by English critic John Ruskin to identify writing that falsely endows nonhuman things with human intentions and feelings, such as "angry clouds" and "sad trees." The pathetic fallacy is a required convention in the classical poetic form of the pastoral elegy, and it is used in the modern poetry of T. S. Eliot, Ezra Pound, and the Imagists. Also known as Poetic Fallacy.

Pelado: Literally the "skinned one" or shirtless one, he was the stock underdog, sharp-witted picaresque character of Mexican vaudeville and tent shows. The *pelado* is found in such works as Don Catarino's *Los effectos de la crisis* and *Regreso a mi tierra*.

Pen Name: See *Pseudonym*

Pentameter: See *Meter*

Persona: A Latin term meaning "mask." *Personae* are the characters in a fictional work of literature. The *persona* generally functions as a mask through which the author tells a story in a voice other than his or her own. A *persona* is usually either a character in a story who acts as a narrator or an "implied author," a voice created by the author to act as the narrator for himself or herself. *Personae* include the narrator of Geoffrey Chaucer's *Canterbury Tales* and Marlow in Joseph Conrad's *Heart of Darkness*.

Personae: See *Persona*

Personal Point of View: See *Point of View*

Personification: A figure of speech that gives human qualities to abstract ideas, animals, and inanimate objects. William Shakespeare used personification in *Romeo and Juliet* in the lines "Arise, fair sun, and kill the envious moon,/ Who is already sick and pale with grief." Here, the moon is portrayed as being envious, sick, and pale with grief—all markedly human qualities. Also known as *Prosopopoeia*.

Petrarchan Sonnet: See *Sonnet*

Phenomenology: A method of literary criticism based on the belief that things have no existence outside of human consciousness or awareness. Proponents of this theory believe that art is a process that takes place in the mind of the observer as he or she contemplates an object rather than a quality of the object itself. Among phenomenological critics are Edmund Husserl, George Poulet, Marcel Raymond, and Roman Ingarden.

Picaresque Novel: Episodic fiction depicting the adventures of a roguish central character ("picaro" is Spanish for "rogue"). The picaresque hero is commonly a low-born but clever individual who wanders into and out of various affairs of love, danger, and farcical intrigue. These involvements may take place at all social levels and typically present a humorous and wide-ranging satire of a given society. Prominent examples of the picaresque novel are *Don Quixote* by Miguel de Cervantes, *Tom Jones* by Henry Fielding, and *Moll Flanders* by Daniel Defoe.

Plagiarism: Claiming another person's written material as one's own. Plagiarism can take the form of direct, word-for-word copying or the theft of the substance or idea of the work. A student who copies an encyclopedia entry and turns it in as a report for school is guilty of plagiarism.

Platonic Criticism: A form of criticism that stresses an artistic work's usefulness as an agent of social engineering rather than any quality or value of the work itself. Platonic criticism takes as its starting point the ancient Greek philosopher Plato's comments on art in his *Republic*.

Platonism: The embracing of the doctrines of the philosopher Plato, popular among the poets of the Renaissance and the Romantic period. Platonism is more flexible than Aristotelian Criticism and places more emphasis on the supernatural and unknown aspects of life. Platonism is expressed in the love poetry of the Renaissance, the fourth book of Baldassare Castiglione's *The Book of the Courtier*, and the poetry of William Blake, William Wordsworth, Percy Bysshe Shelley, Friedrich Holderlin, William Butler Yeats, and Wallace Stevens.

Play: See *Drama*

Plot: In literary criticism, this term refers to the pattern of events in a narrative or drama. In its simplest sense, the plot guides the author in composing the work and helps the reader follow the work. Typically, plots exhibit causality and unity and have a beginning, a middle, and an end. Sometimes, however, a plot may consist of a series of disconnected events, in which case it is known as an "episodic plot." In his *Aspects of the Novel,* E. M. Forster distinguishes between a story, defined as a "narrative of events arranged in their time- sequence," and plot, which organizes the events to a "sense of causality." This definition closely mirrors Aristotle's discussion of plot in his *Poetics.*

Poem: In its broadest sense, a composition utilizing rhyme, meter, concrete detail, and expressive language to create a literary experience with emotional and aesthetic appeal. Typical poems include sonnets, odes, elegies, *haiku,* ballads, and free verse.

Poet: An author who writes poetry or verse. The term is also used to refer to an artist or writer who has an exceptional gift for expression, imagination, and energy in the making of art in any form. Well-known poets include Horace, Basho, Sir Philip Sidney, Sir Edmund Spenser, John Donne, Andrew Marvell, Alexander Pope, Jonathan Swift, George Gordon, Lord Byron, John Keats, Christina Rossetti, W. H. Auden, Stevie Smith, and Sylvia Plath.

Poetic Fallacy: See *Pathetic Fallacy*

Poetic Justice: An outcome in a literary work, not necessarily a poem, in which the good are rewarded and the evil are punished, especially in ways that particularly fit their virtues or crimes. For example, a murderer may himself be murdered, or a thief will find himself penniless.

Poetic License: Distortions of fact and literary convention made by a writer—not always a poet—for the sake of the effect gained. Poetic license is closely related to the concept of "artistic freedom." An author exercises poetic license by saying that a pile of money "reaches as high as a mountain" when the pile is actually only a foot or two high.

Poetics: This term has two closely related meanings. It denotes (1) an aesthetic theory in literary criticism about the essence of poetry or (2) rules prescribing the proper methods, content, style, or diction of poetry. The term poetics may also refer to theories about literature in general, not just poetry.

Poetry: In its broadest sense, writing that aims to present ideas and evoke an emotional experience in the reader through the use of meter, imagery, connotative and concrete words, and a carefully constructed structure based on rhythmic patterns. Poetry typically relies on words and expressions that have several layers of meaning. It also makes use of the effects of regular rhythm on the ear and may make a strong appeal to the senses through the use of imagery. Edgar Allan Poe's "Annabel Lee" and Walt Whitman's *Leaves of Grass* are famous examples of poetry.

Point of View: The narrative perspective from which a literary work is presented to the reader. There are four traditional points of view. The "third person omniscient" gives the reader a "godlike" perspective, unrestricted by time or place, from which to see actions and look into the minds of characters. This allows the author to comment openly on characters and events in the work. The "third person" point of view presents the events of the story from outside of any single character's perception, much like the omniscient point of view, but the reader must understand the action as it takes place and without any special insight into characters' minds or motivations. The "first person" or "personal" point of view relates events as they are perceived by a single character. The main character "tells" the story and may offer opinions about the action and characters which differ from those of the author. Much less common than omniscient, third person, and first person is the "second person" point of view, wherein the author tells the story as if it is happening to the reader. James Thurber employs the omniscient point of view in his short story "The Secret Life of Walter Mitty." Ernest Hemingway's "A Clean, Well-Lighted Place" is a short story told from the third person point of view. Mark Twain's novel *Huck Finn* is presented from the first person viewpoint. Jay McInerney's *Bright Lights, Big City* is an example of a novel which uses the second person point of view.

Polemic: A work in which the author takes a stand on a controversial subject, such as abortion or religion. Such works are often extremely argumentative or provocative. Classic examples of polemics include John

Milton's *Aeropagitica* and Thomas Paine's *The American Crisis.*

Pornography: Writing intended to provoke feelings of lust in the reader. Such works are often condemned by critics and teachers, but those which can be shown to have literary value are viewed less harshly. Literary works that have been described as pornographic include Ovid's *The Art of Love,* Margaret of Angouleme's *Heptameron,* John Cleland's *Memoirs of a Woman of Pleasure; or, the Life of Fanny Hill,* the anonymous *My Secret Life,* D. H. Lawrence's *Lady Chatterley's Lover,* and Vladimir Nabokov's *Lolita.*

Post-Aesthetic Movement: An artistic response made by African Americans to the black aesthetic movement of the 1960s and early '70s. Writers since that time have adopted a somewhat different tone in their work, with less emphasis placed on the disparity between black and white in the United States. In the words of post-aesthetic authors such as Toni Morrison, John Edgar Wideman, and Kristin Hunter, African Americans are portrayed as looking inward for answers to their own questions, rather than always looking to the outside world. Two well-known examples of works produced as part of the post-aesthetic movement are the Pulitzer Prize-winning novels *The Color Purple* by Alice Walker and *Beloved* by Toni Morrison.

Postmodernism: Writing from the 1960s forward characterized by experimentation and continuing to apply some of the fundamentals of modernism, which included existentialism and alienation. Postmodernists have gone a step further in the rejection of tradition begun with the modernists by also rejecting traditional forms, preferring the anti-novel over the novel and the anti-hero over the hero. Postmodern writers include Alain Robbe-Grillet, Thomas Pynchon, Margaret Drabble, John Fowles, Adolfo Bioy-Casares, and Gabriel Garcia Marquez.

Pre-Raphaelites: A circle of writers and artists in mid nineteenth-century England. Valuing the pre-Renaissance artistic qualities of religious symbolism, lavish pictorialism, and natural sensuousness, the Pre-Raphaelites cultivated a sense of mystery and melancholy that influenced later writers associated with the Symbolist and Decadent movements. The major members of the group include Dante Gabriel Rossetti, Christina Rossetti, Algernon Swinburne, and Walter Pater.

Primitivism: The belief that primitive peoples were nobler and less flawed than civilized peoples because they had not been subjected to the tainting influence of society. Examples of literature espousing primitivism include Aphra Behn's *Oroonoko: Or, The History of the Royal Slave,* Jean-Jacques Rousseau's *Julie ou la Nouvelle Heloise,* Oliver Goldsmith's *The Deserted Village,* the poems of Robert Burns, Herman Melville's stories *Typee, Omoo,* and *Mardi,* many poems of William Butler Yeats and Robert Frost, and William Golding's novel *Lord of the Flies.*

Projective Verse: A form of free verse in which the poet's breathing pattern determines the lines of the poem. Poets who advocate projective verse are against all formal structures in writing, including meter and form. Besides its creators, Robert Creeley, Robert Duncan, and Charles Olson, two other well-known projective verse poets are Denise Levertov and LeRoi Jones (Amiri Baraka). Also known as Breath Verse.

Prologue: An introductory section of a literary work. It often contains information establishing the situation of the characters or presents information about the setting, time period, or action. In drama, the prologue is spoken by a chorus or by one of the principal characters. In the "General Prologue" of *The Canterbury Tales,* Geoffrey Chaucer describes the main characters and establishes the setting and purpose of the work.

Prose: A literary medium that attempts to mirror the language of everyday speech. It is distinguished from poetry by its use of unmetered, unrhymed language consisting of logically related sentences. Prose is usually grouped into paragraphs that form a cohesive whole such as an essay or a novel. Recognized masters of English prose writing include Sir Thomas Malory, William Caxton, Raphael Holinshed, Joseph Addison, Mark Twain, and Ernest Hemingway.

Prosopopoeia: See *Personification*

Protagonist: The central character of a story who serves as a focus for its themes and incidents and as the principal rationale for its development. The protagonist is sometimes referred to in discussions of modern literature as the hero or anti-hero. Well-known protagonists are Hamlet in William Shakespeare's *Hamlet* and Jay Gatsby in F. Scott Fitzgerald's *The Great Gatsby.*

Protest Fiction: Protest fiction has as its primary purpose the protesting of some social injustice, such as racism or discrimination. One example of protest fiction is a series of five novels by Chester Himes, beginning in 1945 with *If He Hollers Let Him Go* and ending in 1955 with *The Primitive.* These works depict the destructive effects of race and gender stereotyping in the context of interracial relationships. Another African American author whose works often revolve around themes of social protest is John Oliver Killens. James Baldwin's essay "Everybody's Protest Novel" generated controversy by attacking the authors of protest fiction.

Proverb: A brief, sage saying that expresses a truth about life in a striking manner. "They are not all cooks who carry long knives" is an example of a proverb.

Pseudonym: A name assumed by a writer, most often intended to prevent his or her identification as the author of a work. Two or more authors may work together under one pseudonym, or an author may use a different name for each genre he or she publishes in. Some publishing companies maintain "house pseudonyms," under which any number of authors may write installments in a series. Some authors also choose a pseudonym over their real names the way an actor may use a stage name. Examples of pseudonyms (with the author's real name in parentheses) include Voltaire (Francois-Marie Arouet), Novalis (Friedrich von Hardenberg), Currer Bell (Charlotte Bronte), Ellis Bell (Emily Bronte), George Eliot (Maryann Evans), Honorio Bustos Donmecq (Adolfo Bioy-Casares and Jorge Luis Borges), and Richard Bachman (Stephen King).

Pun: A play on words that have similar sounds but different meanings. A serious example of the pun is from John Donne's "A Hymne to God the Father": Sweare by thyself, that at my death thy sonne Shall shine as he shines now, and hereto fore; And, having done that, Thou haste done; I fear no more.

Pure Poetry: poetry written without instructional intent or moral purpose that aims only to please a reader by its imagery or musical flow. The term pure poetry is used as the antonym of the term "didacticism." The poetry of Edgar Allan Poe, Stephane Mallarme, Paul Verlaine, Paul Valery, Juan Ramoz Jimenez, and Jorge Guillen offer examples of pure poetry.

Q

Quatrain: A four-line stanza of a poem or an entire poem consisting of four lines. The following quatrain is from Robert Herrick's "To Live Merrily, and to Trust to Good Verses": Round, round, the root do's run; And being ravisht thus, Come, I will drink a Tun To my *Propertius.*

R

Raisonneur: A character in a drama who functions as a spokesperson for the dramatist's views. The *raisonneur* typically observes the play without becoming central to its action. *Raisonneurs* were very common in plays of the nineteenth century.

Realism: A nineteenth-century European literary movement that sought to portray familiar characters, situations, and settings in a realistic manner. This was done primarily by using an objective narrative point of view and through the buildup of accurate detail. The standard for success of any realistic work depends on how faithfully it transfers common experience into fictional forms. The realistic method may be altered or extended, as in stream of consciousness writing, to record highly subjective experience. Seminal authors in the tradition of Realism include Honore de Balzac, Gustave Flaubert, and Henry James.

Refrain: A phrase repeated at intervals throughout a poem. A refrain may appear at the end of each stanza or at less regular intervals. It may be altered slightly at each appearance. Some refrains are nonsense expressions—as with "Nevermore" in Edgar Allan Poe's "The Raven"—that seem to take on a different significance with each use.

Renaissance: The period in European history that marked the end of the Middle Ages. It began in Italy in the late fourteenth century. In broad terms, it is usually seen as spanning the fourteenth, fifteenth, and sixteenth centuries, although it did not reach Great

Britain, for example, until the 1480s or so. The Renaissance saw an awakening in almost every sphere of human activity, especially science, philosophy, and the arts. The period is best defined by the emergence of a general philosophy that emphasized the importance of the intellect, the individual, and world affairs. It contrasts strongly with the medieval worldview, characterized by the dominant concerns of faith, the social collective, and spiritual salvation. Prominent writers during the Renaissance include Niccolo Machiavelli and Baldassare Castiglione in Italy, Miguel de Cervantes and Lope de Vega in Spain, Jean Froissart and Francois Rabelais in France, Sir Thomas More and Sir Philip Sidney in England, and Desiderius Erasmus in Holland.

Repartee: Conversation featuring snappy retorts and witticisms. Masters of *repartee* include Sydney Smith, Charles Lamb, and Oscar Wilde. An example is recorded in the meeting of "Beau" Nash and John Wesley: Nash said, "I never make way for a fool," to which Wesley responded, "Don't you? I always do," and stepped aside.

Resolution: The portion of a story following the climax, in which the conflict is resolved. The resolution of Jane Austen's *Northanger Abbey* is neatly summed up in the following sentence: "Henry and Catherine were married, the bells rang and every body smiled."

Restoration: See *Restoration Age*

Restoration Age: A period in English literature beginning with the crowning of Charles II in 1660 and running to about 1700. The era, which was characterized by a reaction against Puritanism, was the first great age of the comedy of manners. The finest literature of the era is typically witty and urbane, and often lewd. Prominent Restoration Age writers include William Congreve, Samuel Pepys, John Dryden, and John Milton.

Revenge Tragedy: A dramatic form popular during the Elizabethan Age, in which the protagonist, directed by the ghost of his murdered father or son, inflicts retaliation upon a powerful villain. Notable features of the revenge tragedy include violence, bizarre criminal acts, intrigue, insanity, a hesitant protagonist, and the use of soliloquy. Thomas Kyd's *Spanish Tragedy* is the first example of revenge tragedy in English, and

William Shakespeare's *Hamlet* is perhaps the best. Extreme examples of revenge tragedy, such as John Webster's *The Duchess of Malfi,* are labeled "tragedies of blood." Also known as Tragedy of Blood.

Revista: The Spanish term for a vaudeville musical revue. Examples of *revistas* include Antonio Guzman Aguilera's *Mexico para los mexicanos,* Daniel Vanegas's *Maldito jazz,* and Don Catarino's *Whiskey, morfina y marihuana* and *El desterrado.*

Rhetoric: In literary criticism, this term denotes the art of ethical persuasion. In its strictest sense, rhetoric adheres to various principles developed since classical times for arranging facts and ideas in a clear, persuasive, appealing manner. The term is also used to refer to effective prose in general and theories of or methods for composing effective prose. Classical examples of rhetorics include *The Rhetoric of Aristotle,* Quintillian's *Institutio Oratoria,* and Cicero's *Ad Herennium.*

Rhetorical Question: A question intended to provoke thought, but not an expressed answer, in the reader. It is most commonly used in oratory and other persuasive genres. The following lines from Thomas Gray's "Elegy Written in a Country Churchyard" ask rhetorical questions: Can storied urn or animated bust Back to its mansion call the fleeting breath? Can Honour's voice provoke the silent dust, Or Flattery soothe the dull cold ear of Death?

Rhyme: When used as a noun in literary criticism, this term generally refers to a poem in which words sound identical or very similar and appear in parallel positions in two or more lines. Rhymes are classified into different types according to where they fall in a line or stanza or according to the degree of similarity they exhibit in their spellings and sounds. Some major types of rhyme are "masculine" rhyme, "feminine" rhyme, and "triple" rhyme. In a masculine rhyme, the rhyming sound falls in a single accented syllable, as with "heat" and "eat." Feminine rhyme is a rhyme of two syllables, one stressed and one unstressed, as with "merry" and "tarry." Triple rhyme matches the sound of the accented syllable and the two unaccented syllables that follow: "narrative" and "declarative." Robert Browning alternates feminine and masculine rhymes in his "Soliloquy of the Spanish Cloister": Gr-r-r—there go, my heart's abhorrence! Water your damned flower-pots, do! If hate killed men, Brother Lawrence, God's blood, would not mine kill you! What? Your myrtle-bush wants trimming? Oh, that rose has prior claims— Needs its leaden vase filled brimming? Hell dry you up with flames! Triple rhymes can be found in Thomas Hood's "Bridge of Sighs," George Gordon Byron's satirical verse, and Ogden Nash's comic poems.

Rhyme Royal: A stanza of seven lines composed in iambic pentameter and rhymed *ababbcc*. The name is said to be a tribute to King James I of Scotland, who made much use of the form in his poetry. Examples of rhyme royal include Geoffrey Chaucer's *The Parlement of Foules,* William Shakespeare's *The Rape of Lucrece,* William Morris's *The Early Paradise,* and John Masefield's *The Widow in the Bye Street.*

Rhyme Scheme: See *Rhyme*

Rhythm: A regular pattern of sound, time intervals, or events occurring in writing, most often and most discernably in poetry. Regular, reliable rhythm is known to be soothing to humans, while interrupted, unpredictable, or rapidly changing rhythm is disturbing. These effects are known to authors, who use them to produce a desired reaction in the reader. An example of a form of irregular rhythm is sprung rhythm poetry; quantitative verse, on the other hand, is very regular in its rhythm.

Rising Action: The part of a drama where the plot becomes increasingly complicated. Rising action leads up to the climax, or turning point, of a drama. The final "chase scene" of an action film is generally the rising action which culminates in the film's climax.

Rococo: A style of European architecture that flourished in the eighteenth century, especially in France. The most notable features of *rococo* are its extensive use of ornamentation and its themes of lightness, gaiety, and intimacy. In literary criticism, the term is often used disparagingly to refer to a decadent or over-ornamental style. Alexander Pope's "The Rape of the Lock" is an example of literary *rococo*.

Roman à clef: A French phrase meaning "novel with a key." It refers to a narrative in which real persons are portrayed under fictitious names. Jack Kerouac, for example, portrayed various real-life beat generation figures under fictitious names in his *On the Road*.

Romance: A broad term, usually denoting a narrative with exotic, exaggerated, often idealized characters, scenes, and themes. Nathaniel Hawthorne called his *The House of the Seven Gables* and *The Marble Faun* romances in order to distinguish them from clearly realistic works.

Romantic Age: See *Romanticism*

Romanticism: This term has two widely accepted meanings. In historical criticism, it refers to a European intellectual and artistic movement of the late eighteenth and early nineteenth centuries that sought greater freedom of personal expression than that allowed by the strict rules of literary form and logic of the eighteenth-century neoclassicists. The Romantics preferred emotional and imaginative expression to rational analysis. They considered the individual to be at the center of all experience and so placed him or her at the center of their art. The Romantics believed that the creative imagination reveals nobler truths—unique feelings and attitudes—than those that could be discovered by logic or by scientific examination. Both the natural world and the state of childhood were important sources for revelations of "eternal truths." "Romanticism" is also used as a general term to refer to a type of sensibility found in all periods of literary history and usually considered to be in opposition to the principles of classicism. In this sense, Romanticism signifies any work or philosophy in which the exotic or dreamlike figure strongly, or that is devoted to individualistic expression, self-analysis, or a pursuit of a higher realm of knowledge than can be discovered by human reason. Prominent Romantics include Jean-Jacques Rousseau, William Wordsworth, John Keats, Lord Byron, and Johann Wolfgang von Goethe.

Romantics: See *Romanticism*

Russian Symbolism: A Russian poetic movement, derived from French symbolism, that flourished between 1894 and 1910. While some Russian Symbolists continued in the French tradition, stressing aestheticism and the importance of suggestion above didactic intent, others saw their craft as a form of mystical worship, and themselves as mediators between the supernatural and the mundane. Russian symbolists include Aleksandr Blok, Vyacheslav Ivanovich Ivanov, Fyodor Sologub, Andrey Bely, Nikolay Gumilyov, and Vladimir Sergeyevich Solovyov.

S

Satire: A work that uses ridicule, humor, and wit to criticize and provoke change in human nature and institutions. There are two major types of satire: "formal" or "direct" satire speaks directly to the reader or to a character in the work; "indirect" satire relies upon the ridiculous behavior of its characters to make its point. Formal satire is further divided into two manners: the "Horatian," which ridicules gently, and the "Juvenalian," which derides its subjects harshly and bitterly. Voltaire's novella *Candide* is an indirect satire. Jonathan Swift's essay "A Modest Proposal" is a Juvenalian satire.

Scansion: The analysis or "scanning" of a poem to determine its meter and often its rhyme scheme. The most common system of scansion uses accents (slanted lines drawn above syllables) to show stressed syllables, breves (curved lines drawn above syllables) to show unstressed syllables, and vertical lines to separate each foot. In the first line of John Keats's *Endymion,* "A thing of beauty is a joy forever:" the word "thing," the first syllable of "beauty," the word "joy," and the second syllable of "forever" are stressed, while the words "A" and "of," the second syllable of "beauty," the word "a," and the first and third syllables of "forever" are unstressed. In the second line: "Its loveliness increases; it will never" a pair of vertical lines separate the foot ending with "increases" and the one beginning with "it."

Scene: A subdivision of an act of a drama, consisting of continuous action taking place at a single time and in a single location. The beginnings and endings of scenes may be indicated by clearing the stage of actors and props or by the entrances and exits of important characters. The first act of

William Shakespeare's *Winter's Tale* is comprised of two scenes.

Science Fiction: A type of narrative about or based upon real or imagined scientific theories and technology. Science fiction is often peopled with alien creatures and set on other planets or in different dimensions. Karel Capek's *R.U.R.* is a major work of science fiction.

Second Person: See *Point of View*

Semiotics: The study of how literary forms and conventions affect the meaning of language. Semioticians include Ferdinand de Saussure, Charles Sanders Pierce, Claude Levi-Strauss, Jacques Lacan, Michel Foucault, Jacques Derrida, Roland Barthes, and Julia Kristeva.

Sestet: Any six-line poem or stanza. Examples of the sestet include the last six lines of the Petrarchan sonnet form, the stanza form of Robert Burns's "A Poet's Welcome to his love-begotten Daughter," and the sestina form in W. H. Auden's "Paysage Moralise."

Setting: The time, place, and culture in which the action of a narrative takes place. The elements of setting may include geographic location, characters' physical and mental environments, prevailing cultural attitudes, or the historical time in which the action takes place. Examples of settings include the romanticized Scotland in Sir Walter Scott's "Waverley" novels, the French provincial setting in Gustave Flaubert's *Madame Bovary,* the fictional Wessex country of Thomas Hardy's novels, and the small towns of southern Ontario in Alice Munro's short stories.

Shakespearean Sonnet: See *Sonnet*

Signifying Monkey: A popular trickster figure in black folklore, with hundreds of tales about this character documented since the 19th century. Henry Louis Gates Jr. examines the history of the signifying monkey in *The Signifying Monkey: Towards a Theory of Afro-American Literary Criticism,* published in 1988.

Simile: A comparison, usually using "like" or "as," of two essentially dissimilar things, as in "coffee as cold as ice" or "He sounded like a broken record." The title of Ernest Hemingway's "Hills Like White Elephants" contains a simile.

Slang: A type of informal verbal communication that is generally unacceptable for formal writing. Slang words and phrases are often colorful exaggerations used to emphasize the speaker's point; they may also be shortened versions of an often-used word or phrase. Examples of American slang from the 1990s include "yuppie" (an acronym for Young Urban Professional), "awesome" (for "excellent"), wired (for "nervous" or "excited"), and "chill out" (for relax).

Slant Rhyme: See *Consonance*

Slave Narrative: Autobiographical accounts of American slave life as told by escaped slaves. These works first appeared during the abolition movement of the 1830s through the 1850s. Olaudah Equiano's *The Interesting Narrative of Olaudah Equiano, or Gustavus Vassa, The African* and Harriet Ann Jacobs's *Incidents in the Life of a Slave Girl* are examples of the slave narrative.

Social Realism: See *Socialist Realism*

Socialist Realism: The Socialist Realism school of literary theory was proposed by Maxim Gorky and established as a dogma by the first Soviet Congress of Writers. It demanded adherence to a communist worldview in works of literature. Its doctrines required an objective viewpoint comprehensible to the working classes and themes of social struggle featuring strong proletarian heroes. A successful work of socialist realism is Nikolay Ostrovsky's *Kak zakalyalas stal* (*How the Steel Was Tempered*). Also known as Social Realism.

Soliloquy: A monologue in a drama used to give the audience information and to develop the speaker's character. It is typically a projection of the speaker's innermost thoughts. Usually delivered while the speaker is alone on stage, a soliloquy is intended to present an illusion of unspoken reflection. A celebrated soliloquy is Hamlet's "To be or not to be" speech in William Shakespeare's *Hamlet*.

Sonnet: A fourteen-line poem, usually composed in iambic pentameter, employing one of several rhyme schemes. There are three major types of sonnets, upon which all other variations of the form are based: the "Petrarchan" or "Italian" sonnet, the "Shakespearean" or "English" sonnet, and the "Spenserian" sonnet. A Petrarchan sonnet consists of an octave rhymed *abbaabba* and a "sestet" rhymed either *cdecde, cdccdc,* or *cdedce.* The octave poses a question or problem, relates a narrative, or puts forth a proposition; the sestet presents a solution to the problem, comments upon the narrative, or applies the proposition put forth in the octave. The Shakespearean sonnet is divided into three quatrains and a couplet rhymed *abab cdcd efef gg.* The couplet provides an epigrammatic comment on the narrative or problem put forth in the quatrains. The Spenserian sonnet uses three quatrains and a couplet like the Shakespearean, but links their three rhyme schemes in this way: *abab bcbc cdcd ee.* The Spenserian sonnet develops its theme in two parts like the Petrarchan, its final six lines resolving a problem, analyzing a narrative, or applying a proposition put forth in its first eight lines. Examples of sonnets can be found in Petrarch's *Canzoniere,* Edmund Spenser's *Amoretti,* Elizabeth Barrett Browning's *Sonnets from the Portuguese,* Rainer Maria Rilke's *Sonnets to Orpheus,* and Adrienne Rich's poem "The Insusceptibles."

Spenserian Sonnet: See *Sonnet*

Spenserian Stanza: A nine-line stanza having eight verses in iambic pentameter, its ninth verse in iambic hexameter, and the rhyme scheme ababbcbcc. This stanza form was first used by Edmund Spenser in his allegorical poem *The Faerie Queene.*

Spondee: In poetry meter, a foot consisting of two long or stressed syllables occurring together. This form is quite rare in English verse, and is usually composed of two monosyllabic words. The first foot in the following line from Robert Burns's "Green Grow the Rashes" is an example of a spondee: Green grow the rashes, O.

Sprung Rhythm: Versification using a specific number of accented syllables per line but disregarding the number of unaccented syllables that fall in each line, producing an irregular rhythm in the poem. Gerard Manley Hopkins, who coined the term "sprung rhythm," is the most notable practitioner of this technique.

Stanza: A subdivision of a poem consisting of lines grouped together, often in recurring patterns of rhyme, line length, and meter. Stanzas may also serve as units of thought in a poem much like paragraphs in prose.

Examples of stanza forms include the quatrain, *terza rima, ottava rima,* Spenserian, and the so-called *In Memoriam* stanza from Alfred, Lord Tennyson's poem by that title. The following is an example of the latter form: Love is and was my lord and king, And in his presence I attend To hear the tidings of my friend, Which every hour his couriers bring.

Stereotype: A stereotype was originally the name for a duplication made during the printing process; this led to its modern definition as a person or thing that is (or is assumed to be) the same as all others of its type. Common stereotypical characters include the absent-minded professor, the nagging wife, the troublemaking teenager, and the kind-hearted grandmother.

Stream of Consciousness: A narrative technique for rendering the inward experience of a character. This technique is designed to give the impression of an ever-changing series of thoughts, emotions, images, and memories in the spontaneous and seemingly illogical order that they occur in life. The textbook example of stream of consciousness is the last section of James Joyce's *Ulysses.*

Structuralism: A twentieth-century movement in literary criticism that examines how literary texts arrive at their meanings, rather than the meanings themselves. There are two major types of structuralist analysis: one examines the way patterns of linguistic structures unify a specific text and emphasize certain elements of that text, and the other interprets the way literary forms and conventions affect the meaning of language itself. Prominent structuralists include Michel Foucault, Roman Jakobson, and Roland Barthes.

Structure: The form taken by a piece of literature. The structure may be made obvious for ease of understanding, as in nonfiction works, or may obscured for artistic purposes, as in some poetry or seemingly "unstructured" prose. Examples of common literary structures include the plot of a narrative, the acts and scenes of a drama, and such poetic forms as the Shakespearean sonnet and the Pindaric ode.

Sturm und Drang: A German term meaning "storm and stress." It refers to a German literary movement of the 1770s and 1780s that reacted against the order and rationalism of the enlightenment, focusing instead on the intense experience of extraordinary individuals. Highly romantic, works of this movement, such as Johann Wolfgang von Goethe's *Gotz von Berlichingen,* are typified by realism, rebelliousness, and intense emotionalism.

Style: A writer's distinctive manner of arranging words to suit his or her ideas and purpose in writing. The unique imprint of the author's personality upon his or her writing, style is the product of an author's way of arranging ideas and his or her use of diction, different sentence structures, rhythm, figures of speech, rhetorical principles, and other elements of composition. Styles may be classified according to period (Metaphysical, Augustan, Georgian), individual authors (Chaucerian, Miltonic, Jamesian), level (grand, middle, low, plain), or language (scientific, expository, poetic, journalistic).

Subject: The person, event, or theme at the center of a work of literature. A work may have one or more subjects of each type, with shorter works tending to have fewer and longer works tending to have more. The subjects of James Baldwin's novel *Go Tell It on the Mountain* include the themes of father-son relationships, religious conversion, black life, and sexuality. The subjects of Anne Frank's *Diary of a Young Girl* include Anne and her family members as well as World War II, the Holocaust, and the themes of war, isolation, injustice, and racism.

Subjectivity: Writing that expresses the author's personal feelings about his subject, and which may or may not include factual information about the subject. Subjectivity is demonstrated in James Joyce's *Portrait of the Artist as a Young Man,* Samuel Butler's *The Way of All Flesh,* and Thomas Wolfe's *Look Homeward, Angel.*

Subplot: A secondary story in a narrative. A subplot may serve as a motivating or complicating force for the main plot of the work, or it may provide emphasis for, or relief from, the main plot. The conflict between the Capulets and the Montagues in William Shakespeare's *Romeo and Juliet* is an example of a subplot.

Surrealism: A term introduced to criticism by Guillaume Apollinaire and later adopted by Andre Breton. It refers to a French literary and artistic movement founded in the 1920s.

The Surrealists sought to express unconscious thoughts and feelings in their works. The best-known technique used for achieving this aim was automatic writing—transcriptions of spontaneous outpourings from the unconscious. The Surrealists proposed to unify the contrary levels of conscious and unconscious, dream and reality, objectivity and subjectivity into a new level of "super-realism." Surrealism can be found in the poetry of Paul Eluard, Pierre Reverdy, and Louis Aragon, among others.

Suspense: A literary device in which the author maintains the audience's attention through the buildup of events, the outcome of which will soon be revealed. Suspense in William Shakespeare's *Hamlet* is sustained throughout by the question of whether or not the Prince will achieve what he has been instructed to do and of what he intends to do.

Syllogism: A method of presenting a logical argument. In its most basic form, the syllogism consists of a major premise, a minor premise, and a conclusion. An example of a syllogism is: Major premise: When it snows, the streets get wet. Minor premise: It is snowing. Conclusion: The streets are wet.

Symbol: Something that suggests or stands for something else without losing its original identity. In literature, symbols combine their literal meaning with the suggestion of an abstract concept. Literary symbols are of two types: those that carry complex associations of meaning no matter what their contexts, and those that derive their suggestive meaning from their functions in specific literary works. Examples of symbols are sunshine suggesting happiness, rain suggesting sorrow, and storm clouds suggesting despair.

Symbolism: This term has two widely accepted meanings. In historical criticism, it denotes an early modernist literary movement initiated in France during the nineteenth century that reacted against the prevailing standards of realism. Writers in this movement aimed to evoke, indirectly and symbolically, an order of being beyond the material world of the five senses. Poetic expression of personal emotion figured strongly in the movement, typically by means of a private set of symbols uniquely identifiable with the individual poet. The principal aim of the Symbolists was to express in words the highly complex feelings that grew out of everyday contact with the world. In a broader sense, the term "symbolism" refers to the use of one object to represent another. Early members of the Symbolist movement included the French authors Charles Baudelaire and Arthur Rimbaud; William Butler Yeats, James Joyce, and T. S. Eliot were influenced as the movement moved to Ireland, England, and the United States. Examples of the concept of symbolism include a flag that stands for a nation or movement, or an empty cupboard used to suggest hopelessness, poverty, and despair.

Symbolist: See *Symbolism*

Symbolist Movement: See *Symbolism*

Sympathetic Fallacy: See *Affective Fallacy*

T

Tale: A story told by a narrator with a simple plot and little character development. Tales are usually relatively short and often carry a simple message. Examples of tales can be found in the work of Rudyard Kipling, Somerset Maugham, Saki, Anton Chekhov, Guy de Maupassant, and Armistead Maupin.

Tall Tale: A humorous tale told in a straightforward, credible tone but relating absolutely impossible events or feats of the characters. Such tales were commonly told of frontier adventures during the settlement of the west in the United States. Tall tales have been spun around such legendary heroes as Mike Fink, Paul Bunyan, Davy Crockett, Johnny Appleseed, and Captain Stormalong as well as the real-life William F. Cody and Annie Oakley. Literary use of tall tales can be found in Washington Irving's *History of New York*, Mark Twain's *Life on the Mississippi*, and in the German R. F. Raspe's *Baron Munchausen's Narratives of His Marvellous Travels and Campaigns in Russia*.

Tanka: A form of Japanese poetry similar to *haiku*. A *tanka* is five lines long, with the lines containing five, seven, five, seven, and seven syllables respectively. Skilled *tanka* authors include Ishikawa Takuboku, Masaoka Shiki, Amy Lowell, and Adelaide Crapsey.

Teatro Grottesco: See *Theater of the Grotesque*

Terza Rima: A three-line stanza form in poetry in which the rhymes are made on the last word of each line in the following manner: the first and third lines of the first stanza, then the second line of the first stanza and the first and third lines of the second stanza, and so on with the middle line of any stanza rhyming with the first and third lines of the following stanza. An example of *terza rima* is Percy Bysshe Shelley's "The Triumph of Love": As in that trance of wondrous thought I lay This was the tenour of my waking dream. Methought I sate beside a public way Thick strewn with summer dust, and a great stream Of people there was hurrying to and fro Numerous as gnats upon the evening gleam, . . .

Tetrameter: See *Meter*

Textual Criticism: A branch of literary criticism that seeks to establish the authoritative text of a literary work. Textual critics typically compare all known manuscripts or printings of a single work in order to assess the meanings of differences and revisions. This procedure allows them to arrive at a definitive version that (supposedly) corresponds to the author's original intention. Textual criticism was applied during the Renaissance to salvage the classical texts of Greece and Rome, and modern works have been studied, for instance, to undo deliberate correction or censorship, as in the case of novels by Stephen Crane and Theodore Dreiser.

Theater of Cruelty: Term used to denote a group of theatrical techniques designed to eliminate the psychological and emotional distance between actors and audience. This concept, introduced in the 1930s in France, was intended to inspire a more intense theatrical experience than conventional theater allowed. The "cruelty" of this dramatic theory signified not sadism but heightened actor/audience involvement in the dramatic event. The theater of cruelty was theorized by Antonin Artaud in his *Le Theatre et son double* (*The Theatre and Its Double*), and also appears in the work of Jerzy Grotowski, Jean Genet, Jean Vilar, and Arthur Adamov, among others.

Theater of the Absurd: A post-World War II dramatic trend characterized by radical theatrical innovations. In works influenced by the Theater of the Absurd, nontraditional, sometimes grotesque characterizations, plots, and stage sets reveal a meaningless universe in which human values are irrelevant. Existentialist

themes of estrangement, absurdity, and futility link many of the works of this movement. The principal writers of the Theater of the Absurd are Samuel Beckett, Eugene Ionesco, Jean Genet, and Harold Pinter.

Theater of the Grotesque: An Italian theatrical movement characterized by plays written around the ironic and macabre aspects of daily life in the World War I era. Theater of the Grotesque was named after the play *The Mask and the Face* by Luigi Chiarelli, which was described as "a grotesque in three acts." The movement influenced the work of Italian dramatist Luigi Pirandello, author of *Right You Are, If You Think You Are*. Also known as *Teatro Grottesco*.

Theme: The main point of a work of literature. The term is used interchangeably with thesis. The theme of William Shakespeare's *Othello*—jealousy—is a common one.

Thesis: A thesis is both an essay and the point argued in the essay. Thesis novels and thesis plays share the quality of containing a thesis which is supported through the action of the story. A master's thesis and a doctoral dissertation are two theses required of graduate students.

Thesis Play: See *Thesis*

Three Unities: See *Unities*

Tone: The author's attitude toward his or her audience may be deduced from the tone of the work. A formal tone may create distance or convey politeness, while an informal tone may encourage a friendly, intimate, or intrusive feeling in the reader. The author's attitude toward his or her subject matter may also be deduced from the tone of the words he or she uses in discussing it. The tone of John F. Kennedy's speech which included the appeal to "ask not what your country can do for you" was intended to instill feelings of camaraderie and national pride in listeners.

Tragedy: A drama in prose or poetry about a noble, courageous hero of excellent character who, because of some tragic character flaw or *hamartia*, brings ruin upon him- or herself. Tragedy treats its subjects in a dignified and serious manner, using poetic language to help evoke pity and fear and bring about catharsis, a purging of these emotions. The tragic form was practiced extensively by the ancient Greeks. In the Middle

Ages, when classical works were virtually unknown, tragedy came to denote any works about the fall of persons from exalted to low conditions due to any reason: fate, vice, weakness, etc. According to the classical definition of tragedy, such works present the "pathetic"—that which evokes pity— rather than the tragic. The classical form of tragedy was revived in the sixteenth century; it flourished especially on the Elizabethan stage. In modern times, dramatists have attempted to adapt the form to the needs of modern society by drawing their heroes from the ranks of ordinary men and women and defining the nobility of these heroes in terms of spirit rather than exalted social standing. The greatest classical example of tragedy is Sophocles' *Oedipus Rex*. The "pathetic" derivation is exemplified in "The Monk's Tale" in Geoffrey Chaucer's *Canterbury Tales*. Notable works produced during the sixteenth century revival include William Shakespeare's *Hamlet, Othello,* and *King Lear*. Modern dramatists working in the tragic tradition include Henrik Ibsen, Arthur Miller, and Eugene O'Neill.

Tragedy of Blood: See *Revenge Tragedy*

Tragic Flaw: In a tragedy, the quality within the hero or heroine which leads to his or her downfall. Examples of the tragic flaw include Othello's jealousy and Hamlet's indecisiveness, although most great tragedies defy such simple interpretation.

Transcendentalism: An American philosophical and religious movement, based in New England from around 1835 until the Civil War. Transcendentalism was a form of American romanticism that had its roots abroad in the works of Thomas Carlyle, Samuel Coleridge, and Johann Wolfgang von Goethe. The Transcendentalists stressed the importance of intuition and subjective experience in communication with God. They rejected religious dogma and texts in favor of mysticism and scientific naturalism. They pursued truths that lie beyond the "colorless" realms perceived by reason and the senses and were active social reformers in public education, women's rights, and the abolition of slavery. Prominent members of the group include Ralph Waldo Emerson and Henry David Thoreau.

Trickster: A character or figure common in Native American and African literature who uses his ingenuity to defeat enemies and escape difficult situations. Tricksters are most often animals, such as the spider, hare, or coyote, although they may take the form of humans as well. Examples of trickster tales include Thomas King's *A Coyote Columbus Story,* Ashley F. Bryan's *The Dancing Granny* and Ishmael Reed's *The Last Days of Louisiana Red*.

Trimeter: See *Meter*

Triple Rhyme: See *Rhyme*

Trochee: See *Foot*

U

Understatement: See *Irony*

Unities: Strict rules of dramatic structure, formulated by Italian and French critics of the Renaissance and based loosely on the principles of drama discussed by Aristotle in his *Poetics*. Foremost among these rules were the three unities of action, time, and place that compelled a dramatist to: (1) construct a single plot with a beginning, middle, and end that details the causal relationships of action and character; (2) restrict the action to the events of a single day; and (3) limit the scene to a single place or city. The unities were observed faithfully by continental European writers until the Romantic Age, but they were never regularly observed in English drama. Modern dramatists are typically more concerned with a unity of impression or emotional effect than with any of the classical unities. The unities are observed in Pierre Corneille's tragedy *Polyeuctes* and Jean-Baptiste Racine's *Phedre*. Also known as Three Unities.

Urban Realism: A branch of realist writing that attempts to accurately reflect the often harsh facts of modern urban existence. Some works by Stephen Crane, Theodore Dreiser, Charles Dickens, Fyodor Dostoyevsky, Emile Zola, Abraham Cahan, and Henry Fuller feature urban realism. Modern examples include Claude Brown's *Manchild in the Promised Land* and Ron Milner's *What the Wine Sellers Buy*.

Utopia: A fictional perfect place, such as "paradise" or "heaven." Early literary utopias were included in Plato's *Republic* and Sir Thomas

More's *Utopia,* while more modern utopias can be found in Samuel Butler's *Erewhon,* Theodor Herzka's *A Visit to Freeland,* and H. G. Wells' *A Modern Utopia.*

Utopian: See *Utopia*

Utopianism: See *Utopia*

V

Verisimilitude: Literally, the appearance of truth. In literary criticism, the term refers to aspects of a work of literature that seem true to the reader. Verisimilitude is achieved in the work of Honore de Balzac, Gustave Flaubert, and Henry James, among other late nineteenth-century realist writers.

Vers de societe: See *Occasional Verse*

Vers libre: See *Free Verse*

Verse: A line of metered language, a line of a poem, or any work written in verse. The following line of verse is from the epic poem *Don Juan* by Lord Byron: "My way is to begin with the beginning."

Versification: The writing of verse. Versification may also refer to the meter, rhyme, and other mechanical components of a poem. Composition of a "Roses are red, violets are blue" poem to suit an occasion is a common form of versification practiced by students.

Victorian: Refers broadly to the reign of Queen Victoria of England (1837-1901) and to anything with qualities typical of that era. For example, the qualities of smug narrowmindedness, bourgeois materialism, faith in social progress, and priggish morality are often considered Victorian. This stereotype is contradicted by such dramatic intellectual developments as the theories of Charles Darwin, Karl Marx, and Sigmund Freud (which stirred strong debates in England) and the critical attitudes of serious Victorian writers like Charles Dickens and George Eliot. In literature, the Victorian Period was the great age of the English novel, and the latter part of the era saw the rise of movements such as decadence and symbolism. Works

of Victorian literature include the poetry of Robert Browning and Alfred, Lord Tennyson, the criticism of Matthew Arnold and John Ruskin, and the novels of Emily Bronte, William Makepeace Thackeray, and Thomas Hardy. Also known as Victorian Age and Victorian Period.

Victorian Age: See *Victorian*

Victorian Period: See *Victorian*

W

Weltanschauung: A German term referring to a person's worldview or philosophy. Examples of *weltanschauung* include Thomas Hardy's view of the human being as the victim of fate, destiny, or impersonal forces and circumstances, and the disillusioned and laconic cynicism expressed by such poets of the 1930s as W. H. Auden, Sir Stephen Spender, and Sir William Empson.

Weltschmerz: A German term meaning "world pain." It describes a sense of anguish about the nature of existence, usually associated with a melancholy, pessimistic attitude. *Weltschmerz* was expressed in England by George Gordon, Lord Byron in his *Manfred* and *Childe Harold's Pilgrimage,* in France by Viscount de Chateaubriand, Alfred de Vigny, and Alfred de Musset, in Russia by Aleksandr Pushkin and Mikhail Lermontov, in Poland by Juliusz Slowacki, and in America by Nathaniel Hawthorne.

Z

Zarzuela: A type of Spanish operetta. Writers of *zarzuelas* include Lope de Vega and Pedro Calderon.

Zeitgeist: A German term meaning "spirit of the time." It refers to the moral and intellectual trends of a given era. Examples of *zeitgeist* include the preoccupation with the more morbid aspects of dying and death in some Jacobean literature, especially in the works of dramatists Cyril Tourneur and John Webster, and the decadence of the French Symbolists.

Cumulative Author/Title Index

Cumulative
Nationality/Ethnicity Index

Argentinian

Asian American

Cumulative Nationality/Ethnicity Index

Subject/Theme Index

118.00

5/23/11

LONGWOOD PUBLIC LIBRARY
800 Middle Country Road
Middle Island, NY 11953
(631) 924-6400
mylpl.net

LIBRARY HOURS

Monday-Friday	9:30 a.m. - 9:00 p.m.
Saturday	9:30 a.m. - 5:00 p.m.
Sunday (Sept-June)	1:00 p.m. - 5:00 p.m.